Information
Technology
for Management

Advancing Sustainable, Profitable
Business Growth

9th Edition

Information Technology for Management

Advancing Sustainable, Profitable Business Growth

EFRAIM TURBAN

LINDA VOLONINO, Canisius College

GREGORY R. WOOD, Canisius College

contributing author:

JANICE C. SIPIOR, Villanova University

WILEY

VP & EXECUTIVE PUBLISHER:	Don Fowley
EXECUTIVE EDITOR:	Beth Lang Golub
ASSISTANT EDITOR:	Katherine Willis
MARKETING MANAGER:	Christopher Ruel
MARKETING ASSISTANT:	Ashley Tomeck
PHOTO EDITOR:	Lisa Gee
DESIGNER:	Kenji Ngieng
SENIOR PRODUCTION MANAGER:	Janis Soo
ASSOCIATE PRODUCTION MANAGER:	Joyce Poh

This book was set by Aptara, Inc. Cover and text printed and bound by Courier Kendallville.

This book is printed on acid free paper.

Founded in 1807, John Wiley & Sons, Inc. has been a valued source of knowledge and understanding for more than 200 years, helping people around the world meet their needs and fulfill their aspirations. Our company is built on a foundation of principles that include responsibility to the communities we serve and where we live and work. In 2008, we launched a Corporate Citizenship Initiative, a global effort to address the environmental, social, economic, and ethical challenges we face in our business. Among the issues we are addressing are carbon impact, paper specifications and procurement, ethical conduct within our business and among our vendors, and community and charitable support. For more information, please visit our website: www.wiley.com/go/citizenship.

Evaluation copies are provided to qualified academics and professionals for review purposes only, for use in their courses during the next academic year. These copies are licensed and may not be sold or transferred to a third party. Upon completion of the review period, please return the evaluation copy to Wiley. Return instructions and a free of charge return mailing label are available at *www.wiley.com/go/returnlabel*. If you have chosen to adopt this textbook for use in your course, please accept this book as your complimentary desk copy. Outside of the United States, please contact your local sales representative.

Library of Congress Cataloging-in-Publication Data

Printed in the United States of America

10 9 8 7 6 5 4 3 2 1

BRIEF CONTENTS

CONTENTS

Mega-forces in Information Technology (IT) are creating an exciting new world. Leading technology trends—namely *social, mobile, cloud, big data,* and *analytics*—offer unprecedented business opportunities. When these technologies converge, organizations are able to gain a competitive edge, to expand market reach, to build brands, and to develop innovative features or ways of doing business. Today's managers, leaders, entrepreneurs and knowledge workers need to know how to leverage the power of innovative technologies, media, networks, platforms, services, and devices. They now need talents and skills that were not part of our vocabulary five years ago—or maybe five months ago.

In this 9th edition, students learn, explore and analyze the latest information technologies and their impact on, well, *almost everything*. Students learn how strategy, operations, supply chains, customer and supplier relationships, collaboration, reporting, recruiting, financing, performance, growth, productivity, and their career success are driven by and dependent on IT-capabilities. Here are a few examples of influential IT developments as well as disruptive impacts of IT covered in this book:

- **Big data, or databases so large they can't be handled with traditional software,** is the next frontier for innovation, competition, and productivity. Big data is produced by companies that track all of our Internet activity, online purchases, and social media interactions. Big data analytics turns ambiguity into clarity and action.

- Financing is a core component of any business. **Crowdfunding, raising small amounts of money from many people,** grew from a $32 million market in May 2010 to a $123 million market by May 2012. **Kickstarter** transformed the investment process for investors and entrepreneurs by providing a funding alternative to turn good business ideas into reality.

- From customer service and qualitative research to promotional support and reinforcing a brand, **Facebook** is a tremendous marketing tool. The value of **social media** lies in the fact that it is the most pervasive form of 2 way communication ever created. Social media helps grow business and create meaningful customer relationships.

- **Twitter** enables direct contact with customers. Brands can chat with existing customers and jump into conversations to grow their fan base.

- **Mobility** and **cloud computing** are changing how people and companies interact with information. Mobile technology has a huge impact on customer behavior and expectations.

- **Sustainability** and green business are smart business.

- With **data visualization, dashboards,** and **enterprise mashups,** users can better prepare for and respond to unanticipated events and make more effective decisions in complex, dynamic situations.

Engaging Students to Assure Learning

Information Technology for Management 9th edition engages students with up-to-date coverage of the most important IT trends today. Over the years, this leading IT textbook had distinguished itself with an emphasis on illustrating the use of cutting edge business technologies for achieving managerial goals and objectives. The 9th edition continues this tradition with more hands-on activities and analyses.

Each chapter contains numerous case studies and real world examples illustrating how businesses increase productivity, improve efficiency, enhance communication and collaboration, and gain a competitive edge through the use of ITs. Faculty will appreciate a variety of options for reinforcing student learning, that include:

3 Cases
- *Case #1,* Opening case
- *Case #2,* Business case
- *Case #3,* Video case

Within chapter learning aids
- Vocabulary in the margins
- Videos references
- Tech notes

End-of-Chapter learning aids
- "Evaluate and Expand Your Learning" sections

  1. IT and Data Management Decisions
  2. Questions for Discussion & Review
  3. Online Activities
  4. Collaborative Work

- Data Analysis & Decision Making sections

Other pedagogical features

- **Quick Look.** The chapter outline provides a quick indication of the major topics covered in the chapter.
- **Learning Outcomes.** Learning outcomes listed at the beginning of each chapter help students focus their efforts and alert them to the important concepts that will be discussed.
- *IT at Work.* The *IT at Work* boxes spotlight real-world cases and innovative uses of IT.

New and Enhanced Features of 9th Edition

The textbook consists of 14 chapters organized into four parts. Chapters 1 and 11 are new. All other chapters have new sections as well as updated sections, as shown in Table P-1.

TABLE P-1	Overview of New and Expanded IT Issues; and Several of the Innovative Organizations that are Discussed in the Chapters	
Chapter	New & Expanded Issues	Innovative Organizations
1: A Look Toward the Future of Information Technology	Crowdfunding Cloud computing The Internet of Things IT consumerization	Kickstarter.com
2: Information Management and IT Architecture	Enterprise mashups Information management Cloud services Virtualization Virtual machines (VM)	PaulMcCartney.com
3: Database, Data Warehouse, and Data Mining	Big data Operational intelligence Data ownership Compliance	msnNow
4: Networks, Collaboration, and Sustainability	Mobile infrastructure Sustainability Machine-to-machine communication Near-field communication SharePoint	Evernote iMindmap Online
5: CyberSecurity, Compliance, and Business Continuity	BYOD Hacktivism IT consumerization Advanced persistent threats *Do not carry* policies IT governance	Anonymous & LulzSec AT&T Toggle
6: E-Business & E-Commerce Models and Strategies	International e-business Internet Advertising Search engine marketing (SEM)	Google, Inc. Realtor.com
7: Mobile Technologies and Commerce	Consumer use of mobile tech Innovation in traditional and web-based retail Location-based marketing In-store mobile payments	Chegg.com Shopkick
8: Web 2.0 and Social Media	Social media platforms & services Feature convergence Application Programmint Interfaces (APIs) Social semantic web services	Bottlenose Poolparty.biz Google+
9: Functional Area and Compliance Systems	Customer touchpoints Tag management Interactive data	SquareUp AdWeek
10: Enterprise Systems and Applications	On-demand CRM Enterprise application integration	Joint Munitions Command Kissmetrics.com

(continued)

TABLE P-1	Overview of New and Expanded IT Issues; and Several of the Innovative Organizations that are Discussed in the Chapters *(continued)*	
Chapter	**New & Expanded issues**	**Innovative Organizations**
11: Performance Management using Data Visualization, Mashups, and Mobile Intelligence	Data visualization Mobile dashboards User experience D3—data driven documents	Roambi.com Tableau software AlphaVision WeDo Technologies SoftwareFX
12: IT Strategy, Sourcing, and Vendor Relationships	Transparency High-end analytics SOA Business processing outsourcing IT vendor relationships	Mint.com Prosper.com Firescope.com
13: Business Process and Project Management	BPM mashups Who's accountable for IT failures	BlueWorksLive.com AutoTrader.com ARIS Express BPM.com
14: IT Ethics and Responsible Conduct	Social discrimination Responsible conduct	JobVite.com Social Intelligence

- ***Solid theoretical foundations.*** Throughout the book, students learn the theoretical foundation necessary for understanding IT.

- ***Up-to-date.*** Every topic in the book has been researched to find the most up-to-date information and features.

- ***Economic justification.*** With the sluggish economic recovery, IT costs and proofs of concept are being demanded prior to investments. Students learn about various cost factors, including total cost of ownership and service level agreements.

- ***IT Ethics, sustainability, and responsible conduct.*** IT has become so pervasive, invasive, prevalent, and a power-guzzler that ethics, sustainability and responsible conduct need to be addressed. For example, we clearly explain how contributions from the field of IT can lead to reduced carbon emissions and global warming, improving quality of life on the plant now and for future generations. We also help students to understand the critical issues related to cyber security, privacy invasion and other data-related abuses so that students can and assess characteristics of responsible conduct.

Supplementary Materials

An extensive package of instructional materials is available to support this 9th edition.

- ***Instructor's Manual.*** The Instructor's Manual presents objectives from the text with additional information to make them more appropriate and useful for the instructor. The manual also includes practical applications of concepts, case study elaboration, answers to end-of-chapter questions, questions for review, questions for discussion, and Internet exercises.

- ***Test Bank.*** The test bank contains over 1,000 questions and problems (about 75 per chapter) consisting of multiple-choice, short answer, fill-ins, and critical thinking/essay questions.

- ***Computerized Test Bank.*** This electronic version of the test bank allows instructors to customize tests and quizzes for their students.

- ***PowerPoint Presentation.*** A series of slides designed around the content of the text incorporates key points from the text and illustrations where appropriate.

- ***Video Series.*** A collection of video clips provides students and instructors with dynamic international business examples directly related to the concepts introduced in the text. The video clips illustrate the ways in which computer information systems are utilized in various companies and industries.

- ***Textbook Web Site.*** (*wiley.com/college/turban*). The book's Web site greatly extends the content and themes of the text to provide extensive support for instructors and students. Organized by chapter, it includes Chapter Resources: tables, figures, link libraries, exercises, and downloadable media-enhanced PowerPoint slides.

Acknowledgments

Many individuals participated in focus groups or reviewers. Our sincere thanks to the following reviewers who provided valuable feedback, insights, and suggestions that improved the quality of this text.

Joni Adkins, Northwest Missouri State University
Karlyn Barilovits, Walden University
Nathan Boyer, Grantham University
Dr. Lewis Chasalow, The University of Findlay
Kuan Chen, Purdue University Calumet
Henry D. Crockett, Tarleton State University
Amir Dabirian, CSU, Fullerton
Norzaidi Mohd Daud, Universiti Teknologi MARA
Michael Donahue, Towson University
Richard Egan, NJIT
Samuel Elko, Seton hill university
Jerry Fjermestad, NJIT
Robert Gordon, Molloy College
Raj Heda, Boston University
Robert Hofkin, Walden University
Lionel M. Holguin Jr., Athens State University
Laurence Laning, Xavier University
Hiram Marrero, Universidad Del Turabo
Stew Mohr, Rutgers University
Barin Nag, Towson University

Mike O'Dowd, Colorado Technical University
Dee Piziak, Concordia University Wisconsin
Mahesh Raisinghani, TWU School of Management
Lisa Rich, Athens State University
Tricia Ryan, Laureate Education/ Walden University
Nancine Vitale, Dowling College
Minhua Wang, SUNY Canton
Charles Wankel, St. John's University
Gene Wright, UW Milwaukee

We are very thankful for help of Graidi Ainsworth, our assistant, who carried out countless research, editorial and record keeping tasks.

We are grateful for the expert and encouraging leadership of Christopher Ruel, Beth Golub, and Katherine Willis. Our sincere thanks for their guidance, patience and support during the development of this most recent version of the book.

Efraim Turban
Linda Volonino
Gregory R. Wood
Janice C. Sipior

Chapter

1

A Look Toward the Future of Information Technology

Quick Look

Learning Outcomes

❶ Describe IT and management issues, opportunities, and challenges.

❷ Identify management's top concerns and the most influential ITs.

❸ Assess the role of IT agility, IT consumerization, and changes in competitive advantage in the second part of the Information Age.

❹ Explain the strategic planning process, SWOT analysis, and competitive models.

❺ Realize how IT impacts your career and the positive outlook for IS management careers.

In this opening chapter, you read about management's top concerns and the information systems (ISs) they consider most influential to their organizations. Understanding senior management's priorities is a smart starting point for your career. You learn about the latest information technology (IT) trends that are important across all industry sectors—small and medium businesses (SMB), multinationals, government agencies, healthcare, and nonprofits. Faced with business challenges, as a manager you need to implement IT solutions and track how well they improve performance. Faced with the latest new technology, as a manager you need to be able to determine whether to invest in it and how to acquire or implement it.

The power of IT to turn challenges into opportunities, to create new markets and industries, to disrupt the way work is done, and to make commerce more social and mobile stems from the creativity and talent of managers—not the capabilities of technology. Managers and workers now need talents and skills that weren't part of our vocabulary five to ten years ago—or maybe five to ten months ago.

The opening case describes how *Kickstarter* responded to a universal business challenge facing entrepreneurs and artists—getting enough start-up cash—with crowdfunding.

CASE 1 OPENING CASE

Need Start-Up Cash? Try Crowdfunding at Kickstarter.com

Crowdfunding is a way to raise money (capital) for new projects by asking for contributions from a large number (crowd) of people via the Web. It's peer-to-peer funding. Also known as **crowdsource funding** or **crowdfinancing**.

Kickstarter is the world's largest crowdfunding platform for creative projects.

Project creator is the creative person who posts his or her project with a video, a description of the concept, and target dollar amount on *Kickstarter.com*.

Backer pledges money to a project, in effect making a financial vote of confidence in the project and creator.

Funding goal is the amount of money requested by the project creator. If this goal is not reached, the deal is off.

If you have a brilliant idea for a film, music album, street art, or cool tech gadget, where would you get start-up money to make it happen? *Hint:* It's unlikely that you'd get a bank loan and certainly not easily. Huge numbers of cash-challenged entrepreneurs and artists could not achieve their visions because of the lack of financing options available to them.

That is, until **crowdfunding.** In simplest terms, people who need money ask for donations to reach their financial goal and explain what they will produce if they reach that goal; and citizens of the Internet—the "crowd"—decide whether to donate and how much.

Kickstarter is the world's largest crowdfunding site for creative projects. Kickstarter is to crowdfunding as eBay is to auctions. They're IT platforms with payment systems that became fun and popular social commerce sites.

Crowdfunding Opportunities for Cash-Challenged Artists and Entrepreneurs

Crowdfunding bypasses banks, family, and friends as funding sources. Crowdfunding needs an IT platform that makes it easy and secure to request, donate, and collect online contributions.

© D. Hurst/Alamy Limited

Figure 1.1 *Kickstarter.com* gives entrepreneurs and those in creative industries online access to money to fund their artistic or business ideas.

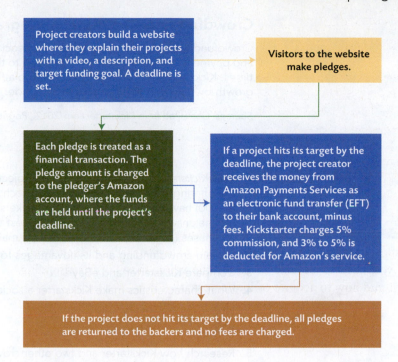

Figure 1.2 The crowdfunding process.

Anyone with a creative project—called project creator—can post an online pitch to potential backers across the world on *Kickstarter.com*. Every week, tens of thousands of people (the crowd) pledge typically from $1 to $1,000—totaling millions of dollars—to film, music, art, technology, design, food, publishing, and other creative projects. The crowd decides which projects are worth their investments by pledging funds. Project creators keep 100% ownership and control over their work. Figure 1.2 shows how crowdfunding at Kickstarter works.

Social Commerce and Incentives

Kickstarter provides the IT platform and payment systems that enable people-to-people commerce, or **social commerce.** Clever incentives and exclusive memberships are offered to backers, which provide the forum for social commerce. Here are three examples:

1. Two California design students in their early twenties, Jesse Genet and Stephan Angoulvant, set a $12,000 goal to launch Lumi Co., a new textile printing technology. They raised $13,597 from 188 backers. To entice backers to pledge $500 or more, they offered a personalized leather envelope, invitations to their launch party and an exclusive event at their Los Angeles offices for the fashion line release, and exclusive newsletters and discounts.

2. TikTok+LunaTik kits turn an iPod nano into a multitouch watch. Project creators asked for $15,000; but raised nearly $1 million from 13,512 backers. Backers who pledged $500 were offered a LunaTik Kickstarter Backer Edition including an 8GB iPod Nano that was laser-signed by designer Scott Wilson. It's now a real product and for sale in the Apple store.

3. Designers of PID-Controlled Espresso Machine, which brings the consistency of expensive espresso machines to a low-cost machine, set a $20,000 goal. They raised $369,569 by its January 20, 2012, deadline. The $1,000 backers were offered a free custom-built machine. Every Kickstarter backer was able to buy the $400 machine for only $200.

In 2012, Kickstarter reported that $100 million was pledged into projects in 2011 with $84 million going into projects that were actually funded. Movies and music projects were the largest funded areas. Over $32 million was pledged for films and video—leading to 3,284 successful projects. For music, backers pledged close to $20 million for 3,653 successful projects. These 2011 stats roughly tripled the 2010 stats.

Crowdfunding—a Creative Integrated IT Solution

Crowdfunding—which is an integration of social networking, e-commerce, and financing and payment systems—clearly is responsive to the needs of the market. In tough economic times, Kickstarter and other crowdfunding platforms offer the ability to support economic growth by funding project creators worldwide.

Sources: Compiled from *Kickstarter.com* (2012), Pogue (2012), *lumi.co* (2012), and *lunatik.com/* (2012).

Discuss

1. Visit *Kickstarter.com* and review the "Project of the Day." What is the project? Review the offerings and number of backers in each level. Which two pledge levels ($1 through $1,000) have the highest number of backers? Which pledge levels are sold out, if any? Do the answers to these questions suggest that backers are actually *customers* making purchases (pre-sales) rather than *donors* making selfless contributions?
2. Explain crowdfunding and its advantages to new entrepreneurs.
3. Compare Kickstarter and eBay.
4. What characteristics make Kickstarter a social commerce site?

Decide

5. Research how Kickstarter and two other crowdfunding sites manage or provide for the collection and transfer of pledges. Based on what you learn, is there a site that you would recommend. Explain why or why not.

Debate

6. Crowdfunding could be viewed as a technology that disrupts the financing industry. Or it could be viewed as so unique that it has created a new industry. Create two teams, and have each team select one of these views. Debate which of view better reflects the impact of crowdfunding.

1.1 IT and Management Opportunities and Challenges

The first section provides background on IT (information technology) and management trends, issues, challenges, and/or opportunities discussed in this chapter.

LIKE, FOLLOW, FAN, SNAP, SHARE, JOIN, SIGN UP, WATCH

Consider how often and in how many ways companies or brands ask you to connect with them, as shown in Figure 1.3. Why do businesses ask you to like, follow, fan, snap, share, sign up, watch, join, or download?

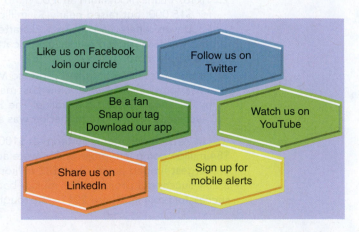

Figure 1.3 Common requests from companies and brands to connect with consumers and prospects via social media or mobile devices.

© digitallife/Alamy Limited

Figure 1.4 *Overstock.com* uses data analytics to discover what their customers want, whether they like a product, and how they can sell it better.

The short answer is to get access to consumers and data about them to improve performance. Three examples are:

1. *Overstock.com.* Jonathan Johnson, a retail executive at *Overstock.com*, explained: "We're not trying to use social media as a sales piece as much as an information-gathering piece. Finding out what our customers want; whether they like a product; how could we sell it better" (Jopson et al., 2011). See Figure 1.4.

2. **Best Buy.** Electronics retailer Best Buy learned how unpopular its restocking fees were through social media. The company changed its product-return policies eliminating those fees that were hurting sales.

3. **Starbucks.** Coffee retailer Starbucks prepared to monitor customers' tweets about a new coffee flavor on the day it was introduced. Managers were surprised to learn that a huge majority of tweets were not about the coffee's intense taste, but were complaints about the higher price. By the next day, they had dropped the price.

Like many companies, Overstock, Best Buy, and Starbucks are making every effort *to learn* how to improve performance. Several examples of learning efforts to improve performance are listed in Table 1.1.

NEXT BIG TECH TRENDS FOCUSED ON COMPETITION, GROWTH, AND INNOVATION

Four current technology trends that offer valuable business opportunities are *social, mobile, cloud,* and *data analytics.* These ITs are often used in combination to gain a competitive edge, to expand market reach, and to develop new features or ways of doing business. They make it easier and cheaper to connect with customers and suppliers, to work with others from anywhere, and to manage files and data.

Tech Note 1-1

The state of Wyoming switched to cloud computing in 2011. This was done by putting 10,000 employees on **Google Apps for Government.**

The financial impact of *mobility* because employees could work from anywhere and better *collaboration* among employees led to a savings of over $1 million per year.

A short video about *Wyoming's Story* is posted on the *Google Apps for Government* site *google.com/apps/intl/en/government/.*

TABLE 1.1	Common Learning Efforts to Improve Performance

- Which marketing campaigns are the most and least effective and why
- What products to develop
- What customers value and dislike
- How to appeal to key customer groups
- How to select and implement enterprise apps that will make a competitive difference
- What perks strengthen customer loyalty most cost-effectively

DATA ANALYTICS—FIGURING OUT WHAT THE DATA MEANS

Simply collecting data has no effect on performance. Data needs to be analyzed. **Data analytics** refers to the specialized software, capabilities, and components all geared toward exploring huge volumes of data to provide greater insight and intelligence—and doing so quickly. Why is it important to analyze quickly? One reason is to be able to know how a particular sale or marketing campaign has influenced sales.

The processes needed to prepare for and conduct data analytics are complex and expensive—and require expertise in statistics and modeling. Data analytic processes include:

1. Locating and collecting reliable data from multiple sources that are in various formats.

2. Preparing the data for analysis. Collected data is not usable until it has been organized, standardized, duplicates are removed (called *deduping*), and other data-cleansing processes are done.

3. Performing the correct analyses, verifying the analyses, and then reporting the findings in meaningful ways.

In the early 2000s, the ability to perform data analytics in real time, or near-real time, improved when vendors and consulting companies started offering it as a service. In the 2010s, vendors offered pre-built, hosted analytics and advanced analytics solutions that reduced total cost of ownership (TCO) and made it feasible for companies to implement data analytics.

Macys' and other large retailers used to spend weeks reviewing their last season's sales data. With data analytic capabilities, they can now see instantly how an e-mailed discount code or flash sale for athletic wear played out in different regions. Charles W. Berger, CEO of ParAccel (*ParAccel.com*), a data analytics provider said: "We have a banking client that used to need four days to make a decision on whether or not to trade a mortgage-backed security. They do that in seven minutes now." Data analytics is used by Wal-Mart stores to adjust its inventory levels and prices; and by FedEx for tweaking its delivery routes. *IT at Work 1.1* identifies other users of data analytics.

IT at Work 1.1

Watson *Wins Jeopardy, Leaving Human Champions in its Silicon Dust*

Data analytics have interesting applications. Here is one famous example of data analytics in action.

Watson is a computer system created by a team of 25 IBM scientists over four years. In 2011, Watson competed against Ken Jennings for Brad Rutter on the game show Jeopardy (see Figure 1.5) in a three-day tournament and won. Watson received the clues as electronic texts at the same time they were made visible to Ken and Brad. Watson would then parse the clues into different keywords and sentence fragments in order to find statistically related phrases. Watson won by using its ability to quickly execute thousands of language analysis algorithms simultaneously to compile potential answers and determine its level of confidence in any given answer.

Figure 1.5 Using data analytics, *Watson* beats Ken and Brad playing Jeopardy.

Questions

1. Explain how Watson figured out the most likely response to win the tournament.

2. View the IBM demo, "Turning insight into outcomes," at *ibm.com/smarterplanet/us/en/business_analytics/article/outperform_with_smarter_analytics.html*.

3. Discuss how companies in various industries are using the insights from analytics to achieve significant outcomes in customer satisfaction and retention, operational efficiency, financial processes, and/or risk, fraud, and compliance management.

Data analytics can help companies achieve these business outcomes:

- Grow their customer base
- Retain the most profitable customers.
- Continuously improve operational efficiency.
- Transform and automate financial processes.
- Detect and deter fraud.

One example is Florida Power and Light (FPL). Mark Schweiger, a senior business analyst at FPL, helped implement a data analytics program to detect electricity theft. Theft was being detected using visual inspection by meter readers and field investigators. FPL knew that an advanced metering infrastructure system would provide data that could flag suspicious accounts for closer examination. In 2009, FPL began implementing a meter data analytics program with the help of vendor DataRaker (*dataraker.com*) estimated for use by 2013.

FPL feeds its vendor meter and customer data, which the vendor crunches to create meaningful red flags indicating electricity theft. The program helps detect when someone is using an unauthorized meter, is bypassing an approved meter, is using a powerful magnet to suppress usage (and billing) data, and has reconnected service without authorization.

MESSY DATA

As you know from your own experience, a lot of data is now text—and text is messy. **Messy data** is the term used to refer to data (e.g., tweets, posts, click streams, images, including medical images) that cannot be organized in a way that a computer can easily process. Data sources include smartphones, social networks, microblogs, click streams from online activities, location-aware mobile devices, scanners, and sensors that automatically collect everything from inventory movement to heart rates. Michael Olson, CEO of Cloudera (*cloudera.com*) explained:

> The old days were about asking, "What is the biggest, smallest, and average?" Today it's, "What do you like? Who do you know? "It's answering these complex questions.

In 2012, research firm Gartner predicted that data will grow 800 percent over the next five years, and 80 percent of the data will be unstructured.

BIG DATA ANALYTICS—THE NEXT FRONTIER OF OPPORTUNITIES

Huge sets of messy data from sources such as multi-petabyte data warehouses, social media, and mobile devices are called **big data.** Research by the McKinsey Global Institute found that **big data analytics,** which is the ability to analyze big data sets, is the next frontier of opportunities for competition, productivity growth, and innovation (Manyika, 2011). Most other research and consulting firms agree that data analytics to gain insights and a competitive edge is one of the biggest opportunities and challenges facing managers.

Questions

1. Why do businesses ask you to like, follow, fan, or interact with them via social networks or web sites?
2. Why is data analytics challenging for companies?
3. Explain messy data.
4. What are the sources of messy data?
5. Explain big data analytics.

1.2 Top Management Concerns and Influential ITs

What do managers consider the most critical building blocks to improving their ability to do their jobs and organizational performance? What ITs are most influential? You will read answers to these questions in this section.

TABLE 1.2	Summary of Characteristics of High-Quality Information
Quality Characteristic	**Description**
Relevant	Information is either relevant or irrelevant to a decision. Irrelevant information interferes with the process—no matter how interesting it is—because it wastes time or causes confusion or delay. Irrelevant information is a persistent problem because ISs are good at generating lots of it.
Timely	This characteristic means that the decision maker receives the information when he or she needs it—that is, when it would be meaningful to the decision.
	For example, the manager of a retail chain needs daily information on stores' performance and products that are selling unusually high or low, so that immediate corrective action can be taken. Receiving performance information at the end of the month leaves thirty-day gaps in corrective actions.
Reliable, accurate	This characteristic means that the information can be trusted and that the decision maker has confidence that information is free from errors, to the extent possible. For example, calculations are correct and data are in correct categories. When information is trusted, it eliminates wasting time having to verify it. Typically, it is more important for the information to be timely than to be perfect.
Easy to understand and use	This characteristic means that information is presented clearly, and concisely, and is well-documented.

BUSINESS PERFORMANCE DEPENDS ON QUALITY INFORMATION AND IT CAPABILITIES

Business performance is directly related to the quality of information. Table 1.2 describes the key characteristics of high-quality information.

An important principle is that what a company can accomplish or achieve depends on what its ITs can do. And for many, business survival depends on IT innovation. Oana Garcia, vice president and Chief Data Officer at Citigroup New York, pointed out that "business and technology teams need to work together and understand the benefits of smart, cost-effective, and collaborative data management, and the implementation of this knowledge is key (*McKinsey Quarterly,* 2011).

Managers of a large U.S. retailer experienced this principle in 2011 as they struggled to understand why their sales were dropping. They had been implementing new online promotions, yet continued losing market share in several profitable segments to a major competitor. When senior managers researched their competitor's practices, they discovered that their problem ran deeper than they had imagined. The competitor had invested heavily in ITs to develop capabilities to collect, integrate, and analyze data from each store and every sales unit. Data was used to run real-world experiments prior to making business decisions. In addition, the competitor had linked its databases to suppliers' databases, which made it possible to adjust prices in real time, to reorder hot-selling items automatically, and to shift items from store to store easily. Their rival's agility and flexibility enabled them to gain an edge and market share.

Despite potential benefits, managers must be careful to avoid "paralysis of analysis." They should not lose agility and flexibility in the hope of gathering perfect data when making time-sensitive decisions.

PRIORITIES DRIVE INVESTMENTS

Another well-known principle states *what's important gets done.* With economic and business conditions recovering slowly, but not steadily, from the worldwide 2008–2011 recessions, budgets and resources are tight. Investment options are

Figure 1.6 Top 5 management concerns and 5 most influential ITs. These findings are based on survey responses from 472 organizations—172 U.S., 142 European, 103 Asian, and 55 Latin America—in mid-2010.

Top 5 Management Concerns
- Business productivity and cost reduction
- IT and business alignment
- Business agility and speed to market
- Business process reengineering (BPR)
- IT reliability and efficiency

5 Most Influential ITs
- Business intelligence (BI)
- Cloud computing
- Enterprise resource planning (ERP)
- Software as a service (SaaS)
- Collaboration and workflow tools

© Luftman & Zadeh, 2011, and Luftman & Ben-Zvi, 2010)

scrutinized to determine their value potential. With limited resources available, priorities (those with the highest payoff potential) get funded, while non-priorities get cut when budget decisions are made.

A helpful way to understand business priorities, issues, challenges, and trends is to look at what managers in the United States, Europe, Asia, and Latin America have reported as their top concerns and the ITs that are most influential to success. Refer to Figure 1.6. The two top 5 lists summarize the Society for Information Management (SIM) survey responses from 472 organizations—172 U.S., 142 European, 103 Asian, and 55 Latin American—in mid-2010. In previous economic downturns, business executives typically had cut back on IT budgets (as well as advertising and new product development) to reduce costs. But in the latest recession, which was worse than prior ones, the opposite has occurred. Taking both top 5 lists into consideration indicates that executives are relying on IT to help cut costs and boost productivity. You read about the ITs listed in Figure 1.6 in the next sections and chapters.

TOP 5 MANAGEMENT CONCERNS

Business productivity and cost reduction. Business productivity and cost reduction were the top concerns by a wide margin. **Productivity** is a measure of efficiency and can be represented by the following model (formula).

$$productivity = \frac{outputs}{inputs}$$

Types of outputs depend on the industry. Outputs can be the number of units manufactured or sold, the number of customers serviced, or the value of new deposits. Inputs are the resources used to produce the outputs. Examples are the number of labor hours, amount of raw materials, and technology. Productivity gains can be achieved by:

- Increasing output, while maintaining the same level of inputs
- Maintaining output, while reducing the level of inputs
- A combination of the above

IT and Business Alignment. Aligning IT with business means leveraging opportunities for IT to support business strategy and improve success. IT-business alignment depends on the IT department understanding strategy, risks, opportunities; and the business understanding IT's potential and limitations.

Business Agility and Speed to Market. Boom economic conditions typically provide companies with plenty of opportunities to improve performance. But during downturns and global financial crises, opportunities are harder to find, and the risk of failure rises. As markets recover from a worldwide recession, managers are exploring new strategies to improve business performance, or profitability. One approach is to develop the *agility* needed to identify and capture opportunities more quickly than rivals. The importance of being an **agile enterprise,** which is one that has the ability to adapt and respond rapidly, has never been greater because of struggling economic recoveries and advances in mobile and social technologies.

Business Process Reengineering (BPR). A **business process** is a series of tasks performed by people or systems that are designed to produce a specific output or achieve a predetermined outcome. Tasks are carried out according to certain rules, standards, or policies. Examples of business processes are customer order processing, credit approval, opening a new account, order fulfillment, processing an insurance claim, and shipping a product. The credit approval process involves a series of steps and decisions to determine whether or not to extend credit and the terms of the loan. Processes range from fully-automated to manual. For additional examples of business processes, view Video 1-1. In a business process, electronic or hard copy business records or documents are created, used, and changed.

Video 1-1
Business Processes
youtube.com/watch?v=JUInjQvz IkE&feature=related

The goal of **business process reengineering (BPR)** is to eliminate the unnecessary non–value added processes, then to simplify and automate the remaining processes to significantly reduce **cycle time,** labor, and costs. Cycle time is the time required to complete a given process. For example, reengineering the credit approval process can cut time from several days or hours to minutes or less. Simplifying processes naturally reduces the time needed to complete the process, which also cuts down on errors.

IT Reliability and Efficiency. Managers and others need to know that they can trust the data—be able to rely on the accuracy, availability, security, and accessibility of data and information systems. Federal and state regulations have made data privacy and protection a legal requirement and impose huge fines for violations.

5 MOST INFLUENTIAL ITs

Business Intelligence (BI). You're familiar with the importance and role of intelligence in national security and the military. Intelligence activities also improve the success of business strategy and operations. BI technologies can help to run the business more efficiently, identify trends and relationships in organizational data, and create or take advantage of business opportunities. Implementing BI successfully is extremely challenging technically because it requires the integration, computation, and analysis of massive data repositories, which is not easy to do. Chapter 11 covers BI in depth.

Cloud Computing. The **cloud** is a term for networked computers, including the public Internet. Often "cloud" means "Internet." **Cloud computing** (or cloud infrastructure or cloud services) does not refer to a specific arrangement, but rather to various computing and network arrangements. To maximize the benefits of cloud computing, companies can build a private cloud, public cloud, or leverage their current IT environment to build a hybrid cloud. See Tech Note 1-2 for more details.

Cloud computing makes it possible for almost anyone to deploy tools that can scale on demand to serve as many users as needed. Many users can access the same apps and from any networked location because they are stored (hosted) on a powerful shared infrastructure in the cloud.

Tech Note 1-2

Companies may lease a cloud computing solution from a service provider. This is known as a **public cloud.** A public cloud allows companies to avoid purchasing and managing certain hardware and software while still delivering their IT services.

For other companies, the most effective way to deliver IT services is to leverage existing IT infrastructure alongside public and private cloud resources to build a *hybrid cloud.* By building a hybrid cloud, companies get the benefits of a public cloud while maintaining control and security.

IT at Work 1.2

Federal Cloud Computing Strategy

In 2011, the U.S. government issued the *Federal Cloud Computing Strategy* that describes cloud computing as a:

> profound economic and technical shift (with) great potential to reduce the cost of Federal Information Technology (IT) systems while . . . improving IT capabilities and stimulating innovation in IT solutions.

The strategy is designed to facilitate federal agencies' adoption of cloud computing, support the private sector, and improve the information available to decision makers.

The chart in Figure 1.7 shows the government estimates shifting $20 billion of IT spending to cloud computing from its current environment. The benefits of the shift are listed in Figure 1.8.

Questions

1. Why did the federal government shift to the cloud?

2. What external pressures are motivating the shift to cloud computing?

3. What three types of benefits did they expect?

4. In your opinion, was this shift to the cloud a smart decision for taxpayers? Explain.

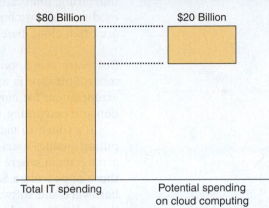

Figure 1.7 Estimated portion of Federal IT spending that is able to be moved to cloud computing.

1. Based on agency estimates as reported to the Office Management and Budget (OMB).

© *Federal Cloud Computing Strategy*, February 8, 2011, cio.gov/documents/Federal-Cloud-Computing-Strategy.pdf

EFFICIENCY	
Cloud Benefits	**Current Environment**
• Improved asset utilization (server utilization > 60–70%)	• Low asset utilization (server utilization < 30% typical)
• Aggregated demand and accelerated system consolidation (e.g., Federal Data Center Consolidation Initiative)	• Fragmented demand and duplicative systems
• Improved productivity in application development, application management, network, and end-user	• Difficult-to-manage systems
AGILITY	
Cloud Benefits	**Current Environment**
• Purchase "as-a-service" from trusted cloud providers	• Years required to build data centers for new services
• Near-instantaneous increases and reductions in capacity	• Months required to increase capacity of existing services
• More responsive to urgent agency needs	
INNOVATION	
Cloud Benefits	**Current Environment**
• Shift focus from asset ownership to service management	• Burdened by asset management
• Tap into private sector innovation	• De-coupled from private sector innovation engines
• Encourages entrepreneurial culture	• Risk-adverse culture
• Better linked to emerging technologies (e.g., devices)	

Figure 1.8 Three categories of cloud benefits are efficiency, agility, and innovation.

© *Federal Cloud Computing Strategy*, February 8, 2011, cio.gov/documents/Federal-Cloud-Computing-Strategy.pdf.

Enterprise Resource Planning (ERP). ERP also refers to technology infrastructure and/or apps that support essential business processes and operations. ERP systems are commercial software packages that are bought as modules. Examples of modules are accounting, inventory management module, supply chain management manufacturing, financial, human resources, budgeting, sales, and customer service. The modules that are bought are integrated—and the result is an ERP. ERP solutions are often cloud-based, as you read in Chapter 10.

Software as a Service (SaaS). Software-as-a-service (SaaS) is pay-per-use arrangement. Software is available to users when they need it. Since pay-per-use is the arrangement for most utilities (electricity, water, gas) other terms for SaaS are on-demand computing, utility computing, and hosted services.

It's tough to understand how SaaS differs from cloud computing. Cloud computing enables users to access data, software, or services via the Internet. SaaS is an arrangement where instead of buying and installing enterprise apps, users access those apps from a SaaS vendor over a network via a browser. Usually there is no hardware and software to buy since apps are used over the Internet and paid for through a fixed subscription fee, or on a pay-per-use basis such as electricity or gas.

Collaboration and Workflow Tools. These tools help people work together in an organized way and manage their tasks more effectively regardless of their location. Employees and managers expect to be able to do work from their mobile and digital devices. Hendrick Motorsports is one of the most famous and highest-winning NASCAR racing teams. For details on how the crew uses Group Chat to collaborate on racetracks, view Video-1-2.

These sets of five business priorities and influential ITs provide a helpful foundation and framework for understanding the strategic and operational role of IT in small and medium businesses (SMB), multinationals, government agencies, healthcare, and nonprofits. *IT at Work 1.3* describes not a single IT, but a concept made possible by a group of ITs.

Video-1-2
Collaboration NASCAR and Hendrick Motorsports
microsoft.com/casestudies/ Microsoft-Lync-Server/Hendrick-Motorsports/NASCAR-racing-team-uses-Lync-to-put-themselves-in-a-position-to-win-the-race/4000011091

Questions

1. What are the top five concerns of management? Briefly explain each.
2. What are the five most influential ITs? Briefly explain each.
3. Describe a business process.
4. Explain the Internet of things.

IT at Work 1.3

The Internet of Things

The **Internet of things** refers to a set of capabilities emerging because of physical things being connected to the Internet or networked via sensors. Networks link data from products or operations, which can generate better information and analysis. These networks capture huge volumes of data that flow to computers for analysis.

Application of the Internet of things: Embedded sensors

When devices or products are embedded with sensors, companies can track their movements or monitor interactions with them. Business models can be fine-tuned to take advantage of this behavioral data. How a company generates revenue from its assets is determined by its business model. A **business model** describes how a company actually operates—how work is done, the degree of automation, the pricing and design of products or services, and how the company generates sales revenue and profit to sustain itself.

For example, an insurance company offers to install location-sensors in customers' cars. By doing so, the company develops the ability to price the drivers' policies on how a car is driven and where it travels. Pricing is customized to match the actual risks of operating a vehicle rather than based on general proxies—driver's age, gender, or place of residence.

Objects are becoming embedded with sensors and gaining the ability to communicate. The resulting information networks promise to create new business models, improve business processes, and reduce costs and risks. For example, sensors and network connections can be embedded in rental cars. Zipcar has pioneered this business model, which includes renting cars by the hour. See Figure 1.9. Cars are leased for short time spans to registered members making rental centers unnecessary. Traditional car rental agencies are starting to experiment with sensors so that each car's use can be optimized for higher revenues.

© Wiskerke/Alamy Limited

Figure 1.9 A Zipcar reserved parking sign in Washington, DC.

Opportunities for improvement

Other applications of embedded physical things are:

- In the oil and gas industry, exploration and development can rely on extensive sensor networks placed in the earth's crust to produce more accurate readings of the location, structure, and dimensions of potential fields. The payoff would be lower development costs and improved oil flows.
- In health care, sensors and data links can monitor patient's behavior and symptoms in real time and at low cost, allowing physicians to better diagnose disease and prescribe tailored treatment regimens. Sensors have been embedded in patients with heart or chronic illnesses so that their conditions can be monitored continuously as they go about their daily activities. Sensors placed on congestive heart patients can now monitor many of these signs remotely and continuously, giving practitioners early warning of conditions that could lead to expensive emergency care. Better management of congestive heart failure alone could reduce hospitalization and treatment costs by $1 billion per year in the U.S.

- In retail, sensors can capture shoppers' profile data stored in their membership cards to help close purchases by providing additional information or offering discounts at the point of sale.
- Farm equipment with ground sensors can take into account crop and field conditions, and adjust the amount of fertilizer that is spread on areas that need more nutrients.
- Billboards in Japan scan passersby, assessing how they fit consumer profiles, and instantly change the displayed messages based on those assessments.
- The automobile industry is developing systems that can detect imminent collisions and take evasive action. Certain basic applications, such as automatic braking systems, are available in high-end autos. The potential accident reduction savings resulting from wider deployment of these sensor systems could exceed $100 billion annually.

Questions and online activity

1. Research Zipcar. How does this company's business model differ from traditional car rental companies, such as Hertz or Avis?
2. Think of two physical things in your home or office that, if they were embedded with sensors and linked to a network, would improve the quality of your work or personal life. Describe these two scenarios.
3. What demands does the Internet of things place on IT budgets or data centers?
4. What are some privacy concerns?

1.3 IT Agility, Consumerization, and Competitive Advantage

Agility means being able to respond quickly. In Figure 1.8, a benefit of a scalable cloud IT infrastructure is that the IT function can be more responsive to urgent agency needs. **Responsive** means that IT capacity can be easily scaled up or down as needed. In contrast, with a traditional non-cloud environment, it took months to increase the capacity of existing IT services because of the need to acquire and install additional hardware and software. Agora Games had the same time lag before transitioning to cloud storage. The benefit of IT agility to business operations is being able to take advantage of opportunities faster or better than competitors.

Closely related to IT agility is flexibility. **Flexible** means having the ability to quickly integrate new business functions or to easily reconfigure software or apps. For example, mobile networks are flexible—able to be set up, moved, or removed easily, without dealing with cables and other physical requirements of wired networks. Mass migration to mobile devices from PCs has expanded the scope of IT beyond traditional organizational boundaries—making *location* irrelevant for the most part.

IT agility, flexibility, and mobility are tightly interrelated and fully dependent on an organization's IT infrastructure and architecture, which are covered in greater detail in Chapter 2.

IT CONSUMERIZATION   With mobile devices, apps, platforms, and social media becoming inseparable parts of work life and corporate collaboration and with more employees work from home, the result is the rapid consumerization of IT.

IT consumerization is the migration of consumer technology into enterprise computing environments. This shift has occurred because personally-owned IT is as capable and cost-effective as its enterprise equivalents.

COMPETITIVE ADVANTAGE

Two key components of corporate profitability are:

1. **Industry structure:** An industry's structure determines the range of profitability of the average competitor and can be very difficult to change.
2. **Competitive advantage:** This is an edge that enables a company to outperform its average competitor. Competitive advantage can be sustained only by continually pursuing new ways to compete.

IT plays a key role in competitive advantage, but that advantage is short-lived if competitors quickly duplicate it. Research firm Gartner defines **competitive advantage** as a difference between a company and its competitors that matters to customers. *IT at Work 1.4* describes changes in opportunities for leadership.

It is important to recognize that some types of IT are **commodities,** which do not provide a special advantage. Commodities are basic things that companies need to function, like electricity and buildings. Computers, databases, and network services are examples of commodities. In contrast, how a business applies IT to support business processes transforms those IT commodities into competitive assets. Critical business processes are those that improve employee performance and profit margins.

The next section focuses on technology issues and provides an overview of core IS and IT concepts.

Questions

1. What are the characteristics of an agile organization?
2. Explain IT consumerization.
3. What are two key components of corporate profitability?
4. Define competitive advantage.
5. What is a business model?

IT at Work 1.4

Radical Change in Opportunities to Gain a Competitive Advantage

The Information Age is in its second half, according to Gartner, Inc., which differs significantly for the first half. In the Information Age's first 80 years, the primary focus was the technology itself. This led to enormous growth and profits for IBM, Microsoft, and other giant IT providers. To a large extent, organizations gained competitive advantages from access to ITs from these providers: for instance, by investing more capital in IT or by having better skills at installing IT in their businesses. The opportunities to gain a competitive edge in these ways don't exist anymore.

Mark Raskino, vice president and Gartner Fellow predicted:

In the second half of the age, as technology becomes ubiquitous, consumerized, cheaper and more equally available to all, the focus for differentiation moves to exploitation of the technology and to the information it processes.

It is already noticeable that the great fortunes of the second half of the age are being made by companies like Google and Facebook, which are not traditional makers of technology.

In this period, the majority of companies that enjoy competitive advantage will gain it from a differential ability to see and exploit the opportunities of new kinds of information (Gartner, December 2011)

Despite the weak and uncertain economic situation, no dramatic cuts to enterprise IT budgets were expected through the mid-2010s. Budgets are being scrutinized closely, and companies have conservative business plans, but IT investments are looked at as critical for ongoing business success.

Questions and Online Activity

1. Explain the differences in the first and second halves of the Information Age, according to Gartner.

2. Register for a free account at *gartner.com*. Search for the latest webinar on hot IT trends, such as *The Gartner Hype Cycle Special Report*. Watch the webinar. In a report, identify the title and URL of the webinar; then describe three important trends and their impacts that were covered in the webinar.

1.4 Strategic Planning and Competitive Models

Strategy planning is critical for all organizations, including government agencies, health care, education, military, and other nonprofit ones. We start by discussing strategic analysis and then explain the activities or component parts of strategic planning.

Strategic technologies are those with the potential for significant impact on the enterprise during the next three years.

WHAT IS STRATEGIC (SWOT) ANALYSIS?

There are many views on strategic analysis. In general, **strategic analysis** is the scanning and review of the political, social, economic, and technical environment of the organization. For example, any company looking to expand its business operations into a developing country has to investigate that country's political and economic stability and critical infrastructure. That strategic analysis would include reviewing the U.S. Central Intelligence Agency's (CIA) *World Factbook* (*cia.gov/library/publications/the-world-factbook/*). The *World Factbook* provides information on the history, people, government, economy, geography, communications, transportation, military, and transnational issues for 266 world entities. Then the company would need to investigate competitors and their potential reactions to a new entrant into their market. Equally important, the company would need to assess its ability to compete profitably in the market and impacts of the expansion on other parts of the company. For example, having excess production capacity would require less capital than if a new factory needed to be built.

The purpose of this analysis of the environment, competition, and capacity is to learn about the strengths, weaknesses, opportunities, and threats (SWOT) of the expansion plan being considered. **SWOT analysis,** as it is called, involves the evaluation of strengths and weaknesses, which are internal factors; and opportunities and threats, which are external factors. Examples are:

- **Strengths:** Reliable processes; agility; motivated workforce
- **Weaknesses:** Lack of expertise; competitors with better IT infrastructure
- **Opportunities:** A developing market; ability to create a new market or product
- **Threats:** Price wars or other fierce reaction by competitors; obsolescence

SWOT is only a guide. The value of SWOT analysis depends on how the analysis is performed. Here are several rules to follow:

- Be realistic about the strengths and weaknesses of your organization
- Be realistic about the size of the opportunities and threats
- Be specific and keep the analysis simple, or as simple as possible
- Evaluate your company's strengths and weaknesses in relation to those of competitors (better than or worse than competitors)
- Expect conflicting views because SWOT is subjective, forward-looking, and based on assumptions

SWOT analysis is often done at the outset of the strategic planning process. Now you will read answers to the question, "what is strategic planning?"

WHAT IS STRATEGIC PLANNING?

Strategic planning is a series of processes in which an organization selects and arranges its businesses or services to keep the organization viable (healthy or functional) even when unexpected events disrupt one or more of its businesses, markets, products, or services. Strategic planning involves environmental scanning and prediction, or SWOT analysis, for each business relative to competitors in that business' market or product line. The next step in the strategic planning process is strategy.

WHAT IS STRATEGY?

Strategy defines the plan for how a business will achieve its mission, goals, and objectives. It specifies the necessary financial requirements, budgets, and resources. Strategy addresses fundamental issues such as the company's position in its industry, its available resources and options, and future directions. A strategy addresses questions such as:

- What is the long-term direction of our business?
- What is the overall plan for deploying our resources?
- What trade-offs are necessary? What resources will it need to share?
- What is our position compared to our competitors?
- How do we achieve competitive advantage over rivals in order to achieve or maximize profitability?

Two of the most well-known methodologies were developed by Porter. Their essentials are presented next.

PORTER'S COMPETITIVE FORCES MODEL AND STRATEGIES

Michael Porter's **competitive forces model,** also called the **five-forces model,** has been used to identify competitive strategies. The model demonstrates how IT can enhance competitiveness. Professor Porter discusses this model in detail in a 13-minute YouTube video from the Harvard Business School.

The model recognizes five major forces (think of them as *pressures* or *drivers*) that could influence a company's position *within a given industry* and therefore, the strategy that management chooses to pursue. Other forces, such as those cited in this chapter, including new regulations, affect all companies in the industry, and therefore may have a rather uniform impact on each company in an industry. Although the details of the model differ from one industry to another, its general structure is universal.

According to Porter, an industry's profit potential is largely determined by the intensity of competitive forces within the industry, shown in Figure 1.10. A good understanding of the industry's competitive forces and their underlying causes is a crucial component of strategy formulation, which is the building of defenses against the competitive forces, or finding a viable position in an industry where the forces are weaker.

Basis of the Competitive Forces Model. Before examining the model, it's helpful to understand that it is based on the fundamental concept of profitability and profit margin.

PROFIT = TOTAL REVENUES minus TOTAL COSTS. Profit is increased by increasing total revenues and/or decreasing total costs. Profit is decreased when total revenues decrease and/or total costs increase.

PROFIT MARGIN = SELLING PRICE minus COST OF THE ITEM. Profit margin measures the amount of *profit per unit of sales*, and does not take into account all costs of doing business.

Five Industry Forces. According to Porter's competitive forces model, the five major forces in an industry affect the degree of competition, which impact profit margins and ultimately profitability. These forces interact so while you read about them individually, their interaction determines the industry's profit potential. For example, while profit margins for pizzerias may be small, the ease of entering that industry draws new entrants into that industry. Conversely, profit margins for delivery services may be large, but the cost of the IT to support the service is a huge barrier to entry into the market.

Here is an explanation of the five industry (market) forces.

1. Threat of entry of new competitors. Industries that have large profit margins attract others (called *entrants*) into the market to a greater degree than small margins. It's the same principle as jobs—people are attracted to higher-paying jobs, provided that they can meet or acquire the criteria for that job. In order to gain market share, entrants typically sell at lower prices or offer some incentive. Those companies already in the

Video-1-3

Five Competitive Forces That Shape Strategy, by Michael Porter *youtube.com/watch?v= mYF2_FBCvXw*

industry may be forced to defend their market share by lowering prices, which reduces their profit margin. Thus, this threat puts downward pressure on profit margins by driving prices down.

This force also refers to the strength of the **barriers to entry** into an industry, which is how easy it is to enter an industry. The threat of entry is lower (less powerful) when existing companies have ISs that are difficult to duplicate or very expensive. Those ISs create barriers to entry that reduce the threat of entry.

2. Bargaining power of suppliers. Bargaining power is high where the supplier or brand is powerful, such as Apple, Microsoft, and auto manufacturers. Power is determined by how much a company purchases from a supplier. The more powerful company has the leverage to demand better prices or terms, which increase its profit margin. Conversely, suppliers with very little bargaining power tend to have small profit margins.

3. Bargaining power of customers or buyers. This force is the reverse of the bargaining power of suppliers. Examples are Dell Computers, Wal-Mart, and governments. This force is high where there a few, large customers or buyers in a market.

4. Threat of substitute products or services. Where there is product-for-product substitution, such as Kindle for Nook or e-mail for fax, there is downward pressure on prices. As the threat of substitutes increases, profit margin decreases because sellers need to keep prices competitively low.

5. Competitive rivalry among existing firms in the industry. Fierce competition involves expensive advertising and promotions, intense investments in research and development (R&D), or other efforts that cut into profit margins. This force is most likely to be high when entry barriers are low; threat of substitute products is high, and suppliers and buyers in the market attempt to control. That's why this force is placed in the center of the model.

The strength of each force is determined by the industry's structure. Existing companies in an industry need to protect themselves against these forces. Alternatively, they can take advantage of the forces to improve their position or to challenge industry leaders. The relationships are shown in Figure 1.10.

Companies can identify the forces that influence competitive advantage in their marketplace and then develop a strategy. Porter (1985) proposed three types of strategies—cost leadership, differentiation, and niche strategies.

In Table 1.3, Porter's three classical strategies are listed first, followed by a list of nine other general strategies for dealing with competitive advantage. Each of these strategies can be enhanced by IT, as will be shown throughout the book.

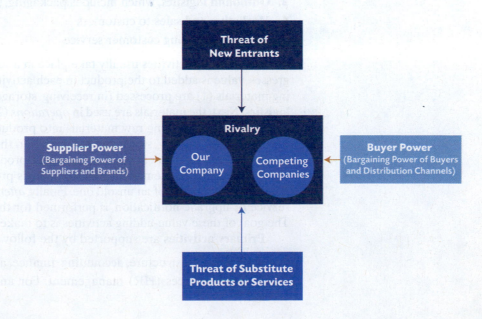

Figure 1.10 Porter's competitive forces model.

TABLE 1.3 | **Strategies for Competitive Advantage**

Strategy	Description
Cost leadership	Produce product/service at the lowest cost in the industry.
Differentiation	Offer different products, services, or product features.
Niche	Select a narrow-scope segment (*market niche*) and be the best in quality, speed, or cost in that segment.
Growth	Increase market share, acquire more customers, or sell more types of products.
Alliance	Work with business partners in partnerships, alliances, joint ventures, or virtual companies.
Innovation	Introduce new products/services; put new features in existing products/services; develop new ways to produce products/services.
Operational effectiveness	Improve the manner in which internal business processes are executed so that the firm performs similar activities better than rivals.
Customer orientation	Concentrate on customer satisfaction.
Time	Treat time as a resource, then manage it and use it to the firm's advantage.
Entry barriers	Create barriers to entry. By introducing innovative products or using IT to provide exceptional service, companies can create entry barriers to discourage new entrants.
Customer or supplier lock-in	Encourage customers or suppliers to stay with you rather than going to competitors. Reduce customers' bargaining power by locking them in.
Increase switching costs	Discourage customers or suppliers from going to competitors for economic reasons.

Primary activities are those business activities through which a company produces goods, thus creating value for which customers are willing to pay. Primary activities involve the purchase of materials, the processing of materials into products, and delivery of products to customers. Typically, there are five primary activities:

1. Inbound logistics, or acquiring and receiving of raw materials and other inputs

2. Operations, including manufacturing and testing

3. Outbound logistics, which includes packaging, storage, delivery, and distribution

4. Marketing and sales to customers

5. Services, including customer service

The primary activities usually take place in a sequence from 1 to 5. As work progresses, value is added to the product in each activity. To be more specific, the incoming materials (1) are processed (in receiving, storage, etc.) in activities called **inbound logistics.** Next, the materials are used in *operations* (2), where significant value is added by the process of turning raw materials into products. Products need to be prepared for delivery (packaging, storing, and shipping) in the **outbound logistics** activities (3). Then *marketing and sales* (4) attempt to sell the products to customers, increasing product value by creating demand for the company's products. The value of a sold item is much larger than that of an unsold one. Finally, *after-sales service* (5), such as warranty service or upgrade notification, is performed for the customer, further adding value. The goal of these value-adding activities is to make a profit for the company.

Primary activities are supported by the following support activities:

1. The firm's infrastructure, accounting, finance, and management.

2. Human resources (HR) management. For an IT-related HR trend, see *IT at Work 1.5*.

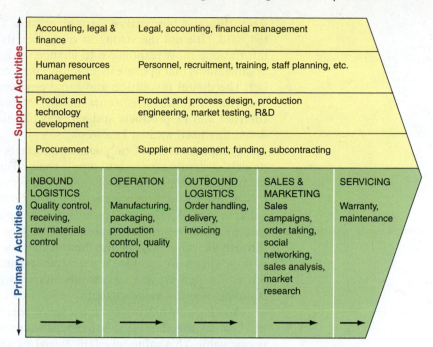

		Accounting, legal & finance	Legal, accounting, financial management

Figure 1.11 A firm's value chain. The arrows represent the flow of goods, services, and data.

	Support Activities		
	Accounting, legal & finance	Legal, accounting, financial management	
	Human resources management	Personnel, recruitment, training, staff planning, etc.	
	Product and technology development	Product and process design, production engineering, market testing, R&D	
	Procurement	Supplier management, funding, subcontracting	

INBOUND LOGISTICS	OPERATION	OUTBOUND LOGISTICS	SALES & MARKETING	SERVICING
Quality control, receiving, raw materials control	Manufacturing, packaging, production control, quality control	Order handling, delivery, invoicing	Sales campaigns, order taking, social networking, sales analysis, market research	Warranty, maintenance

Primary Activities

3. Technology development, and research and development (R&D).

4. Procurement, or purchasing.

Each support activity can be applied to any or all of the primary activities. Support activities may also support each other, as shown in Figure 1.11.

Innovation and adaptability are **critical success factors,** or CSFs, related to Porter's models. CSFs are those things that must go right for a company to achieve its mission.

IT at Work 1.5

Finding Qualified Talent

Managers at a global energy services company could not find or access their best talent to solve clients' technical problems because of geographic boundaries and business unit barriers. The company's help desks supported engineers well enough for common problems, but not for difficult issues that needed creative solutions. Using Web technologies to expand access to experts worldwide, the company set up new innovation communities across its business units, which have improved the quality of its services.

Dow Chemical set up its own social network to help managers identify the talent they need to carry out projects across its diverse business units and functions. To expand its talent pool, Dow extended the network to include former employees and retirees.

Other companies are using networks to tap external talent pools. These networks include online labor markets, such as Amazon Mechanical Turk and contest services, such as InnoCentive that help solve business problems.

- **Amazon Mechanical Turk** (*http://aws.amazon.com/mturk/*) is a marketplace for work that requires human intelligence. Their web service enables companies to access a diverse, on-demand workforce.

- **InnoCentive** (*http://www.innocentive.com/*) is an "open innovation" company that takes R&D problems in a broad range of areas such as engineering, computer science, and business and frames them as "challenge problems" for anyone to solve them. It gives cash awards for the best solutions to solvers who meet the challenge criteria.

Sources: Compiled from McKinsey Global Institute (*mckinsey.com/insights/mgi.aspx*), Amazon Mechanical Turk (*aws.amazon.com/mturk/*), and InnoCentive (*Innocentive.com/*).

Questions and Online Activities

1. Visit and review the Amazon Mechanical Turk web site. Explain HITs. How do they provide an on-demand workforce?

2. Visit and review the InnoCentive web site. Describe what they do and how.

Adaptive and Innovative Organizations. Charles Darwin, the renowned scientist, said, "It's not the strongest of species that survives, nor the most intelligent; but the one most responsive to change." What is true in nature is true today for organizations that operate in a rapidly changing environment, as you have read earlier. The digital revolution and rapid environmental changes bring opportunities and risks. Bill Gates is aware of this. Microsoft is continually developing new Internet and IT products and services to defend itself against Google. Google is defending itself against Facebook.

Competition is not only among products or services, but also among business models, customer service, and supply chains. The concept of value chain has been supplemented by the concepts of *value system* and *value network*.

A firm's value chain is part of a larger stream of activities, which Porter calls a value system. A **value system** includes the suppliers that provide the inputs necessary to the firm and their value chains. Once the firm creates products, they pass through the value chain of distributors, all the way to the buyers (customers). All parts of these chains are included in the value system. Gaining and sustaining a competitive advantage, and supporting that advantage by means of IT—this requires an understanding of entire value system.

A *value network* is a complex set of social and technical resources. Value networks work together via relationships to create social goods (public goods) or economic value. This value takes the form of knowledge and other intangibles and/or financial value.

Real-time, On-Demand IT Support. Eliminating blind spots requires *real-time systems*. A **real-time system** is an IS that provides fast-enough access to information or data so that an appropriate decision can be made, usually before the data or situation changes (operational deadlines from event to system response). Fast enough may mean less than a second if you are buying a stock, or before a business opens in the morning when you determine a price. It can be a day or two in other situations. When a patient is admitted to the hospital, the patient's medical records must be readily accessible. The longer the wait, the greater the risk to the patient. The real-time enterprise is a necessity since the basis of competition is often time or speed. Web-based systems (such as tracking stocks online) provide us with these capabilities. Some examples are the following:

• Salespeople can check to see whether a product is in inventory by looking directly into the inventory system.

• Suppliers can ensure adequate supplies by looking directly into the forecasting and inventory systems.

• An online order payment by credit card is checked for the balance and the amount of the purchase is debited all in one second. This way authorization is given "fast enough" for both a seller and a buyer.

Questions

1. Describe strategic planning.
2. Describe SWOT analysis.
3. Explain Porters' five forces model, and give an example of each force.
4. Describe adaptive organization.
5. Describe real-time business.

1.5 Why IT is Important to Your Career, and IT Careers

Executives, managers, and workers depend on IT in order to make informed decisions, collaborate, communicate, and carry out other activities discussed in this chapter and that you do on a regular basis with your mobiles. A survey of 4,000 employees by the consulting firm Accenture (2011) found that a large proportion of them make their own technology decisions, and one-fourth use their own devices to access enterprise apps and databases (McKendrick, 2011).

The latest trend (or over-hyped term) is "consumerization of IT." As with cloud computing, the term is somewhat ambiguous. In *CIO Magazine,* Bernard Golden (2011) points out, "Consumerization of IT isn't about employees using consumer devices; it's about consumers becoming the primary users of internal IT applications." The greater volume and variety of application access, as consumers tap into what used to be internal IT systems from any device and location will have huge implications for companies and IT architecture. With IT consumerization and the *bring your own device* (BYOD) trend, many of today's businesses are being run by employees on their own devices, rather than on equipment specified and purchased by the IT department.

Next-generation (next gen) digital enterprises are being driven by business managers and individual employees who know what IT they need, how to acquire them, and how to use them. This movement frees up the IT function to develop enterprise systems and innovative solutions. Cloud computing is changing many job descriptions, as you read in *IT at Work 1.6.*

Software engineers are in high demand because of the growth of the cloud. Consider the fact that in 2011, CareerCast determined software engineers to be the best job to have in today's economy, thanks largely to the rise of cloud computing. For details, visit *careercast.com/jobs-rated/10-best-jobs-2011.*

THE NETWORK IS THE BUSINESS

For most organizations, if their computer network goes down, so does the business. Imagine not having Internet access for 24 hours—no texting, e-mail, downloads, ebooks, Facebook, Twitter, data access, status reports, and so on. Looking at what you could still accomplish without IT gives a clear perspective of its importance and ubiquity.

IT at Work 1.6

Cloud Computing Is Changing the Nature of Jobs

Cloud computing is not only driving changes in organizations, it is also changing the nature of jobs—not only within the IT department—but throughout the enterprise as well.

IT Takes on More Strategic and Executive Roles

For chief information officers (CIOs) and other chief executives, cloud-driven changes reflect the more strategic role IT plays in setting the direction of businesses. For businesses, cloud storage, services, and other computing arrangement have led to more reliable and predictable supporting IT.

IT and other managers recognize that the best and most cost-effective solutions—including IT solutions—are those that may have been built, tested, and verified elsewhere.

Being able to identify and leverage from a public cloud or company-owned data centers is becoming a key part of IT leaders' responsibilities. The ability to introduce and develop valuable cloud computing engagements or infrastructure may even be the career path to the corner office, according to a study from CA Technologies (*ca.com/*). About 54% of 685 CIOs surveyed, believe that cloud computing has enabled them to spend more time on business strategy and innovation. Approximately 71% who have adopted cloud computing see their position as a viable path to pursue other management roles, compared to only 44% of non–cloud adopting CIOs.

Growing Demand for Cloud Professionals and Managers

Because of the shift to the cloud, there is growing demand for professionals and managers who are more focused on business development than they are in application development. There are greater opportunities for enterprise architects, cloud architects, cloud capacity planners, cloud service managers, and business solutions consultants. Jobs being created may not always bear the term *cloud* in their titles, but cloud is at the core of their job descriptions.

Cloud-Related Job Descriptions—a few examples

Here are two excerpts from the titles and descriptions posted on online job sites. Notice that each job deeply engages the person with business strategy or operations.

- **Cloud Computing Architect:** Serves a critical role to drive the architect/design and implementation for [our] cloud-based solutions. Interact effectively with CTO, product manager, and engineering managers to drive an optimized solution under known constraints. Provide innovative idea or direction to our product.

- **Lead Software Developer—Cloud Computing Focused:** This position is a great opportunity for someone who is motivated by building high business value applications and working with smaller teams to directly influence company growth.

IT DEFINES AND CREATES BUSINESSES AND MARKETS

IT creates markets, businesses, products, and careers. As you continue to read throughout this book, exciting IT developments are changing how organizations and individuals do things. New technologies and IT-supported functions, such as the 4G networks, embedded sensors, on-demand work forces, and e-readers point to ground-breaking changes. CNN.com, one of the most respected news media, has created a new market whose impacts are yet to be realized. Visit iReport at *ireport.com/*, where a pop-up reads "iReport is the way people like you report the news. The stories in this section are not edited, fact-checked or screened before they post."

CNN.com invites everyone to become a reporter and to "take part in the news with CNN. Your voice, together with other iReporters, can help shape what CNN covers and how. At CNN we believe that looking at the news from different angles gives us a deeper understanding of what's going on. We also know that the world is an amazing place filled with interesting people doing fascinating things that don't always make the news" (*ireport.com/about.jspa*, 2010).

BUREAU OF LABOR STATISTICS (BLS), OCCUPATIONAL OUTLOOK FOR IS MANAGERS

The *Occupational Outlook Handbook*, published by the U.S. Bureau of Labor Statistics, published the occupations that have the most projected growth—2010–2020—and have a bachelor's degree as the typical level of education needed to enter the occupation. Figure 1.12 shows the occupations and their median wages.

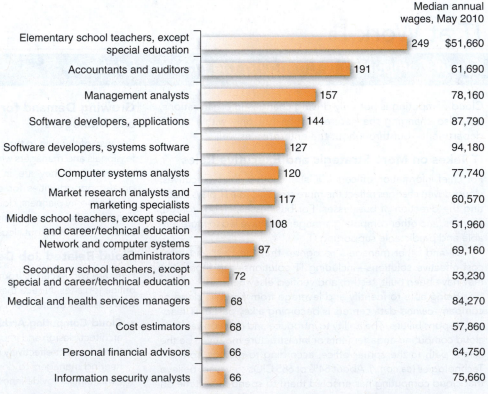

Figure 1.12 Top 13 growth occupations, 2010–2020. The highest mean annual incomes, as May 2010, are in computer, software, and systems occupations.
© U.S. Bureau of Labor Statistics, *bls.gov/opub/ooq/2011/winter/art01.pdf*

IT as a Career: The Nature of IS and IT Work. In today's workplace, it is imperative that ISs work effectively and reliably. IS managers play a vital role in the implementation and administration of technology within their organizations. They plan, coordinate, and direct research on the computer-related activities of firms. In consultation with other managers, they help determine the goals of an organization and then implement technology to meet those goals. They oversee all technical aspects of an organization, such as software development, network security, and Internet operations.

Chief technology officers (CTOs) evaluate the newest and most innovative technologies and determine how they can be applied for competitive advantage. CTOs develop technical standards, deploy technology, and supervise workers who deal with the daily IT issues of the firm. When innovative and useful new ITs are launched, the CTO determines implementation strategies, performs cost-benefit or SWOT analysis, and reports those strategies to top management, including the chief information officer (CIO).

IT project managers develop requirements, budgets, and schedules for their firm's information technology projects. They coordinate such projects from development through implementation, working with their organization's IT workers, as well as clients, vendors, and consultants. These managers are increasingly involved in projects that upgrade the information security of an organization.

IT Job Prospects. Prospects for qualified IS managers should be excellent. Workers with specialized technical knowledge and strong communications and business skills, as well as those with an MBA with a concentration in ISs, will have the best prospects. Job openings will be the result of employment growth and the need to replace workers who transfer to other occupations or leave the labor force (Bureau of Labor Statistics, 2012–2013).

Questions

1. Why is IT a major enabler of business performance and success?
2. Explain why it is beneficial to study IT today.
3. Why are IT job prospects so strong?

Key Terms

agile enterprise *10*

agility *13*

barriers to entry *17*

big data *7*

business intelligence (BI) *10*

business model *12*

business process *10*

business process reengineering (BPR) *10*

cloud computing *10*

commodity *14*

competitive advantage *14*

competitive forces model *16*

critical success factor (CSF) *19*

cycle time *10*

data analytics *6*

enterprise resource planning (ERP) *12*

inbound logistics *18*

Internet of Things *12*

IT consumerization *14*

messy data *7*

outbound logistics *18*

primary activities *18*

productivity *9*

profit margin *16*

real-time system *20*

Software-as-a-service (SaaS) *12*

support activities *19*

SWOT analysis *15*

You find clickable Link Libraries for each chapter on the Companion website.

Google Apps for Government google.com/apps/intl/en/government/

McKinsey Global Institute mckinsey.com/insights/mgi.aspx

IBM demo, "Turning insight into outcomes" ibm.com/smarterplanet/us/en/business_analytics/article/outperform_with_smarter_analytics.html

Manage All Unstructured Data with SAS Text Analytics youtube.com/watch?v=NHAq8jG4FX4

Text Analytics video from SAS software youtube.com/watch?v=NHAq8jG4FX4&feature=channel_video_title

Analysis of economic conditions, from the Federal Reserve federalreserve.gov/monetarypolicy/default.htm

Federal Cloud Computing Strategy cio.gov/documents/Federal-Cloud-Computing-Strategy.pdf

NASCAR and Hendrick Motorsports microsoft.com/casestudies/Microsoft-Lync-Server/Hendrick-Motorsports/NASCAR-racing-team-uses-Lync-to-put-themselves-in-a-position-to-win-the-race/4000011091

Five Competitive Forces That Shape Strategy, by Michael Porter youtube.com/watch?v=mYF2_FBcvXw

U.S. Bureau of Labor Statistics bls.gov/

Evaluate and Expand Your Learning

IT and Data Management Decisions

1. Visit Government Apps at *https://www.apps.gov/* and click on *Social Media Apps*. Four of the categories that you find are (1) Analytics and Search Tools, (2) Blogs and Microblogs, (3) Bookmarking/Sharing, and (4) Idea Generation/General Discussion.
   a. Select one of these four categories. Within that category, select 3 apps by clicking ENROLL for each app.
   b. Click on the URL to load the web site for the app. Then research and review its features and functions.
   c. Using a table to organize the results of your research, compare the features and functions of the three apps.
   d. Assume you have been asked to recommend one of the apps in the category to senior management. You need to decide which app provides the best overall features and functions.
   e. Prepare a one-page report that clearly explains your recommendation.

Questions for Discussion & Review

1. Select five companies you do business with. Does each one need to engage their customers, as shown in Figure 1.1? Explain why or why not.
2. What are the next big tech trends?
3. Under what conditions does cloud storage reduce costs?
4. Why is messy data important?
5. Refer to Figure 1.6. Select and explain two of the top five management concerns.
6. How can productivity be improved?
7. Consider how much time you waste trying to find a file, message, data, or other information that you know you've saved somewhere. What IT could decrease the time you waste? Explain.
8. Consider truck tires. How can embedded sensors—the Internet of things—create a competitive advantage for a transportation company?
9. Refer to your answer in #10. Which of Porter's 5 competitive forces would be impacted by the use of embedded sensors in the fleet of trucks?
10. Why or how would understanding the latest IT trends influence your career?

Online Activities

1. Visit the U.S. Department of Commerce Bureau of Economic Analysis (BEA) web site at *http://www.bea.gov/*.
   a. Review the BEA home page to learn the types of information, news, reports, and interactive data available. Search for the page that identifies *who uses BEA measures*. Identify two users of Industry Data and two users of International Trade and Investment Data.
   b. Click on the Glossary. Use the Glossary to explain GDP in your own words.
   c. Under the NEWS menu, select *U.S. Economy at a Glance*. The URL is *http://www.bea.gov/newsreleases/glance.htm*.
      (1) Review the *GDP, Current Numbers* for that last two reported quarters. How did GDP change in each of those two quarters?
      (2) Click on "View Larger Image." Review the Gross Domestic Product (GDP) Graph, which shows

the Quarter-to-Quarter Growth in Real GDP. *http://www.bea.gov/newsreleases/national/gdp/gdp_glance.htm*. Based on quarterly GDP data, are business conditions improving, stagnant, or deteriorating? Explain your answer.

2. Visit the web site of UPS (*ups.com*), Federal Express (*fedex.com*), or a comparable logistics and delivery company. Select your country.
   a. Find out what information is available to customers before they send a package.
   b. Find out about the "package tracking" system; be specific.
   c. Compute the cost of delivering a $10'' \times 20'' \times 15''$ box, weighing 20 pounds, from your location to another location. Compare the fastest delivery against the least cost.
   d. Prepare a spreadsheet for two different types of calculations available on the site. Enter data and solve for two different calculators. Use Excel.

3. Visit *YouTube.com* and search for two videos on Michael Porter's strategic or competitive forces models. For each video, report what you learned. Specify the complete URL, video title, who uploaded the video and the date, video length, and number of views.

4. Visit *Dell.com* and *Apple.com* to simulate buying a laptop computer. Compare and contrast the selection process, degree of customization, and other buying features. What are the barriers to entry into this market, based on what you learned from this exercise?

Collaborative Work

1. Your team has been tasked with researching and reporting on the growing importance of big data analytics. Your team needs to use online collaborative tools for storing and organizing the content and then writing and editing the report.
   a. Each person researches the features and benefits of one online collaborative platform or software; and distributes the analysis to all members.
   b. Using e-mail or texting, the team reviews and selects a *collaborative work space*—composed of one or more of those collaborative platforms or software.
   c. Implement your work space selected in (b).
   d. Now, each person researches and posts four big data analytics articles, PDFs, or presentations; and bookmarks several web sites to the workspace.
   e. In a report, describe the collaborative work space and the value of using that space to store and share content.

CASE 2 BUSINESS CASE

Building a Sustainable Big City with a Competitive Edge

Large cities with growing populations need to sustainably balance their social, economic and environmental resources. Two environmental concerns for urban areas are that they consume huge amounts of energy and generate 60 percent of the global carbon emissions.

Charlotte's Sustainability Plan Gives it a Competitive Edge Over Other Large Cities

In mid-2011, a public-private collaboration named *Envision Charlotte* was announced among businesses in the City of Charlotte in North Carolina, Duke Energy, and Cisco to change energy-use habits and consumer behavior. This first-of-its kind collaboration is making commercial buildings in Charlotte's urban core, known as the I-277 loop, more energy efficient—and ultimately the most sustainable urban core in the U.S.

Michael Smith, the president of Charlotte Center City Partners, explained that "Charlotte differentiates itself by taking a very 'private sector' approach to city-building through the action of corporate leadership. With *Envision Charlotte*, we are once again setting a priority (environmental sustainability) and creating an architecture that aligns infrastructure investments, policy and commerce to achieve a shared goal."

Behavioral Feedback Loops Facilitating Energy Improvements

Envision Charlotte will cut energy use in Uptown Charlotte by 20 percent and avoid approximately 220,000 metric tons of greenhouse gases by 2016. Unlike other eco-cities or smart-grid

(see *smartgridnews.com*) projects, *Envision Charlotte* provides behavioral feedback loops that show people how their behavior affects energy-usage and how to modify their actions accordingly. Feedback that is gathered is helping Duke Energy and other stakeholders develop strategies to promote energy-efficient behaviors to building occupants.

Envision Charlotte's IT Infrastructure

Verizon Wireless provided the telecommunications network that connects the digital meters, signs, and media players used in *Envision Charlotte*—creating its IT infrastructure.

As of fall 2011, large interactive screens from Cisco were installed in the lobbies of all buildings participating in *Envision Charlotte*. Using digital energy technologies connected by Verizon Wireless' 4G LTE (fourth generation) network, Duke Energy collects and processes energy usage data from about 70 participating buildings and streams it to the screens in lobbies.

Building tenants see the near real-time commercial energy consumption data for the community and suggested actions they can take to reduce their personal energy usage in the office. Having near real-time energy usage information keeps people aware and is a first step toward proactive human engagement to reduce wasted energy in commercial buildings.

Machine-to-Machine IT Supports Sustainability

Envision Charlotte is important because of its environment benefits and the application of the latest 4G technology to sustainability. Mark Bartolomeo, a Verizon Wireless vice president, pointed out: "This is a real-life example of how machine-to-machine (M2M) technology is an effective way to empower people as they become stewards for energy savings."

Sources: Compiled from *envisioncharlotte.com/(2012)*, Pentland (2011), *duke-energy.com* (2012).

Questions and Activities

1. Why was Charlotte a good candidate for this project to reduce energy waste? For your answer, research Charlotte's economic condition as of 2010–2011.

2. What competitive edge does *Envision Charlotte* provide the I-277 loop over other urban centers?

3. How is near real-time information the substitute for energy use?

4. Explain the role of the behavioral feedback loop.

5. What core technologies were needed for this project?

6. Visit the *Smart Energy Now* web site at *duke-energy.com/SmartEnergyNow/*.
   a. What information is made available to the public?
   b. In what ways does the site try to engage visitors?
   c. What might this real-time information impact or influence achieving Charlotte's goal of sustainability?

CASE 3   VIDEO CASE, PUBLIC SECTOR

ACCESS NYC—IT Strategy and Transformation

ACCESS NYC is a powerful tool that is transforming the way human services are delivered to New York City's (NYC) neediest people and families.

Under the leadership of Mayor Michael Bloomberg, NYC is using IT to increase the transparency, accountability, and accessibility of city government, focused on providing city services to an ever-broader constituency. To accelerate this objective, Mayor Bloomberg created the Integrated Human Services System (IHSS) Task Force to examine issues facing NYC's human services agencies and identify ways in which technology might be employed to enhance and streamline service delivery, while making services more efficient and responsive to residents' needs.

To do:

1. Visit: *http://www.accenture.com/us-en/Pages/success-access-nyc-it-strategy-transformation.aspx* where you find four tabs: Overview, Business Challenge, How We Helped, and High Performance Delivered.

2. From the *Overview* site
   • View the Video
   • Download and read the PDF
3. Read the Business Challenge.
4. Read How We Helped.
5. Read the High Performance Delivered.

Questions

1. Explain why disparate information systems severely limited NYC government's ability to coordinate and deliver services to residents.

2. What other challenges did the NYC agencies face trying to serve residents in need?

3. Discuss the IT issues that were addressed or solved by the NYC partnership with Accenture.

4. Describe the ACCESS NYC and performance improvements.

5. What contributed to the success of ACCESS NYC?

Data Analysis & Decision Making

Evaluating Cost-Savings from Switching to the Cloud

1. Visit *Your Company Goes Google* at *http://www.gonegoogle.com* to access the Cost Savings Calculator.
   a. Input a company name and number of employees. You will see an estimated savings per year. On that web page, you will see *Assumptions* in the upper-right corner. Click onto EDIT, and then do a screen capture or print the Assumptions. You will use this data later. Click *return* to site.
   b. Continue through the interactive demo.
   c. When complete, click *Generate my unique URL*. Copy, paste, and save your *unique URL* so you can return and edit the assumptions.
   d. Download the file as a pdf and review your results.
   e. Download the file as a pdf spreadsheet and review your results.
   f. Using your *unique URL*, return to the interactive demo and edit 5 of the values—decreasing each of them. Record which items you edited and the first values and the new values.
   g. Repeat steps (b) through (e).

h. Again using your *unique URL,* return to the interactive demo and edit the same 5 values—but this time increase each of them above the original values. Record the new values.

i. Repeat steps b through e.

j. Compare the differences in cost savings—original values, decreased values, and increased values. What is the difference in cost-savings? Explain how changes in your values impacted the cost-savings.

k. Would you recommend that the company invest in this Google solution? Explain.

l. Which report format is more useful to you, the pdf or spreadsheet? Explain why.

Resources on the Book's Web site

More resources and study tools are located on the Student web site. You'll find additional chapter materials and useful web links. In addition, self-quizzes that provide individualized feedback are available for each chapter.

References

Accenture. "Rising Use of Consumer Technology in the Workplace Forcing IT Departments to Respond, Accenture Research Finds," December 12, 2011.

Bureau of Labor Statistics (2012–2013), U.S. Department of Labor, Occupational Outlook Handbook.

Central Intelligence Agency (CIA) World Factbook, *cia.gov/library/publications/the-world-factbook/*.

Eaton, K. "Facebook More Popular Than Google? Let the Ad Wars Begin," *Fast Company,* March 16, 2010.

Envision Charlotte, *envisioncharlotte.com/*.

Gartner. Gartner Says Second Half of the Information Age to Focus on Exploitation of Technology and the Information It Processes, December 15, 2011.

Gartner. Market Trends: Gaming Ecosystem, June 10, 2011.

Golden, B. "Cloud CIO: What 'Consumerization of IT' Really Means to CIOs." *CIO Magazine,* August 12, 2011.

GoneGoogle.com

iReport, *ireport.com/*.

Jopson. B, D. Gelles, and A. Dembosky. "Retailers wait for Facebook to deliver," *The Financial Times (ft.com),* December 23, 2011.

Luftman, J., and H.S. Zadeh. "Key information technology and management issues 2010–11: An international study," *Journal of Information Technology* 26(3), September 2011.

Luftman, J.; and T. Ben-Zvi. "Key Issues for IT Executives 2010: Judicious IT Investments Continue Post-Recession," *MIS Quarterly Executive* 9(1), March 2010.

Manyika, J., et al. "Big data: The next frontier for innovation, competition, and productivity." *McKinsey Global Institute (MGI) Report,* May 2011.

McKendrick, J. "End users becoming accidental IT managers: survey." *ZDnet.com.* December 14, 2011.

McKinsey Quarterly, January 2011. *mckinseyquarterly.com*

Pentland. W. "How Charlotte Businesses Are Tackling Energy Waste Through Data." *Forbes,* December 22, 2011. *Forbes.com*

Pogue, D. "Embracing the Mothers of Invention." *New York Times.* January 25, 2012.

Porter, M. E. "Strategy and the Internet." *Harvard Business Review*, March 2001.

U.S. Government Apps, 2012. *apps.gov/*.

Quick Look

Learning Outcomes

❶ Identify current information management challenges and evaluate potential solutions.

❷ Recognize the role of IT architecture and how it guides and governs IT growth and maintenance.

❸ Map the functions of various types of information systems to the type of support needed by business operations and decision makers.

❹ Evaluate cloud-computing solutions and services.

❺ Explain the characteristics and assess the benefits of virtualization and virtual machines (VM).

You are experienced in *information management* and its benefits and challenges. You manage online accounts across multiple mobile devices and computers—and social media, texts, photos, videos, music, docs, address books, events, downloads, and other content that make up your digital library. Not being able to transfer and synchronize whenever you add a device or app is annoying and inefficient. To simplify add-ons, upgrades, sharing, and access, you might leverage cloud services such as iTunes, Instagram, Diigo, and Box.net. At some point, a user may want to start over with the latest mobile device—and re-organize everything to make dealing with information and devices easier. That's a glimpse at the information management situations facing organizations today—and why a plan is needed to guide, control, and govern IT growth. As with building construction (e.g., Figure 2.1), blueprints and models help guide and govern IT assets.

To better reflect organizational content, the term **information management** is used instead of *data management*. The most potentially valuable and challenging type is **human information**—the semistructured or unstructured content generated by humans from social media, mobile devices, search engines, and sensors as well as texts, images, audio, and video.

Figure 2.1 Blueprints and models, like those used for building construction, are needed to guide and govern an enterprise's IT assets.

To function in the *big, cloudy, mobile and social* world, companies need a well-designed set of plans—a blueprint—to guide and govern software add-ons and upgrades, hardware, systems, networks, cloud services, and other IT. These blueprints are known as **IT architectures, or enterprise architectures.** Having the right architecture in place cuts IT costs significantly and increases productivity by giving decision makers access to information, insights, and ideas where and when they need them.

CASE 1 OPENING CASE

Paul McCartney's Artistic Legacy (and Its IT Architecture)

Paul McCartney is one of the top entertainers of all time. Formerly of The Beatles (1960–1970) and Wings (1971–1981), he is listed in *Guinness World Records* as the most successful musician and composer in popular music history.

Five Decades and 1 Million+ Artifacts

McCartney has over five decades worth of recordings, videos of live concerts, short video clips, handwritten lyrics, photos, rolls of film, original works of art, and memorabilia in his personal collection. At the start of 2011, his personal collection of over 1 million artifacts was not organized or cataloged. And a large portion was in paper or analog (non-digital) format.

In 2011, McCartney's MPL Communications (McCartney Productions Ltd.) started planning a new interactive portal, *paulmccartney.com*, to provide a fun and exciting experience for fans. MPL is the holding company for his post-Beatles business interests and work (Figure 2.2).

Figure 2.2 Sir Paul McCartney's live concerts are accessible from his new interactive portal, *paulmccartney.com*

Private Collection Transformed into a Digital Library

During 2011, MPL partnered with technology company HP (*hp.com*) to develop the IT architecture needed for the content-rich interactive portal (web site). The foundation of the IT architecture is the digital library that houses Paul's collection. To create the digital library, HP collected artifacts from multiple warehouses, converted them from multiple formats—some obsolete—in digital format, then organized and cataloged them. The digital library was built using HP servers, storage, networking, and management software.

Portal and Digital Library

The web site is the portal that fans see and interact with that feeds content from the massive library. The digital library is stored on a private cloud and plugs directly into the back end of the portal. With this IT architecture, as soon as new content from concerts and other events is added to the library, it is pushed immediately to the site for fans to view.

Once the McCartney digital library was in place, HP worked with him and MPL to replace all aspects of the existing *paulmccartney.com* site, its platform, and the underlying infrastructure.

paulmccartney.com Portal

The *paulmccartney.com* portal leverages the functionality of the underlying digital library to create an engaging and immersive experience for the music community. Through the use of metatags, related content is identified and linked. For example, if a fan searches the *Rubber Soul* album, other content with "Rubber Soul" metatags such as the lyrics, photography, and videos, is displayed, too.

IT Architecture Supports Paul's Vision

McCartney wanted to "make it something really exciting." A really exciting portal was made possible by the IT architecture that powers his media business, making it simpler and more efficient for fans to identify, locate, and use assets in the huge collection. McCartney explained his vision saying:

> The idea is to intrigue people and bring them into our world with new facts, new photographs, news of what's happening, accounts of what happened, backstage moments and all the stuff we can give that nobody else can. The website really brings the digital library to life by constantly pulling new content from my personal collection so there's always a new experience for visitors (HP, 2012).

The portal also features a unique music player—The Jukebox—that fans use to listen to songs and build personal playlists with music pulled from the digital library.

At *paulmccartney.com* you can find all of McCartney's post-Beatles albums, listen to songs before buying an album, and listen to others' playlists. The *Rude Studio* lets you create your own playlist using McCartney songs, and then post the list on the site for other members to listen to and comment on. You can see all the albums a song was recorded on, the first time and location a song was played in concert, the number of times a song was played in concert, the date and location of every concert where each song was played and the set list for each of the concerts.

Jan Zadak, an HP executive vice president, said: "This is an exciting journey as we continue to work closely with Paul McCartney to develop technology solutions that will preserve and extend his legacy."

Sources: Compiled from *Mashable.com* (2012), Reuters (2012), *UltimateGuitar.com* (2011), and *hp.com* (2012).

Discuss

1. Explain the state or condition of McCartney's private collection before this visionary project began in 2011.
2. Using your answer to #1, what had to be done to get McCartney's collection ready for the digital library?
3. What are the benefits to fans of the new *paulmccartney.com* portal?
4. Why is it important to be able to offer real-time content from McCartney's concerts or other events on the portal?
5. As new content was created, how did it get to the portal?

Decide

6. Visit and review the features of *paulmccartney.com*. Consider what Jan Zadak, an HP executive vice president, said: "Fans expect a richer and deeper experience than ever before." Do you agree with this statement? Explain. What features of the portal created a richer and deeper fan experience?

Debate

7. According to MPL, the online music player Jukebox is unique. Not only can fans listen to songs and build their own playlists, but they can gain access to all information related to any particular song or album. Fans can listen to full tracks, buy albums, make dedications, and download Jukebox to their desktops. To encourage return visits, the site lets fans create a custom personal page with their profile, playlists, blogs, private messaging, and videos. Based on these features, debate whether or not the *paulmccartney.com* portal is a competitor of Facebook. Your debate should include the issue of whether or not it is a social media site.

2.1 Information Management in the 2010s

Business and career success depends on understanding and leveraging all types of data—from structured transaction data to unstructured texts. As data types and sources have changed so have information management technologies. **Information management** deals with how information is stored and organized; and the speed at which it is captured, analyzed, and reported. **Mashups** are a familiar example of information management technology. **Consumer mashups** are applications that collect and combine data from multiple public sources and then organize them through a browser-user interface. For instance, Housing Maps (*http://www.housingmaps.com*) combines Craigslist rental listings with Google Maps to show the locations of apartments available for rent.

Enterprise mashups, also referred to as business mashups, combine data from multiple internal and public sources and publish the results to enterprise portals, dashboards, or the cloud. Enterprise mashups are widely used in social media (described in Chapter 7) and to support performance management and reporting (described in Chapter 11).

In the past few years, information has increased in volume, velocity, variety, and complexity. Images, audio, video, location data, and social data from within and outside the enterprise are being captured for business purposes. These trends have major implications for information management. You'll be managing in a world that's mobile, connected, interactive, immediate and fluid—and dependent on how well information is managed.

Enterprise mashups are an information management tool that collects and integrates structured and unstructured content for business purposes.

IT (Enterprise) architecture defines the enterprise's mission, the information necessary to perform the mission, and the processes for implementing new ITs in response to business changes.

CIO Chief Information Officer, the executive in charge of IT.

INFORMATION MANAGEMENT FOR HIGH PERFORMANCE

The overall goal of information management is the design and implementation of a well-planned out IT architecture, policies, and procedures needed to effectively and efficiently support the information and decision needs of an organization. Business information is generally scattered throughout an enterprise, in separate ISs dedicated to specific purposes such as enterprise resource planning, supply chain optimization, or customer relationship management.

Major organizations have over 100 repositories (storage areas) of information. In many companies, the integration of these disparate ISs is limited—as is users' ability to access all the information they need. Providing easy access to large volumes of information is just one of the challenges facing organizations. Managing information effectively is an equally tough task. Despite all the information flowing through companies, executives, managers, and workers throughout the organization often struggle to find the information they need to make sound decisions or do their jobs.

The days of simply managing structured data are over. Now, organizations must manage semi- and unstructured content, which may be of questionable data quality, from external sources—mostly social media and the Internet.

CIOs must ensure data security and compliance with continually evolving regulatory requirements, such as the Sarbanes–Oxley Act, Basel III, the Computer Fraud and Abuse Act (CFAA), the USA PATRIOT Act, and the Health Insurance Portability and Accountability Act (HIPAA).

Issues of information access, management, and security must also deal with information degradation and disorder—where people do not understand what data means or how it can be useful.

REASONS FOR INFORMATION DEFICIENCIES

Companies' information and decision support technologies have developed over many decades. During that time span, there have been different management teams with their own priorities and understanding of the role of IT; technology

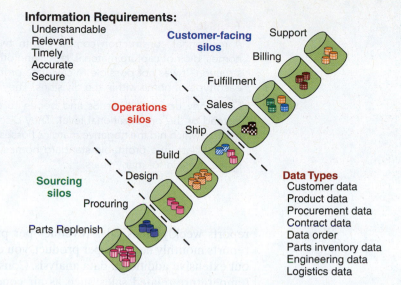

Information Requirements:
Understandable
Relevant
Timely
Accurate
Secure

Customer-facing silos

Support
Billing
Fulfillment
Sales

Operations silos

Ship
Build

Sourcing silos

Design
Procuring
Parts Replenish

Data Types
Customer data
Product data
Procurement data
Contract data
Data order
Parts inventory data
Engineering data
Logistics data

Figure 2.3 Data (or information) silos are ISs that do not have the capability to exchange data with other ISs making timely coordination and communication across functions or departments difficult.

advanced significantly and in unforeseeable ways, and IT investments were cut or increased based on competing demands on the budget. These are some of the contributing factors. Other common reasons why information deficiencies are still a problem include:

1. Data silos. Information can be *trapped* in departments' data silos (also called information silos), such as marketing or production databases. They are called silos because their data are not accessible by other ISs that need it or outside that department. Data silos are illustrated in Figure 2.3. Since silos are unable to share or exchange data, they cannot consistently be updated. When data are inconsistent across multiple enterprise applications, data quality cannot (and should not) be trusted without extensive verification. Data silos exist when there's no overall IT architecture to guide IS investments, data coordination, and communication. Data silos support a single function, and as a result, do not support an organization's cross-functional needs.

For example, most health care organizations are drowning in data, yet cannot get reliable, actionable insights from this data. Physician notes, registration forms, discharge summaries, documents, and more are doubling every five years. Unlike structured machine-ready data, this is messy data that takes too much time and effort for healthcare providers to include in their business analysis. So valuable messy data are routinely left out. Millions of patient notes and records sit inaccessible or unavailable in separate clinical data silos because historically there's been no easy way to analyze it.

2. Lost or bypassed. Data can get lost in transit from one IS to another. Or data might never get captured because of inadequately tuned data collection systems, such as those that rely on sensors or scanners. Or the data may not get captured in sufficient detail, as described in Tech Note 2.1.

3. User-fierce formats. Despite all the talk about user-friendly interfaces, some ISs are horrible to deal with. Poorly designed interfaces or formats that require extra time and effort to figure out increase the risk of errors from misunderstanding the data or ignoring it.

4. Nonstandardized. Data formats are not displayed in a uniform way or standardized format. These situations can make data analysis and comparisons difficult or impossible and increase the risk of errors. For example, if the Northeast division reports weekly gross sales revenues per product line and the Southwest division reports monthly net sales per product, you cannot compare their performance without extensive additional data analysis. Consider the extra effort needed to compare temperature-related sales, such as air conditioners, when some temperatures are expressed in Fahrenheit degrees and others in Centigrade degrees.

5. Moving targets. The information that decision makers want keeps changing—and changes faster than ISs can respond to because of the first four reasons in this list. Tracking tweets, YouTube hits, and other human information requires expensive investments—which managers find risky in an economic downturn.

These situations persist when investing in information management—done correctly—is not a priority. Companies undergoing fast growth or merger activity or those with decentralized systems (each division or business unit manages its own IT) end up with a patchwork of reporting processes. As you'd expect, patchwork systems are more complicated to modify, too rigid to support an agile business, and yet are expensive to maintain.

FACTORS DRIVING THE SHIFT FROM SILOS TO SHARING AND COLLABORATION

Senior executives and managers know about their data silos and information management problems, but they also know about the huge cost and disruption from converting to newer IT architectures. A 2011 Tech CEO Council Report (*techceocouncil.org*) highlighted that Fortune 500 companies waste $480 billion every year on inefficient business processes. However, changes are planned or

IT at Work 2.1

When ISs Fail, The Problem May Be the IT Architecture

Executives of a large chemical company were supported by an information system specifically designed for their needs—called an **executive information system (EIS)**. EISs help top management easily access relevant internal and external data for managing a company, but the value of an EIS depends on data quality.

EIS: Only Half of the Data Is Relevant

Even though it was designed for their needs, the executives found that only 50 percent of the data generated from the EIS was relevant to corporate-level decision making; and not all relevant data were available when and how they wanted it. For example, they needed current detailed sales revenue and cost data to compare the performances of strategic business units (SBU), product lines, and operating businesses. But data were not in standardized format as is needed for comparisons and accurate analysis. The cause of the problem was that SBUs were reporting sales revenues in different time frames, and many reports were delayed. Management could not get a *trusted* current view of the company's overall performance and couldn't know for sure which products were profitable. Two reasons for the failure of the EIS were:

1. **IT architecture was not designed for customized reporting.** The design of the IT architecture had been based on financial accounting rules to facilitate the preparation of financial statements and reporting to regulatory agencies, such as the SEC (Securities and Exchange Commission). This financial reporting design restricted the EIS's reporting formats. That is, it was nearly impossible to generate customized sales performance (nonfinancial) reports or do ad hoc analyses, such to evaluate inventory turnover rates by product for each region by sales quarter. Because of data inconsistencies, executives questioned the reliability of the underlying data.

When executives doubt that the numbers are current and accurate, they are not likely to use it.

2. **Complicated user interface.** Executives could not easily review and focus on key performance indicators (KPIs). Tech Note 2.2 describes KPIs. Instead, executives had to sort through a jumble of on-screen data—some useful and some irrelevant. To compensate for poor interface design, several IT analysts had to extract KPI-related data and perform analyses that executives wanted—delaying response time and driving up the cost of reporting.

Solution: New IT Architecture with Standardized Data Formats

The CIO worked with a task force to design and implement an entirely new IT architecture. Data formats were standardized company-wide to eliminate inconsistencies and provide reliable KPI reports on inventory turns, cycle times, and profit margins of all SBUs.

The new IT architecture was business-driven (instead of financial reporting driven). It was easy to modify reports—eliminating the costly and time-consuming ad hoc analyses. Fewer IT resources are needed to maintain the system. Because the underlying data are now relatively reliable, EIS use by executives increased significantly.

Questions

1. What problems did executives have with the EIS?
2. What were the two reasons for those EIS problems?
3. How did the CIO improve the EIS?
4. What are the benefits of the new IT architecture?

---

being made. An IBM study of more than 3,000 CIOs showed more than 80 percent of respondents plan to lead projects to simplify internal processes. They are struggling to integrate thousands of siloed global applications and align them with business operations.

Greater investments in collaboration technologies have been reported by research firm Forrester (*forrester.com*). Forrester identified three factors driving the trend toward collaboration and information sharing technology:

1. **Global, mobile workforce.** An estimated 62 percent of the workforce works outside an office at some point. This number is increasing.

2. **Mobility-driven consumerization.** There is a growing number of cloud-based collaboration solutions that making it easier to collaborate and share from anywhere.

3. **Principle of "any."** There is growing need to connect any body, any time, any where on any device.

BENEFITS OF INFORMATION MANAGEMENT

Benefits of information management are:

1. Improves decision quality. Improving the timeliness and quality of decision making through access to a more comprehensive set of information sources.

2. Improves predictions. The ability to predict new opportunities or challenges through pattern seeking, matching, and discovery.

3. Reduces risk. Improving enterprise compliance with regulations and policies through improved information quality and governance.

4. Reduces cost by reducing the number of repositories and time spent locating and mashing (integrating) information.

Questions

1. Explain information management.
2. Why are information deficiencies still a problem in organizations?
3. What is a data silo?
4. Explain KPIs and give an example.
5. What three factors are driving collaboration and information sharing?
6. What are the benefits of information management?

2.2 IT Architecture

As ISs become more complex, they require long-range planning. Adding new storage, applications or databases *as needed* is not sufficient. The relationship between complexity and planning is easier to see in physical things such as skyscrapers and transportation systems. If you are constructing a simple cabin in a remote area, there's no need to devise a detailed plan for expansion or to make sure that the cabin fits in its environment. If you are building a simple, single-user, nondistributed IS, you won't need a growth plan either. However, with complex electronic and social commerce, something needs to control the future direction of IT investments. The roadmap or blueprint that guides the build out of IT capabilities, acquisition of networks, cloud services, ISs, software, and hardware is referred to as **IT architecture,** or **enterprise architecture**. The basic components of IT architecture are shown in Table 2.1.

NEED FOR LONG-TERM PLANNING TO MANAGE GROWTH

The IT architecture defines the vision, standards, and roadmap that guide the priorities, operations, and management of the ITs supporting the business. Recall that the top five management concerns, as you read in Chapter 1 and Figure 1.6, are the following:

1. Business productivity and cost reduction

2. IT and business alignment

3. Business agility and speed to market

4. Business process reengineering (BPR)

5. IT reliability and efficiency

TABLE 2.1	Components of IT Architecture
Business architecture	The processes the business uses to meet its goals.
Application architecture	How specific applications are designed and how they interact with each other.
Data architecture	How an enterprise's data stores are organized and accessed.
Technical architecture	The hardware and software infrastructure that supports applications and their interactions.

TABLE 2.2 | Uses and Benefits of IT Architecture

- Maintain a close alignment between IT deliverables and business requirements.
- Improve ability to respond quickly to business changes.
- Develop closer partnerships between business and IT groups.
- Reduce the risk of failed or unnecessary ISs.
- Reduce complexity of existing ISs.
- Improve agility of new IT systems.
- Ensure that legal and regulatory requirements are being met.

According to MIT Sloan School of Management professor Michael A. Cusumano, business agility comes in different forms, but basically it's the ability to anticipate, adapt quickly to, and lead change (Hopkins, 2011). The uses and benefits of the IT architecture, as shown in Table 2.2, address all five of those concerns. Success of IT architecture can be measured in financial terms of profitability and return on investment (ROI), and in terms of customer satisfaction, speed to market, and employee turnover.

IT ARCHITECTURE: THE PLAN TO MAINTAIN IT-BUSINESS ALIGNMENT

The IT architecture reduces the risk of buying or building ISs that are incompatible and unnecessarily costly to maintain and integrate—and continuously evolves toward the desired or target architecture, as shown in Figure 2.4. The **target architecture** is a vision of the future that evolves *in advance of it being achieved*. Therefore, at no time will a specific target architecture ever be achieved.

An IT architecture defines the following:

1. The organization's mission, business functions, and future direction
2. Information and information flows needed to perform the mission
3. Processes for implementing new ITs in response to business changes
4. The current baseline architecture
5. The desired target architecture
6. The sequencing plan, which consists of the short- and long-term strategies for managing the change from baseline to target architecture

POSSIBLE CONFLICT

In an organization, there may be a culture of distrust between the technology and business folks. No enterprise-architecture methodology can bridge this divide unless there is a genuine commitment to change. That commitment must come from the highest level of the organization. Methodologies cannot solve people problems; they can only provide a framework in which those problems can be solved.

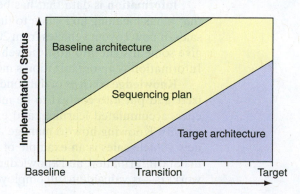

Figure 2.4 IT architecture transition plan to maintain the IT-business alignment. Changes in priorities and business are reflected in the target architecture to help keep IT aligned with them.
© Practical Guide to Federal Enterprise Architecture, *gao.gov/bestpractices/bpeaguide.pdf*, p. 66.

IT at Work 2.2

Gartner's View of Enterprise Architecture

Enterprise architecture is a verb, not a noun. What does it mean to say that architecture is a verb, not a noun? It means that enterprise architecture is the ongoing process of creating, maintaining, and leveraging IT, according to consulting firm Gartner.

Starts with a Shared Vision of the Future

Enterprise architectures must start with where an organization is going—*its target*—not with where it is. Gartner recommends that an organization begin by telling the story of where its strategic direction is heading and the business drivers that they are responding to. The goal is making sure that everybody understands and shares a single vision. As soon as managers have defined this single shared vision of the future, they then consider the implications of this vision on the business, technical, information, and solutions architectures of the enterprise. The shared vision of the future will dictate changes in all of these architectures,

assign priorities to those changes, and keep those changes grounded in business value.

Focus Is on Strategy

Enterprise architecture is about strategy, not about engineering. It is focused on the destination. The two things that are most important are *where an organization is going* and *how it will get there*. There are two problems that the IT architecture is designed to address:

1. **IT systems complexity.** IT systems have become unmanageably complex and expensive to maintain.

2. **Poor business alignment.** Organizations find it difficult to keep their increasingly expensive IT systems aligned with business need.

Questions

1. Explain the relationship between complexity and planning. Give an example.
2. Explain IT architecture.
3. What are the four components of IT architecture?
4. What are the uses and benefits of IT architecture?
5. How are baseline architecture, sequencing plan, and target architecture related?
6. Why should the organization's target architecture never be achieved?

2.3 Information Systems and IT Infrastructure

Information systems are built to achieve specific goals, such as processing customer orders and payroll. In general, ISs process data into information and knowledge.

DATA, INFORMATION, AND KNOWLEDGE

Data, or raw data, refers to a basic description of products, customers, events, activities, and transactions that are recorded, classified, and stored. Data are the raw material from which information is produced; and the quality, reliability, and integrity of the data must be maintained for the information to be useful. Examples are the number of hours an employee worked in a certain week or the number of new Toyota vehicles sold in the first quarter of 2013.

A **database** is a repository that consists of stored data organized for access, search, retrieval, and update.

Information is data that has been processed, organized, or put into context so that it has meaning and value to the person receiving it. For example, the quarterly sales of new Toyota vehicles from 2010 through 2014 is information because it would give some insight into how the vehicle recalls during 2009 and 2010 impacted sales. Information is an organization's most important asset, second only to people.

Knowledge consists of data and/or information that have been processed, organized, and put into context to be meaningful, and to convey understanding, experience, accumulated learning, and expertise as they apply to a current problem or activity. Knowing how to manage a vehicle recall to minimize negative impacts on new vehicle sales is an example of knowledge. Figure 2.5 illustrates the differences in data, information, and knowledge. Organizational knowledge—the expertise of its workers—is valuable to all employees and the bottom line.

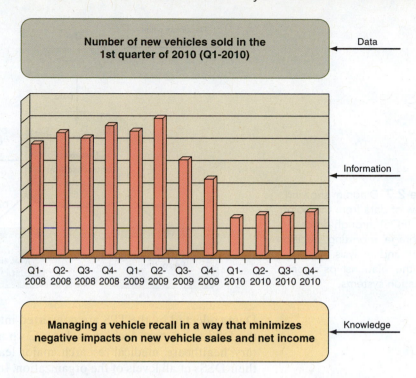

Figure 2.5 Examples of data, information, and knowledge.

The collection of computing systems used by an organization is termed **information technology (IT).** In its broadest sense, IT describes an organization's collection of information systems, their users, and the management that oversees them. Often the term *information technology* is used interchangeably with *information system (IS).*

ISs collect (input) and process data, distribute reports (outputs), and support decision making and business processes. Figure 2.6 shows the input-processing-output (IPO) model.

Figure 2.7 shows how major types of ISs relate to each other and how data flows among them. In this example,

1. Data from online purchases are captured and processed by the TPS, or transaction processing system and then stored in the transactional database.

2. Data needed for reporting purposes are extracted from the database and used by the MIS, management information system, to create periodic, ad hoc, or other types of reports.

3. Data are output to a decision-support system (DSS) where they are analyzed using formulas, financial ratios, or models.

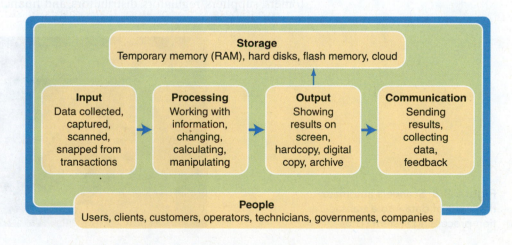

Figure 2.6 Input-processing-output model of ISs.

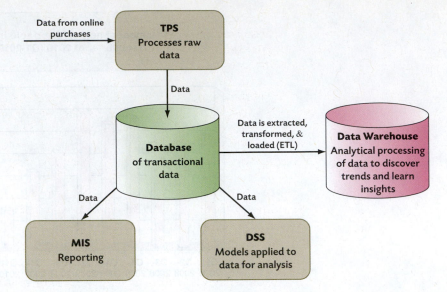

Figure 2.7 Diagram showing the flow of data from the point of sale (POS) through processing, storage, reporting, decision support, and analysis. Also shows the relationships among information systems.

Data collected by the TPS are converted into reports by the MIS and analyzed by the DSS to support decision making. Corporations, government agencies, the military, healthcare, medical research, major league sports, and nonprofits depend on their DSSs at all levels of the organization. Innovative DSSs create and help sustain competitive advantages. DSSs reduce waste in production operations, improve inventory management, support investment decisions, and predict demand. The **model** of a DSS consists of a set of formulas and functions, such as statistical, financial, optimization, and/or simulation models.

Customer data, sales, and other critical data are selected for additional analysis, such as trend analysis or forecasting demand. These data are extracted from the database, transformed into a standard format, and then loaded into a data warehouse.

Transaction Processing Systems (TPS). **Transaction processing systems** are designed to process specific types of data input from ongoing transactions. TPSs can be manual, as when data are typed into a form on a screen, or automated by using scanners or sensors to capture data. Figure 2.8 shows input of barcode data via a handheld scanner.

Organizational data are processed by a TPS—sales orders, payroll, accounting, financial, marketing, purchasing, inventory control, and so forth. Transactions are either:

- **Internal transactions** that originate within the organization or that occur within the organization. Examples are payroll, purchases, budget transfers, and payments (in accounting terms, they're referred to as *accounts payable*).

- **External transactions** that originate from outside the organization, e.g., from customers, suppliers, regulators, distributors, and financing institutions.

Figure 2.8 Scanners automate the input of data into a transaction processing system (TPS).

TPSs are critical systems. Transactions that do not get captured can result in lost sales, dissatisfied customers, and many other types of data errors with financial impacts. For example, if the accounting department issued a check to pay an invoice (bill) and it was cashed by the recipient, but information about that transaction was not captured, then two things happen. One, the amount of cash listed on the company's financial statements is wrong because there was no deduction for the amount of the check. Second, the accounts payable (A/P) system will continue to show the invoice as unpaid, so the accounting department might pay it a second time. Likewise, if services are provided, but the transactions are not recorded, the company will not bill for them and not collect that service revenue.

Batch vs. Online Real-Time Processing. Data captured by a TPS are processed and stored in a database, and then is available for use by other systems. Processing of transactions is done in one of two modes:

1. **Batch processing:** A TPS in batch processing mode collects all transaction for a day, shift, or other time period, and then processes the data and updates the data stores. Payroll processing done weekly or bi-weekly is an example of batch mode.

2. **Online transaction processing (OLTP) or real-time processing:** The TPS processes each transaction as it occurs, which is what is meant by the term *real-time processing*. In order for OLTP to occur, the input device or web site must be directly linked via a network to the TPS. Airlines need to process flight reservations in realtime to verify that seats are available.

Batch processing costs less than real-time processing. A disadvantage is that data are inaccurate because they are not updated immediately, in real time.

Data Quality. The more efficiently and thoroughly an organization gathers, stores, processes, retrieves and uses its data, the more productive it is.

Processing improves data quality, which is important because reports and decisions are only as good as the data they are based upon. As data are collected or captured, they are validated to detect and correct obvious errors and omissions. For example, if a customer sets up an account with a company, such as *Amazon.com*, to purchase from their web site, the TPS will validate that the address, city, and postal code are consistent and also that those data items match the address, city, and postal code of the credit card. If required fields of the online form are not completed or they have obvious errors, the customer is required to make the corrections before the data is processed any further.

Data errors detected later may be difficult to correct, expose the company to legal action, or may never be detected and corrected. You can better understand the difficulty of detecting and correcting errors by considering identity theft. Victims of identity theft face enormous challenges and frustration trying to correct data about them stored in databases.

MANAGEMENT INFORMATION SYSTEMS

The functional areas or departments—accounting, finance, production/operations, marketing and sales, human resources, and engineering and design—are supported by ISs designed for their particular reporting needs. General-purpose reporting systems are referred to as management information systems (MIS). Their objective is to provide reports to managers for tracking operations, monitoring, and control.

Typically, a functional system provides reports about such topics as operational efficiency, effectiveness, and productivity by extracting information from databases and processing it according to the needs of the user. Types of reports are the following:

• **Periodic:** These reports are created or run according to a pre-set schedule. Examples are daily, weekly, and quarterly. Reports are easily distributed via e-mail, blogs, internal web sites (called *intranets*), or other electronic media. Periodic reports are also easily ignored if workers don't find them worth the time to review.

Figure 2.9 Sample report produced by an MIS.

- **Exception:** Exception reports are generated only when something is outside the norm, either higher or lower than expected. Sales in hardware stores prior to a hurricane may be much higher than the norm. Or sales of fresh produce may drop during a food contamination crisis. Exception reports are more likely to be read because workers know that some unusual event or deviation has occurred.

- **Ad hoc:** Ad hoc reports are unplanned reports. They are generated to a screen or in print on an *as needed* basis. They are generated on request to learn more about a situation, problem, or opportunity.

Reports can include tables of data and data charts, as shown in Figure 2.9. With easy-to-use multimedia technology, reports can also include video, audio, and links to other reports.

Functional information systems that support business analysts and other departmental employees can be fairly complex, depending on the type of employees supported. The following examples show the support that IT provides to major functional areas.

1. Bolsa de Comercio de Santiago, a large stock exchange in Chile, is now able to process high-volume trading in microseconds using IBM software. The stock exchange increased its transaction capacity by 900 percent by 2011. By improving the speed that its system operates and applying analytics, the exchange significantly improved order routing, giving its traders visibility in to business activity in real time.

The Chilean stock exchange system can do the detective work of analyzing current and past transactions and market information, learning and adapting to market trends and connecting its traders to business information in real time. Ultrafast throughput in combination with analytics allows traders to make more accurate decisions. As a result, the company is more competitive in the financial services industry.

2. According to the *New England Journal of Medicine*, one in five patients suffer from preventable readmissions, which cost taxpayers an extra $17.4 billion per year. Beginning in 2012, hospitals are penalized for high readmission rates with cuts in the payments they receive from the government. Using a DSS and predictive analytics, the healthcare industry can leverage unstructured information in new ways not possible before, according to Charles J. Barnett, President/CEO of Seton Health care Health care Family. "With this solution, we can access an integrated view of relevant clinical and operational information to drive more informed decision making. For example, by predicting which patients might be readmitted, we can reduce costly and preventable readmissions, decrease mortality rates, and ultimately improve the quality of life for our patients."

3. Army Trains Soldiers with Virtual Worlds. The U.S. Army enlists video games and virtual worlds to teach soldiers interpersonal skills and cultural awareness for combat environments such as Iraq and Afghanistan. The IT supports computerized exercises that can sharpen physical reflexes and shooting skills. It prepares soldiers for a war and with the desire to win. The new systems train for difficult communication situations abroad (Gonsalves, 2008). For example, negotiation skills are heavily dependent on culture. Soldiers learn how to think and communicate under pressure and stress. The system is a multiplayer simulation game with up to 64 players on the networked computer system over an intranet. Players direct their avatars through the realistic war zone cyberspace. The interactions practiced in the game help soldiers deal with local customs, build trust with natives in foreign war zones, and equip and train locals to aid U.S. military efforts.

DECISION SUPPORT SYSTEMS (DSS)

Decision support systems are interactive applications that support decision making. Configurations of a DSS range from relatively simple applications that support a single user to complex enterprise-wide systems, as at Western Petro described in *IT at Work 2.1*. A DSS can support the analysis and solution of a specific problem, to evaluate a strategic opportunity, or to support ongoing operations. These systems support unstructured and semi-structured decisions, such as whether to make or buy products, or what new products to develop and introduce into existing markets.

Degree of Structure of Decisions.

Decisions range from structured to unstructured. Structured decisions are those that have a well-defined method for solving and the data needed to reach a decision. An example of a structured decision is determining whether an applicant qualifies for an auto loan, or whether to extend credit to a new customer—and the terms of those financing options. **Structured decisions** are relatively straightforward, are made on a regular basis, and an IS can insure that they are done consistently.

At the other end of the continuum are **unstructured decisions** that depend on human intelligence, knowledge, and/or experience—as well as data and models to solve. Examples include deciding which new products to develop or which new markets to enter. Semistructured decisions are in the middle of the continuum. DSSs are best suited to support these types of decisions, but they are also used to support unstructured ones. To provide such support, DSSs have certain characteristics to support the decision maker and the decision making process.

Three Defining DSS Characteristics.

Three characteristics of DSSs are:

1. An easy-to-use interactive interface

2. Models or formulas that enable sensitivity analysis, *what if* analysis, goal seeking, and risk analysis

3. Data from multiple sources—internal and external sources plus data added by the decision maker who may have insights relevant to the decision situation.

Having models is what distinguishes DSS from MIS. Some models are developed by end users through an interactive and iterative process. Decision makers can manipulate models to conduct experiments and sensitivity analyses, for example *what if* and *goal seeking*. **What-if analysis** refers to changing assumptions or data in the model to see the impacts of the changes on the outcome. For example, if sale forecasts are based on a 5 percent increase in customer demand, a what if analysis would replace the 5 percent with higher and/or lower estimates to determine *what* would happen to sales *if* demand changed. With **goal seeking,** the decision maker has a specific outcome in mind and needs to figure out how that outcome could be achieved and whether it's feasible to achieve that desired outcome. A DSS can also estimate the risk of alternative strategies or actions.

California Pizza Kitchen (CPK) uses a DSS to support inventory decisions. CPK has 77 restaurants located in various states in the U.S. Maintaining optimal inventory levels at all restaurants was challenging and time consuming. A DSS was built to make it easy for the managers to keep records updated and make decisions. Many CPK restaurants increased sales by 5 percent after implementing a DSS.

Building DSS Applications. **Planners Lab** is an example of software for building DSSs. The software is free to academic institutions and can be downloaded from *plannerslab.com*. Planners Lab includes:

- An easy-to-use model building language
- An easy-to-use option for visualizing model output, such as answers to what-if and goal-seeking questions to analyze the impacts of different assumptions

These tools enable managers and analysts to build, review, and challenge the assumptions upon which their decision scenarios are based. With Planners Lab, decision makers can experiment and play with assumptions to assess multiple views of the future.

DATABASE VOLATILITY AND DATA WAREHOUSING

Given the huge number of transactions, the data in databases are constantly in use and/or undergoing change. This characteristic of databases—referred to as **volatility**—makes it impossible to use them for complex decision making and problem-solving tasks. For this reason, data are extracted, transformed, and loaded (ETL) into a warehouse where it is better formatted for simple to advanced analyses. Real-time and near-real-time analyses need sophisticated systems, IT platforms, and data repositories, such as data warehouses.

Example: Withdrawing Cash from an Automatic Teller Machine, ATM. When cash is withdrawn from an ATM, a TPS processes the data by verifying the available funds, subtracting the withdrawal amount, and then updating and storing the output data to a database. Data are extracted from the database, organized, and reported by an MIS.

ISs EXIST WITHIN A CULTURE

ISs do not exist in isolation. ISs have a purpose and a social (organizational) context. A common *purpose* is to provide a solution to a business problem. The *social context* of the system consists of the values and beliefs that determine what is admissible and possible within the culture of the organization and people involved. For example, a company may believe that superb customer service and on-time delivery are critical success factors. This belief system influences IT investments among other things.

The business value of IT is determined by the people who use them, the business processes they support, and the culture of the organization. That is, IS value is determined by the relationships among ISs, people, and business processes—all of which are influenced strongly by organizational culture, as shown in Figure 2.10.

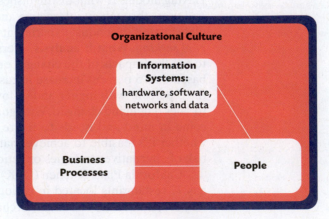

Figure 2.10 Organizational culture plays a significant role in the use and benefits of information systems.

ISs Extend Organizations and Disrupt Ways of Doing Business. The mass migration of users from PCs to mobile devices has expanded ISs beyond the organization and made *location* practically irrelevant. Perhaps equally significant, mobile technology has integrated our business and personal lives.

IT innovations are shaking-up or disrupting the ways companies do business, the jobs of managers and workers, the design of business processes, and the structure of markets. *IT at Work 2.3* describes how an IS that provided feedback to call center operators at 1-800-CONTACTS disrupted how they performed their jobs, and motivated performance improvements, and ultimately sales revenues.

IT at Work 2.3

Feedback and Incentives Improve Performance at 1-800-Contacts

The company 1-800-Contacts transformed and disrupted the way to buy contact lenses and became the world's largest contact lens store. Their business model is to make millions of customers happy with convenient ordering, great value, fast delivery, 100 percent satisfaction guarantee, and the best customer service.

The company stocks more than 20 million contact lenses, and delivers over 150,000 replacement contact lenses every day directly to customers. As a result of its extensive inventory, the company is able to ship 95 percent of its orders within one business day. High volume, cost-efficient operations enable 1-800 CONTACTS to offer products at competitive prices while delivering a high level of customer service.

New Reporting Systems Needed by Call Centers Managers and Operators

The company grew to the point where its ISs could not provide the call center managers and business analysts with quick and easy access to real-time (up-to-date) sales data. For example, when business analysts wanted to review the average number of contact lens boxes shipped per order, they had to get the data from the IT department. Response time was several days. Managers faced an information bottleneck that created *blind spots* (a blind spot means not knowing what's going on as it's going on) about sales and inventory levels until IT provided the reports.

Dashboard Reporting Tools

Information dashboard—easy-to-understand reporting tools as shown in Figure 2.11—were implemented in the call centers. Each call center operator could monitor his performance by looking at the on-screen dashboards.

Operators' and Business Performance Increased

Dashboards are updated every 15 minutes. At a glance, operators know their closing ratio, average sales, calls-per-hour—and how their performance compares to other operators. They are also evaluated in terms of customer satisfaction, which is critical to customer loyalty, sales growth, and profitability. At month's end, operators are ranked; and those in the top 80 percent receive bonuses. Top-ranked operators earn monthly bonuses of $1,000 or more, which is a motivating-sized bonus.

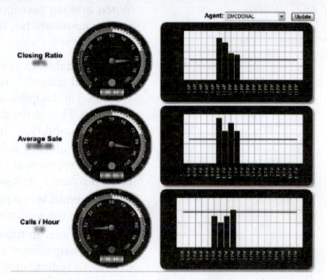

Figure 2.11 Dashboards keep operators informed of their sales performance in 15-minute intervals.

By linking operators' pay to performance, sales increased by $50,000 per month. Once operators could see that their performance tied into their bonus, their overall quality has improved.

Sources: Compiled from Microsoft SQL Server Case Study and Watson and Hill (2009).

Questions

1. What were the information and reporting problems the company faced?
2. How did business analysts get the data they needed?
3. What was the effect of linking operators' pay to business performance? That is, how did feedback at the operator's level lead to improved performance at the organizational level?
4. Why do you think the dashboards updated frequently (every 15 minutes) instead only at the end of the operator's workday?

IT INFRASTRUCTURE

The role of the IT department, or **IT function** as it's sometimes called, is to insure the reliability of the enterprise's IT infrastructure. What an organization's IT infrastructure can support is determined by five major components: (1) hardware; (2) software; (3) networks and communication facilities, including the Internet and intranets; (4) databases and data workers; and (5) information management personnel.

The design of the IT infrastructure determines the ability to efficiently store, protect, and manage data so that they can be made accessible, searchable, shareable, and, ultimately, actionable.

In the past, IT managers only had two options—to build or buy the technology. Now they also have the option of **cloud computing,** in which the technology is rented or leased on a regular or as-needed basis. Cloud computing gets its name from the Internet, which you usually see represented as a cloud. Examples are data storage and computing hardware that are accessed via the Internet instead of being company-owned and on-site in a data center. Cloud computing delivers IT capabilities as *services* over the Internet, allowing them to be managed and accessed via the Internet. Cloud computing services are many times more cost effective than traditional data centers.

ACQUIRING INFRASTRUCTURE COMPONENTS

When making decisions about how to acquire hardware, software, or any of these five components, the following four characteristics of an IT infrastructure need to be considered.

1. Dependable. Dependability means that the infrastructure meets availability, reliability, and scalability requirements of the company's information systems (TPS, MIS, DSS, etc.) and applications. Applications inherit their dependability from the IT infrastructure. That is, the dependability of applications is limited by (is only as good as) the dependability of the IT architecture.

2. Manageable. IT infrastructure determines the complexity of managing the hardware and software that are required to deliver dependable applications. A wireless infrastructure is necessary for interactivity and mobile computing applications.

3. Adaptable. When additional application capacity is needed, organizations are able to scale up the infrastructure as needed.

4. Affordable. In today's IT reality, dependability, manageability, and adaptability are not as significant as affordability. For example, older infrastructures may need expensive redundancy, or backup systems, to ensure these characteristics.

With this understanding of IT infrastructure, we can intelligently examine the reasons why enterprises are investing in cloud computing and virtualization.

Speed and Reliability. When employees log into the company network or e-mail accounts, or access data or documents to perform their jobs, the speed of the response and the reliability of the hardware are critical factors. Delays due to heavy network traffic or system crashes waste time and are frustrating. Of course, everyone wants fast response, quick processing, and rapid access to information or files from various ISs and databases. It is the company's IT infrastructure that determines the workload that ISs, apps, and mobile computing devices can handle and their speed, as you will read in the next section on cloud computing and services.

Questions

1. Contrast data, information, and knowledge.
2. Define TPS and give an example.
3. When is batch processing used?
4. When is real-time processing needed?
5. Explain why TPSs need to process incoming data before storing it in a database.
6. Define MIS and DSS and give an example of each.
7. Why are databases inappropriate for doing data analysis?
8. Define IT infrastructure.

2.4 Cloud Computing and Services

In a business world where first movers gain the advantage and IT is central to every decision, IT responsiveness and agility provide a competitive edge. Yet many IT infrastructures are exorbitantly expensive to manage and too complex to easily adapt. A common solution is cloud computing. *Cloud computing* is the general term for infrastructures that use the Internet and private networks to access, share, and deliver computing resources, as shown in Figure 2.12. The National Institute of Standards and Technology (NIST, *nist.gov*) more precisely defines cloud computing as "a model for enabling convenient, on-demand network access to a shared pool of configuration computing resources that can be rapidly provisioned and released with minimal management effort or service provider interaction" (NIST, 2012).

CLOUD INFRASTRUCTURE

The design of the IT infrastructure determines how data is stored, protected, and managed—and the degree to which it is accessible, searchable, shareable, and, actionable. When the infrastructure cannot meet current data needs or when better, improved performance is needed, companies are turning to cloud computing options.

The cloud has greatly expanded the options for enterprise IT infrastructures because any device that accesses the Internet can access, share, and deliver data. Cloud computing is an important infrastructure because it:

1. Provides a dynamic infrastructure that makes apps and computing power available on demand. Apps and power are available on demand because they are provided *as a service*. For example, any software that's provided on demand is referred to as **software as a service,** or **SaaS.** Typical SaaS products are Google Apps and Salesforce Sales CRM. See Tech Note 2.3.

2. Helps companies become more agile and responsive while significantly reducing IT costs and complexity through improved workload optimization and service delivery.

Tech Note 2.3

Software-as-a-Service (SaaS) is an increasingly popular IT model in which software is available to users as needed. Other terms for SaaS are *on-demand computing*, *utility computing*, and *hosted services*. The idea is basically the same: instead of buying and installing expensive packaged enterprise applications, users can access software apps over a network, with an Internet browser being the only absolute necessity. Usually, there is no hardware and software to buy, since the apps are used over the Internet and paid for through a fixed subscription fee, or payable per an actual usage fee. The SaaS model was developed to overcome the common challenge to an enterprise of being able to meet fluctuating demands on IT resources efficiently.

Figure 2.12 Cloud computing using the Internet and private networks to access, share, and deliver computing resources.

WHY USE THE CLOUD?

Optimizing IT infrastructure at low cost became especially critical after the 2008 financial crises when cost cutting became a priority. During recessions, making the most of IT assets becomes more of a concern for competitive advantage and ultimately, survival. The cloud offers a steep drop in IT costs because apps are hosted by vendors and provided on demand (as services), rather than via physical installations or seat licenses (Han, 2011).

MOVE TO ENTERPRISE CLOUDS

A majority of large organizations have hundreds or thousands of software licenses that support business processes, such as licenses for Microsoft Office, Oracle database management, IBM CRM (customer relationship management), and various network security software. Managing software and their licenses involves deploying, provisioning, and updating them—all of which are time consuming and expensive. Cloud computing over comes these problems. Procuring a physical machine can take days or weeks, but a VM can be provisioned in one business day.

All large software vendors either have offerings in cloud space or are in the process of launching one. In addition there are many startups that have interesting products in cloud space. Cloud services can free companies from having to pay for their own software, hardware, facilities, maintenance, and management. Major software vendors who are also cloud services vendors are listed in Table 2.3.

Other large companies in the cloud services market are Google and Amazon. Google Apps provides common business apps that are accessed from a web browser, while the software and data are stored on the servers. Google's online word-processing apps are accessed online through a browser instead of stored on a computer. Companies pay to use Amazon's e-commerce and order fulfillment infrastructure, in effect, renting it, rather than building their own. *The New York Times* uses Amazon cloud service to upload images of archived newspapers and convert them into a more readable format. Nasdaq OMX Group Inc. uses Amazon's service to provide historical trading information. Both companies pay only for the computing resources or services they use.

PRIVATE CLOUDS

The cloud idea is to store apps and data in the vendors' data centers, rather than on local company-owned servers. Of course, that means data is stored *outside a customer's internal network*. Companies or government agencies that need greater security and data confidentiality set up their own clouds, called **private clouds,** on servers that they own.

TABLE 2.3	Five Major Cloud Vendors
Oracle (*oracle.com*)	Oracle is considered to be a major arms dealer for public and private clouds. Oracle Public Cloud includes database as a service (DaaS), platform as a service (PaaS), Oracle Social Network (OSN), Fusion CRM, and the RightNow cloud customer service products.
IBM (*ibm.com*)	IBM is another arms dealer to the cloud and an infrastructure and platform vendor. Cloud offerings include Smart Business Storage Cloud and Computing on Demand (CoD).
SAP (*sap.com*)	SAP moved Business One, its small business solution, to the cloud. For joint customers of SAP and IBM, IBM cloud computing solutions offers on-demand SAP apps.
Salesforce.com	*Salesforce.com* offers CRM apps, PaaS, and social networking with Chatter, sales force automation with the Sales Cloud, and a marketplace for cloud apps with App Exchange.
Microsoft Windows Azure (*Microsoft.com*)	In 2011, Microsoft made one major cloud acquisition, Skype. From a cloud perspective, Microsoft has focused on its infrastructure and platform offerings called Azure.

IT at Work 2.4

Cloud Pro Leverages iPad's touch: Benefits Start-Ups

The trend in cloud hosting by a vendor increased with the introduction of helpful apps. Rackspace (*rackspace.com*) launched Cloud Pro in April 2010. Cloud Pro leverages iPad's touch interface to enable its customers to manage their servers. Using iPad, network administrators (admins) can turn on backups for a server; create new servers from backups; manage backup scheduling; and reboot, rename, resize, and delete servers. Network admins can perform these functions anytime and from anywhere using their mobiles. The app is available at no additional charge through Apple's iTunes store. A list of latest features is posted on *rackspacecloud.com/ipad*.

This arrangement is of enormous benefit to start-up companies. The iPad tablet and Rackspace Cloud servers lower the entry barriers for Web start-ups because they no longer have to make large investments in hardware to get their businesses going.

App developer Mike Mayo who developed the Rackspace Cloud app for the iPhone and Cloud Pro for theiPad, pointed out the significance of this service:

It's amazing to think that racks of servers in corporations once managed by entire IT teams can now be handled by one person with the touch of a finger using an iPad tablet from anywhere. . . . I believe the mobility and functionality made possible by the Apple iPad and The Rackspace Cloud has the potential to transform the way business applications are managed.

Questions

1. Consider this statement: *Cloud computing is about the flexible delivery of services at the point of need.* Explain how Cloud Pro offers flexible delivery of network management (the service). Explain how it offers that service to network admins at the *point of need* (e.g., while on vacation or away from the office).

2. Discuss one benefit and one disadvantage of Cloud Pro for network admins.

3. Search and view a video demo of Rackspace's Cloud Pro for the iPad. Does the app have amazing features, as Mike Mayo described?

Issues in Moving Workloads from the Enterprise to the Cloud. Building a cloud strategy is a challenge, and moving existing apps to the cloud is stressful. Despite the business and technical benefits, there is the risk of disrupting operations or customers in the process. With the cloud, the network and WAN (wide area network) become an even more critical part of the IT infrastructure. Network bandwidth is needed to support the increase in network traffic. And putting part of the IT architecture or workload into the cloud requires different management approaches—and different IT skills.

Strategic Issues. Strategy questions include deciding:

1. Which workloads should be exported to the cloud.
2. Which set of standards to follow for cloud computing.
3. How to resolve issues of privacy and security as things move out to the cloud.
4. How departments or business units will get new IT resources. Should they help themselves, or should IT remain a gatekeeper?

Vendor Management Issues. There are different vendor management skills. Staff experienced in managing outsourcing projects have some of the needed expertise for managing work in the cloud, such as defining and policing **service-level agreements (SLAs)** with vendors. An SLA is a negotiated agreement between a customer and service provider that can be a legally binding contract or an informal contract. Google Apps SLA is posted at *google.com/apps/intl/en/terms/sla.html*.

Infrastructure Issues. There's a big difference because cloud computing runs on a shared infrastructure, so the arrangement is less customized to a specific company's requirements. A comparison to help understand the challenges is that outsourcing is like renting an apartment while the cloud is like getting a room at a hotel.

With cloud computing, it may be more difficult to get to the root of performance problems, like the unplanned outages that occurred with Google's Gmail and Workday's human resources apps. The trade-off is cost vs. control.

Increasing demand for faster and more powerful computers, and increases in the number and variety of applications is driving the need for more capable IT architectures.

Questions

1. Describe cloud computing.
2. What are the benefits of cloud computing?
3. Describe software-as-a-service (SaaS) and its benefits.
4. How can cloud computing ease the problems of managing software licenses?
5. List five major cloud vendors.
6. When are private clouds used instead of public clouds?
7. Explain three issues that need to be addressed when moving to cloud computing or services.

2.5 Virtualization and VM (Virtual Machines)

Computer hardware had been designed to run a single operating system (OS) and a single app, leaving most computers vastly underutilized. **Virtualization** is a technique that creates a virtualization layer and multiple virtual machines (VM) to run on a single physical machine. The virtualization layer makes it possible for each VM to share the resources of the hardware. Figure 2.13 shows the relationship among the VMs and hardware.

WHAT IS A VIRTUAL MACHINE?

A **virtual machine** is a software layer (virtualization layer) that runs its own OS and apps as if it were a physical computer as shown in Figure 2.13. A VM behaves exactly like a physical computer and contains its own virtual—that is software-based—CPU, RAM (random access memory), hard drive, and network interface card (NIC). An OS cannot tell the difference between a VM and a physical machine, nor can apps or other computers on a network tell the difference. Even the VM thinks it is a "real" computer. Just like a physical computer, a VM hosts its own guest OS and app, and has all the components found in a physical computer (motherboard, VGA card, network card controller, etc.). Yet, a VM is composed

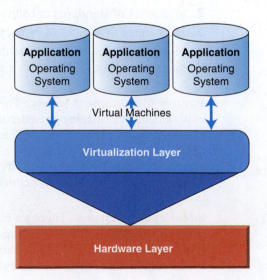

Figure 2.13 Virtual machines running on a simple hardware layer (computer).

entirely of software and contains no hardware components whatsoever. As a result, VM offer advantages over physical hardware.

Virtualization is a concept that has several meanings in IT and therefore several definitions. The major type of virtualization is hardware virtualization, which remains popular and widely used. Virtualization is often a key part of an enterprise's disaster recovery plan. In general, virtualization separates business applications and data from hardware resources. This separation allows companies to pool hardware resources—rather than dedicate servers to applications—and assign those resources to applications as needed.

The major types of virtualization are the following:

- *Storage virtualization* is the pooling of physical storage from multiple network storage devices into what appears to be a single storage device that is managed from a central console.

- *Network virtualization* combines the available resources in a network by splitting the network load into manageable parts, each of which can be assigned (or reassigned) to a particular server on the network.

- *Hardware virtualization* is the use of software to emulate hardware or a total computer environment other than the one the software is actually running in. It allows a piece of hardware to run multiple operating system images at once. This kind of software is sometimes known as a virtual machine.

VIRTUALIZATION CHARACTERISTICS AND BENEFITS

Virtualization increases the flexibility of IT assets, allowing companies to consolidate IT infrastructure, reduce maintenance and administration costs, and prepare for strategic IT initiatives. Virtualization is not primarily about cost-cutting, which is a

IT at Work 2.5

Liberty Wines Improves Business Continuity with Virtualization

Recipient of multiple international wine awards—including the International Wine Challenge On Trade Supplier of the Year for two years running—Liberty Wines is one of the United Kingdom's foremost wine importers and distributors. Liberty Wines supplies to restaurants, supermarkets, and independent retailers from its headquarters in central London.

IT Problems and Business Needs

As the business expanded, the existing servers did not have the capacity to handle increased data volumes, and maintenance of the system put a strain on the IT team of two employees. Existing systems were slow and couldn't provide the responsiveness employees expected.

Liberty Wines needed to speed up business processes to meet the needs of customers in the fast-paced world of fine dining. To provide the service their customers expect, employees at Liberty Wines need quick and easy access to customer, order, and stock information. In the past, the company relied on 10 physical servers for apps and services, such as order processing, reporting, and email.

Virtualized Solution

Liberty Wines deployed a virtualized server solution incorporating Windows Server 2008 R2. The 10 servers were replaced with three physical servers, running 10 virtual servers. An additional server is used as part of a backup system, further improving resilience and stability.

By reducing the number of physical servers from 10 to 4, power use and air conditioning costs were cut by 60 percent. Not only is the bottom line improved, but the carbon footprint is reduced, which is good for the environment.

The new IT infrastructure cut hardware replacement costs by £45,000 (US$69,500) while enhancing stability with the backup system. Apps run faster, so employees can provide better customer service with improved productivity. When needed, virtual servers can be added quickly and easily to support business growth.

Questions

1. What business risks had Liberty Wines faced?

2. How does Liberty Wines' IT infrastructure impact its competitive advantage?

3. How did server virtualization benefit Liberty Wines and the environment?

tactical reason. More importantly, for strategic reasons, virtualization is used because it enables flexible sourcing, and cloud computing.

Characteristics and benefits of virtualization are:

1. **Memory-intensive.** VMs need a huge amount of memory.
2. **Energy-efficient.** Minimizes energy consumed running and cooling servers in the data center—up a 95 percent reduction in energy use per server.
3. **Scalability and load balancing.** When a big event happens, such as the Super Bowl, millions of people hit a web site at the same time. Virtualization provides load balancing to handle the demand for requests to the site. The VMware infrastructure automatically distributes the load across a cluster of physical servers to ensure the maximum performance of all running VMs. Load balancing is key to solving many of today's IT challenges.

Virtualization consolidates servers, which reduces the cost of servers, makes more efficient use of data center space, and reduces energy consumption. All of these factors reduce the total cost of ownership (TCO). Over a three-year lifecycle, a VM costs approximately 75 percent less to operate than a physical server.

Questions

1. How does a virtual machine (VM) function?
2. Explain virtualization.
3. What are the characteristics and benefits of virtualization?
4. When is load balancing important?
5. Explain how software as a service (SaaS) reduces IT costs.
6. How does virtualization reduce TCO (total cost of ownership)?

Key Terms

You find clickable Link Libraries for each chapter on the Companion website.

Blog on cloud computing *http://infoworld.com/blogs/david-linthicum*
Planners Lab, for building a DSS *http://plannerslab.com*
Salesforce.com cloud demos *http://salesforce.com*
Rackspace CloudPro *rackspacecloud.com/ipad.*
Google Apps SLA (service level agreement) *google.com/apps/intl/en/terms/sla.html*
U.S. Defense Information Systems Agency *http://www.disa.mil/*
eWeek's cloud computing news and reviews *eweek.com/c/s/Cloud-Computing/*
Case 3, Video case *soatothecloud.com/2011/10/video-three-cloud-computing-case.html*

Evaluate and Expand Your Learning

IT and Data Management Decisions

1. When selecting a cloud hosting vendor, you need to evaluate the service level agreement (SLA).
   a. Research the SLAs of two cloud hosting vendors. Either Rackspace at *http://www.rackspace.com/cloud/legal/sla/#files* and Amazon. Or Google and Microsoft.
   b. For the vendors you selected, what are the SLAs uptime percent? Expect them to 99.9 percent or less.
   c. Does each vendor count BOTH scheduled downtime and planned downtime toward the SLA uptime percent?
   d. Compare the SLAs on two other criteria.
   e. Decide which SLA is better based on your comparisons.
   f. Report your results and explain your decision.

Questions for Discussion & Review

1. Describe the relationship between IT architecture and organizational performance.
2. Discuss how it's possible to have information deficiencies given today's powerful information technologies and devices.
3. Assume a bank's data are stored in silos based on financial product—checking accounts, saving accounts, mortgages, auto loans, and so on. What problems do these data silos create for the bank's managers?
4. Identify four KPIs for a major airline (e.g., American, United, Delta) or an automobile manufacturer (e.g., GM, Ford, BMW). Which KPI would be the easiest to present to managers on an online dashboard? Explain why.
5. What factors are driving the trend toward collaboration and information sharing technology?
6. Discuss how IT architecture can support management's top business concerns.
7. Why is it important for data to be standardized? Given an example of unstandardized data.
8. Why are TPSs critical systems?
9. Explain what is meant by data volatility. How does it affect the use of databases for data analysis?
10. Discuss why the cloud is considered the *great IT delivery frontier.*
11. What are the benefits of cloud computing?
12. Explain virtualization and virtual machines.
13. How does virtualization reduce IT costs while improving performance?

Online Activities

14. Visit *eWeek.com* Cloud Computing Solutions Center for news and reviews at *eweek.com/c/s/Cloud-Computing/*. Select one of the articles listed under Latest Cloud Computing News. Prepare an executive summary of the article.
15. Visit Rackspace at *rackspace.com/* and review the company's Cloud Pro products. Describe what Cloud Pro does. Explain how Rackspace Cloud Pro leverages the iPad's interface. What are the benefits of the iPad Cloud App?
16. Visit *oracle.com*. Describe the types of virtualization services offered by Oracle.
17. Visit *oncloudcomputing.com*. Click on one of the featured or recommended vendors. Review the vendor's cloud computing offerings. In a one-page report, explain what you learned.
18. Visit *YouTube.com* and search for two videos on virtualization. For each video, report what you learned. Specify the complete URL, video title, who uploaded the video and the date, video length, and number of views.

Collaborative Work

19. Many of the cloud computing and virtualization vendors include case studies of some of their customer.
   a. Each person on the team selects one vendor that posts recent case studies of customers.
   b. Review the cases and select the one you consider most informative.
   c. In a table, identify the business challenges facing the company; what the cloud or virtualization solution consisted of; and the benefits.
   d. Integrate the tables into a single table ranking them in terms of benefits—from highest to lowest.

CASE 2 BUSINESS CASE

Online Gamers' Statistics Stored in the Cloud

Agora Games (*agoragames.com*) hosts online video game competitions and tournaments for amateurs and professionals. Over 60 million Nintendo, SONY, and Xbox gamers worldwide compete in Agora's game communities, such as Mortal Kombat Online (*mortalkombatonline.com*). They provide gamers with individual profiles that record and display what they've just played, their scores, rankings, achievements, and other statistics (stats).

Huge Professional and Amateur Online Video Game Market

The professional and recreational online video games market is huge and growing worldwide. It's projected to hit $70 billion by 2015, according to market researcher DFC Intelligence (*dfcint.com/*). Taking into account all game-related spending, industry revenues might exceed $112 billion in 2015, according to Gartner (*gartner.com*, 2011).

Gamers' Satisfaction Determines Business Success

A game's online community must perform perfectly or it will fail. If a game's online performance or reporting is slow or features don't work correctly, frustrated players leave and rarely return. Since there are many competing games to choose from, online performance is critical to the video game's success.

Data Management Is Crucial

Given the nature of the business and number of customers, Agora's data storage needs fluctuate unpredictably. Without sufficient data storage capacity, gamers' performance suffers—and so does their business. But having too much capacity leads to idle capacity, which increases costs. The solution was cloud storage.

Criteria for Selecting an Enterprise Cloud Storage Solution

Brian Corrigan, Agora's chief technology officer (CTO), said: "We don't want to have to manage hardware, but we do need control over the systems." He evaluated the cloud storage solutions of various vendors based on three criteria.

1. **Multi-platform support.** The storage solution had to support both Ubuntu Linux and Microsoft Windows platforms. Microsoft Xbox is a leading game console.
2. **Guaranteed uptime.** Zero hardware downtime is critical to systems supporting online gaming. Agora needed a vendor or service provider that would manage and insure uninterrupted availability. Not all vendors offer guaranteed system uptime.
3. **Superior tech support.** Agora needed a service provider that was ready and able to fix problems whenever they happened.

The CTO and his team selected Terremark's Enterprise Cloud (*terremark.com*).The Enterprise Cloud resides in **top-tier data centers**—that is, data centers that provide the highest standards of security, availability, and power. Backups provide security and availability. Additional server capacity is available without service interruption. The Enterprise Cloud gives Agora complete control over its systems without having to manage hardware and provisioning. The company only pays for what it uses. Now the IT staff can focus on their core competency—building gaming environments.

Sources: Compiled from *agoragames.com* (2012), *terremark.com/*, *canonical.com*, and *datacenterknowledge.com*.

Questions & Activities

1. Visit and review the Mortal Kombat Online community at *mortalkombatonline.com/* and Section 8 at *s8stats. timegate.com/xbox*. What did you learn about Agora Games' customers?
2. What factors influence Agora Games' business performance?
3. Explain how cloud storage can cut Agora's data storage costs.
4. What changes occurred at Agora Games as a result of investing in enterprise cloud storage?
5. Research two enterprise cloud storage vendors or service providers that provide sufficient information on the Web to assess them meaningfully. Compare and contrast at least four characteristics of these vendors or service providers.

CASE 3 VIDEO CASE

Three Cloud Computing Case Studies

When organizations say they are "using the cloud," they can mean a number of very different things. Using an IaaS service such as Amazon EC2 or Terremark is different from using Google Apps for outsourced email, which is different again from exposing an API into Facebook.

A video shows three Cloud Computing case studies from Vordel's customers. The cases cover SaaS, IaaS, and PaaS. In first two examples, customers are connecting to the Cloud; first to Google Apps (for single-sign-on to Google Apps email) and second to Terremark to manage virtual servers. In the third example, the connection is from the Cloud using a Facebook app to a company's APIs. You might spot *Animal House* references.

To do:

1. Visit *SOAtoTheCloud.com/2011/10/video-three-cloud-computing-case.html*.

2. View the 11-minute video of the 3 case studies.

3. Explain the value or benefits of each organization's cloud investment.

Data Analysis & Decision Making

DSS to Control and Manage Gasoline Costs

Notes: For this analysis, go to the Student Companion Website for the textbook on *Wiley.com* to download the Excel file.

The price of gasoline remains high, and demand for energy is increasing. Individuals, corporations, and governments are involved in solving this issue. It is very likely that you are, too. You will develop a DSS using Excel to calculate gasoline costs and decide what action to take. This assignment may help you learn how to reduce your carbon footprint.

To do:

1. Using the spreadsheet that you download, calculate and compare the costs of driving a hybrid automobile and non-hybrid SUV from your location to a location 600 miles away.

2. You need external data. You need to know the gas prices in your starting and destination locations. *Automotive.com* provides a free application (a widget), a real-time, continually updated tool that monitors gas prices.

3. You have just been promoted to a fleet manager in a food company that uses 300 cars of different sizes. Prepare a DSS using Excel to show top management how to reduce gasoline costs if the price is at $4.00, $4.50, $4.75, and $5.00 per gallon.

Resources on the Book's Web Site

More resources and study tools are located on the Student Web Site. You'll find additional chapter materials and useful Web links. In addition, self-quizzes that provide individualized feedback are available for each chapter.

References

DISA (Defense Information Systems Agency), U.S. Department of Defense, 2010. *disa.mil/services/*

EARF (Enterprise Architecture Research Forum), 2012. *earf.meraka.org.za/earfhome/our-projects-1/completed-projects*

GAO (Government Accountability Office), *Practical Guide to Federal Enterprise Architecture,* February 2001, *gao.gov/bestpractices/bpeaguide.pdf*

Han, Y. "Cloud Computing: Case Studies and Total Costs of Ownership," *Information Technology and Libraries.* Vol. 30, no. 4. December 2011.

Hasson, J. "Will the Cloud Kill the Data Center?" FierceCIO, August 9, 2009. *fiercecio.com/story/will-cloud-kill-data-center/2009-08-09*

Hopkins, M.S. "How to Innovate When Platforms Won't Stop Moving." *MIT Sloan Management Review.* Vol. 52, no. 4. Summer 2011.

HP Delivers Enhanced Fan Experience by Extending Access to Paul McCartney's Digital Library, January 12, 2012.

Keefe, P. "Smart Call," *Teradata Magazine.* Vol. 10, no. 1, Q1 2010. *teradata.com/tdmo/Article.aspx?id=13384*

King, R. "HP builds Paul McCartney's digital library; sets precedent for other artists?" *ZDNet.com,* May 26, 2011.

NIST, National Institute of Standards and Technology Cloud Computing Program. 2012. *nist.gov/itl/cloud/index.cfm*

Rackspace, *rackspace.com/*

Reuters, "HP Delivers Enhanced Fan Experience by Extending Access to Paul McCartney's Digital Library." *Reuters.com,* January 12, 2012.

UltimateGuitar.com, "Paul McCartney Gets A Giant Digital Library." May 27, 2011.

Learning Outcomes

❶ Describe the functions of database technology, the differences between centralized and distributed database architecture, how data quality impacts performance, and the role of a master reference file in creating accurate and consistent data across the enterprise.

❷ Evaluate the tactical and strategic benefits of data warehouses, data marts, and data centers; describe their data volatility and decision-support characteristics; and understand the process of building and using a data warehouse.

❸ Describe data and text mining, and give examples of mining applications to find patterns, correlations, trends, or other meaningful relationships in organizational data stores.

❹ Explain the operational benefits and competitive advantages of business intelligence and analytics, and how forecasting can be improved.

❺ Describe digital and physical data and document management, and how it helps companies meet their compliance, regulatory, and legal obligations.

With organizations collecting a broader variety of data at greater velocity, the technologies for storing, analyzing, and reporting data must be powerful and fast enough to do so. According to a study by McKinsey Global Institute (2011), organizations capture trillions of bytes of information about their customers, suppliers, and operations through digital systems. This represents a 40 percent projected annual growth in the volume of data generated. Fifteen out of 17 sectors in the U.S. economy had more data stored per company than the U.S. Library of Congress, which had collected more than 235 terabytes of data in April 2011 alone.

Databases, data warehouses and marts, and BI make it possible for managers to make decisions and act with clarity, speed, and confidence.

In our iPad era, you might think that physical pieces of paper are a relic of the past, but in most offices the opposite is true. Aberdeen's (2012) survey of 176 organizations worldwide found that the volume of physical documents is growing by up to 30 percent per year. **Document management** technology archives digital and physical data to meet business needs, as well as regulatory and legal requirements.

CASE 1 OPENING CASE

Zero-Downtime at BNP Paribas

Global financial institutions need fault tolerant data management technologies to support their 24/7 operating environments. **Fault tolerant** means zero-downtime, zero data loss, and continuous access to data, analytics, and reporting. Put simply, downtime equals lost revenue, as shown in Table 3.1. Downtime costs vary by industry and the scale of business operations. Global financial institutions such as BNP Paribas invest heavily in fault tolerant database, data warehouse, and business intelligence (BI) technologies because their actual downtime costs could reach into millions of dollars per hour.

Global and financial institutions must have high-performance IT infrastructures to do business. Their IT platforms for the build out of data management and analysis tasks are cutting-edge, as at global bank BNP Paribas (*bnpparibas.com*).

BNP Paribas, The Bank for a Changing World

BNP Paribas is a leader in global banking and financial services, and one of the strongest banks in the world. With a presence in 80 countries, including every major financial market, BNP Paribas has one of the most extensive global banking networks. Its customers include major investment banks, broker-dealers, and institutional investors and issuers.

TABLE 3.1	The Financial Impacts of Down Time of Business Applications	
Industry or Business Application	**Average cost-per-hour of downtime**	**Average cost-per-minute of downtime**
Financial markets	$6.5 million	$109,000
Credit card sales	$2.6 million	$ 44,000
E-commerce	$ 600,000	$ 10,000
Pay-per-view TV	$ 150,000	$ 2,500
Airline reservations	$ 90,000	$ 1,500
Teleticket sales	$ 70,000	$ 1,200
Shipping	$ 30,000	$ 500

Sources, Oracle: Information Management, Dunn & Bradstreet, 2012.

(a)   (b)

Figure 3.1a & b BNP Paribas slogan is "The bank for a changing world."

BNP Paribas implements an Oracle Exadata Database Machine

BNP Paribas invested in Oracle Exadata database platform, data warehousing, and Sybase IQ and SAP BI systems to manage the massive growth of electronic trading data and other transactions. A data warehouse can be the critical tool for maximizing the organization's investment in data it collects or has stored throughout the enterprise.

The Oracle Exadata Machine is a complete package of servers, storage, networking, and software. It provides extreme performance for data warehousing—which BNP Paribas needed because its data warehouse has to manage billions of messages in real time, processing one terabyte (TB) of raw data daily. Many older ITs were simply not designed to efficiently handle today's data and user volumes. For example, BNP Paribas and other enterprises upgrade to SAP BI when they face technical challenges created by exploding volumes of data, growing demand for data among business users, and strict regulatory and legislative requirements.

Sybase IQ (*Sybase.com*) is a high performance analytics server that integrates with SAP BI (*sap.com*). The combination of Sybase IQ and SAP BI helps BNP Paribas integrate data from within and outside; and to perform analyses that transform the data into valuable information for employees and clients. See *Tech Note* 3-1 for a discussion of operational intelligence.

Tech Note 3-1

Sybase IQ is especially designed for *operational intelligence*—capable of query and reporting performance up to 100 times faster than traditional databases. **Operational intelligence** refers to an organization's ability to get information to the people who need it to make decisions or react appropriately to business events. **Queries** are a method to retrieve information from a database or warehouse. Many database management systems use the **Structured Query Language (SQL)** standard query format.

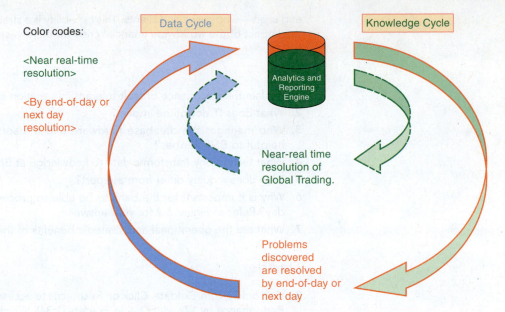

Color codes:

<Near real-time resolution>

<By end-of-day or next day resolution>

Data Cycle

Knowledge Cycle

Analytics and Reporting Engine

Near-real time resolution of Global Trading.

Problems discovered are resolved by end-of-day or next day

Figure 3.2 BNP Paribas relies on its analytics and reporting database engine to resolve global trades in near–real time worldwide; and to detect and resolve problems within a day. The analytics and reporting engine convert trading data into knowledge to support decision making and planning.

In July 2010, the database migration process from its old system onto Oracle Exadata was completed; and a data warehouse was in production and running on the new hardware setup. Hardware maintenance and operating system support is taken care of by Oracle, while BNP Paribas database administrators manage the software.

24/7 Data Access, Analysis, and Query Capabilities

This Oracle database platform provides 24/7 data accessibility to global traders, analysts, and customers. Analytic reports and BI systems are used continuously by financial analysts on the trading floor throughout the world. These systems must process huge data volumes in near real time or within one business day with no downtime.

Figure 3.2 shows the functions of the Oracle analytics and reporting database engine. The engine transforms data into knowledge in two ways:

1. It processes and resolves trading transactions in near real time.
2. It is able to detect and resolve problems quickly.

Delays in error resolution are extremely costly and harmful to customer relationships and the bank's reputation.

Operational and Strategic Benefits

Database machines optimize software and hardware to deliver the best possible performance, allowing database administrators (DBAs) to spend more time on business requirements rather than on technology issues.

The new database platform resulted in a 17 times (17x) increase in data throughput—that is, from the time data is collected through to analysis and reporting. The 17x increase in throughput was achieved in part by compression—that is, compressed data requires less storage and is easier to analyze. IT performance increased, and data storage costs decreased despite huge increases in data and messages. The new database platform has provided other key benefits for BNP Paribas and its financial clients. These benefits include:

- **Queries:** Online client scan generate many more ad hoc queries with faster response times.
- **Reports:** The bank and clients depend on reports and analysis. The new platform provides customized financial portfolio reports at tripled report generation speeds.
- **Transactions:** Of course, online transaction processing (OLTP) is much faster.

Database Machine Investment Criteria

Overall, BNP Paribas achieved significant operational benefits. But the new Oracle database platform was not selected primarily as a way to cut costs or increase efficiency. Rather it was selected as a strategic instrument to improve the productivity and achievements of end users—employees and clients. This capability is a strategic advantage, particularly given the impact of the worldwide financial crisis on the investment and securities industry.

Discuss

1. Explain the importance of fault tolerant information systems.
2. What does IT downtime impact?
3. Who manages the database hardware and the software? Why is this arrangement helpful to BNP Paribas?
4. What technology transforms data to knowledge at BNP Paribas?
5. How does a query differ from a report?
6. Why is it important for the bank to be able to process in near real time or within one day? Refer to Figure 3.2 for your answer.
7. What are the operational and strategic benefits of the new database platform?

Decide

8. Visit *oracle.com/Exadata*. Click on Resources to access the video *BNP Paribas Improves Performance by 17x with Oracle Exadata* (1:34). Which was considered more important to BNP Paribas—the cost savings or time savings? Explain why. Is there a predictable relationship between these two types of savings? Explain.

Debate

9. Does BNP Paribas' investment in Oracle Exadata, data warehousing, and BI provide the global bank with a strategic advantage? Or was the investment necessary for operational survival—in effect, the cost of continuing to do business?

3.1 Database Technology

Today's computing hardware is capable of crunching through huge datasets that were considered impossible a few years back. And data management vendors, such as Oracle, IBM, Microsoft, and Teradata, have been responding with more powerful software and hardware. Data management technologies discussed in this chapter are:

Databases are collections of records stored in a systematic way.

Volatile refers to the fact that the data are constantly changing.

Queries are ad hoc user requests for specific data.

Database management systems (DBMS) are computer programs used to manage the additions, updates, and deletions of data as transactions occur; and support data queries and reporting. They are OLTP systems.

Online transaction processing (OLTP) systems are designed to manage transaction data, which are volatile.

- **Databases** store data generated by business apps, sensors, and transaction processing systems (TPS).
- **Data warehouses** integrate data from multiple databases and data silos and organize them for complex analysis, knowledge discovery, and to support decision making.
- **Data marts** are small-scale data warehouses that support a single function or department. Organizations that are unable to invest in data warehousing may start with one or more data marts.
- **Business intelligence (BI)** tools and techniques process data and do statistical analysis for insight and discovery—that is, to discover meaningful relationships in the data, keep informed of real time, gain insight, detect trends, and identify opportunities and risks.

When most business transactions occur—for instance, an item is sold or returned, an order is sent or cancelled, a payment or deposit is made—changes are made immediately to the database. See Figure 3.3. These online changes are additions, updates, or deletions. **Database management systems (DBMS)** record and process transactions in the database; and support queries and reporting. Given their functions, DBMSs are referred to as **online transaction processing (OLTP)** systems. OLTP is a database

© Vladislav Kochelaevskiy/Alamy Limited

Figure 3.3 Data generated by transactions via computers, handhelds, and other input devices are stored in databases. DBMS support data queries and reports by extracting data from the database and delivering it to a screen or other output device.

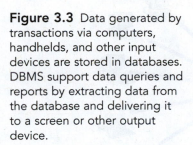

Tech Note 3-2

The most widely used enterprise DBMSs are Oracle, IBM DB2, Microsoft SQL Server, PostgreSQL, and MySQL.

Oracle, which was introduced in 1979, was the first commercially available relational database management system. Oracle is the database leader, holding 48.8 percent market share (Gartner, 2012).

DB2 is widely used in data centers. DB2 runs on Linux, UNIX, Windows, and mainframes and competes directly with Oracle.

SQL Server's ease of use, availability, and tight Windows operating system integration make it an easy choice for firms that choose Microsoft products for their enterprises.

PostgreSQL is the most advanced open source database, often used by online gaming applications and Skype, Yahoo! and MySpace.

MySQL, which was acquired by Oracle in January 2010, powers hundreds of thousands of commercial websites and a huge number of internal enterprise applications. Although MySQL's adopters had reservations about Oracle's ownership of this popular open source product, Oracle has publicly declared its commitment to ongoing development and support.

---

design that breaks down complex information into simple data tables. This design is very efficient for analyzing and reporting captured transactional data. OLTP databases are capable of processing millions of transactions every second.

CENTRALIZED AND DISTRIBUTED DATABASE ARCHITECTURE

There are two basic types of databases: centralized and distributed. For both types of databases, multiple backups or data archives are maintained on-site and off-site.

Centralized Database Architecture. A centralized database stores all related files in a central physical location, as shown in Figure 3.4. For decades the main database platform consisted of centralized database files on large, mainframe computers, primarily because of the enormous capital investment and operating costs associated with alternative systems. Benefits of centralized database configurations include:

1. Better quality. Data consistency is easier when data are physically kept in one location because data additions, updates, and deletions can be made in a supervised and orderly fashion.

2. Better security. Data are accessed via the centralized host computer, where they can be protected more easily from unauthorized access or modification.

A major disadvantage of centralized databases, like all centralized systems, is transmission delay when users are geo-dispersed.

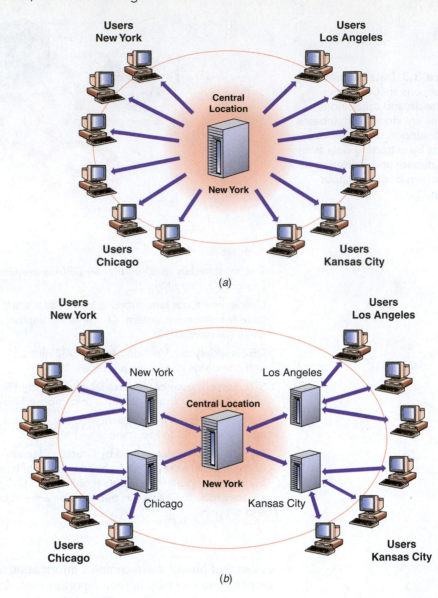

Figure 3.4 (a) Centralized database. (b) Distributed database.

DISTRIBUTED DATABASE ARCHITECTURE

A distributed database system allows apps on computers and mobiles to access data from local and remote databases, as diagrammed in Figure 3.5. Distributed databases use a client/server architecture to process information requests. Computers and mobile devices accessing the servers are called clients. The databases are stored on servers that reside in the company's data centers, a private cloud, or a public cloud.

DATABASE MANAGEMENT SYSTEMS (DBMS) FUNCTIONS

Major data functions performed by a DBMS include:

- **Data filtering and profiling:** Inspecting the data for errors, inconsistencies, redundancies, and incomplete information.
- **Data integrity:** Correcting, standardizing, and verifying the integrity of the data.
- **Data synchronization:** Integrating, matching, or linking data from disparate sources.
- **Data enrichment:** Enhancing data using information from internal and external data sources.
- **Data maintenance:** Checking and controlling data integrity over time.

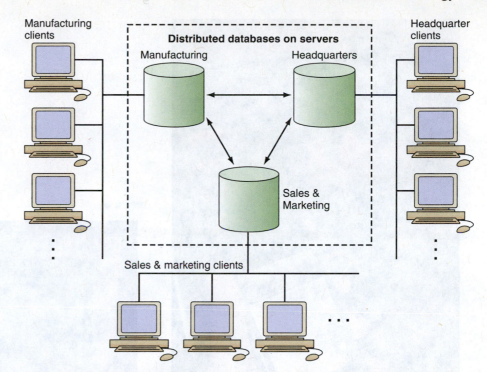

Figure 3.5 Distributed database architecture for headquarters, manufacturing, and sales and marketing.

DATABASES ARE OPTIMIZED FOR TRANSACTIONS AND QUERIES

Data entering the databases from POS (point-of-sale) terminals, scanners, online sales, and other sources are stored in a structured format, depending upon the type of DBMS. Figure 3.6 illustrates the concept of structured data. Traditional databases are not well suited for managing messy data such as tweets and other comments.

Databases are optimized for extremely fast processing of **queries**—or ad hoc user requests for specific data. Query results are formatted for screen displays, as shown in Figure 3.7. Thus, databases need to strike a balance between transaction processing efficiency and query efficiency. Given these functions, databases cannot be optimized for data mining, complex online analytics processing (OLAP), and decision support. These database limitations led to the introduction of data warehouse technology, which you will read about in the next section. Data warehouses and data marts are optimized for OLAP, data mining, BI, and decision support.

GARBAGE-IN, GARBAGE OUT

Data collection is a highly complex process that can create problems concerning the quality of the data that are being collected. Therefore, regardless of how the data are collected, they need to be validated so that users know they can trust them. Classic expressions that sum up the situation are "garbage in, garbage out" (GIGO) and the

Figure 3.6 Illustration of structured data format. Numeric and alpha-numeric data are arranged into rows and pre-defined columns similar to an Excel spreadsheet.

(a)

© Focus Technology/Alamy Limited

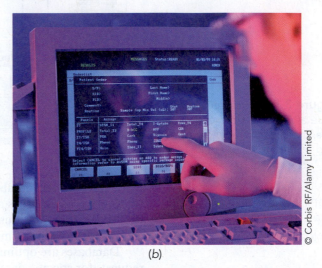

(b)

© Corbis RF/Alamy Limited

Figure 3.7 a & b Database queries are processed in real time and results are transmitted via wired or wireless networks to computer screens or handhelds.

potentially riskier "garbage in, gospel out." In the latter case, poor quality data are trusted and used as the basis for planning. You have encountered data safeguards, such as integrity checks, to help improve data quality when you fill in an online form. For example, the form will not accept an e-mail address that is not formatted correctly.

Dirty Data Costs and Consequences. **Dirty data**—that is, poor quality data—lack integrity and cannot be trusted. Too often managers and information workers are actually constrained by data that cannot be trusted because they are incomplete, out of context, outdated, inaccurate, inaccessible, or so overwhelming that they require weeks to analyze. In those situations, the decision maker is facing too much uncertainty to make intelligent business decisions. The cost of poor quality data may be expressed as a formula.

$$\begin{matrix} Cost\ of\ Poor \\ Quality\ Data \end{matrix} = \begin{matrix} Lost \\ Business \\ Value \end{matrix} + \begin{matrix} Cost\ to \\ Prevent \\ Errors \end{matrix} + \begin{matrix} Cost\ to \\ Correct \\ Errors \end{matrix}$$

Examples of these costs include:

• **Lost business.** Business is lost when sales opportunities are missed, orders are returned because wrong items were delivered, or errors frustrate and drive away customers.

• **Preventing errors.** If data cannot be trusted, then employees need to spend more time and effort trying to verify information in order to avoid mistakes.

- **Correcting errors.** Database staff need to process corrections to the database. For example, the costs of correcting errors at K&D Corporation are estimated as follows:

  a) Two database staff people spend 25 percent of their work day processing and verifying data corrections each day. [2 people * 25 percent of 8 hours/day = 4 hours/day correcting errors]

  b) Hourly salaries are $50 per hour based on pay rate and benefits. [$50/hour * 4 hours/day = $200/day correcting errors]

  c) 250 workdays per year. [$200/day * 250 days = $50,000/year to correct errors]

This cost of the poor quality data spreads throughout the company affecting systems from shipping and receiving to accounting and customer service. Data errors typically arise from the functions or departments that generate or create the data—and not within the IT department. When all costs are considered, the value of finding and fixing the causes of data errors becomes clear. In a time of decreased budgets, some organizations may not have the resources for such projects and may not even be aware of the problem. Others may be spending most of their time fixing problems leaving no time to work on preventing them.

Bad data is costing U.S. businesses hundreds of billions of dollars a year and is affecting their ability to ride out the tough economic climate, according to the technology research firm Ovum. In a 2010 report, Ovum estimated that incorrect and outdated values, missing data, and inconsistent data formats cost businesses $700 billion a year as the result of the inefficiency it causes; lost customers, sales, and revenue; misallocation of resources; and flawed pricing strategies (Sheina, 2010).

For a particular company, it is difficult to calculate the full cost of poor data quality and its long-term effects. Part of the difficulty is the time delay between the mistake and when it is detected. Errors can be very hard to correct, especially when systems extend across the enterprise. Another concern is that the impacts of errors can be unpredictable or serious. For example, the cost of errors due to unreliable and incorrect data alone is estimated to be as high as $40 billion annually in the retail sector (Zynapse, 2010). And one health care company whose agents were working with multiple ISs, but were not updating client details in every IS, increased annual expenses by $9 million.

Data Ownership and Organizational Politics. Despite the need for high-quality data, organizational politics and technical issues make that difficult to achieve. The source of the problem is **data ownership.** That is, who owns or is responsible for the data. Data ownership problems exist when there are no policies defining responsibility and accountability for managing data. Inconsistent data formats of various departments create an additional set of problems as organizations try to combine individual applications into integrated enterprise systems.

The tendency to delegate data quality responsibilities to the technical teams, who have no control over data quality, as opposed to business users who do have such control, is another common pitfall that stands in the way of accumulating high-quality data.

Those who manage a business or part of a business are tasked with trying to improve business performance and retain customers. Compensation is tied to improving profitability, driving revenue growth, and improving the quality of customer service. These key performance indicators (KPIs) are monitored closely by senior managers who want to find and eliminate defects that harm performance. It is strange then, that so few managers take time to understand how performance is impacted by poor-quality data. Two examples make a strong case for investment in high-quality data.

Retail banks: For retail bank executives, risk management is the number one issue. Disregard for risk contributed to the 2008 financial services meltdown. Despite risk management strategies, many banks still incur huge losses. Part of the problem in many banks is that their ISs enable them to monitor risk only at the product level—mortgages, loans, or credit cards. Product-level risk management ISs monitor a customer's risk exposure for mortgages, or for loans, or for credit cards, and so forth—but not for a customer for all products. With product-level ISs, a bank cannot see the full risk exposure of a customer. The limitations of these siloed product-level risk have serious implications for business performance because bad-risk customers cannot be identified easily, and customer data in the various ISs may differ. For example, consider what happens when each product-level risk management IS feeds data to marketing ISs. Marketing may offer bad-risk customers incentives to take out another credit card or loan that they cannot repay. And since the bank cannot identify its best customers either, they may be ignored and enticed away by better deals offered by competitors. This scenario illustrates how data ownership and data quality management are critical to risk management. Data defects and incomplete data can quickly trigger inaccurate marketing and mounting losses. One retail bank facing these problems lost 16 percent of its mortgage business within 18 months while increasing losses in its credit card business (Ferguson, 2012).

Manufacturing. Many manufacturers are at the mercy of a powerful customer base—large retailers. Manufacturers want to align their processes with those of large retail customers to keep them happy. This alignment makes it possible for a retailer to order centrally for all stores or to order locally from a specific manufacturer. Supporting both central and local ordering makes it difficult to plan production runs. For example, each manufacturing site has to collect order data from central ordering and local ordering systems to get a complete picture on what to manufacture at each site. Without accurate, up-to-date data, orders may go unfilled, or manufacturers may have excess inventory. One manufacturer who tried to keep its key retailer happy by implementing central and local ordering could not process orders correctly at each manufacturing site. No data ownership and lack of control over how order data flowed throughout business operations had negative impacts. Conflicting and duplicate business processes at each manufacturing site were causing data errors leading to mistakes in manufacturing, packing, and shipments. Customers were very dissatisfied.

These two examples represent the consequences of a lack of data ownership and data quality. Understanding the impact of mismanaged data makes data ownership and accurate, timely integrated data a higher priority in helping improve business performance.

Compliance with numerous federal and state regulations relies on rock-solid data and trusted metrics used for regulatory reporting. Data ownership, data quality, and formally-managed data are high on the agenda of CFOs and CEOs who are held personally accountable if their company is found to be in violation of regulations.

Data Life Cycle. The data life cycle is a model that illustrates the way data travel through an organization, as shown in Figure 3.8. The data life cycle begins with storage in a database, to being loaded into a data warehouse for analysis, then reported to knowledge workers or used in business apps. Supply chain management (SCM), customer relationship management (CRM), and e-commerce are enterprise applications that require up-to-date readily accessible data to function properly.

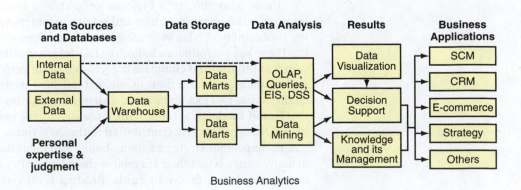

Figure 3.8 Data life cycle.

Three general data principles relate to the data life cycle perspective and help to guide IT investment decisions.

1. **Principle of Diminishing Data Value.** The value of data diminishes as they age. This is a simple, yet powerful, principle. Most organizations cannot operate at peak performance with blind spots (lack of data availability) of 30 days or longer. Global financial services institutions, like BNP Paribas, need near real time data for peak performance.

2. **Principle of 90/90 data use.** According to the 90/90 data-use principle, a majority of stored data, as high as 90 percent, is seldom accessed after 90 days (except for auditing purposes). That is, roughly 90 percent of data lose most of their value after three months.

3. **Principle of data in context.** The capability to capture, process, format, and distribute data in near real time or faster requires a huge investment in data architecture (Chapter 2) and infrastructure to link remote POS systems to data storage, data analysis systems, and reporting apps. The investment can be justified on the principle that data must be integrated, processed, analyzed, and formatted into "actionable information."

As data become more complex and their volumes explode, database performance degrades. One solution is the use of master data and master data management (MDM), which are discussed next.

MASTER DATA AND MASTER DATA MANAGEMENT (MDM)

Master data management (MDM) is a set of processes to integrate data from various sources or enterprise applications to create and maintain a more unified view of a customer, product, or other core data entity that is shared across systems. Figure 3.9 shows how **master data** serves as a layer between transactional data in a database and analytical data in a data warehouse.

More Unified View, but Not a Single View. Although vendors may claim that their MDM solution creates "a single version of the truth," this claim is probably not true. In reality MDM cannot create a single unified version of the data because constructing a completely unified view of all master data is simply not possible.

Master Reference File and Data Entities. Realistically, MDM consolidates data from various data sources into a **master reference file,** which then feeds data back to the applications, thereby creating accurate and consistent data across the enterprise. In *IT at Work 3.1*, participants in the health care supply chain were essentially developing a master reference file to obtain a more unified version of the data. A master data reference file is based on data entities.

A **data entity** is anything real or abstract about which a company wants to collect and store data. **Master data entities** are the main entities of a company, such as customers, products, suppliers, employees, and assets. Each organizational department has distinct

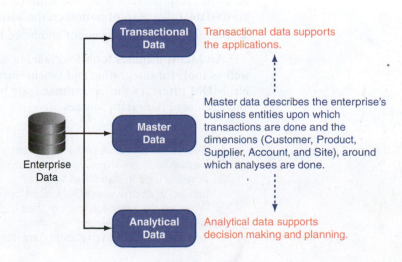

Figure 3.9 An enterprise has three kinds of actual data: transactional, master, and analytical.

Enterprise Data

Transactional Data — Transactional data supports the applications.

Master Data — Master data describes the enterprise's business entities upon which transactions are done and the dimensions (Customer, Product, Supplier, Account, and Site), around which analyses are done.

Analytical Data — Analytical data supports decision making and planning.

IT at Work 3.1

Data Errors Increase Cost of Care by Billions of Dollars and Risk Lives

Every day, health care administrators and others throughout the health care supply chain waste 24 to 30 percent of their time correcting data errors. Each incorrect transaction costs $60 to $80 to correct. In addition, about 60 percent of all invoices among supply chain partners have errors, and each invoice error costs $40 to $400 to reconcile. Altogether, errors and conflicting data increase supply costs by 3 to 5 percent. In other words, each year billions of dollars are wasted in the health care supply chain because of supply chain data disconnects, which refer to one organization's IS not understanding data from another's IS. Unless the health care system develops a data synchronization tool to prevent data disconnects, any attempts to streamline supply chain costs by implementing new technologies, such as data transmission using radio waves (known as radio frequency identification [RFID]) to automatically collect data, will be sabotaged by dirty data.

Consider the problems created by the lack of data consistency in the procurement process. Customers of the Defense Supply Center Philadelphia (DSCP) health care facility were receiving wrong health care items, wrong quantities, or inferior items at higher prices. Numerous errors occurred whenever a supplier and DSC Preferred to the same item (e.g., a surgical instrument) with different names or item numbers.

For three years, efforts were made to synchronize DSCP's medical/surgical data with data used by medical industry manufacturers and distributors. The health care industry developed data standards or codes for each item, which enable organizations to accurately share electronic data. A data synchronization tool provided data consistency. Results from this effort improved DSCP's operating profit margin and freed personnel to care for patients. Other benefits are the following:

- Accurate and consistent item information enables easier and faster product sourcing. (Product sourcing means finding products to buy.)
- Matching of files to ensure lowest contracted price for purchases for quicker, automatic new item entry.
- Significantly reduced unnecessary inventories and amount of fraudulent (unauthorized) purchasing.
- Leveraged purchasing power to get lower prices because purchase volumes were now apparent.
- Better patient safety.

Sources: Compiled from Barlow (2007), Chisholm (2008), and Levine (2007).

Questions

1. What are two examples of waste in the health care supply chain as a result of dirty data in an organization?
2. Why was data synchronization necessary to reduce inefficiency?
3. How can accurate data and verification systems deter fraudulent (unauthorized) purchases?

---

master data needs. Marketing, for example, is concerned with product pricing, brand, and product packaging, whereas production is concerned with product costs and schedules. A customer master reference file can feed data to all enterprise systems that have a customer relationship component, thereby providing a unified picture of the customers. Similarly, a product master reference file can feed data to all of the production systems within the enterprise. Three benefits of a unified view of customers are the following:

1. Better, more accurate customer data to support marketing, sales, support, and service initiatives
2. Better responsiveness to ensure that all employees who deal with customers have up-to-date, reliable information on the customers
3. Better revenue management and more responsive business decisions

An MDM includes tools for cleaning and auditing the master data elements as well as tools for integrating and synchronizing data to make the data more accessible. MDM offers a solution for managers who are frustrated with how fragmented and dispersed their data sources are.

Questions

1. Describe a database and a database management system (DBMS).
2. Explain what an online transaction processing (OLAP) system does.
3. Why are data in databases volatile?
4. Explain what processes DBMSs are optimized to perform.
5. What are the business costs or risks of poor data quality?
6. Describe the data life cycle.
7. What is the function of master data management (MDM)?

3.2 Data Warehouse and Data Mart Technology

A data warehouse is a specialized database containing data that are summarized in various ways so that they are ready for quick responses to inquiries. Data warehouses that integrate data from databases across an entire enterprise are called enterprise data warehouses (EDW). A data mart is smaller and serves a specific department or function, such as finance, marketing, or operations. Tech Note 3-3 summarizes key characteristic of these data stores.

Consider a bank's database. Every deposit, withdrawal, loan payment, or other transaction adds or changes data. The volatility caused by the constant transaction processing makes data analysis difficult—and the demands to process millions of transactions per second consume the database's processing power. To overcome this problem, data are extracted from designated databases, transformed, and loaded into a data warehouse. Significantly, in a data warehouse, data are read-only; that is, they are not subject to change until the next ETL. Unlike databases, warehouse data are not volatile. Thus, data warehouses are designed as **online analytical processing (OLAP) systems,** meaning that the data can be queried and analyzed much more efficiently than OLTP application databases. OLAP is a term used to describe the analysis of complex data from the data warehouse.

REAL-TIME SUPPORT FROM ACTIVE DATA WAREHOUSE (ADW)

The trend is toward real-time data warehousing and analytics—that is, an active data warehouse (ADW). In the past, data warehouses primarily supported strategic applications, which did not require instant response time, direct customer interaction, or integration with operational systems. ETL might have been done once per week or once per month. Today, businesses increasingly use information in the moment to support real-time customer interaction. Companies with an ADW are able to interact appropriately with a customer to provide superior customer service, which in turn improves revenues. With an ADW, retailers can eliminate disconnects by improving communication among merchants, vendors, customers, and associates throughout the day, enabling them to respond to business events in near real time.

Companies, such as credit card company Capital One, track each customer's profitability and use that score to determine the level of customer service. For example, when a customer calls Capital One, that customer is asked to enter the credit card number, which is linked to a profitability score. Low-profit customers get a voice response unit only; high-profit customers get a live person—a customer service representative (CSR).

Data warehouse content can be delivered to decision makers throughout the enterprise via the Internet and a company's own intranets. Users can view, query, and

---

Tech Note 3-3

Comparison of Databases, Data Warehouses, and Data Marts

Databases are:

- Designed and optimized to ensure that every transaction gets recorded and stored immediately.
- Volatile because data are constantly being updated, added, or edited.
- Online transaction processing (OLTP) systems because transactions must be recorded and processed as they occur, that is, in real time.

Data warehouse and data marts are:

- Designed and optimized for analysis and quick response to queries.
- Are nonvolatile, which means that when data are stored, they can be read only and never deleted so that they can be used for comparison with newer data.
- Online analytic processing (OLAP) systems [pronounced: oh-lap].
- Subject-oriented, which means that the data captured is organized to have similar data linked together.

analyze the data and produce reports using web browsers. This is an extremely economical and effective method of delivering data.

INTELLIGENT AND SELECTIVE CUSTOMER SERVICE MADE POSSIBLE WITH ADW

Consider, for example, the case of Charles, a dissatisfied customer who calls the customer service center because of frequent dropped cell calls. Through the call center application attached to the ADW, the CSR accesses not only the complete history of Charles's calls to the company but also a full view of all the services to which he subscribes—TV, video-on-demand, Internet, and cell—along with his customer profitability score, which lets the CSR know how profitable he is to the company. Intelligent and selective customer service is possible because all service lines and calls to customer service are stored in the ADW. The CSR uses the data to determine the best action or offer to resolve this issue to Charles's satisfaction. Additionally, the CSR will have the insight to cross-sell or up-sell additional services based on the customer profile. In this example, the ADW provided a view of the customer that indicated what intervention to take based on the customer's profitability score. Because Charles subscribes to the company's high–profit-margin services, the company wants to minimize the risk of losing him as a customer.

BENEFITS OF DATA WAREHOUSING

Many organizations built data warehouses because they were frustrated with inconsistent decision support data, or they needed to improve reporting applications or better understand the business. Viewed from this perspective, data warehouses are infrastructure investments that companies make to support ongoing and future operations, such as:

- **Marketing and sales.** A data warehouse is used to keep informed of the status of products, marketing program effectiveness, and product line profitability; and to make intelligent decisions to maximize per-customer profitability.
- **Pricing and contracts.** Data is used to calculate costs accurately in order to optimize pricing of a contract. Without accurate cost data, prices may be below or too near to cost; or prices may be uncompetitive because they are too high.
- **Forecasting.** Supports estimating customer demand.
- **Sales performance.** A data warehouse is used to determine sales profitability and productivity for all territories and regions; can obtain and analyze results by geography, product, sales group, or individual.
- **Financial.** Financial management relies on near real-time data, as you have read in Case 1, BNP Paribas.

BUILDING A DATA WAREHOUSE

Figure 3.10 diagrams the process of building and using a data warehouse. The organization's data are stored in operational systems (left side of the figure). Not all data are transferred to the data warehouse. Frequently only summary data are transferred. The warehouse organizes the data in multiple ways—by subject, functional area, vendor, and product.

As shown in Figure 3.10, data warehouse architecture defines the flow of data that starts when data are captured by transaction systems; the source data are stored in transactional (operational) databases; data extract, transformation, and load (ETL) processes flow data from databases into data warehouses and data marts, where the data is available for access, reporting and analysis by business intelligence tools.

Applications. Table 3.2 summarizes several successful applications of data warehouses. Many organizations, sustained by the success of their data warehouse efforts, are taking the data warehouse public. One example is Wells Fargo. Its development effort uses the resources of a Teradata warehouse to provide an online tool that collects and summarizes transactions for consumers—credit card, debit card, online bill payments, checking account—and generates an analysis of online banking sessions. Consumers are better able to understand their spending patterns, and they have reported a higher level of customer satisfaction.

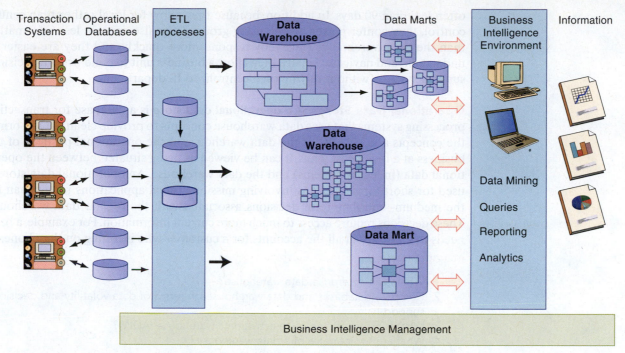

Figure 3.10 Database, data warehouse and marts, and BI architecture.

DATA MARTS, OPERATIONAL DATA STORES, AND MULTIDIMENSIONAL DATABASES

Organizations also implement data marts, operational data stores, and multidimensional databases either as supplements or substitutes for data warehouses.

Data Marts. The high costs of data warehouses can make them too expensive for a company to implement. As an alternative, many firms create a lower-cost, scaled-down version of a data warehouse called a data mart. Data marts are designed for a strategic business unit (SBU) or a single department.

In addition to lower costs (less than $100,000 versus $1 million or more for data warehouses), data marts require significantly shorter lead times for implementation,

TABLE 3.2	Data Warehouse Applications
Industry	**Applications**
Airline	Crew assignment, aircraft deployment, analysis of route profitability, customer loyalty promotions
Banking and financial services	Customer service, trend analysis, product and service promotions, reduction of IS expenses
Credit card	Customer service, new information service for a fee, fraud detection
Defense contracts	Technology transfer, production of military applications
E-Business	Data warehouses with personalization capabilities, marketing/ shopping preferences allowing for up-selling and cross-selling
Government	Reporting on crime areas, homeland security
Health care	Reduction of operational expenses
Investment and insurance	Risk management, market movements analysis, customer tendencies analysis, portfolio management
Retail chain	Trend analysis, buying pattern analysis, pricing policy, inventory control, sales promotions, optimal distribution channel decisions

often less than 90 days. In addition, because they allow for local rather than central control, they confer power on the using group. They also contain less information than the data warehouse. Thus, they respond more quickly, and they are easier to understand and navigate. Finally, they allow a business unit to build its own decision-support systems without relying on a centralized IS department.

Operational Data Stores. An **operational data store** is a database for transaction processing systems that uses data warehouse concepts to provide clean data. It brings the concepts and benefits of the data warehouse to the operational portions of the business at a lower cost. Thus, it can be viewed as being situated between the operational data (in legacy systems) and the data warehouse. An operational data store is used for short-term decisions involving mission-critical applications rather than for the medium- and long-term decisions associated with the regular data warehouse. These decisions require access to much more current information. For example, a bank needs to know about all the accounts for a customer who is calling on the phone.

Questions

1. What is an enterprise data warehouse?
2. Compare databases and data warehouses in terms of data volatility and decision support.
3. What is an advantage of an active data warehouse (ADW)?
4. What are two benefits of a data warehouse?
5. Explain why a company might invest in a data mart.
6. What is an operational data store?

3.3 Data and Text Mining

Data mining tools are specialized software used to analyze data to find patterns, correlation, trends, or other meaningful relationships. Data mining, which is also called **data discovery,** is the process of analyzing data from different perspectives and summarizing it into information that can be used to increase revenues, decrease costs, or both. Data mining software allows users to analyze data from various dimensions or angles, categorize it, and find correlations or patterns among fields in the data warehouse. A data mining example is Nexus 7 deployed by DARPA, as described in *IT at Work 3.2.*

TEXT MINING

Up to 75 percent of an organization's data are nonstructured word processing documents, social media, text messages, audio, video, images and diagrams, fax and memos, call center or claims notes, and so on. **Text mining** is a broad category that involves interpreting words and concepts in context. Any customer becomes a brand advocate or adversary by freely expressing opinions and attitudes that reach millions of other current or prospective customers on social media. Text mining helps companies to tap in to the explosion of customer opinions expressed online. Social commentary and social media are being mined for sentiment analysis or to understand consumer intent. Innovative companies know they could be more successful in meeting their customers' needs, if they just understood them better. Text analytics is proving to bean invaluable tool in doing this. Tools and techniques for analyzing text, documents, and other nonstructured content are available from several vendors.

Combining data and text mining can create even greater value. Palomäki and Oksanen (2012) pointed out that mining text or nonstructural data enables organizations to forecast the future instead of merely reporting the past. They also noted that forecasting methods using existing structured data and nonstructured text from both internal and external sources provide the best view of what lies ahead.

IT at Work 3.2

U.S. Military Uses Data Mining Spy Machine for Cultural Intelligence

The Defense Advanced Research Projects Agency (DARPA) was established in 1958 to prevent strategic surprise from negatively impacting U.S. national security and create strategic surprise for U.S. adversaries by maintaining the technological superiority of the U.S. military. One DARPA office is the Information Innovation Office (I2O). I2O aims to ensure U.S. technological superiority in all areas where information can provide a decisive military advantage. This includes intelligence, surveillance, reconnaissance, and operations support. Figure 3.11 is an example. Nexus 7 is one of DARPA's intelligence systems.

Figure 3.11 The U.S. military has long relied on intelligence for national security

Nexus 7, Data Mining System

Nexus 7 is a massive new data mining system put into use by the U.S. military in Afghanistan to understand Afghan society, and to look for signs of weakness or instability. The classified program ties together "everything from spy radars to fruit prices" in order to read the Afghan social situation and help the U.S. military plot strategy. DARPA describes Nexus 7 as both a breakthrough data analysis tool and an opportunity to move beyond its traditional, long-range research role into a more active wartime mission.

Cultural Intelligence

On the military's classified network, DARPA technologists describe Nexus 7 as far-reaching and revolutionary, taking data from many agencies to produce population-centric, cultural intelligence. For example, Nexus 7 searches the vast U.S. spy apparatus to figure out which communities in Afghanistan are falling apart and which are stabilizing; which are loyal to the government in Kabul and which are falling under the influence of militants.

A small Nexus 7 team is currently working in Afghanistan with military-intelligence officers, while a much larger group in Virginia with a "large-scale processing capacity" handles the bulk of the data crunching, according to DARPA. "Data in the hands of some of the best computer scientists working side by side with operators provides useful insights in ways that might not have otherwise been realized."

Sources: Compiled from *DARPA.mil* (2012), Schachtman (2011) and *Defense Systems* (2011).

Questions

1. What is Nexus 7?
2. How does data mining help I2O achieve its mission?
3. What are Nexus 7's data sources?
4. According to DARPA, what benefit does Nexus 7 provide that could not be realized without it?

Text Analytics Procedure. With **text analytics,** information is extracted out of large quantities of various types of textual information. The basic steps involved in text analytics include:

1. **Exploration.** First, documents are explored. This might be in the form of simple word counts in a document collection, or manually creating topic areas to categorize documents by reading a sample of them. For example, what are the major types of issues (brake or engine failure) that have been identified in recent automobile warranty claims? A challenge of the exploration effort is misspelled or abbreviated words, acronyms, or slang.

2. **Preprocessing.** Before analysis or the automated categorization of the content, the text may need to be preprocessed to standardize it to the extent possible. As in traditional analysis, up to 80 percent of the time can be spent preparing and standardizing the data. Misspelled words, abbreviations, and slang may need to be transformed into a consistent terms. For instance, BTW would be standardized to "by the way" and "left voice message" could be tagged as "lvm."

3. **Categorizing and Modeling.** Content is then ready to be categorized. Categorizing messages or documents from information contained within them can be achieved using statistical models and business rules. As with traditional model development, sample documents are examined to train the models. Additional documents are then

Tech Note 3-4

msn Now *now.msn.com/*

Microsoft pushed out a product under the MSN brand called **msnNow.** It is a combination of data mining for trends and topics and editorial content. Surfacing trends has long been a part of the real-time web and social media. Twitter trends, for example, tend to be less than informative and more of a reflection on the constraints and structure of the twittersphere; msnNow has the potential to take trending seriously.

processed to validate the accuracy and precision of the model, and finally new documents are evaluated using the final model (scored). Models can then be put into production for automated processing of new documents as they arrive.

Text analytics can help identify the ratio of positive/negative posts relating to the promotion. It can be a powerful validation tool to complement other primary and secondary customer research and feedback management initiatives. Companies that improve their ability to navigate and text mine the boards and blogs relevant to their industry are likely to gain a considerable information advantage over their competitors.

IT at Work 3.3

Are There Places Not to Use Analytics?

Between 2008 and 2011, an estimated 25 percent of all newsroom employees were laid off or accepted buyouts, and over 100 free local papers went out of business. Why? During that time, newspaper advertising revenues nose-dived. One exception was AOL, which had hired many journalists. According to the AOL's CEO Tim Armstrong, the most valuable part of AOL is its collection of over 90 blogs and news sites that it manages. AOL relies much more on IT than traditional news-gathering organizations do. In 2010, AOL was using Seed to attract readers through search engines.

Seed: Mining Data and Text

Seed is a system based on the concept that editors can figure out what stories to assign to AOL writers by mining data and text from search engines and social networks. The writings are designed to appeal more to search engines than to readers. The results of data and text mining plus analytics are used to determine what AOL will feature on its blogs and news sites—that is, the results are used by AOL to *remake online news.*

Bad Use of Data/Text Mining and Analytics?

Many journalists and reporters believe the correct answer to the question of whether analytics should be applied to their industry is no. One critics states that AOL has "designed a system called Seed, a hybrid of journalism and engineering . . . Seed is based on the idea that editors can figure out what stories to assign by mining data from search engines like Google and social networks like Facebook. If algorithms can tell you what people are talking about, and what they're searching for, then you know what they want to read."

Seed's Potential Implications and Concerns

While Seed can help editors know what interests people, the results are a lot of stories along the lines of "Confessions of a

Personal Assistant" and "Insane Customer Service Calls: They Called about WHAT?"

Seed guidelines tell writers to maximize keyword density, which is the number of times that certain phrases appear in a piece. Increasing keyword density helps with SEO, search engine optimization, which in turn increases a page's ranking in web search results.

Two major concerns are:

1. **Reporting integrity:** Will Seed lead to online news coverage that's mostly gossip and weird drama?

2. **Reporting quality:** Will Seed's approach to "write to SEO's keyword density algorithm" lead to bad writing?

Having to target a story for search bots infuriates some journalists. One AOL reporter told *The New Yorker*, "When I started here, it was all about getting more page views. Then they decided on a different metric, SEO. What they never realized is that you can't build a real journalistic brand that way."

Sources: Compiled from Auletta (2011) and Brokaw (2011).

For Debate

1. In your opinion, who might benefit from Seed and what are those benefits?

2. To what extent, if any, do you agree about the concern for reporting integrity?

3. To what extent, if any, do you agree about the concern for reporting quality?

4. Do you detect other new media organizations following a similar strategy to attract readers—and remain in business? Identify those organizations and their similarity to AOL's use of Seed.

> 1. Describe data mining.
> 2. How does data mining generate or provide value? Given an example.
> 3. What is text mining?
> 4. Explain the text mining procedure.

3.4 Business Intelligence (BI) and Analytics

What products were bought in the last six months? Who purchased them? Which sales agents were involved? What type of cross-selling potential is there? How does the sales trend break down by product group over the last five years? What do daily sales look like in each of my sales regions?

Companies are using BI solutions to know what questions to ask and find answers to them. BI tools integrate and consolidate data from various internal and external sources and then process them into information to make smart decisions. According to The Data Warehousing Institute (TDWI) and *Business Intelligence Journal*, BI "unites data, technology, analytics, and human knowledge to optimize business decisions and ultimately drive an enterprise's success. BI programs usually combine an enterprise data warehouse and a BI platform or tool set to transform data into usable, actionable business information" (TDWI, 2012).

For many years, managers have relied on business analytics to make better-informed decisions. Multiple surveys and studies agree on BI's growing importance in analyzing past performance and identifying opportunities to improve future performance. Complex and competitive business conditions don't leave much slack for mistakes. To minimize mistakes, managers rely on business analytics technology to predict trends accurately and know how to respond to them early.

BI TRANSFORMS DATA TO DECISIONS

What started as a tool to support sales, marketing, and customer service departments has widely evolved into an enterprise-wide strategic platform. While BI systems are used in the operational management of divisions and business processes, they are also used to support strategic corporate decision making. The dramatic change that has taken effect in the last few years is the growth in demand for operational intelligence across multiple systems and businesses—increasing the number of people who need access to increasing amounts of data.

Business specialists need complex, multidimensional analyses, but businesses are also in search of KPIs that can be used by both departmental users and management. In addition, users want real-time access to this data so that they can monitor processes

---

Tech Note 3-5

Big Data, Also Known as Business Analytics and as the New Intelligent Enterprise

Big data, business analytics, and what the *MIT Sloan Management Review* calls new intelligence enterprise all refer to the ways that companies use the huge amounts of information they're generating (Brokaw, 2012). Business analytics is in high demand based on the following estimates:

- As of mid-2012, the data and analytics marketplace was worth an estimated $64 billion (McKinsey Global Institute).
- Venture capital firms invested an estimate $1 billion in data companies from 2008 through 2010 (451 Research).
- 90 percent of data stored on hard drives, on Internet servers, or in big databases has been collected in just the past two years (IBM).

Demand in the U.S. for people with deep expertise in data analysis could be greater than its projected supply in 2018 (McKinsey Global Institute, 2011).

with the smallest possible lag and intervene rapidly whenever KPIs deviate from their target values. To link strategic and operational perspectives, users must be able to drill down from highly consolidated or summarized figures into the detail numbers from which they were derived to perform in-depth analyses.

BI TECHNOLOGICAL ADVANCES

BI architecture is undergoing technological advances in response to big data and the performance demands of end users (Watson, 2012). BI vendors are facing the challenges of social, sensor, and other newer data types that must be managed and analyzed. One technology advance that can help handle big data is BI in the cloud. BI can be hosted on a public or private cloud. With a public cloud, a service provider hosts the data and/or software that are accessed via an Internet connection. For private clouds, the company hosts its own data and software, but uses cloud-based technologies.

For cloud-based BI, a popular option offered by a growing number of BI tool vendors is software-as-a-service (SaaS). MicroStrategy offers MicroStrategy Cloud, which offers fast deployment with reduced project risks and costs. This cloud approach appeals to small and midsize companies that have limited IT staff and want to carefully control costs. The potential downsides include slower response times, security risks, and backup risks.

BI in the cloud may be a smart option for all companies because the cloud is good for developing proofs of concept for a vendor's software or hardware before making a greater financial investment. For short-term projects, using the cloud can result in time and cost savings because it eliminates the need to buy and install new servers (Watson, 2012).

BUSINESS ANALYTICS

The driver of the business analytics trend is the need to be able to use data to create not just business value, but also competitive advantage. What are indicators of the trend? In 2011, 58 percent of the 4,500+ respondents to a survey conducted by *MIT Sloan Management Review* and IBM Institute for Business Value said their companies were gaining competitive value from analytics (Kiron & Shockley, 2011). To put the situation into perspective, look at Figure 3.12. In 2010, only 37 percent of respondents reported that gain from analytics.

IT at Work 3.4

BI for Finance

Office Depot, an office products supplier, implemented a BI initiative to standardize data used for decision making. In 2011, the company had a 20 TB (terabyte) global data warehouse that integrated data from all functional areas. The data warehouse supports 4,000 corporate, retail, and field sales users in North America and Europe.

Common Language Improves Communication

Prior to implementing the data warehouse and BI, those in the finance department had to piece together data from multiple ISs. Now their data is in a single repository. The data warehouse aligns financial and product data with a shared set of facts, providing finance and merchandising with a common language of terms so that departments can communicate clearly about product profitability issues.

Better Intelligence Improves Profit Margins

Financial analysts discovered lower profit margins on black-and-white copiers than color copiers. Working with the business managers, they shifted inventory to color copiers. When financial managers discovered that pricing discounts were higher than expected in several locations, business managers were notified and took corrective action.

According to Greg Thompson, director of financial systems," Because we now report immediately the cost of production and product margins, we have been able to help the business change its strategies more quickly."

Source: Eckerson (2011).

Percent of companies (n = 4,500+) gaining competitive value from analytics

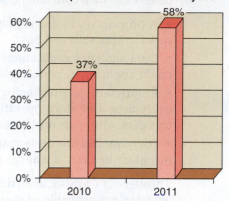

Figure 3.12 Percent of companies gaining a competitive advantage from business analytics increased from 37 percent in 2010 to 58 percent in 2011.
© Kiron & Shockley (2011).

MIT and IBM's key findings included:

1. Top-performing organizations use analytics five times more than lower performers.

2. There is widespread belief that analytics offers value.

3. Half of their respondents said that improvement of information and analytics was a top priority in their organizations.

It's important to point out that the increase came entirely from companies that were already using data analytics for more than financial forecasting, budgeting, and supply chain management. These financial uses represent the baseline (minimum) for analytics use in today's organizations. Companies that focused only on baseline uses of analytics were lagging behind leading-edge companies that rely on analytics to guide strategy as well as day-to-day activities in marketing and operations. Leading-edge companies had more experience with analytic tools and advanced modeling techniques.

Competitive Analytics in Practice: CarMax. CarMax, Inc. is the largest U.S. specialty retailer of used cars, with $9 billion in 2011 revenues. CarMax also sells vehicles that do not meet its retail standards to licensed dealers through on-site wholesale auctions; sells new vehicles under franchise agreements; and provides customers financing through its finance operation, CarMax Auto Finance (Figure 3.13).

CarMax had been the fastest retailer in U.S. history to reach $1 billion in revenues. They grew rapidly because of their compelling customer offer—no-haggle prices and quality guarantees backed by a 125-point inspection that became an industry benchmark—and auto financing.

Figure 3.13 CarMax is the United States' largest used-car retailer and a Fortune 500 company. The first CarMax was started in 1993 and grew to over 100 locations by 2012.

© Bloomberg via Getty Images

CarMax continues to enhance and refine its information systems, which it believes to be a core competitive advantage. CarMax's IT includes:

• A proprietary IS that captures, analyzes, interprets, and distributes data about the cars CarMax sells and buys.

• Data analytics applications that track every purchase; number of test drives and credit applications per car; color preferences in every demographic and region.

• Proprietary store technology that provides management with real-time data about every aspect of store operations, such as inventory management, pricing, vehicle transfers, wholesale auctions, and sales consultant productivity.

• An advanced inventory management system helps management anticipate future inventory needs and manage pricing.

Throughout CarMax, analytics are used as a strategic asset and insights gained from analytics are available to everyone who needs them.

Questions

1. What value does BI offer organizations?
2. What is the value of business analytics?
3. What does it mean to drill down, and why is it important?
4. What were MIT and IBM's key findings about analytics?
5. What ISs helped CarMax achieve record-setting growth?

3.5 Digital and Physical Document Management

As you read in the Quick Look, in 2012 Aberdeen's survey of 176 organizations worldwide found that the volume of physical documents is growing by up to 30 percent per year. Paper documents are a familiar sight, as you see in Figure 3.14.

Figure 3.14 Offices are still paper-intensive and dependent on document management systems.

© Yuri Arcurs/Alamy Limited

BUSINESS RECORDS

All companies create **business records,** which are documents that record business dealings such as contracts, research and development, accounting source documents, memos, customer/client communications, and meeting minutes. **Document management** is the automated control of imaged and electronic documents, page images, spreadsheets, voice and e-mail messages, word processing documents, and other documents through their life cycle within an organization, from initial creation to final archiving or destruction.

Document management systems (DMS) consist of hardware and software that manage and archive electronic documents and also convert paper documents into e-documents and then index and store them according to company policy. For example, companies may be required by law to retain financial documents for at least seven years, whereas e-mail messages about marketing promotions would be retained for a year and then discarded. DMS have query and search capabilities so that they can be identified and accessed like data in a database. These systems range from those designed to support a small workgroup to full-featured, web-enabled enterprise-wide systems.

Departments or companies whose employees spend most of the day filing or retrieving documents or warehousing paper records can reduce costs significantly with DMS. These systems minimize the inefficiencies and frustration associated with managing paper documents and paper workflows. Significantly, however, they do not create a paperless office as had been predicted.

A DMS can help a business to become more efficient and productive by:

- Enabling the company to access and use the content contained in the documents
- Cutting labor costs by automating business processes
- Reducing the time and effort required to locate information the business needs to support decision making
- Improving the security of the content, thereby reducing the risk of intellectual property theft
- Minimizing the costs associated with printing, storing, and searching for content

The major document management tools are workflow software, authoring tools, scanners, and databases. When workflows are digital, productivity increases, costs decrease, compliance obligations are easier to verify, and green computing becomes possible. Green computing is an initiative to conserve our valuable natural resources by reducing the effects of our computer usage on the environment. You can read about green computing and the related topics of reducing an organization's carbon footprint, sustainability, and ethical and social responsibility in Chapter 14.

Businesses also use a DMS for disaster recovery and business continuity, security, knowledge sharing and collaboration, and remote and controlled access to documents. Because DMS have multilayered access capabilities, employees can access and change only the documents they are authorized to handle. Visit altimate.ca/flash/viewer.html to see how files can be opened directly within the web browser without the file's native application installed locally on the user's computer. When companies select a DMS, they ask the following questions:

1. Does the software meet the organization's needs? For example, can the DMS be installed on the existing network? Can it be purchased as a service?
2. Is the software easy to use and accessible from web browsers, office applications, and e-mail applications? If not, people won't use it.
3. Does the software have lightweight, modern web and graphical user interfaces that effectively support remote users?

IT at Work 3.5 describes how several companies currently use DMS.

MEETING COMPLIANCE REQUIREMENTS

Simply creating backups of records is not sufficient because the content is not organized in a way to make it accurately and easily retrieved. The requirement to manage records—regardless of whether they are physical or digital—is not new.

IT at Work 3.5

How Companies Use Document Management Systems

Examples of how companies use DMS are:

- The Surgery Center of Baltimore stores all medical records electronically, providing instant patient information to doctors and nurses anywhere and at any time. The system also routes charts to the billing department, who can then scan and e-mail any relevant information to insurance providers and patients. The DMS helps maintain the required audit trail, including providing records when they are needed for legal purposes. How valuable has the DMS been to the center? Since it was implemented, business processes have been expedited by more than 50 percent, the costs of these processes have been significantly reduced, and the morale of office employees in the center has improved noticeably.

- American Express (AMEX) uses TELEform, a DMS developed by Alchemy and Cardiff Software, to collect and process more than 1 million customer satisfaction surveys every year. The data are collected in templates that consist of more than 600 different survey forms in 12 languages and 11 countries. AMEX integrated TELEform with AMEX's legacy system, which enables it to distribute processed results to many managers. Because the survey forms are now readily accessible, AMEX has reduced the number of staff who process these forms from 17 to 1, thereby saving the company more than $500,000 a year.

- The University of Cincinnati provides authorized access to the personnel files of 12,000 active employees and tens of thousands of retirees. The university receives more than 75,000 queries about personnel records every year and then must search more than 3 million records to answer these queries. Using a microfilm system to find answers took days. The solution was a DMS that digitized all paper and microfilm documents, without help from the IT department, making them available via the Internet and the university's intranet. Authorized employees access files using a browser.

Questions

1. What types of waste can DMS reduce?
2. How do DMS reduce waste?
3. What is the value of providing access to documents via the Internet or corporate network?

What is new is the volume that must be reviewed to determine whether they should be retained or destroyed. Properly managed, records are strategic assets. Improperly managed or destroyed, they are liabilities.

Companies need to be prepared to respond to an audit, federal investigation, lawsuit, or any other legal action against it. Types of lawsuits against companies include patent violations, product safety negligence, theft of intellectual property, breach of contract, wrongful termination, harassment, discrimination, and many more.

Questions

1. What are business records?
2. What is the difference between a document and a record?
3. What are document management systems (DMS)?
4. Why is creating backups an insufficient way to manage an organization's documents?
5. With respect to documents, what must companies be prepared to respond to?

Key Terms

You find clickable Link Libraries for each chapter on the Companion website.

Oracle demos *http://www.oracle.com*

> *oracle.com/pls/ebn/swf_viewer.load?p_shows_id=9758640&p_referred=0&p_width=1000&p_height=675*

> *oracle.com/pls/ebn/swf_viewer.load?p_shows_id=8143184&p_referred=0&p_width=1000&p_height=675*

Sybase IQ *sybase.com*

SAP BI *sap.com*

McKinsey Global Institute *mckinsey.com*

IBM *Ibm.com*

msnNow *http://now.msn.com/*

Analysis Factory, gallery of custom solutions *http://www.analysisfactory.com/gallery/custom-solutions/*

SAS Enterprise Miner, data mining solution *http://www.sas.com/technologies/analytics/datamining/miner/*

Case #3: video *http://video.ca.msn.com/watch/video/privacy-vs-convenience-how-we-enable-data-mining/17ytv84iw*

MSN Privacy vs. Convenience video

Evaluate and Expand Your Learning

IT and Data Management Decisions

1. Visit *http://sas.com/technologies/analytics/datamining/miner/* to assess the features and benefits of SAS Enterprise Miner.
   a. Click the *Demos & Screenshots* tab.
   b. View the SAS Enterprise Miner Software demo, which is about 7 minutes.
   c. Based on what you learn in the demo, what skills or expertise are needed to build a predictive model?
   d. At the end of the demo, you hear the presenter say that "SAS Enterprise Miner allows end-users to easily develop predictive models and to generate scoring to make better decisions about future business events." Do you agree that SAS Enterprise Miner makes it easy to develop models? Explain.
   e. Do you agree that if an expert had developed predictive models that they would help managers make better decisions about future business events? Explain.
   f. Based on your answers to c, d, and e, under what conditions would you recommend SAS Enterprise Miner?

Questions for Discussion & Review

1. Given three examples of business processes or operations that would benefit significantly from having detailed real-time or near real-time data and identify the benefits.

2. Select an industry. Explain how an organization in that industry could improve consumer satisfaction through the use of data warehousing.
3. List three types of waste or damages that data errors can cause.
4. Explain the principle of 90/90 data use.
5. Why is master data management (MDM) important in companies with multiple data sources?
6. Distinguish between operational databases, data warehouses, and data marts.
7. Discuss the factors that make document management so valuable. What capabilities are particularly valuable?
8. Why do data and text management matter?
9. Why is data mining important?
10. How can document management decrease costs? How can it increase customer satisfaction and ultimately customer retention?

Online Activities

1. Visit *Oracle.com*. Click the *Products and Services* tab to open the menu; then click *Oracle Database*. The links are posted in the Chapter 3 Link Library.
   a. Click *Demos* and select *Oracle Database Management Solutions*. What are the benefits of Oracle's Database Management Packs? How do the Packs improve manageability and automation?

b. Click *Demos* and select *Storage Management*. View the *Storage Management with Oracle Database 11g* demo video. What are the benefits of data compression? What are the benefits of this storage solution?

2. Visit the Microsoft SQL Server website at *Microsoft.com/sqlserver*. Click the *About SQL Server* tab and select Customer Stories from the pop-up window. Select one of the customer stories. Describe the challenges or opportunities facing the customer and the business benefits of SQL Server.

3. Visit *Teradata.com*. Click Video News, and select one of the videos. Write an executive summary of the video.

Collaborative Work

1. Each person on the team interviews at least two managers or knowledge workers in various industries. Find the data problems they have encountered and the IT solutions that were selected to solve them. How successful were the IT solutions? Compile the results of the interviews. What do the results suggest about today's data problems? What do the results suggest about IT solutions?

2. Read IT at Work 3-2: U.S. Military Uses Data Mining Spy Machine for Cultural Intelligence. Discuss and answer the questions.

CASE 2   BUSINESS CASE

Global Defense Contractor Gains Competitive Edge with Analytics

BAE Systems (*baesystems.com*) is a global defense and security company with approximately 100,000 employees worldwide. The company delivers a full range of products and services for air, land, and naval forces; and advanced electronics, security, IT solutions, and support services.

BAE Systems had used business analytics for basic costs and financial analysis. When the contractor became involved in long-term performance-based contracts for its military and technical services, it needed more powerful analytical capability. With performance-based contracts, BAE Systems is responsible and liable for equipment availability. If the contract terms are not met, the company does not get paid.

Business Challenge

Michael Peters, Head of Business and Solution Modeling, explained that the business challenge was to answer:

- How do we know we can guarantee the availability of the particular system we're offering?
- How do we know we will make revenue on this and can actually perform against the KPIs in the contract?
- What should the KPIs be?

Deciding the terms of a contract requires that managers understood the relationship between cost, performance, revenue, and risk. With support from the company's analytics team, managers now make data-driven decisions about contract terms and commitments.

Peters estimates that the return on the investment in analytics is at least 20-to-1 or as high as 50-to-1. Much of the cost savings is passed on to customers. Using analytics to reduce performance risk and passing some of the cost savings to customers, gives BAE Systems a significant advantage over its competitors.

Sources: Compiled from BAE Systems (2012), Kiron et al. (2011)

Questions & Activities

1. What change triggered BAE Systems' interest in analytics?
2. Was reducing cost the primary driver of this investment? Explain why or why not.
3. What risk did the company face for poor performance?
4. Assuming that government contracts are awarded to a large extent on cost with the lowest bid the winner, how did BAE Systems gain a competitive edge on its competitors?

CASE 3   VIDEO CASE

Privacy vs. Convenience: How We Enable Data Mining

1. View the *MSN.com* video Privacy vs. Convenience: How we enable data mining. Duration is 7:41. Find the link in the Chapter 3 Link Library *http://video.ca.msn.com/watch/video/privacy-vs-convenience-how-we-enable-data-mining/17ytv84iw* or do a search for it.

2. Discuss the big issue, namely privacy vs. convenience, from the perspective of consumers or individuals. What are the benefits? What are the risks?

3. Discuss the big issue, namely privacy vs. convenience, from the perspective of marketing. What are the benefits? What are the ethical issues?

4. How does your data get captured and used to target ads to individuals?

5. Why do shoppers give their information to retailers such as Amazon and Banana Republic?

6. What other data issues do you think are (or should be) a concern to managers?

Data Analysis & Decision Making

Calculating Document Management Costs

Spring Street Company (SSC, a fictitious company) wanted to reduce the "hidden costs" associated with its paper-intensive processes. Employees jokingly predicted that if the windows were open on a very windy day, there would be total chaos as the papers started flying. If a flood, fire, or windy day occurred, the business would grind to a halt.

The company's accountant, Sam Spring, decided to calculate the costs of their paper-driven processes to identify their impact on the bottom line. He recognized that several employees spent most of their day filing or retrieving documents. In addition, there were the monthly costs to warehouse old paper records. Sam measured the activities related to the handling of printed reports and paper files. His average estimates are as follows:

a) **Dealing with a file:** It takes an employee 12 minutes to walk to the records room, locate a file, act on it, re-file it, and return to his desk. Employees do this 4 times per day (5 days per week).

b) **Number of employees:** 10 full-time employees perform these functions described in (a).

c) **Lost document replacement.** Once per day a document gets "lost" (destroyed, misplaced, or covered with massive coffee stains) and must be re-created. The total cost of replacing each lost document is $200.

d) **Warehousing costs:** Currently, document storage costs are $75 per month.

Sam would prefer a system that lets employees find and work with business documents without leaving their desks. He's most concerned about the human resources and accounting departments. These personnel are traditional heavy users of paper files and would greatly benefit from a modern document management system. At the same time, however, Sam is also risk averse. He would rather invest in solutions that would reduce the risk of higher costs in the future. He recognizes that the U.S. PATRIOT Act's requirements that organizations provide immediate government access to records apply to SSC. He has read that manufacturing and government organizations rely on efficient document management to meet these broader regulatory imperatives. Finally, Sam wants to implement a disaster recovery system.

Your Mission

Prepare a report that provides Sam with the data he needs to evaluate the company's costly paper-intensive approach to managing documents. You will need to conduct research to provide data to prepare this report. Your report should include the following information:

1. How should SSC prepare for a DMS if they decide to implement one?

2. Using the data collected by Sam, create a spreadsheet that calculates the costs of handling paper at SSC based on average hourly rates per employee of $28. Add the cost of lost documents to this. Then, add the costs of warehousing the paper, which increases by 10 percent every month due to increases in volume. Present the results showing both monthly totals and a yearly total. Prepare graphs so that Sam can easily identify the projected growth in warehousing costs over the next three years. Download the spreadsheet to help you get started from the textbook's website.

3. How can DMS also serve as a disaster recovery system in case of fire, flood, or break-in?

4. Submit your recommendation for a DMS solution. Identify two vendors in your recommendation.

Resources on the Book's Website

More resources and study tools are located on the Student Website. You'll find additional chapter materials and useful web links. In addition, self-quizzes that provide individualized feedback are available for each chapter.

References

Auletta, K. "You've got news." *The New Yorker.* January 24, 2011.

Brokaw, L. "Ken Auletta on the Dark Side of Applying Analytics to Journalism." *MIT Sloan Management Review, Improvisations.* January 26, 2011.

Brokaw, L. "'Mapping the TV Genome' at Bluefin Labs and Big Data's Big Stats." *MIT Sloan Management Review, Improvisations.* February 2, 2012.

BusinessWire, "Wendy's Selects Clarabridge's Text Analytics Solution to Enhance Customer Feedback Program." March 22, 2010.

Clarabridge, Press Release, March 22, 2010, *clarabridge.com/.*

DARPA, 2012. darpa.mil/.

Defense Systems. "DARPA intell program sent to Afghanistan to spy." July 21, 2011.

Eckerson. W. "Financial Transformation." *Teradata Magazine*, Q1 2011.

Ferguson, M. "Data Ownership and Enterprise Data Management: Is Your Data Under Control?" *DataFlux.com,* 2012.

Gartner, "Market Share: All Software Markets, Worldwide 2011." March 29, 2012.

Kable, B. "Police to be issued with mobile fingerprinting devices," *ZDNet UK,* March 5, 2010.

Kiron, D. & R. Shockley. "Creating Business Value with Analytics." *MIT Sloan Management Review.* September 15, 2011.

Kiron, D. R. Shockley, N. Kruschwitz, G. Finch & M. Haydock. "BAE Systems: A New Business Model Takes Flight. *MIT Sloan Management Review.* November 7, 2011.

LaValle, S., M. Hopkins, E. Lesser, R. Shockley and N. Kruschwitz. "Analytics: The new path to value." *MIT Sloan Management Review* and *IBM Institute for Business Value.* October 2010.

Levine, L., "In Sync: Getting the Supply Chain Act Together," *Health care Purchasing News*, April 2007. *hpnonline.com/inside/2007-04/0704-DataSynch2.html.*

McKinsey Global Institute. "The challenge—and opportunity—of 'big data.'" May 2011.

NPIA (National Policing Improvement Agency), "Science and Innovation in the Police Service, 2010-2013." 2010.

Oracle, "Zero-Downtime Database Upgrades Using Oracle GoldenGate." February 2010.

Palomäki, P., & M. Oksanen, "Do We Need Homegrown Information Models in Enterprise Architectures?" *Business Intelligence Journal.* Vol. 17, no. 1, March 19, 2012.

Savvas, A. "BNP Paribas deploys Oracle Exadata database." *ComputerWorld UK,* January 3, 2012.

Shachtman, N. "Inside Darpa's Secret Afghan Spy Machine." *Wired,* July 21, 2011.

Sheina, M. "Bad data costing US businesses $700 billion a year." *Ovum*, October 5, 2010.

Silva, V. "Focus on application deployments urgent: Informatica." *NetworkWorld.* April 8, 2010.

Snow, C., "Embrace the Role and Value of Master Data Management." *Manufacturing Business Technology*, 26(2). February 2008.

TDWI (The Data Warehousing Institute), 2012. *tdwi.org/portals/business-intelligence.aspx.*

Thurston, T. "Police to get mobile fingerprint-checking tech." *ZDNet UK,* March 25, 2010.

Watson, H. J. "This Isn't Your Mother's BI Architecture." *Business Intelligence Journal.* Vol. 17, no. 1, First Quarter 2012.

Whitehouse.gov, 2012.

Worthen, B. "IT versus Terror," *CIO*, August 1, 2006.

Zynapse, "New Strategies for Managing Master Data." *zynapse.com.* September 10, 2010.

Quick Look

Learning Outcomes

❶ Describe network systems and their quality-of-service issues, how high-speed data and voice networks function, and opportunities to improve operational efficiency and business models.

❷ Describe wireless applications, mobile network infrastructure, and how they support worker productivity, business operations, and strategy.

❸ Explain the business value of intranets, extranets, and other network portals and their role in improving relationships with employees, customers, and supply chain partners.

❹ Evaluate performance improvements from virtual collaboration and communication technologies, and explain how they support group work.

❺ Describe how companies can contribute to sustainability, green, social, and ethical challenges related to the use and operations of IT networks.

IT networks are critical infrastructures and a huge expense for organizations. Business runs on high-capacity (broadband) data and voice networks. Business performance depends on wired and wireless network connectivity, mobility, and collaboration. And even for companies in non-Internet industries, it has long been known that their strategic advantage comes from network capabilities for communication and collaboration. For example, when the Ford Motor Company began relying on UPS's complex IT networks to track its inventory of millions cars and trucks, they reduced annual vehicle inventory by $1 billion and inventory holding costs by $125 million a year (Rapp & Subramanian, 2004). Recent research shows that web server response times can impact e-commerce sales revenues. For instance, users get impatient and are less likely to revisit a website if the time it takes to load is longer than competitors by 250 milliseconds (Lohr, 2012). Figure 4.1 puts that time into perspective.

Users have the same intolerance for other types of network delays. For the most part, networks are transparent until service is degraded or the unthinkable happens—a crash.

Exciting developments and disruptions are occurring in networks and collaboration. The latest 4G networks, multitasking mobile operating systems, and collaboration platforms are revolutionizing work, business processes, and other things not yet imagined. Wired and wireless networks carry an environmental price tag because of their huge energy consumption, contribute to health risks, and challenge personal privacy.

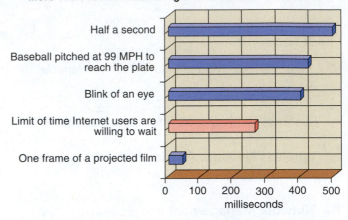

Internet Users' Are Impatient With Web Pages That Take More Than 250 Millisecs Longer To Load Than Other Sites

Figure 4.1 Internet users are intolerant of slow responses to their requests for service.

CASE 1 OPENING CASE

Mobile Network Gives Haneda Airport Its Competitive Edge

Tokyo has two competing airports, Narita International Airport (NIA), which handles mostly international air traffic, and Haneda Airport with mostly domestic air traffic. Haneda Airport is the world's fifth-busiest airport with 18 domestic and foreign airlines handling more than 60 million passengers a year—and countless customer service challenges. Haneda's FLY TO THE WORLD logo (Figure 4.2) represents its strategic goal—to be a hub for global travel. Management of Haneda wanted to significantly increase the number of international flights and attract more travelers—putting it into direct competition with NIA.

Figure 4.2 Haneda Airport gained a competitive advantage by deploying a wireless network that keeps travelers connected and improves baggage handling. *Fly to the World* is its logo.

© Jeff Greenberg/Alamy Limited*

Competitive International Aviation Industry

The international aviation industry is a major economic force composed of approximately 2,000 airlines operating more than 23,000 aircraft and providing service to over 3,700 airports. Huge revenues are generated from airport and airline operations and their related industries, primarily aircraft manufacturing and tourism. Not only is there fierce competition among the airlines, the airports also compete for connecting traffic, cargo traffic, and destination traffic. The quality, cost, and scope of service offered by an airport have an impact on the attractiveness of the destination, which in turn influences the destination's ability to attract the convention market. In fact, convention planners have ranked air service as the second-most-important factor for selecting a convention's location.

Investment in Instant-On Connectivity Pays Off

Tokyo International Airport Terminal Corporation (TIAT) is responsible for the new construction and operation of the Haneda international airport terminal (*haneda-airport.jp/inter/en/mobile/*). TIAT knows that continually driving innovation and improving passenger service are critical success factors in the competitive aviation industry. TIAT decided to provide *instant-on connectivity* to travelers in the international terminal lounges and departure zones. Why? Because when flight delays, cancellations, and other disruptions stress out stranded passengers, they are most in need of access to reliable information via their mobiles to resolve their problems fast. In addition, mobile networks support baggage management, which has reduced lost or misdirected luggage.

TIAT implemented a wireless network infrastructure from HP (*hp.com*). A secured wireless local area network (WLAN) covers roughly 500,000 square feet (150,000 square meters) of the terminal. Wireless access points (APs), typically routers, are base stations for the wireless network. See Figure 4.3.

If any wireless access point (AP) fails, an alternative AP is automatically found and the connection is instantly recovered. This configuration minimizes network downtime, improves the stability of the wireless network, and gives travelers uninterrupted connectivity as they move throughout the international terminal. The investment in wireless connectivity has Haneda Airport management achieve its strategic goal of increased international traffic.

Discuss

1. Why is free, easy instant-on wireless connectivity an important service at an airport?
2. How does the WLAN impact customer service?
3. How can wireless connectivity reduce customer service costs for the airlines that use Haneda Airport's international terminal?
4. What do international airports compete for? Why?
5. What components are needed for a WLAN?

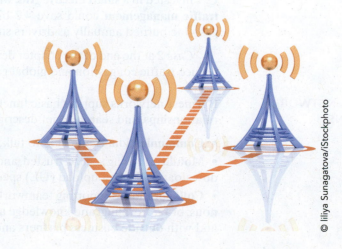

Figure 4.3 A wireless local area network (LAN) is created by multiple wireless access points (AP). Most wireless LANs are based on IEEE 802.11- standards, also known as Wi-Fi. Wi-Fi connectivity uses radio frequencies (RF).

© liliya Sunagatova/iStockphoto

Decide

6. Visit the Haneda Airport, International Flight Passenger Terminal at *haneda-airport.jp/inter/en/*. Click on MOBILE TIAT. What other mobile IT-based services are offered to travelers? How might these mobile technologies make it easier and less expensive to manage airport operations?

Debate

7. What are Haneda Airport's competitors?
8. Does TIAT's investment in the WLAN to provide *instant-on connectivity* to customers in the international terminal provide Haneda Airport with a strategic advantage? Or is the WLAN an expense—that is, the cost of doing business today?

4.1 Business IT Networks and Components

High-speed data and voice networks determine (or restrict) how commerce is conducted and business gets done. Innovative uses of network capabilities create opportunities for more efficient operations and new business strategies, as the cases in this chapter illustrate. For example, machines increasingly communicate and interact directly with other machines over a variety of wireless and wired networks. These **machine-to-machine (M2M)** communications use sensors to relay signals or data through the network to an application, which initiates an action such issuing a traffic alert or closing a valve.

CHANGES BEING DRIVEN BY BROADBAND NETWORKS

Demand for high-capacity networks is growing at unprecedented rates. Examples of high-capacity networks are wireless mobile, satellite, wireless sensor, and VoIP (voice over Internet Protocol) such as Skype. **Voice over IP (VoIP)** networks carry voice calls by converting voice (analog signals) to digital signals. Network capacity is measured in terms of its throughput, or **bandwidth.** The term **broadband** is short for broad bandwidth and means high capacity.

Consulting firm Booz & Co. (*booz.com*) estimated that within the next decade:

1. One trillion sensors will be deployed globally in the form of **smart dust,** gathering and digitizing trillions of gigabytes of data and transmitting it wirelessly to a growing number of big data machines for storage and analysis.

2. The CO_2 (carbon dioxide) equivalent of 53 million cars could be eliminated if the U.S. invested in a **smart electric grid,** which is also called **smart grid** technology. **Smart traffic management** could save 4.2 billion work-hours and 2.64 billion gallons of gasoline burned annually as drivers sit in cars idle in traffic.

Case 2 at the end of the chapter describes how smart mobile networks could help reduce traffic congestion and global gridlock.

BUSINESS NETWORK FUNCTIONS

Business networks support basic functions: communication, mobility, collaboration, relationships, and search. Brief descriptions of these functions are:

- **Communication:** Being able to talk, text, tweet, fax, send messages, etc.
- **Mobility:** Having secure, trusted, and reliable access from anywhere at satisfactory download (DL) and upload (UL) speeds.
- **Collaboration:** Supporting teamwork activities that are synchronous and asynchronous; brain storming; and knowledge and document sharing with in the organization and with outside business partners and interests.

Tech Note 4.1

Internet Protocol (IP) is the method by which data is sent from one device to another via a private network, cellular network, or public Internet. A device's **IP address** uniquely identifies it to the network.

Network **switches** and **routers** are devices that transmit data to their destination based on IP addresses. Switches and routers are the building blocks for all business communications—data, voice, video, and wireless. A switch acts as a controller, enabling networked devices to talk to each other efficiently. Business networks use switches to connect computers, printers and servers within a building or campus. Switches create a network. Routers connect networks. A router links computers to the Internet, so that users can share the connection. Routers act like a dispatcher, choosing the best paths for signals or packets to travel so that they are sent and received quickly.

- **Relationships:** Managing interaction with customers, supply chain partners, shareholders, employees, regulatory agencies, etc.
- **Search:** Locating data, contracts, documents, spreadsheets, diagrams, messages, and other knowledge within an organization easily and efficiently.

Selecting and implementing the correct networks are important because they can improve profitability by increasing productivity, reducing business expenses, and improving security and customer service.

Digital Transmissions. The transmission of the signal by the switches and routers is called **switching.** The two types of switching are:

- **Circuit switching:** A circuit is a dedicated connection between a source and destination, such as when a call is placed between two landline phones. Circuit switching is older technology that originated with telephone calls; and is inefficient for digital transmission.
- **Packet switching:** Packet switching transfers data in small blocks called packets based on the destination IP address in each packet. When received at the destination, the packets are reassembled into their proper sequence.

Wireless networks use packet switching and wireless routers whose antennae transmit and receive packets. At some point, wireless routers are connected by cables to wired networks, as shown in Figure 4.4. *IT at Work 4.1* describes the gains from a wireless network infrastructure.

An important management decision concerns the network's quality of service (QoS), especially for delay-sensitive data such as real-time voice and high-quality video. The higher the required QoS, the more expensive the technologies needed to manage

Video 4-1
Connect for Success
This video from Cisco (*cisco.com*) describes how Fresh Direct Produce uses network technology to connect employees, suppliers, and customers. (2:50 minutes) *http://www.cisco.com/cisco/web/solutions/small_business/solutions/connect_employees_offices/index.html.*

QUALITY OF SERVICE (QoS)

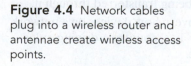

Figure 4.4 Network cables plug into a wireless router and antennae create wireless access points.

IT at Work 4.1

Hospital of the Future Built on Mobile Network Infrastructure

Rockingham Memorial Hospital (RMH) Health care, located in Harrisonburg, VA, is a 238-bed community hospital providing health care services since 1912. RHS serves seven counties—admitting more than 16,000 inpatients and treating nearly 200,000 outpatients.

When hospital's management began planning a move to a new facility, they saw an opportunity to design the *hospital of the future*. Their goal was to use state-of-the-art clinical, information, and mobile network technologies to provide safer, more effective patient care. That meant an accessible electronic medical record (EMR) system, a picture archiving and communications system (PACS) capable of transmitting massive imaging files throughout the facility, networked clinical devices, and VoIP communications systems. Health care providers needed to have access to medical data to treat and monitor patients at any time and location.

Robust Next-Gen Wireless Network

To support their health care vision, RMH needed a next-generation hospital network that provided high-speed wireless coverage across the entire new hospital. The wireless network had to support both voice and data communications and as robust as a wired infrastructure, according to Michael Rozmus, RMH's chief information officer (CIO). The most critical requirement for the new hospital network was that it provide a flexible foundation for future

applications. For example, the network had to be able to adapt to rapidly changing health care technology, such as biomedical technology.

Network Solution and Benefits

RMH management believed that they would benefit most from a single-vendor approach. They invested in a Cisco wireless and unified communications network solution. Specifically, the solution consisted of Cisco Borderless Networks with Cisco routers, switches, security, and wireless infrastructure. Key benefits are:

- Improved emergency response times by 50 to 60 percent
- Enhanced clinician responsiveness to patients and other clinicians
- Achieved 100 percent compliance with regulatory standards

Sources: Compiled from Cisco (2010) and RMHonline.com (2012).

Questions

1. What capabilities did RMH management envision for the hospital of the future?
2. Why was an adaptable network solution so critical to RMH?
3. What were the main components of the hospital's network?
4. In your opinion, how do the hospital's network-enabled capabilities influence quality of health care and health care costs?

---

organizational networks. Bandwidth-intensive apps are important to business processes, but they also strain network capabilities and resources. Regardless of the type of traffic, networks must provide secure, predictable, measurable, and sometimes guaranteed services for certain types of traffic. For example, QoS technologies can be applied to create two-tiers of traffic:

- **Prioritize traffic:** Data and apps that are time-delay sensitive or **latency-sensitive apps,** such as voice and video are given priority on the network.

- **Throttle traffic:** In order to give latency-sensitive apps priority, other types of traffic need to be held back (throttled).

The ability to prioritize and throttle network traffic is referred to as traffic shaping and forms the core of the hotly debated Net Neutrality issue, which is discussed in *IT at Work 4.2.*

NETWORK TERMINOLOGY To be able to evaluate networks and the factors that determine their functionality, you need to be familiar with the following network basics.

- **Bandwidth:** Bandwidth is a measure of the speed at which data is transmitted. Bandwidth depends on the network protocol. Common wireless protocols are 802.11b. 802.11g, 802.11n, and 802.16. For an analogy to bandwidth, consider a pipe used to transport water. The larger the diameter of the pipe, the greater the throughput (volume) of water that flows through it and the faster water is being transferred through it.

- **Protocol:** Protocols are rules and standards that govern how devices on a network exchange data and talk to each other. An analogy is a country's driving rules—whether to drive on the right or left side of the road.

IT at Work 4.2

Net Neutrality vs. Traffic Shaping

Traffic shaping is the practice of managing data transfer to ensure a certain level of performance or QoS. Specifically, traffic is shaped by delaying the flow of less-important network traffic (e.g., bulk data transfers, P2P (peer-to-peer) file-sharing programs, BitTorrent traffic) and giving priority to more important data. Traffic shaping creates a two-tier system that is used for a number of purposes. Two purposes are:

1. Time-sensitive data may be given priority over traffic that can be delayed briefly with little-to-no adverse effect.

2. In a corporate environment, business-related traffic may be given priority over other traffic.

Traffic shaping is hotly debated by those in favor of **net neutrality.** They want a one-tier system in which all Internet data packets are treated the same, regardless of their content, destination or source. In contrast, those who favor the two-tiered system argue that there have always been different levels of Internet service and that a two-tiered system would enable more freedom of choice and promote Internet-based commerce.

Net Neutrality Debate

The concept of net neutrality holds that Internet service providers (ISPs) should treat all sources of data equally. It has been the center of a debate over whether ISPs can give preferential treatment to content providers who pay for faster transmission, or to their own content, in effect creating a two-tier Web, and about whether they can block or impede content representing controversial points of view.

Federal Communications Commission's (FCC) 2010 Decision

On December 21, 2010, the FCC approved a compromise that created two classes of Internet access, one for fixed-line providers and the other for the wireless Net. In effect, the new rules are **net semi-neutrality.** They ban any outright blocking and any "unreasonable discrimination" of web sites or applications by fixed-line broadband providers. But the rules do not explicitly forbid "paid prioritization," which would allow a company to pay an ISP for faster data transmission. Despite the FCC ruling, the debate over net neutrality continues.

Sources: Complied from Federal Communications Commission (*fcc.gov*), Byars (*2010*), and various blog posts.

Questions

1. What is net neutrality?

2. Why is net neutrality such a hotly debated issue?

3. Did the FCC's ruling favor either side of the debate? Explain.

- **TCP/IP:** TCP/IP (transmission control protocol/Internet protocol) is the basic communication protocol of the Internet. This protocol is supported by every major network operating system (OS) to ensure that all devices on the Internet can communicate. It is used as a communications protocol in a company's private network for internal uses.
- **Fixed-line broadband:** Describes either cable or DSL Internet connections.
- **Mobile broadband:** Describes various types of wireless high-speed Internet access through a portable modem, telephone, or other device.
- **3G:** Short for *third generation* of cellular networks. 3G networks support multimedia and broadband services, do so over a wider distance, and at faster speeds than prior 1G and 2G generations. 3G networks have far greater ranges because they use large satellite connections to telecommunication towers.
- **4G:** Short for *fourth generation*. 4G mobile network standards enable faster data transfer rates. 4G networks are digital, or IP, networks.

3G AND 4G

4G technologies represent the latest stage in the evolution of wireless data technologies. 4G delivers average *realistic* download rates (as opposed to *theoretical rates which are much higher*) of 3Mbps or higher. In contrast, today's 3G networks typically deliver average download speeds about one-tenth of that rate. Even though individual networks, ranging from 2G to 3G, started separately with their own purposes, soon they will be converted to the 4G network.

What is significant about 4G networks is that they do not have a circuit-switched subsystem, as do current 2G and 3G networks. Instead, 4G is based purely on the

> **Tech Note 4.2**
>
> **Origin of the Internet, e-Mail, and TCP/IP**
>
> ARPAnet (Advanced Research Projects Agency network) was the first real network to run on packet switching technology. In October 1969, computers at Stanford University, UCLA, and two other U.S. universities connected for the first time—making them the first hosts on what would become the Internet. ARPAnet was designed for research, education, and government agencies. ARPAnet provided a communications network linking the country in the event that military attack or nuclear war destroyed conventional communications systems.
>
> In 1971, e-mail was developed by Ray Tomlinson, who used the @ symbol to separate the username from the network's name, which became the domain name.
>
> On January 1, 1983, ARPAnet computers switched over to the TCP/IP protocols developed by Vinton Cerf. A few hundred computers were affected by the switch. The original ARPAnet protocol had been limited to 1,000 hosts, but the adoption of the TCP/IP standard made larger numbers of hosts possible. By the end of 2012, the number of Internet hosts was near 1 billion.

packet-based IP. Users can get 4G wireless connectivity through one of the following standards:

1. WiMAX is based on the IEEE 802.16 standard and is being deployed by Clearwire for wholesale use by Sprint, Comcast, and Time-Warner Cable to deliver wireless broadband. WiMAX has theoretical speeds of 128 Mbps, with actual download speeds of only 4 Mbps.

2. LTE (Long-Term Evolution) is a GSM-based technology that is deployed by Verizon, AT&T, and T-Mobile. LTE has theoretical speeds of 100 Mbps or more, but actual download speeds range from 10 to 15 Mbps on Verizon.

Improved network performance, which is measured by its *data transfer capacity*, provides fantastic opportunities for mobility, mobile commerce, collaboration, supply chain management, remote work, and other productivity gains.

BUSINESS USES OF NEAR-FIELD COMMUNICATION

Near-field communication (NFC) is an umbrella term that applies to various location-aware technologies, such as **radio-frequency identification (RFID)**. RFID is a location-aware system that transmits the identity (in the form of a unique serial number) of an object or person using radio waves. RFID is used to track items in a supply chain or equipment in a hospital.

NFC technology allows devices to communicate securely with each other over short distances. Location-aware NFC technology can be used to make purchases in restaurants, resorts, hotels, theme parks and theaters, at gas stations, and on buses and trains. Here are examples.

• ASSA ABLOY, a Swedish company, is testing NFC smartphones for remote hotel check-ins and as wireless hotel room keys at Clarion Hotels.

• A major resort chain is evaluating NFC's ability to create instant ski lift passes for guests.

• Passengers on public transportation systems can pay fares by waving an NFC smartphone as they board.

• Banks, credit card issuers, and other financial organizations can benefit from NFC smartphones, as password-protected smartphones send data over encrypted wireless networks and can be much more secure than conventional credit and debit cards.

With millions of NFC-equipped smartphones set to reach users over the next few years and the technology's advantages for shoppers and businesses, NFC looks destined to emerge as a major force in the coming decade.

One popular implementation is pay-by-mobile systems. Near-field will allow users to swipe their smartphone in front of an NFC terminal and pay for almost anything.

Mashup of GPS and Bluetooth.   Advances in GPS positioning and short-range wireless technologies, such as Bluetooth and Wi-Fi, can provide unprecedented intelligence. They could, for example, revolutionize traffic and road safety. Intelligent transport systems being developed by car manufacturers allow cars to communicate with each other and send alerts about sudden braking. In the event of a collision, the car's system could automatically call emergency services. The technology could also apply the brakes automatically if it was determined that two cars were getting too close to each other.

Advancements in networks, devices, and RFID sensor networks are changing enterprise information infrastructures and business environments dramatically. The preceding examples and network standards illustrate the declining need for a physical computer, as other devices provide access to data, people, or services at anytime, anywhere in the world, on high-capacity networks using IP technology. Slow wireless speeds, compared to wireline speeds, had been a constraint. 4G networks and advanced handsets operating on multiple network standards offer universal connectivity/mobility.

Questions

1. What is the difference between circuit switching and packet switching?
2. What is the difference between 3G and 4G?
3. Define bandwidth and broadband.
4. Briefly described the basic network functions.
5. Explain how the FCC settled the net neutrality debate.
6. What are the mobile network standards?
7. Explain near-field communication (NFC).

4.2 Wireless Network Applications and Mobile Infrastructure

In the 21st century global economy, advanced wireless networks are a foundation on which global economic activity takes place. Current 3G and 4G networks and technologies provide that foundation, moving entire economies. For any nation to stay competitive and prosperous, it is imperative that investment and upgrades in these technologies continue to advance to satisfy demand. Mobile data traffic is forecasted to grow 18-fold in size and speed through 2016, according to *Cisco Visual Networking Index (VNI) Mobile Data Traffic Forecast, 2011–2016*. Several key forecasts for 2016 are:

• **More users are using more bandwidth.** By 2016, there will be 5.1 billion mobile users, up from 4.1 billion in 2011. Also by 2016, the majority of global mobile users (60 percent, or 3 billion people) will belong to the *Gigabyte Club* generating more than one gigabyte of mobile data traffic per month, typically by viewing data-intensive video content.

• **More users have more mobile devices.** By 2016, there will be 10 billion mobile devices and connections equal to one-and-a-half devices for each person on Earth.

• **More powerful mobiles.** By 2016, smartphones will represent 82 percent of all handsets, up from just 12 percent in 2011. Mobile traffic originating from tablets will grow 62-fold from 2011 to 2016. That's the highest growth rate of any device category tracked in the Mobile VNI forecast. Just a few years ago, tablets didn't even exist as a category.

• **Wireless networks serving mobiles are getting faster.** By 2016, 36 percent of mobile data traffic will be on a 4G network (*The Network*, 2011)

In addition to feeding mobile users' habits, increased bandwidth is needed to support the numerous industrial applications that leverage wireless technologies. Two leading apps are the smart grid and health care segments.

IT at Work 4.3

Mobile and Virtual Care

In the U.S., Verizon Wireless is developing a suite of digital health care solutions that include chronic care management and virtual care.

- Its **digital care management solution** will leverage a cloud platform and connected medical devices. This solution will integrate biometric devices and deliver personalized care plans to people on their mobile devices.
- The **virtual care solution** will leverage advances in 4G LTE technology by utilizing smartphones, tablets, and video technology.

The resulting tool will virtualize a health care visit, eliminating the need to physically visit a doctor's office for many routine consults.

Sources: Compiled from Friedrich (2011) and Verizon Wireless.

Questions

1. What are the benefits of digital health care solutions?

2. What technologies are needed for virtual health care?

With a combination of smart meters, wireless technology, sensors, and software, the smart grid allows utilities to accurately track power grids and cut back on energy use when the availability of electricity is stressed. And consumers get insight into their power consumption to make more intelligent decisions about how they use energy.

Wireless hospitals and remote patient monitoring, for example, are growing trends. Tracking medical equipment and hospital inventory, such as gurneys, are done with RFID tagging at a number of hospitals. Remote monitoring apps are making health care easier and more comfortable for patients while reaching patients in remote areas, as discussed in *IT at Work 4.3*.

STRATEGIC PLANNING OF BUILD-OUT OF MOBILE CAPABILITIES

Enterprises are moving away from ad hoc adoption of mobile devices and network infrastructure to a more strategic planning build-out of their mobile capabilities. As technologies that make up the mobile infrastructure evolve, identifying strategic technologies and avoiding wasted investments require more extensive planning and forecasting. Factors to consider are the network demands of multitasking mobile devices, more robust mobile OSs, and their applications.

Mobile Infrastructure. Mobile infrastructure consists of the integration of technology, software, support, security measures, and devices for the management and delivery of wireless communications.

WI-FI

Wi-Fi technology allows devices to share a network or Internet connection without the need to connect to a commercial network. Wi-Fi networks beam large chunks of data over short distances using part of the radio spectrum, or they can extend over larger areas, such as municipal Wi-Fi networks. However, municipal networks are not common because of their huge costs. See Figure 4.5 for an overview of how Wi-Fi works.

WIRELESS WIDE AREA NETWORKS (WWANS)

There are three general types of mobile networks: wide area networks (WANs), WiMAX, and local area networks (LANs). WANs for mobile computing are known as **WWANs (wireless wide area networks).** The range of a WWAN depends on the transmission media and the wireless generation, which determines which services are available. Two components of wireless infrastructures are wireless LANs and WiMAX.

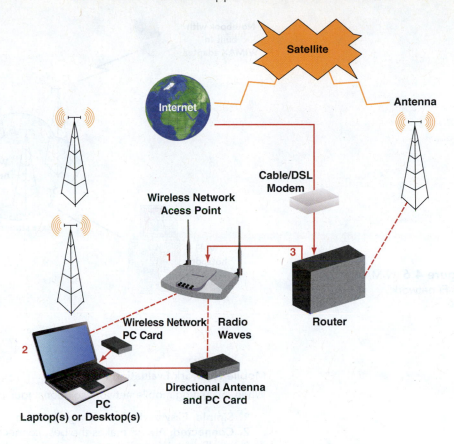

1 Radio-equipped access point connected to the Internet
   (or via a router). It generates and receives radio waves
   (up to 400 feet).
2 Several client devices, equipped with PC cards, generate
   and receive radio waves.
3 Router is connected to the Internet via a cable or
   DSL modem, or is connected via a satellite.

Figure 4.5 Overview of Wi-Fi.

Wireless LAN. Wireless LANs use high-frequency radio waves to communicate between computers, devices, or other nodes on the network. A wireless LAN typically extends an existing wired LAN by attaching a wireless AP to a wired network.

WiMAX–Wireless Broadband. WiMAX transmits voice, data, and video over high-frequency radio signals to businesses, homes, and mobile devices. It was designed to

---

Tech Note 4.3

Wi-Fi networking standards are:

- **802.11b.** This standard shares spectrum with 2.4 GHz cordless phones, microwave ovens, and many Bluetooth products. Data are transferred at distances up to 300 feet.
- **802.11a.** This standard runs on 12 channels in the 5 GHz spectrum in North America, which reduces interference issues. Data are transferred about 5 times faster than 802.11b, improving the quality of streaming media. It has extra bandwidth for large files. Since the 802.11a and b standards are not interoperable, data sent from an 802.11b network cannot be accessed by 802.11a networks.
- **802.11g.** This standard runs on three channels in 2.4 GHz spectrum, but at the speed of 802.11a. It is compatible with the 802.11b standard.
- **802.11n.** This standard improves upon the previous 802.11 standards by adding multiple-input multiple-output (MIMO) and many other newer features. Frequency ranges from 2.4 GHz to 5GHz with a data rate of about 22 Mbps, but perhaps as high as 100 Mbps.

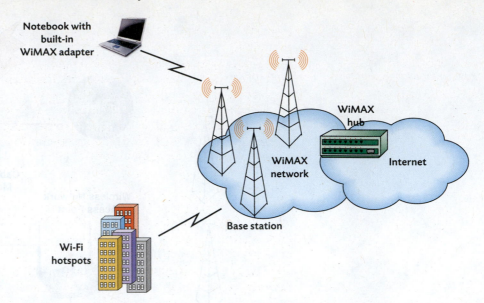

Figure 4.6 WiMAX/
Wi-Fi network.

Tech Note 4.4

Mobile Network Evaluation Factors

When evaluating mobile network solutions, four factors to consider are:

1. **Simple:** Easy to deploy, manage and use.
2. **Connected:** Always makes the best connection possible.
3. **Intelligent:** Works behind the scenes, easily integrating with other systems.
4. **Trusted:** Enables secure and reliable communications.

bypass traditional telephone lines and is an alternative to cable and DSL. WiMAX is based on the IEEE 802.16 set of standards and the metropolitan area network (MAN) access standard. Its range is 20 to 30 miles and does not require a clear line of sight to function. Figure 4.6 shows the components of a WiMAX/Wi-Fi network.

Questions

1. What factors are contributing to mobility?
2. Why is strategic planning of mobile networks important?
3. How does Wi-Fi work?
4. What is a WLAN?
5. Why is WiMAX important?
6. What factors should be considered when selecting a mobile network?

4.3 Network Management and Search

With few exceptions, when the network goes down or access is blocked, so does the ability to operate or function normally. Imagine a network meltdown in which you could not access text messages, apps, the Internet, software, and data files. At most companies, employees would have nothing to do—or an extremely horrible time trying to do work—without network connectivity. Obvious damages of network downtime include lost sales and productivity, financial consequences from not being able to send and receive payments, and inability to process payroll and inventory.

MODEL OF THE NETWORK, COLLABORATION, AND PERFORMANCE RELATIONSHIP

Figure 4.7 presents a model of key network and collaboration factors that influence profitability, sales growth, and ability to innovate. As the model illustrates, an enterprise's network capability depends on proper planning, maintenance, management, upgrades, and bandwidth of the network to insure that it has sufficient capacity and connectivity to link people, locations, and data. It also requires that those who need to access the network are equipped with the devices making it possible to do so. As a comparison, a highway system needs to be planned carefully to support peak traffic demands, monitored for compliance with driving rules, cleaned and maintained regularly, and expanded (upgraded) when it no longer meet the needs of those who rely on it.

When problems inevitably occur (e.g., a network crash or car crash), trained staff are needed to restore the network promptly or to switch to a backup system to minimize disruption during the restoration. *IT at Work 4.4* illustrates the importance of these factors and the consequences of bad planning and the lack of testing of up-to-date disaster recovery plans.

The network architecture is certainly critical because it provides the infrastructure for collaborative work within the company and with external partners and customers, regardless of their location. Often overlooked is the fact that capability and willingness to collaborate depend on a corporate culture that people trust and that gives them the information, tools, and authority to plan and make decisions. When knowledge workers have such authority, the organization has a decentralized (also called *flatter*) organizational structure. A decentralized organization is more responsive to opportunities and problems than a centralized organization where top-level managers, who are typically less involved in day-to-day operations, make decisions.

The purpose of this model is to illustrate that network infrastructure alone does not improve business performance. Rather, it is how network capabilities combine with collaboration technologies to support employees and cross-functional work, connect remote locations, service customers, and coordinate with supply chain partners.

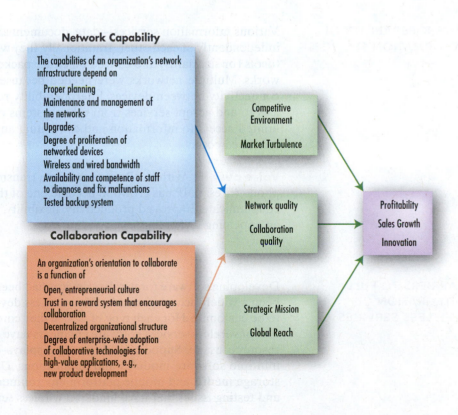

Figure 4.7 Model of network, collaboration, and performance relationship.

Network Capability

The capabilities of an organization's network infrastructure depend on

- Proper planning
- Maintenance and management of the networks
- Upgrades
- Degree of proliferation of networked devices
- Wireless and wired bandwidth
- Availability and competence of staff to diagnose and fix malfunctions
- Tested backup system

Collaboration Capability

An organization's orientation to collaborate is a function of

- Open, entrepreneurial culture
- Trust in a reward system that encourages collaboration
- Decentralized organizational structure
- Degree of enterprise-wide adoption of collaborative technologies for high-value applications, e.g., new product development

Competitive Environment

Market Turbulence

Network quality

Collaboration quality

Strategic Mission

Global Reach

Profitability

Sales Growth

Innovation

IT at Work 4.4

U.S. Customs' Network Crash Strands Passengers

In August 2007, more than 20,000 international travelers were stranded for up to eleven hours because the U.S. Customs and Border Protection (CBP) Agency could not process passengers due to a network crash. A network crash brings immigration to a halt. The crash and long outage was blamed on the cumulative effect of poor network planning, insufficient disaster preparation, a malfunctioning router and network interface card (NIC), mistakes in diagnosing the cause of the outage, and the lack of staff available to repair the network.

Immediate Causes of the Crash and Crisis. The outage started with a malfunctioning NIC on a single workstation on the CBP's LAN. Instead of simply failing, the NIC began sending a huge number of packets through the network causing a "data storm" that crashed the LAN. Later, a switch on the network crashed also, compounding the problem. Misdiagnosing the problem and blaming it on routers provided to Sprint wasted about six hours. Sprint tested the lines remotely, then sent a Sprint technician on site to run more tests, and finally concluded after six hours that the routers were fine, and that it was a LAN issue.

Policy Remained in Force, but Not a Backup System. Because of a zero-tolerance policy, all travelers must be processed and screened through national law-enforcement databases located in Washington, D.C. There was a backup system consisting of a local copy of the database in case of a loss of connectivity to Washington, but the backup system ran on the same LAN, and there was no backup system for a LAN failure.

Human or Machine Error? Human errors were a bigger part of the outage than technological ones. Michael Krigsman, the CEO of Asuret (asuret.com), a Massachusetts-based software and consulting company, wrote on his blog that the cause was a breakdown common in low-cost equipment and gross incompetence. Some experts were baffled that a single NIC could have caused so much trouble. However, a single NIC can take down an older network such as the CBP's, but not updated ones. Furthermore, if a network is not well managed, it increases the number of hours offline while the problem is identified and fixed. Newer networks are a lot more intelligent and able to self-diagnose.

CBP's Plan to Avoid Another Crash. The CBP recognized the need to improve its IT staff, equipment, and infrastructure. They planned to improve diagnostic capabilities at both the human and technological levels to prevent such a head-scratching incident from happening again. They also will get the right technology and staff in place at LAX and other ports.

Sources: Complied from Krigsman (2007) and Poeter (2007).

Questions

1. What are the risks of a legacy network?
2. What were the technical factors that contributed to the failure of the backup system?

INTEROPERABILITY OF INFORMATION SERVICES

Various information services—data, documents, voice, and video—have functioned independently of each other. Traditionally, they were transmitted using different protocols (or standards) and carried on either packet-switched or circuit-switched networks. Multiple networks were needed because of the lack of **interoperability** or connectivity between devices. Interoperability refers to the ability to provide services to and accept services from other systems or devices. Lack of interoperability limited access to information and computing and communications resources—and increased costs.

Voice over IP. With VoIP, voice and data transmissions travel in packets over telephone wires. VoIP has grown to become one of the most used and least-cost ways to communicate. Improved productivity, flexibility, and advanced features make VoIP an appealing technology.

BARRIERS TO FULL INTEGRATION OF WIRELESS SERVICES

Developing software for wireless devices had been challenging because there has not been a widely accepted standard for wireless devices. Therefore, software apps need to be customized for each type of device they communicated with. To keep down the cost of wireless services, software engineers have had to develop code that optimizes resource usage. Supporting different displays can force painstaking changes to multiple software modules and applications. Different CPUs, operating systems, storage media, and mobile platform environments create time-consuming porting and testing issues that have hindered wireless service integration.

COMPUTER NETWORKS

Intranets, extranets, virtual private networks, and enterprise search engines are widely used computer networks.

Intranets. An intranet is a network serving the internal informational needs of a company, using Internet tools. Intranets are portals (also called gateways) that provide easy and inexpensive browsing and search capabilities. Colleges and universities rely on intranets to provide services to students and faculty. Enterprise search engines are discussed later in this section. Using screen sharing and other groupware tools, intranets can be used to facilitate collaboration.

IT at Work 4.5 describes Canada's Labatt Brewing Company use of an intranet portal, named The Pub, for enterprise collaboration and search. The Pub was built using Microsoft Office SharePoint Server (MOSS) and Microsoft SharePoint Services (MSS). **SharePoint** is an integrated suite of capabilities that provides content (unstructured information) management and enterprise search to support collaboration. An enterprise search system provides extensive capabilities for searching structured and unstructured data sources easily. The enterprise search system

IT at Work 4.5

Canada's Labatt Brewer Builds "The Pub," an Intranet for Enterprise Collaboration and Search

How does an enterprise ensure that its employees get the information they need when they need it? For Labatt Brewing Company, the solution was to leverage the power of the SharePoint platform to build a world-class intranet portal. Labatt Breweries of Canada is one of the nation's oldest companies. Labatt is part of Belgium-based Interbrew S.A., one of the largest brewing groups in the world with more than 180 types of beer available in over 110 countries worldwide. And Labatt Blue is the best-selling Canadian beer in the world.

Traditionally, the company used employee meetings and postings on bulletin boards to keep employees informed, but with Labatt employees spread across Canada, the company was faced with the challenge of delivering information to employees in a consistent and timely manner. Much of Labatt's corporate information had been tough to share because it was housed in silos belonging to various business units, meaning employees had difficulty finding up-to-date, pertinent information.

Labatt's Intranet's Architecture and Benefits. After determining Labatt's business and technology requirements, the Labatt IT team decided that an intranet would provide the most efficient way of delivering the single point of access to employees. The intranet would also provide document management and collaboration. The intranet, which was named The Pub, was built using Microsoft Content Management Server, Microsoft Office SharePoint Portal Server, and SharePoint Team Services.

Using The Pub, Labatt rolled out new programs to its employees, such as the Innovation Database. Labatt wanted innovative ways to improve every aspect of the business, and the Innovation Database provides a forum for employees to submit ideas and receive recognition and rewards for ideas that are implemented. Through the seamless deployment of Microsoft technology as the infrastructure for Labatt's intranet, The Pub, the company has been able to empower employees, improve employee communication, and create efficiencies with the IT department, while making a significant impact on employee productivity and collaboration. About 70 percent of Labatt's employees use the portal, which has significantly improved productivity and collaboration across the board. With the robust search function within The Pub, employees are able to quickly locate the documents they need and obtain the information they require to make better business decisions.

Using Microsoft SharePoint Services, a team website was designed to significantly improve the way teams manage information and activities. Team workspaces provides a common point of access for project or departmental information, including, documents, contacts, tasks, and discussions. A summary of the benefits of The Pub are:

- Empower employees
- Help improve overall employee communication
- Create efficiencies with the IT department
- Help make a significant impact on employee productivity and collaboration

Sources: Compiled from *Labatt.com*, Microsoft case study *Labatt Breweries of Canada*, and Imason (2010).

Questions

1. How do information silos impact productivity?

2. Why was a single point of access an important feature?

3. How has sharing information via The Pub improved collaboration at Labatt?

4. Why might workers not be in favor of document and data sharing?

Figure 4.8 Example of an AT&T extranet used by a customer to access account information.

provides fast query response times and consolidated, ranked results (like the results of a Google search) that help users easily locate the information they need. Other descriptions of SharePoint are:

- Browser-based collaboration and document management platform.
- Content management system that allows groups to set up a centralized, password-protected space for document sharing. Documents can be stored, downloaded, and edited, and then uploaded for continued sharing.
- Web-based intranet that can improve management of and access to data.
- Enterprise information portal that can be configured to run intranet, extranet and Internet sites.

Extranets and VPNs. An extranet is a private, company-owned network that can be logged into remotely via the Internet. Typical users are suppliers, vendors, partners, or customers (Figure 4.8). Basically, an extranet is a network that connects two or more companies so they that can securely share information. Since authorized users remotely access content from a central server, extranets can drastically reduce storage space on individual hard drives.

A major concern is the security of the transmissions that could be intercepted or compromised. One solution is to use virtual private networks (VPNs), which encrypt the packets before they are transferred over the network. VPNs consist of encryption software and hardware that encrypt, send, and decrypt transmissions, as shown in Figure 4.9. In effect, instead of using a leased line to create a dedicated, physical

Figure 4.9 Virtual private networks (VPN) create encrypted connections to company networks.

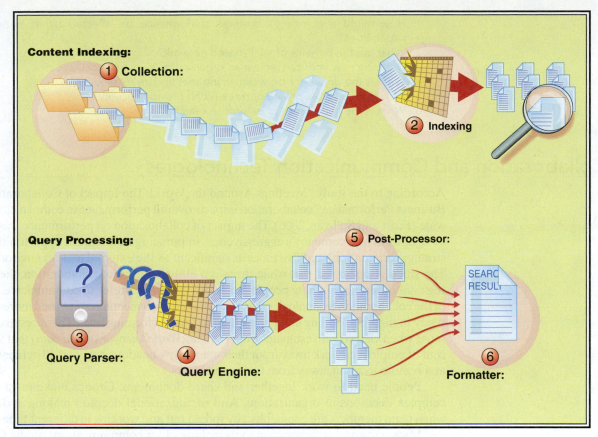

Figure 4.10 Components of enterprise search.

connection, a company can invest in VPN technology to create virtual connections routed through the Internet from the company's private network to the remote site or employee. Extranets can be expensive to implement and maintain because of hardware, software, employee training costs if hosted internally rather than by an application service provider (ASP).

ENTERPRISE SEARCH

Finding your own files and information can be tough, so you can imagine how tough it is to find content created by others in an organization. Too often data, big data, files, and documents are difficult to find and access. The volume of data stored in many organizations reached the point where it actually interferes with productivity rather than contributes to it. One solution is **enterprise search.**

Enterprise search (Figure 4.10) starts with **content indexing,** which is created by software that crawls through directories and websites to extract content from databases and other repositories. Content indexing is done on a regular basis, so if one of those repositories is updated, the search engine will have some sort of procedure that enables it to go in and source and index that updated content.

Content that's been collected is *indexed.* That is, a searchable index of all the content is created. Additional processing, such as metadata extraction, and also auto-summarization might be done, depending on the search engine that is used.

Once the index is created, it can be queried—just as users do Google searches of the Internet. For example, to query an enterprise, a user enters his search terms into a search box on the intranet screen. Of course, what matters is not how searchable the enterprise's content is, but finding the content that is needed.

1. How might a company's business performance be affected by its network's capabilities?
2. What are the benefits of an IP-based network?
3. Describe how VoIP can reduce an organization's communication costs.
4. What is the difference between an intranet and an extranet?
5. How does a virtual private network (VPN) provide security?
6. What is the importance of enterprise search?

4.4 Collaboration and Communication Technologies

According to the study "Meetings Around the World: The Impact of Collaboration on Business Performance," collaboration impacts overall performance in companies worldwide (Frost and Sullivan, 2006). The impact of collaboration on performance was twice as significant as a company's aggressiveness in pursuing new market opportunities (its strategic orientation) and five times as significant as the external market environment. The study also showed that while there is a global culture of collaboration, there are regional differences in how people in various countries prefer to communicate. Of all of the collaboration technologies that were studied, web meetings were used more extensively in high-performing companies than in low-performing ones. These results make sense when viewed with estimates from *NetworkWorld* (*networkworld.com*) that 90 percent of employees work away from their company's headquarters and 40 percent work at a remote location, away from their supervisors.

People need to work together and share documents. Groups make most of the complex decisions in organizations. And organizational decision making is difficult when team members are geographically spread out and working in different time zones.

Messaging and collaboration tools include older communications media such as e-mail, videoconferencing, fax, and texts—and newer media such as blogs, podcasts, RSS, wikis, VoIP, web meetings, and torrents for sharing very large files. As media move to IP, there will not be much left that is not converged onto data networks. One of the biggest components of many Web 2.0 sites and technologies is collaboration. Much of Web 2.0 is about harnessing the knowledge and work of many people. You read about Web 2.0 in greater detail in Chapter 8.

VIRTUAL COLLABORATION

Leading businesses are moving quickly to realize the benefits of virtual collaboration. Here are several examples.

Information Sharing Between Retailers and Their Suppliers: P&G and Wal-Mart. One of the most publicized examples of information sharing is between Procter & Gamble (P&G) and Wal-Mart. Wal-Mart provides P&G access to sales information on every item Wal-Mart buys from P&G. The information is collected by P&G on a daily basis from every Wal-Mart store, and P&G uses the information to manage the inventory replenishment for Wal-Mart.

Retailer-Supplier Collaboration: Asda Corporation. Supermarket chain Asda (*asda.com*) has begun rolling out web-based electronic data interchange (EDI) technology to 650 suppliers. Web-EDI technology is based on the AS2 standard, an internationally accepted HTTP-based protocol used to send real-time data in multiple formats securely over the Internet. It promises to improve the efficiency and speed of traditional EDI communications, which route data over third-party value-added networks (VANs).

Lower Transportation and Inventory Costs and Reduced Stockouts: Unilever. Unilever's 30 contract carriers deliver 250,000 truckloads of shipments annually. Unilever's web-based database, the Transportation Business Center (TBC), provides these carriers with site specification requirements when they pick up a shipment at a manufacturing or distribution center or when they deliver goods to retailers. TBC gives carriers all of the vital information they need: contact names and phone numbers, operating hours, the number of dock doors at a location, the height of the dock doors, how to make an appointment to deliver or pick up shipments, pallet configuration, and other special requirements. All mission-critical information that Unilever's carriers need to make pickups, shipments, and deliveries is now available electronically 24/7.

Reduction of Product Development Time: Caterpillar, Inc. Caterpillar, Inc. (*caterpillar.com*) is a multinational heavy-machinery manufacturer. In the traditional mode of operation, cycle time along the supply chain was long because the process involved paper-document transfers among managers, salespeople, and technical staff. To solve the problem, Caterpillar connected its engineering and manufacturing divisions with its active suppliers, distributors, overseas factories, and customers, through an extranet-based global collaboration system. By means of the collaboration system, a request for a customized tractor component, for example, can be transmitted from a customer to a Caterpillar dealer and on to designers and suppliers, all in a very short time. Customers also can use the extranet to retrieve and modify detailed order information while the vehicle is still on the assembly line.

GROUP WORK AND DECISION PROCESSES

Managers and staff continually make decisions as they develop and manufacture products, plan social media marketing strategies, make financial and IT investments, determine how to meet compliance mandates, design software, and so on. By design or default, group processes emerge, referred to as **group dynamics,** and those processes can be productive or dysfunctional.

Group Work and Dynamics. Group work involves can be quite complex depending on the following factors:

• Group members may be located in different places or work at different times.
• Group members may work for the same or different organizations.
• Needed data, information, or knowledge may be located in many sources, several of which are external to the organization.

Despite the long history and benefits of collaborative work, groups are not always successful.

Online Brainstorming in the Cloud. Brainstorming ideas is no longer limited to a room full of people offering their ideas that are written on a whiteboard or posters. Companies are choosing an alternative—online brainstorming apps in the cloud. An advantage is avoiding travel expenses if members a geographically dispersed, which often restricts how many sessions the company can afford to hold. Two examples of online brainstorming apps are:

1. Evernote (*evernote.com/*) is a cloud-based tool that helps users gather and share information, and brainstorm ideas. One function is Synch, which keeps Evernote notes up to date across a user's computers, phones, devices and the web. See Figure 4.11. A free version of Evernote is available for download.
2. iMindmap Online, from UK-based Think Buzan (*thinkbuzan.com*), relies on mind mapping and other well-known structured approaches to brainstorming. iMindmap Online helps streamline work processes, minimize information overload, generate new ideas, and boost innovation.

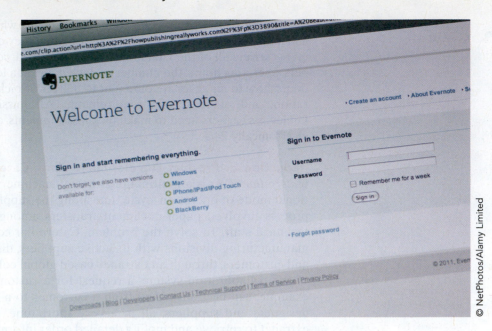

Figure 4.11 Evernote brainstorming, note taking and archiving software website.

Questions

1. What is virtual collaboration?
2. Why is group work challenging?
3. What are the benefits of working in groups?
4. What might limit the use of in-person brainstorming?
5. How can online brainstorming tools overcome those limits?

4.5 Sustainability and Ethical Issues

This section brings attention to the impacts of always-connected and networked lives. No easy or convenient answers exist. And every IT user plays a role in the solution.

MOBILE, CLOUD, SOCIAL, AND GLOBAL LEAVE A FOOTPRINT ON THE ENVIRONMENT

The use of androids, iPhones and other mobiles for everything from social networking to cloud-based apps has raised data consumption dramatically—and with it energy consumption. The surge in energy used to power data centers, cell towers, base stations, recharge mobiles, and so onis damaging the environment. To reduce damaging emissions, companies have implemented new green initiatives. An example is discussed in *IT at Work 4.6*.

Sustainability Solutions. Communications technology accounts for approximately 2 percent of global carbon emissions, a figure that is predicted to double by 2020 as end-user demand for high-bandwidth services with enhanced quality of experience explodes worldwide. Innovative solutions hold the key to curbing these emissions and reducing environmental impact.

Network service providers as well as organizations face the challenges of energy efficiency, smaller carbon footprint, and eco-sustainability. To deal with these challenges, wired and wireless service providers and companies need to upgrade their networks to next-generation, all-IP infrastructures that are optimized and scalable. The network must provide eco-sustainability in traffic transport and deliver services more intelligently, reliably, securely, efficiently, and at the lowest cost.

For example, Alcatel-Lucent's High Leverage Network (HLN) can reduce total cost of ownership by using fewer devices to do more with less, creating an eco-sustainable

IT at Work 4.6

Eco-Sustainable Networks Cut Carbon Emissions by 42 Percent

Mobile network operators worldwide have embarked on bold initiatives to improve the energy efficiency of their wireless networks and reduce the carbon footprint and greenhouse gas (GHG) emissions associated with network operations. According to a Pike Research report (*pikeresearch.com/*), these green network initiatives reduced network carbon emissions by 42 percent by 2013. Mobile operators in Asia Pacific are leading carbon emissions reduction, followed by Europe and North America.

Sustainability Incentives

Four incentives are driving mobile network operators (carriers) to develop greener mobile networks. The four incentives are:

1. **To reduce costs.** Energy consumption is one of the biggest operating costs for both fixed and mobile networks.

2. **To overcome limited availability of reliable electricity.** Many developing countries are high-growth markets for telecommunications, but they have limited reliable access to electricity.

3. **To be more socially responsible.** Many organizations have adopted corporate social responsibility initiatives with a goal of reducing their networks' carbon footprints.

4. **To gain competitive advantage.** Network infrastructure vendors are striving to gain competitive advantage by reducing the power requirements of their equipment. All of these factors will continue to converge over the next several years, creating significant market potential for greener telecom networks.

In 2010, Clearwire Communications, the largest 4G service provider in the U.S., outlined a series of advancements in network architecture to increase capacity, enhance data speeds, and help reduce the environmental impact of the company's growing wireless data network. Clearwire started trials of its first high-efficiency "green" base station cabinets in Chicago. This new generation of base station cabinets is capable of up to a 90 percent reduction in electrical operating expenses, in part because they do not require air conditioning.

Questions

1. Rank the four incentives according to how you believe they motivate a company to invest in greener IT.

2. Explain the reasons for your ranking.

3. Review predictions of global warming and related issues. Consider the expected surge in the use of 4G networks that will increase electricity consumption to power the networks and cool the equipment. Based on your research, estimate the impact on the environment if mobile network operators did not invest in greener networks.

4. Bottom line: Is it profitable for operators to go green? Explain.

---

choice for service providers. Fewer devices mean less power and cooling, which reduces carbon footprint. For example, the HLN can handle large amounts of traffic more efficiently. That's because both bandwidth and intelligence are designed-in to send traffic only where it needs to go, at the highest speed and in the most efficient way.

ETHICAL CONSIDERATIONS OF A CONNECTED WORKFORCE

Managers need to consider ethical and social issues, such as quality of working life. Workers will experience both positive and negative impacts from being linked to a 24/7 workplace environment, working in computer-contrived virtual teams, and being connected to handhelds whose impact on health can be damaging. A 2008 study by Solutions Research Group found that always being connected is a borderline obsession for many people. According to the study, 68 percent of Americans may suffer from *disconnect anxiety*—feelings of disorientation and nervousness when deprived of Internet or wireless access for a period of time. Technology addiction has gone so far that U.S. psychiatrists are considering adding this "compulsive-impulsive" disorder to the next release of the DSM (Diagnostic and Statistical Manual of Mental Disorders).

Consider these developments and their implications:

Driving while distracted is a crime. Texting while driving is quickly becoming the new "driving under the influence," according to safety experts. Several studies show use of mobile devices is a leading cause of car crashes. At any given moment, more than 10 million U.S. drivers are talking on handheld cell phones, according to the National Highway Traffic Safety Administration (*NHTSA.dot.gov*). Why is this a problem? Mobiles are a known distraction, and the NHTSA has determined that driver inattention is a primary or contributing factor in as many as 25 percent of all police-reported traffic accidents. This doesn't include the thousands of accidents that are not reported to the authorities.

In most or all states, distracted driving is a crime that carries fixed fines. For example, in California and New York State, drivers charged with this crime face fines of at least $150 and points on their driving records. If driving while distracted causes injury or death to others, violators face up to 14 years in prison. Fines and penalties will increase if these levels are not strong enough deterrents. (See Figure 4.12.)

Health risks. The U.S. Food and Drug Administration (FDA) recommends minimizing potential risk by using hands-free devices and keeping mobile phone talk to a minimum. A few studies have indicated that using a mobile phone for an hour each day over a 10-year period can increase the risk of developing a rare brain tumor and that those tumors are more likely to be on the side of the head used to talk on the phone. More research is needed in this area.

RF emissions and SAR. According to the Cellular Telecommunications Industry Association (*ctia.org/*), specific absorption rate, or **SAR,** is "a way of measuring the quantity of radio frequency (RF) energy that is absorbed by the body." For a phone to pass Federal Communications Commission (FCC) certification and be sold in the U.S., its maximum SAR level must be less than 1.6 watts per kilogram (1.6 W/kg). Canada has the same (1.6 W/kg) cap as the U.S. In Europe, the maximum level is 2 watts per kilogram. The SAR level that is reported shows the highest SAR level measured with the phone next to the ear as tested by

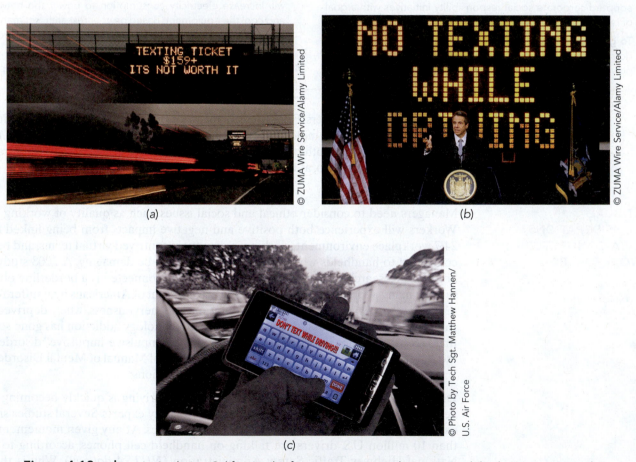

(a)   (b)

(c)

Figure 4.12 a, b, c In Anaheim, California, the freeway sign warns that *texting while driving is not worth it* during *National Distracted Driving Awareness* Month. In Manhattan, New York, Governor Cuomo signed the *Distracted Drivers Bill* that fines distracted drivers $150 and 2 points. The U.S. Air Force runs "A message to die for" awareness campaign.

the FCC. Keep in mind that SAR levels can vary between different transmission bands (the same phone can use multiple bands during a call), and that different testing bodies can obtain different results. Also, it's possible for results to vary between different models of the same phone, such as a handset that's offered by multiple carriers. In March 2010, Apple had banned an iPhone app that measures cell phone radiation (*news.cnet.com/8301-17852_3-10464388-71.html*), but other online sources of SAR are available.

The importance of understanding ethical issues has been recognized by the Association to Advance Collegiate Schools of Business (AACSB International, *aacsb.edu*). For business majors, the AACSB International has defined Assurance of Learning Requirements for ethics at both the undergraduate and graduate levels. In Standard 15: Management of Curricula (AACSB Accreditation Standards, 2006), AACSB identifies general knowledge and skill learning experiences that include "ethical understanding and reasoning abilities" at the undergraduate level. At the graduate level, Standard 15 requires learning experiences in management-specific knowledge and skill areas to include "ethical and legal responsibilities in organizations and society" (AACSB International Ethics Education Resource Center, 2006). Ethical issues are discussed after the social impacts of social networks are examined.

Life Out of Control. The technologies covered in this chapter blur work, social, and personal time. IT keeps people connected with no real off-switch. Tools that are meant to improve the productivity and quality of life in general can also intrude on personal time. Managers need to be aware of the huge potential for abuse by expecting 24/7 response from workers.

Key Terms

3G *91*
4G *91*
bandwidth *88*
broadband *88*
carbon footprint *105*
circuit switching *89*
content indexing *101*
digital care management solution *94*
enterprise search *101*
extranet *100*
fixed-line broadband *91*
group dynamics *103*
Internet Protocol (IP) *89*
interoperability *98*
intranet *99*
IP address *89*
latency-sensitive apps *90*

machine-to-machine (M2M) *88*
near-field communication (NFC) *92*
net neutrality *91*
net semi-neutrality *91*
packet *89*
packet switching *89*
protocol *90*
radio-frequency identification (RFID) *92*
router *89*
SAR (specific absorption rate) *106*
SharePoint *99*
smart dust *88*
smart electric grid *88*
smart grid *88*
smart traffic management *88*
switch *89*

switching *89*
TCP/IP *91*
traffic shaping *91*
virtual care solution *94*
virtual private network (VPN) *100*
voice over IP (VoIP) *88*
WAN (wide area network) *94*
WiMAX *92*
wireless access point *89*
Wi-Fi *94*
Wireless LAN *95*
WiMAX *92*
Wireless WAN *95*
WWANs (wireless wide area networks) *94*

You find clickable Link Libraries for each chapter on the Companion website.

International CTIA Wireless Tradeshows *http://ctiawireless.com/*

Cisco *http://cisco.com*

Microsoft SharePoint 2010 *http://sharepoint.microsoft.com/Pages/Default.aspx*

Cellular Telecommunications Industry Association *http://ctia.org/*

WiMAX Forum *http://wimaxforum.org*

Packet switching flash demo *http://pbs.org/opb/nerds2.0.1/geek_glossary/ packet_switching_flash.html*

Cell phone radiation levels (SAR) *http://reviews.cnet.com/2719-6602_7-291-2.html?tag=*

Goodwill Tacoma Industries *http://h20621.www2.hp.com/video-gallery/us/en/ cb97f9e516dc2062c5945cb4e6bec0b706c13aa5/r/video*

Google Green *http://www.google.com/green/the-big-picture.html*

A conversation on eco-sustainability with Godfrey Chua, IDC *http://www.alcatel-lucent.com/ eco/strategy/eco-networks.html.*

Evernote, Sharing notebooks in Evernote *http://www.evernote.com/about/video/ #QtPCyV62zRM|1|2*

Evaluate and Expand Your Learning

IT and Data Management Decisions

1. Visit the Alcatel-Lucent website, *http://www.alcatel-lucent.com/eco/strategy/eco-networks.html.*
   a. View the video titled: "A conversation on eco-sustainability with Godfrey Chua, IDC."
   b. How are consumers and enterprises the drivers of eco-sustainability or green efforts by service providers?
   c. What is a holistic approach? That is, what does a holistic approach to going green involve?
   d. Given today's economic conditions, do you agree with Godfrey Chua's opinion that consumers and enterprises will demand eco-sustainability or green efforts by service providers? Explain your answer.
   e. Consider the same question in (d) except assume that eco-sustainable network service providers charged higher prices. How does that change your answer, if at all? Explain your reasons.

Questions for Discussion & Review

1. Why are Internet users' impatient with slow response time?
2. What is the value of M2M communications?
3. Explain how network capacity is measured.
4. How are devices identified to a network?
5. Explain how digital signals are transmitted.
6. Explain the functions of switches and routers.
7. Why are different quality of service (QoS) levels on a network important?

8. QoS technologies can be applied to create two tiers of traffic. What are those tiers? Give an example of each type of traffic.
9. Typically, networks are configured so that downloading is faster than uploading. Explain why.
10. What issues are significant about 4G wireless networks?
11. What are two 4G wireless standards?
12. How is network performance measured?
13. Discuss two applications of near-field communication (NFC).
14. There is growing demand for video to handheld devices. Explain two factors enabling or driving this demand.
15. Why attend class if you can view or listen to the podcast of the class (assuming one is available)?
16. Describe the components of a mobile communication infrastructure.
17. Discuss the impact of wireless computing on emergency response services.
18. Describe a LAN, WAN, and wireless LAN.
19. What is the range of WiMAX? Why does it not need a clear line of sight?
20. Which of the current mobile computing limitations do you think will be minimized within two years? Which ones will not?
21. Why are VPNs used to secure extranets?
22. How can group dynamics improve group work? How can it disrupt what groups can accomplish?

23. What are the benefits of using software to conduct brainstorming in the cloud (remotely)?

24. How do mobile devices contribute to carbon emissions?

25. Discuss the ethical issues of anytime-anywhere accessibility.

26. What health and quality-of-life issues are associated with social networks and a 24/7 connected lifestyle?

27. Is distracted driving an unsolvable problem? Explain.

Online Activities

1. Visit the *HP.com* website and click Products, Product Videos to find the Instant-On World video. The direct link is *http://h20621.www2.hp.com/video-gallery/us/en/cb97f9e516dc2062c5945cb4e6bec0b706c13aa5/r/video*.
   a. Describe how the Instant-On airline can avert chaos.
   b. How can an Instant-On city help avoid traffic congestion?
   c. What is a capability of Instant-On government?

2. Visit the Google Apps website. Identify three types of collaboration support and their value in the workplace.

3. Compare the various features of broadband wireless networks (e.g., 3G, Wi-Fi, and WiMAX). Visit at least three broadband wireless network vendors.
   a. Prepare a list of capabilities of each network.
   b. Prepare a list of actual applications that each network can support.

c. Comment on the value of such applications to users. How can the benefits be assessed?

4. View the iMindMap Online tutorial on YouTube at *http://www.youtube.com/watch?v=EuB0zyV_lJY*. Describe the potential value of sharing maps online and synching maps with other computers or devices. What is your opinion of the ease or complexity of the iMindMap interface?

5. Visit Google Green at *http://www.google.com/green/the-big-picture.html*. Describe Google's efforts to minimize the environmental impact of their services. Do you believe that Google can reduce its carbon footprint beyond zero, as they claim? Explain your answer.

Collaborative Work

1. Each team member needs to download and install the free version of Evernote at *evernote.com/*. View the video titled "Sharing notebooks in Evernote" at *evernote.com/about/video/#QtPCyV62zRM\1\2*. Use the Evernote app to research global warming. Try to share your notes with each other. Did Evernote add value to the process?

2. Each team member downloads and installs the free trial version of GoToMeeting, or any other video conferencing software. Conduct a video meeting to answer the questions of *IT at Work 4.5*. Based on your experiences, do you recommend the software you used. Did the software improve group dynamics? What problems did the team encounter—and how did you solve them?

CASE 2 BUSINESS CASE

Avoiding a Future of Crippling Car Congestion

Speaking at the 2012 Mobile World Congress, Bill Ford, the executive chairman of Ford Motors, outlined a plan for "connected cars" to help avoid crippling traffic congestion by mid-21st century. **Connected cars** are vehicles linked to various mobile networks and intelligent systems and capable of M2M communication.

Need for Intelligence on the Road

Imagine roads with four times as many vehicles. That's the forecast—an increase in the number of cars on the world's roads from one billion in 2013 to four billion by 2050. To avoid the global risk of overcrowded roads, Bill Ford proposes creating an intelligent global transportation network that integrates communication between vehicles, a transport infrastructure, and individual mobile devices. He said:

> If we do nothing, we face the prospect of "global gridlock," a never-ending traffic jam that wastes time, energy and resources and even compromises the flow of commerce and health care.

Cross-Industry Collaboration Needed for Success

In order for his proposed solution to succeed, the automotive and telecommunications industries need to cooperate; and their engineers and IT experts will need to collaborate. New networking technologies and business relationships are critical to success. Ford explained:

> No one company or industry will be able to solve the mobility issue alone and the speed at which solutions take hold will be determined largely by customer acceptance of new technologies. The telecommunications industry is critical in the creation of an interconnected transportation system where cars are intelligent and can talk to one another as well as the infrastructure around them. Now is the time for us all to be looking at vehicles on the road the same way we look at smartphones, laptops and tablets; as pieces of a much bigger, richer network.

IT solutions are already tackling traffic congestion problems and shaping what transportation will look like in 2025 and beyond.

Ford's "Blueprint for Mobility" Plan

Under the banner "Blueprint for Mobility," Bill Ford detailed what it will take to make congestion-free motoring—or at least congestion-controlled—a reality in the coming decades, utilizing a combination of connected cars, connected roadways, and a totally redesigned mobile infrastructure.

In the short term, within five to seven years, Ford Motors will be developing more intuitive in-car mobile communications options and driver interfaces that alert drivers to traffic jams, accidents, and other road conditions warranting attention. The company is also working on M2M communication projects, such as vehicle-to-vehicle warning systems.

In the long term, Ford sees a radically different transportation landscape where pedestrian, bicycle, private car, commercial, and public transportation traffic will be woven into a single mobile network to save time, conserve resources, lower CO_2 emissions, and improve safety.

Bill Ford also suggests that connected cars should be about making journeys more efficient by providing alternative transportation options if congestion is unavoidable.

Sources: Compiled from *Mobileworldcongress.com/* (2012) and various blogs (2012).

Questions

1. Explain the concept of connected cars.
2. Why does Bill Ford see a need for connected cars?
3. What does Ford mean by "global gridlock"?
4. Brainstorm a few other ways in which an IT network could help to reduce global gridlock. Do not limit yourself to current mobile network capabilities.
5. If no action is taken far in advance of the forecasted car congestion, what do you foresee will happen?

CASE 3   VIDEO CASE

Advocate Health Care Achieves Fast ROI with Business Video

Advocate Health Care became one of the top health care systems in the U.S. by creating innovations in the medical community. Those innovations led to holistic health care focused on mind, body, and spirit. Advocate relies on the network to foster communication and collaboration around advancing patient care. With Cisco business video solutions, Advocate is achieving measurable ROI. A single TelePresence meeting almost paid for the entire investment, while Digital Signage is saving the company $200 for every 200 feet of printed signs. With Cisco Services, Advocate not only accelerated the adoption of TelePresence and Digital Signs, but also customized the solutions to better meet the company's needs.

Questions

1. Visit the Cisco Newsroom video of "Advocate Health Care" at *http://newsroom.cisco.com/video-content?type=video&videoId=114006.*
2. How does Advocate Health Care (AHC) get a message of sharing across its wide, complex organization?
3. What challenges does AHC face?
4. How does telepresence support AHC's mission?
5. Who was the point person on the telepresence project, and how did he help AHC?
6. In your opinion, why was AHC able to get such a quick ROI? Did high salaries of specialized surgeons have a major impact on ROI? Explain.

Data Analysis & Decision Making

Cost Comparison of Web Conferencing

The two owners of Spinner Media Services Inc. wanted to cut travel costs and productivity losses (wasted time) and maintain the benefits of person-to-person collaboration. They decided to use Web conferencing internally for collaboration and externally for sales demonstrations to customers. Their two options were (1) a pay-per-use basis or (2) a per user licensing plan based on the number of seats or participants. The decision would depend on cost comparisons based on these data estimates:

- Approximately 400 meetings per year
- An average of 12 participants per meeting

- Each meeting lasting about one hour, which takes into consideration the need to get the meeting set up at least 15 minutes in advance and 45-minute meetings
- 250 unique participants, consisting of 50 employees and 200 customers

To do:

1. Research the costs of a pay-per-use basis to a per user licensing plan based on the number of seats or participants for Microsoft's LiveMeeting and Cisco's WebEx. Or evaluate two other pieces of web-based meeting software. Precise cost comparisons are difficult because there are so

many variables, but a general cost analysis between LiveMeeting and WebEx or other software is feasible.

2. Design a spreadsheet that shows cost comparisons of the vendors' licensing options and the pay-per-usage option using the data estimates.

3. Identify other criteria that should be taken into account when making such a decision (for example, vendor support or the ability to integrate with Outlook).

4. Based on your analysis, make a fully documented recommendation to the owners.

Resources on the Book's Web Site

More resources and study tools are located on the Student Web Site. You'll find additional chapter materials and useful web links. In addition, self-quizzes that provide individualized feedback are available for each chapter.

References

AACSB Accreditation Standards. Management of *Curricula. aacsb.edu/eerc/std-15.asp.*

AACSB International, Ethics Education Resource Center, Accreditation Standards. *aacsb.edu/resource_centers/EthicsEdu/standards.asp.*

Booz & Co. *booz.com*

Byars, N. "The Prospect of Internet Democracy." *Journalism and Mass Communication Quarterly,* Vol. 87, no. 2. Summer 2010.

Cisco, "State-of-the-Art New Hospital Builds Borderless Connectivity." December 2010.

Cisco. *Cisco Visual Networking Index (VNI) Mobile Data Traffic Forecast, 2011–2016.* February 2012. *blogs.cisco.com/.*

Evernote. *evernote.com/.*

Federal Communications Commission (FCC). *fcc.gov/.*

Friedrich, N. "Top Application Trends of 2011." *Microwaves & RF.* December 2011.

Imason, Inc. "How Imason Helped Labatt Build a World-Class Intranet with SharePoint." 2010. *imason.com.*

Krigsman, M. LAX IT Failure: Leaps of Faith Don't Work." *ZDNet,* August 15, 2007. *blogs.zdnet.com/projectfailures/?p=346.*

Lohr, S. "For Impatient Web Users, an Eye Blink Is Just Too Long to Wait." *The New York Times,* February 29, 2012.

Mobileworldcongress.com/. 2012.

Poeter, D., "NIC Card Soup Gives LAX a Tummy-Ache." *ChannelWeb.* August 17, 2007.

Rapp, W.V., & H. Subramanian. "Leveraging IT as a Core Competency to Enter New Businesses: The UPS Case." *Business Review, Journal of the American Academy of Business.* Cambridge, October 2004.

Reed, B. "4G Nets on the Way, But They'll Take Time," *Network World.* Vol. 27, no.5. March 8, 2010.

RMH Healthcare, RMHonline.com, 2012.

The Network. http://thenetwork.cisco.com/. 2012.

Learning Outcomes

❶ Describe the types of cybercrimes facing organizations and critical infrastructures, explain the motives of cybercriminals, and evaluate the financial value of cybersecurity.

❷ Explain both low-tech and high-tech methods used to gain access to a company's networks and databases, the vulnerabilities of information systems, and cybercrime symptoms. Describe the critical role of senior management, acceptable use policies, security procedures, and IT for defense-in-depth.

❸ Describe types and characteristics of fraud, the role of corporate governance, and IT tools to detect fraudulent activities.

❹ Explain general, administrative, and endpoint controls needed to secure information systems, networks, and wireless devices; and to manage risk.

❺ Describe network security measures needed to protect the endpoints or wired and wireless networks and deny unauthenticated access.

❻ Describe the role of the internal control environment in deterring fraud and complying with regulations.

❼ Explain the benefits of business continuity and disaster recovery planning methods and why audits are an important part of control systems.

Since 2010, damaging cyberattacks targeting classified and confidential information, trade secrets, and other intellectual property have worsened. Hacking or malware (short for *malicious software*) were linked to almost every data breach, and organized criminals were behind the majority of breaches. Cyberspies and criminals had robbed tens of billions of dollars' worth of data from U.S. companies each year. Hacktivists destroyed brand images and customer relationships and forced the shutdown of the CIA's (Central Intelligence Agency) web site. The always-on world was victimized by mobile malware and infected apps posted by cybercriminals on iTunes (in violation of their policy) to lure users into downloading rogue applications—which then spread from smartphones into corporate networks. U.S. officials reported that combating electronic espionage against corporate America by hackers in China and other countries is a matter of national and economic security.

As you read in this chapter, the mobile, social, connected infrastructures of this decade are more vulnerable to cyberattack. International, federal, and state laws and industry regulations mandate that organizations invest in cybersecurity defenses, audits, and internal controls to secure confidential data and defend against fraud and unauthorized transactions, such as money laundering. Inarguably, everyone needs to understand cybersecurity vulnerabilities, threats, exploits, and defenses.

CASE 1 OPENING CASE

Managing BYOD Security Risks

BYOD (bring your own device) means that employees are using many different types of personal devices to store and process enterprise data, and connect to enterprise networks.

People wanting to use their mobile devices at work has led to the practice of **bring your own device (BYOD)**—which is part of the **consumerization of information technology (COIT)** trend. The BYOD practice for smartphones is seeing enterprises take risks they would not consider taking for conventional computing devices (Dunn, 2012). Many smartphones are not being managed as secure devices, with fewer than one in five adding anti-malware and only half using data encryption.

Trying to Hold Back the BYOD Movement

Previously, employers provided employees with computers that were more advanced than personal ones—and not convenient to carry. Then Androids and iPhones, tablets, e-readers, and other mobile devices flipped that relationship. Figure 5.1 shows that the number of non-PC devices sold (425 million) had exceeded PC sales (390 million) in 2011.

Employees wanted to know "Why can't I use my devices at work?" Many expected instant approval and support for their new iPads within hours of its release. Actually BYOD

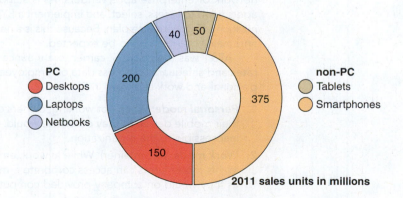

Figure 5.1 Number of units of PC and non-PC devices sold, in millions, in 2011.
Source: Deloitte, 2011.

PC
- ● Desktops
- ● Laptops
- ● Netbooks

non-PC
- ● Tablets
- ● Smartphones

2011 sales units in millions

raises several legitimate areas of concern. New vulnerabilities are created when personal and business data and communications are mixed together. Also, the mobile infrastructure may not be able to support the increase in mobile network traffic and data processing—causing unacceptable delays or requiring additional investments.

Gaining Control of the BYOD Megatrend

Forrester Research, Inc. estimated that 60 percent of companies had begun allowing BYOD by 2012. Chip-manufacturer Intel projects that 70 percent of its employees will use personal devices for some aspect of their job by 2014. No longer was it a question of whether to allow employees to use their own devices, but how to gain control over devices that employees were using at work. The four challenges that have to be resolved are device control costs, security threats, compliance, and privacy.

1. **Device control costs.** One potential benefit of BYOD is saving on costs associated with company-owned equipment. But these cost savings can be wiped out by increased IT costs—mostly for IT personnel who struggle to maintain control over new and existing mobile devices. Every personal device needs to be properly accounted for all as well as the apps they run. With the number of mobile apps hitting 1.3 million in mid-2012–compared to only 75,000 apps for PCs—managing employee-owned devices is more complex and expensive.

2. **Security threats.** Mobile devices and the networks they run can be cybersecurity landmines—capable of compromising confidential, sensitive, or classified data. A major security hole stems from the fact that the latest tablets, smartphones, and other handhelds often rely on unsecured wireless networks—and users don't use encryption or strong password controls. Consequences for data breaches or other compromises include damaged brand or reputation, lost customers, and multi-million-dollar fines.

   Data and ISs need to be protected from unauthorized access, including when an employee's device is lost or stolen, or an employee leaves the company. All **cybersecurity controls**—authentication, access control, data confidentiality, and intrusion detection—implemented on corporate-owned resources over the last decade can be rendered useless on an employee-owned device.

3. **Compliance.** Organizations are subject to national and international regulations and standards that specify how data can or cannot be collected and stored, as well as how it must be made available in the event of an audit or legal action. Companies need to insure and be able to prove that enterprise data stored on personal devices are in compliance, e.g., encrypted, password protected, unaltered, etc.

4. **Privacy.** Controls placed on employee-owned devices can infringe on personal privacy. For instance, organizations could know what sites were visited or movies were watched, what was done on sick days, what texts were sent/received, and all social media activities during work hours and off-hours.

Example of BYOD Solution: AT&T Toggle

It's inevitable that companies will invest in BYOD solutions, most likely from their mobile network or enterprise apps vendors. As is standard with cybersecurity investments, managers need to assess, select, and implement a BYOD solution that is aligned with their organization's IT governance plan. Because this is a new software market, there is no clear leader, and major changes are to be expected.

AT&T was the first U.S. carrier to announce a BYOD application. **AT&T Toggle** separates and safeguards business data on employees' mobile devices by creating two modes: personal and work as shown in Figure 5.2.

1. *Personal mode:* When not working, owners can text, watch videos, and play games on their mobile device as they otherwise would. Personal activities remain segregated and inaccessible to the organization.

2. *Work mode* (or container): While at work, employees switch to their work environment. In this mode, users can access corporate e-mail, applications, calendars and more, just as they would on company-provided computing resources.

Figure 5.2 AT&T Toggle is a BYOD app and service.

Access to business data is managed via a mobile device client installed on the employee's device. This client creates a **work container** that is a "walled off" area on the device where employees can access corporate content securely. All corporate data is fully encrypted and compliant with company policy. Company visibility is limited to the work container only. The company does not have access to the personal side. Employees keep control of that personal mode.

AT&T Toggle offers a web portal that IT administrators use to:

- Manage and monitor employee access to company resources.
- Add, update, and delete business applications on employees' personal devices.
- Wipe all corporate data stored in work mode if an employee leaves the company or loses the device.

The initial version of AT&T Toggle can be used on devices running Android 2.2 or higher, and with any service provider.

Discuss

1. Explain the pressures driving the BYOD trend.
2. Why had organizations initially rejected the idea?
3. What contributed to BYOD acceptance?
4. Identify and discuss four key challenges of BYOD.
5. How does AT&T Toggle attempt to resolve the challenges you identified in question #4?
6. With just a smartphone, users can conduct nearly all their banking business at any time. The level of flexibility and convenience opens up new avenues for fraud and cybercrime. To what extent are users willing to give up convenience for their own security? And for the security of their companies?

Decide

7. View the brief video titled "Learn More About AT&T Toggle." Find the link in the Chapter 5 Link Library on the book's web site, or visit *wireless.att.com* and search for the title (*wireless.att.com/businesscenter/popups/video/learn-more-about-toggle.jsp*).
   a. How is access to the work container protected? What determines the strength of this protection?
   b. Would you feel confident that your privacy was protected using Toggle?

Debate

8. How do you achieve the right balance to protect the enterprise's security and the employee's privacy? What is the right balance of security and privacy?

5.1 Up Close Look at Cybercrimes, Criminals, and Motivations

Critical infrastructure is defined as "systems and assets, whether physical or virtual, so vital to the U.S. that the incapacity or destruction of such systems and assets would have a debilitating impact on security, national economic security, national public health or safety, or any combination of those matters."

The U.S. has 18 critical infrastructure sectors. See Figure 5.3.

During the five months between October 2011 and February 2012, there were 86 reported attacks on computer systems in the U.S. that control national **critical infrastructure**, according to the Department of Homeland Security (DHS, dhs.gov/). Over the same period a year earlier, there had been only 11 such serious attacks. These infrastructure attacks did not cause significant damage, but the eightfold spike is alarming to DHS, Congress, and private sector. Congress reacted by working on legislation that requires stronger cybersecurity standards to defend against increasingly harmful cyberattacks.

Attacks on critical infrastructure could significantly disrupt the functioning of government and business—and trigger cascading effects far beyond the targeted sector and physical location of the incident (see Figure 5.3.)

New cybersecurity dangers are emerging and overtaking familiar threats—viruses, lost disks, and DoS attacks. Experts believe the greatest cybersecurity dangers in the next few years involve **persistent threats** (discussed in *IT at Work 5.1*), mobile computing, and the use of social media for **social engineering.** Social engineering tactics are used by hackers and corporate spies to trick people into revealing login information or access codes. Two social engineering methods are:

1. Pretexting is the use of a story that convinces someone into revealing secret information. For instance, a hacker uses readily available phone numbers and names to call a worker claiming to be the systems administrator who needs to reset passwords to protect the company from hacking. The hacker has the employee re-log into the network say everything he is typing to get the username and password.

2. Baiting is the use of an incentive to get a user to perform an insecure action. A common bait is to offer a free app or video for clicking a link in a text message and voting for best video game. Clicking the link downloads malware.

Many cyber threats and cybersecurity challenges that organizations face today were unimaginable 10 years ago, such as the BYOD issues discussed in the Opening Case #1. And longstanding threats such as of fraud and identity theft still remain. Cyber threats will continue to emerge, evolve, and worsen over the next 10 years and beyond. *IT at Work 5.1* provides an overview of results of the *2012 Global State of Information Security Survey*.

Figure 5.3 Six of the 18 national critical infrastructures (from upper-left, clockwise): commercial facilities; defense industrial base; transportation systems; national monuments and icons; banking and finance; and agriculture and food. *Photos courtesy of United States Department of Homeland Security.*

Source: Homeland Security, "Critical Infrastructure Protection," *http://www.dhs.gov/files/programs/critical.shtm.*

© Werner Nick/Age Fotostock America, Inc. (top, left); © alptraum/Age Fotostock America, Inc. (top, center); © Philip Lange/Age Fotostock America, Inc. (right); © Blakeley/Age Fotostock America, Inc. (bottom, right center); © Zoonar/unknown/Age Fotostock America, Inc. (bottom, left center); © Zoonar/NREY/Age Fotostock America, Inc. (bottom, left)

IT at Work 5.1

Global State of Information Security Survey

The *2012 Global State of Information Security Survey* is conducted by the consulting firm PwC US (*PricewaterhouseCoopers. pwc.com*) and *CIO* and *CSO* magazines (PWC, 2012). According to this 9th annual survey of almost 10,000 security executives from 138 countries, only 72 percent of respondents were confident that their organization's information security defenses were effective. Confidence in their defenses' effectiveness had dropped significantly since 2006. Mark Lobel, a principal in PwC's Advisory practice, explained: "Companies now have greater insights than ever before into the landscape of cybercrime and other security events—and they're translating this information into security investments specifically focused on three areas: prevention, detection, and operational web technologies."

Advanced Persistent Threat (APT) Attacks

A significant percent of respondents across industries agreed that one of the most dangerous cyber threats is an **advanced persistent threat (APT) attack**. APT is a stealth network attack in which an unauthorized person gains access to a network and remains undetected for a long time. APTs are designed for long-term espionage. Skilled hackers launch APT attacks to steal data continuously (for example, daily) over months or years—rather than to cause damage that would reveal their presence. APT attacks target organizations with high-value information, such as national defense, manufacturing, and financial. APT threats are driving organizations' cybersecurity spending because only 16 percent are prepared to defend against them.

Cloud, mobile, and social expand exposure

Cloud computing has complicated cybersecurity. For 23 percent of organizations, cloud technologies have worsened their exposure primarily because they cannot enforce or verify their cloud providers' cybersecurity policies. In addition, mobile devices and social media expose organizations to new and significant threats.

Questions

1. What three areas are organizations focusing their infosec investments on?
2. Explain APT attacks.
3. What industries are at greatest risk of APT attacks? Why?
4. What is the largest perceived risk of cloud computing?

According to the 2012 Data Breach Investigations Report (DBIR), a global study of data theft at companies and government agencies, it takes a long time for victims to find out they have been hacked. In 2011, 92 percent of data breaches were discovered by a third party and not the company being breached. The Ponemon Institute (*ponemon.org*), an information security research firm, has found that a data breach typically costs an organization from $5 million to $8 million—from fines imposed by government agencies, legal fees, mandated improvements in defenses, and costs of notifying and compensating individuals whose data was exposed.

Why then are cyberattacks getting worse? Because networks are used by **hacktivists** (hacker-activists or *hacking for a cause*) looking for media attention; by hackers looking to steal **credentials** such as banking PINS and passwords; by industrial spies looking for trade secrets; by employees performing their jobs, or gaming or gambling online; and by customers buying products and services. The obvious problem is how to identify and block all malicious traffic while allowing legitimate traffic into a network. Such reliable precision and power may never exist.

Apps and other software have holes that hackers exploit—and users often do not know about unless they keep tabs on the latest cyber vulnerabilities. And these vulnerabilities appear almost daily.

TOP DOWN SECURITY

The 2012 Data Breach Investigations Report (DBIR, 2012) revealed that in most cases it is not IT that will keep users safe; rather it is a combination of management and best practices. The DBIR also revealed that 97 percent of data breaches evaluated in the study were avoidable and did not require hackers to possess special skills, resources, or customization. Approximately 30 percent of breaches impacting 84 percent of records breached were the result of stolen login credentials—usernames and passwords.

Complying with regulations is considered one of the primary business risks for highly-regulated industries such as energy utilities, health care, and financial firms. For example, the North American Electric Reliability Corporation (*NERC.com*) can fine a company up to $1 million a day for non-compliance (Chickowski, 2012). Large financial institutions have to comply with dozens of regulations by building information security programs with controls that are appropriate to protect the business and data.

Advanced persistent threat (APT) attackers want to remain unnoticed so that they can continue to steal data, as described in *IT at Work 5.1*. Profit-motivated cybercriminals often operate in stealth mode. In contrast, hackers and hacktivists with personal agendas carry out high-profile attacks.

Hacktivists' Motivations and Dangerous Pranks. These types of cybercriminals seemed to take on everyone from Sony and security firm RSA to the CIA (Central Intelligence Agency) and a Mexican drug cartel throughout 2011 and 2012. During the Arab Spring (Arab Revolutions), hacktivists **LulzSec** and **Anonymous** showed how vulnerable anyone's online presence was, even that of major governments. LulzSec and Anonymous even have logos, as shown in Figures 5.4 and 5.5. One of LulzSec's specialties is finding web sites with poor security, and then stealing and posting information from them online. Their attacks may seem more like Internet pranks than serious cyberwarfare, but they are still illegal.

Hacktivist Attacks and Victims. Hackers committed daring data breaches, compromises, data leaks, thefts, threats, and privacy invasions in 2012. Here are several of those cases.

Combined Systems Inc. Proudly displaying its hacktivist flag (shown in Figure 5.5), Anonymous took credit for knocking Combined Systems Inc. offline and stealing

HIGH-VISIBILITY CYBERCRIMINALS AND HACKTIVISTS

LulzSec is a hacker group and spin-off of the loosely organized hacking collective **Anonymous.** Lulz is slang that can be interpreted as *laugh (LOLs).* They claimed responsibility for several high-profile attacks, including the compromise of user accounts from Sony Pictures in 2011. LulzSec does not appear to hack for financial profit. At times, they act as **hacktivists.**

Hacktivist is short for hacker-activists, or *hacking for a cause.*

Denial of service (DoS) is a type of attack where a web site or network is bombarded with traffic to make them crash.

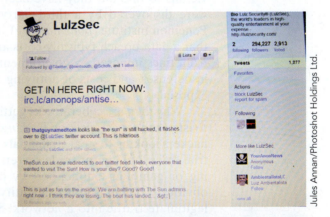

Figure 5.4 LulzSec.

Figure 5.5 Anonymous is represented by a flag with imagery of the "suit without a head" to represent its leaderless organization and anonymity.

personal data from its clients. Anonymous went after Combined Systems, which sells tear gas and crowd-control devices to law enforcement and military organizations, to protest war profiteers.

CIA. In February 2012, for the second time in less than a year, Anonymous launched a denial of service (DoS) attack that forced the CIA web site offline. The CIA takedown followed a busy week for the hacktivists. Within 10 days, the group also went after Chinese electronics manufacturer Foxconn, American Nazi groups, anti-virus firm Symantec, and the office of Syria's president, which are described next.

Foxconn. Apple was facing worldwide scrutiny over questionable working conditions at Foxconn, a Chinese company that assembles iPhones, iPads, and devices for Dell, Sony, IBM, Microsoft, and others. Hacktivists SwaggSec took up the cause by stealing staff's e-mail logins and credentials.

American Nazi Party. To protest hate speech, Anonymous defaced and took down the American Nazi Party web site and white supremacist site, Whitehonor. The attacks were part of Anonymous' Operation Blitzkrieg campaign.

Symantec. Hacker YamaTough posted the source code to Symantec's pcAnywhere software used by customers to access remote PCs. The leak came when YamaTough's extortion attempt against Symantec failed.

Office of the Syrian President. Anonymous leaked e-mails from Syrian President Bashar Assad's office, including a candid e-mail in which one of Assad's media advisers prepped him for an interview with Barbara Walters and told him that the "American psyche can be easily manipulated."

Hamas. Israeli hacking group IDF Team (Israeli Defense Force) launched an attack against a Hamas web site knocking it offline to protest the site's anti-Israeli position. Israeli and Arab hackers battled for over a month. Saudi Arabian hacker 0xOmar posted 15,000 Israeli credit-card numbers. IDF Team retaliated by posting Arabs' credit-card credentials. After 0xOmar disrupted the Tel Aviv Stock Exchange, Israel's El Al Airlines, and two major Israeli banks, the IDF Team countered by hitting the Saudi Stock Exchange and Abu Dhabi Securities Exchange.

Scotland Yard and the FBI. Police had arrested several high-ranking Anonymous hackers, including Ryan Cleary, the British teenager charged with launching DoS attacks against British and U.S. targets. Anonymous intercepted and posted the audio of a 17-minute conference call in which the two agencies discussed plans to track down and prosecute Anonymous hackers.

OnGuardOnline. To protest the controversial Stop Online Piracy Act (SOPA), Anonymous took down OnGuardOnline.gov, the U.S. government's cybersecurity guidance web site. Anonymous defaced the site with a message threatening to destroy dozens of government and corporate web sites if SOPA was passed.

STEALTH, PROFIT-MOTIVATED CYBERCRIMES

Most hack activities do not become headline-grabbers until after the incidents are detected and reported. However, victimized companies are reluctant to discuss them, so statistics are scarce. Most data breaches go unreported, according to cybersecurity experts, because corporate victims fear that disclosure would damage their stock price, or because they never knew they were hacked in the first place.

Theft of Trade Secrets and Other Confidential Information. Theft of trade secrets has always been a threat from corporate moles, disgruntled employees, and other insiders. Of course, now it is easier to steal information remotely, mostly because of smartphones and the BYOD trend. Hackers' preferred *modus operandi* is to break into employees' mobile devices and leapfrog into employers' networks—stealing secrets without a trace.

U.S. cybersecurity experts and government officials are increasingly concerned about breaches from other countries into corporate networks, either through mobile devices or by other means. Mike McConnell, a former director of national intelligence, warned: "In looking at computer systems of consequence—in government, Congress, at the Department of Defense, aerospace, companies with valuable trade secrets—we've not examined one yet that has not been infected by an advanced persistent threat." In the meantime, companies are leaking critical information, often without realizing it. Scott Aken, a former FBI agent who specialized in counter-intelligence and computer intrusion. "In most cases, companies don't realize they've been burned until years later when a foreign competitor puts out their very same product — only they're making it 30 percent cheaper."

Do-Not-Carry Rules. Now, U.S. companies and government agencies are imposing **do-not-carry rules**, which are based on the assumption that devices will inevitably be compromised," according to Mike Rogers, chairman of the House Intelligence Committee. Members could bring only "clean" devices and are forbidden from connecting to the government's network while abroad. Rogers said he travels "electronically naked" to insure cybersecurity during and after a trip. *IT at Work 5.2* describes the reasons following do-not-carry rules.

The types and scope of cyberthefts and other profit-motivated attacks are illustrated by the following incidents.

U.S. Chamber of Commerce and Member Organizations Hacked. The U.S. Chamber of Commerce is headquartered in Washington, D.C. (Figure 5.6). The Chamber did not learn that it and its member organizations were the victims of a cybertheft for months until the FBI informed them that servers in China were stealing data from four of their Asia policy experts, who travel to Asia frequently (Perloth, 2011). It's possible that the experts' mobile devices had been infected with malware that was transmitting information and files back to the hackers. By the time the Chamber hardened (secured) its network, hackers had stolen at least six weeks of e-mails, most of which were with the largest U.S. corporations. Even later, the Chamber learned that its office printer and a thermostat in one of its corporate apartments were communicating with an Internet address in China. The Chamber did not disclose how hackers had infiltrated its systems, but its first step after the attack was to implement do-not-carry rules.

IT at Work 5.2

Traveling Electronically-Clean

When Kenneth G. Lieberthal, an expert at the Brookings Institution, travels to other countries, he follows a routine that seems straight from a secret agent movie. He leaves his smartphone and laptop at home. Instead he brings loaner devices, which he erases before he leaves the U.S. and wipes clean the minute he returns. While traveling, he disables Bluetooth and Wi-Fi and never lets his phone out of his sight. While in meetings, he not only turns off his phone, but also removes the battery for fear his microphone could be turned on remotely.

Lieberthal connects to the Internet only through an encrypted, password-protected channel. He never types in a password directly, but copies and pastes his password from a USB thumb drive. By not typing his password, he eliminates the risk of having it stolen if key-logging software got installed on his device.

Questions

1. Many travelers might consider Lieberthal's method too inconvenient. Clearly, his electronically clean methods are time consuming and expensive. In your opinion, is there a tradeoff between cybersecurity and convenience? Explain.

2. Create a list of best cybersecurity practices for travelers based on Lieberthal's methods.

© Kristoffer Tripplaar/Alamy Limited

Figure 5.6 The United States Chamber of Commerce was hacked over several months.

Hackers Put Hijacked Web Views Up for Sale for Web Fraud. In a new twist on web site exploits for profit, web hackers have begun to turn sites they have exploited (infected with malware) into sources of fraudulent web traffic for anyone willing to pay. The hackers use inline frames (iframes) injected into the HTML code of a web site to redirect visitors from the legitimate site to anywhere on the Web. According to RSA's security blog, the site is operated by a Russia-based group of hackers who created the capability for their own use first. They then realized its potential profitability as a larger service to others who want to profit from web advertising fraud, launch drive-by download attacks on users' browsers, or run other scams based on illegitimately gained page views.

Tech Note 5.1

iframes load and execute web pages within the body of another page. Legitimate web sites use iframes to redirect to content while concealing its source. iframes are widely used in various Facebook apps to deliver content within the Facebook environment. But they're also used by marginally ethical search engine optimization hackers, and are a standard element of most web fraud.

Sony. Sony suffered over a dozen data breaches in 2011 stemming from attacks that compromised over 100 million customer records and gained access to their passwords. Sony-owned web sites were hacked including Sony PlayStation Network (PSN), Sony Online Entertainment (SOE), and Sony Pictures. The hacker attack on its PSN cost the company about $170 million. On the PlayStation (PS3) menu, Sony highlighted a system update option with news of the PS3 software hack, as shown in Figure 5.7. According to a notice posted on the SOE web site (*soe.com/securityupdate/*) on May 2, 2011, Sony temporarily suspended all online multiplayer SOE games "until we could verify their security."

Sony reported that there was no evidence that their main credit card database was compromised, which is in a completely separate and secured environment. However, Sony's customers who reuse their passwords were at risk from attackers using the stolen password data to access their accounts on other sites. Sony faced ongoing customer relations fallout and class-action lawsuits for failing to protect confidential information.

OBJECTIVES OF CYBERSECURITY

As these hacker, hacktivist, and intrusion examples indicate, cybersecurity is a never-ending process of insuring the availability and integrity of data and other computing resources for legitimate users and uses; and defending against threats to

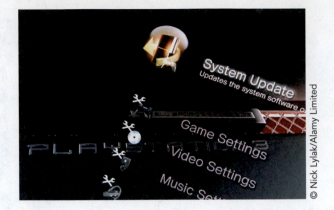

Figure 5.7 A Sony PS3 menu highlighting the system update option with recent news stories of users hacking into the PS3 software.

data, information systems, networks, privacy, commerce, national security, financial stability, and more.

Cybersecurity needs to accomplish the following:

- Make data and documents available and accessible 24/7 while simultaneously restricting access
- Implement and enforce procedures and acceptable use policies (AUPs) for data, networks, hardware, and software that are company-owned or employee-owned as discussed in the opening case
- Promote secure and legal sharing of information among authorized persons and partners
- Insure compliance with government regulations and laws
- Prevent attacks by having network intrusion defenses in place
- Detect, diagnose, and respond to incidents and attacks in real time
- Maintain internal controls to prevent unauthorized alteration of data and records
- Recover from business disasters and disruptions quickly

Business policies, procedures, training, and disaster recovery plans as well as hardware and software technologies play critical roles in cybersecurity.

Questions

1. Define national critical infrastructure. Give three examples.
2. Why are cyberattacks on critical infrastructure particularly dangerous?
3. Explain why hackers and corporate spies use social engineering.
4. Explain why advanced persistent threat (APT) attacks are one of the most dangerous cyber threats.
5. What are the motives of LulzSec and Anonymous?
6. Why do most data breaches go unreported?
7. Why are government agencies and organizations imposing do-not-carry rules?

5.2 IS Vulnerabilities and Threats

Every enterprise has data, files, communications, and business records that profit-motivated criminals (who may be across the globe or be trusted employees) want. Those risks can stem from insiders, outsiders, criminal organizations, or malware. **Malware** are viruses, worms, trojan horses, spyware, and any other type of disruptive, destructive, or unwanted programs. Threats range from high-tech exploits to gain access to a company's networks and databases to non-tech tactics to steal laptops and whatever is available. Because security terms, such as *threats* and *exploits*, have precise meanings, the key terms and their meanings are listed in Table 5.1.

TABLE 5.1	Cybersecurity Terms
Term	**Definition**
Threat	Something or someone that may result in harm to an asset
Risk	Probability of a threat exploiting a vulnerability
Vulnerability	A weakness that threatens the confidentiality, integrity, or availability (CIA) of an asset
CIA triad (confidentiality, integrity, availability)	Three key cybersecurity principles
Exploit	Tool or technique that takes advantage of a vulnerability
Risk management	Process of identifying, assessing, and reducing risk to an acceptable level
Exposure	Estimated cost, loss, or damage that can result if a threat exploits a vulnerability
Access control	Security feature designed to restrict who has access to a network, IS, or data.
Audit	The process of generating, recording, and reviewing a chronological record of system events to determine their accuracy
Encryption	Transforming data into scrambled code to protect it from being understood by unauthorized users
Plaintext or clear-text	Readable text
Ciphertext	Encrypted text
Authentication	Method (usually based on username and password) by which an IS validates or verifies that a user is really who he or she claims to be
Biometrics	Methods to identify a person based on a biological feature, such as a fingerprint or retina
Firewall	Software or hardware device that controls access to a private network from a public network (Internet) by analyzing data packets entering or exiting it
Intrusion detection system (IDS)	A defense tool used to monitor network traffic (packets) and provide alerts when there is suspicious traffic, or to quarantine suspicious traffic
Fault tolerance	The ability of an IS to continue to operate when a failure occurs, but usually for a limited time or at a reduced level
Botnet (short for Bot network)	A network of hijacked computers that are controlled remotely—typically to launch spam or spyware. Also called software robots. Botnets are linked to a range of malicious activity, including identity theft and spam.

VULNERABILITIES

Vulnerabilities are weaknesses that threaten the confidentiality, integrity, or availability (CIA) of an asset.

- **Confidentiality** is the avoidance of the unauthorized disclosure of information. Confidentiality involves the protection of data, providing access for those who are allowed to see it while disallowing others from learning anything about its content.
- **Integrity** is the property that data or files have not been altered in an unauthorized way.
- **Availability** is the property that data is accessible and modifiable when needed by those authorized to do so.

Passwords. The function of a password together with a username is to **authenticate** a user's identity to verify that the person has the right to access a computer or network. Weak passwords create vulnerabilities. Passwords that are shared or not kept secret are useless. Unfortunately, too many people are lazy or unaware of the dangers and choose passwords that are easily guessable, short, common, or a word in the dictionary. Their disregard for this security measure makes it easy for hackers to break into many accounts simply by trying common passwords such as "password," "12345678," "qwerty" or "abc123." Strong passwords contain a combination of upper- and lower-case letters, numbers, and punctuation marks, and at least eight characters long although ten characters is better.

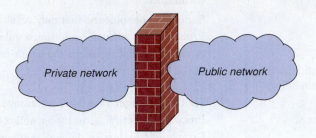

Figure 5.8 Firewalls create barriers to separate insecure public networks from private networks.

Internal Threats. Threats from employees, referred to as **internal threats,** are a major challenge largely due to the many ways an employee can carry out malicious activity. Insiders may be able to bypass physical security (e.g., locked doors) and technical security (e.g., passwords) measures that organizations have in place to prevent unauthorized access. Why? Because technology defenses such as firewalls, intrusion detection systems (IDS), and locked doors mostly protect against external threats.

A **firewall** is an integrated collection of security measures designed to prevent unauthorized access. A network firewall is similar to firewalls in buildings that are designed to isolate one network from another, as shown in Figure 5.8. To protect private networks and devices from external cyberthreats, a firewall inspects incoming or outgoing traffic—allowing in legitimate traffic and denying suspicious traffic. If a hacker learns an employee's password, the firewall offers no defense because the hacker would be using legitimate credentials.

IDS are sensors or tools that monitor traffic on a network after it has passed through the firewall. An IDS is designed to detect a number of threats, including:

- An attacker who is using the identity or credentials of a legitimate user to gain access to an IS, device, or network
- A legitimate user who performs actions he is not authorized to do
- A user who tries to disguise or cover up his actions by deleting audit files or system logs.

Cloud Computing and Social Network Risks. Social networks and cloud computing increase vulnerabilities by providing a single point of failure and attack. Critical, sensitive, and private information is at risk, and like previous IT trends, such as wireless networks, the goal is connectivity, often with little concern for security. As social networks increase their services, the gap between services and cybersecurity also increases. E-mail viruses and malware have been declining for years as e-mail security has improved. This trend continues as communication shifts to social networks and newer smartphones. Unfortunately, malware finds its way to users through security vulnerabilities in these new services and devices. Web filtering, user education, and strict policies are necessary to help prevent widespread outbreaks.

In Twitter and Facebook, users invite in and build relationships with others. Cybercriminals hack into these trusted relationships using stolen log-ins. Fake antivirus and other attacks that take advantage of user trust are very difficult to detect.

An overriding reason why these networks and services increase exposure to risk is the **time-to-exploitation** of today's sophisticated spyware and mobile viruses. Time-to-exploitation is the elapsed time between when vulnerability is discovered and when it's exploited. That time has shrunk from months to minutes so IT staff have ever-shorter timeframes to find and fix flaws before being compromised by an attack. Some attacks exist for as little as two hours, which means that enterprise IT security systems must have real-time protection.

When new vulnerabilities are found in operating systems, applications, or wired and wireless networks, patches are released by the vendor or security organization. **Patches** are software programs that users download and install to fix the vulnerability. Microsoft, for example, releases patches that it calls **service packs** to update and fix vulnerabilities in its operating systems, including Vista, and applications, including Office 2010. Service packs are made available at Microsoft's web site.

Left undetected or unprotected, vulnerabilities provide an open door for IT attacks and business disruptions and their financial damages. Despite even the best technology defenses, infosec incidents will occur mostly because of users who do not follow secure computing practices and procedures.

Phishing and Web-Based Threats. Companies increasingly adopt external, web-based applications, and employees bring consumer applications into the enterprise. Criminal enterprises are following the money on the Internet where that have a global market of potential victims.

Phishing is a deceptive method of stealing confidential information by pretending to be a legitimate organization, such as PayPal, a bank, credit card company, or other trusted source. Phishing messages include a link to a fraudulent phish web site that looks like the real one. When the user clicks the link to the phish site, he or she is asked for a credit card number, social security number, account number, or password. Phishing remains successful and profitable for criminals.

Criminals use the Internet and private networks to hijack large numbers of PCs to spy on users, spam them, shake down businesses, and steal identities. But why are they so successful? The Information Security Forum (*securityforum.org*), a self-help organization that includes many Fortune 100 companies, compiled a list of the top information problems and discovered that 9 of the top 10 incidents were the result of 3 factors:

1. Mistakes or human error

2. Malfunctioning systems

3. Misunderstanding the effects of adding incompatible software to an existing system

Unfortunately, these factors can too easily defeat cybersecurity technologies that companies and individuals use to protect their information. A fourth factor identified by the Security Forum is motivation, as described in *IT at Work 5.3*.

IT at Work 5.3

Money Laundering, Organized Crime, and Terrorist Financing

According to the U.S. Department of State (*state.gov*), organized crime rings rely on money laundering to fund their operations. This practice poses international and national security threats. It undermines free enterprise by crowding out the private sector, and it threatens the financial stability of nations.

Funds used to finance terrorist operations are very difficult to track. Despite this obscurity, by adapting methods used to combat money laundering, such as financial analysis and investigations, authorities can significantly disrupt the financial networks of terrorists and build a paper trail and base of evidence to identify and locate leaders of terrorist organizations and cells.

International organized crime syndicates, al-Qaeda groups, and other cybercriminals steal hundreds of billions of dollars every year. Cybercrime is safer and easier than selling drugs, dealing in black market diamonds, or robbing banks. Online gambling offers easy fronts for international money-laundering operations.

GOVERNMENT REGULATIONS

IT defenses must satisfy ever-stricter government and international regulations. Primary regulations are the Sarbanes–Oxley Act (SOX), Gramm-Leach-Bliley Act (GLB), Federal Information Security Management Act (FISMA), and USA Patriot Act in the U.S. Canada's Personal Information Protection and Electronic Document Act (PIPEDA); and Basel III (global financial services) all mandate the protection of personally identifiable information (PII). The director of the Federal Trade Commission (FTC) bureau of consumer protection warned that the agency would bring enforcement action against small businesses lacking adequate policies and procedures to protect consumer data.

Two accepted models for IT governance are **enterprise risk management (ERM)** and **COBIT (Control Objectives for Information and Related Technology).** ERM is a risk-based approach to managing an enterprise that integrates internal control, the Sarbanes–Oxley Act mandates, and strategic planning. ERM is intended to be part of routine planning processes rather than a separate initiative. The ideal place to start is with buy-in and commitment from the board and senior leadership COBIT, which is described in *IT at Work 5.4*, is an internationally accepted IT governance and control framework for aligning IT with business objectives, delivering value, and managing associated risks. It provides a reference for management, users, and IS audit, control, and security practitioners.

INDUSTRY STANDARDS

Industry groups imposed their own standards to protect their customers and their members' brand images and revenues. One example is the **Payment Card Industry Data Security Standard (PCI DSS)** created by Visa, MasterCard, American Express, and Discover.

PCI is required for all members, merchants, or service providers that store, process, or transmit cardholder data. PCI DSS mandates that retailers ensure that Web-facing applications are protected against known attacks by applying either of the following two methods:

1. Have all custom application code reviewed for vulnerabilities by an application security firm.

2. Install an application layer firewall in front of Web-facing applications. Each application will have its own firewall to protect against intrusions and malware.

IT at Work 5.4

COBIT and IT Governance Best Practices

IT governance is the supervision, monitoring, and control of the organization's IT assets. The IT Governance Institute (*itgi.org*) publishes Control Objectives for Information and Related Technology (COBIT), which many companies use as their IT governance guide. COBIT can be downloaded from isaca.org.

The Sarbanes–Oxley Act requires that companies provide proof that their financial applications and systems are controlled (secured) to verify that financial reports can be trusted. This requires that IT security managers work with business managers to do a risk assessment to identify which systems depend on technical controls rather than on business process controls. To meet COBIT, IT systems should be based on the following three principles:

Principle of economic use of resources: This principle acknowledges that the cost of infosec needs to be balanced with its benefits. It's the basic cost/benefit principle that you're familiar with. For example, you wouldn't spend more to protect your auto, home, or other asset than they are worth. Because it's possible, for instance, for companies to set a very low value on the confidential data of customers and employers and therefore avoid basic infosec defenses, the next two principles try to make sure that doesn't happen.

Principle of legality: This principle requires that companies invest in infosec to meet minimum legal requirements. This is a basic security principle, just like having hand railings on stairways, fire extinguishers, and alarm systems.

Accounting principles: These principles require that the integrity, availability, and reliability of data and information systems be maintained.

The purpose of the PCI DSS is to improve customers' trust in e-commerce, especially when it comes to online payments, and to increase the web security of online merchants. To motivate following these standards, the penalties for noncompliance are severe. The card brands can fine the retailer, and increase transaction fees for each credit or debit card transaction. A finding of noncompliance can be the basis for lawsuits.

CompTIA Infosec Survey. In its 2012 information security survey, the Computing Technology Industry Association (CompTIA, *comptia.org*), reported that only 22 percent of organizations have a formal policy in place governing use of mobile devices at work. The online survey of 500 business and IT professionals from various industries found that 70 percent of IT staff believed that security considerations are the greatest risk involved in supporting mobility.

The respondents identified a number of security risks from mobile devices: downloading unauthorized apps (48 percent), lost or stolen devices (42 percent), mobile-specific viruses and malware (41 percent), open Wi-Fi networks (41 percent), USB flash drives (40 percent), and personal use of business devices (40 percent).

The survey found that tablets are the top mobile device choice for purchase in the next year. Currently, smartphones are used at more organizations than standard cell phones; 84 percent of respondents use their smartphones for light work, such as e-mail or web browsing, while tablets are used for note taking, giving presentations, and as a communications device.

Organizations have to balance business objectives and security objectives, which may not always be in synch.

DEFENSE-IN-DEPTH MODEL

Defense-in-depth is a multi-layered approach to infosec. The basic principle is that when one defense layer fails, another layer provides protection. For example, if a wireless network's security was compromised, then having encrypted data would still protect the data provided that the thieves could not decrypt it.

The success of any type of IT project depends on the commitment and involvement of executive management, also referred to as the "tone at the top." The same is true of IT security. When senior management shows its commitment to IT security, it becomes important to others too. This infosec *tone* makes users aware that insecure practices and mistakes will not be tolerated. Therefore, an IT security and internal control model begins with senior management commitment and support, as shown in Figure 5.9. The model views infosec as a combination of people, processes, and technology.

Step 1: Senior management commitment and support. Senior managers' influence is needed to implement and maintain security, ethical standards, privacy practices, and internal control. The Committee of Sponsoring Organizations of the Treadway Commission (COSO, *coso.org/key.htm*) defines **internal control** as a *process* designed to provide *reasonable* assurance of effective operations and reliable financial reporting. Internal control is discussed later in this chapter.

Figure 5.9 Cybersecurity defense-in-depth model.

Step 2: Acceptable use policies and IT security training. The next step in building an effective IT security program is to develop security policies and provide training to ensure that everyone is aware of and understands them. The greater the understanding of how security affects production levels, customer and supplier relationships, revenue streams, and management's liability, the more security will be incorporated into business projects and proposals.

Most critical is an **acceptable use policy (AUP)** that informs users of their responsibilities. An AUP is needed for two reasons: (1) to prevent misuse of information and computer resources; and (2) to reduce exposure to fines, sanctions, and legal liability. To be effective, the AUP needs to define users' responsibilities, acceptable and unacceptable actions, and consequences of noncompliance. E-mail, Internet, and computer AUPs should be thought of as an extension of other corporate policies, such as those that address physical safety, equal opportunity, harassment, and discrimination.

Step 3: IT Security Procedures and Enforcement. If users' activities are not monitored for compliance, the AUP is useless. Therefore, the next step is to implement monitoring procedures, training, and enforcement of the AUP. Businesses cannot afford the infinite cost of perfect security, so they calculate the proper level of protection. The calculation is based on the digital assets' risk exposure. The risk exposure model for digital assets is comprised of the five factors shown in Table 5.2.

Another risk assessment method is the **business impact analysis (BIA)**. BIA is an exercise that determines the impact of losing the support or availability of a resource. For example, for most people, the loss of a smartphone would have greater impact than loss of a digital camera. BIA helps identify the minimum resources needed to recover, and prioritizes the recovery of processes and supporting systems. A BIA needs to be updated as new threats to IT emerge. After the risk exposure of digital assets has been estimated, then informed decisions about investments in infosec can be made.

Step 4: Hardware and Software. The last step in the model is implementation of software and hardware needed to support and enforce the AUP and secure practices.

Keep in mind that security is an ongoing unending process, and not a problem that can be solved with hardware or software. Hardware and software security defenses cannot protect against irresponsible business practices.

One of the biggest mistakes managers make is underestimating IT vulnerabilities and threats. Most workers use their laptops and mobiles for both work and leisure, and in an era of multitasking, they often do both at the same time. Yet off-time or off-site use of devices remains risky because, despite policies, employees continue to engage in dangerous online and communication habits. Those habits make them a weak link in an organization's otherwise solid security efforts. These threats can be classified as *unintentional* or *intentional*.

TABLE 5.2	Risk Exposure Model for Digital Assets
Factor	**Cost and Operational Considerations**
1. Asset's value to the company	What are the costs of replacement, recovery, or restoration? What is the recoverability time?
2. Attractiveness of the asset to a criminal	What is the asset's value (on a scale of low to high) to identity thieves, industrial spies, terrorists, or fraudsters?
3. Legal liability attached to the asset's loss or theft	What are the potential legal costs, fines, and restitution expenses?
4. Operational, marketing, and financial consequences	What are the costs of business disruption, delivery delays, lost customers, negative media attention, inability to process payments or payroll, or a drop in stock prices?
5. Likelihood of a successful attack against the asset	Given existing and emerging threats, what is the probability the asset will be stolen or compromised?

UNINTENTIONAL THREATS

Unintentional threats fall into three major categories: human errors, environmental hazards, and computer system failures.

1. Human errors can occur in the design of the hardware or information system. They can also occur during programming, testing, or data entry. Not changing default passwords on a firewall or failing to manage patches create security holes. Human errors also include untrained or unaware users responding to phishing or ignoring security procedures. Human errors contribute to the majority of internal control and infosec problems.

2. Environmental hazards include volcanoes, earthquakes, blizzards, floods, power failures or strong fluctuations, fires (the most common hazard), defective air conditioning, explosions, radioactive fallout, and water-cooling-system failures. In addition to the primary damage, computer resources can be damaged by side effects, such as smoke and water. Such hazards may disrupt normal computer operations and result in long waiting periods and exorbitant costs while computer programs and data files are recreated.

3. Computer systems failures can occur as the result of poor manufacturing, defective materials, and outdated or poorly maintained networks (recall the network crash at LAX airport in Chapter 4). Unintentional malfunctions can also happen for other reasons, ranging from lack of experience to inadequate testing.

INTENTIONAL THREATS

Examples of intentional threats include theft of data; inappropriate use of data (e.g., manipulating inputs); theft of mainframe computer time; theft of equipment and/or programs; deliberate manipulation in handling, entering, processing, transferring, or programming data; labor strikes, riots, or sabotage; malicious damage to computer resources; destruction from viruses and similar attacks; and miscellaneous computer abuses and Internet fraud.

Botnets. A **botnet** is a collection of bots (computers infected by software robots). Those infected computers, called **zombies**, can be controlled and organized into a network of zombies on the command of a remote botmaster (also called bot herder). Botnets expose infected computers, as well as other network computers, to the following threats:

- **Spyware:** Zombies can be commanded to monitor and steal personal or financial data.
- **Adware:** Zombies can be ordered to download and display advertisements. Some zombies even force an infected system's browser to visit a specific web site.
- **Spam:** Most junk e-mail is sent by zombies. Owners of infected computers are usually blissfully unaware that their machines are being used to commit a crime.
- **Phishing:** Zombies can seek out weak servers that are suitable for hosting a phishing web site, which looks like a legitimate web site, to trick the users into inputting confidential data.

Botnets are extremely dangerous because they scan for and compromise other computers, and then can be used for every type of crime and attack against computers, servers, and networks.

Questions

1. Explain confidentiality, integrity, and availability.
2. What is the purpose of passwords, firewalls, and intrusion-detection systems (IDS)?
3. Give an example of a weak and a strong password.
4. What is time-to-exploitation?
5. What is a service pack?
6. Explain phishing.
7. Why is money laundering a national security threat?
8. What is an acceptable use policy (AUP)?
9. Why do companies need an enforced AUP?
10. Define and give two examples of an unintentional threat.
11. Define and give two examples of an intentional threat.
12. Define botnet and explain its risk.

5.3 Defending Against Fraud

According to the 2011 LexisNexis True Cost of Fraud Study, retail merchants incur over a $100 billion in fraud losses due to unauthorized transactions, fees, and interest linked to chargebacks (funds returned to the credit card company)—almost 10 times the amount incurred by banks (LexisNexis, 2011). These losses are only customer-related—and do not include fraud committed by employees or in other industries. The number of fraudulent transactions decreased between 2010 and 2011, but average dollar value of a completed fraudulent transaction is increasing. Challenges for U.S. merchants who ship internationally include delay in payment confirmation, verification of customer identity, limited jurisdiction, and ability to reclaim merchandise and costs.

Crimes fall into two categories depending on the tactics of the criminal: violent and nonviolent. Fraud is a nonviolent crime because instead of a gun or knife, fraudsters use deception, confidence, and trickery—all are types of social engineering. Fraudsters carry out their crimes by abusing the power of their position or by taking advantage of the trust, ignorance, or laziness of others.

INSIDER FRAUD

Insider fraud is a term referring to a variety of criminal behaviors perpetrated by an organization's own employees or contractors. Other terms for this crime are *internal, employment,* or *occupational* fraud. **Internal fraud** refers to the deliberate misuse of the assets of one's employer for personal gain. Internal audits and internal controls are essential to the prevention and detection of occupation frauds. Several examples are listed in Table 5.3.

Experts estimate that on average it costs companies 3 percent to 5 percent of revenue each year (ACFE, 2012). When profit margins are thin, internal fraud can put companies out of business. The truth is that companies often are unaware of all the frauds committed within their company.

INTERNAL FRAUD PREVENTION AND DETECTION

The single-most-effective fraud prevention technique is the perception of detection and punishment. If a company shows its employees that it can find out everything that every employee does and will prosecute to the fullest extent anyone who commits fraud, then the feeling that "I can get away with it" drops drastically. The Catch-22 is that companies may have limited resources that hinder a proper fraud diagnosis or forensic accounting investigation, even though they cannot afford unrecoverable losses either.

TABLE 5.3	Types and Characteristics of Organizational Fraud	
Type of Fraud	**Does This Fraud Impact Financial Statements?**	**Typical Characteristics**
Operating management corruption	No	Occurs *off the books.* Median loss due to corruption: over 6 times greater than median loss due to misappropriation ($530,000 vs. $80,000)
Conflict of interest	No	A breach of confidentiality, such as revealing competitors' bids, often occurs with bribery
Bribery	No	Uses positional power or money to influence others
Embezzlement or misappropriation	Yes	Employee theft: employees' access to company property creates the opportunity for embezzlement
Senior management financial reporting fraud	Yes	Involves a massive breach of trust and leveraging of positional power
Accounting cycle fraud	Yes	This fraud is called "earnings management" or earning engineering, which are in violation of GAAP (Generally Accepted Accounting Principles) and all other accounting practices. See *aicpa.org*

Corporate Governance. IT has a key role to play in demonstrating effective corporate governance in order to prevent fraud. Regulators look favorably on companies that can demonstrate good corporate governance and best practice operational risk management. Management and staff of such companies will then spend less time worrying about regulations and more time adding value to their brand and business.

Internal fraud prevention measures are based on the same controls used to prevent external intrusions—perimeter defense technologies, such as firewalls, e-mail scanners, and biometric access. They are also based on human resource (HR) procedures, such as recruitment screening and training.

Intelligent Analysis, Audit Trails, and Anomaly Detection. Much of this detection activity can be handled by intelligent analysis engines using advanced data warehousing and analytics techniques. These systems take in audit trails from key systems and personnel records from the HR and finance departments. The data are stored in a data warehouse where they are analyzed to detect anomalous patterns, such as excessive hours worked, deviations in patterns of behavior, copying huge amounts of data, attempts to override controls, unusual transactions, and inadequate documentation about a transaction. Information from investigations is fed back into the detection system so that it learns. Since insiders might work in collusion with organized criminals, insider profiling is important to find wider patterns of criminal networks.

Identity Theft. One of the worst and most prevalent crimes is identity theft. Such thefts where individuals' Social Security and credit card numbers are stolen and used by thieves are not new. Criminals have always obtained information about other people—by stealing wallets or dumpster digging. But widespread electronic sharing and databases have made the crime worse. Because financial institutions, data processing firms, and retail businesses are reluctant to reveal incidents in which their customers' personal financial information may have been stolen, lost, or compromised, laws continue to be passed that force those notifications.

Questions

1. Define fraud and insider occupational fraud.
2. How can internal fraud be prevented?
3. How can internal fraud be detected?
4. Explain why data on laptops and computers should be encrypted.
5. Explain how identity theft can occur.

5.4 Information Assurance and Risk Management

The objective of IT security management practices is to defend all of the components of an information system, specifically data, software applications, hardware, and networks. Before they make any decisions concerning defenses, people responsible for security must understand the requirements and operations of the business, which form the basis for a customized defense strategy. In the next section, we describe the major defense strategies.

DEFENSE STRATEGY

The defense strategy and controls that should be used depend on what needs to be protected and the cost-benefit analysis. That is, companies should neither under-invest nor over-invest. The SEC and FTC impose huge fines for data breaches to deter companies from under-investing in data protection. The following are the major objectives of defense strategies:

1. Prevention and deterrence. Properly designed controls may prevent errors from occurring, deter criminals from attacking the system, and, better yet, deny access to unauthorized people. These are the most desirable controls.

2. Detection. Like a fire, the earlier an attack is detected, the easier it is to combat, and the less damage is done. Detection can be performed in many cases by using special diagnostic software, at a minimal cost.

3. Contain the damage. This objective is to minimize or limit losses once a malfunction has occurred. This process is also called *damage control*. This can be accomplished, for example, by including a **fault-tolerant system** that permits operation in a degraded mode until full recovery is made. If a fault-tolerant system does not exist, a quick and possibly expensive recovery must take place. Users want their systems back in operation as fast as possible.

4. Recovery. A recovery plan explains how to fix a damaged information system as quickly as possible. Replacing rather than repairing components is one route to fast recovery.

5. Correction. Correcting the causes of damaged systems can prevent the problem from occurring again.

6. Awareness and compliance. All organization members must be educated about the hazards and must comply with the security rules and regulations.

A defense strategy is also going to require several controls, as shown in Figure 5.10. **General controls** are established to protect the system regardless of the specific application. For example, protecting hardware and controlling access to the data center are independent of the specific application. **Application controls** are safeguards that are intended to protect specific applications.

GENERAL CONTROLS

The major categories of general controls are physical controls, access controls, data security controls, communication network controls, and administrative controls.

Physical Controls. Physical security refers to the protection of computer facilities and resources. This includes protecting physical property such as computers, data centers, software, manuals, and networks. It provides protection against most natural hazards as well as against some human hazards. Appropriate physical security may include several controls such as the following:

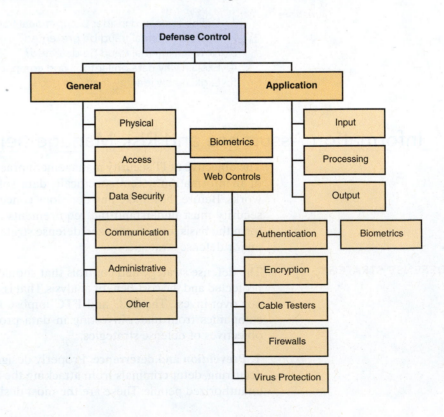

Figure 5.10 Major defense controls.

- Appropriate design of the data center. For example, the data center should be non-combustible and waterproof.
- Shielding against electromagnetic fields
- Good fire prevention, detection, and extinguishing systems, including sprinkler systems, water pumps, and adequate drainage facilities
- Emergency power shutoff and backup batteries, which must be maintained in operational condition
- Properly designed and maintained air-conditioning systems
- Motion-detector alarms that detect physical intrusion

Access Controls. Access control is the management of who is and is not authorized to use a company's hardware and software. Access control methods, such as firewalls and access control lists, restrict access to a network, database, file, or data. It is the major defense line against unauthorized insiders as well as outsiders. Access control involves authorization (having the right to access) and authentication, which is also called user identification (proving that the user is who he claims to be).

Authentication methods include:

- Something only the user knows, such as a password
- Something only the user has, for example, a smart card or a token
- Something only the user is, such as a signature, voice, fingerprint, or retinal (eye) scan; implemented via biometric controls, which can be physical or behavioral

Biometric Controls. A **biometric control** is an automated method of verifying the identity of a person, based on physical or behavioral characteristics. For example, fingerprint scanners are used for identification, as shown in Figure 5.11.

Most biometric systems match some personal characteristic against a stored profile. The most common biometrics are:

- **Thumbprint or fingerprint.** Each time a user wants access, a thumbprint or fingerprint (finger scan) is matched against a template containing the authorized person's fingerprint to identify him or her.
- **Retinal scan.** A match is attempted between the pattern of the blood vessels in the back-of-the-eye retina that is being scanned and a prestored picture of the retina.

Biometric controls are now integrated into many e-business hardware and software products. Biometric controls do have some limitations: they are not accurate in certain cases, and some people see them as an invasion of privacy.

Administrative Controls. While the previously discussed general controls are technical in nature, administrative controls deal with issuing guidelines and monitoring compliance with the guidelines. Examples of such controls are shown in Table 5.4.

Figure 5.11 Biometric scanner.
Source: Department of Homeland Security, *http://www.dhs.gov/files/programs/usv.shtm.*

UPPA/Photoshot Holdings Ltd.

TABLE 5.4	Administrative Controls

- Appropriately selecting, training, and supervising employees, especially in accounting and information systems
- Fostering company loyalty
- Immediately revoking access privileges of dismissed, resigned, or transferred employees
- Requiring periodic modification of access controls (such as passwords)
- Developing programming and documentation standards (to make auditing easier and to use the standards as guides for employees)
- Insisting on security bonds or malfeasance insurance for key employees
- Instituting separation of duties, namely, dividing sensitive computer duties among as many employees as economically feasible in order to decrease the chance of intentional or unintentional damage
- Holding periodic random audits of the system

Endpoint Security and Control. Many managers underestimate business risk posed by unencrypted portable storage devices—which are examples of *endpoints*. Business data is often carried on thumb drives, smartphones, and removable memory cards without IT's permission, oversight, or sufficient protection against loss or theft. Handhelds and portable storage devices put sensitive data at risk. According to the market research firm Applied Research-West, three out of four workers save corporate data on thumb drives. According to their study, 25 percent save customer records, 17 percent store financial data, and 15 percent store business plans on thumb drives, but less than 50 percent of businesses routinely encrypt those drives and even less consistently secure data copied onto smartphones.

Portable devices that store confidential customer or financial data must be protected no matter who owns them—employees or the company. If there are no security measures to protect handhelds or other mobile/portable storage, data must not be stored on them because it exposes the company to liability, lawsuits, and fines. For smaller companies, a single data breach could bankrupt the company.

Questions

1. What are the major objectives of a defense strategy?
2. What are general controls?
3. Define access control.
4. What are biometric controls? Give two examples.
5. What is endpoint security?

5.5 Network Security

As a defense, companies need to implement network access control (NAC) products. NAC tools are different from traditional security technologies and practices that focus on file access. While file-level security is useful for protecting data, it does not keep unauthorized users out of the network in the first place. NAC technology, on the other hand, helps businesses lock down their networks against criminals.

Network security measures involve three types of defenses, which are referred to as *layers*.

1. First layer: Perimeter security to control access to the network. Examples are antivirus software and firewalls.

2. Second layer: Authentication to verify the identity of the person requesting access to the network. Examples are usernames and passwords.

3. Third layer: Authorization to control what authenticated users can do once they are given access to the network. Examples are permissions and directories.

Details of these three defense layers are shown in Figure 5.12.

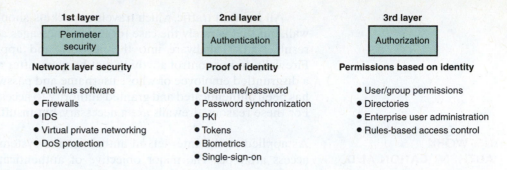

Figure 5.12 Three layers of network security measures.

1st layer	2nd layer	3rd layer
Perimeter security	Authentication	Authorization
Network layer security	**Proof of identity**	**Permissions based on identity**
• Antivirus software	• Username/password	• User/group permissions
• Firewalls	• Password synchronization	• Directories
• IDS	• PKI	• Enterprise user administration
• Virtual private networking	• Tokens	• Rules-based access control
• DoS protection	• Biometrics	
	• Single-sign-on	

PERIMETER SECURITY AND FIREWALLS

The major objective of perimeter security is access control. The technologies used to protect against malware (e.g., firewalls, IDS, and IDP) also protect the perimeter. A firewall enforces an access-control policy between two networks. Firewalls need to be configured to enforce the company's security procedures and policies. A network has several firewalls, but they still cannot stop all malware. See Figure 5.13. For example, each virus has a signature, which identifies it. Firewalls and antivirus software that have been updated—and know of that virus' signature—can block it. But viruses pass through a firewall if the firewall cannot identify it as a virus. For example, a newly released virus whose signature has not been identified or that is hidden in an e-mail attachment could be allowed into the network. That's the reason why firewalls and antivirus software require continuous updating.

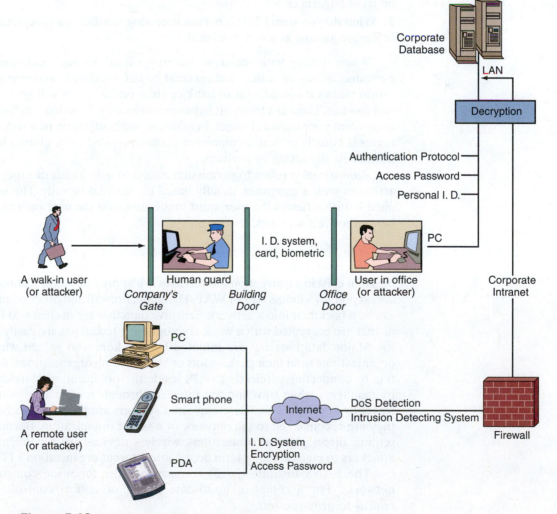

Figure 5.13 IT security mechanisms locations.

All Internet traffic, which travels as packets, should have to pass through a firewall, but that is rarely the case for instant messages and wireless traffic, which, as a result, "carry" malware into the network and applications on host computers. Firewalls do not control anything that happens after a legitimate user (who may be a disgruntled employee or whose username and password have been compromised) has been authenticated and granted authority to access applications on the network. For these reasons, firewalls are a necessary, but insufficient defense.

NETWORK AUTHENTICATION AND AUTHORIZATION

As applied to the Internet, an authentication system guards against unauthorized access attempts. The major objective of authentication is proof of identity. The attempt here is to identify the legitimate user and determine the action he or she is allowed to perform.

Because phishing and identity theft prey on weak authentication, and usernames and passwords do not offer strong authentication, other methods are needed. There are **two-factor authentication** (also called multifactor authentication) and two-tier authentication. With two-factor authentication, other information is used to verify the user's identity, such as biometrics.

There are three key questions to ask when setting up an authentication system:

1. **Who are you?** Is this person an employee, a partner, or a customer? Different levels of authentication would be set up for different types of people.

2. **Where are you?** For example, an employee who has already used a badge to access the building is less of a risk than an employee or partner logging on remotely. Someone logging on from a known IP address is less of a risk than someone logging on from Nigeria or Kazakhstan.

3. **What do you want?** Is this person accessing sensitive or proprietary information or simply gaining access to benign data?

When dealing with consumer-facing applications, such as online banking and e-commerce, strong authentication must be balanced with convenience. If authentication makes it too difficult to bank or shop online, users will go back to the brick and mortars. There is a trade-off between increased protection and turning customers away from your online channel. In addition, authentication of a web site to the customer is equally critical. e-commerce customers need to be able to identify if it is a fraudulent site set up by phishers.

Authorization refers to permission issued to individuals or groups to do certain activities with a computer, usually based on verified identity. The security system, once it authenticates the user, must make sure that the user operates within his or her authorized activities.

SECURING WIRELESS NETWORKS

Wireless networks are more difficult to protect than wired ones. All of the vulnerabilities that exist in a conventional wired network apply to wireless technologies. Wireless access points (wireless APs or WAPs) behind a firewall and other security protections can be a backdoor into a network. Sensitive data that are in clear text (not encrypted) or that are encrypted with a weak cryptographic technique are easily breached.

Major data breaches are initiated by attackers who gained wireless access to organizations from their parking lots or by bypassing organizations' security perimeters by connecting wirelessly to APs inside the organization. Wireless devices used by managers while traveling are infected through remote exploitation during air travel or in cyber cafes. These exploited systems are then used as backdoors when they are reconnected to the network of a target organization. Because they do not require direct physical connections, wireless devices are a convenient vector for attackers to maintain long-term access into a target organization's IT infrastructure.

The SANS Institute (2012) recommends the following controls for wireless networks. For a complete up-to-date listing of critical controls, visit *sans.org/critical-security-controls*.

• Organizations should ensure that each wireless device connected to the network matches an authorized configuration and security profile, with a documented owner of the connection and a defined business need. Organizations should deny access to those wireless devices that do not have such a configuration and profile.

• Organizations should ensure that all wireless APs are manageable using enterprise management tools. APs designed for home use often lack such enterprise management capabilities, and should therefore be avoided in enterprise environments.

• Network vulnerability scanning tools should be configured to detect wireless access points connected to the wired network. Identified devices should be reconciled against a list of authorized wireless access points. Unauthorized or rogue APs should be deactivated.

• Organizations should use Wireless Intrusion Detection Systems (WIDS) to identify rogue wireless devices and detect attack attempts and successful compromises. In addition to WIDS, all wireless traffic should be monitored by a wired IDS as traffic passes into the wired network.

• Organizations should regularly scan for unauthorized or misconfigured wireless infrastructure devices, using techniques such as "war driving" to identify APs and clients accepting peer-to-peer connections. Such unauthorized or misconfigured devices should be removed from the network, or have their configurations altered so that they comply with the security requirements of the organization.

Questions

1. What are network access control (NAC) products?
2. Define perimeter security.
3. Define authorization.
4. What can firewalls not protect against?
5. How can wireless APs put a company at risk?
6. What should organizations do to reduce risks from wireless networks?

5.6 Internal Control and Compliance

The **internal control environment** is the work atmosphere that a company sets for its employees. Internal control is a process designed to achieve:

• Reliability of financial reporting
• Operational efficiency
• Compliance with laws
• Regulations and policies
• Safeguarding of assets

INTERNAL CONTROLS NEEDED FOR COMPLIANCE

The Sarbanes–Oxley Act (SOX) is an antifraud law. It forces more accurate business reporting and disclosure of GAAP (generally accepted accounting principles) violations, thus making it necessary to find and root out fraud. A system of strong internal controls is essential to preventing fraud.

Section 302 deters corporate and executive fraud by requiring that the CEO and CFO verify that they have reviewed the financial report, and, to the best of their knowledge, the report does not contain an untrue statement or omit any material fact. To motivate honesty, executive management faces criminal penalties including long jail terms for false reports. Table 5.5 lists the symptoms, or red flags, of fraud that internal controls can be designed to detect.

Section 805 mandates a review of the Sentencing Guidelines to ensure that "the guidelines that apply to organizations . . . are sufficient to deter and punish organizational criminal conduct." The Guidelines also focus on the establishment of "effective compliance and ethics" programs. As indicated in the Guidelines, a precondition

TABLE 5.5	Indicators of Fraud That Can Be Detected by Internal Controls

- Missing documents
- Delayed bank deposits
- Holes in accounting records
- Numerous outstanding checks or bills
- Disparity between accounts payable and receivable
- Employees who do not take vacations or go out of their way to work overtime
- A large drop in profits
- A major increase in business with one particular customer
- Customers complaining about double billing
- Repeated duplicate payments
- Employees with the same address or telephone number as a vendor

to an effective compliance and ethics program is promotion of "an organizational culture that encourages ethical conduct and a commitment to compliance with the law."

Among other measures, SOX requires companies to set up comprehensive internal controls. There is no question that SOX, and the complex and costly provisions it requires public companies to follow, has had a major impact on corporate financial accounting. For starters, companies have had to set up comprehensive internal controls over financial reporting to prevent fraud and catch it when it occurs. Since the collapse of Arthur Andersen, following the accounting firm's conviction on criminal charges related to the Enron case, outside accounting firms have gotten tougher with clients they are auditing, particularly regarding their internal controls.

SOX and the SEC are making it clear that if controls can be ignored, there is no control. Therefore, fraud prevention and detection require an effective monitoring system.

Approximately 85 percent of insider fraud could have been prevented if proper IT-based internal controls had been designed, implemented, and followed.

SOX requires an enterprise-wide approach to compliance, internal control, and risk management because these issues cannot be dealt with from a departmental or business-unit perspective. However, fraud also requires a worldwide approach, as many incidents have indicated, such as the crime server in Malaysia.

WORLDWIDE ANTI-FRAUD REGULATION

Well-executed insider fraud or money-laundering operations can damage the financial sector, capital markets, and, as a result, a nation's economy. A capital market is any market where a government or a company can raise money to finance operations and long-term investment. Examples are the stock and bond markets.

Preventing internal fraud is high on the political agenda, with the Financial Services Authority (FSA) in the United Kingdom and the SEC in the U.S. both requiring companies to deal with the issue.

Managing risk has become the single most important issue for the regulators and financial institutions. Over the years, these institutions have suffered high costs for ignoring their exposure to risk. However, growing research and improvements in IT have improved the measurement and management of risk.

Questions

1. What is the purpose of an internal control?
2. How does SOX Section 302 attempt to deter fraud?
3. List three symptoms or red flags of fraud that can be detected by internal controls.

5.7 Business Continuity and Auditing

Fires, earthquakes, floods, power outages, and other types of disasters hit data centers. Yet business continuity planning and disaster recovery capabilities can be a tough sell because they do not contribute to the bottom line. Compare them to an insurance policy: if and only if a disaster occurs, the money has been well-spent. And spending on business continuity preparedness can be an open-ended proposition—there is always more that could be done to better prepare the organization.

Ninety-three percent of companies that suffer a significant data loss often go out of business within five years. Disasters may occur without warning, so the best defense is to be prepared. An important element in any security system is the **business continuity plan**, also known as the disaster recovery plan. Such a plan outlines the process by which businesses should recover from a major disaster. Destruction of all (or most) of the computing facilities can cause significant damage. It is difficult for many organizations to obtain insurance for their computers and information systems without showing a satisfactory disaster prevention and recovery plan. IT managers need to estimate how much spending is appropriate for the level of risk an organization is willing to accept.

BUSINESS CONTINUITY PLANNING

Disaster recovery is the chain of events linking the business continuity plan to protection and to recovery. The following are some key thoughts about the process:

- The purpose of a business continuity plan is to keep the business running after a disaster occurs. Each function in the business should have a valid recovery capability plan.
- Recovery planning is part of *asset protection*. Every organization should assign responsibility to management to identify and protect assets within their spheres of functional control.
- Planning should focus first on recovery from a total loss of all capabilities.
- Proof of capability usually involves some kind of what-if analysis that shows that the recovery plan is current.
- All critical applications must be identified and their recovery procedures addressed in the plan.
- The plan should be written so that it will be effective in case of disaster, not just in order to satisfy the auditors.
- The plan should be kept in a safe place; copies should be given to all key managers, or it should be available on the intranet. The plan should be audited periodically.

Disaster recovery planning can be very complex, and it may take several months to complete. Using special software, the planning job can be expedited.

Disaster avoidance is an approach oriented toward prevention. The idea is to minimize the chance of avoidable disasters (such as fire or other human-caused threats). For example, many companies use a device called uninterrupted power supply (UPS), which provides power in case of a power outage.

AUDITING INFORMATION SYSTEMS

An **audit** is an important part of any control system. Auditing can be viewed as an additional layer of controls or safeguards. It is considered as a deterrent to criminal actions, especially for insiders. Auditors attempt to answer questions such as these:

- Are there sufficient controls in the system? Which areas are not covered by controls?
- Which controls are not necessary?
- Are the controls implemented properly?
- Are the controls effective? That is, do they check the output of the system?
- Is there a clear separation of duties of employees?
- Are there procedures to ensure compliance with the controls?
- Are there procedures to ensure reporting and corrective actions in case of violations of controls?

Auditing a web site is a good preventive measure to manage the legal risk. Legal risk is important in any IT system, but in web systems it is even more important due to the content of the site, which may offend people or be in violation of copyright laws or other regulations (e.g., privacy protection). Auditing EC is also more complex since, in addition to the web site, one needs to audit order taking, order fulfillment, and all support systems.

COST-BENEFIT ANALYSIS

It is usually not economical to prepare protection against every possible threat. Therefore, an IT security program must provide a process for assessing threats and deciding which ones to prepare for and which ones to ignore or provide reduced protection against.

Risk-Management Analysis. Risk-management analysis can be enhanced by the use of DSS software packages. A simplified computation is shown here:

$$\text{Expected loss} = P_1 \times P_2 \times L$$

where:

P_1 = probability of attack (estimate, based on judgment)
P_2 = probability of attack being successful (estimate, based on judgment)
L = loss occurring if attack is successful

Example:

$$P_1 = .02, P_2 = .10, L = \$1,000,000$$

Then, expected loss from this particular attack is

$$P_1 \times P_2 \times L = 0.02 \times 0.1 \times \$1,000,000 = \$2,000$$

The amount of loss may depend on the duration of a system being out of operation. Therefore, some add duration to the analysis.

Ethical Issues. Implementing security programs raises many ethical issues. First, some people are against any monitoring of individual activities. Imposing certain controls is seen by some as a violation of freedom of speech or other civil rights. Handling the privacy versus security dilemma is tough. There are other ethical and legal obligations that may require companies to "invade the privacy" of employees and monitor their actions. In particular, IT security measures are needed to protect against loss, liability, and litigation. Losses are not just financial, but also include the loss of information, customers, trading partners, brand image, and ability to conduct business, due to the actions of hackers, malware, or employees.

Liability stems from two legal doctrines: *respondeat superior* and duty of care. *Respondeat superior* holds employers liable for the misconduct of their employees that occurs within the scope of their employment. With wireless technologies and a mobile workforce, the scope of employment has expanded beyond the perimeters of the company.

Under the doctrine of duty of care, senior managers and directors have a fiduciary obligation to use reasonable care to protect the company's business operations. Litigation, or lawsuits, stem from failure to meet the company's legal and regulatory duties.

Questions

1. Why do organizations need a business continuity plan?
2. List three issues a business continuity plan should cover.
3. Identify two factors that influence a company's ability to recover from a disaster.
4. Explain why business continuity/disaster recovery (BC/DR) is not simply an IT security issue.
5. Why should Web sites be audited?
6. How is expected loss calculated?
7. What is the doctrine of due care?

Key Terms

acceptable use policy (AUP) *128*
administrative controls *133*
advanced persistent
   threat (APT) attack *117*
adware *129*
Anonymous *118*
application controls *132*
AT&T Toggle *114*
audit *139*
authentication *134*
authorization *134*
availability *123*
baiting *116*
biometrics *123*
botnet *129*
bring your own device
   (BYOD) to work *133*
business continuity plan *139*
business impact analysis (BIA) *128*
COBIT (Control Objectives for
   Information and Related
   Technology) *126*

credentials *117*
confidentiality *123*
consumerization of information
   technology (COIT) *113*
corporate governance *131*
critical infrastructure *116*
cybersecurity controls *114*
denial of service (DoS) attack *118*
do-not-carry rules *120*
enterprise risk
   management (ERM) *126*
fault-tolerant system *132*
firewall *124*
general controls *132*
hacktivist *117*
insider fraud *130*
integrity *123*
internal control *127*
internal control environment *137*
internal fraud *130*
internal threats *124*

intrusion detection
   system (IDS) *124*
IT governance *126*
LulzSec *118*
malware *122*
money laundering *125*
patches *125*
Payment Card Industry Data Security
   Standard (PCI DSS) *126*
perimeter security *134*
persistent threats *116*
phishing *125*
pretexting *116*
service pack *125*
social engineering *116*
spam *129*
spyware *129*
time-to-exploitation *124*
two-factor authentication *136*
work container *115*
zombies *129*

Chapter 5 LINK LIBRARY

You find clickable Link Libraries for each chapter on the Companion website.

Dark Reading *Darkreading.com*

The *Wall Street Journal* interactive graphic of "China Hackers Hit U.S. Chamber, Attacks Breached Computer System of Business-Lobbying Group; E-mails Stolen," 12/21/2011 *http://online.wsj.com/article/SB10001424052970204058404577110541568535300.html#project%3DCHAMBER122111%26articleTabs%3Dinteractive*

"Video of China Hackers Attack U.S. Chamber of Commerce," 12/21/2011 *http://online.wsj.com/video/china-hackers-attack-us-chamber-of-commerce/A4DF072E-BD65-4063-ABFF-ECB6A9C0312C.html*

Case #3, Cars, Appliances Could Be Hack Targets, 9/9/2011 *http://online.wsj.com/video/cars-appliances-could-be-hack-targets/C1D18429-0F15-4A92-A0B7-418D7760A432.html*

Anti-Phishing Working Group web site *antiphishing.org*

AT&T Toggle video *wireless.att.com/businesscenter/popups/video/learn-more-about-toggle.jsp.*

Government Computer News (GCN) *gcn.com/*

CompTIA *comptia.org/*

SANS Top CyberSecurity Risks *sans.org/top-cyber-security-risks/*

Social engineering *symantec.com/connect/articles/social-engineering*

SANS Institute *20 Critical Controls* *http://www.sans.org/critical-security-controls/*

Evaluate and Expand Your Learning

IT and Data Management Decisions

1. Managers need to determine how much their companies need to invest in cybersecurity to meet their legal obligations. Since there is no such thing as perfect security (i.e., there is always more that you can do), some degree of risk will remain.
   a. When are a company's security measures sufficient to comply with its obligations? For example, does installing a firewall and using virus detection software satisfy a company's legal obligations?
   b. Assume your company has implemented a BYOD solution. Does your company have to encrypt all data that is accessible on employees own devices?

2. Assume that the daily probability of a major earthquake in Los Angeles is .07 percent. The chance of your computer center being damaged during such a quake is 5 percent. If the center is damaged, the average estimated damage will be $1.2 million.
   a. Calculate the expected loss (in dollars).
   b. An insurance agent is willing to insure your facility for an annual fee of $15,000. Analyze the offer, and discuss whether to accept it.

3. Should an employer notify employees that their computer usage and online activities are being monitored by the company? Why or why not?

4. Twenty-five thousand messages arrive at an organization each year. Currently there are no firewalls. On the average there are 1.2 successful hackings each year. Each successful hack attack results in loss to the company of about $130,000. A major firewall is proposed at a cost of $66,000 and a maintenance cost of $5,000. The estimated useful life is 3 years. The chance that an intruder will break through the firewall is 0.0002. In such a case, the damage will be $100,000 (30 percent), or $200,000 (50 percent), or no damage. There is an annual maintenance cost of $20,000 for the firewall.
   a. Would you invest in the firewall? Explain.
   b. An improved firewall that is 99.9988 percent effective and that costs $84,000, with a life of 3 years and annual maintenance cost of $16,000, is available. Should this one be purchased instead of the first one?

Questions for Discussion & Review

1. What are the dangers of BYOD to work, and how can they be minimized?

2. Many firms concentrate on the wrong questions and end up throwing a great deal of money and time at minimal security risks while ignoring major vulnerabilities. Why?

3. Discuss the shift in motivation of criminals.

4. How can the risk of insider fraud be decreased?

5. Why should information control and security be a top concern of management?

6. Explain what firewalls protect and what they do not protect.

7. Why is cybercrime expanding rapidly? Discuss some possible solutions.

8. Some insurance companies will not insure a business unless the firm has a computer disaster recovery plan. Explain why.

9. Explain why risk management should involve the following elements: threats, exposure associated with each threat, risk of each threat occurring, cost of controls, and assessment of their effectiveness.

10. Discuss why the Sarbanes–Oxley Act focuses on internal control. How does that focus influence infosec?

Online Activities

1. Review the *Wall Street Journal* interactive graphic of "China Hackers Hit U.S. Chamber, Attacks Breached Computer System of Business-Lobbying Group; E-mails Stolen" dated December 21, 2011. The link is posted in the Chapter 5 Link Library and is shown here: *http://online.wsj.com/article/SB10001424052970204058404 577110541568535300.html#project%3DCHAM-BER122111%26articleTabs%3Dinteractive*.
   a. Explain the importance and the role of social engineering in this intrusion and cybertheft.
   b. What can be done to prevent this type of intrusion from occurring again?

2. View the video "China Hackers Attack U.S. Chamber of Commerce" dated December 21, 2011. The WSJ details a cyber attack against the U.S. Chamber of Commerce in which e-mails were stolen. *http://online.wsj.com/video/ china-hackers-attack-us-chamber-of-commerce/ A4DF072E-BD65-4063-ABFF-ECB6A9C0312C.html*.
   a. Briefly describe the key issues about the intrusion mentioned in the video.
   b. Draft a list of 3 cybersecurity warnings based on the video.
   c. How serious was the intrusion, and when did it occur?
   d. What or whom did the hackers focus on? Why?
   e. What information could the hackers have gleaned from the intrusion of the Chamber?
   f. What did the Chamber do to increase cybersecurity after learning of the intrusion and cybertheft?
   g. Explain why cars and appliances can be hack targets.
   h. What other resources are at risk?
   i. Does this incident indicate about how widespread hacking is? Explain your answer.

Collaborative Work

1. Research a botnet attack. Explain how the botnet works and what damage it causes. What preventive methods are offered by security vendors?

2. The SANS Institute publishes the Top CyberSecurity Risks at *sans.org/top-cyber-security-risks/*.
   a. Which risks would be most dangerous to financial institutions?
   b. Which risks would be most dangerous to marketing firms?
   c. Explain any differences.

3. Access the Anti-Phishing Working Group Web site (*antiphishing.org*) and download the most recent Phishing Activity Trends Report.
   a. Describe the recent trends in phishing attacks.
   b. Explain the reasons for these trends.

4. Research vendors of biometrics. Select one vendor, and discuss three of its biometric devices or technologies. Prepare a list of major capabilities. What are the advantages and disadvantages of its biometrics?

CASE 2 BUSINESS CASE

Army Deploys Androids, Securely

The U.S. government's most IT-security sensitive organizations are the Army and National Security Agency (NSA). The Army and NSA decided to no longer reject mobile technologies or BYOD. Instead these Department of Defense (DoD) organizations looked for secure ways in which commercially available smartphones can be used to access IT systems. Performance and usability are also key concerns particularly because encryption caused latency (delays). Rather than build special handsets that are hardwired with secure components, the DoD choose to install its software on commercially available phones. This approach minimizes costs and allows the government to stay up to date with the latest phones on the market.

Army Selects Customized Androids, Securely

The Army does not permit any type of smartphone. The Army installs its own software on Android phones. Androids were selected because Google allows its code to be modified. The Androids are reengineered to store classified documents, but not to transmit data over a cell network. This approach costs less than building special handsets and makes it easier for the Army to use the latest phones on the market.

The Android needs to be customized to prevent apps from seeking more information than needed to function. For example, a weather or clock app with GPS capabilities identifies a user's location. The Army does not want to support apps that transmit locations over the network.

NSA

Due to the highly classified nature of its work, the NSA has some of the strictest requirements in government, including whole buildings that are labeled as Sensitive Compartmentalized Information Facilities, which have additional requirements.

To comply with strict security requirements, most NSA employees had to leave their mobiles in their cars in the parking lot rather than bringing them in to work. In 2012, the agency worked on a plan to introduce secure, commercially available mobile devices and an architecture that enables other agencies to use mobiles with classified data. Troy Lange, NSA's mobility mission manager explains: "This is about bringing efficiencies and capabilities that people are used to in their everyday lives and extending that to our national security mission."

Questions

1. In your opinion, will the outcome of these Army and NSA projects have a big impact throughout government? On the private sector as well?
2. What are the top three concerns of the DoD?
3. Do you agree that the Army and NSA deciding to allow the use of mobile technologies and to figure out how best to limit risks is encouraging news to the private sector? Explain your answer.
4. Research and describe the latest developments in the Army or NSA's mobile strategy. Does the Army still restrict their mobile strategy to Androids?

CASE 3 VIDEO CASE

Cars, Appliances Could Be Hack Targets

View the video "Cars, Appliances Could Be Hack Targets" on the online *Wall Street Journal* (September 9, 2011; 4 minutes, 44 seconds). *http://online.wsj.com/video/cars-appliances-could-be-hack-targets/C1D18429-0F15-4A92-A0B7-418D7760A432.html*. Officials warn that computers and mobiles are not the only devices vulnerable to hack attacks. Information security risks are expanding to anything attached to a digital network. Vulnerable devices now include cars, appliances, and electricity meters—and will continue to grow. According to the Data Breach Investigations Report (Verizon, Business 2012), most corporate data breaches occur through some type of network device, which makes all networked devices and appliances subject to attack.

Questions

1. Explain why cars, appliances, and other devices not commonly associated with hacking can be hack targets.
2. What other resources are at risk? Why?
3. What are the concerns of the Department of Homeland Security (DHS)?
4. Why is encryption needed?
5. Explain how the capability to remotely control machines creates a vulnerability or a problem in cyberwarfare?

Data Analysis & Decision Making

Financial Impact of Breached Protected Health Information

1. Visit the *HealthDataManagement.com* web site to access the: "Report Assesses the Cost of PHI Breaches," *http://www.healthdatamanagement.com/news/breach-notification-hipaa-privacy-security-44142-1.html*. This report examines the financial impact of breaches of protected health information.

2. Download the free report, which is a collaborative effort of the American National Standards Institute, The Santa Fe Group, and the Internet Security Alliance, with input from more than 100 members of 70 organizations.

3. The report offers "PHIve," a five-step method to calculate the potential or actual cost of a breach. "In addition to the legal and ethical obligations to protect PHI, there is another, very real and equally important reason for protecting it," according to the report. "It is called 'goodwill'—the intangible advantages that a company has in its market, including strategic locations, business connections, and, relevant to this matter, an excellent reputation."

4. Using the five-step method, calculate the potential cost of a breach.

Resources on the Book's Website

More resources and study tools are located on the Student Web Site. You will find additional chapter materials and useful web links. In addition, self-quizzes that provide individualized feedback are available for each chapter.

References

ACFE (Association of Certified Fraud Examiners). acfe.com/. 2012.

Aftergood, S. "Former Official Indicted for Mishandling Classified Info," FAS, April 15, 2010. *fas.org/blog/secrecy/2010/04/drake_indict.html*.

Antilla, S. "Red flags Were There All Along: Suspicious Activities Largely Unquestioned." *Gazette* (Montreal), December 16, 2008.

Chabrow, E. "U.S. Government Takes Up Mobile Challenge." Bankinfosecurity.com, February 7, 2012.

Chickowski, E. "Compliance Policy Development Do's and Don'ts." *Dark Reading*, April 23, 2012.

Dunn, J.E. "Mobile malware up as enterprises take BYOD risks." *Techworld*, April 12, 2012.

Gold, L. "Forensic Accounting: Finding the Smoking E-mail: E-discovery Is Now a Critical Part of Forensics—and of Firm Policy." *Accounting Today* 22(8), May 5, 2008.

Gorman, S. "China Hackers Hit U.S. Chamber." *The Wall Street Journal Online*, December 21, 2011.

Higgins, K. J., "Security's New Reality: Assume the Worst." *Dark Reading*, March 15, 2012.

Hoover, J. N. "National Security Agency Plans Smartphone Adoption." *InformationWeek Government*, February 3, 2012.

Milan, M. "U.S. government, military to get secure Android phones." CNN.com, February 3, 2012. *cnn.com/2012/02/03/tech/mobile/government-android-phones*.

Perloth, N. "Hacked Chamber of Commerce Opposed Cybersecurity Law." *bits.blogs.nytimes.com*, December 21, 2011.

PWC, The 2012 Global State of Information Security Survey. pwc.com/giss2012.

SANS Institute. *20 Critical Controls*, 2012. *http://www.sans.org/critical-security-controls/*.

Verizon Business, "Data Breach Investigations Report (DBIR)." 2012. A study conducted by the Verizon RISK Team with cooperation from the Australian Federal Police, Dutch National High Tech Crime Unit, Irish Reporting and Information Security Service, Police Central e-Crime Unit, and United States Secret Service. *verizonbusiness.com/about/events/2012dbir/index.xml*.

Chapter

6

E-Business & E-Commerce Models and Strategies

Learning Outcomes

❶ Explain how e-business processes improve productivity, efficiency and competitive advantage for business organizations and the public sector (government and nonprofit organizations.)

❷ Describe five key challenges faced by online retail businesses in the business-to-consumer (B2C) marketplace.

❸ Identify various ways that e-businesses are facilitating trade between buyers and sellers in the business-to-business (B2B) marketplace.

❹ Describe how government agencies are making use of cloud computing and mobile technologies to enhance government services.

❺ Identify some of the ethical and legal issues that regularly confront e-businesses.

Electronic business (e-business) is business that uses the Internet and online networks as the **channel** to consumers, supply chain partners, employees, and so on. During the early web era, the online channel was stand-alone. Typically, retailers rushed to build business-to-consumer (B2C) web sites, and set up online business units that were independent and separated from their traditional (offline) channels. Those e-business units were managed and evaluated according to different performance metrics, incentives, and operating models. Why? Because e-commerce was treated as something so fundamentally different, strange, or high-tech that traditional financial metrics did not apply. When dot-coms started failing on a massive scale in 2000, managers learned that financial principles and marketing concepts applied to e-commerce. Since then, numerous other e-commerce models have emerged, been implemented, and then been replaced by newer ones as web and wireless technologies and applications emerged.

Today, as you know from personal experience, companies are **multichanneling**—integrating online and offline channels for maximum reach and effectiveness. As shown in Figure 6.1, the once purely online eBay added a traditional channel—a store named *eBay@57th* in New York City that opened in November 2009.

In the 2010s, organizations continue to radically rethink their approach to e-business process, the Internet, and how mobile technologies might impact their business. Here are several types of changes impacting companies directly or indirectly.

- Retailers are advertising and selling through social channels, such as Facebook, Twitter, RSS feeds, blogs, and via **comparison shopping engines.** Consumers use Google Product Search, Shopzilla, TheFind, and NexTag comparison shopping engines to compare prices and find great deals for certain brands and products.

- Consumers are using mobile handheld devices to research brands, products, and services from multiple sources. What's important is the extent to which consumers are exploring and challenging the information they've found, and creating and posting their own opinions and detailed experiences. *TripAdvisor.com* is an example.

- Often B2B sites lacked helpful features and capabilities of **business-to-consumer (B2C)** sites. Now manufacturers and distributors are revising their online business-to-business (B2B) capabilities to meet the time-critical requirements of their buyers. With the growth of lean manufacturing and just-in-time inventory management,

Figure 6.1 eBay added a traditional offline channel when it opened a physical store called eBay@57th in New York on November 20, 2009. The store offers previews of select items and Internet kiosks for consumers who want to shop online.

© Richard Levine/Alamy Limited

industrial buyers need on-demand access to supply, and they want well-designed, fast, and full-featured sites.

- Governments and agencies are expanding and refining their **government-to-citizen** (G2C) web sites to improve services and outreach at reduced cost, as shown in Figure 6.3.

- Security issues are a chief concern for e-businesses and e-government agencies. In this chapter, you will read about efforts the federal government is taking to increase **cyber security** and defend against cyber threats to the nation's information infrastructure.

In this chapter, you learn about B2C, B2B, and G2C e-business models and specific e-commerce applications used by businesses and government agencies.

The chapter opens with a larger than usual case study of Google, Inc. Google provides myriad examples of the opportunities and challenges faced by e-businesses today. You will read about what makes Google so popular as an IT employer and why Google is under constant pressure by regulators, both in the U.S. and in the European Union (EU), over potential violations of privacy and antitrust rules. Google also faces challenges as global e-businesses, attempt to satisfy customers from a wide variety of cultures, attempt to remain in compliance with many different legal systems, and struggle to figure out how to balance its profit motive with its famous motto "Don't Be Evil."

CASE 1 OPENING CASE
The Google Universe

In any discussion about e-business, it would be hard not to mention Google, Inc. (Figure 6.2). While Google ranks lower on Forbes Global 500 listing than other notable tech companies like Cisco, Microsoft, Apple, and Intel, its name recognition and consumer favorability ratings make it one of the most popular technology companies (Reisinger, 2012). Once known only for its search engine business, today Google is a mega e-business empire that offers products and services in a wide range of categories. While Internet search continues to be its most well-known service, several other Google products have become leaders in their respective categories.

A Better Way to Search the Web

Google was started in 1998 by Larry Page and Sergey Brin (see Figure 6.3), two students in Stanford University's Ph.D. program. Page and Brin's academic work focused on innovative ways of understanding the structure of the Internet based on how web pages linked to each other. This ultimately led to the development of the Google search engine which was different from other popular search engines of the time (e.g., Yahoo, Excite, Lycos, and AltaVista among others). Many of these early search engines emphasized web page content. So-called **key words** built into web pages were a key determinant of search results. Page and Brin's approach used web page content, but prioritized search rankings by the number of other Internet pages that linked back to a page. Page and Brin reasoned that the number of **backlinks** a page has is a good indicator of its popularity or importance. Their PageRank™ algorithm turned out to be an important innovation as people began finding

Figure 6.2 Google's Mountain View California Office in Silicon Valley. Google maintains offices in over 40 countries around the world.

Figure 6.3 Larry Page (L), Co-Founder and President, Products, and Sergey Brin, Co-Founder and President, Technology, at Google's campus headquarters in Mountain View. They founded the company in 1998.

results from Google's search engine more helpful than other sites. Google's increasing popularity with search engine users led to an opportunity for generating revenue from advertising, which continues to be its primary source of income today. By June 2000, Google became the world's largest search engine.

While continuing to refine and improve its core search (and advertising) business, Google has steadily expanded into other products and services through acquisition and/or the creative efforts of its own R&D teams. Some of its most popular offerings include:

- **Gmail**—a free, advertising supported e-mail service.
- **Blogger**—a blog publishing service.
- **Google Maps**—a web mapping service that powers many map-based services such as the Google Maps web site, Google Maps mobile apps, and many third-party mashup applications through the Google Maps API, the most popular Application Programming Interface on the Internet today. (You read more about mashups and APIs in Chapter 8.)
- **Google Earth**—a global mapping service that combines satellite imagery, 3D images of buildings and terrain, street-level photographs, user-submitted photos, and Google search.
- **Google Analytics**—a program for tracking and monitoring metrics and analytics associated with web site traffic.
- **YouTube**—acquired in 2006, YouTube is now the largest video-sharing site on the Internet.
- **Google Docs**—a web-based document editor and collaboration tool.
- **Google Reader**—one of the most popular RSS aggregators for subscribing to blogs and other syndicated web content.
- **Picasa**—a photo organizing, editing and sharing service
- **Android Mobile Operating System**—developed in partnership with other companies that form the Open Handset Alliance. Android is the most popular mobile OS globally (See Chapter 7).
- **Google+** and **Orkut**—two social networking services. Orkut is very popular in countries like India and Brazil. Google+ is viewed by many as a direct competitor to Facebook (read more about Google+ in Chapter 8).

The list above includes some of Google's most popular products. For a complete list, see *google.com/intl/en/about/products/index.html.*

Google Culture: Massages, Free Food and "Don't Be Evil"

Besides its success in a wide range of e-business ventures, Google distinguishes itself by its unusually open and progressive corporate culture. Since the beginning, Google sought to develop a culture that inspires creativity, diversity, and a determined work ethic. Google is also known for its ethical values, summarized by its famous motto "Don't be evil." A list of 10 guiding principles developed during Google's early days continues to frame strategy and decision making at the company (see Table 6.1).

Google's popularity as an employer is well known. It is regularly listed as one of the most desirable places to work. Google employees enjoy unusual perks like free food in cafeterias, game rooms, health club facilities, fitness classes, subsidized massages, free haircuts, and laundry service.

Google's Business Models and Markets

Business-to-Business Market (B2B)

Unlike many other companies that started during the heady days of the dot-com bubble (see section 6.1), Google has enjoyed a prosperous financial history. In this chapter you will read about various types of e-business markets and models. Most of Google's revenue comes from an **advertising business model.** This means that despite its popularity with individual Internet users around the world, Google is part of a business-to-business (B2B) market with most of its revenue coming from organizations that pay Google to display advertisements to those of us who use its many services for free.

TABLE 6.1 | **Ten Things Google "Knows to Be True"**

1. **Focus on the user and all else will follow.**

   Google focuses on providing the best user experience possible.

2. **It's best to do one thing really, really well.**

   While Google offers a vast array of products and services, *Search* continues to be the foundation of its business and its primary source of revenue.

3. **Fast is better than slow.**

   Google knows that products and services that do things faster are valued by their customers.

4. **Democracy on the web works.**

   Google's *Search* results are based in part, on its PageRank™ algorithm, which identifies sites that have been "voted" to be the best sources of information by other pages across the web.

5. **You don't need to be at your desk to need an answer.**

   Google believes the world is increasingly mobile and is making its many products and services available through mobile devices.

6. **You can make money without doing evil.**

   Google strives to run its business in ways that are profitable, but also ethical, transparent, honest, and fair to all of its customers, despite sometimes competing agendas.

7. **There's always more information out there.**

   Google continues to look for new ways to provide information to Internet users. Their goal is make all of the world's information available to people seeking answers.

8. **The need for information crosses all borders.**

   Google operates in a global market with offices in more than 60 countries around the world. More than half of all Google searches are delivered to people living outside the U.S. Google offers their search engine in more than 130 languages as well as translation tools that make it so people can discover information in languages they don't speak.

9. **You can be serious without a suit.**

   Google understands that creativity and hard work are more likely to result in a culture that is fun and rewards both individual achievements as well as team successes. The Google office environment is casual and creates spaces for collaboration, encouraging people to work and play together.

10. **Great just isn't good enough.**

    Google is constantly pushing the envelope, looking for new and better ways of doing things; sometimes things that nobody else thought was even possible. One of the reasons there are so many Google products is because they see so many opportunities to do things better than other companies.

Google also sells a variety of enterprise-level IT products to business organizations. Many of these services, including Gmail, Search Tools, and mapping solutions are similar in nature to the advertising-supported versions available to the general public. These enterprise solutions however, are designed to be deployed and managed by corporate IT personnel, often integrating with existing IT systems like corporate Intranets. Unlike the advertising-supported products, Google typically charges companies for the use of its enterprise applications and tools. However, Google's business model for its enterprise products is not as clear as it is for consumer products. Google clearly operates B2B e-commerce sites that follow the **"Manufacturer/Direct Sales"** business model whereby the company provides products and services directly to enterprise customers for a fee. But Google also distributes some products, specifically Google Apps for business, through authorized resellers or brokers. It appears that Google recognizes that some business customers require more support than the company is prepared to provide and has created a Google Apps Reseller program where authorized resellers offer Google products along with a range of IT installation, support and maintenance services. This channel is sometimes referred to as the **Value Added Reseller Model.**

Business-to-Consumer (B2C) Market

Like any advertising business, Google must have a sharp focus on the needs of the end user, those of us who use its services. After all, it is this large market of individuals using Google's free products that help it attract fee-paying advertisers. As a result, Google still needs to practice marketing and branding from a business-to-consumer (B2C) perspective, competing with companies like Microsoft, Apple, Facebook and others to entice people to use its products.

Business-to-Government (B2G) Market

Google actively promotes its enterprise solutions to a variety of government agencies in the U.S. and abroad. As a result, the company is actively engaged in Business-to-Government (B2G) marketing. For instance, the U.S. Department of Interior recently became one of Google's largest government customers of cloud-based services, providing e-mail and collaboration tools to the large federal agency. Many government agencies utilize Google's *Search Appliance* product. Once installed on an agency web site, the tool makes it easy for government employees and citizens to locate a wide variety of documents, forms, and other information that has been placed online. One difference that users might notice when using the Search Appliance installed on a government web site is that search results do not include paid ads like those at Google.com. (Try the tool on the City of Calgary's web site, Calgary.ca) The company promotes *Google Apps for Government*, an enterprise suite that includes Gmail, Google Calendar, Google Docs and video sharing among other things. This reduces the need for governments to develop these tools on their own, saving millions of tax payer dollars. *Google Apps* meet all the standards of the **Federal Information Security Management Act (FISMA),** a requirement for all federal agencies. Google competes with a number of other companies to meet the growing IT needs of government agencies (see the *e-government* case at the end of this chapter.) As part of its ever expanding list of ventures, Google has begun working with select municipalities on infrastructure projects, building a fiber optic network in Kansas City in order to increase network speeds for residents in Kansas and Missouri.

Domestic and International Business Challenges

Because the Internet is a global network, Google's products and services are technically accessible to most computer users around the world. Google has offices in over 40 different countries, and its products are available in as many as 130 languages. However, the company faces significant challenges navigating myriad cultural, legal, and language differences around the globe, and must maintain a vigilant international strategy in order sustain its competitive advantage in so many different countries. Most of the challenges Google encounters are based on a few significant issues that draw criticism both at home and abroad.

Privacy

Google compiles information about everyone who uses its products and builds individual profiles that allow it to sell targeted advertising services to businesses. In March 2012, Google consolidated 60 different privacy policy statements, written for different services, into a single, companywide policy. Almost immediately, the new policy came under fire from privacy critics and government agencies around the world (Figure 6.4). It remains to be seen if Google can operate with a single privacy policy that satisfies the laws, regulatory agencies, and consumer expectations in each and every country.

Google is not alone with respect to this challenge. Any cloud-based e-business that collects personal information about its users must contend with a multitude of different standards imposed by each country. Not too long ago, Internet advertising companies were able to operate more freely because the industry and technology were so new; it's not clear, however, that many governments fully understood how companies like Google, Apple, Facebook and others operated. It also took time before countries were able to create laws regulating privacy issues. Increasingly, however, governments around the world are imposing much stricter privacy rules, and they expect Google and others to comply. Companies that make their money from targeted advertising, like Google and Facebook, represent particularly

GEORGES GOBET/AFP/Getty Images, Inc.

Figure 6.4 EU Justice, Fundamental Rights and Citizenship Commissioner Viviane Reding presents proposals to revamp data privacy law across the European Union. She has been critical of Google's privacy policies and practices.

large targets for regulatory agencies in places like the European Union that impose stricter privacy rules than the U.S. For these companies, personal information about users is what drives their business. Information is the currency in which they trade. As a result, Google receives a lot more scrutiny than other e-businesses, whose basic challenge is to simply protect user information from unauthorized access. Without the ability to leverage user information for creating targeted advertising, companies like Google aren't much more effective than traditional media (e.g., television, radio, and print media) companies.

These issues, both ethical and legal, are complex and far from being resolved. See Table 6.2 for a list of specific privacy related challenges faced by Google.

What these and other cases illustrate is the ongoing challenge Google faces as it attempts to create policies and practices that comply with the varying laws and the consumer cultures throughout the world.

TABLE 6.2	**A Sample of Privacy Complaints Associated with Google**

The European Union's Justice Commissioner, Vivian Reding, says Google's revised privacy policies "are in breach of European law."

Officials in France's data protection authority also object to the new Google policy and claim it violates European legal rules regarding transparency.

Officials in Japan and Korea have expressed reservations about the new policy.

In 2011, French regulators targeted Google over issues related to data-gathering practices associated with its online mapping service. Google ultimately admitted guilt in the case involving the collection of e-mail, computer passwords, and other information from private Wi-Fi networks by workers roaming French cities in automobiles collecting photos for its Street View mapping service.

Street View Data collection operations are under investigation in more than two dozen other countries including Canada and Spain (*Streitfeld & O'Brien*, 2012; *Carr*, 2010) (see Figure 6.5).

In 2010, officials from France, Germany, Ireland, Israel, Italy, the Netherlands, New Zealand, Spain, and the United Kingdom issued a joint statement objecting to privacy rights violations associated with Google Buzz, a social networking platform that Google ultimately discontinued in 2011.

U.S. congressmen, along with consumer groups, called on the Federal Trade Commission in 2012 to investigate Google for knowingly bypassing the privacy settings of people who used Apple's Safari web browser on phones and computers. Google has reported that it has since ceased the practice.

Figure 6.5 A car equipped with special cameras records images for *Google Street View*, the 3D mapping application available on Google Maps. In this picture, the car is taking pictures of private homes in a residential UK neighborhood.

Conflicts with Totalitarian Governments

Access to information and freedom of speech represent a special challenge for Google. The company must sometimes contend with foreign governments that strictly control the information their citizens have access to. The country that has tested Google's business model (providing information to attract users) and its corporate values (e.g., "Don't be evil") more than any other is China. When Google first launched its Chinese search engine, *Google.cn*, in 2006, it voluntarily conformed to strict Chinese censorship rules that blocked information on key words or topics objectionable to the Beijing government. By 2009, however, Google announced its Gmail system had been the target of a series of cyber-attacks, which they all but blamed on the Chinese government. The hackers had attempted to access the accounts of Chinese human rights activists. In that same year, the Chinese government began blocking YouTube and intermittently blocking other Google services. By 2010, Google stopped censoring results on their search engine, and instead redirected searches from mainland China to their Hong Kong–based search page, which operated without the same government censorship rules (Figure 6.6).

The move enraged mainland Chinese officials who set about restricting access to the Hong Kong–based search engine and threatened not to renew Google's license to operate in China. The conflict with China is costly to Google. In the west, critics say that Google's early attempt to appease the Chinese government represents a violation of its "Don't be Evil" policy, making Google a complicit partner in human rights violations. On the other hand, alienating the Chinese government carries the risk that Google will miss out on one of the largest markets in the world. By January 2012, the *Wall St. Journal* reported that Google was exploring ways of continuing its work in China. It still maintains offices in mainland China and Hong Kong, and is exploring ways to leverage the popularity of the Android mobile operating system, which powers about 60 percent of Chinese smartphones. Google is also developing services that help advertisers target Chinese users through non-Google

Figure 6.6 Bouquets of flowers are placed in front of Google's Beijing China headquarters as a display of support after Google announced in January 2010 that it was considering closing its China operations after China-based hackers launched a cyber-attack on the company. Google continues to operate in China on a limited basis.

web sites. The market in China is too large for Google to ignore, but it could still face many of the same censorship issues that caused it trouble before. The *Android Market* (now called "Google Play") offers many mobile apps that would violate Chinese regulations. Will Google censor those apps if it launches a Chinese version of its app market? Apple faces similar challenges in regard to its iOS mobile operating systems. *TheGeek.com* (2009) reports that Apple deleted a number of mobile apps featuring quotes and teachings from the Dali Lama from its Chinese app store. The Dalai Lama is Tibet's popular spiritual leader known for his criticism of China's human rights violations and its occupation his country.

Anticompetitive Issues

Most developed countries have recognized that competition is good for business and consumers, and have **antitrust laws** designed to discourage companies from using anticompetitive practices.

According to the U.S. Department of Justice (2012),

> Competition in a free market benefits American consumers through lower prices, better quality and greater choice. Competition provides businesses the opportunity to compete on price and quality, in an open market and on a level playing field. . . .

Globally, the U.S. and the European Union have the most well developed antitrust laws. Google's dominant position in the industry makes it a target for agencies charged with upholding antitrust laws. Google is not the only e-business company to face charges of uncompetitive behavior. Apple, Microsoft, Amazon, Intel, Yahoo, and others have at one time or another faced antitrust scrutiny for business practices, both domestically and in the European Union. Google's sheer size, power, and unusually large breadth of services almost ensure that it will be scrutinized for antitrust violations. One challenge that legal experts face when deciding if Google has violated antitrust laws is based in part on its advertising business model. Google gives away services for free in order to attract users it can then offer to its advertising clients. However, by giving away these services, Google looks as though they are trying to drive other companies out of business through a practice called **predatory pricing,** offering goods and services at prices that don't cover the costs of producing these services. When used as an anticompetitive practice, it is applied for a short period of time, creating a price war that eventually eliminates competitors. In Google's case, however, free services are provided as a long-term strategy for attracting Internet users. Regardless, France recently found Google guilty of harming a French firm, Bottin Cartographies, which charges for its mapping services (Barth, 2012).

According to Fairsearch.org, an advocacy group supported by a number of popular e-commerce businesses, Google has engaged in a variety of anticompetitive practices. In a 2011 report issued by the group, the organization claims that Google is guilty of:

- "Deceptive display: Steering users toward its own products by displaying them at the top or in the middle of the results page in ways that suggest to consumers that they are natural search results, rather than links to Google's own sites;
- Search manipulation: Manipulating its search algorithm to exclude or penalize competing sites, effectively "disappearing" them from the Internet;
- Unauthorized content scraping: Stealing content developed by other web sites, such as user reviews, without permission and displaying that content on its own pages, sometimes even without attribution;
- Unfair treatment of advertisers: Manipulating advertisers' quality scores to inflate ad prices and placing restrictions on its "must buy" ad platform that inhibit customers from using competing platforms; and
- Exclusionary conduct in mobile: Buying up companies in the mobile search area that present a nascent competitive threat, and imposing exclusivity restrictions in its Android licensing agreements to maintain and expand its dominance."

(Quoted from *Fairsearch.org*, 2011).

Web Analytics

One advantage that e-businesses have over traditional **brick-and-mortar companies** is the ability to track consumer behavior. This allows companies to evaluate user responses to a variety of marketing strategies. Brick-and-mortar businesses are unable to generate similar metrics without spending considerable amounts of money. Google offers e-businesses and web site owners a number of tools for tracking web site traffic and monitoring online behaviors.

Google Analytics—a powerful web site traffic analytics tool that tracks the number of visitors to a web site, identifies geographic location of users, evaluates how users interact with a site and how they respond to specific promotional tactics. These and many other metrics are used by managers to make decisions about marketing strategy and web site design.

Google Alerts—reports new online Internet content based on predefined search terms. The service allows businesses to monitor stories about their company, products, competitors or other issues that may affect the business.

Google Trends—analyzes Internet user search trends on specific topics. This allows businesses to evaluate interest in their company, products, and competitors over time.

Google Insights—offers more detailed analysis of user search trend behavior. Businesses can evaluate Internet user search activity based on category, seasonality, geographic distribution, and other properties.

Blogger Statistics—a subset of Google Analytics metrics available to people who create blogs on Google's blogging platform.

Ethical and Legal Issues

On the surface, you might think that helping Internet users find information on the web is a mission with relatively few ethical challenges. However, you have already read about a number of situations where Google's business practices have led to legal problems and exposed it to charges that it does not always adhere to its own "Don't be evil" mantra. Google faces situations regularly where it must determine the most ethical course of action:

Privacy—Does Google's street view mapping service violate people's privacy when, without permission, it takes pictures of:

* Minor children?
* People sunbathing?
* People urinating, picking their noses, or engaged in other embarrassing behaviors?
* People whose faces, license plates or other information is identifiable?

Google says it responds to requests to remove pictures like those above, but privacy advocates say that's not good enough. They say Google shouldn't post such pictures in the first place.

Google claims that it resists government requests to identify users based on how they use the company's search engine. Many people use the search engine to find pornography, including images that exploit children. The Google's Insight tool can be used to review trends in search behavior. From a privacy and free speech perspective, Google's actions are to be applauded. However, Google's resistance to government requests might also be interpreted as protecting individuals who engage in illegal behavior and, in some cases, prey on young, innocent victims. Google has also been accused of resisting government requests for this kind of information as a way of making its search engine more attractive to consumers of pornography. Is Google protecting First Amendment rights or simply protecting its business interests?

Google's initial decision to cooperate with China by censoring search engine results is viewed by many as a capitulation of its corporate ethical values. In effect, Google's censorship practices aided and abetted China's policy of restricting speech, a basic human freedom. To what extent is Google acting unethically when it cooperates with governments that are violating human rights by restricting freedom of expression and blocking access to information?

Google's ad pricing practices have also come under fire for their lack of transparency and misleading portrayal as auctions. Critics argue that the price Google charges to advertisers for key words are not based on the highest bidder, but rather on what will make Google the most money.

Copyright Infringement—some of Google's practices raise questions about its ethical use of other people's intellectual property. For instance, *Google Books* is a program aimed at digitizing the full text of books and storing that information in a Database (Figure 6.7).

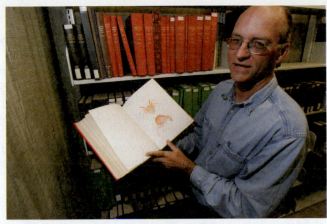

© ZUMA Wire Service/Alamy Limited

Figure 6.7 *May 27, 2010, San Diego, California*, Peter Brueggeman, director of the Scripps Institution of Oceanography Library and Archives, is working with Google in the scanning of 100,000 volumes from the library at the institution.

Content from this database can appear in Google search results. While Google makes the full text of books available only if they are in the public domain, some authors and writers' associations object to Google making any use of their intellectual property to gain commercially without providing compensation to the writers or publishers of the original work.

There is also concern about Google's attempt to become the global repository for books and digitized printed matter. Pam Samuel, a professor at UC Berkley Law School cites some critical issues:

- Unlike modern public libraries, Google Books is a for-profit venture, and the profit motive may impact decisions about how Google decides to share the world's book collection with the rest of us. While Google Books currently exists as a free (advertising supported) service, that doesn't mean that Google will always offer it for free.

- Google might claim that its digitized collection is proprietary and restrict what is known as the "fair use," rule which allows people to use copyrighted material for limited, noncommercial purposes (e.g., education)

- Libraries have traditionally guarded patron privacy to a much greater extent than what Google has ever agreed to, leaving the door open to the possibility that Google may share individual reading behavior with governments and/or advertisers.

According to the Open Book Alliance, Google requires that ". . . libraries must deploy "technological measures" to prevent other libraries, digital archives, researchers, competing search engines, and others from downloading and analyzing the content of those public domain books. In other words, once a public domain book is scanned into Google's database, the new digitized version ceases to be in the public domain. This is designed to prevent other companies from creating similar digital collections of books that could compete with Google's collection (*Openbookalliance.org*, 2011).

Conclusion

As a large, multifaceted e-business, Google has enjoyed tremendous success in spite of the complexities associated with serving global B2B, B2C, and B2G markets. At the same time, it faces an ever-evolving set of legal and ethical challenges around the world. The company has been praised for its stimulating and rewarding work environment designed to attract creative, intelligent, and hardworking employees. Its progressive corporate culture and stated desire to balance the profit motive with important ethical values have made it one of the most popular e-businesses worldwide. However, critics are quick to point out that Google doesn't always live up to its own values and that its power and dominant role in the marketplace is not in the best interest of the global community. The company's response to critics of its privacy policies and copyright infringement appears to be self-serving. On a more positive note, Google continues to pioneer innovative products and services that are increasingly popular with Internet users. Because of its size and dominant position in the market, it is sometimes difficult to remember that Google is still a relatively young company that has managed a complex set of technology, business and ethical challenges better than many others.

Discuss

1. How does Google's advertising business require it to operate from the perspective of both a B2B and a B2C company?
2. Explain how Google's PageRank™ algorithm led to search results that users found more helpful that those from earlier search engines.
3. Describe how Google's advertising model offers advertisers superior targeting capabilities compared to traditional advertising channels (e.g., television, radio, and print media).
4. Why is Google increasingly blamed for antitrust violations? Cite examples of business practices that are of concern to antitrust regulators around the world.

Debate

5. Is Google's collection of data for its Street View program unethical? What specific Street View data collection actions have created concern for users and regulatory agencies around the world?
6. When Google cooperates with governments like China by restricting access to information available through its search engine, is it guilty of human rights violations (e.g., freedom of speech)? Is Google contradicting its own motto, "Don't be Evil," in these situations?
7. Is Google infringing on the rights of authors and publishers when it includes their copyrighted work in its searchable database of books?
8. Is Google wrong to set limits on the use of public domain books it has digitized and stored in its database? Is this an example of anticompetitive behavior? Is it unethical?

Discussion

Read Google's new, consolidated privacy policy: *google.com/policies/privacy/*.

9. What kinds of information were you surprised to learn that Google collected about users?
10. Does the policy clearly describe the way Google uses the information it collects?
11. Do you feel that the policy describes practices that are a violation of personal privacy?
12. Finally, what actions can users take to limit the information that Google collects about them and do you think options to limit information collection by Google are adequate?

Sources: Compiled from Efrati & Chao (2012), Branigan (2009), Wilson, Ramos & Harvey (2007), Evans (2008), Gross (2012), Chertoff (2012), Zibreg (2009), BBC News (2012), Pfanner (2011, 2012), Reisinger (2012), Valentino-Devries (2012), Waugh (2012), *Carr (2010),* Hunton & Williams (2010), Streitfeld & Wyatt (2012), Barth (2012), Wikipedia (2012), Humphries (2012), Openbookalliance.org (2009), Marshall (2006), Woollacott (2012), Shankland (2011), Government Computers News (2012).

6.1 E-Business Challenges and Strategies

The popularity of Internet and mobile technologies has created an environment where consumers enjoy greater control over where and how they interact with a business or a brand through a mix of online channels and media. To successfully compete in this online environment, managers need to understand and respond to changing consumer expectations and behavior as well as the evolving needs of business customers and emerging supply chain systems that were not in existence just a few years ago. In some cases, nontraditional suppliers of IT services and products have risen to challenge once-dominant companies in the industry.

The opening case describes how, in a relatively short period of time, Google, Inc. has become a powerful, global e-business, supplying products to consumers, businesses, and governments. Google and other e-business are redefining traditional channels. Consumers and companies used to purchase software that ran on their computers. Now many companies use products and services that are distributed based on the software as service (SaaS) or cloud computing model. As in the case of Google, many of these cloud-based consumer services are free (or advertising supported). Enterprise products and services are frequently less expensive than they used to be.

A key to success in today's competitive environment is having a clear understanding of the business model your company is following and making sure that managers from various functional areas—marketing, IT, operations, logistics, and accounting, all operate in a manner consistent with that model.

To better understand the importance of sound models and strategies, in the next section you read about the dot-com era.

DOT-COM ERA, 1995 TO 2002

Companies rushed into e-commerce in the 1990s. Many far-fetched predictions and management assumptions were made that led to poor decisions and e-business failures. There were numerous debates, with one side arguing that *business over the Internet* had its own set of rules that differed (mysteriously) from traditional business models that valued positive earnings and cash flow. The opposing side argued that adding the prefix "e" to business did not eliminate the need to earn a profit, but risk-taking investors generally ignored this logic for several years.

From the mid-1990s to 2002, the media and Internet stock analysts hyped the *new economy* and the growth of dot-com businesses. (A few of those stock analysts were later arrested and/or fined for fraud and misleading investors.) The concept of a new economy helped fuel the theory that Internet companies were different (had new rules). In terms of the stock market, old economy companies like Procter & Gamble were out. New economy companies like Yahoo.com (and many that went bankrupt within a few years), were in.

Dot-Com Bubble Inflates. The new economy was the economy of the **dot-com era** (or **dot-com bubble**), which extended from roughly 1995 to 2000. In 1995, the number of Internet users sharply increased. Pure-play companies, nicknamed dot-coms, existed only on the Internet without a physical brick-and-mortar presence. These Internet-channel companies were set up to capture the new marketspace. *Marketspace* was the term used instead of the old economy's *marketplace*. (The new economy had a new vocabulary, furthering the divide between traditional and e-business.)

Unrestrained by business models that required making a profit and having huge sums of money from venture capitalists (private investors), many dot-coms engaged in daring and sometimes fraudulent business practices. According to many dot-com business models, the objective was to build up a customer base (market share), even if it meant selling at a loss in the short term (which many did) hoping they'd become profitable in the long run. Investors bought into these irrational business models, and the stock prices of dot-coms skyrocketed, attracting more investors. In reality, the dot-com bubble was a stock market bubble. That is, stock prices were significantly inflated and continued to rise (see Figure 6.8), inflating the size of the bubble until March 2000.

Dot-com Bubble Bursts and Deflates. Most dot-coms were listed on the Nasdaq, or National Association of Securities Dealers Automated Quotation System (*nasdaq.com*). On March 10, 2000, the Nasdaq Composite index reached its peak of 5,048.62 points. From March 11, 2000, to October 9, 2002, the Nasdaq lost 78 percent of its value by dropping from 5046.86 to 1114.11 points as dot-com stock prices fell or lost all value. Figure 6.8 shows changes in the Nasdaq from the start of the bubble to 2003. March 10, 2000, is called the day the bubble burst because it was the turning point. The steady decline ended most debate over whether or not positive earnings, cash flow, and other financial metrics of brick-and-mortar (physical) commerce applied to e-commerce.

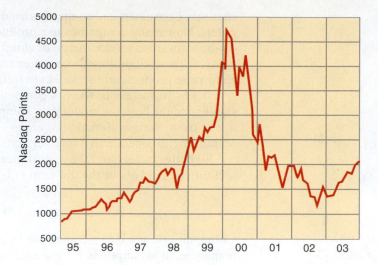

Figure 6.8 Changes in the Nasdaq during the dot-com era, which burst (started to decline) on March 10, 2000, and declined until October 2002.

Lessons are still being learned about B2C and B2B commerce as companies experiment with new features to gain even a slight or temporary competitive advantage. As you read in the chapter's introductory case, companies that can combine strong product ideas, like Google's superior search engine, with sound business models and practices, can quickly rise to become powerful and financial prosperous.

Fundamental capabilities and challenges of e-commerce are briefly discussed next.

E-BUSINESS AND E-COMMERCE FUNDAMENTALS

An **e-business process** involves the use of electronic or digital technologies, often based on the Internet or World Wide Web, to accomplish some business task. For example, a company that advertises job openings on its web site is using an e-business process for the purpose of recruiting new employees.

An **e-business** is a company where a significant or substantial part of its business is based on the utilization of e-business processes. Obviously companies vary in their use of e-business processes. Some companies are more or less traditional businesses that use a small number of e-business processes, while at the other extreme, pure play e-businesses operate almost completely online.

E-commerce refers to the use of e-business process for the specific purpose of buying or selling goods and services. In other words, e-commerce is a form of e-business. Increasingly, companies that have not traditionally identified themselves as e-businesses are finding that adoption of e-business practices increases productivity, efficiency, and competitive advantages. In addition to e-commerce, Internet or web-based technologies have been used for developed for the following:

E-BUSINESS APPLICATIONS

Internal Communications. Companies discover that various kinds of communication can be carried out more efficiently using e-business processes. Internet telephony (voice communication over the Internet) is replacing traditional telecommunications. Businesses documents are created and shared via electronic methods such as e-mail and through cloud-based platforms (e.g., Google Docs and *box.net*). Employees, business partners, and customers are communicating using social networks, web-based video conferencing (e.g., Skype), instant messaging, e-mail and other Internet (or Intranet) based tools. The availability of broadband wireless and wired networks, as well as laptops and mobile/handheld devices, increases the availability of all these e-business communication methods.

Service. Self-service features reduce inefficiencies and costs of providing service to customers, clients, patients, citizens, and so on. For example, the Federal Express web site lets customers track their shipments, calculate shipping costs, schedule pickups, and print their own labels. Airlines encourage travelers to print board passes before arriving at the airport.

Collaboration and training. *Telepresence* refers to a set of technologies that allow people to mimic face-to-face interactions. Telepresence minimizes the limitations of having to be physically present in a single location to collaborate, or give and receive live online training or education. Video conferencing technologies and even virtual world platforms are widely used by companies today to hold meetings and conduct training with employees who are geographically scattered. (For example, check out the web site for a unique virtual meeting company called *Venuegen.com*). The web abounds with collaboration tools that facilitate team work, brain storming, media sharing, project management, scheduling and other aspects of the collaborative process.

Community. Social networks such as Facebook and Twitter provide e-businesses the ability to build communities on a scale not previously possible prior to the emergence of the World Wide Web. You will read about social media in the Chapter 8.

Supply Chain Management. Many administrative aspects of supply chain management are more efficiently handled using web-based tools and technologies. Certain B2B e-commerce platforms offer more efficient marketplaces for suppliers and buyers, and non-transactional tasks (supplier identification, inventory management, contracts, etc.) can be more effectively carried out on the web as well.

Research, Information Gathering and Web Analytics. As the introductory case to this chapter illustrated, many professionals utilize the web to search for information on a wide range of topics. Use of the web as an alternative to physical books, scientific and trade journals, industry newsletters and other publications represents a significant advantage. Many types of marketing research and secondary data analysis have replaced traditional methods, often providing firms with higher quality information, faster results, and lower data acquisition costs. Many companies offer cloud-based web site traffic analysis tools and social media monitoring services so that businesses can evaluate the quantity and quality of brand-related discussions occurring on social media sites. You read more about Web Analytic tools later in this section.

Marketing Communications. Increasingly, e-businesses are finding that several different web-based options exist for communicating with potential customers. Brands can use online advertising to create awareness, develop favorable brand attitudes, generate leads, stimulate sales, and achieve a wide range of other marketing communications objectives (see section 6.5).

As previously discussed, some companies may use only a few of the e-business processes listed above. Other companies will use all of the above and more. As a general rule, anytime a company can increase its productivity while reducing its costs by implementing an e-business process, it makes sense to do so. Someday, we expect that the distinction of a traditional vs. an e-business will become moot because all companies will be practicing some combination of online and traditional business practices based on their particular needs and business goals.

Types of E-Business Markets. There are several different types of markets that e-businesses participate in. The following definitions describe terms that have been used throughout the text.

Business-to-business (B2B). In B2B markets, both the sellers and the buyers are business organizations. Over 85 percent of e-commerce volume is B2B—far exceeding B2C commerce.

Business-to-consumers (B2C). In B2C markets, the sellers are organizations, and the buyers are individual end users. B2C is sometimes called **e-tailing** (electronic retailing).

Consumers-to-business (C2B). In C2B markets, consumers make known a particular need for a product or service, and then suppliers compete to provide that product or service at the requested price. An example is Priceline.com, where the customer names a product or service and the desired price, and Priceline tries to find a supplier to fulfill the stated need.

Government-to-citizens (G2C) and others. In these markets, a government agency provides information and services to its citizens via e-commerce technologies. Government units can engage in e-commerce with other government units—**government-to-government (G2G)** or with businesses—**government-to-business (G2B).**

Business-to-government (B2G). In B2G markets, businesses sell goods and services to government agencies. Businesses that service government agencies must often follow special rules or regulations governing product specifications and marketing practices. In the introductory case, you read how *Google Apps for Government* must meet standards specified by the Federal Information Security Management Act (FISMA) because federal agencies are required to use products that meet certain IT security standards.

Mobile commerce (m-commerce). Any of the above markets can take on an additional characteristic if the buyer and/or seller is using a mobile, handheld device. Transactions and activities are conducted using wireless networks and mobile apps.

E-BUSINESS WEB SITE REQUIREMENTS AND CHALLENGES

As a consumer, you've most likely had direct experience with an e-commerce web site and are familiar with common "front end" features for site navigation, product search, "shopping basket," and check-out procedures. However, a number of integrated systems, networks, database and accounting tools, dynamic page display systems and maintenance tools needed to support e-business operations are less widely understood by the typical user. The complex logistical systems responsible for fast and efficient order fulfillment (getting the correct items to the customer in a reasonable amount of time) remain a mystery to many (and in some cases may be considered proprietary trade secrets.) The following sections provide summary descriptions of many e-business and e-commerce capabilities that are considered essential in today's competitive environment.

Availability. Availability relates to the server-side of e-business. An "always on" facility is needed to maintain these business critical apps. Web sites need to be hosted on servers (specialized large-capacity hard drives) that are capable of supporting the volume of requests for access, or traffic, to the site. Figure 6.9 shows an example of web-hosting servers. Servers need to be connected to the Internet via huge capacity

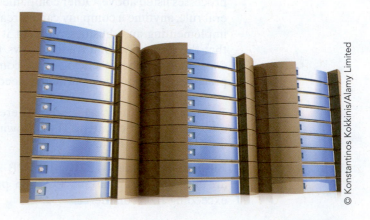

Figure 6.9 Web hosting servers.

transmission (telecommunication) lines. Servers need to be taken offline for service or replacement, at which time hosting is switched to other servers or, if the business can tolerate it, the web site is taken offline during the maintenance.

Hosting on a third-party's server is done if the company lacks infrastructure to host it themselves or the IT expertise to manage it. Another reason or benefit of third-party hosting is **scalability**—being able to add-on additional capacity incrementally, quickly, and as needed.

Accuracy and Quick Response. Not only must web servers be available, the e-commerce software and databases need to respond quickly. Web software must be capable of searching, sorting, comparing product features; checking availability, balances, and/or delivery times; check out; processing promotions and payments; verifying that the credit card number belongs to the person trying to use it; and confirmation of the purchase in real time. Speed is even more important in time-sensitive, B2B commerce where errors that delay delivery are intolerable. Recall that in Google's list of ten things it knows to be true (see Table 6.1); one of the items specifically referred to the importance of being fast. Consumers have come to expect apps and web pages to function quickly. Failure on this issue generally means customers will go to a competing vendor.

Security and PCI DSS Compliance. All of the servers, transmission lines, application software, databases, and connections must be secured; and confidential data often must be protected with another layer of defense, typically encryption. For web sites accepting credit cards, an additional security standard is imposed by the payment card industry (PCI).

PCI DSS compliant and certified. All e-commerce and brick-and-mortar merchants, regardless of size and sales volume, need to be PCI DSS compliant to accept, hold, process, or exchange credit cardholder information of the major credit cards. The **PCI DSS (Payment Card Industry Data Security Standard)** is a set of information security requirements to help prevent credit card fraud. The PCI DSS was developed by the **Payment Card Industry Security Standards Council (PCI SSC),** an organization founded by American Express, Discover Financial Services, JCB International, MasterCard Worldwide, and Visa, Inc.

Table 6.3 lists the PCI DSS principles and twelve accompanying requirements, around which the specific elements of the DSS are organized. The PCI Council publishes a list of Validated Payment Applications on its *pcisecuritystandards.org* web site. Web sites built for e-commerce need to be hosted on software platforms that are PCI certified. Certification to verify that the credit card handling processes and Internet systems comply with PCI DSS must be done annually.

Building Competitive Advantage. No competitive innovation remains unique for long. Leading companies are always looking for next-generation capabilities to develop new competitive advantage. One approach is to integrate social networks. Companies can implement their own social networks and associated services; or leverage Facebook or other existing ones. Operating a private social network provides companies with increased control and monitoring capabilities, but requires considerably greater financial resources and human resources. Increasingly, companies are learning to make use of strategies that take advantage of public social networks like Facebook and Twitter.

Integration of e-Commerce Systems with Enterprise systems. Another huge challenge is integrating e-commerce systems with legacy and other enterprise systems. There is growing interest in allowing better integration across all customer points of interactions. This challenge intensifies when companies are merged or acquired because then multiple web sites that are built on a variety of technology platforms need to be integrated.

TABLE 6.3	PCI DSS Principles and Requirements

The core of the PCI DSS is a group of principles and accompanying requirements, around which the specific elements of the DSS are organized

Build and Maintain a Secure Network

Requirement 1: Install and maintain a firewall configuration to protect cardholder data

Requirement 2: Do not use vendor-supplied defaults for system passwords and other security parameters

Protect Cardholder Data

Requirement 3: Protect stored cardholder data

Requirement 4: Encrypt transmission of cardholder data across open, public networks

Maintain a Vulnerability Management Program

Requirement 5: Use and regularly update antivirus software

Requirement 6: Develop and maintain secure systems and applications

Implement Strong Access Control Measures

Requirement 7: Restrict access to cardholder data by business need-to-know

Requirement 8: Assign a unique ID to each person with computer access

Requirement 9: Restrict physical access to cardholder data

Regularly Monitor and Test Networks

Requirement 10: Track and monitor all access to network resources and cardholder data

Requirement 11: Regularly test security systems and processes

Maintain an Information Security Policy

Requirement 12: Maintain a policy that addresses information security

Web Analytics and Intelligence Software. Web site activities, such as what was clicked, how long a visitor viewed a page, the IP address of the visitor's computer, and items put into the shopping cart are captured and stored in a log file. Log data is analyzed to learn how visitors navigate the site, to assess advertising campaigns, and other factors of interest. Many vendors offer web analytics and intelligence software so that managers can analyze web traffic and other activities of visitors, as described in Table 6.4.

TABLE 6.4	Web analytics and intelligence software tools and solutions	
Software	**Features and Functions**	**URL**
ClickTracks	Provides products, visualization tools, and hosted services for web site traffic analysis, including visitor behavior.	*clicktracks.com*
Coremetrics	A platform that captures and stores customer and visitor clickstream activity to build LIVE (Lifetime Individual Visitor Experience) profiles, which serve as the foundation for e-business initiatives.	*coremetrics.com*
Google Analytics	Offers free web analytics services with integrated analysis of Adwords and other keyword-based search advertising.	*goggle.com/analytics*
SAS Web Analytics	Automatically turns raw web data into business information.	*sas.com/solutions/ webanalytics/*
Webtrends	Measures campaign performance, search engine marketing, web site conversion, and customer retention.	*webtrends.com*

INTERNATIONAL E-COMMERCE

Too often international online shoppers have to work through several hurdles to buy from U.S. e-commerce companies. They face the challenge of finding out whether a site will ship to their country. Shipping costs tend to be higher than necessary, and delivery can be slow and unpredictable. In addition, prices are not converted into the shopper's native currency. The total cost of delivery for international customers is often too vague and incorrect. Customers may learn that they have to pay additional unexpected customs fees and taxes to receive their order, to return their order, or to correct errors.

As you read in the introductory case, global e-commerce can present considerable challenges for many businesses because of the difficulty associated with complying with myriad differences in laws and regulations around the world.

E-BUSINESS MODELS

To better understand how e-business works, look at Figure 6.10. A company such as Dell (labeled "Our Company") provides products and/or services to customers, as shown on the right side. To do so, the company buys inputs such as raw materials, components, parts, or services from suppliers and other business partners in the procurement process. Processing the inputs is done in its production/operations department. Finance, marketing, IT and other departments support the conversion of inputs to outputs and the sale to customers.

An objective of e-business is to *streamline* and *automate* as many processes as possible. A few examples of processes are credit card verification, production, purchasing, delivery, inventory management, or providing CRM (customer relationship management). This is done by e-commerce mechanisms such as e-markets, e-procurement, and e-CRM as shown in Figure 6.10. Note that processes in the figure involve several types of transactions.

Recall that business models are the methods by which a company generates revenue. For example, in B2B one can sell from catalogs or in auctions. The major e-business models are summarized in Table 6.5. Forward and reverse auctions are explained in *IT at Work 6.1*.

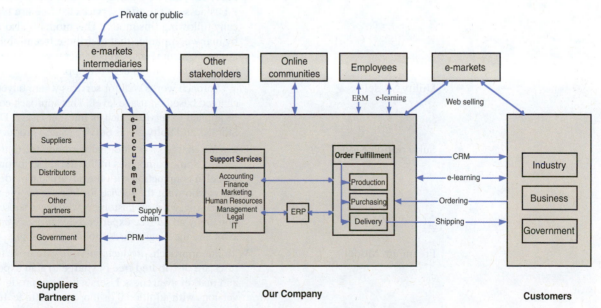

Figure 6.10 An Example of an e-commerce Company.

TABLE 6.5 | e-Business Models

e-business Model	Description
Comparison shopping engines	TheFind, NexTag, and Google Product Search engines find products, compare prices, and find great deals—and are paid a commission.
Affiliate marketing	Vendors ask partners to place logos or banner ads on their sites. If customers click the logo, go to vendor's site, and buy, then vendor pays a commission to partners.
Online Shopping	Transactions are conducted efficiently (more information to buyers and sellers, less transaction cost) in virtual marketplaces (private or public).
Information brokers and matching services	Brokers provide services related to e-commerce information, such as trust, content, matching buyers and sellers, evaluating vendors and products.
Membership	Only members can use the services provided, including access to certain information, conducting trades, etc.
Forward auctions	Sellers put items up for bid to many potential buyers, and the highest bid wins, as in eBay.
Reverse auctions	Buyers put notices of items or services they want to buy on an auction site. Those notices are called requests for quotes (RFQ). The lowest qualified bid wins.
Name-your-own-price	Customers decide how much they are willing to pay. An intermediary (e.g., *Priceline.com*) tries to match a provider.
E-procurement	Buying and selling of B2B and B2G goods and services, oftentimes utilizing special software platforms that integrate with company ERP systems that provide efficiencies in transaction process (e.g., invoicing, payment, order tracking, etc.).
Online direct marketing	Manufacturers or retailers sell directly online to customers. Very efficient for digital products and services.
Advertising	Supply free or low-cost services online to users, attracting them to the platform where they are exposed to targeted advertising messages. Google, Facebook, online gaming sites, and other popular e-businesses that offer services for free are typically following this model. This model is also used by many companies that distribute free mobile apps to consumers. Advertisements are displayed when the customers uses the app.
Utility Model	This approach works well for services where buyers are charged based on usage levels. This approach could be applied to services such as Internet Usage, Data Storage, and Software as Service (SaaS) products.
Subscription Model	Users are charged a periodic subscription fee to use a service. Some companies utilize the subscription model in conjunction with the advertising model. Users who want the service for free are exposed to advertising, whereas customers who pay a subscription enjoy an ad-free experience (examples: *Pandora.com* and the Angry Birds mobile game app.)
Freemium Model	With this approach, products/services with basic features are distributed free of charge to gain exposure and market awareness. Users who want product versions with additional or more powerful features "upgrade" to the full product by paying a fee.

(continued)

TABLE 6.5	e-Business Models *(continued)*
Bricks and Clicks	The national association of retailers is advocating an "omni-channel" strategy for its members that promote integration of traditional brick-and-mortar stores with Internet and Mobile marketing channels, creating a seamless brand experience for customers. (See Chapter 7 for additional information.)

IT at Work 6.1

Online Auctions for Commerce

An **auction** is a competitive process in which either a seller solicits bids from buyers or a buyer solicits bids from sellers. The primary characteristic of auctions, whether offline or online, is that prices are determined dynamically by competitive bidding. Auctions have been an established method of commerce for generations, and they are well-suited to deal with products and services for which conventional marketing channels are ineffective or inefficient. Electronic auctions generally increase revenues for sellers by broadening the customer base and shortening the cycle time of the auction. Buyers generally benefit from online auctions by the opportunity to bargain for lower prices and the convenience of not having to travel to an auction site to participate in the auction.

Auctions are used in B2C, B2B, C2B, and C2C commerce, and are becoming popular in many countries. Auctions can be conducted from the seller's site, the buyer's site, or from a third party's site. Auctions are divided here into two major types: forward auctions and reverse auctions.

Forward Auctions

Forward auctions are auctions that sellers use as a channel to attract many potential buyers. The most popular forward auction site is eBay. Like many e-commerce sites, eBay offers mobile apps that allow customers to participate in auctions from their handheld devices (see Figure 6.11.) Usually, items are placed at an auction site, and buyers can bid on items or services until the deadline. The highest bidder wins the items. Sellers and buyers can be individuals or businesses. The popular auction site eBay.com conducts mostly forward auctions, but there are many B2C and B2B online auctions. Forward online auctions are used to liquidate excess inventory or to increase the scope of customers, particularly for unique products or services. For example, see liquidation.com as an example of an online liquidator.

Reverse Auctions

In reverse auctions, a company or government agency that wants to buy items places a *request for quote* (RFQ) on its web site or third-party bidding marketplace. Once RFQs are posted, sellers or pre-approved suppliers submit bids electronically. Reverse auctions can attract large pools of willing sellers, who may be manufacturers, distributors, or retailers. The bids are routed via the buyer's intranet to the engineering and finance departments for

Figure 6.11 Mobile eBay app for iPhone.

© incamerastock/Alamy Limited

evaluation. Clarifications are made via e-mail, and the winner is notified electronically.

The reverse auction is the most common auction model for large-quantity purchases or high-priced items. Everything else being equal, the lowest-price bidder wins the auction. Governments and large corporations frequently mandate this RFQ approach for procurements because competition among sellers leads to considerable savings.

For Further Exploration: Why are auctions an efficient online sales channel? Visit *liquidation.com*. What types of items are sold via this auction site?

Review Questions

1. What was the dot-com bubble? What lessons were learned from it?
2. List some benefits of operating as an e-business.
3. What are the requirements and challenges of e-business?
4. What is the importance of PCI DSS compliance?
5. Define the term "business model" and list five e-business models.

6.2 Business-to-Consumer (B2C) e-Commerce

Just a short time ago, the idea of purchasing things online was a novel concept. People who purchased books and other low-priced items from web sites were seen as innovators. Nowadays, shopping for things online and finding the best deal by comparing online prices with those in brick-and-mortar stores is a common consumer practice. In the past decade, the variety of goods and services available through e-commerce sites has sky rocketed. If you look through older textbooks in the IT field, you'll find authors predicting that e-commerce will be mainly successful with low-priced consumer goods. But we know now that's simply not the case. People today purchase everything from toothpaste to cars and diamond rings online.

Retail sales via online channels, financial services, travel services, and digital products (e.g., music and movie streaming services) are widely popular forms of B2C commerce. The most well-known B2C site is Amazon.com, whose IT developments received U.S. patents that keep it ahead of competition and are described in *IT at Work 6.2*.

Several of the leading online service industries are banking, trading of securities (stocks, bonds), employment, travel, and real estate services.

IT at Work 6.2

Amazon.com's *IT Patents Create Competitive Edge*

Entrepreneur and e-tailing pioneer Jeff Bezos envisioned the huge potential for retail sales over the Internet and selected books for his e-tailing venture. In July 1995, Bezos started Amazon.com, offering books via an electronic catalog from its web site. Key features offered by the Amazon.com mega e-tailer were broad selection, low prices, easy searching and ordering, useful product information and personalization, secure payment systems, and efficient order fulfillment. Early on, recognizing the importance of order fulfillment, Amazon.com invested hundreds of millions of dollars in building physical warehouses designed for shipping small packages to hundreds of thousands of customers.

Amazon has continually revised its business model by improving the customer's experience. For example, customers can personalize their Amazon accounts and manage orders online with the patented "One-Click" order feature. This personalized service includes an electronic wallet, which enables shoppers to place an order in a secure manner without the need to enter their address, credit card number, and so forth, each time they shop. One-Click also allows customers to view their order status and make changes on orders that have not yet entered the shipping process. Amazon's other registered trademarks are EARTH'S BIGGEST SELECTION and IF IT'S IN PRINT, IT'S IN STOCK.

In addition, Amazon added services and alliances to attract more customers and increase sales. In January 2002, Amazon.com declared its first-ever profit—for the 2001 fourth quarter; 2003 was the first year it cleared a profit in each quarter.

Amazon has invested heavily in its IT infrastructure, many features of which it had patented. The selected list of patents give a glimpse into the legal side of the company, and explain why numerous major retailers, such as Sears and Sony, have used Amazon.com as its sales portal.

- 6,525,747—Method and system for conducting a discussion relating to an item.
- 6,029,141—Internet-based customer referral system, also known as the Affiliate program.

- 5,999,924—Method for producing sequenced queries.
- 5,963,949—Method for data gathering around forms and search barriers.
- 5,960,411—Method and system for placing a purchase order via a communications network (One-Click purchase).
- 5,826,258—Method and apparatus for structuring the querying and interpretation of semi-structured information.
- 5,727,163—Secure method for communicating credit card data when placing an order on a nonsecure network.
- 5,715,399—Secure method and system for communicating a list of credit card numbers over a nonsecure network.

Amazon launched the e-reader Kindle in 2007. Its success proved the viability of the e-book market and led to the entry of numerous competitors, such as Barnes & Noble's Nook and the Apple iPad. Some analysts estimated the Kindle accounted for about 60 percent of the e-reader market in 2010.

In mid-2010, Amazon started rolling out a software upgrade for Kindle, adding the ability for users to share e-book passages with others on Facebook and Twitter. The new social networking feature in version 2.5 adds another web link to the standard Kindle and the larger Kindle DX, as Amazon finds itself in an increasingly competitive market because of the iPad's features. The iPad is designed for reading digital books, watching online video, listening to music, and web browsing.

Sources: Compiled from Gonsalves (2010), Rappa (2010), and *amazon.com*.

Discussion Questions

1. Why is order fulfillment critical to Amazon's success?
2. Why did Amazon patent One-Click and other IT infrastructure developments?
3. How has Amazon adapted the Kindle to new technologies?
4. Why would other retailers form an alliance with *Amazon.com*?

Online Banking. Online banking includes various banking activities conducted via the Internet instead of at a physical bank location. Online banking, also called direct banking, offers capabilities ranging from paying bills to applying for a loan. Customers can check balances and transfer funds at any time of day. For banks, it offers an inexpensive alternative to branch banking. Transaction costs are about 2 cents per transaction versus $1.07 at a physical branch.

Most brick-and-mortar conventional banks provide online banking services and use e-commerce as a major competitive strategy. Customers are aware that if they are banking exclusively with a brick-and-mortar institution they may be missing out on high-paying investment options or competitive loan rates that easily undercut many traditional banking entities. One of the high-interest online-only banks is ING Direct. With prominent and sophisticated marketing, ING Direct has become one of the most successful direct banks, as you read in *IT at Work 6.3*.

IT at Work 6.3

ING Direct, The Largest Online Bank

ING Direct, a division of the Dutch financial-services giant ING Group, surpassed E*Trade Bank to become the largest online bank. ING Direct first opened for business in Canada in 1997. By 2007, ING Direct had become the most successful direct bank in the world with more than 17 million customers in nine countries. Within five years of opening in the U.S., ING had acquired 2.2 million U.S. customers and $29 billion in deposits.

High Rates, High-Volume, Low-Margin, and High Profits

ING had paid the highest rates on savings accounts, which were 2.6 percent compared to the 0.56 percent average rate being paid for money-market accounts at traditional banks. The bank invested heavily in online and offline marketing efforts to steal customers away from other banks. ING Direct's strategy of simple products and aggressive rates and marketing campaigns (see Figure 6.12), has created clear differentiation from its competitors. One of their successful marketing tactics was a $25 check for signing up.

Despite its high rates and huge marketing expenditures, ING Direct profits soared. For example, the U.S. division earned a

Figure 6.12 Woman Inside Bank Paris France, Exhibit of ING Direct Internet Bank.

pretax profit of $250 million in 2004, more than double its pretax profit of $110 million in 2003. More recently, the company has been impacted negatively by the global economic meltdown that started in 2008 and problems associated with the European economy. The Amsterdam-based company had to be bailed out twice by the Dutch government and is considering selling its U.S. operations to Capital One. In spite of these problems related to the economy, ING is still held in high regard by consumer groups, receiving high marks from *Consumer Reports* and the *Kiplinger Personal Finance Magazine*. News that the company would be selling its U.S. operations to Capital One sparked frustration and concern by its customers across a variety of social media sites. The sell-off was required as a condition of ING's earlier bail out deals. Customers have grown very loyal to ING and are fearful that their online banking experience would suffer under new management.

One reason that ING is likely to withstand the global economic chaos better than some of its competitors is that this high-volume, low-margin business uses online efficiencies to offer a bare-bones service to low-maintenance customers. Originally, the bank did not offer checking accounts because they cost too much, but added checking a few years later. ING Direct has almost no bricks-and-mortar other than eight cafés to in large U.S. cities that serve to promote its business to customers unfamiliar with its name. Its U.S. headquarters is a converted Wilmington warehouse rather than an expensive high-cost office building. ING now faces a much different and more competitive environment than it did just a few years ago. Based in part on its initial success, many other banks have entered the online arena, which means that ING will need to continue finding innovative ways to differentiate itself from traditional banking institutions.

Sources: Compiled from *INGDirect.com* (2010), Stone (2005), and Ensor (2007), Goldwasser (2010).

Discussion Questions

1. How did ING Direct become the world's largest online bank?
2. Why did ING Direct use both online and offline marketing campaigns?
3. What attracted customers to online banking at ING Direct?
4. What attracted brick-and-mortar banks into the online banking segment?

International and Multiple-Currency Banking. International banking and the ability to handle trading in multiple currencies are critical for international trade. Electronic fund transfer (EFT) and electronic letters of credit are important services in international banking. An example of support for e-commerce global trade is provided by TradeCard.com. TradeCard offers a *software as a service* (SaaS) model that provides supply chain collaboration and a trade finance compliance platform.

Although some international retail purchasing can be done by giving a credit card number, other transactions may require cross-border banking support. For example, Hong Kong and Shanghai Bank (hsbc.com.hk) has developed a special system, HSBC*net*, to provide online banking in 60 countries. Using this system, the bank has leveraged its reputation and infrastructure in the developing economies of Asia to rapidly become a major international bank without developing an extensive new branch network.

Online Job Market. Most companies and government agencies advertise job openings, accept résumés, and take applications via the Internet. The online job market is especially effective and active for technology-oriented jobs. While sites like dice.com and monster.com can still be helpful, job seekers nowadays are employing a variety of social media skills, including the use of LinkedIn.com to develop a network of contacts and establish a personal, online reputation. In many countries, governments must advertise job openings on the Internet. In addition, hundreds of job-placement brokers and related services are active on the web. You can get help from jobweb.com to write your résumé.

ISSUES IN ONLINE RETAILING

Despite the tremendous growth of online retailers, many e-tailers face challenges that can interfere with the growth of its e-tailing efforts. Major issues are described next.

1. **Resolving channel conflict.** Sellers that are **click-and-mortar companies,** such as Levi's or GM, face a conflict with their regular distributors when they circumvent those distributors by selling online directly to customers. This situation is called **channel conflict** because it is a conflict between an online selling channel and physical selling channels. Channel conflict has forced some companies to limit their B2C efforts, or not to sell direct online. An alternative approach is to try to collaborate in some way with the existing distributors whose services may be restructured. For example, an auto company could allow customers to configure a car online, but require that the car be picked up from a dealer, where customers could also arrange financing, warranties, and service.

2. **Resolving conflicts within click-and-mortar organizations.** When an established company sells online directly to customers, it creates conflict within its own offline operations. Conflicts may arise in areas such as pricing of products and services, allocation of resources (e.g., advertising budget), and logistics services provided by the offline activities to the online activities (e.g., handling of returns of items bought online). To minimize this type of conflict, companies may separate the online division from the traditional division. The downside is that separation can increase expenses and reduce the synergy between the two organizational parts.

3. **Managing order fulfillment and logistics.** E-tailers face tough order fulfillment and logistics problems when selling online because of the need to design systems to accept and process a huge volume of small orders, physically pick items from warehouse shelves and put them into boxes, be sure that the correct labels are applied, and the need to accept returns. The return process is referred to as reverse logistics. Logistics is discussed in more detail in section 6.4.

4. **Determining viability and risk of online retailers.** Many purely online e-tailers went bankrupt in the dot-com era, the result of problems with cash flow, customer acquisition, order fulfillment, and demand forecasting. Online competition, especially

in commodity-type products such as CDs, toys, books, or groceries, became very fierce due to the ease of entry to the marketplace. As Porter's five competitive forces model explain, low entry barriers intensify competition in an industry. So a problem most new and established e-tailers face is to determine how long to operate while you are still losing money and how to finance the losses.

5. Identifying appropriate revenue (business) models. One early dot-com model was to generate enough revenue from advertising to keep the business afloat until the customer base reached critical mass. This model did not always work. Too many dot-coms were competing for too few advertising dollars, which went mainly to a small number of well-known sites such as AOL, MSN, Google, and Yahoo. In addition, there was a chicken-and-egg problem: sites could not get advertisers to come if they did not have enough visitors. To succeed in e-commerce, it is necessary to identify appropriate revenue models and modify those models as the market changes.

ONLINE BUSINESS AND MARKETING PLANNING

Online marketing planning is very similar to any other marketing plan. It's strange to have separate plans for online and offline because that is not how customers perceive a business. Here are online business and planning recommendations.

1. Build the marketing plan around the customer, rather than on products

2. Monitor progress toward the one-year vision for the business in order to be able to identify when adjustments are needed, and then be agile enough to respond

3. Identify all key assumptions in the marketing plan. When there is evidence that those assumptions are wrong, identify the new assumptions and adjust the plan.

4. Make data-driven, fact-based plans.

Review Questions

1. Describe how digital content and services can lead to significantly lower costs.
2. What general features make the delivery of online services successful for both sellers and buyers?
3. How has Amazon maintained its competitive edge?
4. How did ING Direct attract customers to become the world's largest online bank?
5. List the major issues relating to e-tailing.
6. List three online marketing planning recommendations.

6.3 Business-to-Business (B2B) e-Commerce and e-Procurement

In business-to-business (B2B) markets, the buyers, sellers, and transactions involve only organizations. B2B comprises about 85 percent of e-commerce dollar volume. It covers applications that enable an enterprise to form electronic relationships with its distributors, resellers, suppliers, customers, and other partners. By using B2B, organizations can restructure their supply chains and partner relationships.

There are several business models for B2B applications. The major ones are sell-side marketplaces and e-sourcing (the buy-side marketplace).

SELL-SIDE MARKETPLACES

In the **sell-side marketplace** model, organizations sell their products or services to other organizations from their own private e-marketplace or from a third-party site. This model is similar to the B2C model in which the buyer is expected to come to the seller's site, view catalogs, and place an order. In the B2B sell-side marketplace, however, the buyer is an organization. The two key mechanisms in the sell-side model are forward auctions and online catalogs, which can be customized for each buyer.

Sellers such as Dell Computer (dellauction.com) use auctions extensively. In addition to auctions from their own web sites, organizations can use third-party auction sites, such as eBay, to liquidate items. Companies such as Overstock.com help organizations to auction obsolete and excess assets and inventories.

The sell-side model is used by hundreds of thousands of companies and is especially powerful for companies with superb reputations. The seller can be either a manufacturer (e.g., IBM), a distributor (e.g., *avnet.com* is an example of a large distributor in IT), or a retailer (e.g., *Walmart.com*). The seller uses e-commerce to increase sales, reduce selling and advertising expenditures, increase delivery speed, and reduce administrative costs. The sell-side model is especially suitable to customization. For example, organizational customers can configure their orders online at cisco.com, and others. Self-configuration of orders results in fewer misunderstandings about what customers want and much faster order fulfillment.

E-SOURCING

E-sourcing refers to many procurement methods. The primary methods are auctions, RFQ processing, and private exchanges. E-sourcing also applies to all other secondary activities, which have added to the cycle time and cost of procurement transactions. Secondary activities include trading partner collaboration, contract negotiation, and supplier selection.

E-Procurement. **Corporate procurement,** also called **corporate purchasing**, deals with the buying of products and services by an organization for its operational and functional needs. Organizations procure materials to produce finished goods, which is referred to as **direct procurement,** and products for daily operational needs, which is referred to as **indirect procurement**. **E-procurement** refers to the re-engineered procurement process using e-business technologies and strategies. Strategies and solutions linked to e-procurement have two basic goals.

1. Control costs: The first goal is to control corporate spending. Organizations want to spend intelligently for procurement activities to maximize the value of their spending, that is, insure that money spent to procure items results in procuring the right products at the best value. Corporate e-procurement constitutes a substantial portion of an organization's operational spending. For example, it is common for large manufacturing organizations to spend millions of U.S. dollars procuring products and services. Organizations thus design e-procurement systems to facilitate and control overall procurement spending.

2. Simplify processes: The second goal is to streamline the procurement process to make it efficient. Inefficiencies in the procurement process introduce delays in ordering and receiving items and tax internal resources.

The two goals of cost control and streamlining can be met in three ways.

1. Streamline the e-procurement process within an organization's value chain. Doing so reduces the number of employees needed to process purchasing, reduces the procurement cycle time to order and receive items, and empowers organization's staff with enough information about the products and services to enable them to make intelligent decisions when procuring items.

2. Align the organization's procurement process with those of other trading partners, which belong to the organization's virtual supply chain. Alignment can be achieved by automating the process from end to end including trading partner's systems, and simplifies the buying process. This enables suppliers to react efficiently to buyers' needs.

3. Use appropriate e-procurement strategies and solutions. Organizations analyze spending patterns in an effort to improve spending decisions and outcomes.

Public and Private Exchanges. Exchanges are sites where many buyers and sellers conduct business transactions. They may be public or private, depending on whether or not they are open to the public.

Vertical exchanges serve one industry (e.g., automotive, chemical), along the entire supply chain. *Horizontal exchanges* serve many industries that use the same products or services (e.g., office supplies, cleaning materials). Four types of exchanges are

1. Vertical exchanges for direct materials. These are B2B marketplaces where *direct materials*—materials that are inputs to manufacturing—are traded, usually in *large quantities* in an environment of long-term relationship known as **systematic sourcing**. An example is PlasticsNet.com, a vertical marketplace for industry professionals.

2. Indirect materials in *one industry* are purchased as-needed using a practice called **spot sourcing.** Buyers and sellers may not even know each other. In vertical exchanges, prices change continuously (like a stock exchange), based on the matching of supply and demand. Auctions are typically used in this kind of B2B marketplace, sometimes done in private trading rooms on these exchanges. Some question exists as to how viable the market is for this type of exchange. Several businesses that have been previously cited as successful indirect material vertical exchanges have gone out of business: *paperexchange.com*, *Chemconnect.com*, *esteel.com*, and Altra Energy Technologies.

3. Horizontal exchanges. These are many-to-many e-marketplaces for indirect materials, such as office supplies, light bulbs, and cleaning materials used by *any industry*. Because these products are used for maintenance, repair, and operations (and not sold to generate revenue), these indirect supplies are called **MRO.** Prices are fixed or negotiated in this systematic exchange. Examples are *Worldbid.com*, *Globalsources.com*, and *Alibaba.com*.

American Express applied its own experience on indirect purchasing to develop tools that improve compliance with established procurement rules on indirect purchases, or MRO supplies. Instead of a pile of catalogs or personal supplier preferences, the system relies on a master catalog, which lists only approved products from authorized vendors. One of the big gains is the elimination of **maverick buying.** Maverick buying is outside the established system. If the procurement process is too complicated, people will go outside the system, and buy from a local vendor. Maverick buying can prove costly not only because that vendor's prices may be high, but it can also keep the company from achieving volume levels that could trigger a new tier of discounts.

Since catalog purchases have high transaction costs, American Express put catalogs from multiple suppliers and from various categories of spending into its master catalog *CatalogPro*. This catalog makes it easier for users to find the right items and purchase at contract rates.

4. Functional exchanges. Needed services such as temporary help or extra space are traded on an as-needed basis. For example, Employease.com can find temporary labor using employers in its Employease Network (*eease.com*). Prices are dynamic, and vary depending on supply and demand.

Another important facet of managing procurement is **demand management**—knowing or predicting what to buy, when, and how much. The best procurement cost is zero, when people aren't buying what they don't need.

Review Questions

1. Briefly differentiate between the sell-side marketplace and e-sourcing.
2. What are the two basic goals of e-procurement? How can those goals be met?
3. What is the role of exchanges in B2B?
4. Explain why maverick buying might take place and its impact on procurement costs.

6.4 E-Government and Public Sector IT Trends

E-commerce models apply to government and the public sector organizations, as you have read in earlier examples in this textbook. Web technologies help public sector agencies to deal with economic, social, and environmental challenges, and to manage their operations and growth the way that for-profits organizations do. Here we examine the application of web technologies to government agencies.

E-government involves the use of Internet technology to deliver information and public services to citizens, business partners, and suppliers of government entities, and people who work in the public sector. Benefits of e-government include the following:

• Improves the efficiency and effectiveness of government functions, including the delivery of public services.

• Enables governments to be more transparent to citizens and businesses by providing access to more of the information generated by government.

• Offers greater opportunities for citizens to provide feedback to government agencies and to participate in democratic institutions and processes.

As a result, e-government may facilitate fundamental changes in the relationships between citizens and governments.

E-government transactions can be divided into three major categories: **Government-to-consumer** (G2C), **government-to-business** (G2B), and **government-to-government** (G2G). In the G2C category, government agencies increasingly are using the Internet to provide services to citizens. An example is *electronic benefits transfer* (EBT), in which governments transfer benefits, such as Social Security and pension payments, directly to recipients' bank accounts or to smart cards.

G2G includes intra-government e-commerce (transactions between different governments) as well as services among different governmental agencies.

In G2B or B2G, governments use the Internet to sell to or buy from businesses. For example, *electronic tendering systems,* using reverse auctions, are often mandatory to ensure the best price and quality for government procurement of goods and services.

The U.S. government (and many state and local governments) serve the business community by making vital information easily accessible to business organizations. Consider, for instance, the census.gov web site. Prior to creation of the Internet and web, businesses that needed to use census data for market analysis had to hire market researchers to visit a limited number of census repositories located around the country (typically at large universities and public libraries in large municipalities). These researchers had to wade through countless paper-bound volumes containing thousands upon thousands of tables detailing the demographic characteristics of the U.S. population. Collecting and analyzing census data to determine market characteristics was a labor-intensive and costly process. Now, with all census data available to users through the *census.gov* web site, any organization, large or small, profit or nonprofit (as well as individual citizens) can easily access this valuable information from any web-connected device. Similar situations exist with regard to many other government agencies that provide data that is essential to business managers who seek to better understand the business environment in the U.S. or want to compete for opportunities to sell goods and services to the government. Providing easy access to vital information is perhaps one of the most significant accomplishments of the federal government during the last decade.

E-GOVERNMENT IN THE CLOUD

Government officials, like corporate managers, did not easily embrace cloud computing. But their concerns about cloud computing have decreased according to a survey of IT decision makers released in mid-2010. The survey conducted by the nonprofit Public Technology Institute (PTI) found that 45 percent of local governments are using some form of cloud computing for applications or services. The findings revealed that an additional 19 percent of local governments planned to implement some form of cloud computing within the year, while 35 percent had no intentions to do so.

Encouraging government agencies to move toward cloud computing solutions was one of the top priorities of the nation's first Chief Information Officer (CIO) Vivek Kundra. (See the E-Government case at the end of this chapter.) According to Kundra, the use of cloud computing tools has already saved the government billions of dollars while at the same time, increasing government productivity and efficiency.

Local governments have several options for cloud computing—a public cloud, private cloud, regional cloud, government-operated cloud, or a cloud operated by a vendor on behalf of a government. Budget pressures are a leading factor moving governments into cloud computing solutions.

Two cases of e-government are the City of Carlsbad (*carlsbadca.gov/*), California, which implemented a cloud computing solution, and the e-government use of smartphone apps to control drunken driving.

THE CITY OF CARLSBAD TURNS TO THE CLOUD

The City of Carlsbad employs 1,100 people and serves more than 100,000 local citizens. The city's workforce devotes a lot of time to team-based projects that depend on communication and collaboration. The city was faced with an outdated e-mail system and no collaboration system—and severe budget constraints. The city needed to replace the aging e-mail system that it managed in-house to provide its employees with improved collaboration.

The city first considered Microsoft Exchange Server 2007 and Microsoft Office Outlook. But the IT department considered whether it would be cost-effective to spend its limited budget on the purchase of hardware, hiring, and training staff to administer Exchange Server 2007. So the city sent out a request for proposal (RFP) to various vendors to compare the costs of a hosted, managed, or on-premises solution. The IT staff explored how to acquire and use IT to get long-term savings. They worked with the consulting company Gartner to understand the value, security, and reliability ramifications of going with a hosted solution, and learned that hosting was a viable option. Therefore, given its limited budget and server expertise, the city decided on a cloud computing solution. This solution avoided on-premises investments with Microsoft's Business Productivity Online Standard Suite, collaboration software hosted at Microsoft data centers. For a low per-user, per-month subscription fee, the suite offers hosted communication and collaboration services that include desktop and mobile e-mail, calendaring and contacts, instant messaging and presence, shared workspaces, and live audio-visual web conferencing applications.

In February 2009, the city began working with Microsoft Services to plan the migration of 880 GroupWise mailboxes to Exchange Online. On all of its desktops, the city installed Microsoft Office 2007 and the Microsoft Online Services client that provides a **single sign-on** to all online services in the suite. With single sign-on, users log in once and have access to all software and data sources that they are authorized to access. The city used a migration tool from Quest Software that facilitates the municipal government's migration from GroupWise directly to Exchange Online.

The City of Carlsbad is the first public sector entity to deploy the Microsoft Business Productivity Online Standard Suite. The city is benefiting from more flexibility in resource allocation, reduced costs, accelerated deployment, and improved employee productivity. Faced with tough economic times, the cloud solution provides the city with the ability to allocate its finite resources where they'll generate the greatest return on investment (ROI).

IT at Work 6.5

Apps for Democracy Community Initiative

In the fall of 2008, the Washington, D.C., Office of the Chief Technology Officer asked iStrategyLabs how it could make DC.gov's Data Catalog (*data.octo.dc.gov/*) useful for the citizens, visitors, businesses, and government agencies. The Data Catalog provides citizens with access to 431 datasets from multiple agencies, featuring real-time crime data feeds, school test scores, and poverty indicators, and is the most comprehensive public data source in the world. The solution was the creation of *Apps for Democracy* (*appsfordemocracy.org/*), a contest that had cost $50,000 and returned 47 iPhone, Facebook, and web applications with an estimated value of $2,600,000 to the city.

The Apps for Democracy contest challenges citizens to make open source applications that can access any of the data sets held by the government. The 2009 winning entry was an iPhone program in which users can submit 311 service requests to the district government. The application also interfaces with Facebook.

Sources: Compiled from Data Catalog (*data.octo.dc.gov/*) and Apps for Democracy (*appsfordemocracy.org*).

Discussion Questions

1. Visit the Data Catalog (*data.octo.dc.gov/*).

2. What value does it provide citizens?

E-GOVERNMENT SERVES CITIZENS WITH APPS TO CURB DRUNKEN DRIVING

With widespread use of smartphone applications, several government agencies and app developers have found a promising way to curb drunken driving. In 2010, two iPhone apps were made available. One app called R-U-Buzzed was released by the Colorado Department of Transportation. R-U-Buzzed estimates blood-alcohol content, and a mashup program called *Stumble Safely* that gives Washington, D.C., pedestrians a safe route home after a night at the bar. The Stumble Safely app was submitted to the Apps for Democracy contest, described in *IT at Work 6.5*.

California's Office of Traffic Safety (OTS) partnered with the popular Taxi Magic app team to promote sober designated drivers, a cab driver in this case. California announced the partnership in May 2010. "It gives those who need to get someplace when they've had too much to drink an easy way to do it," said California OTS Spokesman Chris Cochran. "It's one more tool in the anti-DUI [driving under the influence] tactics we have" (Wilkinson, 2010). The free Taxi Magic app was released in January 2009, and has become one of the top downloaded apps in Apple's iTunes store. Users who are in a metropolitan area where the service is available can use the app's Magic Book feature to tap one button that phones the cab company and arranges pick-up location details.

The state agency's partnership with Taxi Magic came at zero cost and fits its mission to encourage designated drivers and safe driving. The California OTS is the first state agency the company has partnered with, which Taxi Magic did to promote safety.

Review Questions

1. What are the benefits of e-government?
2. What is the advantage of using cloud computing as the platform for e-government?
3. What is the purpose of Apps for Democracy?
4. How do e-government apps help fight drunken driving?

6.5 E-Commerce Support Services and Digital Marketing Communications

Implementation of e-commerce requires support services. B2B and B2C applications require payments and order fulfillment; portals require content. Figure 6.13 shows the major e-commerce services, which include:

- e-infrastructure: technology consultants, system developers, integrators, hosting, security, wireless, and networks
- e-process: payments and logistics

- e-markets: marketing and advertising
- e-communities: citizens, audiences, and business partners
- e-services: CRM, PRM, and directory services
- e-content: supplied by content providers

All of these services support the e-commerce applications in the center of the figure, and all of the services need to be managed.

MARKET RESEARCH FOR E-COMMERCE

The goal of market research is to find information and knowledge that describes the relationships among consumers, products, marketing methods, and marketers. This information is used to discover marketing opportunities, establish marketing plans, better understand the purchasing process, and evaluate marketing performance. On the web, the objective is to turn browsers into buyers. Market research includes gathering information about topics such as the economy, industry, firms, products, pricing, distribution, competition, promotion, and consumer purchasing behavior.

WEB ADVERTISING

One of the problems with traditional advertising channels is that advertisers knew very little about the recipients. Market segmentation by various characteristics (e.g., age, income, gender) helped, but did not solve the problem. The Internet introduced the concept of **interactive marketing,** which has enabled marketers and advertisers to interact directly with customers. In interactive marketing, a consumer can click an

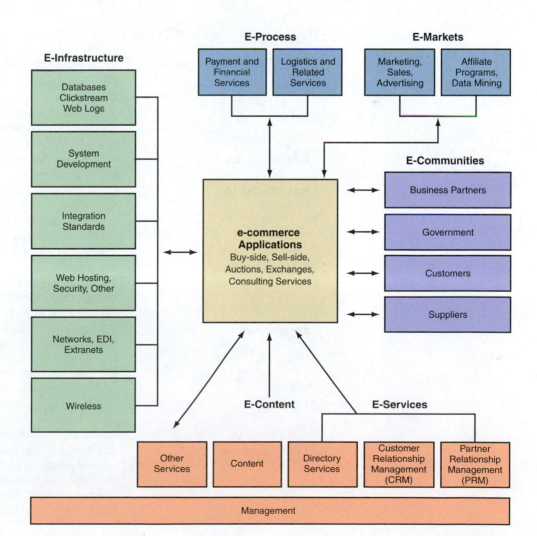

Figure 6.13 A Model of e-commerce support services.

ad to obtain more information or send an e-mail to ask a question. Besides the two-way communication and e-mail capabilities provided by the Internet, vendors also can target specific groups and individuals based on behavior. Several companies like Google, Facebook, and lesser-known ad firms like Right Media and ValueClick track the online behavior of consumers. They use this information to help advertisers direct ads to customers most like to be interested in what the advertisers are promoting.

Television advertising continues to command the greatest amount of ad spending by businesses, but companies are increasing the amount of money they spend on Internet advertising, and reducing what they spend on other traditional media channels. In 2012, spending on Internet advertising exceed print media spending for the first time. Most large companies practice integrated marketing communications, where online and traditional ad campaigns are coordinated to deliver a consistent message. Online advertising comes in a number of forms (see Table 6.6.)

Search Engine Marketing (SEM). Search Engine Marketing is an umbrella term that describes practices associated with increasingly the likelihood that a company will appear in search results when people conduct Internet searches using terms or phrases related to a product or company. There are two basic forms of SEM: **search engine optimization (SEO)** and **pay per click (PPC) advertising.** SEO is a set of practices designed to increase the chances that a company's website will appear in **organic search** results. Organic search results come from a company designing or *optimizing* its web site to appeal to the various algorithms used by search engines to determine

TABLE 6.6	Variations in Online Advertising
Type of Online Advertising	**Definition/Description**
Banner ads	These are a form of display (graphic+text) ads delivered from an ad server. They can appear on a company's own web site or on the web site of other organizations, online publications, or blogs. The actual form of the display ad can vary.
Paid Search Ads	Non-organic listings on search engine results pages (see PPC below).
Rich Media/Video	Use of interactive media and/or video to promote a brand. Many companies get extra mileage from their television ads by placing them on YouTube. Other companies have created entire channels on YouTube to promote their brands.
E-mail Advertising	Advertising campaign content delivered as e-mail. It is the digital equivalent of direct mail delivered through the U.S. Postal service. Unwanted e-mail is referred to as SPAM.
Sponsorships	This category includes a variety of ad formats that support events, web content, online experiences (e.g., games), and so on. The goal is to build favorable brand associations by making the sponsored content available to the viewer.
Classified Ads	Usually categorized, text-based ads, that are often priced-based on the amount of space they fill. Example: *craigslist.com*
Lead Generation	Ads designed to generate leads. Usually require respondents to supply contact information in order to receive information, free subscription, or some other enticement. Advertiser pays on the basis of number of leads generated.

the order of listings in search results. Some search engines base their organic searches on web site content and key words listed on a web page. As described in the case at the beginning of this chapter, Google uses a patented PageRank™ algorithm (among other factors) to determine organic search results. Search engine optimization (SEO) is a constantly evolving discipline, part science, part creative strategy, which attempts to achieve higher search rankings based on the design and content of a web site. Pay per click (PPC) advertising, on the other hand, involves paying search engines to display PPC listings alongside organic search results in areas designated for paid or sponsored ads. Most search engines clearly identify organic vs. PPC search listings through shading, labels, or other identifiers. Google uses a program called Adwords to manage its PPC business. Through Adwords, businesses can bid on search terms they want to influence where their PPC ads appear. Advertisers can manage other aspects of their campaigns by setting budgets and identifying characteristics that further target the kind of customer they want to see their ads. For instance, a computer repair business in Portland, OR, might use Adwords to limit its PPC ads to people who are interested in computers and live within 10 miles of Portland.

Because online behavior and user response to digital advertising can be more easily tracked and measured than advertising in traditional media, some alternative ways of charging for digital advertising have emerged. Some of the most common ways of paying for online advertising include:

Cost Per Impression—advertiser pays for the number of users exposed to the ad, typically expressed as cost per mille (CPM) or cost per thousand (CPT). Both terms base the ad charge on how many thousands of users are exposed to the ad.

Cost per click (or **pay per click**—PPC)—advertiser pays based on how many people take actions by clicking on the ad which often services as a hyperlink to the advertiser's web site or a page promoting the advertiser's brand.

Cost per Action (CPA)—similar to cost per click, but here the qualifying action might be to watch a video, fill out a lead form, purchase a product, visit a web site, make a donation, and so on.

There are many other variations on these three primary payment methods. Understanding the differences between these approaches is important because each method has a different impact on determining the effectiveness of an advertising campaign as well as estimates of Return on Investment (ROI) of ad spending dollars.

ELECTRONIC PAYMENTS

Payments are an integral part of doing business, whether in the traditional way or online. Unfortunately, in several cases traditional payment systems are not effective for e-commerce, especially for B2B. Contrary to what many people believe, it may be less secure for the buyer to use the telephone or mail to arrange or send payment, especially from another country, than to complete a secured transaction on a computer. For all of these reasons, a better way is needed to pay for goods and services in cyberspace. This better way is *electronic payment systems*, such as PayPal.

There are several alternative methods for making payments over the Internet. The major ones are summarized in Table 6.7.

The most common methods, paying with credit cards and electronic bill payments, are discussed briefly here.

Electronic Credit Cards. Electronic credit cards make it possible to charge online payments to one's credit card account. For security, only encrypted credit cards should be used. Credit card details can be encrypted by using the SSL protocol in the buyer's computer (available in standard browsers).

Here is how electronic credit cards work: When you buy a book from Amazon, your credit card information and purchase amount are encrypted in your browser, so the information is safe during transmission on the Internet. Furthermore, when this information arrives at Amazon, it is not opened but is transferred automatically

TABLE 6.7	Electronic Payments Methods
Method	**Description**
Electronic funds transfer	Popular for paying bills online. Money is transferred electronically from payer's account to the recipient's.
Electronic checks	Digitally signed e-check is encrypted and moved from the buying customer to the merchant.
Purchasing e-cards	Corporate credit cards, with limits, work like regular credit cards, but must be paid quicker (e.g., in one week).
e-Cash—smart cards	Cards that contain considerable information can be manipulated as needed and used for several purposes, including transfer of money.
e-Cash—person-to-person	Special online account from which funds can be sent to others is created. PayPal is the best-known company (an eBay company). You can pay businesses as well. Another example is Yahoo Pay Direct.
Electronic bill presentment and payments	Bills are presented for payer's approval. Payment is made online (e.g., funds transfer). Examples: *CheckFree.com*, *Yahoo Bill Pay*.
Pay at ATMs	ATM allows you to pay monthly bills (e.g., to utility companies) by transferring money from your account to the biller.
Micropayments	Payments are too small to be paid with credit cards. Can be paid with stored-value money cards, or with special payment methods, including payments from cell phones.
B2B special methods	Enterprise invoice presentment and payment, wire transfer, and electronic letter of credit are popular methods.

in encrypted form to a clearing house, where the information is decrypted for verification and authorization. The complete process of how e-credit cards work is shown in Figure 6.14. Electronic credit cards are used mainly in B2C and in shopping by SMEs (small-to-medium enterprises).

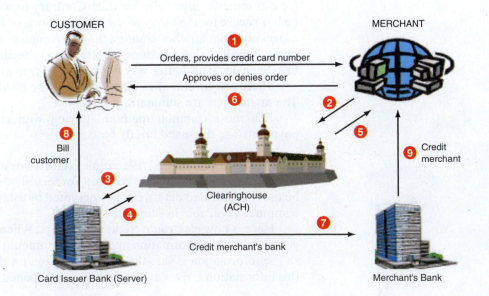

Figure 6.14 The sequence of activities involved in e-credit card processing.

Electronic Bill Payments. There are three major ways to pay bills over the Internet:

1. Online banking. The consumer pays bills from their bank's online banking web site. Some banks offer the service for free with a checking account, or if the account holder maintains a minimum balance.

2. Biller direct. The consumer makes payments at each biller's web site either with a credit card or by giving the biller enough information to complete an electronic withdrawal directly from the consumer's bank account. The biller makes the billing information available to the customer (presentment) on its web site or the site of a billing hosting service. Once the customer views the bill, he or she authorizes and initiates payment at the site. The payment can be made with a credit/debit card or by using the Automated Clearing House (ACH) transfer system. The biller then initiates a payment transaction that moves funds through the payment system, crediting the biller and debiting the customer. This method is known as electronic bill presentment and payments (EBPP).

3. Bill consolidator. The customer enrolls to receive and pay bills for multiple billers with a third-party bill consolidator. The customer's enrollment information is forwarded to every biller that the customer wishes to activate (service initiation). For each billing cycle, the biller sends a bill summary or bill detail directly to the consolidator. The bill summary, which links to the bill detail stored with the biller or the consolidator, is made available to the customer (presentment). The customer views the bill and initiates payment instructions. The consolidator initiates a credit payment transaction that moves funds through the payment system to the biller.

SECURITY IN ELECTRONIC PAYMENTS

Two main issues need to be considered under the topic of payment security: what is required in order to make e-commerce payments safe, and the methods that can be used to do so.

Security Requirements. Security requirements for conducting e-commerce are the following:

- **Authentication.** The buyer, the seller, and the paying institutions must be assured of the identity of the parties with whom they are dealing.

- **Integrity.** It is necessary to ensure that data and information transmitted in e-commerce, such as orders, replies to queries, and payment authorizations, not be accidentally or maliciously altered or destroyed during transmission.

- **Nonrepudiation.** Merchants need protection against the customer's unjustified denial of placing an order. On the other hand, customers need protection against merchants' unjustified denial of payments made. (Such denials, of both types, are called *repudiation*.)

- **Privacy.** Many customers want their identity to be secured. They want to make sure others do not know what they buy. Some prefer complete anonymity, as is possible with cash payments.

- **Safety.** Customers want to be sure that it is safe to provide a credit card number on the Internet. They also want protection against fraud by sellers or by criminals posing as sellers.

ORDER FULFILLMENT

Any time a company sells a product directly to customers, one that must be delivered physically, it is involved in various **order fulfillment** activities. It must perform the following activities: quickly find the products to be shipped; pack them; arrange for the packages to be delivered speedily to the customer's door; collect the money from every customer, either in advance, by COD, or by individual bill; and handle the return of unwanted or defective products.

It is very difficult to accomplish these activities both effectively and efficiently in B2C, since a company may need to ship small packages to many customers quickly. For this reason, both online companies and click-and-mortar companies often have

IT at Work 6.6

E-Money: The Future Currency

You walk through the crowded train station in central Tokyo, heading straight for the entry barriers, and you can ignore the people in queue at the ticket machines. You take out your mobile phone and wave it at a card reader. A beep is heard, and you can pass through, ready for your train.

The growing e-money lifestyle in Japan is making life more convenient for consumers by allowing a number of transactions to be conducted via mobile phone, instead of the traditional paper bills and coins given at the cash register. The system is called Mobile Suica, and it debuted publicly in January 2006, as an offering by NTT DoCoMo, which is the leading Japanese mobile phone provider, and East Japan Railway. Mobile Suica is a cellphone-based smartcard that can be used for buying rail tickets or for accessing buildings. It is based on RFID.

Europe is updated, making money obsolete in places such as France, where Société Générale, in partnership with Visa Europe and Gemalto, introduced a Visa Premier "contactless" bank card in July 2007 for consumers to make small purchases with. In England, the *Evening Standard*, a popular newspaper, is sold at special kiosks where the only contact made is between card and scanner.

The Bank of Japan has not released any figures for e-money, but analysts say e-money represents about 20 percent of the ¥300 trillion (US$2.8 trillion) in Japanese consumer spending. Experts say the new technology will promote the growth of e-money. "With contactless Mobile Suica on your mobile phone, you can check your balance, and upload more money into your account at any time, from anywhere," said an expert (see Figure 6.15).

There are causes for concern, however, especially for security. "Losing my phone would be like losing my money," said a

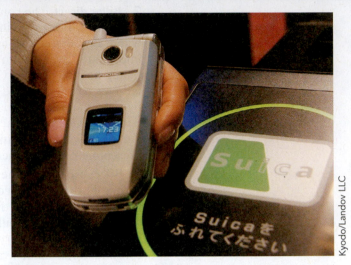

Kyodo/Landov LLC

Figure 6.15 Contactless Mobile Suica on a mobile phone.

consumer. To address these, some mobile phone providers have already introduced biometric security measures that include fingerprint, facial, and voice recognition needed to activate phones. In the U.S., mobile payment options are increasing for retailers and consumers, but are still not commonplace. You will read more about the development of mobile payment options in Chapter 7.

Sources: Compiled from *International Herald Tribune* (2008), *nttdocomo.com* and *slashphone.com*.

---

difficulties in their B2C supply chain, and they outsource deliveries and sometimes packaging. Here, we provide a brief overview of order fulfillment.

Order fulfillment includes not only providing customers with what they ordered and doing it on time, but also providing all related customer service. For example, the customer must receive assembly and operation instructions to a new appliance. In addition, if the customer is not happy with a product, an exchange or return must be arranged. Order fulfillment is basically a part of what are called a company's *back-office operations. Back office* activities are inventory control, shipment, and billing.

Order Fulfillment Process. A typical e-commerce fulfillment process is shown in Figure 6.16. The process starts on the left, when an order is received and after verification that it is a real order. Several activities take place, some of which can be done simultaneously; others must be done in sequence. Demand forecasts and accounting are conducted at various points throughout the process.

• **Activity 1:** Assurance of customer payment. Depending on the payment method and prior arrangements, the validity of each payment must be determined. In B2B, the company's finance department or financial institution (i.e., a bank or a credit card issuer) may do this. Any holdup may cause a shipment to be delayed, resulting in a loss of goodwill or a customer.

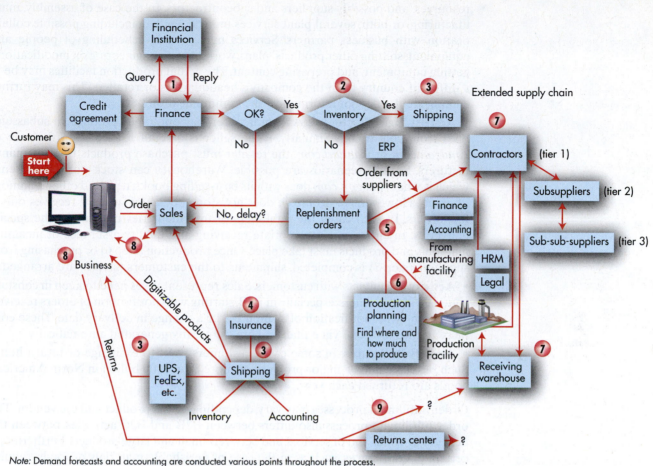

Figure 6.16 Order fulfillment and logistics system.

Note: Demand forecasts and accounting are conducted various points throughout the process.

- **Activity 2:** Check of in-stock availability. Regardless of whether the seller is a manufacturer or a retailer, as soon as an order is received, an inquiry needs to be made regarding stock availability. Several scenarios are possible here that may involve the material management and production departments, as well as outside suppliers and warehouse facilities. In this step, the order information needs to be connected to the information about in-stock inventory availability.

- **Activity 3:** Shipment arrangement. If the product is available, it can be shipped to the customer right away (otherwise, go to step 5). Products can be digital or physical. If the item is physical and it is readily available, packaging and shipment arrangements need to be made. This may involve the packaging or shipping departments and internal shippers or outside transporters

- **Activity 4:** Insurance. Sometimes the contents of a shipment need to be insured. This could involve both the finance department and an insurance company, and again, information needs to flow, not only inside the company, but also to and from the customer and insurance agent.

- **Activity 5:** Replenishment. Customized orders will always trigger a need for some manufacturing or assembly operation. Similarly, if standard items are out of stock, they need to be produced or procured. Production can be done in house or by contractors. The suppliers involved may have their own suppliers (subsuppliers or tier-2 suppliers).

- **Activity 6:** In-house production. In-house production needs to be planned. Production planning involves people, materials, components, machines, financial resources, and possibly suppliers and subcontractors. In the case of assembly, manufacturing, or both, several plant services may be needed, including possible collaboration with business partners. Services may include scheduling of people and equipment, shifting other products' plans, working with engineering on modifications, getting equipment, and preparing content. The actual production facilities may be in a different country from the company's headquarters or retailers. This may further complicate the flow of information and communication.

• **Activity 7:** Contractor use. A manufacturer may opt to buy products or subassemblies from contractors. Similarly, if the seller is a retailer, such as in the case of *Amazon.com* or *walmart.com*, the retailer must purchase products from its manufacturers. Several scenarios are possible. Warehouses can stock purchased items, which is what *Amazon.com* does with its best-selling books, toys, and other commodity items. However, *Amazon.com* does not stock books for which it receives only a few orders. In such cases, the publishers or intermediaries must make the special deliveries. In either case, appropriate receiving and quality assurance of incoming materials and products must take place. Once production (step 6) or purchasing from suppliers (step 7) is completed, shipments to the customers (step 3) are arranged.

• **Activity 8:** Contacts with customers. Sales representatives need to keep in constant contact with customers, especially in B2B, starting with notification of orders received and ending with notification of a shipment or a change in delivery date. These contacts are usually done via e-mail and are frequently generated automatically.

• **Activity 9:** Returns. In some cases, customers want to exchange or return items. Such returns can be a major problem, as more than $100 billion in North American goods are returned each year.

Order fulfillment processes may vary, depending on the product and the vendor. The order fulfillment process also differs between B2B and B2C activities, between the delivery of goods and of services, and between small and large products. Furthermore, certain circumstances, such as in the case of perishable materials or foods, require additional steps.

Review Questions

1. What are the major e-commerce support services?
2. List the security requirements for e-commerce.
3. Describe the issues in e-commerce order fulfillment.
4. Describe the different types of online advertising
5. What are the key differences in the CPM, CPC, and CPA methods of paying for advertising?
6. What is the difference between SEO and PPC search engine marketing?

6.6 E-Business Ethics and Legal Issues

Legal and regulatory standards frequently lag behind technological innovation. As a result, e-businesses must frequently apply ethical principles when questions arise about how their decisions and actions will impact employees, consumers, and the communities in which they operate. We begin by considering ethical issues relating to e-business. We then examine the legal environment in which e-commerce operates.

ETHICAL AND IMPLEMENTATION ISSUES

Many of the ethical and implementation issues related to IT in general apply also to e-business.

Privacy. As discussed in the Google case at the beginning of the chapter, privacy is an issue of concern to many Internet users and has also become the focus of regulatory agencies around the world. While it is clear that individual Internet users are concerned about their privacy, the technology and business practices that impact how individual information is collected and used seem to change faster than the laws of most countries. Therefore it is important that e-businesses carefully evaluate their actions and take steps to safeguard individual privacy. While respecting privacy is clearly the right choice from an ethical stand point, it is also a good business practice. While companies may be able to fool the general public and regulatory agencies for a short time, eventually companies that abuse their power and use personal information inappropriately will, at a minimum, lose favor with consumers, and they could potentially face legal and financial penalties for acting inappropriately.

Web Tracking. Log files are the principal resources from which e-businesses draw information about how visitors use a site. Applying analytics to log files means either turning log data over to an application service provider (ASP) or installing software that can pluck relevant information from files in house. By using tracking software, companies can track individuals' movements on the Internet. Programs such as cookies raise privacy concerns. The tracking history is stored on your PC's hard drive, and any time you revisit a certain web site, the computer knows it. In response, some users install programs such as Cookie Cutter, CookieCrusher, and Spam Butcher, which are designed to allow users to have some control over cookies. Or they delete their cookie files. Many browsers now include features that limit monitoring and tracking of online activity.

Loss of Jobs. The use of e-commerce may result in the elimination of some company employees as well as brokers and agents. The manner in which these unneeded workers are treated may raise ethical issues, such as how to handle the displacement and whether to offer retraining programs.

Disintermediation and Reintermediation. One of the most interesting e-commerce issues relating to loss of jobs is that of intermediation. Intermediaries provide two types of services: (1) matching and providing information, and (2) value-added services such as consulting. The first type of services (matching and providing information) can be fully automated, and therefore these services are likely to be assumed by e-marketplaces and portals that provide free services. The second type of services (value-added services) requires expertise, and these can be only partially automated. Intermediaries who provide only (or mainly) the first type of service may be eliminated, a phenomenon called **disintermediation** (elimination of the intermediaries).

For example, airlines sell tickets directly to customers, eliminating some travel agents. Direct sales from manufacturer to customers may eliminate retailers. On the other hand, brokers who provide the second type of service or who manage electronic intermediation are not only surviving, but may actually prosper. This phenomenon is called **reintermediation.** In reintermediation of travel agents, for example, new activities may include organizing groups that go to exotic places. Intermediaries therefore may fight manufacturers in fear that the traditional sales channel will be negatively affected by online channels. For instance, Wal-Mart and Home Depot warned Black & Decker that they would take its products off their shelves if Black & Decker began to sell its products directly through the Internet. Also, confronted with dealer complaints, Ford executives recently agreed to discontinue plans for future direct online car sales.

LEGAL ISSUES SPECIFIC TO E-COMMERCE

Many legal issues are related to e-commerce. When buyers and sellers do not know each other and cannot even see each other (they may even be in different countries), there is a chance of fraud and other crimes over the Internet. During the first few years of e-commerce, the public witnessed many of these, ranging from the creation of a virtual bank that disappeared along with the investors' deposits, to manipulation of stock prices on the Internet. Unfortunately, fraud on the Internet is increasing.

Antitrust Laws. At one time or another, many well-known technology companies have faced scrutiny over business dealings that appeared to be in conflict with antitrust laws in the U.S. As noted in the Google case at the beginning of the chapter, the European Union also has strict antitrust laws, and companies must contend with regulatory agencies in those markets as well. At one time or another Microsoft, Apple, Google, Intel, Cisco Systems, Oracle, Sun Microsystems, and other large technology companies have had to defend themselves in the U.S. or abroad over charges that they engaged in business practices, or proposed business deals that would have violated antitrust laws.

It's not just government regulators that create antitrust headaches for technology companies. In many cases, competitors use antitrust lawsuits to frustrate companies they fear may gain an edge in the market, or companies feel they must defend themselves when they believe they have suffered from unfair competition. As the technology industry continues to evolve, we can expect to see increasing use of antitrust laws here and abroad to regulate the behavior of some of the industry's largest companies.

Collection of State Sales Tax by Online Merchants. In addition to privacy laws and antitrust laws, perhaps the most hotly debated legal issue associated with e-commerce today is related to **sales tax**. In the early days of e-Commerce, one of the factors that motivated people to purchase products online was the ability to avoid paying sales tax. Over time, various states have stepped up their enforcement efforts and passed laws that more clearly specified sales tax collection requirements. The challenge for e-commerce companies that want to comply with these laws is that sales tax rules vary from state to state, creating a compliance nightmare. Not only does the amount of the tax vary from state to state, but administrative rules for reporting and record keeping are different for each state as well.

The sales tax issue has legal implications for both consumers and online merchants. Consumers who live in states that have sales tax (all but Alaska, Delaware, Montana, New Hampshire, or Oregon) are legally obligated to pay sales tax, even if it is not collected by the online merchant. While the specific rules vary from state to state, consumers are required to pay a **use tax** (usually the same rate as the sales tax) on products they purchase from out-of-state businesses. Most states require consumers to pay this use tax at the same time they pay their income taxes. Even states without income tax have forms that citizens are expected to complete in order to pay the use tax. Most people have ignored this rule, and enforcement has been a challenge for states, but increasingly they are finding ways of increasing enforcement. While most consumers continue to ignore the sales tax and use tax regulations, the fact is, online purchases for most consumers are not "tax free."

From the merchant's perspective, they have always been required to collect tax from customers that live in the state where they do business or have some connection. This is referred to as "the nexus." Nexus is usually defined as the state where the company has an office, business operation, or some other substantial connection. The problem here is that each state has different rules about what constitutes a nexus. Some states define the term so broadly that simply having an employee or even an associate sales person will constitute a nexus, which then requires sales tax collection. For example, Amazon has an associate program where web site owners can post links to Amazon products and collect a small commission on any sales that result from people clicking on the link. By this definition, Amazon would be required to collect sales tax from consumers in any state where someone is part of its associate program.

Now the federal government is threatening to step into the fray. As of 2012, there were three bills before Congress that mandated that all but the smallest online retailers collect and remit sales tax to each state that met certain guidelines for simplifying their sales tax policies. While such laws would be unpopular with voters, there is a strong likelihood that some sort of federal regulation will eventually become law forcing sales tax collection by e-commerce businesses because the vast majority of states are pressing so hard for these rules. Supporting the effort are a majority of traditional brick-and-mortar businesses who feel disadvantaged when competing with online merchants that already enjoy many cost advantages due to the more efficient nature of their e-business operations. We predict that collection of state sales tax by online merchants will become a federal law in the near future.

Review Questions

1. List some ethical issues in e-commerce.
2. List the major legal issues of e-commerce.
3. Define disintermediation. Give an example.
4. Define reintermediation. Give an example.

Key Terms

advertising business model *148*

affiliate marketing *164*

antitrust law *153*

auction *165*

backlinks *147*

brick-and-mortar organizations *153*

business-to-business (B2B) *159*

business-to-consumers (B2C) *160*

channel *146*

channel conflict *168*

click-and-mortar organizations *168*

comparison shopping engine *146*

corporate procurement *170*

corporate purchasing *170*

cost-per-action (CPA) *177*

cost-per-click (CPC) *177*

cost-per-impression (CPI) *177*

cyber-security *146*

demand management *171*

direct procurement *170*

disintermediation *183*

dot-com era (bubble) *157*

e-business process *158*

e-commerce *158*

e-government *172*

e-procurement *170*

e-sourcing *170*

e-tailing *160*

Federal Information Security Management Act (FISMA) *150*

forward auction *165*

government-to-business (G2B) *160*

government-to-citizens (G2C) *160*

government-to-consumer (G2C) *172*

government-to-government (G2G) *160*

indirect procurement *170*

interactive marketing *175*

key words *147*

manufacturer/direct sales business model *149*

mobile commerce (m-commerce) *160*

MRO *171*

multichanneling *146*

order fulfillment *179*

organic search *176*

PCI DSS (Payment Card Industry Data Security Standard) *161*

pay-per-click advertising (PPC) *176*

Payment Card Industry Security Standards Council (PCI SSC) *161*

predatory pricing *153*

reintermediation *183*

reverse auctions *165*

sales tax *184*

scalability *161*

search engine optimization (SEO) *176*

sell-side marketplace *169*

single sign-on *173*

spot sourcing *171*

systematic sourcing *171*

use tax *184*

value added reseller *149*

Chapter 6 LINK LIBRARY

You find clickable Link Libraries for each chapter on the Companion website.

Amazon.com's first web site, August 1995 *digitalenterprise.org/images/amazon.gif*

e-Business forum *ebusinessforum.com*

Google Merchant Center *google.com/merchants*

Google Product Search *google.com/products*

Shopzilla *shopzilla.com*

U.S. Federal Trade Commission, the nation's consumer protection agency *ftc.gov*

PCI Security Standards Council *pcisecuritystandards.org/index.shtml*

Internet statistics *internetworldstats.com*

Many Eyes (beta) data sets and visualization tools *manyeyes.alphaworks.ibm.com/manyeyes/*

Washington, DC, Data Catalog *data.octo.dc.gov/*

Evaluate and Expand Your Learning

IT and Data Management Decisions

A group of students has come to you with an e-commerce idea for setting up an online textbook exchange where students can buy and sell used textbooks. However, they are not quite sure what the best way would be to monetize the site. They have approached you for advice.

1. Identify a set of possible alternative e-business models that could be considered for a textbook exchange site.

2. List the pro's and con's of each e-business model. Consider factors like how each model might impact students' willingness to use the site, the complexity of implementing each model, and the potential for generating revenue.

3. Prepare a brief memo summarizing your findings to #1 and #2 above and then make a recommendation as to the most likely e-business model that would lead to success for the textbook exchange.

Questions for Discussion & Review

4. Discuss the reasons for having multiple e-commerce business models in one company.

5. Distinguish between business-to-business forward auctions and buyers' bids for RFQs.

6. Discuss the benefits to sellers and buyers of a B2B exchange.

7. What are the major benefits of e-government? How are they changing?

8. Discuss the various ways to pay online in B2C.

9. Why is order fulfillment in B2C difficult?

10. Discuss the reasons for e-commerce failures.

11. Describe some key ethical issues related to e-commerce.

12. Why is cyber security a growing concern to business and government agencies? What steps is the government taking to protect the IT infrastructure from cyber-attacks?

13. What are the two different forms of search engine marketing? How are they different?

14. Describe the different ways listed in the chapter for e-businesses to advertise.

Online Activities

15. Assume you're interested in buying a car. You can find information about cars at autos.msn.com or *autobytel.com* for information about financing and insurance. Decide what car you want to buy. Configure your car by going to the car manufacturer's web site. Finally, try to find the car from *autobytel.com*. What information is most supportive of your decision-making process? Was the experience pleasant or frustrating?

16. Visit amazon.com and identify at least three specific elements of its personalization and customization features. Browse specific books on one particular subject, leave the site, and then go back and revisit the site. What do you see? Are these features likely to encourage you to purchase more books in the future from *Amazon.com*? Check the One-Click feature and other shopping aids provided. List the features and discuss how they may lead to increased sales.

17. Go to *nacha.org*. What is the National Automated Clearing House Association (NACHA)? What is its role? What is the ACH? Who are the key participants in an ACH e-payment? Describe the pilot projects currently underway at ACH.

18. Visit *espn.com*. Identify at least five different ways it makes revenue.

19. Visit *manyeyes.alphaworks.ibm.com/manyeyes/*. Select visualizations from the left-side menu bar. Generate two visualizations. How does visualization improve understanding of the data sets?

20. Read Google's new Privacy Policy at *http://www.google.com/policies/privacy/*. What types of information does Google collect about people who use its services? How can people either restrict or avoid having Google collect information about them? How does Google say it uses the information it collects about people who use its services?

Collaborative Work

21. Have each team study a major bank with extensive e-commerce offerings. For example, Wells Fargo Bank is well on its way to being a cyberbank. Hundreds of brick-and-mortar branch offices are being closed. In Spring 2003, the bank served more than 1.2 million cyberaccounts (see *wellsfargo.com*). Other banks to look at are Citicorp, Netbank, and HSBC (Hong Kong). Each team should attempt to convince the class that its e-bank activities are the best.

22. Assign each team to one industry. Each team will find five real-world applications of the major business-to-business models listed in the chapter. (Try success stories of vendors and e-commerce–related magazines.) Examine the problems the applications solve or the opportunities they exploit.

23. Have teams investigate how B2B payments are made in global trade. Consider instruments such as electronic letters of credit and e-checks. Visit *tradecard.com* and examine their services to SMEs. Also, investigate what Visa and MasterCard are offering. Finally, check Citicorp and some German and Japanese banks.

24. Conduct a study on selling diamonds and gems online. Each group member investigates one company such as *bluenile.com, diamond.com, thaigem.com, tiffany.com*, or *jewelryexchange.com*.
    a. What features are used in these sites to educate buyers about gemstones?
    b. How do the sites attract buyers?
    c. How do the sites increase trust for online purchasing?
    d. What customer service features are provided?
    e. Would you buy a $5,000 diamond ring online? Why, or why not?

25. Working in a small group of three or four people, use the Internet to plan a trip to Paris. Have each individual, working independently, use the services of a different online travel site such as *orbitz.com*, *travelocity.com*, *kayak.com*, *Concierge.com* and *expedia.com* (search "online travel sites" for additional options).
    a. Find the lowest airfare.
    b. Examine a few hotels by class.

c. Get suggestions of what to see.
d. Find out about local currency, and convert $1,000 to that currency with an online currency converter.
e. Compile travel tips.

Prepare a report comparing how each site performed in terms of its ease of use, helpfulness and best overall deal.

CASE 2   E-GOVERNMENT

Increasing Productivity and Efficiency with Cloud and Mobile Technologies

Government agencies are increasingly finding that IT solutions can help them deliver critical services and information to citizens and businesses. In the same way that business organizations are learning to streamline their operations through the use of e-business processes, governments are also finding they can accomplish more, on tighter budgets, when applying the right IT solutions.

In the early days of computer and network technology, it was not unusual for government agencies to hire programmers or IT vendors for custom software development. But this approach was expensive and oftentimes led to expensive failures. IT professionals in government have increasingly recognized the need for a more efficient and coordinated

approach. In 2009, President Obama appointed Vivek Kundra as the first U.S. Chief Information Officer (CIO). Under Kundra's leadership, the federal government streamlined its IT efforts and encouraged agencies to move toward cloud computing solutions as a way of reducing IT spending and the need for large, government owned data centers. (Note: Kundra recently left government service to join Salesforce.com, a leading provider of cloud-based enterprise solutions.)

As part of Kundra's efforts to bring transparency to the IT operations of the federal government, an IT Dashboard was created (see Figure 6.17 and *itdashboard.gov/*) so that citizens, government employees, and IT vendors could see

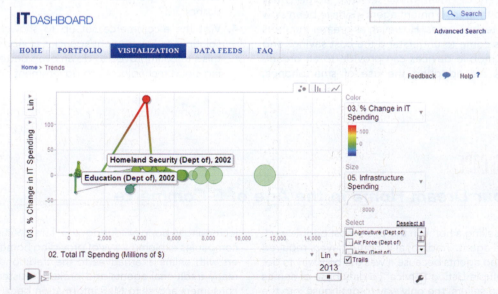

Figure 6.17 A screen shot of the federal government's IT Dashboard, which allows users to view spending on IT projects across the federal government and to see how projects are meeting their completion goals.

how the government was spending its IT budget and observe the progress of various IT projects. The dashboard also brings accountability to agencies, highlighting IT projects that were in trouble or outright failing. According to Kundra, the process of shedding light on these IT projects resulted in a savings of $3 billion and increased completion speed of some projects. As part of the effort to encourage government agencies to adopt cloud computing solutions, the government created *Apps.gov*, an online "store" where government agencies could efficiently explore products and services from a variety of vendors. The *Apps.gov* site, created by the General Services Administration, operates like an e-commerce site, listing cloud-based solutions in a variety of categories. Links to vendor sites make it easy for government employees to find information on the listed products.

As in private industry, security is a key issue facing government agencies that want to enhance their use of Information Technology. According to President Obama, the "cyber threat is one of the most serious economic and national security challenges we face as a nation" and "America's economic prosperity in the 21st century will depend on cybersecurity" (*Whitehouse.gov* 2012). In addition to the kinds of criminal activity discussed earlier in the chapter, the government must also design its enterprise IT systems to resist attacks by terrorists and unfriendly foreign governments. The administration created the Cybersecurity Office and appointed Howard Schmidt to serve as the Cybersecurity Coordinator. His job is to work closely with the new U.S. CIO, Steven VanRoekel, and other federal agencies to develop policies and procedures to protect the nation's IT infrastructure from cyber threats. (See *whitehouse.gov/cybersecurity* for additional information.) The Department of Defense has particularly important needs with regard to cybersecurity and operates a special agency to guide its military cyber defense strategies.

Finally, mobile technologies are playing an increasing role in the delivery of government services. Some critics have complained that government agencies have been slow to adopt mobile technologies. However, as greater numbers of administrators come to understand the cost savings and efficiencies that mobile devices can provide to an organization, agencies are adopting the use of smartphones, tablets, and other handheld devices to reduce paperwork, improve work flow, transmit data from field operations, and enhance interactions with the public. In 2011, the Department of Defense announced it was creating a special online app store for members of the military so that they could download mobile apps that had been vetted for security issues. According to DOD officials, various branches of the military are realizing that mobile technologies are particularly appropriate for their mission because they provide a significant level of computing, mapping and communications power in a small device for soldiers who need to be mobile (Hoover, 2011). The federal government recently created a site (*apps.usa.gov*) where you can find a number of mobile apps developed to provide information and services to citizens, researchers, educational institutions, and business organizations.

In conclusion, government agencies at all levels are realizing the benefits of adopting e-business practices. Cloud and mobile technologies, in particular, are in the forefront of recent efforts to improve productivity and efficiency. New offices and officials have been charged with the responsibility of making sure that the government's IT infrastructure remains safe from cybersecurity threats. The government's use of the Internet and other IT solutions is an important factor in supporting access to information for the nation's citizens and business organizations.

Sources: Compiled from: Hoover (2011), O'Dell (2011), *Whitehouse.gov* (2012), Government Technology (2010).

Questions & Activities

1. Why are government agencies increasingly interested in using cloud and mobile technologies to accomplish their missions?
2. Why is security even more important for government agencies than businesses in the private sector?
3. What is the purpose of the new federal government IT dashboard?
4. Visit the e-commerce set up to showcase cloud-based solutions to government agencies at *Apps.gov.* How could this site be improved to do an even better job of promoting cloud technologies to government agencies?

CASE 3   VIDEO CASE

Finding Your Dream Home in the Age of E-Commerce

When buying or selling a home in the U. S., most people work with a real estate agent. Traditionally, home buyers required the help of licensed agents because it was the only way to get access to the Multiple Listing Service®, a data base of homes for sale. For home sellers, the only way to get house into the database was to sign a listing contract, and agree to a commission payment, with a Realtor®. As the Internet became increasingly popular during the late 1990s, a number of companies explored ways of providing home buyers and sellers with online alternatives to the traditional MLS®. Initially, many traditional agents and brokers resisted efforts to give consumers access to MLS information because they felt that would diminish the value of the real estate agent in the home buying and selling process. However, faced with the prospect

Figure 6.18 In the U.S., home buyers increasingly use the Internet to find information about homes for sale.

Images.com/Alamy Limited

of being replaced by competing online listing services, the National Organization of Realtors® partnered with other companies and created Realtor.com, an online web site for finding information about homes in your area.

Watch this Video about the *Realtor.com* web site: *youtube.com/watch?v=usA1jvv7Y1U.*

While Realtor.com became one of the most popular online listing sites, it has competitors. For this case, let's compare some different online home listing services and see how each uses the power of the Internet to improve the home search process.

Pretend you are a prospective home buyer and want to purchase a home in your area. Select a price range for your home, and make a short list of features you'd like to have in

a new house (e.g., fireplace, number of bedrooms, size of home, and so on).

Next, let's go shopping!

Visit at least two or three different real estate listing sites:

- Zillow: *http://www.zillow.com/*
- Yahoo! Real Estate: *http://realestate.yahoo.com/*
- Realtor.com: *http://www.realtor.com/*
- Trulia: *http://www.trulia.com/*
- Homes.com: *http://www.homes.com/*

Evaluate each of the sites on the following criteria:

A. Ease of navigation and use.
B. Quality of the search engine tool for generating a list of homes that fit your criteria.
C. Features for getting information about homes (e.g., mapping services, photos, videos, price and tax information, etc.).
D. Advice and tips on the home buying process.
E. Social features—does the web site have a blog, discussion board or other ways that home buyers can talk to one another about their experiences and questions?

Questions and Activities

1. Based on your experience, which web site does the best job of helping home buyers identify homes they might like to purchase?
2. What were the biggest strengths of the sites you visited? What were the biggest weaknesses?
3. How well did each site do in terms of educating you about the home buying process? Did the information provided seem objective and helpful, or did it appear to be biased toward getting you to call a real estate agent?
4. Finally, if you were really faced with the prospect of buying a home, would you use one or more of these sites, or would you spend most of your time working with a real estate agent? Explain your answer.

Data Analysis & Decision Making

Analysis Using Visualization

Creating Visualizations Using Public Online Datasets

Visit ManyEyes and click onto data sets:

Link: *manyeyes.alphaworks.ibm.com/manyeyes/*

(Alternative link if the one above does not work:

http://www-958.ibm.com/software/data/cognos/manyeyes/ datasets)

Click on "create visualization" and read how to *create a visualization in 3 easy steps.*

1. Then select recent data set that has been uploaded to Many Eyes. The link in the "data" column takes you to a view of the data set itself. The blue "Visualize" button lets you visualize the data.
2. Read the other sections of "Learn More."
3. Create 4 different visualizations and save each to a file, or print your results. Many Eyes uses Java applet technology. In a few browsers, you may need to download Sun's Java Plugin to see the visualizations.
4. Review and compare your results.
5. What is the value of visualization?

Resources on the Book's web site

More resources and study tools are located on the Student web site. You'll find additional chapter materials and useful web links. In addition, self-quizzes that provide individualized feedback are available for each chapter.

References

Barth, C. "France to Google: You'll Pay For Making That Free!" Forbes.com, February, 2012. *forbes.com/sites/chrisbarth/2012/02/02/france-to-google-youll-pay-for-making-that-free/.*

BBC News, "Google privacy changes 'in breach of EU law.' " BBC.co.uk, March, 2012. *bbc.co.uk/news/technology-17205754.*

Branigan, T. "China blocks YouTube: Attack on video showing security forces beating Tibetans." *Guardian*, March 2009. *guardian.co.uk/world/2009/mar/25/china-blocks-youtube.*

Carr, A. "Canada, Spain Find Google Violated Privacy Laws, Collected Loads of Personal Data, Medical Records." Fastcompany.com, October, 2010, *fastcompany.com/1696302/canada-finds-google-violated-privacy-laws-collected-loads-of-personal-data-medical-records.*

Carrns, A. "Capital One's Response to Outrage Over ING Direct Purchase." *N.Y. Times*, June, 2011. *bucks.blogs.nytimes.com/2011/06/22/capital-ones-response-to-outrage-over-ing-direct-purchase/.*

Chertoff, M. "Cloud computing and the looming global privacy battle." *Washington Post*, February, 2012. *washingtonpost.com/opinions/cloud-computing-sets-stage-for-a-global-privacy-battle/2012/02/06/gIQAhV2V2Q_story.html.*

Efrati, A., & Chao, L. "Google Softens Tone on China: Two Years After Censorship Clash, Company Renews Push to Expand in World's Biggest Internet Market. *Wall St. Journal*, January 12, 2012. *online.wsj.com/article/SB10001424052970203436904577155003097277514.html.*

Ensor, B. "The Sources of ING Direct's Success." *Forrester*, April 25, 2007.

Evans, D. "Antitrust Issues Raised by the Emerging Global Internet Economy." *Northwestern University Law Review: Colloquy,* 2008. *law.northwestern.edu/lawreview/colloquy/2008/13/.*

Goldwasser, J. "Best Online Banks: Bank online and you can avoid the fees and even earn a little interest." *Kiplinger's Personal Finance* Magazine, December 2010. *kiplinger.com/magazine/archives/best-online-banks.html.*

Gonsalves, A. "Amazon Kindle 2.5 Adds Social Networking." *InformationWeek*, May 3, 2010.

Government Computers News. "Google: Privacy changes won't affect government clients." GCN.com, January 27, 2012. *gcn.com/articles/2012/01/27/agg-google-privacy-changes-enterprise-government-contracts.aspx.*

Government Technology. "2010 Year in Review: Mobile Technology and Sustainability Are Among Government Issues." Govtech.com, December, 2010. *govtech.com/education/2010-Year-in-Review.html.*

Gross, D. "How to prepare for Google's privacy changes." CNN.com, February 29, 2012. *cnn.com/2012/02/29/tech/web/protect-privacy-google/index.html.*

Hoover, J.N. "Army Readies Mobile App Store." *Information Week*, October 14, 2011. *informationweek.com/news/government/mobile/231900854?itc=edit_in_body_cross%22.*

Humphries, M. "Free Google Maps API deemed anti-competitive in France." Geek.com February 2, 2012. *geek.com/articles/news/free-google-maps-api-deemed-anti-competitive-in-france-2012022/.*

Hunton & Williams LLP. "International Data Protection Authorities Scold Google Over Privacy Concerns." Hunton Privacy Blog, April 21, 2010. *huntonprivacyblog.com/2010/04/articles/international-data-protection-authorities-scold-google-over-privacy-concerns/.*

Information Assurance Technology Analysis Center (IATAC). Accessed, May, 2012 *iac.dtic.mil/iatac/.*

International Herald Tribune, "Cellphones in Japan Make Wallets Obsolete," February 25, 2008.

Fairsearch.org "Google's Transformation from Gateway to Gatekeeper" 2011, *fairsearch.org/wp-content/uploads/2011/10/Googles-Transformation-from-Gateway-to-Gatekeeper.pdf*

Marshall, J. "Google Ethics, Part I." Ethics Scoreboard.com, April 17, 2006. *ethicsscoreboard.com/list/google1.html.*

O'Dell, J. "U.S. Government Open-Sources IT Dashboard to Help Cut Tech Costs." Mashable.com, March 31, 2011. *mashable.com/2011/03/31/government-it-dashboard/.*

Openbookalliance.org. "Pam Samuelson on Google Books: It's Not A Library," October 2009. *openbookalliance.org/2009/10/pam-samuelson-on-google-books-its-not-a-library/.*

Pfanner, E. "France Says Google Privacy Plan Likely Violates European Law." *New York Times.* February 28, 2012. *nytimes.com/2012/02/29/technology/france-says-google-privacy-plan-likely-violates-european-law.html.*

Pfanner, E. "Google Faces French Fine for Breach of Privacy." *New York Times,* March 21, 2011. *nytimes.com/2011/03/22/technology/22privacy.html.*

Rappa, M. "Case Study: Amazon.com." DigitalEnterprise.com, 2010. *digitalenterprise.org/cases/amazon.html.*

Reisinger, D. " Google's approval ratings best Apple, Facebook, Twitter." Cnet.com, April 10, 2012. *news.cnet.com/8301-1023_3-57411810-93/googles-approval-ratings-best-apple-facebook-twitter/.*

Shankland, S. "Google to government: Let us build a faster Net." Cnet.com, September, 2011. *news.cnet.com/8301-30685_3-20112042-264/google-to-government-let-us-build-a-faster-net/.*

Stone, A. "ING Direct: Bare Bones, Plump Profits." *BusinessWeek,* March 14, 2005.

Streitfeld, D. & O'Brien, K. "Google Privacy Inquiries Get Little Cooperation." N.Y. Times, May 22, 2012. *nytimes.com/2012/05/23/technology/google-privacy-inquiries-get-little-cooperation.html?pagewanted=all*

Streitfeld, D. & Wyatt, E., "U.S. Antitrust Move Has Google Fighting on Two Fronts." *N.Y. Times*, April 27, 2012. *nytimes.com/2012/04/28/technology/us-move-has-google-fighting-on-2-fronts.html?pagewanted=all.*

United States Department of Justice. Mission: Antitrust Laws. 2012 *justice.gov/atr/about/mission.html*

Valentino-Devries, J. "Lawmakers Target Google's Tracking", *Wall St. Journal*, February 18, 2012. *online.wsj.com/article/SB10001424052970204059804577229681587016516.html?mod=WSJ_WSJ_U.S._News_5.*

Waugh, R. "'Unfair and unwise': Google brings in new privacy policy for two billion users—despite EU concerns it may be illegal." *Daily Mail.* March 1, 2012, *dailymail.co.uk/sciencetech/article-2108564/Google-privacy-policy-changes-Global-outcry-policy-ignored.html#ixzz1tmZM9e6q.*

White House National Security Council Web Site. Whitehouse.gov, Accessed May, 2012. *whitehouse.gov/cybersecurity.*

Wikipedia "Criticism of Google," 2012. *en.wikipedia.org/wiki/Criticism_of_Google.*

Wilkinson, K. "States Targeting Drunken Driving With Smartphone Apps." *Government Technology.* May 4, 2010. *govtech.com/gt/759850?topic=117673/.*

Wilson, K., Ramos, Y., & Harvey, D. "Google in China: The Great Firewall", The Kenan Institute for Ethics at Duke University, 2007. *duke.edu/web/kenanethics/CaseStudies/GoogleInChina.pdf.*

Woollacott, E. "Google finally defeats Microsoft in government contract battle." TGDaily.com, May 2, 2012. *tgdaily.com/business-and-law-features/63111-google-finally-defeats-microsoft-in-government-contract-battle.*

Zibreg, C. "Apple bends to Chinese censors, kicks Dalai Lama apps from the App store." TheGeek.com, December 30, 2009. *geek.com/articles/mobile/apple-bends-to-chinese-censors-kicks-dalai-lama-apps-from-the-app-store-20091230/.*

Chapter 7

Mobile Technologies and Commerce

Learning Outcomes

1 Understand the three primary components of mobile technology: mobile devices, mobile operating systems and software, and wireless networks.

2 Describe how mobile technologies are creating opportunities for new forms of commerce in established industries.

3 Recognize how mobile payment methods benefit both consumers and retailers.

4 Describe how location-aware features of mobile devices create opportunities for new services, new approaches to advertising, and valuable benefits for mobile device users.

5 Identify ways that business organizations are using mobile technologies to become more efficient, productive, and profitable.

Mobile computing has changed dramatically in just the last few years. Portable devices that connect wirelessly to the Internet are lighter, smaller, thinner, and much more powerful. Popular smartphones devices are now capable of performing functions like watching full-length movies that weren't even available on desktop computers a few years ago.

New categories of handheld devices, like the Kindle eReader and the Apple iPad are being rapidly adopted. Along with the growth of smartphones, these powerful mobile devices are creating a wide range of new mobile commerce opportunities. Wireless connectivity to the Internet, through Wi-Fi and telecommunications net-works has become ubiquitous. Consumer and enterprise apps for mobile computing and commerce continue to expand the capabilities of this popular technology.

In this chapter, we review the technological founda-tions for mobile computing and commerce, and identify the factors that impact the usability of these tools. You will read how companies in some industries are leverag-ing the benefits of mobile technology and wireless net-works to increase customer loyalty while at the same time, innovative companies in other industries are using mobile technology to disrupt traditional supply chain net-works, developing new products, services and marketing practices.

CASE 1 OPENING CASE

Macy's Races Ahead With Mobile Retail Strategies

Mobile devices, particularly smart phones, have become a key tool in the arsenal of mod-ern day shoppers. Using **barcode** scanner apps, customers in brick and mortar retail stores can quickly compare prices with other stores and online retailers. They can access product information, check expert and consumer product reviews, and even purchase products from online retailers. This practice, called **showrooming**, represents a significant threat to many traditional retailers who continue to ignore the impact of mobile consumer behavior.

Target recently wrote to several of its vendors asking them to create special products, only sold in Target stores, in an attempt to stifle consumer comparison shopping via mobile devices (Zimmerman, 2012). But other retailers, recognizing the pervasive nature of mobile shopping trends, are developing strategies to embrace and engage the mobile shopper.

Department store giant Macy's is recognized as a pioneer when it comes to using mobile technologies to enhance the shopping experience of its customers (see Figure 7.1) Macy's uses in-store displays to encourage customers to use mobile devices while shop-ping. The *Backstage Pass Program* is designed to enhance the in-store shopping experi-ence at Macy's. Using **QR codes** and **Short Message Service (SMS)** technology, customers

Figure 7.1 Macy's attracts shoppers with a well designed mobile web site configured for a variety of handheld devices.

© CJG—Technology/Alamy Limited

can easily access fun and informative 30-second videos that highlight the retailer's celebrity designers and fashion experts (see the videos at youtube.com/Macys). Mobile shoppers can access the videos by scanning the QR codes posted on displays in each department. Shoppers who don't have a QR code scanner can access the videos by texting a special key word to Macy's using codes supplied on the displays. Backstage Pass is an example of what marketers call a **mobile display strategy**. It is supported by an integrated communications campaign involving traditional television and print media advertising. Macy's can measure customer interest in the program by tracking the number of times customers watch the videos. Based on the initial success of the program, Macy's has increased spending on mobile display strategies by 70 percent (Kats, 2012).

SMS Database Strategy. Another key mobile strategy used by Macy's is to grow their list of customers who have opted in to receive discounts and special offers via text message. According to Martine Reardon, executive vice president of national marketing at Macy's, New York, the retailer is including SMS short codes in most of its printed coupons to encourage customers to opt in to receiving coupons and other offers via text message. Macy's customers have responded well to these kinds of promotions, so growing the list of people who opt-in to this program should be easy.

Mobile Check-in Strategy. Macy's has partnered with Foursquare and Shopkick to create check-in programs that reinforce shopping behavior at retail outlets (see Figure 7.2). Mobile customers using the Shopkick app on their phones receive points on their account just for visiting a Macy's store. They may also receive special offers from Macy's via the Shopkick app when they visit particular departments or scan featured merchandise. The points can be redeemed for restaurant vouchers, iTunes gift cards, and gift cards from a variety of participating retailers. Macy's partnered with Foursquare and a charitable foundation created by insurance company Aflac. For every consumer who checks in at Macy's via the Foursquare app, Aflac donates $1 to its charity, The Aflac Cancer Center and Blood Disorders Service of Children's Healthcare of Atlanta. Aflac made the same offer to customers who checked in while watching Macy's famous Thanksgiving Day Parade, using an entertainment check in service called GetGlue.com. These kinds of partnerships and programs not only reinforce store shopping behavior, but enhance Macy's positive brand reputation among target consumers.

Mobile Payment Strategy. Customers can pay for products at Macy's using Google Wallet, a mobile payment app. At the register, customers simply tap their phones on a **near field communications (NFC)** device in order to transfer funds to Macy's. Google Wallet is one of several approaches to mobile payment competing to become the dominant alternative to traditional credit cards. Mobile payment is expected to become widespread in the near future as banks, retailers and telecommunications companies gain experience with the technology. (Read more about mobile payment in section 7.3).

Augmented Reality Strategy. During the Thanksgiving and Christmas holiday season, Macy's runs a program to benefit the Make-A-Wish Foundation. For the past few years,

Figure 7.2 Macy's encourages shoppers to "check-in" to its retail stores using mobile promotional apps like Foursquare and Shopkick.

Macy's has donated $1 for every customer that visited a store and "mailed" a letter to Santa. In 2011, Macy's made that visit even more fun, inviting customers to take pictures of their children in special holiday displays using augmented reality apps that inserted one of the animated characters associated with the campaign into the picture. Pictures could then be uploaded into a holiday card template, shared by email, or posted to the customer's Facebook page.

While other retailers are still trying to understand mobile consumer behavior, Macy's is already adapting to a new retail environment where increasing numbers of consumers are using handheld devices. They have shown that traditional brick-and-mortar retailers can enhance the in-store shopping experience using mobile technologies in a variety of ways.

Sources: Compiled from Zimmerman (2012), Tsirulnik (2011), Macy's (2011), Johnson (2011), Kats (2012).

Discuss

1. Describe how each of Macy's mobile retail strategies enhances the in-store shopping experience for customers.
2. What will most customers think about Target's attempt to make mobile price comparison more difficult?
3. How does Macy's benefit from the use of location-based apps like Foursquare and Shopkick?
4. Why is it important that Macy's get customers to opt in to their program before sending promotional text messages?

Decide

5. Does Macy's Backstage Pass Program really add value to the customer or is it just a gimmick with short-term benefits?

Debate

6. Traditional retailers spend a considerable amount of money to maintain an inventory of products and provide sales people to service in-store customers. Is it unethical for customers to "showroom" these retailers, taking advantage of their services but then ultimately purchasing the product online from a retailer that doesn't provide these services?

7.1 Mobile Computing Technology

The mobile computing landscape has evolved rapidly over the last two decades. Traditionally, users had to go to their computers to run programs or access Internet-based services. Computers were connected via wires to peripheral devices, other computers, and networks. This lack of mobility significantly constrained the performance of people in sales, repair services, education, law enforcement, and similar jobs whose work took place outside of the office.

Wireless technology makes mobile computing and commerce a source of vast opportunities for businesses. In this section, you will read about the three technology foundations of mobile computing: mobile devices, mobile operating systems and software, and wireless networks.

MOBILE COMPUTING DEVICES

Constant innovation in the mobile equipment marketplace makes it difficult to categorize end-user devices. As capabilities and functionality are added to devices, the differences between laptops, tablets, e-readers, and smartphones becomes blurred. For the discussion below, we will rely on current trends in terminology and categorization to discuss these devices, but recognize that as mobile computing hardware evolves, new categories will emerge and traditional categories will become irrelevant.

Laptops, Notebooks, Netbooks, and Tablets. Mobility started when computers became portable. Early mobile devices were only slightly smaller than desktop computers, but had cases so they could be carried. They were still heavy and bulky. Laptops computers are significantly lighter and more practical. Several variations are available:

Standard laptops and desktop replacements. Performs most basic functions of a desktop computer; weighs over 3.6 kg.
Notebooks. Smaller, but less powerful than standard laptops. They weigh from 2.7 to 3.6 kg.
Netbooks (mini-notebook, ultra-portable). Designed for Internet access and cloud computing. Much of their functionality is based on the presumption that the user will be able to connect to a network. They have limited RAM, processing power and storage capabilities; and weigh less than 1.8 kg.
Ultra-thin Laptops. Serve the needs of users who need very light and thin computers. As with notebooks, some processing power and functionality is sacrificed to achieve the size and weight requirements, typically 1.8 to 2.7 kg.
Tablet Computers. Originally, the term *tablet computer* was used to describe a portable PC, similar to a notebook device. The screen was connected to the case with a swivel hinge that allowed users to open the device and use the regular keyboard, or fold the screen down flat on top of the key board and use it as an electronic tablet. Weighing between 1 kg and 1.8 kg, these devices are popular with workers in health care, education, and personal sales. More recently, the term *tablet* has become synonymous devices like the Apple iPad, which use a touch screen or stylus input instead of a keyboard. These smaller devices were originally called **slates** to differentiate them from the tablet computer with the swivel hinge. However, the term never caught on with consumers, and today when most people refer to a tablet, they are talking about the smaller, iPad-like device. Computers with the swivel screen are sometimes called convertible PCs.

Other laptop variations include the UMPC (ultra mobile personal computer), Smartbook (combines features of a netbook and a smartphone), gaming laptop, and rugged computers, designed for industrial settings or for use in challenging climatic conditions.

Google's Project Glass. Are you ready for something different? Check out Google's Project Glass, a new kind of mobile device in the early stages of development. Users wear a hands free-device similar to a pair of glasses that runs voice activated, network-based applications. On the surface, it appears this product concept is the ultimate mobile device. You can watch a video and read further about this futuristic innovation at g.co/projectglass. While we can see tremendous potential for this kind of product if developed correctly, we are also sympathetic to critics who suggest that technology products oftentimes are not as fun and exciting as they appear in promotional videos. For a humorous alternative view of the new product, see *youtube.com/watch?v=_mRF0rBXIeg*.

Smartphones. The first modern cell phone was invented by researchers at Motorola in the mid-1970s. Since that time, mobile phones have evolved from large, simple devices used for two-way communication to small but powerful networked computer systems. The International Telecommunication Union (2011) estimates that 5.9 billion people, or 87 percent of the world's population use mobile phones, a sizable increase from 5.4 billion in 2010 and 4.7 billion in 2009 (mobiThinking, 2012). Mobile phone sales to end users totaled over 440.5 million units worldwide in the third quarter of 2011. Smartphone sales totaled 115 million units during this same period, a 42 percent increase over 2010 figures (Gartner, 2011).

The Nielsen Company (2012) estimates that smartphones now account for almost half (49.7%) of the U.S. cell phone market, up from 36 percent only a year earlier. Smartphones use a computer operating system and are capable of running software apps and connecting to the Internet. There has been an explosion in recent years in the number of mobile apps available for smartphones in spite of significant challenges faced by programmers (see Mobile Computing Software below). Telecommunications vendors like Verizon and AT&T continue to refine ways of packaging and promoting data plans to various sectors of the market place. As people increasingly use smartphones for streaming videos, listening to online music and performing other cloud-based computing functions, the volume of data travelling over wireless networks is increasing.

MOBILE COMPUTING SOFTWARE

There are three dominant PC operating systems (OSs): Microsoft Windows, Apple, and Linux. Most laptops and related devices are also powered by these OSs. Programmers who write software apps target one or more of these platforms for their programs. Writing apps for handheld mobile devices, however, is much more difficult because of the many different devices and OSs. The following list briefly describes the most popular mobile OSs:

1. Android OS (Google/Open Handset Alliance). Android is the most popular operating system with a 46 percent global market share (Nielsen, 2012). Like the Apple **iOS**, its use is not limited to smartphones; it can be found on tablet computers, notebooks, and e-readers (see Figure 7.3).

2. iOS (Apple, Inc.). Formerly called the iPhone OS, this innovative platform is often credited, in part, for spurring growth within the smartphone segment. The iOS is used in Apple's iPhone, iPod Touch, and iPad products. These devices were among the first to utilize a touch screen, a feature now found on devices made by other manufactures. The iOS is the second-most-popular mobile OS globally, accounting for approximately 19 percent of the market (Canalys, 2012).

3. Symbian (Symbian Foundation). Once the dominant smartphone OS globally, its market share is now around 16 percent and negligible in the U.S. It runs mainly on phones manufactured by Nokia. The fourth generation of this OS became available in 2011.

4. Blackberry (RIM). Made by Research in Motion, this was the dominant OS in the U.S. just a few years ago. While still popular with may business users, its share has dropped dramatically to around 15.9 percent as consumers shift toward Android and Apple-based products.

Figure 7.3 Mobiles that run on the Android OS are the most popular on the market.

© Alex Segre/Alamy Limited

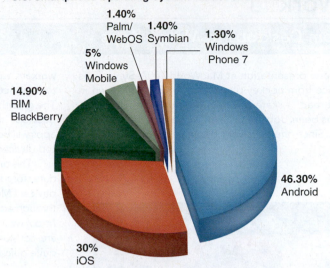

U.S. Smartphone Operating System Market Share—Q4 2011

Figure 7.4 Market shares of smartphone OS in the U.S.

Source: Adapted from the Nielsen Company, 2012.

5. Other Mobile OSs. Windows Mobile (Microsoft), Palm (Palm, Inc.), and Bada (Samsung) are still found on some smartphone devices, though these OSs account for only a small portion of the global market.

Consumers expect to access web sites from their smartphones and other devices and are frustrated when companies do not have web sites that are compatible with their device, OS, and mobile browser configuration. This presents special challenges for business and web site programmers because now they must design web sites to work with multiple configurations. If a company is unable to develop mobile sites for all possible configurations, then knowing the relative market share of mobile OSs will help target the most dominant platforms. Figures 7.4 and 7.5 illustrate the relative share of these platforms in the U.S. and worldwide.

Developers also face the challenge of making sure their mobile web site displays correctly in a variety of mobile browsers. Netmarketshare.com maintains statistics on 15 different mobile browsers, suggesting a highly fragmented market. However, in April, 2012, the Safari browser accounted for over 60 percent of the market, while Android and Opera Mini account for 18 percent and 15 percent respectively (see *Netmarketshare.com*). This means developers can focus their efforts on optimizing mobile web sites for these top three browsers.

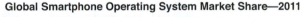

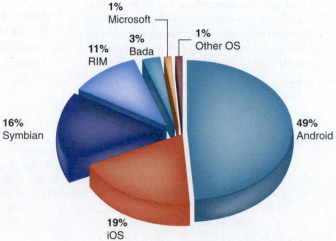

Global Smartphone Operating System Market Share—2011

Figure 7.5 Market shares of smartphone OS worldwide.

Source: Adapted from Canalys Estimates, 2012.

IT at Work *7.1*

Trend: From Desktops to Mobile Apps

During his iPhone presentation at MacWorld 2007, Steve Jobs displayed advice from hockey player Wayne Gretzky, shown in Figure 7.6 that read: *I skate to where the puck is going to be, not where it has been*. Jobs said: "And we've always tried to do that at Apple. Since the very very beginning. And we always will."

Figure 7.6 Wayne Gretsky skating to where the puck's going to be.

Jobs pointed out that Apple always moves toward where they expect the future will be. Apple often shaped the future. For example, Apple's launch of the iTunes store in April 2003 jump-started the digital music industry. iTunes was a significant break-through that forever changed the music industry and was the first representation of Apple's future outside its traditional computing product line. You're familiar with the success of that future-driven business model.

A key direction: business apps for mobiles. The strong move towards feature-rich mobile apps is driving the move away from computer desktops and desktop computers. For example, the increased use of Google Apps may chip away at Microsoft Office's market share. Why? Because users are transitioning to mobile and breaking away from the traditional *desktop and documents era*. The direction is towards highly functional apps that provide

workers with information and answers without having to do tedious actions, such as logging in or doing extensive searches. The growth in app use will be coupled with the further decline in desktops in favor of mobiles. Social networking and collaboration apps will be built first for mobile devices in recognition that desktop devices are secondary to mobiles.

This ongoing *move to mobile* will intensify the need to secure data stored on mobiles plus defend against attacks aimed at these devices. Mobiles are being enhanced with greater functionality through add-ons that are available at Google Apps Marketplace *http://www.google.com/enterprise/marketplace/*. New add-ons are constantly being introduced and often are widely adopted quite quickly.

Figure 7.7 In October 2003, Steve Jobs announced the Windows version of the iTunes store saying "Hell froze over," which brought a big laugh from the audience in San Francisco.

Questions

1. Research the release of Apple's new products and services. Build a timeline showing those releases.

2. Based on your research, discuss how Apple has shaped the future of at least two industries.

Review Questions

1. What are the three technological foundations of mobile computing?
2. List the reasons why it can be difficult to categorize mobile devices.
3. What factors have led to the recent growth of the smartphone market?
4. Why is mobile computing now almost synonymous with wireless computing?
5. Why is developing mobile web sites more difficult than developing standard web sites?

7.2 Mobile Commerce

In 1997, two Coca-Cola vending machines that accepted payment via SMS text message were installed in Helsinki Finland. Ever since, industry experts and pundits have been predicting that mobile commerce, or mCommerce, is about to become "the next big thing" in marketing and the sale of consumer goods. Before we explore how mobile commerce has evolved since 1997, let's define some terms related to this topic:

Mobile Commerce, or **mCommerce,** is the buying or selling of goods and services using a wireless, handheld device such as a cell phone or tablet (slate) computer.
Mobile eCommerce: The use of wireless handheld devices to order and/or pay for goods and services from online vendors. Example—ordering a pair of shoes from Zappos.com using a mobile app, or purchasing music from iTunes from your iPod.
Mobile Retailing: The use of mobile technology to promote, enhance, and add to value to the in-store shopping experience. Example—using a coupon on your cell phone when checking out at the Hard Rock Café, or checking in to a retail location using FourSquare's mobile app.
Mobile Marketing: A variety of activities used by organizations to engage, communicate, and interact over Wi-Fi and telecommunications networks with consumers using wireless, handheld devices. Example—sending special offers to customers who have opted in to receive discounts via SMS text message or advertising a brand on a popular mobile game app like Angry Birds.

These four terms are not mutually exclusive. Mobile eCommerce, Mobile Retailing, and Mobile Marketing are all forms of Mobile Commerce. Mobile eCommerce emphasizes the use of mobile apps and mobile web sites for carrying out transactions and does not necessarily involve interaction with traditional retail stores. Mobile Retailing on the other hand, emphasizes in-store shopping using mobile devices, but could include situations where the customer ultimately orders from a web site or mobile app. Mobile Marketing is the term used to describe promotional strategies and tactics that encourage both Mobile eCommerce and Mobile Retail. This overlap is a reflection of the evolution toward omni-channel mobile commerce (see Figure 7.8).

While there have been some interesting and even successful examples of mCommerce since 1997, predictions about mobile technology becoming a pervasive force in consumer retailing have proven overly optimistic. There are several reasons why consumers and businesses have been slow to embrace mCommerce:

- Relatively primitive mobile devices (compared to modern smartphones and tablets)
- Concerns about privacy and security
- Slow network connection speeds
- Limited market size
- Limited and inconvenient mobile payment options
- Lack of technological standardization (devices, OSs, browsers, etc.)

However, many of these barriers have been reduced or eliminated. As you have read in the previous section, the number of people who now own mobile devices, particularly smartphones, has grown dramatically. According to one widely quoted statistic, more people own cell phones today than own toothbrushes! Telecommunications carriers have expanded their coverage of populated areas using high-speed networks. Modern smartphones and tablet devices have features that make shopping via bright colorful screens fun and easy. While security will always be an evolving concern, consumer comfort with carrying out transactions on mobile devices continues to grow. A number of mobile payment methods are emerging that are more convenient than traditional transaction methods. So after years of waiting, it appears that the stage is finally set for earlier predictions about mCommerce to come true. In this section, we describe some of the many ways businesses and consumers are using mobile technologies to buy and sell goods and services.

SHOPPING FROM WIRELESS DEVICES

Originally, mCommerce was envisioned as a separate channel from traditional brick-and-mortar store operations. In fact, many retailers and customers view mobile commerce as competing with traditional retail channels. As you read in the opening case, Target feels threatened by customers who *showroom* their stores using mobile devices. However, as businesses learn about the full potential of mobile technology, the distinction between mobile eCommerce and in-store retailing are beginning to blur. While most businesses currently operate their eCommerce and mobile channels separately from the traditional retail channel, it is expected that strategies integrating the customer experience across channels will emerge, resulting in what the National Retail Federation (2011) refers to as the **omni-channel** approach to retailing.

As illustrated in Figure 7.8, many businesses operate separate retail channels. For instance, in-store product prices may be different from those the customer finds on the company's eCommerce web site and direct mail catalog. Records of customer purchases from the eCommerce site may not be available to service personnel assisting the customer at the store level. But retail strategy is evolving. The ultimate goal is to offer consumers multiple brand-based touch points that leverage the strengths of each channel. For instance, a company with a truly integrated or **omni-channel strategy** might spark a customer's interest using mobile advertising or direct mail catalogs. The customer then visits a brick-and-mortar store to examine the product firsthand and speak to a sales person. In-store purchases might be made using one of the mobile payment methods discussed later in this chapter. If the store doesn't have the particular size or color of the product desired, the customer might order it by accessing the store's eCommerce site with a smartphone by scanning a QR code placed strategically on an in-store display (see Figure 7.9). The product would then be delivered through the mail. Product returns could be handled through the mail or returned to the store depending on what is most convenient for the customer. Customer service reps in a call center would have a record of the customer's purchase regardless of which channel the transaction had been completed through. The omni-channel strategy will also take into consideration the potential impact of social media, whereby customers interact with the brand on sites like Facebook or Twitter and share brand experiences with others in their social network.

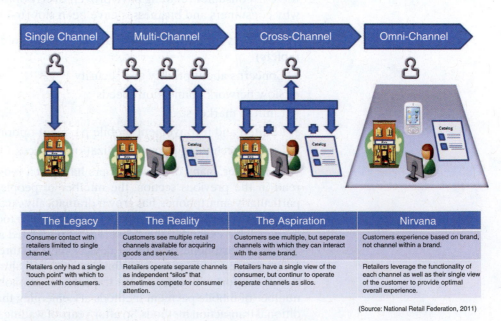

(Source: National Retail Federation, 2011)

Figure 7.8 Trend in mCommerce strategy is toward omni-channel approach.

Figure 7.9 Smartphone users can scan QR codes that help them easily access product information on the Internet without the hassle of typing a URL code into a mobile browser.

© Jochen Tack/Alamy Limited

Information: Competitive Advantage in Mobile Commerce. Integrating mobile technology with a brand's retail and eCommerce strategy provides another important benefit to business: customer information and identification. When customers interact with a brand using a mobile device, information is collected about the customer that can be used to optimize the interaction. For instance, when customers use a brand's mobile app to shop for products, their shopping experience can be customized based on the company's knowledge of previous purchases, payment methods, product preferences, and even location.

In-store Tracking. In-store shopping experiences can be optimized through mobile technology that can track a customer's movement through a retail store. This is analogous to eCommerce sites that track the pages a customer looks at in order to better understand consumer interests and to make decisions about web site design. Tracking how a customer moves through a store, noting what displays the customer looks at or what departments the customer spends the most time in can be extremely helpful for understanding individual consumer preferences as well as creating optimal store layout. Systems for tracking customers based on signals emitted from cell phones and other mobile devices are under development. It is expected that they will be available on a commercial basis in the near future.

While the goal of in-store tracking is to provide an enhanced shopping experience for the consumer, most people are likely to find this kind of monitoring a violation of privacy. In plain language, many will find it creepy. Businesses that are not careful about how they implement these programs will experience customer backlash and may even run afoul of new privacy laws and regulations. Therefore, it is important that brands involved in mobile eCommerce and Mobil Retailing have clear privacy statements and use an opt-in system to obtain permission from customers before tracking their online and off-line shopping behaviors. Customers are generally willing to give up some degree of privacy as long as companies explain how collecting the information will benefit the customer and identify the safeguards used to protect the customer's information. Companies often reward customers for providing information and opting in to monitoring programs. This is often accomplished through loyalty programs that offer discounts and special premiums to customers who opt in.

Few businesses fully utilize mobile tracking and monitoring systems at present. But as brands become more sophisticated with mobile technology, it is expect they will strive to gain a competitive advantage by using this information to provide better service, convenience, and a more enjoyable shopping experience, both online and in traditional stores.

Figure 7.10 Users with a QR app can access additional product information by scanning a Quick Response code in a magazine advertisement.

Quick Response (QR) Codes. In Japan, many products are tagged with QR codes. Consumers in that country frequently scan QR codes to access product information from a mobile device. Using a barcode scanner app and the camera feature of a mobile device, customers scan the QR code containing a link to an Internet web page (see Figure 7.9). In the case at the beginning of this chapter, you read how Macy's uses QR codes on in-store displays to direct customers to promotional videos that feature their products. The QR code is supposed to be an easier alternative to typing a URL address into a mobile browser (see Figure 7.10). While QR codes have not been as popular in the U.S. as they are in Asia, marketers have used them in print advertising and direct mail ads with some success. Charitable organizations use QR codes on the outside of direct mail solicitations. Scanning the code takes the user to a video explaining the mission of the organization and typically makes a more compelling request for donation than what is possible through print media. Additionally, responses to the QR code promotions can be tracked used to evaluate program effectiveness.

Some experts feel, however, that QR code technology is never going to be as popular in the U.S. as it is in Asia. They cite studies that report many smartphone users simply don't know what to do with a QR code. Other research suggests that users think the scanning process is either inconvenient or that QR codes frequently direct users to pages that don't contain anything of interest. For QR codes to become something American consumers use frequently, businesses will have to prove that they help mobile users find content that is interesting and valuable. **Mobile Visual Search** (MVS) technology is emerging as an alternative to QR codes. See Video Case 3 at the end of this chapter for additional information.

MOBILE ENTERTAINMENT

Mobile entertainment is expanding on wireless devices. Most notable are music, movies, videos, games, adult entertainment, sports, and gambling apps.

Sports enthusiasts enjoy a large number of apps and services on their mobile devices. Apps exist to check game scores; track news about specific athletes, teams, or sports; participate in fantasy team contests like fantasy football; and participate in sports-oriented social networking services. A number of sports-related games like mobile golf and sports trivia apps are widely available. There are even apps designed to provide tips and information for improving your own athletic performance. Apps are available to record workout times, schedule training exercises, heart rates, and a variety of other information related to athletic training. The iPhone even has an app that analyzes a person's golf swing and provides advice for improving performance.

ESPN is widely acknowledged as a leader in mobile marketing to the sports fan. They have a number of popular branded mobile apps that deliver information and entertainment to their target audience. They also utilize well designed mobile web sites and have a large database of fans that have opted in to receive sports-related news alerts sent to their phones via text messages.

Industry analysts predict that recent improvements in mobile devices will lead to an even bigger increase in the number of people who watch video clips, movies, and television programming on their mobile devices. The screen size of devices like Apple's iPad make watching video programming more attractive than on a smartphone. However, the number of people viewing video on smartphones seems to be increasing as well (Google, IPSOS OTX MediaCT, 2011). Companies like theChanner.com offer television programming to mobile device users. Popular streaming services like Netflix and Hulu now offer mobile apps for iOS and Android-based devices.

The iTunes Store continues to be a leading in distributor of digital music, movies, TV shows, e-books, and podcasts available to consumers for a fee. While most iTunes content is available to be purchased, there are frequently e-books, movies, and other digital content available for free. Mobile users can also access music from digital streaming sites like *Pandora.com* and *Grooveshark.com*. Both of these services offer free streaming music. Users can upgrade their accounts by paying a subscription fee which then reduces the amount of advertising they are exposed to.

While still relatively small, the mobile gambling industry is expected to grow substantially in the next few years. Some predict this type of mobile commerce could generate as much as $20 billion in the near future. Primary growth of this market is expected to take place in Japan and other Asian countries, such as horse racing in Hong Kong. Current laws in the U.S. prohibit most forms of online gambling; consequently, gambling via mobile devices is restricted as well in the U.S.

Many mobile apps are available for consumers interested in home-based entertainment activities. The Food Network offers an app with tips and recipes for fine dining and entertaining. Martha Stewart's Digital Magazines publish a number of home entertainment and lifestyle mobile apps (see *marthastewart.com/apps*) Mobatech is the maker of a mobile bartending app with numerous recipes for cocktails and party drinks.

HOTEL SERVICES AND TRAVEL GO WIRELESS

In recent years, smartphones and other mobile devices have become essential travel aids. Most major airlines, hotel chains, and Internet travel agencies have developed mobile apps to help travelers manage their arrangements. Airlines frequently give passengers the option of receiving up-to-date information about their flights via SMS text messaging. Google Maps is one of the most popular apps used by travelers, particularly those traveling by automobile. Even AAA, the automobile club, has a mobile app that helps drivers plan their trips and an app for drivers who need roadside assistance (see Figure 7.12.) Other interesting mobile travel tools include apps that translate text when traveling abroad, apps for finding nearby Wi-Fi hotspots, and apps created by a number of popular travel guides.

Most large hotels chains, and many independent hotels and inns offer guests in-room, wireless high-speed Internet connections, although this is not always a free service. Some of these same hotels offer Wi-Fi Internet access in public areas like the lobby and meeting rooms. Larger hotel chains have apps that allow guests to make reservations, check their bill, and locate hotel services using a mobile app. Some hotels are experimenting with mobile check-in programs where guests use their mobile device to gain access to their rooms using NFC or SMS text message technology. This makes it possible to check in to the hotel without having to stop first at the front desk.

MOBILE SOCIAL NETWORKING

People are increasingly using mobile devices to with social networking sites like Facebook and Twitter. According to Nielsen (2011) social media apps are the third-most-popular kind of mobile app (after games and weather apps). Much like web-based social networking, mobile social networking occurs in virtual communities. All of the most popular social networking sites offer apps that allow users to access their accounts from a smartphone or other mobile device. Some experts predict that mobile social media will be continue to be a primary driving force in the growth of the mobile market.

IT at Work 7.2

Angry Birds Make Mobile Game Developers Happy

Have you ever played popular mobile games like Angry Birds (Figure 7.11), Draw Something, or The Sims FreePlay? Media research firm Nielsen (2011) reports that games are the most popular mobile apps in the U.S. While many apps in this category are free, 93 percent of app downloaders are willing to pay for game apps, compared to 76 percent for news apps, another popular category. Mobile gamers spend an average of 7.8 hours a month playing games, but smartphone users appear to be heavier users of this category, with iPhone owners playing 14.7 hours /month and Android owners playing 9.3 hours/month. Reports of market size and growth rates differ on the exact amounts, but they agree that this category is sizable and growing rapidly. Flurry, a mobile app analytics firm estimates that downloads for iOS and Android phones alone, produced revenue of $800 million and $1.9 billion in 2010 and 2011, respectively, an increase of 137 percent in one year (Farago, 2011).

To put this in perspective, in 2009, iOS and Android mobile gaming apps accounted for just 11 percent of the portable (hand-held) gaming market dominated by Sony and Nintendo. By 2011, iOS and Android games accounted for a majority (58 percent) of the market. Clearly, mobile gaming apps have become a disruptive force in the marketplace, displacing two historically strong companies. Even more impressive is the fact that the above statistics are based on revenues produced by paid downloads. Many mobile games are available as free apps supported by advertising revenues. When advertising revenues are taken into account, the amount of money being produced by this app category is quite large. Some analysts estimate that ad revenue produce by mobile games was approximately $65 million in 2011 (eMarketer, 2012).

Compiled from Dotson (2012), Nielsen (2011), Farago (2011), Asante (2012), eMarketer (2012).

Figure 7.11 Angry Birds is such a popular mobile game that it generates additional revenue from sales of clothing, plush toys, posters, lunch boxes, and even bed linens.

Questions

1. Why did established companies like Nintendo and Sony fail to gain an early position in the growing mobile gaming market?

2. How are mobile games different from traditional video games? What advantages do mobile game apps have over traditional game makers?

3. Gaming is the most popular mobile app category in the U.S. Social Media apps are the third-largest category. What do you think this says about the role of mobile devices in the lives of U.S. consumers?

4. Since most gaming apps are free, how do developers make money in this category?

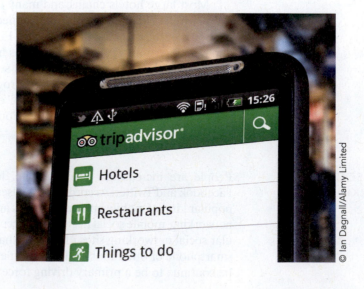

Figure 7.12 Travelers use mobile apps to book reservations, find directions, and find reviews and recommendations for a wide range of travel and hospitality services.

IT at Work 7.3

Wireless Marketing and Advertising in Action

Industry analysts expect advertising in the mobile channel to heat up. Increasing numbers of smartphones, better browsers, enhanced GPS capabilities, and better ways of measuring advertising effectiveness are all factors powering this growth. The following are a few examples of wireless advertising in action.

Location-Based Marketing. *Foursquare.com* is one of the most popular apps in the growing field of mobile advertising (see Figure 7.13). The Foursquare app makes use of the mobile device's GPS system (see section 7.4) to determine the user's location. Part of Foursquare's success is due to the fact that most users don't view it as an advertising program. Structured as a mobile social media game, users "check in" from their phones when they visit retail shops and restaurants. Users provide information and ratings based on their reaction to these outlets. This information is shared with advertisers and friends who are also part of the Foursquare network. Foursquare develops a profile of users based on the

Figure 7.13 The NBC Universal store in Rockefeller Center in New York encourages customers to check-in to the store using the popular foursquare app.

kinds of businesses they frequent and can use this information to better target consumers with advertising messages. Foursquare reinforces member use of the service by awarding *badges* to members for various types and levels of usage. Members who are the most frequent shopper at a particular location are awarded the title of *Mayor* and may receive special attention and discounts from the retailer. The company provides advertisers with information about target customers that they usually don't have: their location. This helps advertisers deliver timely messages that can be more relevant and meaningful to consumers, increasing the chances that the ads will lead to a purchase transaction.

Another popular location-based mobile marketing app is Shopkick. When the Shopkick app is activated, users receive points when they visit a participating retailer. Retailers use the app to encourage and reward specific kinds of shopper behavior. Shopkick points are used to reward consumers for visiting specific locations in a store, purchasing products, scanning featured prod-

ucts, and even participating in brief surveys. Shoppers often receive targeted discounts and promotional offers when they are in a store. Shopkick users can trade in their points for restaurant vouchers, iTunes cards or gift cards from participating retailers.

Augmented Reality (AR) apps utilize a special technology that will become more commonplace in the future. Augmented reality involves computer-generated graphic images that are superimposed on pictures of real things (e.g., people, rooms, buildings, roads, and so on). This technology can be used by advertisers in several ways. For instance, a mobile phone user might point her phone camera at an office building and activate an AR app that generates the logos of all foodservice outlets (e.g., Starbucks, Subway, McDonalds) inside the building. Furniture retailer IKEA offers shoppers an AR app that allows them to project images of its products on to pictures of the rooms in their homes so that they can "visualize" how the products will look (MobiAdNews, 2009). (See Figure 7.14 for an additional example.) Industry experts expect that AR advertising will grow as smartphone users become more familiar with the concept.

Figure 7.14 IBM's augmented reality shopping app automatically delivers personalized coupons, customer reviews, and hidden product details (such as whether packaging is biodegradable) to smartphones as consumers browse store shelves. The app transforms marketing promotions from intrusions into services that customers welcome.

Mobile Directories. Hoping to become the king of location-based web domains, Go2Online (*go2.com*) helps travelers with mobile devices find everything from lodging to automobile repair shops. Partnering with Sprint, Nextel, Verizon, and Boost, Go2 claims its services are available on every web-enabled phone in America. Entering "JiffyLube" or any of hundreds of other brand names into the Go2 system will bring up the nearest location where one can find that product or service. Another popular directory service, Yellow Pages, uses augmented reality as part of their mobile strategy. See an interesting example at *youtube.com/watch?v=tOw8X78VTwg/*.

Sources: Compiled from Moore (2010), Whitfield (2010), and City of Denver (2012).

1. Describe some ways in which people are using mobile devices to shop for products and services

2. What are some ways in which traditional brick-and-mortar retailers can use mobile technology to enhances a customer's in-store shopping experience

3. List types of mobile entertainment available to consumers.

4. List some ways that travelers and travel-related businesses are using mobile technology.

5. How are companies using QR codes to promote products and services to mobile consumers? Why are QR codes not as popular in the U.S. as they are in Asia and other parts of the world?

6. Explain why the mobile gaming market represents such a lucrative market opportunity.

7.3 Mobile Transactions and Financial Services

MOBILE ELECTRONIC PAYMENT SYSTEMS

Consumers use mobile devices for a wide range of shopping or commercial activities. As discussed in the case at the beginning of this chapter, shoppers are using mobile devices to compare prices, research products prior to purchase, and identify alternative product options and alternative retailers. Increasingly, mobile devices are becoming an attractive way to pay for products. According to comScore's *2012 Mobile Future in Focus* report, mobile payment activity during the holiday shopping season (October to December) increased over 80 percent from 2010 to 2011. Other industry reports, like the World Payments Report (Capgemini, et al., 2011) suggest that the overall rate of mobile payments will continue to increase at least 50 percent a year for the next three years. Some forms of mobile payment represent an attractive option for consumers who do not have credit cards. Additionally, retailers may benefit from new payment options that carry lower transaction costs compared to what banks charge when credit cards are used.

As mobile commerce grows, there is a greater demand for payment systems that make transactions from smartphones and other mobile devices convenient, safe, and secure. A number of businesses have attempted to meet this demand using a variety of technologies. There are two basic transaction types of interest: the online purchase of goods and services using a mobile device (e.g., ordering a book from Amazon.com) and using a mobile device to pay for goods and services in a traditional brick-and-mortar store. Here are examples of some approaches that are being developed.

Charge to Phone Bill with SMS confirmation (see *zong.com* and *boku.com*). This eCommerce payment solution is a lot easier than entering credit card and other information on a small mobile handheld device. It requires users to set up an account with a payment company like zong.com. When completing an online transaction, users click the "ZONG—Buy with Mobile" button, and enter their phone number. They receive an SMS text message with a secure PIN number that they enter on the eCommerce web site to complete the transaction. The amount of the charge is then added to the payer's phone bill, and the telecom carrier remits this amount to the payee. Telecom companies may deduct a service charge from the amount paid. (Zong was recently purchased by PayPal.)

Near Field Communications (NFC) (see *Google Wallet and Isis Mobile Wallet*). Another approach to mobile payment is designed for payments in traditional retail stores. At check out, mobile users simply pass or tap their phone on a merchant terminal and payment is transferred. Users receive an SMS text message confirmation. While Google Wallet has received considerable attention in the technology press, in part because of Google's power and influence in the industry, relatively few consumers can use this option. Only a small number of phones have the required NFC feature. Additionally, the program is only available to people with Citi MasterCard with PayPass or Google's Pre-Paid credit card. To be successful, the program will have to expand beyond these limitations.

Phone Displays Barcode That Retailer Scans. A number of companies are developing mobile payment systems that generate a QR code on the user's phone, which is then scanned by the retailer. Starbucks uses this approach with its mobile payment system (Tsirulnik, 2010). Customers create an account with Starbucks as part of the retailer's loyalty program, and transfer money to a pre-paid account. Upon check out, users activate the Starbucks app, which creates a bar code that can be scanned at check out. The funds are deducted from the user's account. Other companies are working on programs that could be used at a variety of retailers, much as you can use a credit card.

Credit Card + Web Form. Using a mobile web browser, buyers make online purchases by entering their credit card number and other identifying information just the way they would if they were using a personal computer. This process can be cumbersome given the smaller screen and key boards on mobile devices, but it is an option.

Transfer Funds from Payment Account Using SMS (see *obopay.com* and *paypal.com*). Using this approach, the user creates an account at a company like obopay.com and transfers money into it from a bank or credit card account. Using a mobile phone and SMS, the user can then transfer money to anyone else with a mobile phone number. The receiver must create an account at the payment company in order to retrieve the funds. See Figure 7.15.

Mobile Phone Card Reader (see *Square.com* and *Paypal.com*). This novel approach requires mobile phone users to insert a small card reader in the audio jack of their mobile device. The card reader, which resembles a small cube (Square) or pyramid (PayPal), allows those with accounts at Square or PayPal to make or receive credit card payments without a merchant account.

User Scans 2D Tags Generated by Retailer (see *Cimbal.com*). This payment system uses QR or 2D tags to identify the merchant or payee. The buyer scans the merchant's tag using a special smartphone app and then approves fund transfer when it shows up on the device. Person-to-person transfers are also possible since the app can generate custom QR tags that individuals can scan from one another's mobile devices.

By "Bumping" iPhones with Payment Applications (see *bumptechnologies.com*). Using an iPhone app called *bump*, two individuals can transfer money to each other simply by tapping their phones together.

Almost all of the payment systems described above are illustrated by videos on Youtube.com. Interested readers are encouraged to view these video resources for a more complete explanation of how the different mobile payment systems work.

Figure 7.15 PayPal is one of several firms attempting to become a leader in the mobile payments industry.

© Ian Dagnall/Alamy Limited

Wireless payment systems transform mobile phones into secure, self-contained purchasing tools capable of instantly authorizing payments over the cellular network. One advantage of many mobile payment systems over traditional credit card systems is the ability to handle **micropayments**, or transactions involving relatively small sums of money. The ability to make micropayments allows individuals to use their mobile devices to do things like purchase a beverage from a vending machine or make a payment to a municipal parking meter. Many cities in Europe, and a growing number in the U.S., have adopted mobile phone payment systems for parking and report dramatic increases in revenue because of the reduction in loss due to theft, broken meters and the reduced expense associated with collecting cash from traditional meters.

Mobile Bill Payments. In addition to paying bills through wireline banking or from ATMs, a number of companies are now providing their customers with the option of paying bills directly from a cell phone. Western Union, HDFC Bank in India, Citibank and several other institutions worldwide now offer mobile bill payment services. This trend is proving particularly attractive to mobile users in developing countries where many people do not have bank accounts.

MOBILE BANKING AND FINANCIAL SERVICES

Mobile banking is generally defined as carrying out banking transactions and other related activities via mobile devices. The services offered include bill payments and money transfers, account administration and check book requests, balance inquiries and statements of account, interest and exchange rates, and so on.

Banks and other financial institutions let customers use mobile devices for a wide range of services (see Table 7.2).

People access financial services using a combination of mobile media channels including Short Message Service (SMS), mobile web browsers, and customized apps. Mobile banking is a natural extension of online banking services, which have grown in popularity over the last decade (see Figure 7.16).

Throughout Europe, the U.S., and Asia, an increasing percentage of banks offer mobile access to financial and account information. In 2009, ABI Research evaluated 29 U.S. banks on accessibility of their mobile banking services. Six of the banks received top marks: BB&T, Eastern Bank, Fifth Third Bank, Northeast Bank, USAA, and Wells Fargo. Bank of American and Chase also received positive evaluations.

In Sweden, Merita Bank has pioneered many services and The Royal Bank of Scotland offers mobile payment services. Banamex, one of Mexico's largest banks, is a strong provider of wireless services to customers. Many banks in Japan allow all banking transactions to be done via cell phone. Experts predict that growth in the mobile banking services sector could reach between 894 million and 1.5 billion customers globally by 2015. The Asia-Pacific region is expected to emerge as the predominant market for mobile banking services (Berg Insights, 2010; Global Industry Analysts, 2010).

TABLE 7.2	Most Common Mobile Banking Services

- Account alerts, security alerts, and reminders
- Account balances, updates, and history
- Customer service via mobile
- Branch or ATM location information
- Bill pay (e.g., utility bills), deliver online payments by secure agents, and mobile phone client apps
- Funds transfers
- Transaction verification
- Mortgage alerts

Figure 7.16 Mobile banking, stock trading, and payment services have increased in recent years.

© blammo/Alamy Limited

Short Codes. Banks and financial service organization have two basic options for providing mobile services. Smartphone users can download dedicated apps to conduct banking transactions. The other option is to provide service through SMS (text message) technology. As you know, text messaging is still widely popular, even with people who use smartphones. Many mobile financial services make use of short codes for sending SMS texts. A short code works like a telephone number, except that it is only 5 or 6 characters long and easier to remember. Businesses lease short codes from the **Common Short Code Association (CSCA)** for $500 to $1,000 a month. The lower price is for randomly assigned codes whereas companies that want a specific short code pay a higher monthly rate. Once a company has leased its short code, it can begin using it in promotions and interactivity with customers.

Short codes are used for a wide variety of SMS text services, not just financial services. For example, voting on the popular television show *American Idol* is done with short codes. Each contestant is assigned a specific short code, and viewers are encouraged to send text messages indicating which performer they like the best. The annual *MTV Movie Awards* also uses short code voting, which allows viewers to pick the winning entry in certain prize categories. On some telecommunications networks, ring tones are sold using short codes and SMS texts.

Security Issues. At present, the benefits associated with mobile banking seem to outweigh potential security threats. However, as the number of people who engage in mobile banking increases, the likelihood that criminals will target mobile financial activity is sure to grow as well. What kinds of threats exist to mobile banking? Table 7.3 lists the most common mobile banking risks.

TABLE 7.3	Mobile Banking Security Risks

Cloning—Duplicating the Electronic Serial Number (ESM) of one phone and using it in second phone, the clone. This allows the perpetrator to have calls and other transactions billed to the original phone.

Phishing—Using a fraudulent communication, such as an e-mail, to trick the receiver into divulging critical information such as account numbers, passwords, or other identifying information.

Smishing—Similar to phishing, but the fraudulent communication comes in the form of an SMS message.

Vishing—Again, similar to phishing, but the fraudulent communication comes in the form of a voice or voicemail message encouraging the victim to divulge secure information.

Lost or Stolen Phone—Lost or stolen cell phones can be used to conduct financial transactions without the owner's permission.

Questions

1. What are the two basic types of mobile payment transactions?
2. Why have e-wallets not been widely adopted, and what will makers of e-wallets need to do to make this payment method more attractive to consumers?
3. What are the most common types of mobile banking activities consumers perform?
4. What are the most common security risks associated with mobile banking?
5. Describe some of the mobile payment systems
6. What is a micropayment, and why is it beneficial to consumers and businesses that mobile payments systems can process these types of transactions.

7.4 Location-Based Services and Commerce

Location-based commerce (l-commerce) or **location-based services (LBS)** refers to the delivery of advertisements, products, or services to customers whose locations are known at a given time. Location-based services are beneficial to both consumers and businesses. From a consumer's viewpoint, l-commerce offers convenience, safety, and productivity. For instance, you can connect to an emergency service with a mobile device and have the service pinpoint your exact location. The services offer convenience because you can locate what is near you without having to consult a traditional directory or map. The services offer increased productivity because you can optimize your travel and time by determining points of interest within close proximity. From a business supplier's point of view, l-commerce offers an opportunity to sell more.

L-commerce services revolve around five key concepts:

1. Location. Determining the basic position of a person or a thing (e.g., bus, car, or boat), at any given time

2. Navigation. Plotting a route from one location to another

3. Tracking. Monitoring the movement of a person or a thing (e.g., a vehicle or package) along the route

4. Mapping. Creating digital maps of specific geographical locations

5. Timing. Determining the precise time at a specific location

L-COMMERCE TECHNOLOGIES

Providing location-based services requires the following location-based and network technologies.

- **Position Determining Equipment (PDE).** This equipment identifies the location of the mobile device either through GPS or by locating the nearest base station. The position information is sent to the mobile positioning center.

- **Mobile Positioning Center (MPC).** The MPC is a server that manages the location information sent from the PDE.

- **Location-based technology.** This technology consists of groups of servers that combine the position information with geographic- and location-specific content to provide an l-commerce service. For instance, location-based technology could present a list of addresses of nearby restaurants based on the position of the caller, local street maps, and a directory of businesses. It is provided via the content center via the Internet.

- **Geographic content.** Geographic content consists of digitized streets, road maps, addresses, routes, landmarks, land usage, Zip codes, and the like. This information must be delivered in compressed form for fast distribution over wireless networks.

- **Location-specific content.** Location-specific content is used in conjunction with the geographic content to provide the location of particular services. Yellow-pages directories showing the location of specific business and services are examples of this type of content.

IT at Work 7.4

The Highway 91 Project

Route 91 is a major eight-lane, east-west highway near Los Angeles. Traffic is especially heavy during rush hours. California Private Transportation Company (CPT) built six express toll lanes along a 10-mile stretch in the median of the existing Highway 91. The express lane system has only one entrance and one exit, and it is totally operated with EC technologies. The system works as follows.

Only prepaid subscribers can drive on the road. Subscribers receive an automatic vehicle identification (AVI) device that is placed on the rearview mirror of the car (see Figure 7.17). The device, which uses RFID technology, about the size of a thick credit card, includes a microchip, an antenna, and a battery. A large sign over the toll-way tells drivers the current fee for cruising the express lanes. In a recent year, it varied from $0.50 in slow traffic hours to $3.25 during rush hours.

Sensors in the pavement let the tollway computer know that a car has entered; the car does not need to slow or stop. The AVI makes radio contact with a transceiver installed above the lane. The transceiver relays the car's identity through fiber-optic lines to the control center, where a computer calculates the fee for that day's trip. The system accesses the driver's account, and the fare is automatically deducted from the driver's prepaid account. A monthly statement is sent to the subscriber's home.

Surveillance cameras record the license numbers of cars without AVIs. These cars can be stopped by police at the exit or fined by mail. Video cameras along the tollway also enable managers to keep tabs on traffic, for example, sending a tow truck to help a stranded car. Also, through knowledge of the traffic volume, pricing decisions can be made. Raising the price as traffic increases ensures that the tollway will not be jammed. In similar systems, nonsubscribers are allowed to enter via special gates where they pay cash.

The system saves commuters between 40 and 90 minutes each day, so it is in high demand. An interesting extension of the system is the use of the same AVIs for other purposes. For example, they can be used in paid parking lots. Someday you may even

Figure 7.17 Mobile Device Used in Highway 91 Project.

Steve Grayson UPI Photo Service/NewsCom

be recognized when you enter the drive-through lane of McDonald's and a voice asks you, "Mr. Jones, do you want your usual meal today?"

Questions

1. What is the role of the wireless component of this system?
2. Outline the consumer benefits described in this story compared to traditional toll road systems. Describe the benefits of the system to the government or agencies operating the toll road.
3. Describe how the technology being used by 91 Express Lanes might be used in other kinds of business situations.

Figure 7.18 shows how these technologies are used in conjunction with one another to deliver location-based services that are managed via the service center. Underlying these technologies are global positioning and geographical information systems.

Global Positioning System (GPS). A global positioning system (GPS) is a wireless system that uses satellites to determine where the GPS device is located anywhere on the earth. GPS equipment has been used extensively for navigation by commercial airlines and ships, and for locating trucks and buses.

GPS is supported by 31 U.S. government satellites, plus 3 to 4 decommissioned (but still functional) satellites that can be reactivated if necessary. The goal is to make sure that at least 24 of these satellites are available to provide service worldwide at least 95 percent of the time. Each satellite orbits the earth once every 12 hours on a precise path, at an altitude of 10,900 miles. At any point in time, the exact position of each satellite is known because the satellite broadcasts its position and a time signal from its onboard atomic clock, which is accurate to

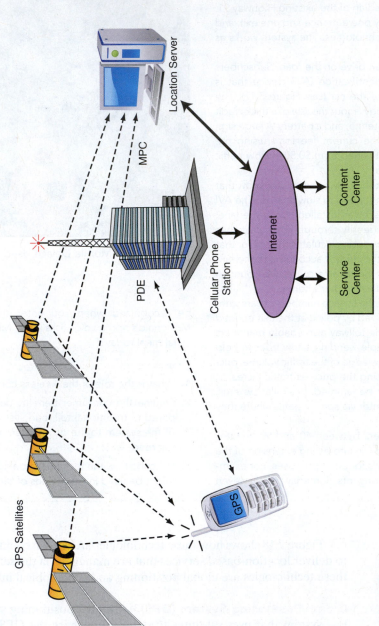

Figure 7.18 Smartphone with GPS in location-based commerce.

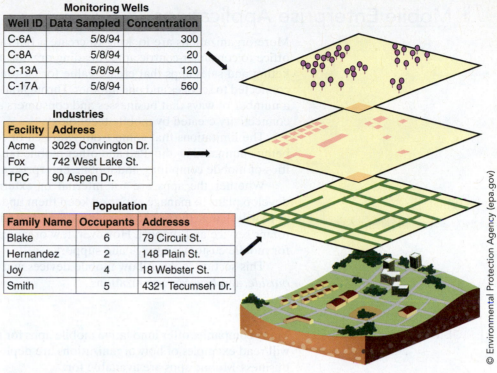

Monitoring Wells

Well ID	Data Sampled	Concentration
C-6A	5/8/94	300
C-8A	5/8/94	20
C-13A	5/8/94	120
C-17A	5/8/94	560

Industries

Facility	Address
Acme	3029 Convington Dr.
Fox	742 West Lake St.
TPC	90 Aspen Dr.

Population

Family Name	Occupants	Addresss
Blake	6	79 Circuit St.
Hernandez	2	148 Plain St.
Joy	4	18 Webster St.
Smith	5	4321 Tecumseh Dr.

© Environmental Protection Agency (epa.gov)

Figure 7.19 Illustrates how GIS systems apply layers of information to a map to create visual representations that aid in decision making.

one-billionth of a second. Receivers also have accurate clocks that are synchronized with those of the satellites.

GPS handsets can be stand-alone units or can be plugged into or embedded in a mobile device. They calculate the position of the handsets, or send the information to be calculated centrally. Knowing the speed of the satellite signals, 186,272, miles per second, engineers can find the location of any receiving station, latitude, and longitude, to within 50 feet by *triangulation*, using the distance from a GPS to *three* satellites to make the computation. GPS software then computes the latitude and longitude of the receiver. This process is called **geocoding.**

Geographical Information System (GIS). The location provided by GPS is expressed in terms of latitude and longitude. To make that information useful to businesses and consumers, it is necessary in many cases to relate those measures to a certain place or address. This is done by inserting the latitude and longitude onto a digital map, which is part of a geographical information system (GIS). The GIS then adds layers of information to the map, which can include things like store names, customer names and locations, traffic pattern data, demographic information, and so on. The integration of information layers with geographic or location data and GIS visualization technology is then used to create digitized map displays (see Figure 7.19). Companies such as Mapinfo, Esri, Autodesk, and others provide core GIS spatial technology, maps, and other data content needed in order to power location-based GIS/GPS services.

Questions

1. What are location-based services?
2. What are some examples of location-based commerce?
3. Describe GPS. What is it used for?
4. Describe GIS and its advantages.
5. Describe how advertisers may take advantage of GIS and GPS information to make their advertising and promotional campaigns more effective.

7.5 Mobile Enterprise Applications

More organizations are looking to create a full range of mobile apps—from back-office to consumer-centric apps. Leading organizations are developing mobile marketing and sales apps that create value for customers who want to be increasingly connected to services and one another. Throughout this chapter, you have read about a number of ways that businesses and consumers are benefiting from the increased connectivity created by mobile technology.

The limitations that come from two-inch or four-inch smartphone screens are being eliminated by the iPad and other mobile tablets—and expanding the possibilities of mobile computing and mobile enterprise applications.

Whether the apps are for internal or external users, organizations need to develop plans to manage apps and keep them updated. Greater adoption of mobile apps will change the way that organizations deal with both internal and external customer service and support. However, few organizations have yet to develop a plan for mobile customer service and support.

This section looks at how mobile devices and technologies can be used *within*, *outside*, and *between* organizations.

MOBILE APPS

Many companies offer innovative mobile apps for the enterprise. In this section, you will read examples of how organizations are deploying mobile solutions to conduct business. Mobile apps are available for:

- Supporting salespeople while they are waiting on customers
- Supporting field employees doing repairs or maintenance on corporate premises or for clients
- Supporting traveling or off-site executives, managers, or other employees
- Supporting employees while they do work inside the enterprise, but where there is no easy access to desktop computers; e.g., in a warehouse, outdoor facilities, or large retail stores
- Employees involved in logistical operations such as driving trucks or delivery vehicles, or working in remote warehouses or storage facilities

Investments in mobile enterprise apps are made to provide employees with communication and collaboration tools, and access to data, information, and people inside the organization.

Mobile POS (Point of Sale). Traditional POS technology involves a computerized cash register connected to a server via a wired local area network (LAN). These stations are fixed and require customers to bring their merchandise to a specific location in the store where they wait in line for their turn to check out. Long lines frustrate customers. Some studies show that at least one in ten customers will abandon a long line and leave the store without completing a purchase.

Mobile POS stations can be set up as needed by using handheld computers, scanners and printers. During periods of high volume, employees can set up temporary mobile check-out stations capable of scanning merchandise bar codes, processing credit card payments, and printing receipts. Employees can even walk through a fixed station line offering to expedite checkout for those customers paying by credit card.

Inventory Management. Inventory management and tracking represent a significant expense for retailers. Using bar codes, NFC, and handheld devices, retailers can record when merchandise enters the store, where it is stored, and when it is moved to the floor. Delivery drivers use mobile devices to enter invoices and

IT at Work 7.5

NextBus: Superb Customer Service

Service Problem

Buses in certain parts of San Francisco have difficulty keeping up with the posted schedule, especially in rush hours. Generally, buses are scheduled to arrive every 20 minutes, but at times, passengers may have to wait 30 to 40 minutes. The schedules become meaningless, and passengers are unhappy because they waste time.

Solution

San Francisco bus riders carrying a smartphone or similar device can quickly find out when a bus is likely to arrive at a particular bus stop. The system tracks public transportation buses in real time. Knowing where each bus is and factoring in traffic patterns and weather reports, NextBus (*nextbus.com*) dynamically calculates the estimated arrival time of the bus to each bus stop on the route. The arrival times are also displayed on the Internet and on a public screen at each bus stop.

The NextBus system has been used successfully in several other cities around the U.S., Finland, and in several other countries. Figure 7.20 shows how the NextBus system works. The core of the NextBus system is a GPS satellite that can tell the NextBus information center where a bus is at any given time. Based on a bus's location, the scheduled arrival time at each stop can be calculated in real time. Users can access the information from their cell phones or PCs anytime, anywhere. NextBus schedules are also posted in real time on passengers' shelters at bus stops and public displays.

NextBus is an ad-free customer service, but in the near future advertising may be added. As the system knows exactly where you are when you request information and how much time you have until your next bus, it could send you to the nearest Starbucks for a cup of coffee, giving you an electronic discount coupon for a cup of coffee as you wait.

Sources: Compiled from en.wikipedia.org/wiki/NextBus, and nextbus.com.

Questions

1. How can NextBus generate revenues?
2. Who might be good sponsors of the service?

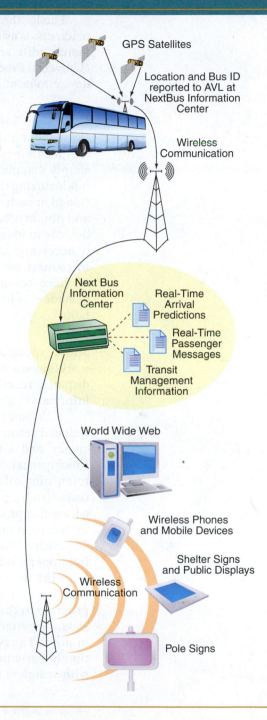

Figure 7.20 NextBus operational model.
Source: nextBus.com, 2008.

other shipping data into the store's database at the point of delivery, making billing and accounting easier. As merchandise is sold, inventory levels are updated, triggering replacement orders and reducing the chances of stock-out situations. The benefits are a reduction in lost sales due to missing or unavailable merchandise and theft.

If a customer asks an employee to help find a particular product, the employee can check its location from a handheld device, or order it and arrange for drop shipping directly to the customer's home. Immediate response reduces the probability that the customer will purchase the product from another business.

Finally, the cumbersome process of changing prices on in-store merchandise is made easier using mobile devices. Employees can walk the aisles of a store, scanning merchandise and checking the posted price against the price in the store's UPC (Universal Product Code) database. Employees who find a discrepancy can use the device to print a new price tag.

Customer Service. Because wireless devices can be quickly set up or moved throughout a store, retailers can position mobile price check devices in convenient locations for customers to verify prices or retrieve product information by simply scanning the UPC code on a product. These devices can be moved without incurring the costs of rewiring the units. Wireless self-help kiosks can be positioned in each department allowing customers to identify the location of products and obtain other information to facilitate their purchase. Stores can program the devices to identify inventory levels of a product at nearby locations in the chain if necessary. Some devices have a voice-activated feature allowing customers to request assistance from store employees carrying handheld devices capable of voice communications. This prevents customers from having to search for someone to help when they need assistance—or leaving because they can't get help.

Job Dispatch. Mobile devices are becoming an integral part of groupware and workflow solutions. For example, nonvoice mobile services can be used to assist in dispatch functions—to assign jobs to mobile employees, along with detailed information about the tasks.

A dispatching handheld for wireless devices allows improved response with reduced resources, real-time tracking of work orders, increased dispatcher efficiency, and a reduction in administrative work. For example, Michigan CAT (michigancat.com), a large vendor of used heavy machinery equipment, offers an interesting solution. Michigan CAT's system uses Cloudberry from Air-Trak (air-traksoftware.com) which supports both cellular and satellite networks. It entails a hybrid approach to the use of a GPS tracking and messaging system that enables information and forms generated by Caterpillar's database (DBS) and Service Technician Workbench (STW) software to be transmitted wirelessly between the field operations staff and service vehicles equipped with laptop. Data gathered from the field can be easily integrated into a back-end system. A simple extraction program was created to move data, service reports, and time sheets from one program to the other, eliminating duplicate keying of the same information into separate systems. Other dispatchers can access the information to add comments or notes. The system's benefits include increased productivity, reduced staff time, timely parts ordering, faster invoicing, and secure, precise service information with seamless integration between the company's systems.

Mobile App Failure. However, not all mobile apps are successful. An example is the U.S. Census Bureau's mobile snafu. For the 2010 census the government allocated $3 billion for handhelds to improve the interviewer's performance in the field. Unfortunately, due to poor program management, poor contract estimate, and hardware and software delays, the program had to be delayed to the 2020 census. The cost of manual data collection and programming increased the cost of the project by $2.2 to $3 billion.

CUSTOMER SUPPORT AND MOBILE CRM

Mobile access extends the reach of customer relationship management (CRM)—both inside and outside the company—to both employees and business partners on a 24/7 basis, to any place where recipients are located.

In the large software suites, such as Siebel's CRM (an Oracle company), the two CRM functions that have attracted the most interest are **sales force automation** and **field service.** For instance, a salesperson might be on a sales call and need to know recent billing history for a particular customer. Or a field service representative on a service call might need to know current availability of various parts in order to fix a piece of machinery. It is these sorts of situations where real-time mobile access to customer and partner data is invaluable. Two popular offerings are Salesforce.com's App Exchange Mobile and Oracle's CRM On Demand (*oracle.com/crmondemand/index.html*).

MOBILE SUPPLY CHAIN MANAGEMENT (MSCM)

Mobile computing solutions are also being applied to B2B and supply chain relationships. Such solutions enable organizations to respond faster to supply chain disruptions by proactively adjusting plans or by shifting resources related to critical supply chain events as they occur. Mobile supply chain apps create efficiencies by reducing delays and improving communications and coordination between supplier and customer. With the increased interest in collaborative commerce comes the opportunity to use wireless communication to collaborate along the supply chain. For this to take place, inter-organizational information systems integration is needed.

Mobile devices can also facilitate collaboration among members of the supply chain. Instead of calling a partner company and asking someone to find certain employees who work with the company, employees can be contacted directly on their mobile devices.

By enabling sales force employees to type orders or queries directly into ERP (Enterprise Resource Planning) systems while at a client's site, companies can reduce clerical mistakes and improve supply chain operations. By allowing salespeople to check production schedules and inventory levels, access product configuration and availability as well as capacity available for production, sales people can obtain quantities and real-time delivery dates. Thus, companies empower their sales force to make more competitive and realistic offers to customers. Today's ERP systems tie into broader supply chain management solutions that extend visibility across multiple tiers in the supply chain. Mobile supply chain management empowers the workforce to leverage these broader systems through inventory management and other functionalities that extend across multiple supply chain partners and take into account logistics considerations.

Questions

1. Describe how mobile devices and apps are being used inside organizations.
2. Describe some ways that sales people are benefiting from mobile technology.
3. Describe how retailers improve the shopping experience for their customers using mobile technology.
4. How is mobile technology being used to improve inventory management within companies?
5. Describe some benefits to companies using Mobile Supply Chain Management (MSCM) programs.

Key Terms

Android OS   *196*
augmented reality   *206*
barcode   *192*
Blackberry OS   *196*
cloning   *211*
Common Short Code Association
   (CSCA)   *210*
disruptive innovation   *220*
field service   *217*
geocoding   *213*
geographical information system
   (GIS)   *213*
global positioning system
   (GPS)   *213*
hotspot   *198*
in-store tracking   *202*

iOS   *196*
location-based commerce
   (l-commerce)   *211*
location-based marketing   *206*
location-based service (LBS)   *211*
mCommerce   *200*
micropayment   *209*
mobile commerce or mobile
   eCommerce   *200*
mobile display strategy   *193*
mobile marketing   *200*
mobile point of sale (MPOS)
   system   *216*
mobile retailing   *216*
mobile supply chain management
   (MSCM)   *217*

mobile visual search (MVS)   *222, 203*
near field communications
   (NFC)   *193, 208*
network access point   *198*
omni-channel strategy   *201*
phishing   *211*
quick response (QR) code   *203*
sales force automation (SFA)   *217*
short codes   *210*
short message service (SMS)   *193*
slate   *195*
smishing   *211*
SMS database strategy   *193*
Symbian OS   *196*
tablet or tablet computer   *195*
vishing   *211*

Chapter 7 LINK LIBRARY

You find clickable Link Libraries for each chapter on the Companion website.

The Future of M-Commerce—Did You Know 4.0   *youtube.com/watch?v=quO-sxqFYcE*

Starbucks Mobile Payment Live Demonstration   *youtube.com/watch?v=or6U0GeZ4j0*

Google Wallet Explained in a Nutshell (What is Google Wallet?)
   youtube.com/watch?v=iuvyN4iZiP8

ASSA ABLOY Mobile Keys Clarion Hotel Video   *youtube.com/watch?v=hNhleCZkpqI*

Shopkick for iPhone Review   *youtube.com/watch?v=jIU1yAquAHw*

Layar - Impactful Augmented Reality in Your Everyday Life
   youtube.com/watch?v=HW9gU_4AUCA

Evaluate and Expand Your Learning

Optimizing Web Sites for Mobile Viewing

The foundation of almost every mobile marketing strategy begins with a web site that is optimized for viewing from a mobile device (e.g., smartphone or tablet).

1. Using a mobile device (e.g., smartphone or tablet) visit your college website and make a list of areas where the site performs poorly when viewed on a mobile device. Look for missing or scrambled content, pages that are

too large for a mobile screen, loss of interactive functionality, etc.

2. Then go to Google's mobile website evaluation service at howtogomo.com/en/d/test-your-site/. Compare the list of shortcomings with those identified by the Google service.

3. Based on your own observations and those identified by the Howtogomo.com web site, prepare a list of recommendations for optimizing your institution's web site when viewed on a mobile device.

Additional Resources: In addition to the Google service identified above, you may also wish to utilize mobile web evaluation tools found at the following web sites:

- *ready.mobi/launch.jsp?locale=en_EN*
- *validator.w3.org/mobile/*
- *opera.com/developer/tools/mini/*
- *mobilemoxie.com/handset-emulators/ phone-emulator/*

Questions for Discussion & Review

1. Explain how mobile computing technology is being used by brick and mortar retailers to enhance the in-store shopping experience.
2. Describe some of the latest advances in mobile computing devices. What trends do you see in the development of this equipment? Speculate on how future devices might look or function.
3. Based on how other industries have developed over time, what do you predict will occur in the area of mobile device operating systems? (Hint: How does this market compare to the operating system market for personal computers?)
4. Describe some of the key developments in wireless network technology that have take place in the last few years.
5. How are people using mobile devices to conduct banking and other financial services?
6. Evaluate the various mobile electronic payment processes described in the chapter. Which ones do you think are likely to emerge as the dominate method for mobile payment? Explain your answer.
7. What are some of the risks faced by consumers who use mobile devices for banking and other financial transactions?
8. What are the key benefits of using a mobile wallet? Do you think new improvements to this mobile application will make it more attractive to end users?
9. How has mobile computing changed the retail shopping behavior of consumers?
10. Describe the mobile entertainment market and ways people can use their mobile devices to have fun.
11. Why is mobile social networking expected to grow dramatically in the next few years?
12. How is mobile computing creating an attractive opportunity for advertisers? Will consumers be receptive to this type of communication? Why or why not?
13. List some location-based services, and explain their value to mobile device users.
14. How are businesses, governments, and other organizations using mobile computing to enhance their productivity, efficiency and profitability?

Online Activities

1. Conduct research on the relative advantages/disadvantages of Apple's iOS vs. Android OS developed by Google and the Open Handset Alliance. Based on your research, predict which system will ultimately become the most popular with mobile device users.
2. Take a poll among your classmates and friends to see how many are using feature phones vs. smartphones. Briefly interview a handful of people in each group to identify their reasons for owning the kind of phone they do. Summarize your findings in a brief report.
3. Investigate how your college or university is using mobile computing technology (note: you make have to speak to several different people). Specific areas you should examine include admissions, instructional uses, operations, and information services. Conduct research to see how other campuses employ mobile technology. Prepare a brief report comparing your campus with others.
4. Prepare a brief report comparing Apple's iPad with various Android-based tablets (e.g., Asus Eee Pad, Samsung Galaxy Tab, Sony Tablet S). How do these products compare with the iPad? What are the strengths and weaknesses of each product?
5. Conduct research on the way telecommunications companies are charging for mobile access to the Internet. Identify providers that offer fixed or flat rate pricing vs. those that charge based on usage.
6. Visit ME, a news site for the mobile entertainment industry (*mobile-ent.biz/*). Select an entertainment category and study recent developments in that area. Prepare a report summarizing the current status and predictions of future development in the category.
7. Using *Youtube.com* or any other video-sharing site, watch examples of augmented reality handhelds and promotional campaigns. Write a brief report describing your reaction to this new technology, and predict if it will become more commonplace in the future.
8. If you have a smartphone and an appropriate mobile network access plan, download handhelds for *Pandora.com* and *Grooveshark.com*. Use these two services for a few days to listen to music. Prepare a presentation that compares the services, listing the strengths and weaknesses of each. (**Caution**—these services use a lot of bandwidth, so you should check with your cell phone carrier prior to using these handhelds to make sure you won't incur unexpected expenses on your phone bill)
9. If you have a smartphone, download the shopping app *Shopkick.com*. Use the app for a few weeks, and then prepare a report or presentation about your experience. Describe how Shopkick uses behavioral reinforcement to encourage specific kinds of shopping behaviors (e.g., store visits, looking for promotional products, participating in marketing surveys, etc.) Explain whether or not you think you will continue using application.
10. If you have a Facebook account, download the Facebook mobile handheld, and use it for approximately one week. Prepare a report describing how your mobile experience on the social networking site compares with your experience using a personal computer. Do you think you could use the

mobile handheld as your primary interface with Facebook? Why or why not?

Collaborative Work

1. Along with a group of students, sign up for an account at *foursquare.com*. Make connections with your group members on the service. Use Foursquare for a week or two, checking into the retail locations you visit. At the conclusion of this experience, meet with your group and compare reactions. Was it fun? Did the group gain valuable information from each other? Was the experience compelling enough that you'll want to maintain your account?

2. *Yelp.com* is a social networking directory service. It helps people find local business based on location, ratings, and recommendations from friends. With a group of students from your class, sign up for an account on Yelp, and download their mobile handheld. Connect with your classmates (and other friends) on

the Yelp service. Use Yelp for two weeks, and then prepare a presentation with your group on the advantages and disadvantages of this new service.

3. Have each member of your group contact their bank to identify what mobile banking services, if any, are offered. Create a table that lists the mobile banking services offered by each bank. Finally, have the team discuss how receptive they are to the idea of banking on their mobile devices. Identify the reasons why people want to engage in mobile banking and reasons why they are reluctant.

4. *Dropbox.com* and *box.net* are two cloud-based document-sharing services that make it easier for collaborative teams to share documents. Each service has a mobile app. Working in a small group of three to five people, experiment using each of these services and prepare a brief report on the strengths and weaknesses of each mobile document-sharing service.

Case 2

Chegg Takes Texbooks Mobile

Mobile technologies are considered a **disruptive innovation** because they have the capability of transforming traditional business practices, creating new value networks, and spawning new markets. Popular examples of disruptive innovation include Apple's iTunes service that replaced music CDs with downloadable digital mp3 files. Netflix and other movie streaming services disrupted the previous model of distributing movies on DVDs through brick-and-mortar retail outlets. Several companies are now exploring the use of mobile technologies as a disruptive innovation in the college textbook market.

End users (college students) have traditionally had very little power in the college textbook market. Textbook publishers promoted their products to college professors who decided what books to require for their courses. Competition at the retail level was almost nonexistent—students almost always had to purchase textbooks from a college book store or a used textbook from another student.

All that began to change, however, with the emergence of eCommerce. Nowadays, students have a range of options for purchasing new and used textbooks, renting textbooks, reading books online, or purchasing textbooks in an e-book format. Publishers and book sellers who once held fairly secure positions in the distribution channel now face competition from a variety of nonconventional sources including online retailers (e.g., Amazon), C2C eCommerce sites (e.g., Craigslist, eBay, half.com), and publishers who sell direct to students (e.g., Flatworld Knowledge).

Chegg.com

As part of this industry restructuring, Chegg.com began renting textbooks to students in 2007, creating an alternative to purchasing from college bookstores and online book sellers like Amazon.com. While renting textbooks was innovative approach at the time, Chegg managers realized that to remain competitive, they needed to position their company in a way that wasn't focused on a particular product form (e.g., printed textbook) or distribution method (e.g., retail bookstore). Instead, Chegg set out to create a learning network for students, offering a range of products and services through various channels that enhance students' educational experience (see Table 7.4).

Mobile technology has been a key component of Chegg's value strategy from the beginning. In 2009, just two years after entering the rental market, Chegg created a mobile web site and an SMS-based service that made it possible for students to check rental prices for textbooks by texting the ISBN number of the book they were interested in. The following year, Chegg launched an app for iPhone and iPad users. Android users can still access services from the company's well designed mobile site. In 2012, Chegg launched a cloud-based eTextbook reader designed to give students access to their textbooks from a wide range of mobile devices. While Chegg is not the first company to make textbooks available online, the eTextbook reader provides powerful features for highlighting text, taking notes, and checking word definitions. Users can view *Key Highlights*, or material crowd-sourced from the highlighting activities of other students using the reader. Finally, readers can access Chegg's *Always on Q&A Service*, where students can ask questions about various academic subjects and often receive an answer back from subject-matter experts within hours.

Despite Chegg's innovative and customer-oriented strategy, it faces an increasingly competitive marketplace. Well funded competitors like Amazon.com and Barnes & Noble now offer textbook rentals and e-textbooks with some of the same features as Chegg's reader. CourseSmart is another online vendor offering digital content from major publishers such as Pearson, Cengage, McGraw Hill, and Wiley & Sons (the publisher of this textbook). CourseSmart offers a number of mobile apps for various devices as well as the capability to read texts through mobile browsers (no app download necessary). Finally, Apple has announced their desire to transform the textbook market in much the same way they did the music business. However, the existing list of companies that are already practicing disruptive innovation may make it more difficult for Apple to have quite the same impact as they did in the music business.

Questions & Activities

1. Evaluate the mobile features of Chegg's textbook program. Do they offer services that are truly helpful to college students, or are they just a gimmick?

2. Go to Chegg.com to view a demo of its e-Textbook reader. After reviewing the service, evaluate if you think the reader will motivate students to obtain their textbooks from Chegg instead of using alternative textbook suppliers.

3. How does Chegg's mobile price comparison service provide benefit to college students? Do you think it helps to increase rentals and purchases from Chegg?

4. What other ways could Chegg use mobile technologies to provide further value to college students?

5. Using a mobile device, check the purchase and/or rental prices of the textbooks you are using this semester. Compare these with prices from alternative vendors (e.g., your college bookstore, Amazon.com, half.com, etc.). Prepare a table comparing your overall cost from each supplier. Based on your findings, do you plan to change the way you obtain textbooks in the future?

Sources: Chegg.com (2010), Conneally (2012), Wired Academic (2012), Crook (2009), Eldon (2012)

TABLE 7.4	The Chegg Learning Network
Purchase New/Used Textbooks (ch 1)	Online, Mobile app or Mobile Website
Renting Textbooks	Online, Mobile app, Mobile Website and College bookstores and rental stands at select colleges
Homework Help Q&A	Online and Mobile Website
eTextbooks	Cloud based Mobile Textbook Reader
Course Reviews, Grade Distributions and Schedule Planning Tools	Online and Mobile Website

Source: Chegg.com (2012).

CASE 3 VIDEO CASE

Future Tech: Searching with Pictures Using MVS

Earlier in the chapter, you read that U.S. consumers were not responding to QR code marketing with the same enthusiasm as Asian consumers. In response, some companies are experimenting with an alternative to QR codes called **mobile visual search (MVS)** technology. MVS is an image recognition technology that proponents claim will be more attractive to consumers.

With an MVS app, users scan pictures they find on product labels, catalogs, or advertisements. This initiates a search function that returns information to the user. Depending on the MVS app used, the search information might be general in nature, similar to what you get when conducting a search on Google. Or the app may return specific information, for instance, a page where the user can order the product.

Figure 7.21 Mobile Visual Search Using Google's Goggles app.

This technology has spawned a new industry of mobile visual search services that include companies like Snaptell (now owned by Amazon), Kooaba, PixlinQ, BuzzAR, TinEye, Pongr and, of course, Google.

To Do

1. Watch videos of three different MVS applications:

MVS Application / Developer	Video
Goggles—Google	*youtube.com/watch?v=bq-hXD33vXs*
Shopgate—PixlinQ	*youtube.com/watch?v=RpPt9wXwc9M*
Shortcut—Kooaba	*youtube.com/watch?v=abWmaNj2BAc*

2. Get the latest news and information about MVS by searching on the phrase "Mobile Visual Search" using Google or some other popular search engine.
3. Compare and contrast MVS with marketing strategies using QR codes.
4. If consumers begin to use MVS on a widescale basis, how should businesses adjust their marketing practices to take advantage of this technology?
5. Based on the videos and additional research, how do the MVS services of Goggles (Google), Shopgate (PixlinQ.com), and Shortcut (Koobaba) differ from one another?

Data Analysis & Decision Making

Notes: For this analysis, go to the Student Companion web site to download the Excel file.

Analysis Using Spreadsheets

Estimating Financial Benefits of Increased Customer Loyalty

Customer loyalty is a bond between a targeted customer and an organization where the customer consistently spends most or all of his or her budget on the supplier's goods or services. Loyal customers add value to a supplier's bottom line by one or more of the following:

- Generating new sales by referring other customers
- Paying a price premium
- Buying a broader mix of goods and services
- Reducing the company's selling and servicing costs

Enhancing loyalty in target customers can lead to sustainable and profitable sales growth. Chegg's mobile commerce strategy, as you read in the Business Case, is aimed at increasing customer loyalty.

You are tasked with completing the analysis using spreadsheet software. Create a spreadsheet with the data shown in Figure 7.22. Then use formulas or functions to calculate the blue-shaded cells. The results represent the NPV and ROI of the mobile commerce campaigns.

Estimating Financial Benefits of Increased Customer Loyalty

		Year 1	Year 2	Year 3	Total	Present Value (PV)
(a)	Benefit	$ 803,300	$ 722,970	$ 650,673		
(b)	Cost	317,060	301,207	286,147		
(a)–(b)	Net Cash Flow					
	Net Present Value (NPV)					
	ROI					

Figure 7.22 Spreadsheet for estimating financial benefits of increased customer loyalty.

Resources on the Book's Web Site

More resources and study tools are located on the Student Web Site. You'll find additional chapter materials and useful web links. In addition, self-quizzes that provide individualized feedback are available for each chapter.

References

ABI Research. "29 US Banks Receive Mobile Banking "Report Card.'" Press Release, ABI Research. September 2009. *abiresearch.com/press/1488-29+US+Banks+Receive+Mobile+Banking+%93Report+Card%94+From++ABI+Research.*

Asante, J. "Mobile Gaming Powers Up: '99 Cents Is the New Quarter.'" NPR.org, April 3, 2012. *npr.org/blogs/alltechconsidered/2012/04/03/149855680/mobile-gaming-powers-up-99-cents-is-the-new-quarter.*

Berg Insight. "Berg Insight predicts 894 million mobile banking users by 2015." Berginsight.com, April 2010. *berginsight.com/News.aspx?m_m=6&s_m=1.*

Canalys. "Smart phones overtake client PCs in 2011." Canalys Newsroom, February 3, 2012. *canalys.com/newsroom/smart-phones-overtake-client-pcs-2011.*

Capgemini. The Royal Bank of Scotland plc (RBS) and Efma. "World Payments Report," 2011. *capgemini.com/insights-and-resources/by-publication/world-payments-report-2011/.*

Chegg.com. "Chegg.com Introduces Two New Ways for College Students to Easily Rent Their Textbooks." PRNewswire, August 11, 2010. *prnewswire.com/news-releases/cheggcom-introduces-two-new-ways-for-college-students-to-easily-rent-their-textbooks-100428194.html.*

City of Denver, "Denver's Augmented Reality Public Art Tour." Accessed April 22, 2012. *denvergov.org/doca2/DenverOfficeofCulturalAffairs/PublicArt/PublicArtTours/AugmentedRealityTours/tabid/436942/Default.aspx.*

comScore, Inc. "Mobile Future in Focus," February, 2012. comscore.com/Press_Events/Presentations_Whitepapers/2012/2012_Mobile_Future_in_Focus.

Conneally, T. "Everything you need to know about e-textbooks before Apple gets involved." Betanews.com. January 17, 2012. *betanews.com/2012/01/17/everything-you-need-to-know-about-e-textbooks-before-apple-gets-involved/.*

Craig, K. "Best cities for free wifi." TechKnowTimes, November 29, 2010. *techknowtimes.com/computing/wireless-internet-computing/best-cities-for-free-wifi/.*

Crook, J. "Chegg adds mobile components to textbook rental service." Mobile Marketer, August 31, 2009. *mobilemarketer.com/cms/news/messaging/4059.html.*

Dotson, C. "How Mobile Games Leapt from Cult to Cultural Phenomenon." Mashable.com, January 20, 2012. *mashable.com/2012/01/30/mobile-gaming-market/.*

Eldon, E. "Chegg Launches Mobile Reader for Online Textbooks." Techcrunch.com, January 18, 2012. *techcrunch.com/2012/01/18/chegg-launches-mobile-reader-for-online-textbooks/.*

eMarketer. "Mobile Video Provides Biggest Growth for Ad Support" eMarketer Digital Intelligence, January 12, 2012. *emarketer.com/Article.aspx?id=1008777&R=1008777.*

Farago, P. "Is It Game Over for Nintendo DS and Sony PSP?" 2011. *blog.flurry.com/bid/77424/Is-it-Game-Over-for-Nintendo-DS-and-Sony-PSP.*

Gartner, Inc. "Gartner Says Sales of Mobile Devices Grew 5.6 Percent in Third Quarter of 2011: Smartphone Sales Increased 42 Percent." November 15, 2011. *gartner.com/it/page.jsp?id=1848514.*

Global Industry Analysts. "Global Mobile Banking Customer Base to Reach 1.1 Billion by 2015, According to New Report by Global Industry Analysts, Inc.," February 2010. *prWeb.com/releases/2010/02/prWeb3553494.htm.*

Google, IPSOS OTX MediaCT. "The Mobile Movement: Understanding Smartphone Users." April 2011. *thinkwithgoogle.com/insights/uploads/23600.pdf.*

Howard, N. "Is it safe to bank by cell phone?" *MSN Money,* July 2009. *articles.moneycentral.msn.com/Banking/FinancialPrivacy/is-it-safe-to-bank-by-cell-phone.aspx?page=2.*

International Telecommunication Union. "The World in 2011: ICT Facts and Figures," 2011. *itu.int/ITU-D/ict/facts/2011/material/ICTFactsFigures2011.pdf.*

Johnson, L. "Macy's, Aflac partner for holiday donation campaign." *Mobile Commerce Daily,* November, 29, 2011. *mobilecommercedaily.com/2011/11/29/macy%E2%80%99s-aflac-partner-for-holiday-donation-campaign.*

Kats, R. "Macy's mobile spend up 70pc: FirstLook keynote." *Mobile Marketer,* January 20, 2012. *mobilemarketer.com/cms/news/messaging/11933.html.*

Macy's "Macy's Backstage Pass." Press Release, February 2011. *macysinc.com/pressroom/macys/press.aspx?cid=5&mkid=589.*

McGee, B. "Mobile Banking Security—Phishing for Answers?" *Netbanker.com,* January 2008. *netbanker.com/2008/01/mobile_banking_security_phishi_2.html*

MobiAdNews.com. "IKEA Uses Mobile Augmented Reality To Engage Shoppers' Imagination," August 2009. *mobiadnews.com/?p=3829.*

Mobile Marketing Association. "Mobile Banking Overview (NA)," January 2009. *mmaglobal.com/mbankingoverview.pdf*

Mobile Marketing Association. "One in Five U.S. Adult Consumers Now Using Mobile Commerce," May, 2010. *mmaglobal.com/news/one-five-us-adult-consumers-now-using-mobile-commerce.*

MobiThinking. "Global mobile statistics 2012: All quality mobile marketing research, mobile web stats, subscribers, ad revenue, usage, trends," February 2012. *mobithinking.com/mobile-marketing-tools/latest-mobile-stats#subscribers.*

Moore, G. "Foursquare leads new mobile advertising model." Masshightech.com, April, 2010. *masshightech.com/stories/2010/04/26/daily10-Foursquare-leads-new-mobile-advertising-model.html.*

National Retail Federation. "Mobile Retailing Blueprint: A Comprehensive Guide for Navigating the Mobile Landscape," January 4, 2011. *nacs.org/LinkClick.aspx?fileticket=soszpbfz-n8%3D&tabid=1382&mid=3483.*

Nielsen. "Smartphones Account for Half of all Mobile Phones, Dominate New Phone Purchases in the US," March 2012. *blog.nielsen.com/nielsenwire/online_mobile/smartphones-account-for-half-of-all-mobile-phones-dominate-new-phone-purchases-in-the-us/.*

Nielsen. "Play Before Work: Games Most Popular Mobile App Category in US." NielsenWire, 2011. *blog.nielsen.com/nielsenwire/?p=28273*.

Tsirulnik, G. "Starbucks rolls out largest mobile payments effort nationwide." *Mobile Marketer,* March 31, 2010. *mobilemarketer.com/cms/news/commerce/5818.html*.

Tsirulnik G. "Macy's is 2011 Mobile Marketer of the Year." *Mobile Marketer*, December, 9 2011. *mobilemarketer.com/cms/resources/mobilegends-awards/11657.html*.

Whitfield, T. "Augmented Reality for Mobile Advertising." Econsultancy.com, February 2010. *econsultancy.com/blog/5397-augmented-reality-for-mobile-advertising/*.

Wired Academic. "Chegg Trots Out Its HTML5 E-Textbook Reader, Challenging Inkling, Cengage, Kno, et al.," January 28, 2012. *wiredacademic.com/2012/01/chegg-trots-out-its-html5-e-textbook-reader-challenging-inkling-cengage-kno-et-al/*.

Zimmerman, A. "Showdown Over 'Showrooming: Target Asks Vendors for Help Keeping Comparison Shoppers." *Wall Street Journal*, January 23, 2012. *online.wsj.com/article/SB10001424052970204624204577177242516227440.html*.

Learning Outcomes

1. Explain the interactive nature of Web 2.0 and its business applications.

2. Identify trends in virtual communities and social networks and assess their impact on business.

3. Describe how organizations use Web 2.0 apps to improve business functions.

4. Explain metrics used to evaluate the effectiveness of social media strategies and tactics.

5. Describe semantic technologies and tools that improving interactivity and interoperability of Web apps.

In his popular 2007 video, *Web 2.0. . . The Machine is Us/ing Us*, cultural anthologist Michael Wesch predicted that enhancements to the Internet, known as **Web 2.0**, would cause us to rethink a lot of our assumptions about things as diverse as ethics, privacy, governance, family, and even love. We would rethink our assumptions because the interactive nature of the Internet allows for social connections between individuals, organizations, governments and other entities that were not previously possible.

In this chapter, you learn about the technologies and capabilities of the social Internet. You examine how **online communities** are evolving into **social networks** and how businesses are responding to this new development. You read about ways that organizations are benefiting from **Enterprise 2.0** applications, using social technologies to run their businesses more effectively. Naturally, the magnitude of change occurring online has created some unease on the part of traditional-minded businesses and individual users.

We explore the use of **social media metrics** that help businesses determine the effectiveness of their communication strategies in this new environment. Finally, we take a quick glance at our crystal ball and speculate on what the future holds for the next evolution of the Internet.

CASE 1 OPENING CASE

Organizations WOW Customers with Social Customer Service

In 2008, a little-known musician by the name of Dave Carroll initiated a social media firestorm of bad publicity for United Airlines, Inc (UAL) after the company refused to pay for damaging his expensive Taylor guitar during a layover at Chicago's O'Hare Airport. After a frustrating year of negotiations with UAL, Carroll became convinced the company had created a system designed to simply wear customers down to avoid paying claims. As a result, he launched what would become a legendary social media attack on UAL's corporate stonewalling by producing three YouTube videos that went viral, attracting millions of viewers and generating countless news stories, blog posts, and even a Harvard Business School (2010) business case. Read the full story and watch the videos at: *davecarrollmusic.com/music/ubg/*.

While Carroll ultimately embarrassed the company into settling his claim, it's clear that UAL continues to struggle, not only with its customer satisfaction levels, but also its ability to manage the airline's online reputation effectively. That's not the case, however, at several other large companies that are increasingly learning to use social media to engage customers, correct problems, and enhance their brand image through social customer service.

Turning Complaints into Happy Customers

While business organizations were initially interested in social media because of its potential for branding and public relations, many organizations have begun to realize its potential for customer service and product support functions. In fact, a recent study by Forrester Research and Cisco (2010) shows that customer service activities are the second-most-common application of social technologies by business organizations (marketing was first.) Even excellent companies sometimes make mistakes or fail to completely satisfy customers. Because the cost of retaining a customer is often less than the cost of acquiring a new customer, many organizations invest in customer service operations to assist customers when problems occur. Traditional customer service channels consist of phone (call centers), mail, and in-store support. Today, customers may also use e-mail, and a wide range of social channels including Facebook, Twitter, and YouTube. Furthermore, customers might not complain directly to the company on its official Facebook or Twitter pages. Companies need to be able to identify unhappy customers that share negative comments outside of "official" channels. Traditional wisdom suggests that when consumers have a negative experience with a company, they share it with as many as 10 people. But now, unhappy customers can potentially share their experience with hundreds of people using a single message on social media. Or, as David Carroll learned, the message might reach tens of millions.

Figure 8.1 Zappos CEO Tony Hsieh and Jenn Lim have worked hard to create a culture of happiness across the company, including the customer service team.

The WOW factor at Zappos

At online shoe retailer, Zappos, customer service through all channels is designed to "WOW" customers. A 10-person team of social customer service agents is trained and empowered to go the extra mile for customers who contact them through their official Twitter channel, @zappos_service. Agents have even gone as far as helping customers find the shoes they want at a competing retailer. Zappos agents strive to personalize their service by talking to customers in a normal "voice," sharing their names, and taking whatever time is necessary to address customer concerns. The company does not use scripted responses or policy documents restricting what agents can or cannot say to customers on the company's Twitter customer service channel. The only objective is to WOW the customer. This helps customers to feel as though they are dealing with a real person who cares about their needs. The absence of scripted guidelines for assisting customers does not mean Zappos takes customer service lightly. After a lengthy and careful screening process, prospective Zappos Agents receive weeks of training and become immersed in its customer-focused culture during their initial stages of employment. Once agents pass the training program, they are actually offered money to quit the company! This is done to insure that only those agents who truly want to excel at Zappos remain with the company. This approach to customer service is one that extends throughout the company, and reflects Zappos corporate culture of happiness (see Figure 8.1). As a result, Zappos has earned one of the best reputations for its ability to please its customers, even when mistakes happen.

Comcast Makes a Turnaround with Social Media

Like UAL, cable giant Comcast was once the target of many social media public relations disasters. YouTube videos of service technicians falling asleep while on hold with their own customer service call center were embarrassing for the company. Now, Comcast is considered a pioneer in the area of using social technologies for customer service. Under the leadership of Frank Eliason (now Senior VP of Social Media at Citibank), Comcast was one of the first corporations to recognize the potential of using Twitter for customer service. Twitter allowed the company to respond more quickly to customer complaints than had been possible with traditional channels. In fact, because of the public nature of Twitter messages, Eliason and his team were able to identify upset customers even when they weren't directly communicating with the company. By monitoring Twitter for all messages that mentioned Comcast, agents are able to offer assistance to sometimes surprised customers who don't realize the company is interested in helping them solve their problems. Despite Comcast's innovations in social customer service, a quick scan of the Internet will produce evidence that lots of people still get frustrated with Comcast's inability to deliver cable and Internet service that meets their expectations. But by using social tools to engage customers on the major social platforms, Comcast has made great strides in helping customers solve problems when they arise.

Figure 8.2 Cisco Systems is the world's largest manufacturer of computer networking equipment and the developer of social customer service software, SocialMiner.

Cisco Systems Creates Social Tools for Customer Service

Cisco Systems, Inc. is an American multinational corporation and a market leader in the design and manufacture of computer networking equipment (see Figure 8.2). Cisco not only uses social channels for customer service, but they've leveraged their expertise in networking and software development to create applications that other companies can use to provide multiple channel support services to customers. Cisco has developed a social customer service app called SocialMiner. This app makes it possible for companies to take a proactive approach to social customer service, monitoring conversations on Twitter, Facebook, blogs, and other social media platforms. SocialMiner helps service agents identify and resolve issues as they emerge across different social media platforms. The app also stores conversations in a database for later analysis, allowing companies to identify systematic problems and take corrective action to prevent problems from happening in the first place.

Sources: Compiled from March (2011), Reisner (2009), Forrester Consulting (2011), and *Davecarrollmusic. com* (2012).

Discuss

1. How does social media represent a threat to companies who limit their support services to traditional channels?

2. When customers have a negative experience with a company, what are the various ways they can use social media to tell others about their experience?

3. Explain why companies can no longer afford to limit their customer service channels to traditional channels (e.g., call centers).

4. What are some of the frustrations customers encounter when seeking customer service support from a company?

5. What are the benefits for companies that offer customer service support through social channels like Twitter and Facebook?

Decide

6. Watch a video demonstration of Cisco's social customer service application: *youtube.com/ watch?v=aRFkNmqep5Y*. What advantages does this approach seem to offer over and above simply monitoring social media sites like Facebook and Twitter directly?

Debate

7. Search YouTube and Twitter for customer complaints about Comcast. Some are straight-forward complaints about service while others can perhaps be described as angry rants, containing profanity, threats, and highly emotional tirades. Debate: Should companies attempt to respond to all types of negative sentiment expressed on social platforms? If no, what should the criteria be for deciding when and when not to respond? If yes, how should companies respond to these highly emotional expressions of customer angst?

8.1 Web 2.0 and Social Media

In your lifetime, there have been dramatic changes in the way people use the Internet. In the early 1990s, many people did not have regular access to the Internet, and those who did typically "dialed up" their network from a home or office telephone. Dial-up access meant long waits as content from web pages "downloaded" onto the screen from slow servers. Some users joked that the letters "www" in a web address stood for "world wide wait." E-mail was the primary mechanism for social interaction. Online communities were often like public bulletin boards where all members of the community could read the messages that others posted. Web sites were static—essentially online billboards for the businesses that created them. Online purchasing (e-commerce) was rare and risky because there were few safeguards protecting your credit card information. But all that has changed.

NEW MODELS DRIVEN BY WEB 2.0

Today, most of us access the Internet using wired or wireless broadband technology, chewing up bandwidth that was unheard of a few years ago. We expect to be able to stream audio and video files, and watch feature-length films over wireless connections and mobile devices. We surf web pages that constantly change their appearance in response to how we interact with them. While e-mail and phone calls are still common forms of communication in business, young people tend to view them with disdain in favor of tweets, texts, or social networking sites like Facebook. We keep track of our world, interests, and hobbies by reading blogs and online newspapers, and sharing them with friends and family by postings on profile pages (see Figure 8.3).

Some people write their own blogs, post videos on YouTube, or share pictures using sites like Flickr or Photobucket. E-commerce continues to grow and evolve, for instance, buying books from Amazon, selling on eBay, downloading music and videos from iTunes, booking travel arrangements on *Travelocity.com*, and buying concert tickets from Ticketmaster.

The transformation has happened so smoothly that we frequently don't recognize many of the implications for businesses, agencies, and individuals. As Michael Wesch notes, we may need to rethink a lot of things.

Figure 8.3 Web 2.0 is also referred to as the Social Web.

BROADCAST VS. CONVERSATION MODELS

Internet interactivity allows for robust social connections between individuals, organizations, governments, and other entities. Organizations previously communicated with their audiences using a **broadcast model,** where messages flowed from the sender to the receiver. Now, organizations must learn to use a **conversation model,** where communication flows back and forth between sender and receiver. The conversation model is becoming the dominant model for communications due to two factors. First, advances in social technologies increasingly offer Internet users new and varied ways to publish their own content online. Second, Internet users are becoming less accepting of organizations and governments that only rely on traditional communication strategies. To survive in today's networked world, organizations of all types must learn to engage people using interactive communications.

In the next section, you will read about the technological aspects of Web 2.0. It's important to recall that while IT provides the platform for this phenomenon, the changing behavior of users represents the biggest challenge and opportunity for businesses today.

Because of Web 2.0, people have different attitudes about how they want businesses to interact with them. They have higher expectations for a company's character, ethical behavior, responsiveness, and ability to meet their individual needs. Customers expect businesses to use Web 2.0 capabilities to satisfy their needs. Not responding is a risk.

Web 2.0 also represents opportunities for those who understand and master the new way of doing things. Managers who invest the time to understand and become proficient in new approaches to identifying, communicating, and building relationships with customers online will have a tremendous advantage over managers who limit themselves to traditional methods.

WHAT IS WEB 2.0?

Experts don't always agree on a definitive definition for Web 2.0. Many writers have identified characteristics that differentiate the new web from what is called Web 1.0 (see Table 8.1). Others maintain that the term *Web 2.0* is simply an inevitable, incremental advance from earlier capabilities. In a 2006 interview, Tim Berners-Lee, originator of the World Wide Web, suggests the term *Web 2.0* is simply ". . . a piece of jargon, nobody even knows what it means." Berners-Lee maintains that the Internet has been about connecting people in an interactive space from the beginning.

While the applications that are labeled as Web 2.0 may simply be an extension of earlier advances, it is the change in user behavior that matters most to businesses around the world. The new technologies dramatically increase the ability of people to interact with businesses and each other, to share and find information, and form relationships. This perspective explains why Web 2.0 is often called the **Social Web**.

TABLE 8.1	Web 1.0 versus Web 2.0	
Web 1.0	**Web 2.0: The Social Web**
Static pages, HTML	Dynamic pages, XML, and Java
Author-controlled content	User-controlled content
Computers	Computers, cell phones, televisions, PDAs, game systems, car dashboards
Users view content	Users create content
Individual users	User communities
Marketing goal: *influence*	Marketing goal: *relationships*
Data: single source	Data: multiple sources, e.g., mashups

WEB 2.0 APPLICATIONS

Each of the following technologies and tools describes a valuable capability commonly associated with Web 2.0:

Blogs. **Blog** is short for *web log* and is a web site where users regularly post information for others to read and comment. Blog authors, or **bloggers**, use this approach to share opinions, commentary, news, technical advice, personal stories, and so on, as shown in Figure 8.4. Blogs are relatively easy to create and are used by individuals and businesses as a way of communicating. Wordpress, Typepad, and Blogger offer easy-to-use software. Because it is a common practice for bloggers to use a special kind of hyperlink called a **trackback** to reference other blogs in their writing, blogs are collectively referred to as the **blogosphere**. In a sense, bloggers and their followers form an online social network.

Blogs are a key tool for **content marketing**, where valuable information is shared with current or prospective customers. Bloggers can establish a lot of credibility for themselves and their organizations by providing helpful information to people who are part of their target market. Politicians practice a similar strategy when they use blogs to communicate with their constituencies. Chief executives and other managers use blogs targeted to their employees to motivate, inspire, and provide information about company goals.

Wikis. A **wiki** is a web site that allows many people to add or update information found on the site. Wikis are a collaborative work that benefits from the efforts of many participants. Wikipedia is an online encyclopedia that is the most popular general reference work on the Internet (Alexa, 2012). Businesses create wikis for a particular product and allow employees and customers to contribute information that will form a knowledge base resource for those who need information about the product.

Social Networking Service. A **social networking service** is a web site where individuals, who are defined by a *profile*, can interact with others. This interaction can take the form of posting messages, sharing photographs or videos, sharing links to online material, instant messaging, and so on. Social networking sites are different from the broader category of *online communities* in that they usually allow individuals to control who can access information they post to the site. For instance, on Facebook, people "friend" one another to gain access to information. An individual's social network consists of all the friends they've acknowledged or *friended* on the site. LinkedIn uses a similar feature, allowing users to add *contacts*, and to approve or deny requests to establish a connection with others.

Sharing Sites. Some sites are dedicated to sharing of various kinds of media including video, audio, and pictures. YouTube, shown in Figure 8.5, is the best known web site

Figure 8.4 WordPress is one of the leading platforms for online blogs.

Figure 8.5 YouTube, a video-sharing site, is the third-most-popular site on the Internet.

for sharing video files. Some sites allow users to load **podcasts**, or audio/video files that people download onto devices like computers and MP3 players. Picture-sharing sites like Flickr and Photobucket have expanded beyond simple photo sharing and now include video capabilities, organization and editing tools, and let people sell photos or order products with their photo images (e.g., calendars, coffee mugs, and T-shirts).

Widgets and Mashups. **Widgets** are standalone programs that can be embedded into web pages, blogs, profiles on social networking sites, and even computer desktops. Common widgets include clocks, visitor counters, weather reporters, and chat boxes. Businesses frequently sponsor the development and distribution of widgets as a way of promoting themselves. For instance, *ESPN.com* offers users a number of widgets that can receive and display sports information such as scores, and news and broadcast schedules. See *IT at Work 8.1: The Value of Mashups* for more details.

RSS (Really Simple Syndication). RSS feeds allow users to aggregate regularly changing data—such as blog entries, news stories, audio, and video—into a single place called a news aggregator or **RSS reader**. RSS pushes content to users so they avoid the hassle of having to visit several different sites to get the information they

IT at Work 8.1

The Value of Mashups

The term **mashup** refers to an application or web page that pulls information from multiple sources, creating a new functionality. For instance, assume that you find a web page with a listing of popular restaurants in your community. By placing the cursor over a particular restaurant's name, a small window opens with a map showing the location of the restaurant as well as summary review information from people who have eaten there before. When you move the cursor away from the restaurant name, the window disappears.

Mashups allow developers to create uses for data that may not have been envisioned by the individuals or organizations that originally created it. So why do companies like Google, Facebook, Twitter, and others make their data and web content available to others? The answer is that companies have found that sharing data leads to increased business, brand recognition, and favorable brand image. For instance, when Google allows mashup developers to

use its mapping data, it increases Google's digital footprint on the Internet, increasing the number of people on a daily basis who will see Google's brand name and have a positive experience with its products and services.

Questions

1. To better understand mashup applications, visit the Tall Eye web site at map.talleye.com/index.php. At that site, use a mashup application to answer such questions as "If I dig a hole all the way through the earth, where will I come out?" and "If I walk a straight line all the way around the globe, what places will I pass through?"

2. In the example above, a mashup was described that used Google Maps data to create a restaurant directory. Can you think of other ways developers could use Google Maps data to create helpful mashups?

Figure 8.6 Users can subscribe to online content using RSS technology.

are interested in. See Figure 8.6. Popular RSS readers include GoogleReader, Feedly and Reeder (for Mac/iOS). RSS enables content management, enabling users to filter and display information in ways they find most helpful. RSS readers are a special kind of mashup application.

Social Bookmarking and Tag Clouds. People have traditionally kept track of sites they wanted to remember by using the bookmark feature or favorites list on their browser. These methods allowed users to store and organize web site addresses in folders they had created. However, as lists become long, this folder system becomes unwieldy and disorganized. Using self-defined **tags**, such as "business partners," "travel," and "IT vendors," users can classify sites, allowing them to be searched using those tags. Online content posted at sites like Flickr and YouTube can also be tagged, which helps other users find that content. *Delicious.com* is perhaps the most popular social bookmarking site, but a newer service, *Diigo.com*, offers a number of attractive social features including the ability for users to form collaborative groups or communities around link sharing and the ability to highlight text on web pages and comment on links.

Social bookmarking sites can serve as alternative search engines. Because links on Delicious and Diigo are tagged by humans instead of computer algorithms, these sites can sometimes yield useful information different from the search results of traditional search engines like Google and Yahoo.

Cloud tags are graphic representations of all the tags that people have attached to a particular page. Figure 8.7 shows three examples of cloud tags. The varying font sizes of tags in a cloud represent the frequency of tags at the site.

Feature Convergence in Social Media Apps. However, YouTube is also a form of social networking site; users interact with one another by leaving comments about videos, post video responses, create and share video playlists, and even create *channels* for their video content.

Sharing sites: Like YouTube, they contain elements of social networking by allowing users to interact and comment on things that are posted to the site.

While *Delicious.com* is positioned as a social bookmarking site, it also maintains a wiki and a blog and uses RSS feeds. This shows that many popular web sites can't be easily categorized by a single technology.

Nowadays, few social media services fit neatly into the categories described above because of **feature convergence.** For instance, Facebook started as a social networking service, but now offers many other features. It is a sharing site used by many to distribute photos. It is increasingly common for people to tag or label photos with the names of people in the picture, making it easy to find and display photos of individuals that have been saved in multiple locations on Facebook. Users can maintain

(a)

(b)

(c)

© Equinox Imagery/Alamy Limited

Figure 8.7 Examples of tag clouds. (a) Tag clouds illustrate the content and frequency of specific words on a webpage, (b) Tag cloud illustration of financial budgeting terms, (c) Tag cloud illustration of supply chain management terms.

blogs on their Facebook page, and Facebook hosts thousands of apps that pull data from sources outside of the social network, making it a huge mashup app.

Twitter was initially positioned as a micro-blogging service, but is now commonly described as a social network. Third-party developers have created a host of apps that add features and functionality to the user's experience. Members of this community share photos and links, and participate in discussion forums using Twitter.

Likewise, YouTube started as a sharing site, making it easy for people to share video clips with others. However, YouTube now contains many features that make it difficult to distinguish from a social networking service. The same is true of Flickr, a photo-sharing site that has really become a community platform for people interested in photography.

Every day, new social media apps spring up that mix and blend different Web 2.0 features and technologies to create apps that meet the needs of different market segments.

AJAX Technologies. AJAX, or **Asynchronous JavaScript and XML,** refers to a group of technologies that create web pages that respond to users' actions without requiring the entire page to reload. AJAX languages are JavaScript, XML, HTML, and CSS, which are defined in Table 8.2. AJAX makes it possible for web developers to create small apps that run on a page instead of running on a server. This capability makes content

TABLE 8.2	AJAX Languages for Web 2.0
Programming Language	**Description**
HTML (Hyper Text Markup Language) *Page Structure*	The predominant language for web pages. It provides a means to create structured documents by denoting structural semantics for text such as headings, paragraphs, lists, etc., as well as for links, quotes, and other items.
XML (Extendable Markup Language) *Page Content*	A set of rules and guidelines for describing data that can be used by other programming languages. It is what makes it possible for data (information) to be shared across the web.
CSS (Cascading Style Sheets) *Page Appearance*	A style sheet language used to enhance the appearance of web pages written in a markup language.
Javascript *Page Behavior/ Functionality*	An object-oriented language used to create apps and functionality on web sites. Some examples of JavaScript applications include popup windows, validation of web form inputs, and images that change when a cursor passes over them.

run much faster and increases the functionality of web sites. Why? Because without AJAX, every time you clicked a hyperlink, you would need to wait for a page to load. AJAX apps run faster because it doesn't involved waiting for an entire page to load in a browser

Social Media. Collectively, these Web 2.0 applications are commonly referred to as **social media** because they have moved the locus of control for mass communications from large organizations to individual users. In other words, people as well as organizations control both the message and the medium. Organizations and individual users can easily share their thoughts, opinions, and experiences interactively with each other. Instead of a large organization broadcasting a single message to a mass audience, a massive number of conversations are taking place across the Internet.

Nobody has complete control over the message or the medium, yet anyone can contribute to the conversation. The challenge for organizations today is to develop social strategies for taking part in these conversations. A new mindset is required. Businesses that used to spend most of their time developing sophisticated ways of getting their message heard must now develop sophisticated strategies for listening and responding to what their consumers are saying.

WEB 2.0 ATTITUDE

As you have read, the availability of Web 2.0 applications is changing not only how people behave, but also the way they think about things. This new way of thinking is captured in a provocative list of 95 statements called the Cluetrain Manifesto (*cluetrain.com*). Perhaps the fundamental principle of the Manifesto is described by its first thesis: *Markets are conversations*. Other excerpts from the Manifesto are listed in Table 8.3. Over time, successful companies will learn to engage customers in conversations as an alternative to the unidirectional or broadcast method of communication. While the Cluetrain Manifesto seemed idealistic, impractical, and revolutionary when it was first written in 2000, we are starting to see more examples of companies finding ways of turning those principles into action.

Most companies still struggle with the concept of *conversation*. Forrester researchers Charlene Li and Josh Bernoff (2008) describe a number of companies who recognize the power of what they call the **groundswell**, "... a spontaneous movement of people using online tools to connect, take charge of their own experience and get what they need—information, support, ideas, products, and bargaining power—from each other."

TABLE 8.3 | **Excerpts from the Cluetrain Manifesto**

Select Cluetrain Theses

- Markets are conversations.
- Markets consist of human beings, not demographic sectors.
- These networked conversations are enabling powerful new forms of social organization and knowledge exchange to emerge.
- As a result, markets are getting smarter, more informed, more organized. Participation in a networked market changes people fundamentally.
- People in networked markets have figured out that they get far better information and support from one another than from vendors. So much for corporate rhetoric about adding value to commoditized products.
- Corporations do not speak in the same voice as these new networked conversations. To their intended online audiences, companies sound hollow, flat, and inhuman.
- Companies need to realize their markets are often laughing. At them.
- Most marketing programs are based on the fear that the market might see what's really going on inside the company.
- Networked markets can change suppliers overnight. Networked knowledge workers can change employers over lunch. Your own "downsizing initiatives" taught us to ask the question: "Loyalty? What's that?"

Source: The Cluetrain Manifesto (2000). *cluetrain.com.*

Businesses are learning to participate in the groundswell by using Web 2.0 tools to implement **integrated social media (ISM)** strategies. Organizations that fail to participate effectively in the groundswell risk becoming irrelevant.

Because of the relatively low cost and ease of use, social media is a powerful democratization force; the network structure enables communication and collaboration on a massive scale. Figure 8.8 shows the emergence and rise of mass social media. The figure compares traditional and social media and illustrates the new tools

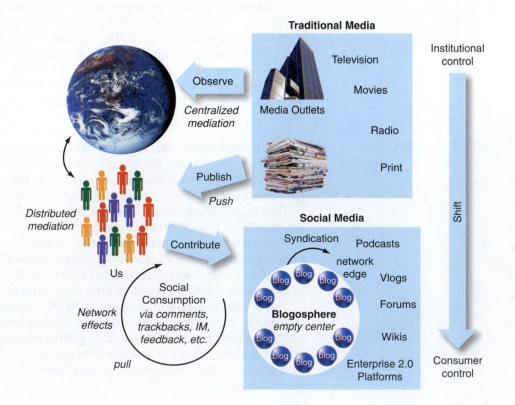

Figure 8.8 The emergence and rise of mass social media.

of social media, such as blogs and video blogs (vlogs), as being in the consumer's control. Social media content is produced and consumed by people whereas traditional media content is typically produced by organizations and pushed to or observed by people who are passive viewers.

Notice that traditional media content goes from the technology to the people, whereas in social media, people create and control the content.

Review Questions

1. How has Web 2.0 changed the behavior of Internet users?
2. What are the basic tools or applications that characterize Web 2.0?
3. Why is Web 2.0 referred to as the Social Web?
4. What are some of the benefits or advantages that web developers gain from using AJAX technologies?
5. What are some of the most important messages for business organizations in the Cluetrain Manifesto?
6. What is feature convergence? Give some examples of this trend with regard to social media apps.

8.2 Virtual Communities and Social Networking Services

Online or virtual communities parallel typical physical communities, such as neighborhoods, clubs, and associations, except that they are not bound by political or geographic boundaries. These communities offer several ways for members to interact, collaborate, and trade. Virtual or online communities have been around for a long time and predate the World Wide Web. The **Usenet** (*usenet.com*) provided the initial platform for online communities by making it possible for users to exchange messages on various topics in public **newsgroups**, which are similar in many ways to online bulletin board systems. While the Usenet is technically not part of the Internet, much of the content can be accessed from Internet sites like Goggle Groups.

Online communities can take a number of forms. For instance, some people view the blogosphere as a community. YouTube is a community of people who post, view, and comment on videos. Epinions (*epinions.com*) is a community of people who share their experiences and opinions about products and companies. Flickr, Photobucket, Webshots, and similar sites are photo-sharing communities. Wikipedia is a community of people who create, edit, and maintain an online knowledge base. Twitter is a community, or perhaps several communities, of people who frequently share short, 140-character messages with one another about a variety of topics. Obviously, social networking sites like Facebook and LinkedIn are communities and have seen tremendous growth in recent years. The mass adoption of social networking web sites points to an evolution in human social interaction (Weaver and Morrison, 2008).

Social network analysis (SNA) is the mapping and measuring of relationships and flows between people, groups, organizations, computers, or other information or knowledge-processing entities. The nodes in the network are the people and groups, whereas the links show relationships or flows between the nodes. SNA provides both a visual and a mathematical analysis of relationships. In its corporate communications, Facebook has begun using the term **social graph** to refer to the global social network reflecting how we are all connected to one another through relationships, as shown in Figure 8.9. Facebook users can access a social graph application that visually represents the connections among all the people they have in their network. Berners-Lee (2007) extended this concept even further when he coined the term **giant global graph**. This concept is intended to illustrate the connections between people and/or documents and pages online. Connecting all points on the Giant Global

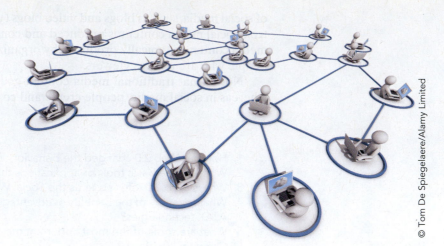

© Tom De Spiegelaere/Alamy Limited

Figure 8.9 A social graph uses nodes and ties to illustrate relationships between individuals and groups of people.

Graph is the ultimate objective goal for creators of the **semantic web**, which you read in section 8.5.

Online communities have received increasing attention from the business community. Online communities can be used as a platform for:

- Selling goods and services
- Promoting products to prospective customers; e.g., advertising.
- Prospecting for customers
- Building relationships with customers and prospective customers
- Identifying customer perceptions by "listening" to conversations
- Soliciting ideas for new products and services from customers
- Providing support services to customers by answering questions, providing information, etc.
- Encouraging customers to share their positive perceptions with others; e.g., word of mouth
- Gathering information about competitors and marketplace perceptions of competitors
- Identifying and interacting with prospective suppliers, partners and collaborators

See Enterprise 2.0 in the next section.

In recent years, several companies have created online communities for the purpose of identifying market opportunities through crowdsourcing. **Crowdsourcing** is a model of problem solving and idea generation that marshals the collective talents of a large group of people. Using Web 2.0 tools, companies solicit, refine, and evaluate ideas for new products and services based on input from their customers. Business organizations that have implemented this approach include Fiat, Sara Lee, BMW, Kraft, Procter & Gamble, and Starbucks. See Openinnovators.net for a list other examples.

SOCIAL NETWORKING SERVICES (SNS)

Social networking services represent a special type of virtual community and are now the dominant form of online community. With social networking, individual users maintain an identity through their profile and can be selective about which members of the larger community they choose to interact with. Over time, users build their network by adding contacts or friends. On some social network platforms, organizations create an identity by establishing discussion forums, group pages, or some other presence. Social networking has increased substantially in recent years. The Nielsen Company (2010) reported that users spent an average of over six hours on social networking sites in March 2010, more than a 100 percent increase over the previous year. Figure 8.10 shows the growth rate of time spent on social networking sites.

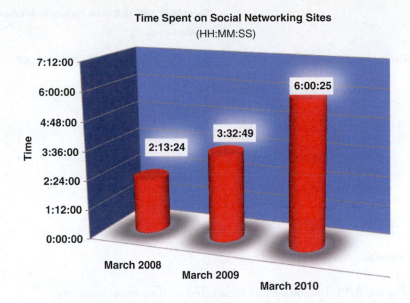

Time Spent on Social Networking Sites
(HH:MM:SS)

Figure 8.10 Increase in time spent on social networking services, March 2008–2010. © Nielsen, 2010.

The number of social networking services has grown tremendously in recent years. It is expected that it will segment and consolidate in the future just like other industries. Among the general purpose SNS platforms, Facebook is the clear leader with over 908 million active users (as of August, 2012). Facebook is the second-most-visited site on the Internet after Google according to *Alexa.com* (2012) and they have publically said they want to be number one (Vogelstein, 2009; Harvey, 2010). Many have observed that if Facebook were a country, it would the third-largest in the world behind India and China. Other large social network services are listed in Table 8.4. For an up-to-date list of popular social networking sites around the world, see *en.wikipedia.org/wiki/List_of_social_networking_sites*.

Comparisons of leading SNSs are shown in Figure 8.11. Note that two relatively new sites, *tumblr.com* and *Pinterest.com*, are small in comparison to other sites, but have high engagement rates as evidenced by the average amount of time users spend using these apps.

While SNS sites share some common features, they are not all alike. As the category matures, sites are differentiating themselves in a variety of ways. For instance, the SNS services in Wikipedia's list differ in terms of:

- Target age group
- Geographic location of users

TABLE 8.4	Large Social Network Services	
Name	**Focus or Market Position**	**Size**
Qzone	Caters to users in mainland China	480 million users
Habbo	Caters to teens in 31 countries.	268 million users
Renren	Considered the "Facebook of China." Caters to college-age users.	160 million users
LinkedIn	Professional networking site	160 million users
Badoo	Social discovery site for meeting new people. Popular in Europe and Latin America	154 million users
Orkut	Popular in Brazil and India	100 million users
Google+	Relatively new, but fast-growing site developed by search engine giant Google.	250 million users

Figure 8.11 Unique visitors to selected leading social networks.

- Language
- Interest area; e.g., music, photography, gaming, travel
- Social vs. professional networking
- Interface; e.g., profile page, micro blog, virtual world, emphasis on graphic vs. text content

Facebook Dominates Social Networking. Facebook is the largest social networking service the world, with more than 901 million monthly and 526 million daily active users. Facebook was launched in 2004 by a former Harvard student, Mark Zuckerberg. Photos, groups, events, marketplace, posted items, and notes are the basic applications already installed in Facebook. Apart from these basic applications, users can develop their own apps or add any of the millions of Facebook apps that have been developed by other users. Facebook was responsible for originating a unique feature called Newsfeed. This app featured a constantly updated stream of status updates from a user's friends. In late 2011, Facebook introduced another major revision to its site called Timeline. The Timeline app is designed to show the chronological progression of key events in people's lives as illustrated by their Facebook status updates, photos, songs they've listen to, bad hair cuts, as well as changes in occupations, locations, relationships, and so on. Facebook says they want to make it easier for people to tell their life story by curating all the content they've shared on the social networking service. Many users, however, were surprised by the radical interface change and are uncomfortable with how easy it became for others to access old, long-forgotten posts and status updates. According to many news reports, the new app has encouraged many to tighten their privacy settings even further to limit the content that is shared with others.

When Zuckerberg created Facebook, he had very strong social ambitions aimed at helping people connect to others on the web. Facebook was initially an online social space for college and high school students. It started by connecting students to all others at the same school. In 2006, Facebook expanded to anyone 13 years or older with a valid e-mail address. The lack of privacy controls (e.g., tools that restrict who sees your profile) was among the biggest reasons why many business people resisted joining Facebook.

In 2008, Facebook introduced new controls that allow users to set different levels of access to information about themselves for each of their groups; for instance, family, friends from school, friends from work, and so on. For example, close friends might see your mobile phone number, music favorites, e-mail address, and so forth, while other friends might see only the basics of your resume (Abram and Pearlman, 2008). Facebook is regularly criticized for its approach to user privacy, highlighting an ongoing tension between the corporate goals of Facebook, which depends on a high level of access to user data, and the desire of individual users to control access to their personal information.

Facebook has expanded to the rest of the world with the help of its foreign language members: Engineers first collected thousands of English words and phrases throughout the site and invited members to translate those bits of text into another language. Members then rate translations until a consensus is reached. The Spanish version was done by about 1,500 volunteers in less than a month. The German version was done by 2,000 volunteers in less than two weeks. In early March 2008, Facebook invited French members to help out. They did the translations in a few days. Facebook exists in over 70 different languages and approximately 70 percent of their members are outside of the U.S. (Facebook, 2010).

In May 2012, Facebook went public with an Initial Public Offering (IPO), selling company shares on the NASDAQ stock exchange. It raised over $16 billion, making it the third-largest IPO in U.S. history. While founder Mark Zuckerberg sold some 30 million shares during the offering (for $1.15 billion), he continues to own approximately 22 percent of the company, but has power over 57 percent of the voting stock, effectively giving him control of the company.

The Open Graph Initiative: A primary reason that Facebook expands is the network effect: more users mean more value. In April 2010, Zuckerberg announced Facebook's new initiative called **Open Graph**. The goal was to connect all the different relationships that exist on the Internet by linking web sites to Facebook. Programmers at external web sites were encouraged to include a Facebook "Like" button on their web sites. That way, when Facebook members visit the web site, they can click the Like button, and their relationship with that web site will be reflected back on their Facebook page for friends to see.

Facebook also encourages other web sites to allow people to use their Facebook user name and password to sign in or create accounts. For instance, if you are a Facebook member and you visit *Pandora.com* (a music service) or *Yelp.com* (a local directory service), you can sign into the sites using your Facebook username and password. Facebook will then share your profile information with those sites. This new initiative is exciting for its potential to enhance the social richness and ease of use of the Internet. On the other hand, this is just one more example of how Facebook creates concerns about how it shares users' information with others.

Figure 8.12 Facebook and other social sites are accessed mostly via mobile devices.

© incamerastock/Alamy Limited

Google Takes on Facebook With G+. Launched in June, 2011, Google+, or G+ as some like to call it, is the latest entrant to the SNS market, and some believe it is capable of becoming a formidable competitor to Facebook. By March 2012, Google+ had over 100 million users.

Like Facebook, Google+ offers building and sharing features, as you read in the Google+ case at the end of this chapter.

It's clear that Mark Zuckerberg is not taking Google+ lightly. Facebook continues to launch new features and apps they hope will help maintain its dominant status. Search "Google+ vs. Facebook" for current news and information.

And Now, for Something Different: Second Life. Second Life is a social network service unlike most others. What makes it unique is that it uses a 3D virtual world interface in which users, called *Residents,* are represented by **avatars**, or cyber bodies that they create.

Developed by Linden Research in 2003, residents communicate with others in the virtual world through chat or voice communications. Residents can create and trade things they make in Second Life including virtual clothes, art, vehicles, houses, and other architectural structures. See Figure 8.13. They can also earn money by providing services such as instruction in a foreign language or serving as a DJ in a virtual club. This has led to the evolution of a Second Life economy with its own currency, the Linden dollar (L$). While most of the economic activity remains in the Second Life world, there are news reports of a few entrepreneurs who have made considerable sums of real money. Residents who make a lot of Linden dollars can exchange them at a rate of about 250 L$ for every U.S. dollar.

Between 2006 and 2008, there was a big spike in interest on the part of businesses who saw great potential for using Second Life. For example, IBM used it as a location for meetings, training, and recruitment. American Apparel was the first major retailer to set up shop in Second Life. Starwood Hotels used Second Life as a relatively low-cost market research experiment in which avatars visit Starwood's virtual Aloft hotel. The endeavor created publicity for the company, and feedback on the design of the hotel was solicited from visiting avatars. This information was used in the creation of the first real-world Aloft hotel which opened in 2008 (Carr, 2007). Starwood subsequently donated their Second Life property to a nonprofit educational organization. Fashion and clothing manufacturers like Reebok, American Apparel, Adidas, and others used Second Life as a place to feature new clothing designs, setting up virtual stores where Second Life citizens could purchase digital clothing for their avatars. The hope was that awareness of fashion products on Second

Figure 8.13 Second Life residents participate in a virtual world beauty contest sponsored by cosmetics manufacturer L'Oreal.

Life would transfer interest and eventual purchase of real-world products. But efforts by these and other businesses, like 1-800-flowers, to get Second Life citizens to purchase real-world products through the virtual community have proven disappointing. Many businesses that were quick to become part of the early excitement around Second Life have left the virtual world community.

Will Second Life eventually replace Facebook and other 2-D SNS platforms? Probably not, in spite of its impressive interface. While Second Life is visually compelling, it requires users to master a much larger range of controls and technology to become fully functional. Its aesthetic similarity to video games may cause some to underestimate its potential for more serious applications. Also, avatars interact in real time, so users need to be online at the same time as their friends and acquaintances in order to interact. That said, there are some niche applications that show promise. Using speakers and microphones, groups of people can conduct meetings in Second Life. Teachers can interact with their students in Second Life. How would you like it if your professor held office hours on a virtual beach? Linden Labs has revamped the special browser that residents use to participate in the virtual world and is actively promoting its use for interesting business applications, but it is unlikely to achieve the same level of attention as Facebook in its present form. We believe, however, that Second Life will continue to provide benefit as a fascinating niche player in the overall SNS marketplace.

One company has attempted to leverage the attractive features of a virtual world interface and tailor its offering to businesses specifically for meetings, web conferences, training, and enterprise collaboration applications. VenueGen offers a social enterprise application using a virtual world interface. They distinguish themselves from Second Life with a focus on business customers and a clear attempt to disassociate from the role playing and gaming culture of Second Life. VenueGen offers virtual online meeting spaces that range from small intimate conference rooms, to professional-looking training centers and large auditoriums. VenueGen offers simpler avatar controls and generally places fewer demands on users' computing equipment. This is important because most businesses do not invest heavily in computer hardware associated with gaming, for instance, powerful graphic cards, fast CPU units, and so on. With the increasing availability of social video tools like Skype and the Google+ Hangouts app, it is unclear if virtual worlds will ever break out of their gaming and role playing space and be taken seriously as a platform for enterprise and eCommerce applications.

Twitter: Microblogging. Twitter is a social networking site where users send short messages called **tweets** of 140 characters or less to their network of *followers*. Started in 2006, Twitter is now among the top 15 web sites in terms of traffic. Like Facebook, it has experienced tremendous growth over the last few years as businesses and individual users discover ways of using the **microblogging** site to meet their needs. At its most basic level, Twitter provides a platform for users to send out frequent status updates to those who follow them. Twitter is used by celebrities as a way of maintaining frequent contact with their fan base and by businesses and bloggers as a way of engaging their customers and directing traffic to updates on web sites. People use Twitter for personal and recreational purposes, as a way of communicating with a network of friends, family, and acquaintances. Increasingly, companies are using Twitter as a quick-response customer service channel. See Figure 8.14 and Case 1.

Breaking news is distributed through Twitter networks by major news organizations and private citizens who witness events firsthand. Twitter has become an integral part of many social media campaigns directed at consumers. Even though sending and receiving tweets is like instant messaging, the site allows individuals to broadcast messages to very large groups of followers. In turn, followers can reply to tweets or forward tweets originally sent by others (called a **retweet**). Groups of users can engage in chats or Twitter Forums on a wide variety of topics. Follow @forums on Twitter to receive notices of upcoming chats.

Figure 8.14 Twitter is a microblogging SNS that limits messages to 140 characters or less.

Basic Twitter service is simple and efficient, but a large segment of the *Twittersphere* use third-party apps that have been developed to enhance the service. Some are considered essential tools in the life of the power Twitter user:

- **TweetDeck** is an advanced, split-screen app that allows users to view messages streaming from followers, people being followed, and people the user might wish to follow. It also makes it easy to quickly reply to incoming tweets, increasing the frequency of Twitter conversations. The TweetDeck interface makes it easy to participate in Twitter Forums.
- **Twitpic** allows users to add photos to their tweets.
- **Twitterfeed** automatically tweets posts published on a blog using RSS technology.
- **Twitterholic** is a service that ranks users by number of followers, friends and updates.

Private SNS Services. Many business and professional organizations have found it desirable to create their own focused social networking services. Several companies offer platforms for just this purpose. One of the most popular is *Ning.com*. Until recently, you could create a private social network service on Ning for free. However, in May 2010, Ning phased out its free service by converting its networks to premium (paid) accounts.

Companies create private social networks to better understand their customers. They get the ability to monitor or listen to customers and identify important issues that they're discussing. Businesses also develop social networks for internal use, limiting access to employees or business partners.

Nonprofit organizations build communities for donors or users interested in particular causes. Li and Bernoff warn that building a private social networking service is not an easy undertaking and requires considerable resources, even when the SNS platform is free. Organizations are cautioned not to enter into the project lightly and to carefully plan their strategy and resource allocations prior to launch. Building a community with all of its social and relationship implications, only to abruptly terminate it because of resource limitations, is likely to create a public relations disaster. For companies that execute this approach properly, the private social network can yield benefits in terms of marketing information and fruitful customer relationships.

Social Networking Services are perhaps the most feature rich applications of Web 2.0. It is expected that growth and innovation in this sector will continue as individual users and business organizations discover its power for building networks and

IT at Work 8.2

Addressing Social Media Privacy Concerns

Privacy rights are too easily abused. Governments and industry associations are trying to control these abuses through legislation and professional standards, but they frequently fail to provide adequate protection. One of the most effective deterrents is fear of backlash from abuses that become public and cause outrage. So it is important to identify privacy issues that pertain to social media and specifically social networking services. Examples of privacy violations include:

- Posting pictures of people on social networking sites without their permission.
- Tricking people into disclosing credit or bank account information or investing in "Work at Home" scams.
- Sharing information about members with advertisers without the users' knowledge or consent.
- Disclosing an employer's proprietary information or trade secrets on social networking sites.
- Posting information on social networking sites that could compromise people's safety or make them targets for blackmail.

Taking Control of Your Privacy

The most important thing that users can do to protect themselves is to understand that they're responsible for protecting their own information. The basic solution is common sense. Unfortunately, most social networking sites create the illusion of privacy and control. This sometimes can lull even the most vigilant users into making mistakes. Sites like Facebook, MySpace, and others make us feel like our information is only going to be seen by those we've allowed to become part of our network. Wrong. Listed below are common sense guidelines:

- Don't post private data. Nothing, absolutely nothing you put on a social networking site is private. You should avoid posting personal information including full birth date, home address, phone number, etc. This information is used for identity theft.
- Be smart about who you allow to become part of your network. It is not uncommon for teenagers to "friend" hundreds of individuals on their Facebook accounts. With this many contacts, there is no way to protect profile or other information.
- Don't rely on current privacy policies. Social networking sites change their privacy policies regularly. Many have accused Facebook of doing this specifically to wear down user vigilance with regard to maintaining desired privacy settings. Regularly review your social network service privacy policies. Set your privacy settings at the level offering maximum protection—operating as if you have no privacy whatsoever.
- Minimize your use of applications, games, and third-party programs on social networking sites until you have carefully investigated them. They can expose you to malicious programs or viruses. Do not automatically click on links that look like they were sent to you by members of your network.

Discussion Questions

1. Which of these guidelines is the easiest to follow? Which is the toughest? Explain why.

---

relationships. We expect that Facebook will continue to dominate the field, but that smaller SNSs will stake out strong positions in niche markets using traditional market segmentation strategies—focusing on the needs of specific geographic, cultural, age or special interest segments.

Questions

1. What are the major differences between Social Networking Services and older online communities?
2. What is the basic difference between the Social Graph and Berners-Lee's concept of the Giant Global Graph?
3. Explain Facebook's Open Graph initiative and how they plan to expand their influence across the World Wide Web.
4. What are some potential ways that business organizations can take advantage of Second Life's unique virtual world interface?
5. Why would a business want to create a private SNS? What are some of the challenges associated with doing this?

8.3 Enterprise 2.0—Social Networks and Tools for Business

The term **Enterprise 2.0** refers to the use of Web 2.0 technologies for business or organizational purposes. According to Harvard professor Andrew McAffee (2008), Enterprise 2.0 applications are valuable because they don't impose artificial constraints on the communications of employees. Social technologies encourage greater collaboration within organizations and allow the formation of teams or groups around issues or problems rather than formal organizational silos. The objective of these tools is to make collaboration and knowledge exchange among employees, consultants, and company partners easier. McAffee is among a growing number of IT experts who advocate using Web 2.0 applications to either supplement or replace the intranet platforms that are widely used by business organizations today.

According to Cecil Dijoux (2009), Enterprise 2.0 is likely to lead to changes in organizational culture the same way that Web 2.0 is creating fundamental changes in the marketplace and culture in general. Dijoux claims that organizations will need to communicate with their employees using a conversation rather than a broadcast model. Important ideas are more likely to come from the bottom up (the workforce) than from managers at the top. Managers won't be able to rely as much on their job title to maintain respect. They'll have to earn it on the **enterprise social network**. Other benefits include greater transparency in the organization, increased agility and simplicity, creation of a sharing culture, and the emergence of more efficient and effective organizational structures.

BUSINESS USE OF WEB 2.0 TECHNOLOGIES

How are businesses using these new technologies? According to a recent KPMG report (2011) over 70 percent of organizations around the world are active in social media to some extent. Interestingly, use of social media appears to be greater in some emerging markets like China, India, and Brazil compared to more developed economies like the UK, Germany, and Canada. The majority of business organizations view social media primarily as a tool for marketing, sales, and business development. However, increasingly businesses are learning that social media can play an important role in recruiting, product development, and customer service. Vollmer and Premo (2011) report that most companies are planning to increase spending on social media in the near future. Facebook (94%), Twitter (77%), and YouTube (42%) are the three most popular platforms used by businesses. Approximately 25 percent of companies communicate with their customers through corporate blogs. In addition to marketing and PR functions, 75 percent of companies use social media for customer support and 56 percent conduct some form of social media market research. Finally, because of the growing role of social media across a variety of business functions, top executives are becoming increasingly involved in social media decisions. Over one third (35%) of companies reported that a senior-level executive is responsible for leading companywide social media activities.

Recruiting and Professional Networking.
Social networking among business professionals has exploded over the last few years. Begun in 2003, LinkedIn is the largest professional networking service with over 150 million users across the globe as of 2012. Most users join LinkedIn for free, but many who wish to use all the benefits and tools of the site upgrade to a premium account by paying a subscription fee. LinkedIn allows users to create profiles that include their resumes, professional affiliations, educational history, and so on. Members can also update their status to let others in their network know what they are doing. LinkedIn allows people to post endorsements of others, which provides a way to share testimonials. Users expand their networks by directly asking to connect with other professionals, or through referrals and introductions from people in their existing network. Savvy recruiters use the popular networking site in a number of ways, as described in *IT at Work 8.3*. Recent studies conducted between 2009 and 2012 suggest that between 70 and 88 percent of employers use LinkedIn as part of their recruiting process.

Just as recruiting strategies are changing, job hunting strategies will change as well. Job hunters need to master various social media tools in order to make contact with and establish relationships with potential employers. LinkedIn provides a way

IT at Work 8.3

Recruiters Use Professional Networking Sites

Susan Heathfield, a Human Resources (HR) expert at About.com, maintains that it is no longer sufficient to post job openings on *monster.com*, *Careerbuilder.com*, and *Craigslist.com*. Job postings on these large sites often generate hundreds of applications from unqualified candidates. This can be overwhelming for recruiters and very inefficient. Instead, many have turned to professional networking sites like LinkedIn. In a blog post, Heathfield identified a number of specific ways that businesses can use on LinkedIn to increase the effectiveness of their recruiting:

- Identify potential candidates among your existing network of professionals.
- Ask your network to identify or recommend candidates for a position.
- Evaluate potential employees based on references and referrals from your existing network.
- Actively search for candidates among LinkedIn users using key words or qualifications from their profiles.
- Ask current employees to search among their LinkedIn Networks for potential candidates.

- For a fee, you can post job openings on LinkedIn.
- Request introductions to potential candidates through your existing network of professionals.
- Use Inmail (the internal LinkedIn e-mail system) to contact potentially qualified individuals.

It is clear that recruiters have come to embrace LinkedIn as an effective and cost-efficient way of generating qualified candidates. As LinkedIn's global presence grows, this will provide an important benefit to companies who need to fill positions internationally.

Sources: Compiled from Heathfield (2012) and *LinkedIn.com*.

Discussion Questions

1. Why have *monster.com*, *Careerbuilder.com* and *Craigslist.com* lost their effectiveness?
2. Why have HR departments turned to professional networking sites like LinkedIn?
3. Why is it so essential for career-minded workers to build a professional social network? What can this network do for you?

for candidates to gain visibility by expanding their network, joining LinkedIn groups, building their reputations by participating in Q&A discussions, generating testimonials, and integrating these activities with other social media tools like blogs and Twitter. See Figure 8.15. While LinkedIn clearly dominates the professional networking space, a number of other professional sites have carved out niche positions in the marketplace. Search on "professional social networking" to generate a current list of alternative sites.

Marketing, Promotion, and Sales. Many companies believe that social media has tremendous potential to boost marketing and sales efforts. They see social media as the new way to communicate with current and potential customers. Throughout this chapter, we have cited several examples of how companies use social media technology to build and enhance customer relationships. Companies use blogs to disseminate information about their products, and they work hard to influence the attitudes and opinions of those who write blogs about them. Business organizations are finding ways

Figure 8.15 LinkedIn is used as a primary recruiting tool by a majority of companies.

© Alex Segre/Alamy Limited

IT at Work 8.4

Blenders Achieve Online Popularity with ISM

Let's say you have a product that costs substantially more than any of your competitors, but your advertising budget is tight. Sound like a recipe for business failure? Not if you are the makers of BlendTec, a high-end brand of kitchen blenders. This company has leveraged a limited marketing budget using an Integrated Social Media (ISM) strategy and in the process has established a huge fan base.

BlendTec achieved enormous success with a series of YouTube videos featuring CEO Tom Dickson using his durable blenders to destroy everything from marbles and hockey pucks to an Apple iPhone. The videos are short and fun to watch, but effectively illustrate the durability and strength of BlendTec's products. What started out as an inside joke at the company has become an Internet sensation. BlendTec hosts its own channel on YouTube with over 50 different "Will it Blend?" segments.

Blendtec Goes Viral

The company had almost zero name recognition prior to its viral campaign, but is now one of the most watched collections of videos on YouTube. Most of the videos on the BlendTec channel have been viewed hundreds of thousands of times and several have been seen by millions. The most popular video, viewed over 13.6 million times, features the blended destruction of an Apple iPad. The Blendtec team has enticed viewers to watch their blender destroy iPhones (10.5 million views), glow sticks (9 million views), and Bic lighters (6 million views).

ISM Strategy

While the YouTube videos are the most visible part of the BlendTec's social media efforts, the company utilizes an ISM strategy with a variety of tactics. The most popular videos are also featured on BlendTec's company web page. Viewers at this site help BlendTec spread the word by sharing videos with their social network by clicking on buttons for Facebook or Twitter. They can even subscribe to the site using RSS technology. The "Will It Blog" is used to provide information about products and upcoming videos. BlendTec regularly updates its followers with new videos and blog posts using Twitter. The company's Facebook page has over 90,000 fans who comment on the videos and request, sometimes plead, for certain objects to be blended in future videos. According to Dickenson, company sales have increased five-fold since the viral campaign was launched. That's a lot of enthusiasm for something as simple as a blender!

Sources: Compiled from: Helm (2006), Dilworth (2007), and *YouTube.com* (2012).

Questions

1. BlendTec's videos are certainly fun to watch, but content isn't the only thing that has led to the viral nature of their campaign. What other elements of social media does the company use to optimize the success of their strategy?

2. How is BlendTec's video campaign any different from a television advertising campaign? What are the advantages for the company and the consumer?

3. Review the varying popularity of BlendTec's videos (YouTube shows the number of times a video has been viewed). Can you identify any factors that might explain why some are more popular than others? What recommendations would you make to the company for future Will it Blend videos?

4. For Further Exploration: Read Dan Ackerman Greenberg's tips on how to make a video go viral (*techcrunch.com/2007/11/22/ the-secret-strategies-behind-many-viral-videos/*), then visit the BlendTec web site. How many of Greenberg's strategies are employed by the blender company?

---

of enhancing their presence on popular SNS sites like Facebook and Google+ to more effectively engage their customers.

YouTube has become a popular way for companies to promote themselves using viral videos. The BlendTec YouTube video, discussed in *IT at Work 8.4*, is an excellent example. Companies monitor blogs and discussion boards in order to *listen* to their customers and even participate in these discussions to build meaningful relationships. Business organizations find that promoting through social media is more effective and often less expensive than traditional advertising and public relations efforts. Every year, more and more companies report that their spending on traditional media is declining, while the resources they plan to devote to social media increase.

Internal Collaboration and Communication. As mentioned previously, most large and medium-sized companies utilize an Intranet for internal collaboration and communication. Businesses exercise a good deal of control over how and what happens on their intranets. According to Toby Ward (2010), most intranets are based on Web 1.0 technology and appear "flat" when compared to modern Web 2.0 capabilities. As a result, traditional intranets lack many social features that would improve communication and collaboration.

Russell Pearson (2010) and James Bennett (2009) believe that intranets need to evolve with the behavior of "social" employees who join companies and expect to be able to communicate as professionals in the same ways they have communicated prior to joining the workforce. This means intranets should include features and tools for file sharing, blogging, social tagging or bookmarking, wikis and so on. As well, managers will need to balance their innate desire for control with the more important goal of enhancing communication with and among the workforce. As you have read earlier, managers will need to learn how to use social technology to engage in conversations with employees, listen to their ideas, and motivate them toward mutually beneficial goals. Sending out paper memos from the head office, or even a mass e-mail, and expecting a desired response from company employees will be increasingly ineffective.

Small companies without formal Intranet platforms can use existing social media services to enhance the performance and collaborative efforts of employee teams:

- Use cloud storage sites like box.net or Dropbox for document sharing and collaborative writing.
- Use *Diigo.com* or *Delicious.com* for curating and sharing links to online content related to company projects.
- Meetings and discussions can be held using video conferencing tools like Skype or Google+ Hangouts. VeneuGen or Second Life can provide platforms for virtual world meetings.
- Idea generation and brain storming can be accomplished using tools like Google Moderator or IdeaScale.
- Sites like Ning, Yammer, and Zoho offer companies of all sizes the ability to create private social networks with a suite of collaboration tools that require little in the way of IT support or custom programming.

In some companies, using social media for collaboration and internal communications may prove more financially rewarding than marketing and promotion applications.

Supply Chain Management 2.0. **Supply chain management** (SCM) refers to the set of activities that support the production and distribution of goods and services to end users. Activities typically associated with SCM include acquisition of raw materials, production processes and scheduling, inventory control, logistics, and coordination of channel members—wholesalers, distributors, and retailers. Supply chains are, by nature, social entities. They include a number of people and organizations that must work together in order to create and deliver goods and services to consumers.

SCM 2.0 involves the use of social media tools to enhance communication and decision making across the supply chain. Consider how enterprise social network systems could aid in the identification of new suppliers or buyers using sites like LinkedIn. Channel members can use blogs to share ideas about best practices and mashup apps to coordinate inventory levels throughout the channel and aid in transportation and shipping decisions. Any tool that increases the ability of channel partners to communicate, coordinate and solidify relationships will make businesses more competitive.

Just as social media is changing things about the social world we live in, it is also changing how businesses behave and operate.

Questions

1. How does a professional social networking service like LinkedIn fundamentally differ from Facebook or MySpace?
2. Identify some specific ways in which managers or leaders of organizations will need to change in response to the opportunities and challenges presented by social media.
3. Explain why social media tools are likely to make supply chains more efficient and productive in the future.
4. What are some specific ways in which workers will rely on social media tools to be more productive in their professions?

8.4 Social Media Metrics: Measuring the Conversation

An important principle is: *You cannot manage what you do not measure.* Management depends on data-driven measurements, or metrics.

Businesses are constantly evaluating the efficiency and effectiveness of their activities. As part of the strategic planning process, companies identify goals, objectives, strategies, and tactics. In this way, they identify and focus on those activities that lead to revenue and profits, and reduce their emphasis on activities that don't support company goals.

WHY MEASURE SOCIAL MEDIA?

While standard **metrics** exist for many traditional business activities, the field of social media and the related issue of **social media metrics** are so new that there are few standard ways of evaluating social media activities. We identify key methods of measuring the effectiveness of social media efforts, but acknowledge that there are many variations on what we describe.

PERFORMANCE DASHBOARDS GUIDE DECISION MAKING AND ACTION

As you have read in Chapter 2, managers keep informed by using performance **dashboards** to summarize the effectiveness of activity and progress toward goals. These graphic representations show how well a company is performing on key metrics. In many cases, data is continuously fed into dashboards so that managers have access to real-time information. This is a significant advantage over using monthly or quarterly reports for assessing progress towards goals and helps to increase organizational responsiveness to a variety of situations. When automated, the dashboard is an example of a business mashup, a Web 2.0 application that pulls data from multiple sources and displays it in one location.

But what should a management team track in terms of social media in its dashboard? In the next section, we discuss metrics that organizations find meaningful and effective.

TYPES OF SOCIAL MEDIA OBJECTIVES

Literally hundreds of metrics exist to track how people respond to social media. The list in Table 8.5 is just a sample of the many factors that can be tracked. New companies are springing up every day to offer tools for tracking social media activity and its impact on other key performance indicators (KPI). There are many different kinds of metrics because social media can be used to do so many things. Therefore, the question of what kind of information a company tracks depends on what it is trying to accomplish with its social media efforts. For instance, if a company wants to increase traffic to its web page, then it would start tracking the number of visitors who arrive at its web site as a result of a tweet, a status update on the company's Facebook page, a YouTube video, or some other social media activity.

On the other hand, if a company wants to learn how customers feel about its products, it would track the number of positive vs. negative blog posts, the sentiment expressed in Twitter messages, positive vs. negative YouTube videos posted by customers, and so on.

Traditionally, business organizations developed media objectives around various models called **response hierarchies.** A common response hierarchy includes the following stages: Awareness, Knowledge, Liking, Preference, and Purchase (Lavidge & Steiner, 1961). Using this model, advertisers set measureable objectives for each stage. For instance, a company might set an objective like:

• Achieve 45 percent brand awareness in our primary market within the first quarter, or

• Increase the conversion rate from preference to purchase by 2 percent over the next 6 months

TABLE 8.5	Examples of Social Media Metrics

Activity Metrics
- Pageviews
- Unique number of visitors
- Posts
- Comments and trackbacks
- Time spent on site
- Contributors
- Frequency: of visits, posts, comments

Survey Metrics
- Satisfaction
- Quality and speed of issue resolution
- Content relevance

ROI Metrics
- Sales and marketing
  - Cost per number of prospects
  - Number of leads per period
  - Cost of lead
  - Conversion of leads to customers
  - Customer lifetime value (CLV)
- Product Development
  - Number of new product ideas
  - Idea to development initiation cycle time
- HR
  - Hiring and training costs
  - Employee attrition
  - Time to hire

General Internet Metrics
- Net Promoter Score (*netpromoter.com*)
- Number of mentions (tracked via web or blog search engines)

Source: Adapted from Happe & Rachel (2008), The Social Organization.

Once these objectives are set, advertisers use marketing research to track their progress toward reaching the objectives and can evaluate the success of their promotional activities.

Businesses could apply response hierarchy models to social media. However, response hierarchy models are based on an advertising or broadcast approach to communication and fail to capture the full potential of the social media environment. The real potential of social media goes far beyond sending messages that influence people. Interactive social media can be used to collect information as well as send it. It can be used to reduce costs associated with customer service. It can be used to gather intelligence on competitors and much more. Because there are so many applications, companies need to be very clear about what they want to accomplish with their social media efforts; and this in turn will drive what information they track to assess the effectiveness of their actions.

At this point, it seems there are four basic approaches to social media metrics: *tool-based metrics, tactical metrics, strategic metrics,* and *ROI metrics.* The four approaches are not mutually exclusive. It is common for some specific metrics to be used in each of the four approaches. The difference between each approach is how a business defines its objectives, or what it is trying to accomplish, as explained next.

Tool-Based Metrics. Metrics are driven by objectives. The metrics a company uses are determined by what the company is trying to achieve. In some cases, a company will define its objectives based on a specific Web 2.0 tool. **Tool-based metrics** are designed to identify information about a specific application. For instance, a company might wish to determine if it should advertise on a popular blog, or sponsor the creation and distribution of a useful widget application. In these situations, the company would probably track number of blog readers or number of widget users. Companies that use Twitter might track the number of followers, number of times other people mention their company in Tweets, or number of times people retweet messages. A 2009 report by the Interactive Advertising Bureau (IAB) specified definitions for three widely used Web 2.0 tools: blog metrics, social network metrics, and widget metrics. Advertisers view these tools as channels for reaching consumers and are therefore interested in both the volume of traffic related to a particular tool as well as the nature of the interaction or "conversations" occurring because of the tool. Examples of specific metrics identified by the IAB for these tools are listed in Table 8.6.

Tactical Metrics. Another way for organizations to select appropriate metrics is based on tactical objectives. For instance, a company may express its tactical objectives as follows:

• Increase traffic to our web site by 10 percent.
• Increase requests for product information via our web site by 15 percent.
• Increase the number of people who create a user account on our web site by 12 percent.
• Increase the number of people who download our informational brochure by 25 percent.

Based on these tactical objectives, companies can develop specific actions that support the objectives and then monitor progress. For instance, in order to increase traffic to the web site, a company might start its own blog, identify and communicate with people who blog about the company or industry, and then begin a Twitter campaign. They can then track the number of visitors to the web site, noting changes in total volume as well as identifying where the traffic is coming from. Using **tactical metrics** of this nature, they can determine the relative impact that each of these specific social media activities is having on their tactical objectives.

TABLE 8.6	Tool Specific Metrics	
Blog Metrics	**Social Networking Service Metrics**	**Widget Metrics**

• Number of Conversation-Relevant Posts on the Site
• Number of Links to Conversation-Relevant Posts on the Site
• Earliest Post Date for Conversation-Relevant Posts
• Latest Post Date for Conversation-Relevant Posts
• Duration between Earliest and Last Post Date for Conversation-Relevant Posts
• Mean-time between Conversation Relevant Posts
	• Unique visitors
	• Cost per unique visitor
	• Page Views
	• Return Visits
	• Proportion of visitors who interact with an ad or application.
	• Time Spent on Site
	• Activity metrics related to:
	  - Contest/Sweeps Entries
	  - Coupons downloaded/redeemed
	  - Uploads (e.g., images, videos)
	  - Messages sent (e.g., Bulletins, Updates, E-mails, Alerts)
	  - Invites sent
	  - Newsfeed items posted
	  - Comments posted
		• Number of application installations
		• Number of Active Users
		• Audience Profile—User demographics from self-reported profile information
		• Unique User Reach
		• Percentage of users who have installed application among the total social media audience
		• Growth of users within a specific time frame
		• Influence—Average number of friends among users who have installed application.

Source: Adapted from Social Media Ad Metrics Definitions (2009) Interactive Advertising Bureau.

IT at Work 8.5

Haley Marketing Group Enhances SEO through Social Media

Haley Marketing Group is a marketing services company, based in western New York, started in 1996 whose mission is to help companies in the staffing services industry develop long-term, profitable relationships with their customers. According to Haley's president David Searns, "In the early days, direct mail was our main communication vehicle for nurturing relationships. That evolved into e-mail marketing. But today, social media allows us and our clients to create, maintain and enhance relationships in ways that were never possible before."

Haley Marketing Group makes strategic use of social media. Everything they do online is part of an integrated plan to accomplish specific business objectives. Chief Operating Officer (COO) Victoria Kenward notes, "While we are a marketing company, we don't have an unlimited marketing budget. Like our clients, we need to maximize the impact of every dollar we spend to promote the company. That's why we don't do anything unless we have a very clear objective and we track everything to make sure that we're getting the return we need on our efforts."

SEO and Social Media

Like many other businesses, Haley Marketing is interested in making sure their company ranks at the top when prospective clients use search engines like Google to identify companies in their industry. **Search engine optimization (SEO)** involves a number of strategies to influence how search engines categorize, rank, and list web pages when people do searches. Google, among others, is particularly influenced by the amount of traffic that flows to a web site. More traffic means a higher ranking on search results.

Increasing Web Traffic via SEO and Social Media

Haley Marketing Group relies on inbound marketing techniques for sales leads. Historically, direct mail and e-mail marketing provided a sufficient quantity of well-qualified sales leads, but in recent years the responses from these lists has declined. The volume of sales leads being produced was insufficient to meet corporate goals.

The Solution: Integrated Social Media

The foundation of Haley Marketing's strategy is the creation and distribution of content. The company web site was re-engineered in 2008 to be a platform for educational resources and information on the marketing services Haley provides for its clients. In 2009, the site was augmented with landing pages offering free webinars, free eBook downloads, and other complimentary resources. In addition, the company produces a monthly e-mail newsletter, called The Idea Club. Searns, along with all other employees, is required to contribute a minimum of two blog posts a month to the *Ask Haley Blog*, which offers marketing tips and advice for staffing industry professionals.

According to Searns, "the greatest challenge we face is getting our target audience to become aware of, and engage with, the content we offer." To drive web traffic, the company employs a variety of channels, including five monthly e-mail communications to an opt-in list of staffing professionals, consistent promotion via social networks, search engine optimization, and online PR.

In terms of integrated social media, Searns, Kenward, and most of the company employees maintain an active presence on LinkedIn, a professional social networking service that has become the primary recruiting tool for many companies. When new content is created or events are scheduled, company employees use their LinkedIn status, LinkedIn events calendar, and LinkedIn groups to notify associates.

The company also maintains a Facebook page. Whenever new content is added to the *Ask Haley Blog*, the corporate Facebook page is automatically updated, and those individuals who have "Liked" Haley Marketing are notified about the new content.

Haley Marketing also uses multiple Twitter accounts as another means of driving traffic to their site. Updates from the *Ask Haley* blog are automatically fed to the Twitter accounts of several employees, and the Twitter feeds are then fed to LinkedIn.

Members of Haley Marketing's network that want to subscribe to the blog can do so using an RSS feed button positioned next to each post. Readers also help promote the *Ask Haley Blog* by sharing links with their Facebook, LinkedIn, or Twitter Networks simply by clicking on a small button next to the post.

Performance Improvements

Traffic to the Haley Marketing Group web site has increased by 344 percent in the 18-month period that they have employed their ISM strategy. Unique visitors to the site have increased 504 percent, and page views have increased by 105 percent as well. Most importantly, the volume of traffic from search engines has steadily increased from about 300 per month to over 1,500.

Source: Gregory R. Wood's personal interviews with David Searns and Victoria Kenward, 2010.

Questions

1. How did Haley Marketing Group define their objectives? What type of metric—for example tool, tactical, strategy, or ROI—did they use to evaluate the success of their ISM strategy?

2. Did Haley Marketing Group use appropriate metrics for evaluating their efforts? What additional metric should they consider?

3. Compare Haley Marketing's traditional approach to communication with its social media tactics. What advantages does the company gain by using social media?

4. While the case discusses Haley Marketing Group's attempt to optimize search engine optimization (SEO), what other social media objectives might they pursue with the tools they are using?

5. Research SEO. Can companies like Haley Marketing Group increase their rankings on popular search engines? Explain.

Strategic Metrics. Various authors have attempted to identify higher-level objectives that more fully capture the potential of social media than what is described by focusing on a specific social media tool or tactical objective. In their influential book on social media strategies Li and Bernoff (2008) identify five strategic objectives that companies can pursue using social media.

1. **Listening:** Learn about your customers by paying attention to what they are saying online to one another or directly to you.
2. **Talking:** Communicate with your customers by engaging in conversations.
3. **Energizing:** Encourage current customers and fans to spread the word through ratings, reviews, and other positive buzz.
4. **Supporting:** Help customers solve problems by providing information and online resources like user forums, knowledge bases, and other tools.
5. **Embracing:** Invite customers to generate ideas for new products and services.

Organizations that seek to optimize their performance in each of these areas will identify and implement social media tactics as well as track related metrics to evaluate progress towards goals. For instance, companies that use crowdsourcing to generate new product ideas might count the number of ideas submitted, the number of people who vote on the ideas, the number of positive vs. negative comments made about each idea, and so on. Companies who want to strategically "listen" to their markets might measure the number of "conversations," identify who is "talking," identify what people are saying, and so forth.

A number of **social media monitoring services** have sprung up in recent years to provide this kind of data to large business organizations and major brands (see Tech Note 8.1). Most of these services use IT to track online content and feed summary statistics into dashboards that can be used by their clients. Subscription rates for these services vary, but can be quite substantial. Fortunately for smaller companies and nonprofit organizations, a number of free or low-cost solutions exist. One such service is *SocialMention.com*, which tracks the volume of social media activity and provides four useful metrics that measure:

1. **Strength:** the likelihood that a brand will be mentioned in social media
2. **Reach:** an influence measure based on the number of unique people who post or tweet about a brand
3. **Passion:** a measure of the likelihood that people will post repeatedly about a brand
4. **Sentiment:** a ratio of positive to negative mentions about a brand.

Google Alerts, Twitter Search, and Addictomatic are other free services that allow users to monitor social media activity. These services do a pretty good job of creating a snapshot of social media activity within a given time frame. Unlike the paid services listed in Tech Note 8.1, they don't usually provide users with easy access to trends or aggregate data in a way that managers can easily use to make quick decisions. For small businesses and nonprofit agencies that decide to regularly monitor social media, the cost of moderately priced services like Sprout Social, Trackur, or uberVU might make more sense. These services offer a solid range of features with scalable pricing plans.

ROI Metrics. Finally, many experts in the field of social media metrics emphasize the importance of what they call **social media ROI** (return on investment). This approach attempts to monetize the return on the cost of implementing social media strategies. The ROI concept has inherent appeal because it addresses the need of the business organization to engage in activities that will contribute to revenue goals. The ROI concept inspires considerable debate, however. Some maintain that the qualitative contributions of social media (e.g., relationships, conversations, trust, etc.) cannot be meaningfully expressed in monetary or quantitative terms. However, despite

Tech Note 8-1

Top Social Monitoring Services

The companies listed below provide sophisticated, full-service monitoring, tracking, and response technology solutions on a subscription basis.

1. Radian 6
2. Collective Intellect
3. Lithium
4. Sysomos
5. Attensity360
6. Alterian SM2
7. Crimson Hexagon
8. Spiral 16
9. Webtrends
10. Spredfast

Source: Lasica & Bale (2011).

the potential difficulty associated with capturing all contributions of social media to a company's bottom line, the attempt must be made. Unless a reasonable link can be established between the costs associated with social media and a company's financial performance, some executives are unlikely to support social media initiatives, particularly in a depressed economy.

Sometimes the calculation of ROI for social media is easy. For instance, if an online retailer can increase traffic to its web site by publishing a blog, then the company can track how many of these customers ultimately make a purchase after reading the blog. That data can be used to determine the blog's contribution to sales revenue. If a company notices an 18 percent drop in calls to its customer service line after implementing an online support forum, the reduction in call center expense can be readily calculated. Companies that see their sales leads increase because of their presence on a social network can estimate the resulting sales volume by applying their *yield rate* to this new set of inquiries (e.g., 1000 new leads times a 7 percent yield rate equals 70 new customers). If a company knows how much each new customer is worth, it can estimate the total revenue produced by its presence on the social network. Each of these is an example of a quantitative or **hard ROI metric**.

Other times, the link between important social media activity and a firm's financial performance is less direct. For instance, what is the relationship between an increase in the number of positive blog postings about a company's product and sales of the product? What is the relationship between the number of users who download a widget application sponsored by the company and company sales performance? To answer questions like these, it is necessary to make assumptions about the conversion rate of customers as they pass through stages similar to the response hierarchy models discussed at the beginning of this section. For instance, a company that wishes to increase awareness for its brand or product may sponsor the distribution of a popular desktop widget or create a viral video for YouTube. While they can track the number of people who use the widget or view the video, they would need to make some assumptions about the conversion rate, or the number of people who ultimately purchase something from the company as a result of increased awareness rates.

Considerable work remains to be done in the area of ROI metrics. However, we believe that companies will be most likely to adopt social media strategies when there is a clear link to financial performance. As managers become comfortable with their capabilities, and experience success in this area, they become less risk averse to engaging in social media activities to support strategic goals even when the link to revenues or costs is difficult to measure.

1. Why should companies use metrics to track social media activity?
2. List examples of tool-based metrics. What questions can an organization answer with this kind of information?
3. List social media strategies that businesses might pursue. What kind of information could they collect to see if they are being effective with social media?
4. Why do businesses find ROI metrics to be so compelling?
5. Why are ROI metrics for social media sometimes difficult to use or identify?

8.5   The Future: Web 3.0

If there's one thing that history has taught us, it's that the future is hard to predict. It might seem silly to try to predict what the future Internet will look like when it's clear that so many people are having trouble trying to understand all the implications of the Internet we have now. However, forward-thinking businesses and individuals are beginning to plan for the next evolution, which is sometimes called **Web 3.0**. In an attempt to predict what the future web will look like, Sramana Mitra (2007) has approached the question differently from others who focus on specific apps or technologies that may emerge as part of the future Internet. Instead, she proposes a model that describes the characteristics of Web 3.0 from the user perspective. According to Mitra (2007), the future web will be defined as:

> **Web 3.0 = (4C + P + VS), where,**
>
> **3C = Content, Commerce, Community**
>
> **4th C = Context**
>
> **P = Personalization**
>
> **VS = Vertical Search**

The current web is disjointed, requiring us to visit different web sites to get content, engage in commerce, and interact with our network of relationships (community). The future web will use context, personalization, and vertical search to make the 3Cs—content, commerce, and community—more relevant.

Context defines the intent of the user; e.g., trying to purchase music, to find a job, to share memories with friends and family.

Personalization refers to the user's personal characteristics that impact how relevant the 3Cs are to the individual.

Vertical Search refers to a search strategy that focuses on finding information in a particular content area, such as travel, finance, legal, and medical.

Future web sites, therefore, will maximize user experience by increasing performance on the factors outlined in this model.

SEMANTIC WEB

Tim Berners-Lee, creator of the technology that made the World Wide Web, is the director of the **World Wide Web Consortium (W3C)**. This group is working on programming standards designed to make it possible for data, information, and knowledge to be shared even more widely across the Internet. In effect, it hopes to turn the Internet into one large database (or rather, a collection of databases) that we can access for wide ranging purposes. The W3C is developing standards for a **metadata** language, or ways of describing data so that it can be used by a wide variety of applications. Much of the world's data is stored in files structured so that they can only be read by the programs that created them. With metadata, the information in these files can be tagged with information describing the nature of the data, where it came from, or how it's arranged. That way, it can be read and used by a wide variety of applications.

It is helpful to think about the **semantic web** against the background of earlier Internet function. According to Jim Hendler and Tim Berners-Lee (2010), leading developers of the semantic web:

The Internet allowed programmers to create programs that could communicate without having to concern themselves with the network of cables that the communication had to flow over. The web allows programmers and users to work with a set of interconnected documents without concerning themselves with details of the computers that store and exchange those documents. The semantic web raises this to the next level, allowing programmers and users to make reference to real-world objects—whether people, chemicals, agreements, stars or whatever else—without concerning themselves with the underlying documents in which these things, abstract and concrete, are described.

THE LANGUAGE(S) OF WEB 3.0

The early web was built using **Hypertext Markup Language (HTML)**. As noted earlier, Web 2.0 was made possible, in part, by the development of languages like XML and JavaScript. The semantic web utilizes additional languages that have been developed by the W3C. These in include **RDF (Resource Description Framework)**, **OWL** and **SPARQL**. RDF is a language used to represent information about resources on the Internet. It will describe these resources using metadata **URI's (uniform resource identifiers)** like "title," "author," "copyright and license information." It is one of the features that allow data to be used by multiple applications.

SPARQL is a Protocol and RDF Query Language. As the name implies, it is used to write programs that can retrieve and manipulate data stored in RDF format. OWL is the W3C Web Ontology Language used to categorize and accurately identify the nature of things found on the Internet. These three languages, used together, will enhance the context element of the web, producing more fruitful and accurate information searches. Work continues by the W3C with input by programmers and the broader Internet community to improve the power and functionality of these languages.

SOCIAL SEMANTIC WEB (S2w)

While the semantic technologies being developed by W3C will greatly enhance our ability to find and utilize information on the web, much of the user-generated content being created on social media platforms remains isolated. Example: You have to go on Facebook to see the pictures your friend posted on Facebook. You need to go to *Delicious.com* to view the social bookmarks that other users have saved on that site. To realize the full potential of information on social sites across the web, additional semantic technologies are being developed that will make it possible to unlock content from platforms of origin so that it can be used and shared by other applications, creating a social semantic web. These social semantic tools make use of the technology previously discussed, RDF, OWL, and SPARQL, as well as additional rules (called ontologies) for describing the relationships between objects, information, and people on the social web. For example, two ontologies used in development of the social semantic web are:

Friend of a Friend (FOAF)—Rules for describing people, their relationships with others and the things they create. (See *foaf-project.org*.)

Semantically-Interlinked Online Communities (SIOC)—A standard set of rules for describing user-generated objects found in different social networks. This ontology makes it possible for content from one or more social platforms to move to other platforms or applications. (See *sioc-project.org/*.)

Applications developed using social semantic technologies will result in a variety of new capabilities:

Enhanced user profiling for marketing purposes. Instead of user profiles based on activity from a single social network, profiles can be developed based on activity across several types of social platforms (e.g., SNS, blogs, social bookmarking sites, etc.). These enhanced profiles will provide marketers with even greater precision in the development of market segmentation and targeting strategies, and the implementation of various targeted promotional activities. As you might guess, this is also likely to intensify concerns regarding privacy.

Enhanced ability to share content and manage Information Streams. Applications based on social semantic technology will allow sharing of objects across platforms. For example, users will have the ability to share pictures originally posted on Facebook, with friends who are members of other social networking services. People will have greater control over the content streaming at them from social media sites.

Enhanced ability to search for and utilize information from social sites. Users will be able to perform more complex searches than are currently available on most search engines. They will be able to conduct searches that require information from multiple sites or conduct searches based on the characteristics of the people who created the information. It will be easier to curate or aggregate content from social sites and display it in a single application and organize it in different ways. Teachers, for instance, will be able to access course content from a variety of sites and curate it in a single space for students in their class

Social Semantic Tools Available Now. While not in widespread use, some interesting tools that integrate semantic and social technologies are already available. To better understand the potential of these new developments, explore the following sites:

DBpedia.org is an online community effort to develop various applications for extracting information from Wikipedia, the online social encyclopedia created by users around the world. The basic Wikipedia search engine allows users to locate individual pages based on search terms. As everyone knows, when you type a word into the Wikipedia search tool, it results in a list of pages that might contain information of interest. However, using a semantic application developed by DBpedia.org, called a Faceted Browser (see *dbpedia.neofonie.de/browse/*), users can ask complex questions requiring the aggregation of information from multiple pages on Wikipedia. For instance, a student looking for a particular kind of college might use this tool to ask, "What private colleges in the U.S. have between 3000 and 5000 students?" Manually looking through all the college pages on Wikipedia to create a list that answers the question would take days. The Faceted Browser tool generates the list in seconds. For a full list of DBpedia applications visit *wiki. dbpedia.org/Applications*.

Bottlenose.com is a social media dashboard that uses semantic technologies to help users effectively process large amounts of social media content. People who have many Facebook friends and/or follow many people on Twitter can easily become overwhelmed by the large volume of tweets, status updates, and other content posted on these sites. Bottlenose applies semantic technologies to filter content from social sites (currently Facebook, Twitter, LinkedIn, and Google Reader) in ways that make it easier to use. For instance, users can sort information into streams based on topics like Technology News, Entertainment News, Sports, Videos, Events, and Pictures. Information enters each of these streams based on the topic or nature of the content, independent of the site it originates from. The application allows users to create their own custom streams based on individual needs. Another interface option in Bottlenose allows users to display social content in a newspaper format, which some users find easier or more entertaining to read. Finally, a futuristic 3D interface called *Sonar* allows users to manage and manipulate content streams based on trending topics, people, and time frame. By using semantic technology, Bottlenose has created an application that is more useful than current applications that simply aggregate social media content, leaving users to struggle with large volumes of data. Visit *Bottlenose.com* and try it for yourself or watch a video demonstration.

While the field of semantic web technology is still relatively new, initial applications are showing much promise, particularly those that aid in the processing of social content. In the not too distant future, most of us will routinely use powerful semantic applications to efficiently and productively process information available from both traditional web sites and social media platforms.

Application Programming Interfaces (API). Another key trend contributing to the evolution of the web is the growing importance of Application Programming Interfaces. An API is essentially a tool that allows programs to talk to or interact with one another. This makes it possible for one program to get information from another program. For instance, the most popular API in current use is the Google Maps API (*code.google.com/apis/maps/*) which allows programmers to embed Google Maps into their own web site applications. Since APIs make it possible for web applications to share data, the new semantic web technologies that clarify the nature and structure of this data have the potential to improve API functionality and enhance the performance of applications that use them.

Recall that earlier in the chapter you read about Facebook's Social Graph initiative, designed to link Facebook with web sites across the Internet. The ability of the Facebook API to seamlessly move a variety of data types between the social network and other web sites will be improved by the semantic technologies described above. Facebook users will enjoy a wider range of features and functionality as a result of these developments. This is just another example of how semantic web technologies will improve the end user experience.

ARTIFICIAL INTELLIGENCE

Some people believe that the future Internet will be an intelligent web. The application of **artificial intelligence (AI)** to our Internet experience could make things even more efficient and effective. Over time, our computers could learn about us, our interests, our information needs, our friends, and so on. This would create searches that produced more relevant information and tools for improving decision making and problem solving. To put it simply, the semantic web will vastly increase the amount of information that is available—so much so that human users are likely to be overwhelmed and unable to find relevant information that meets their specific needs. AI provides a potential solution, detecting the context of our information searches using rules developed over time based on our online activities. The development of AI technologies will be a significant element in the potential success of the semantic web (Hendler and Berners-Lee, 2010).

AI may even change the way we interface with the Internet. Imagine a web browser that can engage in conversation and ask questions to clarify the tasks we ask it to perform? The stage is being set for exactly this kind of experience. Visit *alicebot.org/logo-info.html* and click the "Chat with A.L.I.C.E." link for an example.

MOBILITY

We have already seen tremendous expansion in the kinds of equipment used to access the Internet. It is expected that this phenomenon will continue as web browsers are built into smart phones, PDAs, e-readers, and other wireless devices. Social media apps are among the most popular programs on handheld mobile devices. As smart phones, e-readers, and tablet devices move into the mainstream, web programmers will be increasingly compelled to create sites that display nicely on small screens. Smart phone owners already use their mobile devices in retail stores to compare prices, access product information, and look at reviews from other customers. In the near future, we expect that stores will identify ways of making the shopping experience more social using mobile apps that enhance the retail experience of their customers. You read about several of these trends in Chapter 7.

Figure 8.16 Demand for access to SNS is driving development of new smartphone technology and other wireless devices.

BARRIERS TO BE OVERCOME

Closed Data Sources. Obviously, the key to an information-rich web is information. However, not everyone is particularly interested in having their data made available to anyone who wants it. You can probably think of many of situations where data should be protected to prevent intrusions on privacy, to maintain public safety, and to protect national security. For many businesses, information is a key to their competitive position in the marketplace. The last thing they want to do is give away something of value and get nothing in return.

So what information should be made public? What should be kept private? The truth is that technology will be used to determine who has access to different kinds of information. W3C is working to develop such standards. Once companies are convinced that they can reliably restrict access of their data to an audience they define, they will be more likely to tag the data so that it can be accessed using Web 3.0 technologies by authorized users.

Incompatible Data Structures and Format. While the W3C is working to develop standards for tagging information with metadata labels, we must remember that across the web, data exists in many different forms and structures. It is a formidable undertaking to layer all data files with information that make it possible to be read by everyone. It remains to be seen how long it will be until most commonly used information is appropriately tagged. While we sometimes talk about Web 3.0 as a future evolution, in fact, the new web is already here—it just hasn't gotten very far yet.

Web developers are already hard at work applying Web 3.0 technologies. Search engines like Hakia and iGlue are considered semantic search engines. Microsoft's search engine, Bing, also makes use of semantic technologies. Semantic web technologies have potential for improving the performance of what some developers call "recommendation engines." These apps are used by retail sites to help customers find products that meet their needs. Recommendation engines will help you find a good book to read on Amazon, the perfect hotel for your vacation on Travelocity, a fantastic pair of shoes from *Zappos.com*, and a great movie to watch on Netflix. The apps combine information about past product choices, current preferences, and the behavior of customers who are similar to you in order to make product recommendations that you are likely to find attractive. That said, relatively few businesses have started to explore the potential for leveraging Web 3.0 technologies. It's probably fair to say that most of the business world is still focused on learning to use Web 2.0 technologies.

Interoperability across Mobile Equipment, Web Sites, and Software. As the number of Internet devices and related operating systems proliferates, it becomes difficult for web programmers to maintain compatible variations of their site for each potential configuration. Some companies don't even try to be compatible with more than the top two or three most popular device/OS configurations. This creates what some call a *fractured web*, where each device can only access a portion of the available online content because of incompatibility.

Lack of Net Neutrality. Currently, most Internet content flows freely through networks maintained by large telecom companies. While these companies charge us for access to the Internet, they are not allowed to control the content that flows through the networks. This maintains a level playing field, guaranteeing that all web content is equally accessible. If big telecom companies get their way, however, in the future they will be able to charge organizations for access to a "fast lane" on the Internet. This means that larger companies like Facebook, Microsoft and Google will be able to pay to have their information delivered more quickly to your browser, while smaller companies and individuals with blogs and web sites would be relegated to a relatively slow data pipe.

This might reduce the power of individuals and smaller, innovative companies, changing the democratic and social nature of the Internet. Opponents of net-neutrality argue that they have spent billions to create the infrastructure for high-speed Internet and should be able to manage it without interference from the government. They call concerns that smaller players will be pushed aside unrealistic and alarmist. Between 2008 to 2011, considerable debate and a number of legal battles were waged on the issue of **Net Neutrality**. In December of 2010, the FCC issued rules banning Internet Service Providers (ISPs) from preventing access to certain web sites or competing ISPs. In 2011, the FCC issued a set of rulings that generally supported the concept of neutrality, although critics say the rules fell short of adequate protection. Despite these rulings, the issue remains uncertain as industry lobbyists push legislators in Congress to over-turn the rules and allow ISPs greater control over their networks, making it possible for them to create different tiers of service based on ability to pay. As an Internet user, you should stay informed on this issue and let your representatives in Congress know how you feel about the issue of Net Neutrality.

Questions

1. Independent of any specific technology, what three capabilities does Sramana Mitra predict will become enhanced in Web 3.0.
2. What is the purpose of metadata labels used to tag data files?
3. What is the Semantic Web? How is it different from Web 2.0?
4. How might artificial intelligence play a role in the evolution of the future web?
5. What are some of the barriers or challenges to be overcome in creating Web 3.0?

Key Terms

AJAX (Asynchronous JavaScript and XML) *234*

Application Programming Interface (API) *259*

artificial Intelligence *259*

asynchronous javascript *234*

avatar *242*

blog *231*

bloggers *231*

blogosphere *231*

broadcast model *230*

cloud tag *233*

content marketing *231*

context *256*

conversation model *230*

crowdsourcing *238*

dashboard *250*

Enterprise 2.0 *226*

enterprise social network *246*

feature convergence *233*

Friend of a Friend (FOAF) *257*

giant global graph *237*

groundswell *235*

hangout *264*

hard ROI metrics *255*

HTML (Hypertext Markup Language) *257*

Chapter 8 LINK LIBRARY

You find clickable Link Libraries for each chapter on the Companion website.

Web 2.0. . . The Machine Is Us/ing Us—Michael Wesch
   youtube.com/user/mwesch#p/u/9/NLlGopyXT_g

Social Media Revolution—Is it a fad?   *youtube.com/watch?v=3SuNx0UrnEo*

The Mashable Social Media Guide   *mashable.com/social-media/*

Cluetrain Manifesto   *cluetrain.com/*

O'Reilly Media   *oreilly.com/community/*

World Wide Web Consortium   *w3.org/Consortium/*

Read, Write, Web technology blog   *readwriteweb.com/*

Evaluate and Expand Your Learning

IT and Data Management Decisions

1. You have been hired by your college or university to evaluate how the institution is viewed by people who use social media.
   A. List the names of two or three other colleges/universities that you think are comparable to your school in terms of size, quality, and nature of the school (e.g., liberal arts, tech. school, religious, private vs. public, etc.)
   B. On the web, go to *SocialMention.com*.
   C. Type in the name of your college/university and click the "Search" button. Record how your school performs on the four metrics: Strength, Passion, Sentiment, and Reach. (You can find the definitions of these metrics on the web site.)
   D. For comparison purposes, repeat the process for the other schools you identified in "A" above.
   E. Prepare a brief memo describing how your school performs on these social media metrics. How favorable or unfavorable do people seem to feel about your school relative to the other institutions you evaluated? What other insights can you gain from these metrics? Finally, what recommendations would you make to the administration of your college/university to improve their performance on these metrics?

Questions for Discussion & Review

1. Explain the fundamental differences between Web 1.0 and Web 2.0.

2. Compare the methods that companies used to communicate with their customers using the broadcast model vs. ways that companies can have conversations with their customers using Web 2.0 tools.

3. Describe why it is increasingly difficult to neatly categorize web sites as purely "blogs," "social network services," "sharing sites," "wikis," etc.

4. Is there really any meaningful difference between "Web 2.0" and "Enterprise 2.0"?

5. How will the social web and individual user expectations for communication shape the workplace of the future? What are some specific ways in which managers or business leaders will have to adjust to this new environment?

6. Describe the fundamental changes that need to take place before the semantic web concept becomes widespread.

7. Explain the role of social media metrics in helping organizations track the impact of social media on their business.

8. What role might Artificial Intelligence play in the semantic web? How will AI tools be helpful in the future?

9. How will concern for individual privacy affect the growth and expansion of Social Networking Services and other social web applications?

Online Activities

1. Using online sources, research Facebook's Open Graph initiative. Make a list of pros and cons regarding these changes from the viewpoint of a Facebook user.

2. Visit *searchstories-intl.appspot.com/en-us/creator/* and watch some Google Search Stories made by others. Then, using the tools on the site, make one of your own. Have fun and be creative. Share with your class.

3. If you are a member of Facebook and have over 100 "friends," use the Social Graph Application to map out your Facebook network (*apps.facebook.com/socgraph/*). See if you can identify any patterns or groupings that occur.

4. Using Google's blog search tool, identify some active blogs on a topic of interest to you. Leave comments in the response section (if available). See if the blog author or other readers reply.

5. Set up an account on two different RSS readers (e.g., Google Reader and *Feedly.com*), and use them to subscribe to some blogs that are of interest to you. Prepare a report or presentation comparing the strengths and weakness of each application.

6. Prepare a report on the economic activity that takes place on Second Life. Describe how people make money in the virtual world, and identify the opportunities and challenges associated making a living in Second Life.

7. Set up an account on *Twitter.com*. Also, download Tweetdeck, a useful interface for Twitter. Identify and "follow" people who seem to be sending messages that are of interest to you. Prepare a report on your experiences. Evaluate Twitter as a tool for social networking.

8. Visit the LinkedIn page for college graduates: *grads.linkedin.com/*. Using the information on this page, create a LinkedIn account, and begin building your professional network. Search the Internet for additional tips on using LinkedIn to find jobs and prepare a brief report on your findings.

9. Using a search engine, find four examples of mashup applications. Prepare a report describing each one. If possible, identify the web site(s) where data is pulled from to create the application.

10. Create an account on *diigo.com*, the social bookmarking site. Actively use it to tag and categorize web pages that you want to remember for future viewing. Use the search engine on *diigo.com* to find pages that other users have tagged. Compare the effectiveness of your searches to similar searches using Google and Yahoo.

11. Using a search engine, identify a list of Web 3.0 Companies. Prepare a brief report that describes three or four of these firms, and specifically identify the characteristics or capabilities that associate them with the new semantic web described in the chapter.

Collaborative Work

1. It seems like everyone is on Facebook, but there are other popular social networking services. Divide the class into teams of four or five students. Have each team create accounts on a lesser known SNS. For a period of one week, team members should interact on the new SNS, and prepare a brief presentation on their experience. Be sure to discuss ways that the alternative SNS is better or worse than Facebook.

2. Form a team of four or five people willing to set up accounts on Second Life, the virtual world SNS. Spend a week learning to control your avatar and interacting with your team members in the virtual world. Prepare a report or presentation on your experiences.

3. Have each team identify a topic on Wikipedia that it feels could be updated or enhanced with additional information. Conduct research using credible sources, and carefully make editorial changes to the Wikipedia page. Report back to the class on your experience.

4. Using online sources, have two teams research each side of the Net Neutrality debate. In class, each team should make a 5–10 minute presentation to support their position. At the end of the presentations, allow the rest of the class to ask questions. Conduct a vote to see which team made the most convincing argument.

5. Have each member of your team identify a Social Media Monitoring service and explore the kind of information that companies like these can collect. Working together, prepare a report outlining the kind of data that are available to companies who want to know if their social media activities are effective.

CASE 2 BUSINESS CASE

Is Google+ a Better Social Network?

On June 28, 2011, Google launched its new social networking service Google+, designed to compete directly with Facebook, the dominant SNS on the web. For approximately three months, Google kept the site in beta mode. Invitations to the site were first extended to Google employees and influential people in technology and social media. These people in turn were allowed to invite up to 150 others to join. Demand to join the nascent SNS was so strong that at one point Google had to shut down new memberships for a short period. However, by September 20, 2011, the service was open to anyone who wished to join, and by March 2012 the service claimed 100 million users (compared to Facebook which claims over 800 million users). Google+ ranks 13th on Experian Hitwise's Social Networking and Forums (Perez, 2011). See Figure 8.17.

Figure 8.18 On January 30, 2012, President Barack Obama participated in an online interview held through a Google+ Hangouts, making it the first completely virtual interview from the White House.

Hangouts is a video-conferencing feature that allows users to chat in real time with members of their network, as shown in Figure 8.18. Prior to the launch of Hangouts, other popular free video conferencing applications only allowed video conferencing between two and four individuals. Facebook's video chat feature is limited to conversations between two people.

Google+ also features **Stream** (similar to Facebook's Newsfeed), games, as well as enhanced photo management capabilities (including photo editing).

Figure 8.17 With the launch of Google+, the search engine giant hopes to create a social network that is fully integrated with all of its other services.

Google+ Entices Users with Superior Features

Google+ offers a number of features designed to attract users to its platform. In fact, it appears that one of Google's strategies is to use the SNS as an integrated platform for many of its current stand-alone services. The Circles feature allows users to organize connections into different groups based on relationship (e.g., friends, co-workers, family, customers, etc.). This gives people greater control over who can see the things they share. For instance, the fact that you waited four-hours in line to watch the latest sequel in the *Twilight* series? Probably just friends. On the other hand, news about an upcoming product launch from your company? Probably co-workers and customers. Circles seem to address a longstanding frustration expressed by Facebook users about the dangers of sharing things on the SNS that aren't appropriate for your entire network.

Facebook Responds

While Facebook publically claims to not be very worried about competition from Google+, it did release a number of new features in the months following the launch of the new SNS. Facebook Lists seem to be its answer to Google+ Circles. Lists allow users to control who sees status updates, photos, and wall posts. Facebook also launched a feature called Subscriptions, which allow users to control how much information they get from others in the network. You can use subscriptions to limit, for instance, the number of raging political posts that show up in your newsfeed from all the militant anarchists in your network.

Facebook also introduced **Timeline,** a significant departure from the traditional way that user profiles are displayed. With Timeline, Facebook creates a historical record of photos, status updates, locations you've visited, and significant events. Users are encouraged to fill in the gaps of the timeline, even adding information about dates before they joined Facebook. Reaction to the Timeline feature has been mixed, with some users expressing concern over privacy issues and others claiming that by encouraging users to fill in the gaps, Facebook is simply trying to get people to share more personal data that the company can use to attract advertisers.

A David and Goliath Story?

Some might be tempted to paint this as a classic David and Goliath story, given the relative size of Facebook compared to Google's new entry to the SNS space. However, remember that Googe+'s parent company is the leading Internet brand name and is considerably larger than Facebook in terms of total users and ad revenue (Machlis, 2011). Only time will tell how the competition for users and advertising dollars will play out between these two formidable competitors.

Sources: Compiled from Parr (2011), Bond (2011), Whittaker (2011), Nunez (2011), and Machlis (2011)

Questions & Activities

1. Create an account at *Google.com*. Login to the site. Explore the Google+ social network, by clicking "+" link with your name in the upper left-hand corner of the screen. In Google+, look for the YouTube search button and use it to find a list of Google+ Tutorials that explain the various features of the site.

2. If you have a web cam attached to your computer, arrange to meet other students for a brief video chat using the Google+ Hangouts feature. How does it compare to other video conferencing apps you may have used?

3. Are features the primary motivation for users to join an SNS community? How will this affect the ability of Google+ to attract new users?

4. Is Google+ engaging in direct competition with Facebook, or is it attempting to be something different?

5. If Google+ offers superior features, why aren't more people using it? What steps should Google+ take to attract more people to its new SNS?

CASE 3 VIDEO CASE

Danone Activia Engages Customers Using Social Media

© whiteboxmedia limited/Alamy Limited

Figure 8.19 The Activia brand appeals to people who want a healthy lifestyle and share a concern for the environment.

Groupe Danone is a multinational food processing company (known as Dannon in the U.S.) and the maker of Activia brand yogurt. Danone has worked hard to create a premium, international brand image for Activia that emphasizes healthy lifestyle, natural ingredients, and concern for the environment.

In the spring of 2010, the Slovenian marketing firm Red Orbit helped Danone create a social media campaign to relaunch a yogurt-based drink under the Activia brand name. Watch the video case study using this link: *youtube.com/watch?v=cWXesLRnggw*.

After watching the video, answer the following questions to gain a better understanding of how social media goes beyond simply broadcasting brand messages to engage customers and create excitement around the brand.

Questions and Activities

1. How would you describe Activia's brand objectives as they relate to this campaign? In other words, what was Activia hoping to achieve with regard to its brand image?

2. Successful social media campaigns engage people. What specific things did Activia do to engage customers and generate activity on their Facebook page?

3. Some might say the contest prize (a two-week trek vacation through Indonesia) was a bit unusual. Why do you thing the campaign creators selected this as the prize?

4. Contestants were told to have their friends "vote" for their submissions. What did Activa accomplish with this tactic?

5. While the contest was launched on Facebook, it eventually spread to other social and traditional media channels. How or why did this occur? Was this desirable from Activia's perspective?

6. In terms of social media metrics, what specific outcomes did the campaign produce?

7. One common objective that companies have for social media campaigns is the creation of "brand advocates," people who are so excited about the brand that they freely promote it to others. In what ways did this campaign inspire people to become brand advocates?

Data Analysis & Decision Making

Estimating the ROI of Social Media

Notes: For this analysis, go to the Student Companion Web Site to download the spreadsheet file.

Recall that customer attrition rate is the rate (percent) at which a company loses customers. The opposite is the customer retention rate, which is the percent of customers that stay with the company. Mathematically,

$$\text{customer attrition rate} = 100 \text{ percent} - \text{customer retention rate}$$

Scenario: BravoMedia-2020 has asked you to estimate the ROI of four social media investments.

CCAR. Some customer attrition cannot be controlled and is not relevant to this analysis. Your focus is only on the "controllable customer attrition rate" (CCAR) that is now 6 percent per quarter. By applying four social media campaigns, which are shown in Figure 8.20, the CCAR can be lowered by 4 percent—from 6 percent per quarter to 2 percent per quarter.

ROI Calculation

Number of customers, January 2013	1,500,000
Controllable Customer Attrition Rate (average rate per quarter) [CCAR]	6%

Average profit per customer	$	10

IT-based Strategies to reduce the Controllable Customer Attrition Rate (CCAR)	Percent reduction in CCAR	Estimated Cost of the campaign or app	
#1 - Launch campaign using 2D tags	1.25%	$	700,000
#2 - Create campaign on Facebook	0.50%	$	425,000
#3 - Launch viral marketing campaign	0.75%	$	525,000
#4 - Develop an iPhone app	1.50%	$	350,000
Total reduction in CCAR	4.00%	Total investment $	2,000,000

2013

	Q1	Q2	Q3	Q4
Expected loss of customers, no strategy (6% CCAR)	90,000	84,600	79,524	74,753
Number of customers remaining at end of Quarter	1,410,000	1,325,400	1,245,876	1,171,123
Expected loss of customers, using all 4 marketing campaigns (2% CCAR)	30,000			
Number of customers remaining at end of Quarter	1,470,000			

IMPROVEMENTS DUE TO IT-BASED CAMPAIGNS -- INCREASED # OF RETAINED CUSTOMERS

Improvement in # of customers retained due to campaigns (difference between the Q4 numbers)	
Average profit per customer	$ 10
TOTAL VALUE OF CAMPAIGNS [improvement * $10]	$ -

ROI = (Total Value of Campaigns - Total Investment)/Total investment * 100% =	

Figure 8.20 ROI Spreadsheet for Chapter 8.

Cost. The cost of each of the four social media campaigns is shown in Figure 8.20.

Profit. The average profit for each retained customer is $10.

Improvement. The total value (improvement) of the four campaigns is represented as:

$$IMPROVEMENT = \text{Increase in number of retained customers} * \$10$$

The investment cost is the sum of the four campaign costs.

$$INVESTMENT\ COST = \$2,000,000$$
(see Figure 8.20)

The general formula for ROI is:

$$ROI = (IMPROVEMENT - INVESTMENT\ COST)/ INVESTMENT\ COST * 100\ percent$$

A positive ROI indicates that the investment in the four campaigns improves the bottom line, or profit.

Analysis: Perform the calculations to estimate the ROI. Figure 8.20 illustrates the spreadsheet that you can download from the student companion site. You need to enter formulas or functions in the highlighted cells to calculate the ROI. Based on the results of your ROI analysis, make a recommendation to management. Include your spreadsheet to justify and explain your recommendation.

Resources on the Book's Web Site

More resources and study tools are located on the Student Web Site. You'll find additional chapter materials and useful web links. In addition, self-quizzes that provide individualized feedback are available for each chapter.

References

Abram, C., and Pearlman, L. "*Facebook For Dummies.*" Hoboken, NJ: John Wiley & Sons, 2008.

Alexa Topsites, March 2012. *alexa.com/topsites.*

Bennett, J. "Will social media kill off the intranet in years to come?" *Internalcommshub.com,* 2009. *internalcommshub.com/open/channels/whatsworking/intranetend.shtml*

Berners-Lee, T. Interview with Scott Laningham, developerWorks Interviews, IBM, August 2006.

Berners-Lee, T. "*Giant Global Graph.*" Timbl's blog, Decentralized Information Group, November 2007. *Dig.csail.mit.edu/breadcrumbs/blog/4.*

Bond, M. "Facebook Timeline a New Privacy Test." *USAToday.com,* November 2, 2011.

Carr, D. "Is Business Ready for Second Life?" *Baseline Magazine,* March 2007.

Carroll, D. "United Breaks Guitars." Dave Carroll Music. 2012. *davecarrollmusic.com/music/ubg/*

Dijoux C. "Enterprise 2.0 Explained to Our Managers in 10 Principles." Hypertextual. November 2009.

Dilworth, D. "Blendtec Mixes Online Video to Raise Brand Awareness." *DMNews,* June 6, 2007.

Facebook Statistics, 2010. *facebook.com/press/info.php?statistics.*

Forrester Research. "2008 Forrester Groundswell Awards Winners." 2008.

Forrester Research and Cisco Systems. "Social Networking in the Enterprise: Benefits and Inhibitors," May, 2010. *cisco.com/en/US/prod/collateral/ps10680/ps10683/ps10668/soc_nw_en_tlp.pdf*

Happe, R. "Social Media Metrics." *The Social Organization,* 2008.

Harvard Business School Working Knowledge (HBSWK). First Look, May 4, 2010. *hbswk.hbs.edu/item/6418.html*

Harvey, M. "Facebook sets up Google-war with vast expansion through Open Graph," *Times Online.* 2010.

Heathfield, S. "Use LinkedIn for Recruiting Employees." *Humanresources.com.* 2012.

Helm, B. "As Seen on YouTube. Order Now!" *Bloomberg BusinessWeek.* December 11, 2006: *businessweek.com/the_thread/brandnewday/archives/2006/12/as_seen_on_youtube_order_now.html*

Hendler, J., and Berners-Lee, T. "From the Semantic Web to Social Machines: A Research Challenge for AI on the World Wide Web," *Artificial Intelligence,* 174, 2010.

Hird, J. "20+More Mind Blowing Social Media Statistics." Digital Marketing Blog. August 2009.

KPMG. International Going Social How Business Are Making the Most of Social Media, December, 2011.

Lasica, J., and Bale, K. "Top 20 social media monitoring vendors for business." *Socialmedia.biz,* January 2011.

Lavidge, R. J., and Steiner, G. A. "A Model of Predictive Measurements of Advertising Effectiveness." *Journal of Marketing* 25, no. 6, 1961.

Levine, R., Locke, C., Searls, D., Weinberger, D. *The Cluetrain Manifesto: The End of Business as Usual.* Cambridge, MA: Perseus Books, 2000.

Li, C., and Bernoff. J. *Groundswell: Winning in a World Transformed by Social Technologies.* Boston: Harvard Business Press, 2008.

Lipsman, A. "State of the U.S. Social Networking Market: Facebook Maintains Leadership Position, but Upstarts Gaining Traction." *Comscore.com,* December 2011.

Machlis, S. "Google vs. Facebook by the Numbers." *ComputerWorld.com,* July 7, 2011.

March, J. "Zappos: Delivering WOW Customer Service through Twitter." The Social Customer. 2011.

McAfee, A. "Interview: Andrew McAfee—What is Web/Enterprise 2.0." 2008. [Video File] *youtube.com/watch?v=6xKSJfQh89k.*

Mitra, S. "Web 3.0 = (4C + P + VS)." *Sramanamitra.com,* 2007. *sramanamitra.com/2007/02/14/web-30-4c-p-vs.*

Murguia, A. "Jobvite Index Shows Hiring Patterns in LinkedIn, Facebook and Twitter," *Jobvite.com,* July, 2011.

Nielsen Company. "Facebook and Twitter Post Large Year over Year Gains in Unique Users." May 4, 2010.

Nunez, M. "Google+ Strategy Outlined: Goal is 'Not to Build Something Separate' From Other Google Products." *IBTimes.com,* October 20, 2011.

Parr, B. "Google+. The Complete Guide." *Mashable.com,* July 16, 2011. *mashable.com/2011/07/16/google-plus-guide/.*

Pearson, R. "Imagineering a Windows (Social) Media Player." *The Parallax View.* 2010.

Perez, J. "Hitwise: Google+ traffic up in October over last month." *Computerworld.com.* October 27, 2011. *computerworld.com/s/article/9221280/Hitwise_Google_traffic_up_in_October_over_last_month*

Reisner, R. "Comcast's Twitter Man." *Bloomberg Businessweek*, January 13, 2009.

Social Media Ad Metric Definitions, Interactive Advertising Bureau. 2009.

Thompson, D. "Here Come the Raises." *The Atlantic*, March 2012.

Vogelstein, F. "Great Wall of Facebook: The Social Network's Plan to Dominate the Internet—And Keep Google Out." *Wired Magazine*, June 2009.

Vollmer, C., & Premo, K. "Campaigns to Capabilities: Social Media & Marketing 2011." Booz & Company. *booz.com/media/file/BoozCo-Campaigns-to-Capabilities-Social-Media-and-Marketing-2011.pdf.*

Ward, T. "The Social Intranet." *IntranetBlog.com*, 2010.

Weaver, A., and Morrison, B. "Social Networking." *Computer*, February 2008.

Whittaker, Z. "Facebook Timeline a 'Stalker's Paradise': Mass Exodus on the Way?" *ZDNet.com*, September 27, 2011.

Wesch, M. "Web 2.0 . . . The Machine is Us/ing Us," [video file] March 2007. *youtube.com/watch?v=NLlGopyXT_g.*

Chapter 9

Functional Area and Compliance Systems

Learning Outcomes

❶ Describe various types of functional systems and how they support managers and workers at the operational level.

❷ Define how manufacturing, production, and transportation information systems enable organizational processes and support supply chain operations and logistics.

❸ Explain how sales and marketing information systems support advertising, market research, intelligence gathering, getting products and services to customers, and responding quickly and efficiently to customers' needs.

❹ Describe how accounting, auditing, and finance application systems meet compliance mandates, help deter fraud, and facilitate capital budgeting and forecasting.

❺ Explain how human resources information systems (HRIS) improve business-to-employee (B2E) communications, workforce productivity, and compliance with federal employment laws; and discuss ethical issues related to the use of HRIS data.

As a manager, you'll be involved in the interrelationships among various functions within the organization. Business functions are connected by the data and reports they share or generate. Decisions made in the sales and marketing department, for example, cause ripple effects in accounting, finance, IT, manufacturing, and human resources (HR) departments. In this chapter, you read how various information systems support and integrate business functions to maximize operational performance and to meet compliance with numerous and demanding regulations. Ideally, operational ISs (also called functional area ISs) provide:

- **Transparency:** knowing what's happening in any department or function at any time.
- **Quick response:** responding appropriately to changes in conditions or demand as needed, enabling business units to take advantage of opportunities, to protect against threats, or to improve efficiency.

Ultimately, data from functional ISs are used extensively by enterprise applications, including business intelligence (BI), e-commerce, customer relationship management (CRM), and supply chain management (SCM), as shown in Figure 9.1.

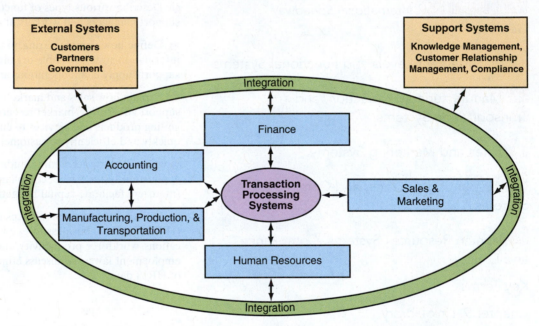

Figure 9.1 Data from functional area ISs support enterprise apps.

CASE 1 OPENING CASE

International Speedway Gets Lean

Lean: The core idea is to maximize value while minimizing waste. Eliminating waste (**going lean**) in a department or along an entire value stream results is carried out by automating and streamlining processes, which reduce process time and errors.

Millions of racing fans attend NASCAR, the Daytona 500, and other motorsport events at International Speedway Corporation (ISC) tracks. Based in Daytona Beach, Florida, ISC is a leading promoter of motorsports entertainment with more than 100 events at 14 racetracks in the U.S. and Canada ISC's corporate mission is to deliver memorable motorsports experiences for guests of all ages at its venues; and to operate efficiently and effectively to maximize shareholder value (*internationalspeedwaycorporation.com*, 2012). The success of its mission depends largely on its ability to fill seats at events and minimize waste in marketing campaigns.

ISC is organized around decentralized business units. Each race venue (see Figure 9.2) is a separate business unit with specific race goers, events, and objectives.

© Edwin Remsberg/Alamy Limited

© ZUMA Wire Service/
Alamy Limited

Figure 9.2 ISC manages huge volumes of fan data compiled from the Daytona 500 and all other NASCAR races.

Customer touchpoints are ways to reach, build, and strengthen relationships with customers. Touchpoints that don't interest or create interest with a customer are a waste of resources, both time and budget.

Mission: Set of outcomes an organization wants to achieve.

Data-Rich, but Insight-Poor

During 2007, customer demand for racing events had flattened out (that is, *no sales growth*). Management decided to introduce targeted marketing campaigns that are based on a clear understanding of current and prospective customers. Management had the data they needed as a result of collecting structured and unstructured data on 4 million race fans through formal surveys, e-mail, phone calls, and social network sites. But they had not been leveraging that data to maximize advertising effectiveness. Too much of the advertising budget was wasted on campaigns advertising to people who were not interested in particular races, while fans who would have been interested in the race were not being contacted.

Targeted Campaigns and Personalizing Customer Touchpoints

To run targeted campaigns, the chief marketing officer (CMO) wanted a 360-degree view of customers, for instance, what, when, how, and why they bought tickets going as far back as 2002. The CMO uses the data to determine how to personalize **customer touchpoints.** Ideally, touchpoints either interest or create interest in customers to maximize return of advertising dollars. Increasing the number and frequency of high-quality touchpoints increases the chance of being top-of-mind with customers when they are deciding on entertainment. Knowing what customers want can be a powerful competitive edge.

Trying to create a complete view of customers was a challenge for ISC for two reasons:

1. Using data dating back to 2002 meant analyzing up to 10 million rows of data, which was beyond the capability of ISC's data infrastructure and analytics apps. Each row corresponds to one person, but a single fan might have been listed 5, 10, or more times in various databases. There was a lot of data redundancy because of various data collection systems.

2. Personalizing touchpoints required a consolidated, up-to-date view of customers, which was not possible because of ISC's data silos and non-integrated data collection methods.

To address these data challenges and launch new sales and marketing initiatives, ISC needed a capable IT infrastructure.

Integrated Marketing Data Solution and Business Outcomes

ISC selected *Marketing Studio*, an integrated IT platform consisting of a marketing database and analysis tools from Aprimo (*aprimo.com*), to be able to segment customers precisely. Managers now know who their fans are—not just the person who bought the tickets. For example, if someone buys four tickets, ISC captures the names and other data about all four fans instead of only the purchaser's name and data. The data are used to personalize e-mails and market to specific fans.

By being able to access transaction data down to a specific seat in a grandstand, each race venue (business unit) develops more profitable, individualized campaigns that are delivered through their consumers' preferred channel. The units efficiently develop and produce

5,000 marketing communications annually. In 2008, prior to using Studio, ISC had four corporate staff members working on 250 campaigns. After 2010, 1.5 full-time-equivalent employees worked 1,000 campaigns. Out of those 1,000 campaigns, only three e-mails might be sent to the wrong list. That level of quality had not been possible before the investment in the marketing database and analysis tools.

Discuss

1. Explain ISC's strategic problem that was making it difficult to achieve their mission.
2. Explain ISC's data challenges.
3. Explain the benefits of being lean.
4. How did its data challenges relate to its strategic problem?
5. Visit *Aprimo.com*; click on "Products," and then click "Aprimo Marketing Studio." Review the features and benefits listed by the vendor. What are three of the benefits offered by the software?
6. Why is it important to use customer touchpoints effectively or correctly?

Decide

7. Does the *efficiency* of marketing depend on the extent to which it is data-driven and fact-based? Does the *effectiveness* of marketing depend on the extent to which it is data-driven and fact-based? Would marketing apps have a great impact on efficiency or effectiveness—or not? Explain your analysis and answers.

Debate

8. Most marketers know this very old quote from John Wanamaker, considered the father of modern advertising, "I know that half of my advertising dollars are wasted … I just don't know which half." This quote can be interpreted to mean:

    a. Marketing programs or campaigns are not easily justified on ROI because they are expensive and direct benefits (increased sales) are difficult to quantify.

    b. Half of the cost of marketing campaigns is wasted.

    Based on ISC's results after implementing campaign management software, debate whether or not either interpretation is still valid. Justify your position.

9.1 Management Levels and Functional Systems

Management levels are modeled as a pyramid shown in Figure 9.3. Starting at the base of the pyramid, the levels are operational, managerial or administrative, and strategic. Each level of management has its concerns, data needs, decision making responsibilities, time horizons, and strategic and tactical questions. Answers to the questions require understanding the capabilities of mundane to complex ITs, which ones to implement, and how to manage them.

• At the **strategic level,** senior or-top level management plan and make decisions that set or impact the long-term direction of the entire organization. These decisions are visionary and future-oriented. External data about the economy, markets, competitors, and business trends are essential to their SWOT (strengths, weaknesses, opportunities, and threats) analysis, planning, and decisions.

• At the **managerial or administrative level,** middle-level managers define business models and make tactical decisions that are shorter range. Examples are how to beat out competitors and generate revenues and profits to fulfill the organization's mission, objectives, and strategy. Control is important at this level. Middle management sets goals for their departments or business units that are consistent with organizational goals set by senior management. External and internal data are important for decision making, which often has a one- to three-year time horizon.

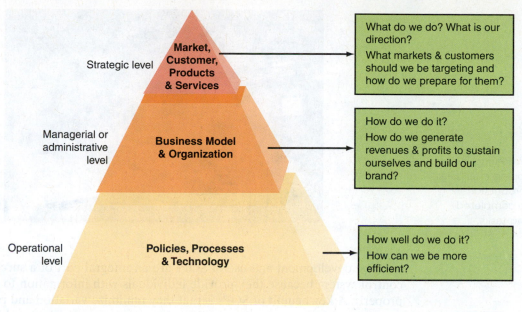

Figure 9.3 Three organizational levels, their concerns, and strategic and tactical questions, planning and control.
Source: Adapted from Booz&Co, 2011.

• At the **operational level,** department managers, supervisors, and workers need detailed data, in real time or near real time, and the ability to respond to what they learn from functional ISs. Decision making is mostly for the short-term, because decisions are made to control ongoing activities and operations. The purpose of control is to identify deviations from goals as soon as possible in order to take corrective action. Tracking sales, inventory levels, orders, and customer support are examples of control activities. A company's internal data are most important at this level.

INFORMATION SYSTEMS DESIGNED TO SUPPORT BUSINESS FUNCTIONS AND PROCEDURES

Originally, ISs were designed to support the accounting function. Later, other functional areas received IS support. This design process led to the creation of data silos that made it difficult to share data needed by cross-functional business processes. For example, when a customer orders a tablet device, the order is processed by the sales department and finance verifies and approves credit. Then order fulfillment or production determines whether the product is in the warehouse; picking and shipping departments pack the product, print the mailing label, and prepare for shipping (see Figure 9.4). When work flows and data flows between departments do not work well or coordination is difficult, they cause delays, errors, and poor customer service. This is why integrating the functional departments via information systems that enable communication, coordination, and control is essential.

The business functions interact by passing data from one to the other. For example, after products are produced and shipped, the production and shipping systems inform the accounting systems, which record the sale and issue an accounts payable (A/P) or charge the buyer's credit card. Business records are generated by each activity, including those needed for product warranties, sales reports, and financial statements. Data requirements of the operational level units are extensive and relatively routine, rarely changing because they depend on fixed sources of input and **standard operating procedures (SOP)**. An SOP is a set of written instructions that document a routine or repetitive activity that is followed by an organization. SOPs are easily automated or supported by functional area information systems.

© API/Alamy Limited

Figure 9.4 Preparing factory orders for shipping after sales, finance, and production functions have completed their processing tasks.

The development and use of SOPs are an integral part of a successful quality control system because they provide individuals with information to perform jobs properly. A key benefit of SOPs is that they minimize variation and promote quality through consistent implementation of a process or procedure within the organization, even if there are temporary or permanent personnel changes. SOPs are written, for example, for handling purchase orders, order fulfillment, customer complaints, recruitment and hiring, emergency response, and disaster recovery. Data that are lost, destroyed, or compromised have financial implications. As such it is critical that businesses have SOPs to ensure that data are secure, accurate, and that integrity is maintained. *IT at Work 9.1* gives an outline of SOPs to secure transaction data.

BASIC FUNCTIONAL AREA SYSTEMS

The basic functional area information systems and examples of their apps are the following.

- **Manufacturing and production:** materials purchasing, quality control, scheduling, shipping, receiving. For example, to produce small appliances, a manufacturer needs to order materials and parts, pay for labor and electricity, create shipment orders, and bill customers.

IT at Work 9.1

Standard Operating Procedures for Securing Transaction Data, an Outline

Data security: Data must be protected from malicious or unintentional corruption, unauthorized modification, theft, or natural causes such as floods.

Data accuracy: Data validation is used to detect and correct data entry errors, such as address data and customer names.

Data Integrity: Data integrity with real-time systems involves the ACID test, which is short for atomicity, consistency, isolation, and durability:

- *Atomicity:* If all steps in a transaction are not completed, then the entire transaction is cancelled.

- *Consistency:* Only operations that meet data validity standards are allowed. For instance, systems that record checking accounts only allow unique check numbers for each transaction. Any operation that repeated a check number

would fail to insure that the data in the database is correct and accurate. Network failures can also cause data consistency problems.

- *Isolation:* Transactions must be isolated from each other. For example, bank deposits must be isolated from a concurrent transaction involving a withdrawal from the same account. Only when the withdrawal transaction is successfully completed will the new account balance be reported.

- *Durability:* Backups by themselves do not provide durability. A system crash or other failure must not cause any loss of data in the database. Durability is achieved through separate transaction logs that can be used to re-create all transactions from a known checkpoint. Other ways include database mirrors that replicate the database on another server.

Figure 9.5 A billboard in New York City's Times Square advertises the services of SquareUp, a credit card reader system for Apple and Android mobile devices.

© Richard Levine/Alamy Limited

• **Accounting:** accounts receivable, accounts payable, general ledger, budgeting. Accounting systems keep account balances up to date, disburse funds, and post statements.

• **Finance:** cash management, asset management, credit management, financial statement reporting to comply with federal and industry-specific regulations and government agencies.

• **IT:** cloud computing services, service level agreement (SLA) management, software license management, user accounts management, information and network security.

• **Sales and marketing:** pricing, social media promotions, market research, demand forecasts, sales campaign management, order tracking, and online and mobile order processing and sales (see Figure 9.5).

• **HR:** payroll, recruitment and hiring, succession planning, employee benefits, training, compensation, performance appraisal, compliance with federal and state employment regulations.

In **online transaction processing (OLTP),** events or transactions are processed as soon as they occur. Data are accessed directly from the database, and reports can be generated automatically (Figure 9.6). *IT at Work 9.2* describes a real-time sales and reporting system.

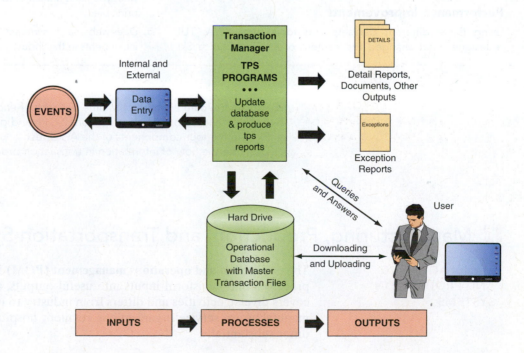

Figure 9.6 Information flows triggered by a transaction or event.

IT at Work 9.2

Real-time Reporting Improves Sales at First Choice Ski

First Choice Ski (*firstchoice-ski.co.uk/*) holds a 14 percent market share of the online UK ski vacation industry. TUI Travel, its parent company, is an international leisure travel group, which operates in 180 countries and serves more than 30 million customers.

In the highly competitive tour operator industry, profit margins are tight. Being lean and responsive is key to maintaining a profitable business. By using Yahoo! Web Analytics (*web. analytics.yahoo.com/*) and real-time reporting, First Choice Ski was able to monitor and quickly respond to the behaviors of visitors on its travel web site. Figure 9.7 is an example of a web analytics interface.

First Choice Ski Tracks Customers' Behaviors

At First Choice Ski, customers spend a lot of time researching and selecting their vacations. Simon Rigglesworth, e-commerce manager, explained: "We see users return multiple times from multiple sources such as paid search, e-mail and even social networking as they try to find the vacation that suits them the best. Capturing as much information as possible allows us to identify the best way to complete the sale and optimize for it."

After experimenting with fee-based analytics packages, First Choice Ski selected Yahoo! Web Analytics (YWA), which is free. Web Analyst Penelope Bellegarde used the *Search Phrases Report* in YWA to leverage factors driving visitors to First Choice Ski. She said: "If we notice a specific destination is driving a lot of visits to the site, then it is very likely we will promote that destination on the homepage."

The *Internal Campaign Report* helps them monitor and manage their many travel promotions. For example, Bellegarde monitors the number of clicks and number of sales generated by each campaign, and when a low ratio of sales to clicks is noticed, they adjust the campaign accordingly.

Performance Improvements

Using these different datasets and tools from YWA, TUI redesigned and changed the content of its First Choice Ski

Figure 9.7 Example of a web analytics interface.

© NAN/Alamy Limited

homepage. Afterwards, the bounce rate (transfer out) from the homepage decreased 18 percent, and the exit rate decreased 13 percent. Most important, the number of sales generated from the home page increased 266 percent. "We are now generating quantifiable, actionable, data-driven processes for prioritizing and reviewing web site developments," says Rigglesworth.

Sources: Compiled from firstchoice-ski.co.uk/ and Yahoo.com/.

Questions

1. How does the ski travel site's quick response to visitors' clickstream behavior relate to its profit margin?
2. Consider this measurement principle: You can't manage what you can't measure. Explain how the case illustrates this principle.
3. Does web analytics impact barriers to entry and rivalry among incumbents in this industry?

Questions

1. Explain the core concerns and time horizons of each level of management.
2. Define standard operating procedure (SOP), and give an example.
3. Explain the four components of the ACID test.
4. Describe the flow of information in transaction processing.

9.2 Manufacturing, Production, and Transportation Systems

MANUFACTURING AND PRODUCTION SYSTEMS

The **production and operations management (POM)** function is responsible for the processes that transform inputs into useful outputs, as shown in Figure 9.8. POM covers diverse activities and differs from industry to industry; for instance, POM of manufacturers, service organizations, retailers, hospitals, and government agencies differ substantially.

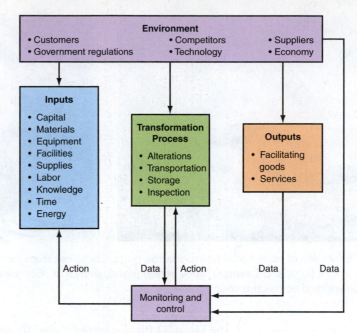

Figure 9.8 Production operations management (POM) systems process and transform inputs into outputs.

TRANSPORTATION MANAGEMENT SYSTEMS

Transportation management systems (TMS) handle transportation planning, which includes shipping consolidation, load and trip planning, route planning and tracking fleet and driver planning, and carrier selection. TMSs also support vehicle management and accounting transactions. Every day in the U.S., the transportation network connects cities, manufacturers, and retailers, moving large volumes of goods and individuals through a complex network of approximately 4 million miles of roadways, more than 140,000 miles of active rail, 600,000 bridges and tunnels, more than 350 maritime ports, hundreds of thousands of miles of pipeline, nearly 30 million trips using mass transit and passenger rail, and more than 450 commercial airports.

In 2012, there was a noticeable increase in the use of TMS. Four factors contributing to the growth of TMS are:

1. Outdated transportation systems need to be upgraded or replaced. Many systems were installed over 10 years ago—before tablet computers and mobile technologies had become widespread in business. Similar to most legacy (old) systems, they are inflexible, difficult to integrate with other newer systems, and expensive to maintain.

2. Growth of intermodal transport. Intermodal transportation refers to the use of two or more transport modes, such as container ship, air, truck, and rail, to move products from source to destination. See Figure 9.9 for examples. Many more companies are shipping via intermodals and their older TMSs cannot support or deal with intermodal movement, according to Dwight Klappich, a research vice president for Gartner.

When brick-and-mortar manufacturers began selling online, for example, they learned that their existing TMSs are inadequate for handling the new line of business. Shippers that expand globally face similar challenges when they try to manage multiple rail, truck, and ocean shipments. Thus, there is a growing need more robust TMSs to handle multidimensional shipping arrangements.

3. TMS vendors add capabilities. The basic functions performed by a TMS include gathering data on a load to be transported and matching those data to a historical routing guide. Then the TMS is used to manage the communication process with the various carriers. New feature-rich TMSs are able to access information services to help the shipper identify optimal routes given all current conditions. For example,

© Randy Duchaine/Alamy Limited

© Robert Quinlan/Alamy Limited

Figure 9.9 Examples of intermodal transportation ports. Container ships from around the world are unloaded in the Brooklyn, New York (left), and Bayonne, New Jersey (right), shipyards. Containers are tracked as they are loaded onto trucks or rail and transported across the country.

the latest TMSs can interact directly with market-data benchmarking services. An automated, real-time market monitoring function saves shippers time, errors, and cuts costs significantly.

4. TMS handle big data. Transportation tends to generate a high volume of transactional data. Managing the data isn't easy. TMS vendors are developing systems that make valuable use of the big data that are collected and stored. By drilling down into specific regions or focusing on particular market trends, for example, shippers can use their big data to make better decisions.

IT at Work 9.3 describes a cloud-based software-as-a-service (SaaS) TMS.

LOGISTICS MANAGEMENT SYSTEMS

Logistics management deals with the coordination of several complex processes, namely ordering, purchasing or procurement, inbound logistics (receiving), and outbound logistics (shipping) activities. The general goals of logistics management systems are to:

- Optimize transportation operations
- Coordinate with all suppliers
- Integrate supply chain technologies
- Synchronize inbound and outbound flows of materials or goods
- Manage distribution or transport networks

IT at Work 9.3

Total Visibility, a SaaS Transportation Management System

In 2012, Agistix (*agistix.com*) introduced Total Visibility, a new cloud-based, SaaS TMS. By providing the TMS in the cloud, shippers have access from any location at any time. SaaS (a leased arrangement) makes it affordable to more shippers.

Total Visibility provides shippers with real-time visibility to eliminate blind spots. Visibility is achieved by capturing shipment estimates so that clients can better forecast spend (costs) and meet compliance reporting requirements. Real-time data allows customers to know what is happening and to analyze big data to ensure that their supply chain is functioning as designed.

Total Visibility aggregates and standardizes a company's shipping activities and provides shippers with a comprehensive view into every shipment they have paid for anywhere in the world. Key benefits of Total Visibility for shippers are real-time visibility to all shipments in transit across all carriers, all service levels, all modes, international and domestic, inbound and outbound.

These systems enable real-time monitoring and tracking of supply chain shipments, schedules, and orders. You read about supply chain management in more detail in Chapter 10.

INVENTORY CONTROL SYSTEMS

The function of **inventory control systems,** which are also called *stock control* or *inventory management systems*, is to minimize the total cost of inventory while maintaining optimal inventory levels. Inventory levels are maintained by re-ordering the quantity needed at the right times in order to meet demand. POM departments keep **safety stock** or **buffer stock** as a hedge against **shortages,** or stockouts. Safety stock is extra inventory in case of unexpected events, such as spikes in demand or longer delivery times.

Managing inventory is important to profit margins because of numerous costs associated with inventory, in addition to the cost of the inventory. Inventory control systems minimize the following three cost categories:

1. Cost of holding inventory: warehousing costs (see Figure 9.10), security costs, insurance, losses due to theft or obsolescence, and inventory financing costs based on the interest rate

2. Cost of ordering and shipping: employees' time spent ordering, receiving, or processing deliveries; and the shipping fees

3. Cost of shortages: production delays and missed sales revenues because of stockouts

To minimize the sum of these three costs, the POM department has to decide when to order and how much to order. One inventory model that is used to answer both questions is the **economic order quantity (EOQ)** model. The EOQ model takes all costs into consideration. For additional information on EOQ, a tutorial is available at *scm.ncsu.edu/public/inventory/6eoq.html*.

Just-in-time (JIT) and lean manufacturing are two widely used methods or models to minimize waste and deal with the complexity of inventory management. Minimizing inventory costs remains a major objective of supply chain management.

Just-in-Time. JIT inventory management attempts to minimize holding costs by not taking possession of inventory until it is needed in the production process. With JIT, costs associated with carrying large inventories at any given point in time are eliminated. But the tradeoff is higher ordering costs because of more frequent orders.

Figure 9.10 Inventory holding and handling costs can significantly increase the cost of goods sold (CGS).

© Huntstock, Inc./Alamy Limited

Because of the higher risk of stockouts, JIT requires accurate and timely monitoring of materials usage in the production.

Everything in the JIT chain is interdependent, so coordination and good relationships with suppliers are critical for JIT to work well. Any delay can be very costly to all companies linked in the chain. Delays can be caused by labor strikes, interrupted supply lines, bad weather, market demand fluctuations, stock outs, lack of communication upstream and downstream in the supply chain, and unforeseen production interruptions. In addition, inventory or material quality is critical. Poor quality causes delays, for example, to fix products or scrap what cannot be fixed and wait for delivery of the re-order.

JIT was developed by Toyota because of high real estate costs in Tokyo, Japan, that made warehousing expensive. It is used extensively in the auto manufacturing industry. For example, if parts and subassemblies arrive at a workstation exactly when needed, there is no need to hold inventory. There are no delays in production, and there are no idle production facilities or underutilized workers, provided that parts and subassemblies arrive on schedule and in usable condition. Many JIT systems need to be supported by software. JIT vendors include HP, IBM, CA, and Steven Engineering.

Despite potential cost-saving benefits, JIT is likely to fail in companies that have:

- Uncooperative supply chain partners, vendors, workers, or management
- Custom or nonrepetitive production

Lean Manufacturing Systems. In a **lean manufacturing system,** suppliers deliver small lots on a daily or frequent basis, and production machines are not necessarily run at full capacity. One objective of lean manufacturing is to eliminate waste of any kind; that is, to eliminate anything that does not add value to the final product. Holding inventory that is not needed very soon is seen as waste, which adds cost but not value. A second objective of lean manufacturing is to empower workers so that production decisions can be made by those who are closest to the production processes.

Oracle, Siemens, and other vendors offer demand-driven lean manufacturing systems. Like any IS, JIT needs to be justified with a cost-benefit analysis. And all JIT success factors apply to lean manufacturing. For example, JIT requires that inventory arrive on schedule and be the right quality. For companies subject to bad weather or labor strikes, lean manufacturing may not be suitable.

Quality Control Systems. **Manufacturing quality control (QC) systems** can be standalone systems or can be part of an enterprisewide **total quality management (TQM) effort.** QC systems provide data about the quality of incoming materials and parts, as well as the quality of in-process semifinished and finished products. These systems record the results of all inspections and compare actual results to expected results.

QC data may be collected by sensors or RFID (radio frequency identification) systems and interpreted in real time, or they can be stored in a database for future analysis. Reports on percentage of defects or percentage of rework needed can keep managers informed of performance among departments. KIA Motors introduced an intelligent QC system to analyze customer complaints so they could more quickly investigate and make corrections.

Other POM Technologies. Many other areas of POM are improved by information systems and tools. Production planning optimization tools, product routing and tracking systems, order management, factory layout planning and design, and other tasks can be supported by POM subsystems. For example, a web-based system at Office Depot matches employee scheduling with store traffic patterns to increase customer satisfaction and reduce costs. Schurman Fine Papers, a manufacturer/retailer of greeting cards and specialty products, uses special warehouse management software to improve demand forecasting and inventory processes. Its two warehouses efficiently distribute products to over 30,000 retail stores.

COMPUTER INTEGRATED MANUFACTURING (CIM) AND MANUFACTURING EXECUTION SYSTEMS (MES)

Computer integrated manufacturing (CIM) systems control the day-to-day shop floor activities. In the early 1980s, companies invested greatly in CIM solutions even though they were complex, difficult to implement, and costly to maintain. They had required the integration of many products and vendors.

Prior to CIM, production managers were given many pieces of information such as time, attendance, receiving reports, inspection reports, and so on to figure out how to accomplish production tasks. The information was late, rarely current or reliable, voluminous, and extremely difficult to assimilate. CIM helps production managers better use information to execute manufacturing plans.

A **manufacturing execution system (MES)** is an online integrated computerized system that consists of methods and tools used to accomplish production. CIM and MES are very similar concepts, but there are differences. MES typically refers to a broader infrastructure than CIM. MES is based much more on standard reusable application software, instead of custom designing software programs on a contract-by-contract basis. MES tries to eliminate the time and information gap of early years on the shop floor by providing the plant with information in real time. Corporate business functions are provided with timely plant information to support business planning decisions. For the most part, the term CIM is more commonly used, and will be used in the rest of this section.

Today's CIM systems provide scheduling and real-time production monitoring and reporting. CIM data-driven automation affects all systems or subsystems within the manufacturing environment; design and development, production, marketing and sales, and field support and service. CIM systems can perform production monitoring, scheduling and planning, statistical process monitoring, quality analysis, personnel monitoring, order status reporting, and production lot tracking. Manufacturer BAE has implemented CIM.

BAE Systems Uses CIM in its Combat Aircraft Facility. BAE Systems (*baesystems. com*) is a global company headquartered in London, England, engaged in the development, delivery, and support of advanced defense, security, and aerospace systems. BAE is among the world's largest military contractors.

In September 2010, BAE opened a titanium-machining facility to manufacture components for the F-35 Lightning II combat aircraft. The facility took 10 months to complete during which time engineers at BAE considered a number of ways to ensure that it would be able to accommodate the high throughput of titanium military aircraft parts cost effectively. According to Jon Warburton, BAE's F-35 program manager, after conducting a thorough examination of numerous potential manufacturing solutions, the BAE team finally decided to deploy a highly automated CIM system (Wilson, 2011). The CIM system ensures that titanium parts for the aircraft can be manufactured on a JIT basis. To do so, it coordinates the orders received into the plant, as well as the movement of raw materials and tooling, and optimizes the use of the machine tools.

A key element of the CIM strategy was the deployment of two **flexible manufacturing systems (FMS)** that can accommodate the manufacture of different parts at different volumes. When an order for a part is received, the data relating to it are passed to the FMS systems, which schedule the manufacture of a part in the most expedient way by examining the current workload across each of eight machine tools. Each FMS can store up to 1,000 cutting tools in a racking system ready to be loaded into the machine tools. A series of twin robot systems deliver the stored cutting tools into each machine, as well as replenishing any worn tools. The biggest challenge faced by the team in the development of the facility was to ensure that the FMS and the machine tools communicated effectively with both one another and with BAE's CIM system.

Goals of CIM. CIM has three basic goals: (1) the simplification of all manufacturing technologies and techniques, (2) automation of as many of the manufacturing processes as possible, and (3) integration and coordination of all aspects of design, manufacturing, and related functions.

The major advantages of CIM are its comprehensiveness and flexibility. These are especially important in business processes that are being completely reengineered or eliminated. Without CIM, it may be necessary to make large investments to change existing ISs to fit the new processes.

Questions

1. What is the function of POM in an organization?
2. What trends are contributing to the growing use of TMS?
3. Define logistics management.
4. What are the three categories of inventory costs?
5. What are the objectives of JIT?
6. Explain the difference between EOQ and JIT inventory models.
7. What is the goal of lean manufacturing?
8. What is CIM?

9.3 Sales and Marketing Systems

Sales and marketing information systems can expand the capacity to create new products, services, channels, and market opportunities that lead to new revenue streams. *IT at Work 9.4* describes such an example.

In general, sales and marketing systems support advertising, market research, intelligence gathering, getting products and services to customers, and responding to customers' needs. Many of these systems are shown in Figure 9.11.

Chapters 7, 8, and 10 cover sales and marketing systems and strategies, including e-commerce and customer relationship management (CRM). This section will focus on data-driven marketing and capabilities of sales and marketing ISs.

DATA-DRIVEN MARKETING

Data-driven, fact-based decision making increasingly relies on data that's *hot*—impacting the business or potential customer right now, or in real-time. One use of hot data is *push-through* pay-per-click (PPC) marketing, which refers to online

IT at Work 9.4

Google's Microsurvey Market Research Offers New Revenue Model for Online Publishers

In 2012, *Adweek.com* reported on a new service called "Google Customer Surveys," which publishers can use to generate revenues from their online content. The service is an alternative to having a paywall for online news content. For example, when users visit web sites of partners like the *New York Daily News* and *Texas Tribune*, they'll find several articles partially blocked. To continue reading the full article, they have to answer a question or microsurvey provided by Google.

Adweek, a Google Partner

Adweek's editors, reporters and designers spend a lot of our time thinking about the transformational impact digital technology is having on the businesses and people they cover. They needed to monetize their digital assets to ensure that the brand continues to be a profitable going concern. To that end, *Adweek* partnered with Google on a new web-based revenue play. By answering a single marketing question per day, readers can continue to get full access to *Adweek.com* and all their reporting, analysis, and video. This method offers a solution to business concerns without blocking or limiting your access via a traditional paywall.

Microsurvey, Market Research

One or two market research multiple-choice questions are asked, for instance, "Which types of candy do you usually buy for your household?" Choices include "None, Chocolate, Hard candies, Gummies, Toffees." Advertisers pay Google to host the surveys, and the sites receive 5 cents per response from Google. To minimize the possibility that people select untruthful answers leading to poor quality data, Google makes the questions as engaging as possible. And if users start to just answer the first question on each page, or answer too quickly, the program notices that behavior and forces readers to answer new questions.

Figure 9.11 Sales and marketing systems and related subsystems.

advertising that "appears" on the screens of consumers' devices based on their location, behavior, interests, or demographic information. Unlike *pull-through* ads that appear based on the user's keyword searches, push-through ads use data about the person to determine whether the ad should appear. This capability creates opportunities for highly targeted advertising programs. For example, Facebook members self-report data about their location, age, interests, and so on. Based on this data, advertisers can request that their ad be pushed to Facebook members who fit a specific profile based on demographic, geographic, or behavioral factors.

SALES AND DISTRIBUTION CHANNELS

Marketers need to determine the optimal ways to distribute their products and services through a combination of electronic, mobile, and physical channels. For example, integrating a PPC advertising campaign with other online and offline advertising initiatives generally provides the best overall results.

Here are representative topics relating to sales and distribution channels.

• In Macy's and many other retailers, customers check the current sales price on digital screens with barcode readers.

• Customers use Exxon Mobil Speedpass to fill their tanks by waving a token, embedded with an RFID device, at a gas-pump sensor. Then the RFID starts an authorization process, and the purchase is charged to the debit or credit card on account.

- Home Depot and many supermarkets installed self-checkout machines. Self-service kiosks cut labor costs for retailers, and can reduce customers' checkout times, as shown in Figure 9.12.

Here are some representative examples of how marketing management is being done.

Pricing of Products or Services. Sales volumes as well as profits are determined by the prices of products or services. Pricing is a difficult decision, particularly during economic recessions. Prices can be changed frequently, as you read in *IT at Work 9.1*. A company may offer flash sales to engage fans or customers and to encourage a quick sale. **Flash sales** work by offering customers an incredible offer for a very short time. This sales method lends itself perfectly to the immediacy of social media, and it's a next stage in social commerce that sees brands using established sales methods, updated for the 21st century.

ZDnet reported that visits to online flash sale sites had increased by over 100 percent in July 2011 compared to July 2010 (King, 2011). Additionally, visits to flash sales come from nearly all household income brackets, with the most actually stemming from those in the $30,000 to $99,999 range. However, an estimated 52 percent of online consumers in the U.S. claimed they were starting to get overwhelmed by the volume of e-mails they are receiving from deals and discount sites.

Tag Management. Tags, such as QR codes or Microsoft tags, need to be managed. Seventy-three percent of marketers using an automated tag management system (TMS) say that it speeds up their ability to run marketing campaigns. And 42 percent say the process as significantly faster (Sullivan, 2012).

The study from Econsultancy and Tealium released in mid-2012 found 69 percent of those using a TMS managed to implement new tags or modify existing ones within the same workday. In contrast, 44 percent of marketers not using TMS said it took longer than a week to do so.

TMS automation can aid marketers who manage ad targeting and other online advertising features. It not only speeds processes, but reduces costs. Almost 75 percent of respondents who use a TMS report the costs associated with tagging are reduced, and 45 percent had significantly lower costs.

With digital marketing becoming more complex, 88 percent of respondents agree that data-driven systems will become standard necessities in the marketing toolkit. Despite growing complexity, digital marketers want to control the process—86 percent say making fast changes to marketing assets without burdening the IT team will be increasingly important. Over 80 percent of users find that marketing can take over the responsibility from IT.

Figure 9.12 Self-checkout kiosks reduce labor costs.

© Marmaduke St. John/Alamy Limited

Those using a TMS had an average of 19 tag-based online marketing solutions, compared to only 10 for those not using TMS. For web site performance, TMS boosted web site speed. Using a TMS also reduced the resource costs compared to not using a TMS.

Meanwhile, privacy concerns will force marketing technologies to offer "do-not-track options." Marketing using a TMS supports privacy initiatives, which is another benefit of TMS.

Salesperson Productivity. The performance of salespeople is collected in the sales and marketing TPS and used to compare performance along several dimensions, such as time, product, region, and even the time of day. Actual current sales can be compared to historical data and to expectations. Multidimensional spreadsheet software facilitates this type of analysis.

Sales productivity can be boosted by web-based call centers. When a customer calls a sales rep, the rep can look at the customer's history of purchases, demographics, services available where the customer lives, and more. This information enables reps to provide better customer service.

Sales automation software is especially helpful to small businesses, enabling them to rapidly increase sales and growth. A leading software is *salesforce.com*, which is a CRM application that is offered as a software as a service (SaaS). You read about *Salesforce.com* in detail in the CRM section of Chapter 10.

Profitability Analysis. In deciding on advertising and other marketing efforts, managers need to know the profit contribution or profit margin (profit margin = sale price minus cost of good) of certain products and services. Profitability metrics for products and services can be derived from the cost accounting system. For example, profit performance analysis software available from IBM, Oracle, SAS, and Microstrategy are designed to help managers assess and improve the profit performance of their line of business, products, distribution channels, sales regions, and other dimensions critical to managing the enterprise. Several airlines, for example, use automated decision systems to set prices based on profitability.

Marketing activities conclude the primary activities of the value chain. Next we look at the functional systems that are *support activities* (also called *secondary activities*) in the value chain: accounting, finance, and human resources management.

Questions

1. Explain push-through marketing and pull-through marketing.
2. List two sales and distribution channels.
3. What are the benefits of tag management systems (TMS)?
4. Describe how a flash sale works.

9.4 Accounting, Finance, and Compliance Systems

Accounting and finance departments control and manage cash flows, assets, liabilities, and net income (profit). Financial accounting is a specialized branch of accounting that keeps track of a company's financial transactions. Because investors, regulators, and others rely on the integrity and accuracy of external financial statements, accounting has common rules—namely, the generally accepted accounting principles (GAAP) and accounting standards. In the U.S., the Financial Accounting Standards Board (FASB) develops the accounting standards and principles.

Corporations whose stock is publicly traded must also comply with the reporting requirements of the Securities and Exchange Commission (SEC), a regulatory agency of the U.S. government. Using standardized guidelines, the transactions are recorded, summarized, and presented in a financial report or financial statement such as an income statement or a balance sheet. However, the objective of financial accounting is not simply to report the value of a company. Rather, its purpose is to provide sufficient and accurate information for others to assess the value of a company for investment or other purposes.

FINANCIAL DISCLOSURE (REPORTING) AND COMPLIANCE

As part of the organization's compliance obligations, the accounting function must attest (verify) that there are no material weaknesses in internal controls. A weakness in an internal control is a major cause of fraud, which is also known as white collar crime. The prevention, detection, and investigation of financial fraud are needed to reduce the risk of publicly reporting inaccurate information. The most significant examples of financial misrepresentations are Bernard L. Madoff Investment Securities, Enron, WorldCom, and the subprime mortgage crisis. The FBI investigates white collar crime and reports on their web site *FBI.gov*.

SEC Financial Disclosure System. At publicly traded firms, the accounting and finance functions are responsible for accurately disclosing (reporting) the firm's financial condition to regulatory agencies. For example, firms must file quarterly and annual financial statements to the SEC. Financial statements include Statements of Financial Position, Comprehensive Income, Changes in Equity, and Cash Flows.

The SEC's financial disclosure system is central to its mission of protecting investors and maintaining fair, orderly, and efficient markets. Since 1934, the SEC has required financial disclosure in forms and documents. In 1984, the SEC began collecting electronic documents to help investors get information, but those documents made it difficult to search and find specific data items To eliminate that difficulty and improve how investors find and use information, the SEC sought a new **data disclosure compliance system**, where data items are tagged to make them easily searchable. The reporting (disclosure) system was based on electronic data tagging, or **eXtensible Business Reporting Language (XBRL)**. As of 2012, the SEC mandated new interactive data reporting requirements as described in *IT at Work 9.5*.

IT at Work 9.5

SEC Requires Interactive Data Reporting Using XBRL

The SEC now requires data reporting in XBRL, and those reports require XBRL software.

New SEC Reporting Requirements

In March 2012, the SEC adopted the U.S. GAAP Financial Reporting Taxonomy. The **taxonomy** is an electronic dictionary of business reporting elements used to report business data. This taxonomy applies to public companies (also referred to as **filers**) that are registered with the SEC. Now filers must create and submit their financial reports as *tagged interactive data files* to comply with SEC reporting rules (*FASB.org*, 2012). Tagged interactive data files are created using eXtensible Business Reporting Language, or XBRL. The SEC has set up a website, as shown in Figure 9.13, to help filers meet their latest disclosure and filing requirements.

The SEC provides XBRL guidance on its portal at *http://xbrl.sec.gov/*. This portal provides information about XBRL in order to facilitate successful compliance with the interactive data rules.

What Is Interactive Data and Who's Using It?

Interactive data can provide investors quicker access to the data they want in a form that's easily used and can help companies prepare the information more quickly and more accurately. In the past, using noninteractive disclosure documents, investors who wanted specific information had to manually search lengthy corporate

Figure 9.13 The Securities and Exchange Commission (SEC) requires publically traded companies to file financial statements as tagged interactive data files using XBRL. Guidance for filing reports is provided at *XBRL.sec.gov*. *Source: http://xbrl.sec.gov/.*

annual reports or mutual fund documents. Searching and extracting particular information in those documents was time consuming.

Using interactive data, an investor can immediately pull out specific information and compare it to information from other companies, performance in past years, and industry averages. As more companies use interactive data, sophisticated analysis tools used by financial professionals are now available to average investors.

Interactive data may help public companies improve their reporting processes. Filers using interactive data may be able to consolidate enterprise financial information more quickly and reliably across operating units within different operating systems.

Banks also submit their *call reports* to the Federal Deposit Insurance Corporation (FDIC) in XBRL format.

XBRL. Data becomes interactive when it is labeled using a **computer markup language** that can be processed by software for sophisticated viewing and analysis. Markup languages use standard sets of definitions, or taxonomies, to enable the automatic extraction and exchange of data. Interactive data taxonomies can be applied—much in the way that bar codes are applied to merchandise—to allow computers to recognize that data and feed it into analytical tools. XBRL is the markup language that was developed for business and financial reporting. Figure 9.14 shows how XBRL documents are created. XBRL helps companies:

- Generate cleaner data, including written explanations and supporting notes.
- Produce more accurate data with fewer errors that require follow-up by regulators.
- Transmit data faster to regulators and meet deadlines.
- Increase the number of cases and amount of information that staffers can handle.

FRAUD PREVENTION AND DETECTION

Fraud is a crime with severe financial consequences. Fighting fraud is an ethical duty—and essential to public trust and the integrity of a company's brand.

    Insider fraud is a term referring to a variety of criminal behaviors perpetrated by an organization's own employees or contractors. Other terms for this crime are *internal*, *employment*, or *occupational* fraud.

Why Fraud Occurs. Fraud occurs because internal controls to prevent insider fraud—no matter how strong—will fail on occasion. **Fraud risk management** is a system of policies and procedures to prevent and detect illegal acts committed by

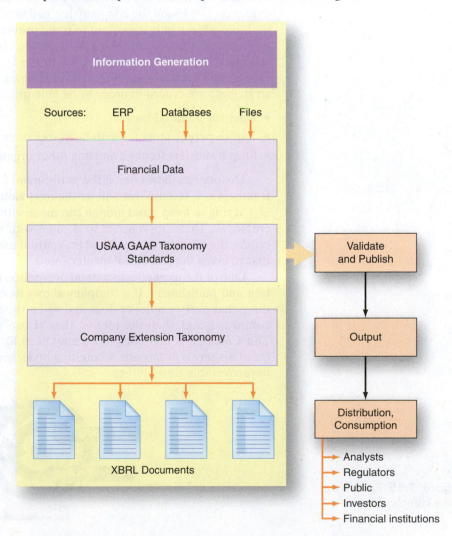

Figure 9.14 Overview of the creation of XBRL documents.

managers, employees, customers, or business partners against the company's interests. Although each corporation establishes its own specific procedures, fraud risk management involves assessing a company's exposure to fraud; implementing defenses to prevent and detect fraud; and defining procedures to investigate, prosecute, and recover losses from fraud. Analyzing why and how fraud could occur is as important as detecting and stopping it. This analysis is used to identify necessary corporate policies to deter insider fraud and fraud detection systems for when prevention fails.

Fraud Risk Factors. Factors that increase a company's exposure to fraud are shown in Figure 9.15. Information systems are implemented to harden against these factors. Companies make themselves targets because of the interaction of these four factors:

1. A high level of trust in employees without sufficient oversight to verify that they are not stealing from the company

2. Relying on informal processes of control

3. A mindset (belief) that internal controls and fraud prevention systems are too expensive to implement

4. Assigning a wide range of duties for each employee giving them opportunities to commit fraud

When a small manufacturer was the victim of theft of intellectual property, the computer network logs identified the computer that had been used to commit the alleged crime. But there was no way to connect that computer to one specific individual. A manager's conviction that he knew who had done it was not sufficient evidence. The lesson the company learned was that the internal control—*separation of duties*—is not only important to fraud prevention, but also essential to fraud prosecution and recovery of their losses. At the company, employees shared computer accounts so they were not able to link the fraud to the person who committed it. Designing effective fraud response and litigation-readiness strategies (post-incident strategies) are crucial in order to be able to:

• Recover financial losses
• Punish perpetrators through lawsuits, criminal charges, and/or forfeited gains
• Stop fraudsters from victimizing other organizations

History has shown that if the punishment for committing fraud is not severe, the fraudster's next employer will be the next victim, as described in *IT at Work 9.6*.

Trying to keep fraud hidden can mean either *doing nothing* or simply firing the employee. These approaches to dealing with fraud are not sustainable because it erodes the effectiveness of fraud prevention measures and produces **moral hazard**—that is, takes the risk out of insider fraud.

One of the most effective fraud prevention techniques is the perception of detection and punishment. If a company shows its employees that it can find out everything that every employee does and will prosecute to the fullest extent anyone who commits fraud, then the feeling that "I can get away with it" drops drastically. The Catch-22 is that companies may have limited resources that hinder a proper fraud diagnosis or forensic accounting investigation, even though they cannot afford unrecoverable losses either.

Figure 9.15 Factors that make companies targets for fraud.

IT at Work 9.6

Employee Is a Serial Fraudster

A dental practice with $4 million in annual revenues had fired its bookkeeper after a tax audit revealed to the owners that she'd been stealing over a $100,000 per year for at least four years. The bookkeeper was responsible for all accounting duties and financial reporting for tax purposes. Her work was not inspected closely by external auditors or the owners. No internal control systems, such as controls that would prevent checks being written to bogus vendors or employees, were implemented.

The classic **red flags** (fraud indicators)—lavish vacations, jewelry, and cars that she could not afford—were evident, but ignored by the owners/managers. The bookkeeper was a serial fraudster having defrauded at least two prior employers—a religious organization and a nonprofit where she'd worked as a volunteer.

The defrauded medical practice decided to keep the incident quiet so they did not take legal action against the bookkeeper. That turned out to be a mistake because the bookkeeper used that situation to her advantage. She filed a wrongful termination lawsuit. For several reasons, including not being able to collect evidence (lax internal controls enabled the bookkeeper to destroy evidence), the practice settled the lawsuit by paying her over $5,000. In effect, the fraudster had turned to extortion knowing that the practice was unprepared to fight back. Inarguably, she's now defrauding her current employer.

Questions

1. How was the fraud detected?
2. How long had it been going on?
3. What were the red flags that suggested the bookkeeper was living beyond her means?
4. What mistakes were made in the handling of the fraud?
5. In your opinion, did the dental practice have an ethical responsibility to prosecute the fraudster?

Financial Meltdowns Triggered by Fraud. In the early 2000s, the U.S. business economy was significantly impacted by fraud scandals that involved senior executives at a number of major corporations. Lawmakers felt that the scope of the crimes undermined the public's confidence in the country's financial systems and markets. A number of laws were passed that heightened the legal responsibilities of corporate management to actively guard against fraud by employees, established stricter management and reporting requirements, and introduced severe penalties for failure to comply. As a result, fraud management became a necessary functional process. These frauds played a role in the SEC's mandate for XBRL data reporting.

Internal Controls. In companies with lax accounting systems, it is too easy for employees to misdirect purchase orders and payments, bribe a supplier, or manipulate accounting data. When senior managers are involved in the fraud, preventing fraud is extremely tough. Consider Bernie Madoff, who committed a record-setting $64 billion fraud scheme for many years after Sarbanes–Oxley was passed to prevent that type of financial fraud.

In a much smaller but still serious fraud case involving a New York-based nonprofit, a volunteer was responsible for counting cash receipts at the annual fundraiser. The volunteer had performed this task for 30 years. One year, an accountant was assigned to assist the volunteer with the count. The volunteer offered the accountant a "cut" of the cash in exchange for her silence about the theft.

Strong internal controls, which depend on IT for their effectiveness, consist of the following:

- **Segregation of duties** tops the list of best practices in control procedures. When handling a company's assets, the work of managers and employees needs to be subject to approval or authorization. For example, any attempt to issue a check to a vendor not in the database of approved vendors will be prevented by the accounting information system.
- **Job rotation.** More than one person should be familiar with each transaction cycle in the business where possible. Rotation of jobs helps prevent overreliance on a single individual—and is a way to expose fraudulent activities.

- **Oversight.** Management—whether a single owner or a team of individuals—must monitor what is actually happening in the business. **Auditing** information systems are part of a strong oversight function. Unannounced periodic walk-throughs of a process or review of how things are really being done can reveal existing or potential problem areas.

- **Safeguarding of assets** is essential to a fraud prevention program. Access to networks, financial systems, and databases must be controlled with strong passwords and other security measures. Similarly, bank checks, petty cash funds, and company credit cards need to be locked up when not in use.

- **IT policies.** Understand your information system. Heavy reliance on IT staff can open up opportunities for fraud. Establish a computer use policy and educate employees on the importance of securing information. Strictly enforce use of separate log-ins and keep passwords confidential.

AUDITING INFORMATION SYSTEMS

Fraud can be easy to commit and hard to detect. Just ask any auditor. The problem may be worse in government and nonprofit entities that do not have adequate accounting and internal control systems. The problem is so bad at the federal level that auditors have been unable to express an opinion on the fairness of the consolidated financial statements of the U.S. For example, NASA, the space agency, had been unable to explain $565 billion in year-end adjustments to its books. It could be bad accounting, fraud, waste, or abuse. Without adequate records, no one really knows. This amount is astounding; especially when one considers that the combined cost of fraud in Enron and WorldCom was less than $100 billion in shareholder equity.

Because physical possession of stolen property is no longer required and it's just as easy to program a computer to misdirect $100,000 as it is $1000, the size and number of frauds have increased tremendously. See *IT at Work 9.7*, which describes a real life case.

FINANCIAL PLANNING AND BUDGETING

Management of financial assets is a major task in financial planning and budgeting. Financial planning, like any other functional planning, is tied to the overall organizational planning and to other functional areas. It is divided into short-, medium-, and long-term horizons, much like activities planning.

Knowing the availability and cost of money is a key ingredient for successful financial planning. Especially important is projecting cash flows, which tells organizations what funds they need and when, and how they will acquire them. In today's tough economic conditions with tight credit and limited availability of funds, this function has become critical to the company's survival.

Inaccurate cash flow projection is the number-one reason why many small businesses go bankrupt. The inability to access credit led to the demise of the investment bank Lehman Brothers in September 2008.

Budgeting. The best-known part of financial planning is the annual budget, which allocates the financial resources of an organization among participants, activities, and projects. The budget is the financial expression of the organization's plans. It allows management to allocate resources in the way that best supports the organization's mission and goals. IT enables the introduction of financial logic and efficiency into the budgeting process. Several software packages, many of which are web-based, are available to support budget preparation and control. Examples are budgeting modules from Oracle (*oracle.com*) and SAP (*sap.com*).

Capital budgeting is the process of analyzing and selecting investments with the highest ROI for the company. The process may include comparing alternative investments; for instance, evaluating private cloud vs. public cloud computing options.

The major benefits of using budgeting software are that it can reduce the time and effort involved in the budget process, explore and analyze the implications of organizational and environmental changes, facilitate the integration of the corporate

IT at Work 9.7

Lax Accounting Systems Enable Employee Fraud

Chris was a compulsive gambler, and she hid it well. Her problem began innocently at work when one day a casino web site popped up on her computer as she surfed the Internet during lunch. She placed a few bets using the free credits offered by the site to entice first-time players. She won, and that gave her a thrilling feeling, she would later explain to fraud investigators.

Two years later, as the payroll manager of a medium-sized manufacturing firm, Chris had defrauded her employer of over $750,000. Why did she do it? To pay off her gambling losses that were costing her an average of $7,000 a week. How did she do it? She took advantage of the lack of controls in her company's payroll and accounting information systems and controls.

Chris' Employment History and Deception

Chris had worked at the company for a decade. Her performance reviews described her as hardworking, reliable, and loyal, but did not mention she felt underpaid. Chris was bitter, thinking her employer didn't treat her fairly. When her gambling began to spiral out of control, she turned to fraud. "As far as I was concerned, they owed me," she told the forensic accountants.

The company's HR manager and comptroller were supposed to review Chris's work. But the HR manager focused on providing her with the correct data for employees' wages and benefits. The comptroller appeared not to have exercised control over payroll processing, which Chris knew.

Chris's primary deception was two phony employees she set up on the company's hourly payroll system as a new and separate cost center. As she processed and received the records sent to and from an external payroll provider (EPP) without effective oversight, she was able to control the scheme without detection. The phantom employees' checks were drawn up manually by EPP, sent to Chris and deposited into an account she had in a bank near her home. Near year-end, she also had EPP make adjustments to the payroll register to eliminate the amounts paid to the phony employees. When she went on vacation, she deactivated the two phony names from the payroll.

Fraud Scheme Based on Lack of Oversight

Chris started paying herself for unauthorized overtime. This plan proved to be a great success—she paid herself for 1,500 hours overtime over two years as opposed to the actually 50 she did work. Chris falsified records and increased the size of her theft until the HR manager finally noticed. When confronted with the evidence, she confessed that she'd gambled the money away and could not repay.

Questions

1. What role did trust play in Chris' ability to commit fraud for so long (that is, the employer's trust in Chris)?
2. What role did weak accounting ISs play in her ability to commit fraud?
3. In your opinion, if Chris had known that strong accounting ISs were in place would that had deterred her from trying to steal from her company?

---

strategic objectives with operational plans, make planning an ongoing continuous process, and automatically monitor exceptions for patterns and trends.

Forecasting. As you have read, a major reason organizations fail is their inability to forecast and/or secure sufficient cash flow. Underestimated expenses, overspending, financial mismanagement, and fraud can lead to disaster. Good planning is necessary, but not sufficient, and must be supplemented by skillful control. Control activities in organizations take many forms, including control and auditing of the information systems themselves. Information systems play an extremely important role in supporting organizational control, as we show throughout the text. Specific forms of financial control are presented next.

Financial Ratio Analysis. A major task of the accounting/finance department is to watch the financial health of the company by monitoring and assessing a set of financial ratios. These ratios are also used by external parties when they are deciding whether to invest in an organization, extend credit, or buy it.

The collection of data for ratio analysis is done by the TPS, and computation of the ratios is done by financial analysis models. Interpretation of ratios and the ability to forecast their future behavior require expertise, which is supported by DSSs (decision support systems).

Profitability Analysis and Cost Control. Companies are concerned with the profitability of individual products or services, product lines, divisions, or the financial health of the entire organization. Profitability analysis DSS software allows accurate computation of profitability and allocation of overhead costs. One way to control cost is by properly estimating it. This is done by using special software. For example, Oracle Hyperion Profitability and Cost Management software (*oracle.com*) is a new performance-management application that provides actionable insights into costs and profitability. This app helps managers evaluate business performance by discovering the drivers of cost and profitability and improving resource alignment. Sophisticated business rules are stored in one place, enabling analyses and strategies to be shared easily across an entire enterprise.

Questions

1. What is eXtensible Business Reporting Language (XBRL)?
2. Why does the SEC mandate data disclosure, where data items are tagged to make them easily searchable?
3. What is insider fraud? What are some other terms for insider fraud?
4. What is fraud risk management?
5. What four factors increase the risk of fraud?
6. Explain how accounting ISs can help deter fraud.
7. Define capital budgeting.
8. What is the purpose of auditing?

9.5 Human Resources Information Systems, Compliance, and Ethics

Companies cannot simply hire a great workforce. They have to find, recruit, motivate, and train employees to succeed in their workplace. Retaining high-performance people requires monitoring how people feel about the workplace, their compensation, value to the company, and chances for advancement—and maintaining workplace health and safety.

HR is a field that deals with employment policies, procedures, communications, and compliance requirements. Effective HR compliance programs are a necessity for all organizations in today's legal environment. HR needs to monitor workplace and employment practices to insure compliance with the Fair Labor Standards Act (FLSA), Occupational Health & Safety Agencies (OSHA), and the antidiscrimination and sexual harassment laws. Seven other employment laws to protect against discrimination are listed in Table 9.1.

TABLE 9.1	HR needs to monitor compliance with anti-discrimination employment laws
Title VII of the Civil Rights Act of 1964	Prohibits discrimination on the basis of race, color, religion, national origin, and sex. It also prohibits sex discrimination on the basis of pregnancy and sexual harassment.
Civil Rights Act of 1966	Prohibits discrimination based on race or ethnic origin.
Equal Pay Act of 1963	Prohibits employers from paying different wages to men and women who perform essentially the same work under similar working conditions.
Bankruptcy Act	Prohibits discrimination against anyone who has declared bankruptcy.
Americans with Disabilities Act	Prohibits discrimination against persons with disabilities.
Equal Employment Opportunity Act	Prohibits discrimination against minorities based on poor credit ratings.
Age Discrimination in Employment Act (ADEA)	Prohibits discrimination against individuals who are age 40 or above.

HUMAN RESOURCES INFORMATION SYSTEMS

Human resources information systems (HRIS) provide a company's HR department with powerful software solutions that reduce the manual workload necessary for HR administration. PeopleSoft Human Capital Management, which is one of the market-leading HRISs, provides a global foundation for HR data and improved business processes.

HRISs have been moved to intranets and clouds—wherein HR apps are leased in software as a service (SaaS) arrangements. Using intranets, HR apps have shifted many routine tasks to employees who log in to manage their benefits, deductions, direct deposits, health care, and so on. When employees manage their own HR services, HR professionals can focus on legal and compliance responsibilities, employee development, talent management, hiring, and succession planning.

SaaS HR. Deloitte Consulting (*deloitte.com*) research shows that 84 percent of surveyed companies are either transforming or planning to transform how they handle HR functions (Deloitte, 2011). Chief motivators are cost savings (85 percent) and greater effectiveness (75 percent). SaaS can be an efficient way to transform and improve HR and at lower cost, as shown in Table 9.2.

Many companies are exploring SaaS options, but as with all new IT, there is a great deal of apprehension. Three major factors holding companies back from HR SaaS investments include:

1. Security. SaaS security may be as effective as security associated with in-house data centers, but many companies don't understand the situation. Some early adopters are keeping highly sensitive applications in house.

2. Quality of service. The lack of formal service-level agreements (SLA) or performance and availability means quality of service may be a risky issue for some organizations.

3. Integration. Many companies have questions about their ability to integrate SaaS applications seamlessly with their in-house applications.

Benefits of using SaaS for HR. Three real-world examples illustrate the benefits of tying SaaS to global HR transformation efforts:

1. A global medical device manufacturer needed to create an independent HR system as it divested from its parent company. Cloud computing was at the core of its new global HR delivery model, which reduced the demand on internal business and IT resources. The company was able to establish fully independent HR operations within 10 months.

TABLE 9.2	Ways SaaS HR technologies can improve delivery of HR services at lower cost
Middle-ground between fully in house and fully outsourced	SaaS can offer a middle option between having an in-house tech staff dedicated to HR and moving to full-scale outsourcing. For example, software can be hosted off-site while HR processes are managed in-house.
Scalability	SaaS can offer scalability so HR organizations can add or remove capacity on demand. This is a cost-saving benefit for organizations with variable workloads. Organizations that are expanding through mergers and acquisitions (M&A) or expanding globally can benefit from scalable SaaS solutions.
Lower costs	Many SaaS and cloud computing options cost less and are faster to implement than large enterprise systems.

2. A national nonprofit foundation with a fast-growing employee population wanted to improve the effectiveness of HR operations. The organization selected a cloud-based solution, which dramatically improved time to value without over-stretching internal IT resources. Because little front-end investment was required, the foundation hit its budget target.

3. A global entertainment company needed a learning management system that could deliver content varying from instructor-based training to 30-second video how-to snippets. They chose to deploy a new learning management system in the cloud. With this approach, they quickly got the new system up and running.

There are now SaaS products and services that can integrate with on-site HR solutions. Many offer scalability so that HR organizations can add or remove capacity on demand. This is especially advantageous for organizations with variable workloads or growth spikes triggered by acquisitions.

Figure 9.16 illustrates how IT facilitates the work of the HR department. The figure summarizes the role HR plays in acquiring and developing talented people in organizations.

Recruitment. Recruitment is the process of finding potential employees with the skills and talent needed by the company, testing them, and deciding which ones to hire. Some companies are flooded with viable applicants, while others have difficulty finding the right people. LinkedIn is one of the primary social media sites used in recruitment, which tends to bring in more qualified applicants at lower cost. For example, the Finish Line Corp. had to process more than 330,000 candidates that applied for employment with the company in a 12-month period. More than 75 percent of them applied online. Using screening software by Unicru, 112,154 candidates were eliminated immediately. More than 60,000 hours of store managers' time were saved because of the reduction in the number of interviews conducted.

MANAGEMENT AND EMPLOYEE DEVELOPMENT

Once recruited, employees become part of the corporate HR pool, which needs to be maintained and developed. Several activities supported by IT are the following.

Performance Evaluation. Most employees are evaluated periodically by their immediate supervisors. Peers or subordinates may also evaluate others.

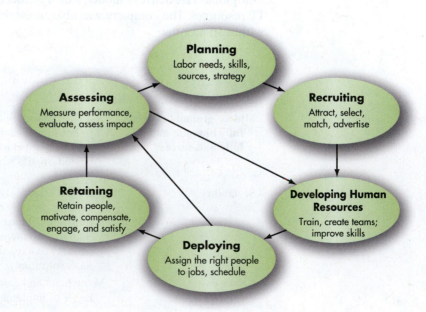

Figure 9.16 HR management activities.

Evaluations are usually recorded on paper or electronic forms. Using such information manually is a tedious and error-prone job. Once digitized, evaluations can be used to support many decisions, ranging from rewards to transfers to layoffs. For example, Cisco Systems is known for developing an IT-based human capital strategy. Many universities evaluate professors online. The evaluation form appears on the screen, and the students fill it in. Results can be tabulated in minutes. Corporate managers can analyze employees' performances with the help of intelligent systems, which provide systematic interpretation of performance over time. Several vendors provide software for performance evaluation, such as *HalogenSoftware.com* and *Capterra.com*.

Training and Human Resources Development. Employee training and retraining is an important activity of the human resources department. Major issues are planning of classes and tailoring specific training programs to meet the needs of the organization and employees. Sophisticated HR departments build a career development plan for each employee. IT can support the planning, monitoring, and control of these activities by using workflow applications.

Some of the most innovative developments are in the areas of live online training (LOT) using WebEx (*webex.com*) or other online meeting software. YouTube, Teradata University Network (TUN), and *CNN.com* offer excellent educational videos.

HR PLANNING, CONTROL, AND MANAGEMENT

In some industries, labor negotiation is an important aspect of HR planning and it may be facilitated by IT. For most companies, administering employee benefits is also a significant part of the human resources function. Here are some examples of how IT can help.

Personnel Planning and HR Strategies. The HR department forecasts requirements for people and skills. In some geographical areas and for overseas assignments, it may be difficult to find particular types of employees. In such cases, the HR department plans how to find sufficient human resources or develop them from within.

Benefits Administration. Employees' contributions to their organizations are rewarded by salary/wage, bonuses, and other benefits. Benefits include those for health and dental care as well as contributions for pensions. Managing the benefits system can be a complex task, due to its many components and the tendency of organizations to allow employees to choose and trade-off benefits. In large companies, using computers for self-benefits selection can save a tremendous amount of labor and time for HR staff.

Providing flexibility in selecting benefits is viewed as a competitive advantage in large organizations. It can be successfully implemented when supported by computers. Some companies have automated benefits enrollments. Employees can self-register for specific benefits using the corporate portal or voice technology. Employees self-select desired benefits from a menu. Payroll pay cards are now in use in numerous companies, such as Payless Shoes, which has 30,000 employees in 5,000 stores. The system specifies the value of each benefit and the available benefits balance of each employee. Some companies use intelligent agents to assist the employees and monitor their actions.

Employee Relationship Management. In their effort to better manage employees, companies are developing human capital management, facilitated by the web, to streamline the HR process. These web applications are more commonly referred to as employee relationship management. For example, self-services such as tracking personal information and online training are very popular in ERM.

Improved relationships with employees results in better retention and higher productivity.

Ethical Challenges and Considerations. HRIS apps raise ethical and legal challenges. For example, training activities that are part of HRM may involve ethical issues in recruiting and selecting employees and in evaluating performance. Likewise, TPS data processing and storage deal with private information about people, their performance, and so forth. Care should be taken to protect this information and the privacy of employees and customers.

The federal law related to workplace substance abuse, the Drug-Free Workplace Act of 1990 requires employers with federal government contracts or grants to ensure a drug-free workplace by documenting and certifying that they have taken a number of steps. Dealing with alcoholism and drugs at work entails legal risks because employees have sued for invasion of privacy, wrongful discharge, defamation, and illegal searches. Employment laws make securing HR information necessary for the protection of employees and the organization.

Questions

1. What are the key HR functions?
2. What are the benefits of moving HRISs to intranets or the cloud?
3. Why have companies implemented SaaS HR?
4. What concerns have deterred companies from implementing SaaS HR?
5. How can companies recruit more qualified applicants at lower cost?
6. Describe IT support for HR planning and control.
7. What are ethical issues related to HRIS apps?

Key Terms

auditing *290*

buffer stock *279*

capital budgeting *290*

computer integrated manufacturing (CIM) *281*

computer makeup language *287*

customer touchpoints *271*

data disclosure compliance system *286*

economic order quantity (EOQ) *279*

eXtensible Business Reporting Language (XBRL) *286*

filers *286*

flash sales *284*

flexible manufacturing system (FMS) *281*

fraud risk management *287*

insider fraud *287*

inventory control systems *279*

just-in-time (JIT) *279*

lean *270*

lean manufacturing system *280*

managerial or administrative level *272*

manufacturing execution systems (MES) *281*

manufacturing quality control (QC) systems *280*

moral hazard *288*

online transaction processing (OLTP) *275*

operational level *273*

production and operations management (POM) *276*

red flag *289*

safety stock *279*

shortage *279*

standard operating procedures (SOP) *273*

strategic level *272*

taxonomy *286*

total quality management (TQM) *280*

transparency *270*

transportation management systems (TMS) *277*

waste *270*

Chapter 9 LINK LIBRARY

You find clickable Link Libraries for each chapter on the Companion website.

Oracle   *oracle.com*

SEC   *Sec.gov*

XBRL   *Xbrl.sec.gov*

Aprimo   *Aprimo.com*

IBM   *IBM.com*

SAP   *Sap.com*

EOQ Tutorial   *scm.ncsu.edu/public/inventory/6eoq.html*

WebEx   *webex.com*

Salesforce software   *salesforce.com*

Superior Manufacturing Group   PDF: *one-point.com/sites/default/files/YTC03356-USEN-00.pdf*
   Website: *http://www.one-point.com/success-stories/superior-manufacturing*

Evaluate and Expand Your Learning

IT and Data Management Decisions

1. Visit the Oracle website at *oracle.com*.
   a. Click Application Integration.
   b. Click the **Demos** tab.
   c. Click **Play the demo** that is featured.
   d. Select your language, and then watch the demo.
   e. What is the app being demonstrated? Describe what was integrated.
   f. What is the value of the app? Why would a company invest in this app?
   g. Return to the Demos tab, and select the **PeopleSoft Overview.**
   h. Play the PeopleSoft demo.
   i. How can companies benefit from using PeopleSoft?
   j. Why would a company invest in PeopleSoft to meet its compliance obligations, such as the Patriot Act?

Questions for Discussion & Review

1. Discuss the need for sharing data among functional areas.
2. Describe waste and give three examples.
3. What is the value of lean manufacturing?
4. What is the objective of EOQ?
5. What are the risks of JIT?
6. Explain the value of being able to respond to hot data.
7. Push-through ads-use data about the person to determine whether the ad should appear. What marketing opportunities does this capability create?
8. Why might a company offer flash sales?
9. Explain why the SEC requires that filers use XBRL.
10. How can internal controls help to prevent fraud?
11. How do companies make themselves targets for insider fraud?

12. What are the benefits of prosecuting an employee who has committed fraud against the company?
13. Why might a company not want to prosecute a fraudster?
14. Explain moral hazard. Give a fraud-related example.
15. Fraudsters typically spend the money they steal on luxury items and vacations. Explain why these items are red flags of fraud.
16. What are three examples of strong internal controls?
17. Discuss how IT facilitates the capital budgeting process.
18. Discuss the role IT plays in auditing.
19. Explain the role and benefits of the SaaS in HR management.
20. How can IT improve the recruitment process?

Online Activities

1. Search for an explanation of EOQ. Explain the formula.
2. Finding a job on the Internet is challenging; there are almost too many places to look. Visit the following sites: *careerbuilder.com, craigslist.org, LinkedIn.com, careermag.com, hotjobs.yahoo.com, jobcentral.com,* and *monster.com.* What benefits do these sites provide you as a job seeker?
3. Visit *sas.com* and access revenue optimization. Explain how the software helps in optimizing prices.
4. Enter *sas.com/solutions/profitmgmt/brief.pdf*, and download the brochure on profitability management. Prepare a summary.
5. Visit *techsmith.com/camtasia/features.asp*, and take the product tour. Do you think it is a valuable tool?
6. Examine the capabilities of two financial software packages. Prepare a table that clearly compares and contrasts their capabilities.

7. Review *salesforce.com*. What functional support does the software provide?

Collaborative Work

1. Each group should visit and investigate a large company in a different industry and identify its channel systems. Then find how IT supports each of those components. Finally, suggest improvements in the existing channel system that can be supported by IT technologies and that are not in use by the company today. Each group presents its findings.

2. Create four groups. Each group member represents a major functional area: production/operations management, sales/marketing, accounting/finance, and human

resources. Find and describe several examples of processes that require the integration of functional information systems in a company of your choice. Each group will also show the interfaces to the other functional areas. For example, accounting students can visit *accountantsworld.com* just to be surprised at what is there, and *1040.com* can be useful to both the accounting and finance areas.

3. Each group investigates a major HR software vendor. Prepare a list of HR functions supported by the software. Make a recommendation.

4. Analyze the financial crisis of 2008. In your opinion, what roles did IT play to accelerate the crisis? Also, how did IT help to rectify some of the problems? Be specific.

CASE 2 BUSINESS CASE

Station Casinos' Loyalty Program

Station Casinos Inc. (*stationcasinos.com/*) is a gaming company that owns 18 properties, most of which are off the Las Vegas Strip. In addition to an extensive gaming floor, a typical property includes a hotel, restaurants, bars, arcades, movie theaters, live entertainment venues, and retail stores. Figure 9.17 shows one of Station Casino's properties, the Palace Station Casino.

Station occupies a valuable niche in the Las Vegas gaming marketplace. Unlike competitors on the Strip that cater primarily to tourists who visit a few times a year, Station sees many of its guests weekly or daily. It is the premier provider of gaming and entertainment for the nearly 2 million people who live in the Las Vegas area.

In June 2011, Station successfully emerged from bankruptcy. Their turnaround strategy included a customer loyalty program and data analytics.

Figure 9.17 Palace Station Casino in Las Vegas, Nevada.

Station Goes *All In* with a Customer Loyalty Program and Customer Analytics

"*Boarding Pass* is a sophisticated loyalty program that generates an amazing amount of data," according to CIO Scott Kreeger. Making sense of the diverse information coming from various touchpoints is a big challenge.

The CIO wanted to be able to analyze the entire value of each guest across all of Station's venues. Managing marketing and operations effectively requires having all data in a central location and using advanced analytics to yield deeper, broader customer and operational insights. An analytics app dubbed *Total Guest Worth* provides a new way to measure customer value to better target promotions.

Despite tough economic conditions in Las Vegas, Station's investment in its *Boarding Pass* customer loyalty program has paid off: Millions of guests have signed up for this loyalty card that tracks their gaming activities and other purchases, and then rewards them with points.

Payoff from System Integration and Data Precision

Implemented in three phases over 18 months, the new loyalty system integrates customer, gaming, and finance data from as many as 500 heterogeneous sources—gaming, lodging, food, beverage, and so on.

By being more precise with slot promotions campaigns, Station cut $1 million per month from its nearly $13 million budget. But campaigns are not just more efficient—they are more effective. Station has achieved a 4 percent increase in total monthly net slot revenue and a 14 percent improvement in guest retention. By monitoring profit per active guest, the higher customer retention rate has improved overall company profits. Designing, developing, and deploying personalized marketing and promotional campaigns is done in days now, compared with weeks previously for less personalized and less effective campaigns. And campaign analysis that once took weeks is now done in hours. Martin and his team have created more than 160 different functional area reports for several hundred internal customers. Users can also run 3,000 to 5,000 ad hoc queries per day to support their Decisions.

Customer Segmentation and Marketing Promotions

Detailed analysis provides a granular view of Station's customer segments, which leads to more effective promotions. Instead of analyzing 14 base segments, marketers can now analyzes 160 subsegments each month. "We can run tests on every single segment to determine who should get an offer and what kind of offer to send," according to the vice president of relationship marketing. Station also knows exactly who responds to what offers and, using the solution, automatically generates the appropriate reward.

Adding to the overall payoff, even though Station was processing more segments and programs, their data production and processing expenses decreased by $500,000 per month. Kreeger explained, "With this solution in place, we can develop those new services quickly and efficiently, and adapt them in near real time as customer needs and behaviors change."

A summary of how Station's profits improved is:

- Cut $1 million in wasted advertising per month from its nearly $13 million budget by being more precise with its promotional campaigns.
- Increased total monthly net slot revenues by 4 percent.
- Increased customer retention by 14 percent.
- Data production and processing expenses decreased by $500,000 per month.

Sources: Station Casinos Inc. (*stationcasinos.com/*), *blog.stationcasinos.com* (2011), *casinoloyaltyprograms.org.*

Questions

1. Explain Station Casino's niche market in Las Vegas.
2. Describe Station's customer base.
3. Why was making sense of the diverse information from various touchpoints a big challenge?
4. Explain the function of the app *Total Guest Worth.*
5. How did *Boarding Pass* and *Total Guest Worth* lead to performance improvements?
6. Describe the ways in which Station is a data-driven, fact-based company.

CASE 3   VIDEO CASE

Superior Manufacturing Wipes the Competition

Superior Manufacturing Group uses real-time sales data for faster decision making. One Point Solutions, an IBM Business Partner, recommended a combination of Informix and IBM Cognos Express as the best way to achieve enterprise-grade reporting at the right budget level for a mid-size corporation.

According to Jim Wood, IT Manager at Superior Manufacturing Group, "Cognos Express contributes directly to our efficiency and profitability.... The self-service capabilities of Cognos Express have helped us release the equivalent of one full-time employee from report writing."

1. Download and read the PDF "Superior Manufacturing gets set to wipe the floor with the competition" at *http://www.one-point.com/sites/default/files/YTC03356-*

USEN-00.pdf. The link is also listed in the Chapter 9 Link Library.

2. Visit *http://www.one-point.com/success-stories/superior-manufacturing* and view the video (5 minutes, 39 seconds).
3. Explain what the MIS director wanted to do and why.
4. What were the data-related and reporting challenges facing Superior?
5. What were the results of the new Cognos Express software?
6. Why can business decisions be made almost instantaneously?

Data Analysis & Decision Making

SunWest Foods' Improved Bottom Line

SunWest Foods is California's second-largest rice producer, milling up to 80 tons of rice per hour at peak season. SunWest has 100 employees in three processing/warehouse facilities in Biggs, California, and a marketing office in Davis, California. SunWest buys rice from 350 farms, then packages, distributes, and sells domestically and internationally.

Non-Integrated Operational Systems and Data Silos

The company's collection of stand-alone marketing, manufacturing, and marketing ISs with their own data formats and stored in

multiple data silos were a constant cause of inefficiency. Customers' orders had to be manually entered up to 10 times to get the data into each IS—wasting time and creating errors. Staff had to work weeks to compile business reports from data spread across their non-integrated ISs with various data formats. Because of inventory blind spots, SunWest held extremely high levels of inventory to ensure they could fulfill orders.

Financial and Operations Clarity

To improve enterprise-wide financial controls, planning, and reporting. SunWest installed Microsoft Dynamics NAV. Jim Errecarte, SunWest President and CEO explained, "We used to have a balance sheet for each company. Now we know P&L

[profit and loss] for every profit center inside every company, plus all six product lines. The 10 to 15 staff-hours per month to assemble necessary reports have dropped to a few minutes."

Errecarte says, "Unequivocally, the impacts of our patchwork system were many extra steps and rushed business decisions based on incomplete reports we couldn't wait for—particularly in our commodity positions. We were overdue for one cohesive, end-to-end solution to encompass purchasing, sales, production, distribution, finances, and trend prediction."

SunWest previously had a generalized price list for each market sector. Now it can offer customer-specific prices, manage them easily, and track the benefits.

Summary of Benefits

Today, staff can focus on their business functions, executives generate their own reports in minutes, managers make smarter commodity buy-sell decisions and operate leaner, and customers almost never call about order mistakes. A summary of benefits achieved through the integration of data silos are:

- Data reentry time dropped 80 percent, which cut out 30 staff hours per week.

- Commodity reports save 5 hours of senior executive time per week.
- Marketing's rice reports that lagged 3 months are now real time saving marketing managers a total of 7 hours per week.
- Panic calls on incomplete orders drop from monthly to less than quarterly, reducing customer service staff's time by 12 hours per week.
- Reductions in inventory levels save SunWest an estimate $200 per month in holding costs and interest charges.
- Revenues have increased net profit by an estimated $150 per month because of high quality order fulfillment.

Analysis to Do

1. Design a spreadsheet to calculate the savings in **labor costs per year.** Use the data from the case to estimate the reduction in wasted time. Assume that the hourly labor rate for staff workers is $15.00 per hour; and the rate for managers and senior executives are $100 per hour.

2. Add the savings in inventory holding costs and interest charges and the increase in net profit to calculate the annual improvement due to the implementation of the new financial and operations system.

Resources on the Book's Web site

More resources and study tools are located on the Student Web Site. You'll find additional chapter materials and useful web links. In addition, self-quizzes that provide individualized feedback are available for each chapter.

References

ACFE, 2013.

blog.stationcasinos.com, 2011.

Booz & Co., 2011. *booz.com/.*

Casinoloyaltyprograms.org

Deloitte Consulting. "HR in the Cloud: It's Inevitable, Human Capital Trends 2011." *deloitte.com.*

FASB. "US GAAP Financial Reporting Taxonomy." *fasb.org*, 2012.

Johnson. P., Volonino, L., & Redpath, I. "Fraud Response and Litigation-Readiness Strategies for Small and Medium Businesses: A Handbook on How to Prepare for Litigation, Prosecution & Loss Recovery in Response to Insider Fraud." *The Institute for Fraud Prevention, theIFP.org*, November 2011.

King, R. "Online flash sales more than double in one year." *ZDNet.com*, August 10, 2011.

Klein, S. "A 'Meaningful' User of an Electronic Health Record System Describes Its Clinical and Financial Benefits." *The Commonwealth Fund*, June/July 2011.

Oracle.com. 2013

Salesforce.com, 2013

SAP. *sap.com*, 2013

SEC. *sec.gov*, 2013

Station Casinos Inc., *stationcasinos.com/*

Sullivan, L. "Econsultancy Releases Study On Tag Management Automation." *Data and Behavioral Insider*. May 16, 2012.

SunWest Foods, Microsoft Case Study, April 30, 2010.

Wilson, D. "Manufacturing Technology: Hard work." *The Engineer* 33, April 25, 2011.

XBRL, *xbrl.sec.gov*, 2013.

Learning Outcomes

❶ Explain the potential executive, managerial, and operational support of enterprise systems, their success factors, and reasons for failure.

❷ Describe enterprise resource planning (ERP) systems and how ERP investments are justified.

❸ Describe supply chain management (SCM) networks and solutions.

❹ Explain the collaborative planning, forecasting, and replenishment (CPFR) functions related to SCM.

❺ Describe customer relationship management (CRM) systems and their role in customer acquisition, retention, and customer lifetime value.

Organizations continue to run older business systems, called **legacy systems.** Legacy systems may be retained because they form the core of mission-critical computing systems. The disadvantages of older systems is that they are expensive to maintain, cannot be updated without significant effort, and lack the flexibility to interface (connect to) and exchange data with newer ITs or to take advantage of Internet-enabled business processes. Because of their challenges, when companies need to update mission-critical legacy systems, they turn to enterprise information system software.

Enterprise information systems, or simply **enterprise systems** (or enterprise software), integrate core business processes and functions that you read about in Chapter 9. Integration is achieved by linking databases and data warehouses so that data can be shared with:

- *Internal functions:* Functions that take place within the company, which are referred to collectively as the **internal supply chain.**
- *External partners:* Business or supply chain partners, such as customers or suppliers. These constitute the **external supply chain.**

In Chapter 10, you learn how cross-functional enterprise systems support the organization's mission and business models.

CASE 1 OPENING CASE

Managing the U.S. Munitions Supply Chain

Legacy systems are older information systems that typically have been maintained over several decades because they fulfill critical needs. Because the time and cost to replace them are too high, companies may stick with their legacy systems, even though new IT exists that would make their processes more efficient.

Enterprise systems are cross-functional or inter-organizational systems that support an organization's strategy.

Supply chain starts with the acquisition of raw materials or the procurement (purchase) of products and proceeds through manufacture, transport, and delivery—and the disposal or recycling of products.

Munitions are the weaponry hardware, vehicles, and equipment and their ammunition.

Munitions Supply Chain Management

The Joint Munitions Command (JMC) is a major part of the U.S. Army Materiel Command (AMC). These Commands are supporting the Army's transformation to an ever more responsive, deployable, agile, versatile, and survivable force. JMC's role is to support U.S. warfighters by managing the *munitions supply chain* to get the right munitions at the right place at the right time. JMC manufactures, procures, stores, and transports tanks, weaponry, howitzers, and other munitions (see Figure 10.1) as well as bullets, artillery shells, and other ammunition to locations worldwide.

The headquarters on Rock Island Arsenal in Illinois is responsible for munitions production plants and storage depots in 16 states. JMC employs 14,000 personnel, has an annual budget of $1.7 billion, and is accountable for $30 billion of munitions and missiles. The motto *Ready–Reliable–Lethal* shown in Figure 10.2, summarizes the Command's support and commitment to those who are in the field.

Supply Chain Challenges

According to the U.S. Army JMC web site (*jmc.army.mil/*):

> JMC provides bombs and bullets to America's fighting forces—all services, all types of conventional ammunition from 500-pound bombs to rifle rounds. JMC manages plants that produce more than 1.6 billion rounds of ammunition annually and the depots that store the nation's ammunition for training and combat.

Clearly, managing the munitions supply chain is extremely complex and critical. Like other supply chains (or networks), it depends on good relationships among suppliers in the network and the quality of supplier information and communication channels.

One of JMC's long-standing challenges was how to efficiently manage its stockpiles of munitions and equipment that were stored in its depots. The depots were operating independently and, as a result, inefficiently. To improve its supply chain efficiency and military readiness, JMC worked with the consulting company Accenture (*Accenture.com*) on several IT initiatives that would streamline operations and integrate logistics. Integrating systems so that supply chain partners are able to share data lowers the cost and the risk of doing business. Supply chain risks include avoidable delivery delays and delivering incomplete orders or the wrong items, which put people's lives and military missions at risk.

JMC Improves Battle Readiness at Reduced Cost

JMC's project began with a focus on efficiency, but has resulted in increased warfighting readiness at reduced cost. After transforming operations, integrating its supply chain,

Figure 10.1 JMC manages the supply chain of materiels used in war (tanks, howitzers, weaponry) and ammunition (bullets, artillery shells).

and improving data management, JMC is now better able to rapidly supply U.S. forces with the highest quality munitions when they need them and to cut transportation costs up to 50 percent—a significant savings per year. These improvements were made possible as a result of greater asset visibility (tracking and monitoring), better forecasting and decision making capabilities, communication, and collaboration along the supply chain.

Sources: Compiled from Schwerin, (2012) *jmc.army.mil/* (2012), *http://www.jmc.army.mil/ Historian/JMCHistory.aspx* and *http://www.accenture.com/us-en/Pages/success-joint-munitions-command-logistics.aspx*

Figure 10.2 *Ready– Reliable-Lethal* motto of the Joint Munitions Command of the U.S. Army.

Source: http://www.jmc.army.mil/

Discuss

1. Explain the role of the munitions supply chain.

2. Discuss how JMC ensures that soldiers receive the highest-quality ammunition, on time, and where needed.

3. Discuss the challenges of managing the munitions supply chain.

4. How did the lack of integration of depots impact costs and efficiency?

5. Why would improvements in munitions supply chain management also improve warfighting readiness?

6. What factors impact the ability to manage the munitions supply chain?

Decide

7. What factors determine the efficiency of a supply chain? For example, does the supply chain depend on the extent to which data is shared? Explain your analysis and answers.
8. For the JMC, where does the munitions supply chain start and where does it end?

Debate

9. Is munitions supply chain management unique, and if so, why? Or is it similar to the management of any supply chains? Explain your positions.

10.1 Enterprise Systems

Enterprise systems refer to a category of information systems that integrate internal business processes and improve collaboration with external business partners. Integration and collaboration enable data sharing to keep workers informed and able to make better decisions. These systems integrate the functional systems that you read about in Chapter 9, such as accounting, finance, marketing, and operations. Major types of enterprise systems are:

- ERP: Enterprise Resource Planning
- SCM: Supply Chain Management
- CPFR: Collaborative Planning, Forecasting, and Replenishment
- CRM: Customer Relationship Management

One or more of these systems can be integrated for maximum benefit. For example, the integration of ERP and SCM improves inventory management and supply chain performance; and by integrating CRM and KM, companies are better able to identify their profitable and unprofitable customers and to calculate **customer lifetime value (CLV).** Roughly defined, CLV is the estimated revenue that a customer will generate during its lifetime with the company.

Another advantage of enterprise systems is that processes become more automated or totally automated, which increases efficiency. For example, by automating finance processes, a company can do things such as accept online orders and do business-to-business (B2B) transactions electronically, instead of via e-mail or offline methods such as telephone or fax.

ENTERPRISE SYSTEMS IMPLEMENTATION CHALLENGES

Implementing an enterprise system is complex, time-consuming, and typically requires help of a consulting firm, vendor, or **value-added reseller (VAR).** VARs add features and services with the software and work with companies to make sure their individual needs are met and they are getting the most value from their software. New enterprise systems can make a significant difference in productivity, but they won't be utilized to their full potential if they are not properly integrated with other systems needed to run the business. Lack of communication between systems can lead to inefficiencies. Integration allows the different systems to talk to one another to automate business processes. Testing the integration to make sure the system and modules are functional and performing the way they should is always necessary.

Despite the complexity of technical issues, the greatest challenges when implementing enterprise systems are process and change management. Companies that have inconsistent or outdated business processes along their supply chains tend to have poor-quality data. To improve data quality, companies reengineer those processes and consolidate them into an integrated enterprise system.

Consider ERP systems. An ERP is central to organizational efficiency by integrating accounting, financial, inventory management, and sales applications. ERP software is complicated because using it effectively involves re-engineering core business functions. Prior to selecting and implementing an ERP or other enterprise system, it's essential that a company identify the problems to be solved, the goals to be achieved, and the type of support the system is to provide. Common goals are real-time or near real-time data and sufficient agility to respond quickly to operational and market conditions. **Agility** is the ability to thrive and prosper in an environment of constant and unpredictable change. Agility is a result of streamlining processes on the shop floor to speed up order fulfillment, which in turn maximizes capacity for increased productivity.

TYPES OF ENTERPRISE SYSTEMS AND THEIR FUNCTIONS

The major enterprise systems are listed and described in Table 10.1. Companies implement most or all of these systems—and not just one.

REASONS WHY COMPANIES MIGRATE TO ENTERPRISE SYSTEMS

Companies tend to migrate to enterprise systems when the limitations caused by their existing legacy systems interfere with performance or their ability to compete. Here are major reasons why companies replace a few or most of their legacy systems with enterprise systems. It's important to realize that many companies do not have the resources to replace all their legacy systems.

- **High maintenance costs.** Maintaining and upgrading legacy systems are some of the most difficult challenges facing CIOs (chief information officers) and IT departments.
- **Business value deterioration.** Technological change weakens the business value of legacy systems that have been implemented over many years and at huge cost.
- **Inflexibility.** Monolithic legacy architectures are inflexible. That is, these huge systems cannot be easily redesigned to share data with newer systems, unlike modern architectures.
- **Integration obstacles.** Legacy systems execute business processes that are hardwired by rigid, predefined process flows. Their hardwiring makes integration with other systems such as CRM and Internet-based applications difficult and sometimes impossible.

TABLE 10.1	Descriptions of Enterprise Systems	
Name	**Abbreviation**	**Description**
Enterprise Resource Planning	ERP	ERP software apps integrate all departments and functions across an organization onto a single information system that can serve each department's particular needs.
		ERP systems are commercial software packages that integrate business processes, including supply chains, manufacturing, financial, human resources, budgeting, sales, and customer service.
Supply Chain Management	SCM	SCM software supports procurement, manufacturing, storage, inventory control, scheduling, and transportation.
Collaborative Planning, Forecasting, and Replenishment	CPFR	CPFR is an extension of SCM and ERP—and focuses on improving *prediction* (or reducing uncertainty). With better prediction, members of the supply chain have the right amount of raw materials and finished goods when they need them.
Customer Relationship Management	CRM	CRM systems create a total view of customers to maximize share-of-wallet and profitability. CRM is also a business strategy to segment and manage customers to optimize customer lifetime value (CLV).

- **Lack of staff.** IT departments find it increasingly difficult to hire staff who are qualified to work on applications written in languages no longer used in modern technologies.
- **The cloud.** The cloud has lowered upfront costs. Cloud-based enterprise systems can be a good fit for companies facing upgrades to their legacy ERP and other enterprise systems.

IMPLEMENTATION CHALLENGES AND BEST PRACTICES

As you read, implementing an enterprise system is challenging because it requires extensive changes in processes, people, and existing systems. Three required changes are:

1. Redesign of business processes. Processes need to be simplified and redesigned so that they can be automated, either totally or partially. Tasks that are no longer necessary are removed from the processes.

2. Changes in how people perform their jobs. Jobs and how they are performed will change to accommodate the new processes. Enterprise systems require retraining of end users, whose productivity will slow initially as they adjust to a new way of doing their jobs.

3. Integration of many types of information systems. Integrating information systems is necessary so that data can flow seamlessly among departments and business partners. Automated data flows are essential to productivity improvements.

A best practice is to examine the inefficiencies in existing processes to find ways to improve on or significantly simplify the process. For example, manual document-intensive processes (such as order entry and billing) create major headaches for workers. These processes require users to manually review documents for approval, enter data from those documents into a back-office system, and then make decisions. Automated order entry systems track customer orders from the time of initial order placement through the completion of those orders; and they perform backorder processing, analysis, invoicing and billing.

Because of their complexity, enterprise systems are leased or licensed from vendors and customized with support from IT personnel who are familiar with their company's business processes. The trend toward *ERP software-as-a-service* continues to increase. In fact, the term *ERP* commonly refers to commercially available software systems. For examples of monthly costs and a comparison of 10 ERP vendors' products, visit *top10erp.org/*. To simplify and reduce the cost of the ERP software selection process (the selection process itself is complex and critical), an annual event called the ERP Vendor Shootout (*erpshootout.com/*) is held and geared toward ERP selection teams and decision makers for companies with manufacturing, distribution, or project-oriented requirements.

ENTERPRISE SYSTEMS INSIGHTS

Here are three other insights related to enterprise systems to better understand the current state of enterprise systems and their potential.

1. One of the IT department's most important roles is to provide and support applications that enable workers to access, use, and understand the data. These applications need to be tightly aligned with well-defined and well-designed business processes—a standard that few enterprises are able to achieve.

2. Customer loyalty helps drive profits, but only for customers who are profitable to the company. Many companies don't know how to recognize or encourage the kind of customer loyalty that's worth having. Using data about buying behaviors (e.g., amount spent per month; purchase of high-margin products; return activity; and demands for customer service) helps a company identify its loyal customers and which ones are profitable.

3. Companies all over the world are spending billions of dollars in the design and implementation of enterprise systems. Huge investments are made in ERP systems from vendors such as SAP, Oracle, JD Edwards (from Oracle), Microsoft Dynamics, and Baan to create an integrated global supply chain. Interorganizational ISs play a major role in improving communication and integration among firms in a global supply chain.

Next you read about ERP systems, which despite the name are not limited to planning functions. Although most types of companies now have an ERP system, ERP evolved from the manufacturing industry.

Questions

1. Explain the purpose of an enterprise system.
2. Describe five types of enterprise systems.
3. What is customer lifetime value (CLV)?
4. What is a value added reseller (VAR)?
5. What are two challenges of legacy systems?
6. Why do companies migrate to enterprise systems?
7. Explain enterprise system implementation challenges.
8. Explain the three types of changes needed when an enterprise system is implemented.

10.2 Enterprise Resource Planning (ERP) Systems

What is an ERP system? From a technology perspective, ERP is the software infrastructure that links an enterprise's internal applications and supports its external business processes. ERP apps are modular, and the modules are integrated with each other to expand capabilities.

An ERP helps managers run the business from front to back. Departments can easily stay informed of what's going on in other departments that impact its operations or performance. Being informed of potential problems and having the ability to work around them improves the company's business performance and customer relations. For example, an ERP enables a manufacturer to share a common database of parts, products, production capacities, schedules, backorders, and trouble spots. Responding quickly and correctly to materials shortages, a spike in customer demand, or other contingency is crucial because small initial problems are usually amplified down the line or over time. Table 10.2 lists the characteristics of ERP apps.

MANUFACTURING ERP SYSTEMS AND LEAN PRINCIPLES

Manufacturers know that their success depends on lower costs, shorter cycle times, and maximum production throughput. A key factor to lowering costs is inventory management—minimizing inventory errors and balancing between having enough material available to keep production running, but not so much that it increases inventory holding costs. ERP systems help manufacturers avoid material shortages through accurate demand forecasting, more precisely manage production and coordinate distribution channels, and as a result improve on-time delivery of products. Engineers, production floor workers, and those in the purchasing, finance, and delivery departments can access and share plans, production status, quality control, inventory, and other data in real time.

TABLE 10.2	Characteristics of ERP Apps

- Integrate data silos to enable managers to really understand what is going on
- Provide data access, integrated business processes, and the IT platform needed to become and remain competitive
- Support most or all of a company's business functions and processes
- Expand the company's reach beyond its internal networks to its suppliers, customers, and partners

IT at Work 10.1

Four Rules for selecting an ERP

ERPs are complex, but they are becoming more user friendly. Other options are hosted ERP solutions, such as ERP Software-as-a-Service (SaaS) and cloud-based ERP. Still, ERPs are expensive, time-consuming implementations that require a lot of planning. Four rules to consider when selecting an ERP solution or software package are:

1. **Select an ERP solution that targets the company's requirements.** ERP packages are tailored for organizations based on their size and industry. Midmarket solutions have more sophisticated capabilities than packages for small businesses; and large enterprise packages are the most complex. It's important to choose an ERP that can support critical functions of the organization, such as accounting or inventory management.

2. **Evaluate potential ERP vendors' strengths and weaknesses.** Check how many customers each vendor has, their

financial health (you don't want a vendor on the brink of bankruptcy), if they have any experience in the industry, and how the ERP can adapt as the company grows.

3. **Meet with each vendor and get a hands-on demo of their ERP solutions.** Demos allow employees to experience the usability of each ERP module and see how well the ERP would support business processes.

4. **Calculate the ERP's total cost of ownership (TCO).** The cost of the ERP or the monthly SaaS fee is only the beginning of the calculation. The TCO also includes implementation, customization, management services, training, additional hardware and networks, additional bandwidth for a Web-based product, and IT staff.

Many ERP systems incorporate **lean manufacturing principles,** which involve minimizing all forms of waste. Firms track detailed supply chain activities from start to finish, so that any procedures and processes that delay the design, creation, or delivery of goods are identified and corrected. Manufacturing ERP software makes it easier to detect and prevent defects, which reduces scrap and rework. Better tracking combined with more accurate demand planning eliminate costly excess inventory. *IT at Work 10.1* lists the rules for selecting an ERP System.

ERP: A STRATEGIC WEAPON FOR FOOD MANUFACTURERS

Food manufacturing is a highly competitive and regulated environment. Major challenges facing food manufacturers are margin pressures, food safety regulations, and changing consumer tastes. An integrated system is essential for controlling costs, managing inventory, and meeting government regulations. Figure 10.3 shows the subsystems that need to share data and support the operations of most manufacturers.

Food Safety and Agri-Food Regulations. In a survey conducted by *Food Engineering* magazine, the top concern of the agri-food industry was food safety in large part because worldwide distribution systems have increased the risk and range of contaminated food entering the food supply. In 2009, the *New York Times* reported that a single hamburger could contain beef products from several slaughterhouses on several continents (Moss, 2009). An estimated 76 million people in the U.S. get sick every year with foodborne illness and 5,000 die, according to the U.S. Centers for Disease Control and Prevention (CDC).

Figure 10.3 A goal of an ERP system is to integrate the various subsystems making it possible for them to share data. The arrows represent data flows—*the transfer of data.*

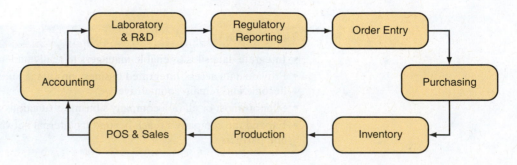

Figure 10.4 The FDA monitors food safety. The farm-to-fork, preventive approach embodied in the 2011 FSMA reflects an established scientific and managerial consensus on how to improve food safety systems.

The threats and potential costs associated with food safety are high and rising. Contaminated spinach, peanut butter, beef, imported seafood, pet food, and many other food products, in addition to life-threatening and ethical issues, result in litigation, bad publicity, and recall costs that damage or destroy companies' reputations.

The European Food Safety Authority (*efsa.europa.eu/*) applies a "From the Farm to the Fork" integrated approach based on transparency, risk analysis and prevention, and consumer protection. The U.S. Congress responded to terrorism by passing the Public Health Security and Bioterrorism Preparedness and Response Act (Bioterrorism Act) in 2002. In January 2011, the Food Safety Modernization Act (FSMA) was signed into law, the most comprehensive reforms to Federal food safety laws since 1938. As the Food and Drug Administration's (FDA) Deputy Commissioner explained, FSMA shifts the focus of FDA activities from "catching food safety problems after the fact to systematically building in prudent preventive measures across the food system, from the farm to the table" (*ers.usda.gov/*, 2011). See Figure 10.4.

For a food manufacturer, the key benefits of an integrated ERP system are improved operational performance and a framework to meet regulatory mandates and reporting requirements, and cost control. Many food manufacturers are replacing multiple software apps with an integrated ERP system to manage complexity and maximize productivity and profitability. Specifically, the ERP gives manufacturers a single point of control for data thereby:

- Eliminating the need to enter data in multiple systems
- Reducing common data entry errors and costs
- Allowing for the posting of transactional data in real time for instant access to up-to-date information
- Being able to respond quickly to food recalls
- Meeting requirements of the Bioterrorism Act, FSMA, and other regulations for accurate record keeping in order to support the discovery and quick response to food chain supply threats

FROM STAND-ALONE DATA SILOS TO AN INTEGRATED ENTERPRISE SYSTEM

Replacing stand-alone or legacy systems with ERP requires migrating databases and applications. Not surprisingly, database vendors such as Oracle and IBM are also enterprise system vendors. Vendors provide tools that help automate both the database migration and the application migration, which occur separately.

Implementing an enterprise system may be a competitive necessity for companies with data management problems. The greater the number of applications and databases, the greater the complexity of data management because of the numerous interfaces needed to exchange data. As you see in the left-side diagram of Figure 10.5,

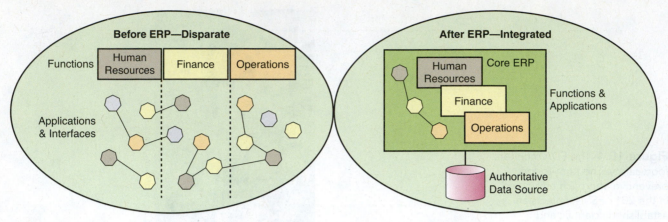

Figure 10.5 Comparison of disparate systems within an enterprise to an integrated ERP system.
Courtesy of U.S. Army Business Transformation Knowledge Center (2009), *army.mil/armyBTKC/.*

disparate functional systems—HR, finance, and operations—involve numerous interfaces. These interfaces increase maintenance efforts and costs, as well as the risk of dirty data. An ERP integrates functions include a suite of IT modules that can be purchased as needed by the company.

Enterprise Application Integration Layer. In Figure 10.6, you see how an ERP fits into an enterprise's IT infrastructure. The core ERP functions are integrated with other systems or modules that are bolted on, including SCM, PLM, CRM, and BI. In the example shown in Figure 10.6, the ERP interfaces with legacy applications through an **enterprise application integration (EAI)** layer, and with external business partners through a B2B gateway (explained in next section). EAI is middleware that connects and acts as a go-between for applications and their business processes. Benefits of EAI are listed in Table 10.3.

B2B Gateway Layer. Business-to-business integration (B2Bi) is vital to ensure the efficient, accurate and timely flow of data across internal ISs and external business partners. (See left-side of Figure 10.6.) Companies that implement B2Bi are realizing enormous competitive advantage through faster time to market, reduced cycle times, and increased customer service. Through integration of business and technical processes, companies are able to strengthen relationships with partners and customers, achieve seamless integration inside and outside the enterprise, gain real-time views of customer accounts, increase operational efficiencies, and reduce costs.

Companies need to be able to safely and securely participate in B2Bi and to securely exchange data over the Internet. **B2B gateways** provide these services. They consist of a suite of software products that support internal and external integration and business processes. B2B gateways provide a backbone for the secure exchange of data, files, and documents—intra-company and with external parties. As such, they increase real-time visibility into business activity and performance.

JUSTIFYING AN ERP

Why are ERP systems worth their cost? Because decisions are only as good as the timeliness and completeness of the data on which they're based. The more complete the data, the less the uncertainty and risk involved in the decision process. An ERP provides the

TABLE 10.3	Benefits of the Enterprise Application Integration (EAI) Middleware Layer

- Reduced IS development and maintenance costs
- Enhanced IS performance and reliability
- Extended life cycle of legacy systems
- Reduced time to market of new IS features or applications

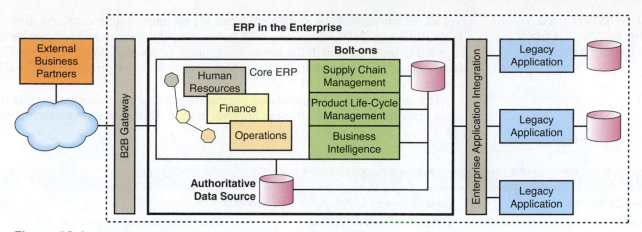

Figure 10.6 How ERP interfaces with other enterprise systems.
Courtesy of U.S. Army Business Transformation Knowledge Center (2009), *army.mil/armyBTKC/*.

integration and automation that makes timely and complete data possible. So it's not surprising that establishing a reliable pipeline of data from internal functions and external business partners is a priority for businesses of all sizes in every industry.

ACQUIRING AN ERP

Typically, ERP systems are acquired by purchasing or leasing packaged software. The purchased or leased ERP software is customized to meet the company's needs by adding modules. ERP systems include modules for manufacturing, order entry, accounts receivable and payable, general ledger, purchasing, warehousing, transportation, and HR. ERPs are not built in house nor built using proprietary software because the costs and time to do so would be staggering. You read more about IS acquisition in Chapter 11.

IT at Work 10.2 illustrates how improved agility can create a competitive advantage. ERP provides the infrastructure needed for the agility for quick correction and response, which can be exploited to improve profitability, market share or customer service.

IT at Work 10.2

ERP Enables Agility, a Competitive Asset for Manufacturers

The first step toward becoming an agile manufacturer is developing the means to monitor the marketplace; for instance, changes in customer demand or competitors' actions, and to respond to it quickly. ERP software brings all areas of the manufacturing operation into a single, real-time database where the actions of one department do not happen in isolation, but rather are known throughout other departments. As a result, all departments are aware of what's going on within the company and are capable of responding quickly to customer demands. Manufacturers that have invested in ERP to become agile are able to leverage their insights into new products and services for their current customers and prospective ones—and to counteract competitors' attempts to steal away their customers.

While agile manufacturing is not widespread, early adopters are reaping the benefits. An example is Humanetics (*humanetics.com*), a Texas-based precision metal works company with four geographically dispersed plants. Humanetics' ERP system serves the following functions:

- Supports estimating and quoting processes

- Supports parts' manufacturing, shipping, invoicing, and payment collection
- Prepares financial statements
- Manages the day-to-day international movement of parts, quality control, and on-time delivery

In a global economy, windows of opportunity open quickly and can close just as fast. The more agile and aware the manufacturer, the greater the rewards from being the first responder to customer needs.

Sources: Compiled from Alexander (2009) and humanetics.com (2009).

Questions

1. What competitive advantages does agility provide to a manufacturing company?

2. Are those competitive advantages sustainable? Why or why not?

UNDERSTANDING ERP SUCCESS AND FAILURE FACTORS

Not all enterprise systems implementations are an immediate success. As shown in Table 10.4, several of the best companies have suffered devastating consequences that have led to multi-million dollar losses, bankruptcy, or lawsuits. Most often, the ERP eventually is fixed and remains in use, which gives the false impression that the ERP was successful from the start.

The success of ERP depends on organizational and technological factors that occur prior to, during, and after the implementation. Knowing what to do and what

TABLE 10.4	ERP Failures and Lawsuits
ERP Customer	**Description of ERP Failures and Lawsuits**
Dillard's, Inc., department store	Dillard's alleged that i2 failed to meet obligations regarding two software-license agreements for which the department-store operator had paid $8 million. In June 2010, JDA Software Group Inc. reported that its i2 Technologies unit lost the software-licensing dispute with Dillard's Inc. and was ordered to pay $246 million in damages.
Hershey Food, manufacturer of chocolates, confectionaries, and beverages	Hershey's spent three years implementing a $115 million ERP system with SAP, Siebel, and Manugistics. The ERP was to replace all legacy systems and to integrate inventory, production, order processing, payroll, accounting, and finance. Hershey's devastating mistake was trying to implement all systems in all departments at the same time and at its busiest time of the year.
	Hershey suffered heavy losses in profits and sales, which led to an 8 percent drop in its stock price; and filed a lawsuit against the vendors.
Dorset County in the UK	Several workers claimed a job that had previously only taken a minute was taking one hour. And the ERP system still has to shut down a few days each month to allow data to be processed.
Nike, athletic shoe and apparel manufacturer	Nike implemented i2's (*i2.com*) demand and supply planner software, which it wanted up and running before introducing an SAP ERP to handle all supply chain and sales order processes.
	The i2 system created duplicate orders, deleted customer orders, and deleted manufacturing requests to Asian factories. Adding to the problems, the ERP was not designed to handle Nike's large number of products. Many legacy systems had been left in use, but they lacked the ability to communicate with the supply chain software causing huge delays and system crashes. The $400 million upgrade to Nike's supply chain and ERP systems caused $100 million in lost sales, a drop of 20 percent in stock price, and class-action lawsuits. Nike blamed the failure on underestimating the needed resources for the i2 system and rolling out the SAP prematurely.
FoxMeyer. Bankrupted; and formerly the fourth-largest pharmaceuticals distributor	FoxMeyer's ERP could not process the transactions needed to supply their customers with their orders. FoxMeyer had been processing 425,000 invoice lines per day on their legacy software. Their ERP was limited to 10,000 invoice lines per day. This decreased order processing capability quickly put the company into bankruptcy protection and ultimately shut down the business.
Waste Management, garbage-disposal giant	Waste Management filed a lawsuit in March 2008 against SAP over an allegedly failed installation of its ERP software. In the lawsuit, Waste Management claimed that SAP executives participated in a fraudulent sales scheme and demo that resulted in the massive failure. Waste Management had claimed it suffered significant damages, including more than $100 million it spent on the project, which it has dubbed "a complete and utter failure," and more than $350 million for benefits it would have realized if the software had been successful.
	SAP counter-sued alleging that Waste Management violated its contract agreement and did not "timely and accurately define its business requirements" nor provide "sufficient, knowledgeable, decision-empowered users and managers" to work on the project.
	The legal matter between Waste Management and SAP was resolved in 2010. Waste Management received "a one-time cash payment" in accordance with the settlement, according to a quarterly earnings filing it made with the SEC in April 2010. The terms of the settlement are confidential.

not to do is important. Both the successes and failures teach valuable lessons too, as you read in this section.

Be aware that reading vendor white papers and viewing webcasts or demos may give you a biased view of the benefits of their software. You need to conduct your own research to learn the full story of an enterprise system implementation. Problems may be skipped over or ignored. While blogs and YouTube posts may be good sources of objective data, many vendors have blogs and YouTube videos that are designed to appear to be neutral, when in fact they're not.

Cases of ERP Failure. ERP implementations are complex, so it's not surprising to learn that there have been horror stories of ERP projects gone wrong. Dell canceled an ERP system after spending two years and $200 million on its implementation. Hershey Food Corp. had widely publicized lawsuits against ERP software vendors because of their failed implementations. Table 10.4 presents cases of ERP failures. In cases of extreme failure, companies have sued their vendors or consulting firms because their ERP software failure made it impossible to ship product or, at the extreme, led to a shutdown of the entire business.

Overall, ERP projects have gone badly for multiple reasons, such as changing internal requirements by the company that slow down system integrator implementation, lack of resources for training and system design, and complexity in the software (Krigsman, 2011).

ERP Success Factors. What factors increase the likelihood of ERP success and minimize the risk of problems? Many managers assume that success or failure depends on the software; and furthermore, that a failure is the fault of the software that's purchased or licensed. In reality, 95 percent of a project's success or failure is in the hands of the company implementing the software, not the software vendor.

The results of a survey to identify what ERP experts had found to be most important to successful ERP projects are shown in Figure 10.7. These ERP experts were given a list of five factors and asked to select only one of them as *most important*. The sixth alternative was *all five factors*. The results (which sum to 100 percent) are:

1. Strong program management: 6 percent
2. Executive support and buy-in: 19 percent

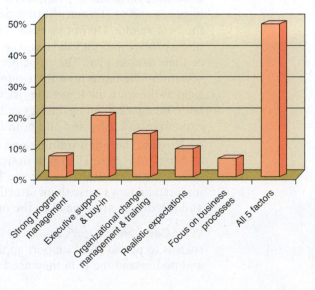

Survey responses to the question:
What is most important to successful ERP projects?

Figure 10.7 Experts identify what's most important to the success of an ERP.

3. Organizational change management and training: 13 percent
4. Realistic expectations: 8 percent
5. Focus on business processes: 5 percent
6. Interaction of all five factors: 49 percent

That is, 49 percent of the ERP experts have found that success depended on all five factors. Stated another way, nearly half of the experts indicated that the failure of any one of these five factors would or could cause the ERP to fail.

The following recommendations explain why ERP success depends on several key factors being done right.

1. **Focus on business processes and requirements.** Too often, companies get caught up in technical capabilities or platforms on which the ERP runs. But compared to business processes, none of this really matters. What matters is how managers want business operations to run and what the key business requirements are. Once management and IT have defined them, they can more effectively choose the software that fits their unique business needs.

2. **Focus on achieving a measurable ROI.** Developing a business case to get approval from upper management or the board of directors is essential, but not sufficient. Establish key performance measures, set baselines and targets for those measures, and then track performance after going live. The performance results are proof of how well the ERP meets the expectations that had been listed in the business case.

3. **Use a strong project management approach and secure commitment of resources.** An ERP project depends on how it is managed. Responsibility for the management of the ERP implementation project cannot be transferred to vendors or consulting firms. Because of the business disruption and cost involved, ERP projects require the full-time attention and support of high-profile champions from the key functions for a long period of time, from 6 to 12 months on average. It's also known that ERP projects cannot be managed by people who *can be spared*. They must be managed by people who are *indispensable* personnel. Without powerful champions and necessary budget (discussed next), expect the ERP to fail.

4. **Insure strong and continuing commitment from senior executives.** Any project without support from top-management will fail. No matter how well-run a project is, there will be problems such as conflicting business needs or business disruptions that can only be resolved by someone with the power and authority to cut through the politics and personal agendas.

5. **Take sufficient time to plan and prepare up front.** An ERP vendor's motive is to close the deal as fast as possible. The company needs to make sure it correctly defines its needs and what it can afford to achieve in order to intelligently evaluate and select the best vendor. Do not be rushed into a decision. Too often, companies jump right into a project without validating the vendor's understanding of business requirements or their project plan. The principle of "measure twice, cut once" applies to vendor selection. The more time the company spends ensuring that these things are done right at the start, the lower the risk of failure and the less time spent fixing problems later. Filing a lawsuit against a vendor (see Table 10.5) is not a fix. Lawsuits are both expensive and risky, and add nothing to the company's performance.

6. **Provide thorough training and change management.** Another key principle to understand is that when you design an ERP, you redesign the organization. ERP systems involve dramatic change for workers. ERPs lose value if people do not understand how to use them effectively. Investing in training, change management, and job design are crucial to the outcome of any large-scale IT project.

Why Companies Don't Invest in ERP. One of the IT department's most important roles is to provide and support applications that insure that workers can access, use, and understand the data they need to perform their jobs effectively. An ERP would seem to be the perfect solution. Despite their potential benefits, not all companies invest in ERP, typically if they are unable to meet or overcome the following requirements:

• Applications must be tightly aligned with well-defined and designed business processes, which is a standard that few enterprises are able to achieve.
• Business processes must be modified to fit the software.
• Initial costs to purchase or lease and set up the ERP may be extremely high.
• Complexity of the applications might make it too difficult for employees to use correctly for maximum efficiency and ROI.

In addition, justifying an ERP becomes more difficult during an economic downturn.

Questions
1. Define ERP and describe its objectives.
2. Briefly describe the challenges of legacy systems that motivate the migration to ERP.
3. Describe how ERP enables agility.
4. Explain manufacturing ERP systems and lean principles.
5. List and briefly describe three ERP implementation success factors.
6. Describe barriers to ERP implementation.

10.3 Supply Chain Management (SCM) Systems

The journey that a product travels, as shown in Figure 10.8, starting with raw material suppliers and then to manufacturers or assemblers, distributors and retail shelves, and ultimately to customers is its **supply chain.** The supply chain is like a pipeline composed of multiple companies that perform any of the following functions:

• Procurement of materials
• Transformation of materials into intermediate or finished products
• Distribution of finished products to retailers or customers
• Recycling or disposal in a landfill

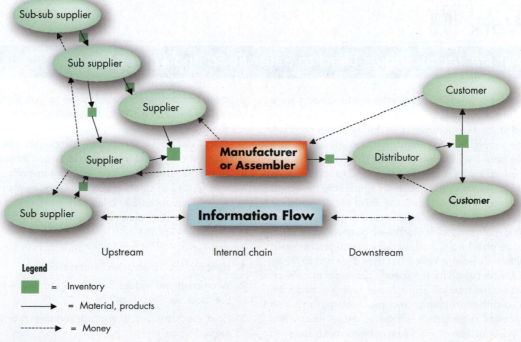

Figure 10.8 Structure of a typical supply chain.

Supply chains vary significantly depending on the type, complexity, and perishability of the product. For example, in a simplified sense, the food supply chain begins with the livestock or farm, moves to the manufacturer (processor), then through the distribution centers and wholesalers to the retailer and final customer. In *IT at Work 10.3*, you read how track and trace technologies are being used to improve food safety and reduce costs.

MANAGING THE FLOW OF MATERIALS, DATA, AND MONEY

Supply chains involve the flow of materials, data, and money. Descriptions of these three main flows are:

1. Material or product flow: This is the movement of materials and goods from a supplier to its consumer. For example, chipmaker Intel supplies computer chips to its customer Dell. Dell supplies its computers to end-users. Products that are returned make up what is called the **reverse supply chain** because goods are moving in the reverse direction.

2. Information flow: This is the movement of detailed data among members of the supply chain, e.g., order information, customer information, order fulfillment, delivery status, and proof-of-delivery confirmation. Most information flows are done electronically, although paper invoices or receipts are still common for non-commercial customers.

3. Financial flow: This is the transfer of payments and financial arrangements, e.g., billing payment schedules, credit terms, and payment via **electronic funds transfer (EFT)**. EFT provides for electronic payments and collections. It is safe, secure, efficient, and less expensive than paper check payments and collections.

Supply chain links are managed. Think of the chain in terms of its links because the entire chain is not managed as a single unit. A company can only manage the links it actually touches. That is, a company will manage only partners who are one-back and one-up because that's the extent of what a company can manage.

ORDER FULFILLMENT AND LOGISTICS

Order fulfillment is the set of complex processes involved in providing customers with what they have ordered on time and all related customer services. Order fulfillment depends on the type of product/service and purchase method (online, in-store,

IT at Work 10.3

Track and Trace Technologies Lead to Safer Food and Lower Costs

Beef patties, pet food, peanut butter, lettuce and spinach are a few of the contaminated food recalls. One solution is to implement track and trace technologies that follow food products throughout their supply chain, primarily through the use of barcodes and radio frequency identification (RFID). Bar coding and RFID enable the tracking of food through the food supply chain from "farm to fork." Without the capability to identify the scope of the contamination and contain it, the food recall would be much more extensive than necessary as a safety precaution. For example, when *E. coli*–tainted spinach was discovered in 2007, using the bar code on a bag of bad spinach, investigators traced its origin to California's Salinas Valley. But then they had to do an intense and expensive search for the specific grower in that Valley. And during that search time, all spinach was being pulled from grocery stores, distribution plants, and processing plants and destroyed. A growers' organization estimates the recall cost the spinach industry $74 million. It would have been much faster to

track the contaminated leaves to the grower if spinach bags and containers had carried RFID tags with complete histories of the contents' origins.

With detailed information, companies can streamline the distribution chain and lower spoilage and contamination rates. Reducing the rates of spoilage and contamination is important for reasons related to safety and costs. Consumer product and retail industries lose about $40 billion annually, or 3.5 percent of their sales, due to supply chain inefficiencies.

Questions

1. How can food be tracked and traced?

2. What costs are reduced during a contaminated food recall if the food has RFID tags?

3. How much money is wasted annually due to supply chain inefficiencies?

catalog, etc.). For example, a customer who has ordered a new appliance via the *Sears.com* web site needs to receive it as scheduled, with assembly and operating instructions, and warranty and return information. The customer can receive a paper manual with the product or download the instructions from the Sears web site. In addition, if the customer is not happy with a product, an exchange or return can be arranged via the web site.

Order fulfillment is a part of **back-office operations,** which are activities that support the fulfillment of orders, such as accounting, inventory management, and shipping. It also is closely related to **front-office operations** or *customer-facing activities*, which are activities, such as sales and advertising that are visible to customers. The key aspects of order fulfillment are the delivery of materials or products at the right time, to the right place, and at the right cost.

Logistics is defined by the Council of Logistics Management as "the process of planning, implementing, and controlling the efficient and effective flow and storage of goods, services, and related information from point of origin to point of consumption for the purpose of conforming to customer requirements" (*Logisticsworld.com*). Note that this definition includes inbound, outbound, internal, and external movements and the return of materials and goods. It also includes *order fulfillment*. The distinction between logistics and order fulfillment is not always clear, and the terms are sometimes used interchangeably because logistics is a large part of order fulfillment.

STEPS IN THE ORDER FULFILLMENT PROCESS

The order fulfillment process consists of the flows of orders, payments, information, materials, and parts, all of which need to be coordinated with various departments and external partners. The order fulfillment process starts when an order is received, and includes the following nine activities that are supported by software or may be automated:

Step 1: Make sure the customer will pay. Depending on the payment method and prior arrangements with the customer, verify that the customer can and will pay and establish the payment terms. This activity is done by the finance department for B2B sales or an external company, such as PayPal or a credit card issuer such as Visa for B2C sales. Any holdup in payment may cause a shipment to be delayed, resulting in a loss of goodwill or a customer. In B2C, the customers usually prepay by credit card, but the buyer may be using a stolen card, so verification is crucial.

Step 2: Check in-stock availability, and re-order as necessary. As soon as an order is received, the stock (inventory) is checked to determine the availability of the product or materials. If there's not enough stock, the ordering system places an order, typically automatically using EDI (electronic data interchange). To perform these operations, the ordering system needs to be connected to the inventory system to verify availability and also to suppliers' ordering systems. Several scenarios are possible that may involve the material management department and production department, as well as outside suppliers and warehouse facilities. Most often buyers can check availability by themselves using the web.

Step 3: Arrange shipments. When the product is available, shipment to the customer is arranged (otherwise, go to step 5). Products can be digital or physical. If the item is physical and it's readily available, packaging and shipment arrangements are made. Both the packaging/shipping department and internal shippers or outside transporters may be involved. Digital items are usually available because their "inventory" is not depleted. However, a digital product, such as software, may be under revision, and thus unavailable for delivery at certain times. In either case, information needs to flow among several partners.

Step 4: Insurance. Sometimes the contents of a shipment need to be insured. Both the finance department and an insurance company could be involved, and again, information needs to flow, not only inside the company, but also to and from the customer and insurance agent.

Step 5: Replenishment. Customized (build-to-order) orders will always trigger a need for some manufacturing or assembly operation. Similarly, if standard items are out of stock, they need to be produced or procured. Production can be done in-house or by contractors.

Step 6: In-house production. In-house production needs to be planned, and actual production needs to be scheduled. Production planning involves people, materials, components, machines, financial resources, and possibly suppliers and subcontractors. In the case of assembly and/or manufacturing, several plant services may be needed, including collaboration with business partners. Production facilities may be in a different country from the company's headquarters or retailers. This may further complicate the flow of information.

Step 7: Use suppliers. A manufacturer may opt to buy products or subassemblies from suppliers. Similarly, if the seller is a retailer, such as in the case of *Amazon.com* or *Walmart.com,* the retailer must purchase products from its manufacturers. In this case, appropriate receiving and quality assurance of incoming materials and products must take place.

Once production (step 6) or purchasing from suppliers (step 7) is completed, shipments to the customers (step 3) are arranged.

Step 8: Contacts with customers. Sales representatives need to keep in close contact with customers, especially in B2B, starting with notification of orders received and ending with notification of a shipment or a change in delivery date. These contacts are usually done via e-mail and are frequently generated automatically.

Step 9: Returns. In some cases, customers want to exchange or return items. The movement of returns from customers back to vendors is *reverse logistics*. Overall, between $50 and $100 billion in U.S. goods are returned each year. Such returns can be a major problem, especially when they occur in large volumes.

We now take a more in-depth look at supply chain management concepts.

SUPPLY CHAIN MANAGEMENT CONCEPTS

Supply chain management (SCM) is the efficient management of the flows of material, data, and money in the supply chain, as shown in Figure 10.9. **SCM software** refers to software that supports the steps in the supply chain—manufacturing, inventory control, scheduling, and transportation. SCM software concentrates on

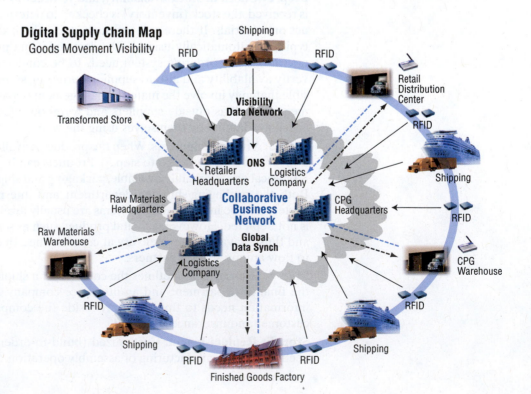

Figure 10.9 Managing a supply chains with RFID.

improving decision making, forecasting, optimization, and analysis. SCM software is configured to achieve the following business goals:

- To reduce uncertainty and variability in order to improve the accuracy of forecasting.
- To increase control over the processes in order to achieve optimal inventory levels, cycle time, and customer service.

The benefits of SCM have long been recognized in business, government, and the military. In today's competitive business environment, efficient, effective supply chains are critical to survival and fully dependent on SCM software, which depends on up-to-date and accurate data. If the network goes down or data are outdated, those managing the supply chain are mostly working blind.

The use of RFID in the supply chain provides a major opportunity to reduce costs and increase operating efficiencies. Figure 10.10 illustrates how RFID can improve the efficiency of a supply chain by improving data quality.

MANAGING ON-DEMAND ACTIVITIES

The current business environment contains the elements of an *on-demand enterprise* with *real-time* operations. To review those concepts:

- **On-demand enterprise.** The concept of an on-demand enterprise is based on the premise that manufacturing or service fulfillment operations will start only after an order is received. We also refer to this approach as *build-to-order*. Enterprises have added this approach to their traditional **produce-to-stock** manufacturing. As the term indicates, *produce-to-stock* is the manufacture of products to stockpile inventory so the company is ready to respond to future demand. An obvious example of produce-to-stock is automobile dealerships, which have huge inventories of vehicles on their lot.

- **On-demand and real-time processes.** An on-demand process in the fulfillment cycle is one that is primed to respond to real-time conditions. There will be no backorders, safety stock, lag time, or excess inventory. This principle is not fully achievable, but it is the direction that high-tech companies are headed in. Laptop and netbook manufacturers build-to-order as much as possible to reduce inventory, holding, and obsolescence costs. Inventory holding costs can greatly add to the cost of a product and narrow the profit margin.

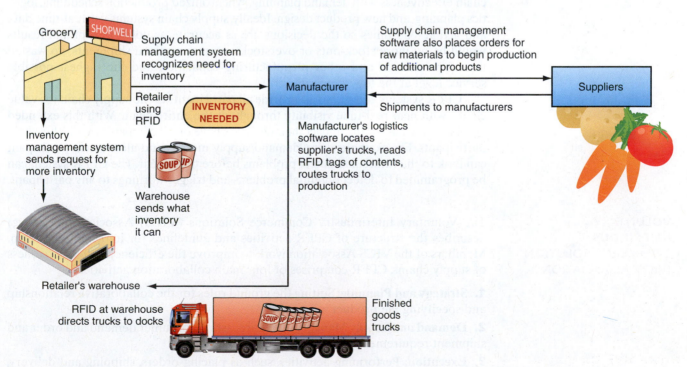

Figure 10.10 How RFID tags provide the data needed to manage the supply chain.

These on-demand concepts have revolutionized the design and management of supply chains. To achieve on-demand and real-time processes, companies must reengineer their supply chain and add SCM to their ERP capabilities.

Questions

1. Define a supply chain.
2. List four functions performed in a supply chain.
3. List and describe the three main flows being managed in a supply chain.
4. Describe SCM.
5. What is order fulfillment?
6. Define logistics.

10.4 Collaborative Planning, Forecasting, and Replenishment (CPFR) Systems

Procter & Gamble (P&G) has been an innovative leader in inventory management for several decades. P&G had convinced Wal-Mart to implement its continuous replenishment software. **Continuous replenishment** is a supply chain relationship in which a vendor continuously monitors the inventory of the retailers and distributors of its products so that it can automatically replenish their inventories when stock levels drop to the re-order point. For example, P&G continuously replenished Pampers baby diapers at Wal-Mart stores. In this **vendor-managed inventory (VMI)** situation, a vendor manages the inventory of its customers eliminating the need for customers to send purchase orders. The advantage to the vendor is having more advanced notice of product demand. The advantage to the retailer or distributor is minimizing inventory costs. Having the correct item in stock when the end-customer needs it benefits all partners.

CPFR, EXTENSIONS OF ERP AND SCM

CPFR is a business practice that pools the knowledge of many trading partners to coordinate demand forecasting, planning, production, and order fulfillment. It is a **demand-driven supply chain.** *Demand-driven* means that decisions about what to produce and in what quantities are based on data-driven forecasts and analytics of customer demand. By following CPFR, companies can dramatically improve supply chain effectiveness with demand planning, synchronized production scheduling, logistics planning, and new product design. Ideally, supply chain systems use real-time data and actual lead times so the decisions are as accurate as possible. Optimal results would be no more stock-outs or overstocks; no more missed shipments; no wasted use of production and other manufacturing capacities; and the highest possible service level at the lowest possible cost.

CPFR systems and networks provide all participants in the supply chain (or value chain) with near real-time visibility throughout the entire chain. With this extended visibility, they can see the impact their decisions have on all companies and value chain participants. For example, using demand/supply models and alerts, each participant can look to the future and detect problems before they occur. The CPFR system can be programmed to detect potential problems and trigger warnings to any participant.

VOLUNTARY INTERINDUSTRY COMMERCE SOLUTIONS (VICS) ASSOCIATION

The Voluntary Interindustry Commerce Solutions (VICS) Association (*vics.org*) describes the structure of CPFR activities and guidelines for implementing them. Members of the VICS Association work to improve the efficiency and effectiveness of supply chains. CPFR comprises of four main collaboration activities:

1. Strategy and Planning: Setting the ground rules for the collaborative relationship and specifying the product mix.

2. Demand and Supply Management: Forecasting consumer demand and order and shipment requirements over the planning horizon.

3. Execution: Performing activities, such as placing orders, shipping and delivery, receiving, stocking, tracking sales transactions, and making payments.

4. Analysis: Monitoring outcomes of planning and execution, assessing results and key performance metrics, sharing insights with partners, and adjusting plans to improve results.

Large manufacturers of consumer goods, such as Warner–Lambert (WL), have improved the efficiency of their supply chains using CPFR. As part of a pilot project, WL shared strategic plans, performance data, and market insights with Wal-Mart. The company realized that it could benefit from Wal-Mart's market knowledge, just as Wal-Mart could benefit from WL's product knowledge. See *IT at Work 10.4* for details.

IT at Work 10.4

Warner-Lambert Collaborates with Retailers

In 2000, Warner-Lambert (WL) was acquired by Pfizer (*pfizer.com*) creating the world's fastest-growing pharmaceutical company. A major product is Listerine mouthwash. The materials for making Listerine come mainly from eucalyptus trees in Australia and are shipped to the WL manufacturing plant in New Jersey. Like all manufacturers, WL wanted answers to "What are we going to sell this week or month?" They forecast overall demand to determine how much Listerine to produce. Once demand is determined, WL calculates how much raw material is needed and when. Forecast errors lead to excess raw material or finished product inventories, or shortages. Excess inventories drive up costs; and stock-outs reduce sales revenues.

WL forecasts demand with the help of JDA Demand Management System (*jda.com/*). Used with other SCM software, JDA analyzes manufacturing, distribution, and sales data against expected demand and business climate information. Its goal is to help WL decide when and how much Listerine and other products to produce. For example, the model can anticipate the impact of

seasonal promotion or a production line being down. WL's supply chain excellence stems from the CPFR program.

WL's demand management system analyzes manufacturing, distribution, and sales data against expected demand and business climate information to help WL decide how much product to make and distribute. Because WL can smooth seasonality in forecasts, it has dramatically cut manufacturing and raw materials inventory costs. Data transfer between companies is done using **electronic data interchange (EDI)** (see Figure 10.11). EDI is a communication standard that enables the electronic transfer of routine documents, such as purchase orders, between business partners. It formats these documents according to agreed-upon standards.

Questions

1. What other supply chain management solutions are offered by JDA?

2. For what industries, besides retailing, would such collaboration be beneficial?

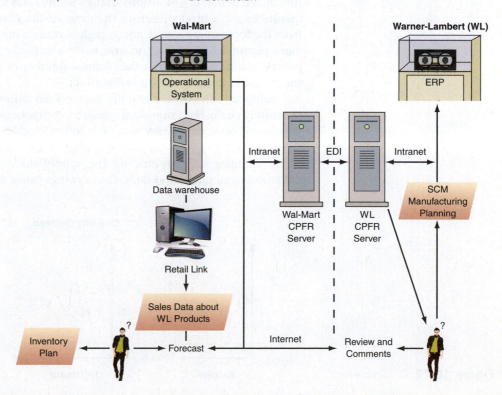

Figure 10.11 Model of CPFR.
Sources: Compiled from *JDA.com* (2009) and *VICS.org.*

Collaboration and the Bull Whip Effect. The supply chain (trading) partners collaborate because of the long lead time needed to make products available for customers and the massive amount of uncertainty in what will be in demand. CPFR goals are:

1. To maximize sales revenues by insuring that there are enough products available to meet demand.

2. To minimize inventory, transportation, and logistics costs.

The common solution to supply chain uncertainties is to build inventories—called **safety stock**—as a buffer. Of course, high safety stock levels increase inventory holding costs. And high inventories at multiple points in the supply chain can result in the **bullwhip effect.**

P&G logistics executives examined the order patterns for one of their best-selling products, Pampers diapers. At retail stores, Pampers sales (which reflect demand) fluctuated, but the variability was not excessive. This demand fluctuation is shown in the left-side graph of Figure 10.12. When they examined the sales orders of distributors, the executives were surprised by the higher degree of variability, as shown in the middle graph of Figure 10.12. Next, when they looked at P&G's orders of materials—the manufacturing level—to their suppliers such as 3M, they discovered that the variability in the size of orders were even greater. Looking across Figure 10.12, you see how the swings in demand look like bullwhips—increasing in variability from retailers to distributors to manufacturers.

At first glance, the variability did not make sense. While the consumers, in this case, babies, consumed diapers at a steady rate, the demand amplified as they moved up the supply chain. The bullwhip effect means that even small increases in demand at the retail level can cause a big increase in the need for parts and materials at the manufacturer level, as explained in the following example.

An example of CPFR and the bullwhip effect. Supply chain systems generate demand forecasts for a planning period, such as a quarter, month, or week. Participating sales representatives generate the sales forecasts. Based on these forecasts, the ERP or supply systems stage, source, and schedule production and distribution facilities to meet forecasted demand. Conditions change so the sales force usually has to adjust order quantities for a product before the close of the planning period. These deviations from the forecast are significant enough to cause a mismatch between what your company planned for production and what is actually needed to meet the amended orders. The deviations from the planned number of sales orders ripple through the supply chain, causing the bullwhip effect.

Adjusted sales orders amplify demand deviations as the information travels up the supply chain. For example, if you are a component supplier one step up the chain, you would order more raw materials to build additional components and increase safety stock. Next, your supplier will add its own safety stock to your adjusted order. These changes will continue up the supply chain, magnifying the original small deviation from planned orders. These swings cause all the firms in the supply chain

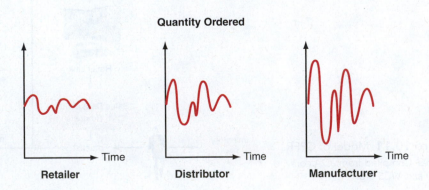

Figure 10.12 Bullwhip effect.

to revamp their sourcing, manufacturing, and distribution plans. They now scramble to get additional raw material, add production lines, and restock distribution lines to meet the amended sales order quantities.

As a result of these swings from the bullwhip effect, firms across the supply chain are saddled with excess inventory, procurement cost overruns, additional warehousing and shipping costs, and most importantly, quality problems. The upstream firms have the option of taking the loss resulting from amended orders or passing on the costs by reducing other product attributes. Component quality is the biggest casualty of rush orders. Distributors or retailers often return products manufactured to meet the amended demand signals, thus placing additional burden on the supply chain.

Low inventory levels increase the risk of stock-outs (insufficient supply) and lost revenues when demand is high or delivery is slow. In either event, the total cost—including the cost of holding inventories, the cost of lost sales opportunities, and bad reputation—can be very high. Thus, companies strive to optimize and control inventories.

BULLWHIP EFFECT IMPLICATIONS

The bullwhip effect has broad implications in 2013 as the economy emerges from a recession and companies rush to fill orders while also restocking warehouse shelves. It touches everyone from retailers to the industrial companies that supply the grease, bolts, and coal needed to manufacture products. The manner in which companies, large and small, respond to market shifts determines which ones emerge first from the slump and start growing again.

A big question as the economy starts to recover is how well suppliers are positioned to ramp up production. Bottlenecks may occur as spot shortages cause unexpected price hikes and hamper companies' ability to meet demand. That's why heavy-equipment manufacturer Caterpillar had taken the unusual step of visiting with key suppliers to ensure they had the resources to quickly increase output. In extreme cases, Caterpillar even is helping its suppliers get financing.

Caterpillar example: Caterpillar says that even if customer demand for its equipment remained the same (that is, no growth), it would still need to boost production in its factories by 10 to 15 percent in order to restock dealers' inventories. Mechanical Devices Co. is already feeling the crack of the whip. The small factory in Bloomington, Illinois, supplies Caterpillar with metal parts. It struggled through 2009, shedding about 100 of its 275 workers and scrounging for other clients to keep its machines running.

One reason that Caterpillar is so attuned to the inventory cycle is its history. The company went through a massive growth spurt in the past decade, fueled by the twin forces of a commodity boom and a housing boom. Sales of the company's iconic yellow machines grew to $54 billion in 2011 from $20 billion in 2002. Its first-quarter profit in 2011 reflected an industrial sector that was growing again, with most of its sales growth coming from the sale of big machines. When the recession hit in 2007, construction and mining companies had cut back their spending on heavy machinery first, according to Mike DeWalt, Caterpillar's director of investors (AP, 2011). For more than two years, companies had held back their investment, but then had no choice but to replace aging machinery, which increased Caterpillar's sales. That means spending is likely to continue as companies replace more vehicles and even expand on growing demand.

COLLABORATION IMPROVES-B2B E-COMMERCE

The promising source of performance improvement in B2B e-commerce is collaboration in the supply chain. Supply chain collaboration can increase profit margins by as much as 3 percent for supply chain partners, which is a significant improvement. For the collaboration effort to succeed, business partners must *trust* each other and each other's information systems.

Questions

1. How does demand uncertainty affect inventory? Give an example.
2. What is continuous replenishment?
3. Define CPFR, and describe how it works.
4. Describe the four main collaboration activities of CPFR as identified by the Voluntary Interindustry Commerce Solutions (VICS) Association.
5. What is the function of safety stock?
6. Explain the bullwhip effect.

10.5 Customer Relationship Management (CRM) Systems

Every company depends on customers for revenues and growth. Intelligently managing relationships with customers can increase revenues and net profits significantly. Similar to managing inventory and supplier relationships, effective customer relationship management (CRM) is data-driven, complex, and continuously changing. The growth of mobile sales channels and social networking makes recognizing customers across multiple touch points a challenge. In addition, many companies have customer data in multiple, disparate systems that are not integrated—until they implement CRM systems. As shown in Figure 10.13, CRM integrates with ERP and other enterprise systems. From a business perspective, CRM involves public relations (PR), marketing, quality control, sales, service, and support, as diagramed in Figure 10.14.

From a technology perspective, CRM refers to the methodologies and software tools to leverage customer information in order to achieve the following:

• Building greater customer loyalty and therefore greater profitability per customer
• Deter customer attrition (loss of a customer)
• Acquire new customers who are most likely to become profitable
• Up-sell (sell more profitable products/services) or cross-sell (sell additional products/services) to unprofitable customers to move them to a profit position.
• Reduce inefficiencies that waste advertising dollars

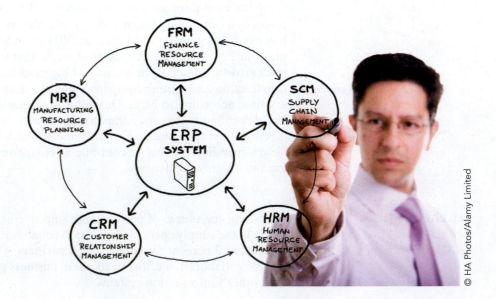

Figure 10.13 Diagram showing how CRM relates to ERP and other enterprise systems.

Figure 10.14 Components of CRM include public relations (PR), marketing, and their supporting systems.

© Stephen VanHorn/Alamy Limited

CUSTOMER ACQUISITION AND RETENTION

CRM technologies help marketing managers run effective campaigns, promotions, commercials, and advertisements to attract new customers, or to increase sales to existing customers, or to do both. Attracting and acquiring new customers is expensive, for instance, it costs banks roughly $100 to acquire a new customer. Newly acquired customers are unprofitable until they have purchased enough products or services to exceed the cost to acquire and service them. Therefore, retaining customers that generate revenues in excess of the costs (e.g., customer service, returns, promotional items, and the like) are critical. The purpose of loyalty or frequent-purchase programs offered by online retailers, coffee shops, airlines, supermarkets, credit card issuers, casinos, and other companies is to track customers for CRM purposes and build customer loyalty to improve financial performance. Loyalty programs rely on data warehouses and data analytics to recognize and reward customers who repeatedly use services or products. The 1-800-FLOWERS.COM loyalty program is described in *IT at Work 10.5*.

IT at Work 10.5

1-800-Flowers.com *Uses Data Mining for CRM*

1-800-FLOWERS.COM is an Internet pioneer. Online sales are a major marketing channel in addition to telephone and fax orders. Competition is very strong in this industry. The company's success was based on operational efficiency, convenience (24/7 accessibility), and reliability. However, all major competitors provide the same features today. To maintain its competitive edge, the company transformed itself into a customer-centric organization, caring for more than 15 million customers.

The company decided to cultivate brand loyalty through customer relationships based on detailed knowledge of customers. How is this accomplished? SAS software spans the entire decision-support process for managing customer relationships. Collecting data at all customer touch points, the company turns those data into knowledge for understanding and anticipating customer behavior, meeting customer needs, building more profitable customer relationships, and gaining a holistic view of a customer's lifetime value. Using SAS Enterprise Miner, 1-800-FLOWERS.COM sifts through purchasing data to discover trends, explain outcomes, and predict results so that the company can increase response rates and identify profitable customers. In addition to selling and campaign management, the ultimate goal is to make sure that when a customer wants to buy, he or she continues to buy from 1-800-FLOWERS.COM and cannot be captured by a competitor's marketing. Their objective is not just about getting customers to buy more. It is about making sure that when they decide to purchase a gift online or by phone, they do not think of going to the competition.

Data mining software helps the company identify the many different types of customers and how each would like to be treated. Customer retention increased by over 15 percent.

Questions

1. Why is being number one in operational efficiency not enough to keep 1-800-FLOWERS.COM at the top of its industry?

2. What is the role of data mining?

3. How is the one-to-one relationship achieved in such systems?

CRM FOR A COMPETITIVE EDGE

According to management guru Peter Drucker, "Those companies who know their customers, understand their needs, and communicate intelligently with them will always have a competitive advantage over those that don't." (Bogatz, 2002). For most types of companies, marketing effectiveness depends on how well they know their customers; specifically, knowing what their customers want, how best to contact them, and what types of offers they are likely to respond to positively. According to the *loyalty effect*, a 5 percent reduction in customer attrition can improve profits by as much as 20 percent. Customer-centric business strategies strive to provide products and services that customers want to buy. One of the best examples is the Apple iPhone and iPod—devices that customers were willing to camp out on sidewalks to buy to guarantee getting one on the day of their release. In contrast, companies with product-centric strategies need to create demand for their products, which is more expensive and may fail.

CRM EXAMPLE: TRAVELOCITY

CRM is best understood by looking at a familiar company's CRM strategy. Consider Travelocity.com, the online travel agency. Travelocity implemented CRM software from Teradata (*teradata.com*) to better understand, target, personalize, and communicate with its 40+ million customers. Michael Hawkins, Travelocity's Director of Data Warehousing and CRM, explained: "We actually know where/what people are shopping for—even if they don't buy. This allows us to craft offers based on people's real-world interests." (*teradata.com/customers/Travel-Travelocity*). Within the first year following its CRM implementation, Travelocity achieved these changes:

- Gross bookings and earnings improved by 100 percent
- Gross profit margins improved 150 percent
- Booker conversion rates rose to 8.9 percent—highest in the online travel services industry

Overall, CRM software has enabled Travelocity to:

- Analyze click stream data and discover how customers use the web site. This information is leveraged to better personalize messages in real time while customers are using the site.
- Test the value of specific messages and offers on various customer segments.
- Identify customers who have booked a flight, but not a hotel or car rental and then make them a compelling offer. Adjusting offers or taking action based on customer behavior is referred to as *event-based marketing*.

Building CRM capabilities takes time and requires a data warehouse for the analytics. Travelocity started with the building blocks to learn about their customers and the best ways to deliver targeted market campaigns to them. In addition, Travelocity can respond quickly to offers from their suppliers. For example, at 8 am a major airline offered travel agencies a special fare from Los Angeles to San Juan, Puerto Rico. Travelocity quickly scanned their customers' browsing behavior, pulled the e-mail addresses of 30,000 people in the Los Angeles area who had browsed but not bought tickets to the Caribbean, and then generated an e-mail message to them. The response rate was incredible—with 25 percent of the recipients who had been e-mail booking flights. This was an effective campaign measured by the response rate or take rate as well as a highly efficient one as measured by the ROI from the profit on sales of those extra tickets.

CRM SUCCESSES AND FAILURES

As with many IT innovations, there have been initially a large number of CRM failures, which have been reported in the media. Some of the major issues relating to CRM failures are the following:

- Difficulty in measuring and valuing intangible benefits. There are only a few tangible benefits to CRM.

- Failure to identify and focus on specific business problems that the CRM can solve.
- Lack of active senior management (non-IT) sponsorship.
- Poor user acceptance. This issue can occur for a variety of reasons, such as usability problems and unclear benefits; that is, CRM is a tool for management, but it may not help a rep sell more effectively.
- Trying to automate a poorly defined business process in the CRM implementation.

Example of a failure: Citizen National Bank's experience is an example of a failure, changing the CRM vendors, and then a success. The lessons learned, at a cost of $500,000 were:

- Be absolutely clear on how the CRM application will add value to the sales process.
- Determine if and why sales people are avoiding CRM.
- Provide incentives for the sales team to adopt CRM.
- Find ways to simplify the use of the CRM application.
- Adjust the CRM system as business needs change.

JUSTIFYING CRM

One of the biggest problems in CRM implementation is the difficulty of defining and measuring success. Additionally, many companies say that when it comes to determining value, intangible benefits are more significant than tangible cost savings. Yet companies often fail to establish quantitative or even qualitative measures in order to judge these intangible benefits.

A formal business plan must be in place before the CRM project begins—one that quantifies the expected costs, tangible financial benefits, and intangible strategic benefits, as well as the risks. The plan should include an assessment of the following:

- **Tangible net benefits.** The plan must include a clear and precise cost-benefit analysis that lists all of the planned project costs and tangible benefits. This portion of the plan should also contain a strategy for assessing key financial metrics, such as ROI, net present value (NPV), or other justification methods.
- **Intangible benefits.** The plan should detail the expected intangible benefits, and it should list the measured successes and shortfalls. Often, an improvement in customer satisfaction is the primary goal of the CRM solution, but in many cases this key value is not measured.
- **Risk assessment.** The risk assessment is a list of all of the potential pitfalls related to the people, processes, and technology that are involved in the CRM project.

Having such a list helps to lessen the probability that problems will occur. And, if they do occur, a company may find that, by having listed and considered the problems in advance, the problems are more manageable than they would have been otherwise.

Tangible and Intangible Benefits. Benefits typically include increases in staff productivity; for instance, closing more deals, cost avoidance, revenues, and margin increases, as well as reductions in inventory costs; due to the elimination of errors, for example. Other benefits include increased customer satisfaction, loyalty, and retention.

ON-DEMAND OR CLOUD CRM

Like several other enterprise systems, CRM can be delivered on-premise or on-demand via the cloud. The traditional way to deliver such systems was on-premise—meaning users purchased the system and installed it on site. This was very expensive, with a large upfront payment. Many SMEs (small and medium enterprises) could not justify it, especially because most CRM benefits are intangible.

The solution to the situation, which appears in several similar variations and names, is to lease the software. Salesforce.com pioneered the concept for its several

CRM products including supporting salespeople, under the name of **on-demand CRM,** offering the software in a cloud arrangement. The concept of on-demand is known also as *utility computing* or *software as a service* (SaaS). One of the biggest benefits companies who use on-demand CRM find is that it's easily accessible. With software, you're tied to a desk. With cloud CRM, it's accessible via mobile devices anywhere and time.

Sales are a multistep process, which providers of on-demand CRM attempt to support. Most CRM services are designed to easily integrate with the programs businesses are already using, such as help desk services, sales force automation, and lead management.

Cloud CRMs, such as *Force.com,* are increasingly popular because in the cloud, CRM apps are never limited by the underlying technology platform. Organizations can customize and make changes in real time, as their business needs evolve. Other benefits on-demand cloud CRM are:

- Improved cash flow
- No need for corporate software experts
- Ease of use with minimal training
- Fast time-to-market
- Vendors' expertise available

Questions

1. Explain CRM from business and technology perspectives.
2. Discuss the role of CRM in customer acquisition and retention.
3. According to Peter Drucker, what does marketing effectiveness depend upon?
4. How can CRM be justified?
5. What are the benefits of on-demand cloud CRM?

Key Terms

You find clickable Link Libraries for each chapter on the Companion website.

Comparison of top 10 ERP vendors *http://top10erp.org /*

ERP Vendor Shootout *http://erpshootout.com /*

New Study on Collaborative Execution Finds Supply Chain Collaboration Can Improve Operational Metrics by 50 Percent or More, (March 27, 2012)
http://www.e2open.com/news/article/new-study-on-collaborative-execution-finds-supply-chain-collaboration-can-improve-operational-metrics-by-50-percent-or-more/

Oracle *http://oracle.com*

SAP *http://sap.com*

SAP Business Objects Supply Chain Performance Management
http://www.sap.com/solutions/sapbusinessobjects/large/industries/supply-chain-operations/supply-chain-performance-management/index.epx

E2Open *http://www.e2open.com*

Microsoft Dynamics *http://microsoft.com/dynamics/en/us/default.aspx*

Teradata *http://Teradata.com*

JDA Software Group, Inc. *http://www.JDA.com*

Evaluate and Expand Your Learning

IT and Data Management Decisions

1. *Consider the following:* In the 1990s, hard disk drive (HDD) makers were among the first industries to move production to lower-cost countries. Beginning in Singapore, these companies shifted manufacturing operations to China and Thailand, in search of ever-lower labor costs. Since then, Thailand has become the second-largest maker of hard drives and a major supplier of parts to the industry worldwide. With the catastrophic Thailand floods in fall 2011, the industry faced shortages of over 30 million drives per quarter. Some executives at HDD companies were forced to explain a glaring oversight: why had they had relied so heavily on a supplier in a country located in a high-flood risk area?

   Also consider that: By the end of the 1990s, most supply chains had become lean by minimizing their inventories and reducing waste, and could schedule deliveries across the globe with incredible precision. Supply chain speed and flexibility were impressive Products that should take months to procure and manufacture were promised within days of customer requests.
   a. What supply chain management lessons can be learned from the experiences of HDD makers?
   b. What are the risks of highly efficient and lean supply chains?
   c. Could one catastrophic supply chain event wipe out years of profits or market share? Explain your answer.
   d. In your opinion, when do cost savings outweigh the risks?
   e. In your opinion, when are cost savings outweighed by the risks?

Questions for Discussion & Review

1. According to "New Study on Collaborative Execution Finds Supply Chain Collaboration Can Improve Operational Metrics by 50 Percent or More" (2012),

   By a ratio of nearly two to one, supply chain professionals agreed that one of the biggest barriers to successful collaboration is a slow issue resolution process. This was identified as a systemic problem related to quality of information flow, in terms of both the granularity (level of detail) and timeliness of data shared.

   And 92 percent of respondents agreed that rapid problem resolution was part of good collaboration. True collaboration can be defined in terms of speed, both in problem solving and in organizational learning. More than half of the responses indicated that speed of response in truly collaborative relationships was twice as fast or faster, with learning curve improvements more than 50 percent greater than in non-collaborative trading partner relationships.

   (See Chapter 10 Link Library for *http://e2open.com/news/article/new-study-on-collaborative-execution-finds-supply-chain-collaboration-can-improve-operational-metrics-by-50-percent-or-more/*).
   a. Discuss why supply chain partners may not be able to resolve issues quickly. Consider *information flows* in your discussion.
   b. What might be the impacts on the supply chain of slow problem (issue) resolution?
   c. Based on your answer to (a), discuss which enterprise systems could speed up problem resolution.
   d. What is meant by *learning curve improvements*?

2. Distinguish between ERP and SCM software. In what ways do they complement each other? Why should they be integrated?

3. State the business value of enterprise systems and how they can be used to make management of the supply chain more effective.

4. What are the problems in implementing ERP systems?

5. Explain how vendor-managed inventory can save costs in the supply chain.

6. Find examples of how two of the following organizations improve their supply chains: manufacturing, hospitals, retailing, education, construction, agribusiness, and shipping. Discuss the benefits to the organizations.

7. It is claimed that supply chains are essentially "a series of linked suppliers and customers; every customer is in turn a supplier to the next downstream organization, until the ultimate end-user." Explain. Use a diagram.

8. Discuss why it is difficult to justify CRM.

9. A supply chain is much more powerful in the Internet marketplace. Discuss how Internet technologies can be used to manage the supply chain.

Online Activities

1. Visit *Teradata.com* and find a podcast or webinar that deals with CRM and supply chains. Identify the benefits cited in the podcast or webinar.

2. Visit *SAP.com* and identify ERM modules.

3. Visit *http://blog.kissmetrics.com/* and click Infographics. Select one of the infographics and review the content. Discuss what you learned.

4. Visit *http://www.teradata.com/podcasts/ADW-CRM-Overstock/*. Listen to the Active Data Warehousing and CRM at Overstock.com podcast. Explain how active data warehousing and CRM benefits Overstock.com's marketing department.

Collaborative Work

1. Each team selects a major enterprise system vendor. Search and read a case study of one of the vendor's customers. Summarize the case and identify the benefits of the implementation.

2. Visit *http://www.salesforce.com/*. Click View Demos. Register for access to the demos. Each person selects and views a different demo. Compile a report that describes the benefits of each application or software solution.

3. Visit *http://www.soffront.com/*. Click *CRM Platform* and select *Screens and Workflow*. Under *Discover More*, click Datasheets & Videos. Watch a few of the videos. Compile a report of how this software supports CRM.

CASE 2 BUSINESS CASE

Supply Chain Collaboration in the Cloud at Lenovo

Lenovo is the world's second-largest maker of PCs, and it nearly doubled its market share between 2009 and 2011. Huge sales growth and expansion via mergers and acquisitions (M&A) forced Lenovo to rethink its global supply chain strategies and operations. Key M&A in 2011 included German PC and consumer electronics company Medion, and a joint venture with NEC to form the leading PC business in Japan.

Global Supply Chain Runs on Legacy Systems

Following its purchase of IBM's Personal Computing Division for $1.75 billion in 2005, Lenovo faced numerous system integration challenges. Without its own IT infrastructure in place to support a worldwide business, Lenovo had to operate its new global supply chain on legacy systems. Outsourcing core systems was too expensive at the time. Because of their inflexibility, the legacy systems could not be scaled to handle the growth in operations—so operations were handled using manual-based processes.

Goal: Build a World-Class Global Supply Chain

The challenge for Lenovo and its global supply chain organization was to design and build a worldwide IT platform to transition from legacy systems as fast as possible and with minimal business disruption. The new platform needed to be able to provide visibility, efficiency, and responsiveness to manage its growing business trading network.

Lenovo's average product innovation cycle is six months, which magnifies the cost of supply chain errors. Supply chain operations had to be flexible and reliable to guarantee fast delivery of the latest products to customers. According to Jon Pershke, vice president of Global Supply Chain, "access to real-time, actionable information—plus the ability to collaborate with partners to resolve exceptions—are critical to achieving this goal."

Key objectives of its overall strategy to build a world-class global supply chain were:

- Leverage cloud-based systems to reduce operating costs, improve IT flexibility, and deliver superior customer experience
- Reduce the cost and time to add new trading partners
- Enable a real-time, consolidated view of processes and operations, providing a "single version of the truth" for Lenovo and its partners
- Eliminate the need for manual intervention
- Enable collaboration for key supply chain processes, including order-to-cash and inventory management

- Converge physical and digital networks to cut costs and improve service levels.

From Legacy Systems to the Cloud

Lenovo partnered with E2open's consulting and deployment teams (.e2open.com) to design and build a cloud-based supply chain solution for seamless information sharing, process management, and collaboration.

The E2open cloud solutions have added significant value to Lenovo's global supply chain operations in a number of key areas:

1. The *any-to-any platform* enabled the company and its partners to exchange data in any preferred format. This platform cut testing and infrastructure maintenance costs.

2. Streamlined procurement processes have improved automation and collaboration; and improved the confidentiality of pricing agreements.

3. The cloud solution has enabled the convergence of physical and digital supply chain networks providing greater security and reducing the risk of error or fraud.

Lenovo's cloud-based supply chain and logistics solutions have improved operations and customer satisfaction at significantly lower cost.

Sources: Compiled from Lenovo (2012), e2Open.com (2012), and Supply Chain Management Review (scmr.com; 2012).

Questions

1. What major changes occurred at Lenovo between 2005 and 2011?
2. How did those changes impact Lenovo?
3. Explain Lenovo's goal for its supply chain.
4. In the transition from legacy to cloud, what were its two requirements?
5. Why is access to real-time, actionable information important?
6. How did the cloud solutions add value to Lenovo's global supply chain operations?

CASE 3   VIDEO CASE

Supply Chain Performance Management

The *SAP BusinessObjects Supply Chain Performance Management* software and services package includes preconfigured metrics, analytics, and dashboards that can help you reduce the cost, complexity, and risk of implementation. Key features and functions of the software include:

- **Business content.** Pre-built data integration and data models allow you to comply with leading frameworks, such as the supply chain operations reference (SCOR) model
- **Data extraction and transformation.** Access data and gain insight more quickly, thanks to prebuilt integration with transactional systems and pre-calculation of metrics
- **Analysis and reporting.** Produce more useful reports with semantically consistent navigation across information
- **Impact analysis.** Understand the relationships among supply chain metrics
- **Ability to react faster** to problems and risks by understanding risks in the supply chain

- **Reduced cycle times** and accelerated problem resolution through identification and resolution of problems.

Questions

1. Visit SAP BusinessObjects Supply Chain Performance Management site at *http://www.sap.com/solutions/sapbusinessobjects/large/industries/supply-chain-operations/supply-chain-performance-management/index.epx*
2. Watch the video demo showing how SAP software allows you to analyze the financial performance of a company's supply chain, analyze the operational performance, and capture actionable information. Then answer the following questions.
   a. What is the purpose of impact analysis?
   b. KPIs (key performance indicators)

Data Analysis & Decision Making

Assessing the Cost/Benefits of Cloud CRM

A large food processing company would like to find the cost/benefit of installing a cloud CRM application. They list both tangible and intangible costs and benefits of the project. Your job is to design a spreadsheet to perform the following analysis:

1. Calculate the tangible costs and benefits.
2. List the intangible costs and risks.
3. List the intangible benefits.

Data for the analysis are:

COSTS

- Cloud CRM system: $44 per user per month
- Technical support and maintenance: $500/month
- Total number of users: 95 (90 sales people and 5 supervisors)
- Training of 90 sales people for 5 days: productivity loss $200/day per person

- Training of 5 supervisors: productivity loss $300/day per person
- Training fees: $4,000
- Additional hardware, networks, and bandwidth: $27,000/month

BENEFITS

- An increase in average sales revenues = $7,000 per month per sales person

- An increase in sales revenues from improvement in customer retention = $5,000/month
- Gross profit from sales revenues = 14 percent

Resources on the Book's Web Site

You'll find additional chapter materials and useful web links. In addition, self-quizzes that provide individualized feedback are available for each chapter.

References

Accenture. "Joint Munitions Command calls on Accenture for integrated logistics and high performance guidance." 2010. *accenture.com/*.

Alexander, D. "How Agile Are You?" Manufacturing Automation, May 2009. *Business Wire*, "Research and Markets: Recent Overview of the Performance Apparel Markets," April 17, 2009.

AP (Associated Press). "Caterpillar Surpasses Earnings Expectations and Raises Its Outlook for the Year." *The New York Times*, April 29, 2011.

Bogatz. G. "Product-centric to Customer-centric: Why CRM is the Business Strategy for School-Market Success." *Marketing Works Inc.* November 2002. *marketingworksinc.com/crmart.htm*

Center for Disease Control (CDC). *CDC.gov/*.

e2Open.com. 2012.

Economic Research Service. *ers.usda.gov/*.

European Food Safety Authority. *efsa.europa.eu/*.

Food and Drug Administration. *FDA.gov*.

Food Safety Modernization Act (FSMA). *fda.gov/Food/FoodSafety/FSMA/default.htm*

Humanetics.com/.

JDA Software Group, Inc. *JDA.com*.

Joint Munitions Command, *jmc.army.mil/*. 2012. *jmc.army.mil/Historian/JMCHistory.aspx*

Krigsman, M. "ERP train wrecks, failures, and lawsuits." *ZD Net.* January 19, 2011.

Lenovo. "Collaboration in the Cloud: How Lenovo is Teaming with e2Open to Improve Global Supply Chain Execution," 2012.

Moss, M. "The Burger That Shattered Her Life," *New York Times*, October 2, 2009.

Rettig, C., "The Trouble with enterprise software," *MIT Sloan Managements Review* (Fall 2007).

Schwerin, C. "Army gears up for next Network Integration Evaluation." U.S. Army, *army.mil*, April 2, 2012.

Supply Chain Management Review. *scmr.com*, 2012.

Ten ERP vendors' products. *top10erp.org/*.

United States Army. *army.mil/*.

Voluntary Interindustry Commerce Solutions, 2012. *vics.org*.

Weier, M.H. "Food Industry Looks To RFID to Avoid Next Catastrophe." *InformationWeek*. February 5, 2007.

Performance Management using Data Visualization, Mashups, and Mobile Intelligence

Learning Outcomes

❶ Describe how data visualization applications, data discovery systems, and interactive reports support organizational functions and decision making, and how visual analytics are helping managers improve financial performance.

❷ Explain data mashup technology as an alternative self-service and end-user systems development approach.

❸ Describe how enterprise dashboards and reporting support executive, managerial, and operational levels by leveraging real-time data and people's natural ability to think visually.

❹ Discuss why a mobilized workforce is best supported by a mobile approach to data, and explain the competitive advantages of mobile intelligence.

In the past, managers usually did not have a convenient way to analyze and develop a good understanding of a lot of data, or to compile data from diverse sources to get reports out fast enough. These limitations make it hard to monitor and manage performance. Ways to combat these problems are **visualization (viz) technologies**—primarily, business dashboards, enterprise mashups, interactive reporting tools, and visualization apps for mobiles. These tools pull data from business intelligence (BI) systems, data warehouses, and other internal and external data stores; then display them in meaningful graphics with drill-down capabilities.

Business dashboards get data into the hands of knowledge workers, giving them an instant view of performance metrics and the ability to analyze data themselves. The term **enterprise mashup** is used to differentiate business-related mashups from web mashups, as you read in Chapter 8. Enterprise mashup technologies extract and combine various types of data from data warehouses, marts, and other sources to produce dashboards and reports.

Visualization technologies create information management efficiencies. Now end-users can do things themselves that previously required a team of IT developers and months of effort. Making connectivity and data mashing accessible to tech-savvy people increases productivity. With visualization tools, workers can better prepare and respond to unanticipated events and make more effective decisions in complex, dynamic situations.

CASE 1 OPENING CASE

Data Viz iPad App Improves America First's Performance

Data visualization, or **data viz,** is the gathering of complicated information into readable graphics. While not new, data viz technologies have matured, providing users with an easy way to display and digest massive amounts of data.

Figure 11.1 shows America First's 2011 and 2010 consolidated earnings in a general ledger-style layout; while Figure 11.2 presents an at-a-glance visualization of three key items for display on a mobile device. By clicking any bar on the chart, the CFO can drill down to increasingly detailed data. With visualization tools, displays of the data or KPIs most vital to each manager's needs can be designed easily.

America First Credit Union is member-owned, nonprofit financial institution with 101 full-service branch locations throughout Utah and online banking services. Founded in 1939, it is the 11th-largest credit union in the U.S. with $5.1 billion (2012) in assets. A problem facing America First Credit Union (*americafirst.com*) was how to convey the company's performance, risk position, and opportunities to executives in a concise and trusted way and at low cost. The solution—use a **data visualization app** for mobile devices, which is also called a **mobile BI app.**

Providing Data Visualization on Tablets Cut Costs

America First's new reporting system delivers data on financial, risk, and loan performance as graphical or visual displays to senior executives on their iPads. The shift to tablets and the mobile visualization system began as a necessary cost-cutting move. The strain of the economic recession had contributed to the $9.3 million net loss in 2010 (Figure 11.1) forcing the credit union to cut costs wherever possible. In November 2010, America First began to replace laptops with Apple iPads starting with the chief financial officer (CFO), controller, and network manager.

How Costs Were Cut

Tablet computers cost less than $700 each, which is at least 50 percent less than the cost of notebooks that America First had deployed. And a tablet's $25 monthly service fee is 40 percent less than broadband service plans for laptops.

How Speed Was Improved

The reporting process was done by e-mailing PDFs of spreadsheets to managers. Spreadsheets were dense, general ledger-style text and line items. It was taking executives too long to make sense of the financial data presented to them this way. This process also caused delays and confusion because of multiple versions of the reports. Managers wasted time trying to verify that they had the latest version of the financials.

Statement of Consolidated Earnings 2011 and 2010

Earnings	2011	2010
Interest on Loans	$ 218,018,324	$ 244,329,244
Interest on Investments	3,264,876	2,606,492
Other Interest Income	2,402,693	260,424
Fees and Other Revenue	133,989,545	128,203,134
Total Earnings	**$ 357,675,438**	**$ 375,399,294**
Expenses		
Interest Expenses	$ 39,285,170	$ 55,116,800
Operating Expenses	204,253,769	194,352,673
Provisions for Loan Loss	92,468,010	123,771,665
Total Expenses	**$ 336,006,949**	**$ 373,241,138**
Net Earnings before NCUA Impairments	21,668,489	2,158,156
NCUA Impairments	11,109,478	11,481,384
Net Earnings after NCUA Impairments	**$ 10,559,011**	**($ 9,323,228)**

Figure 11.1 America First Credit Union's earnings report in table format.

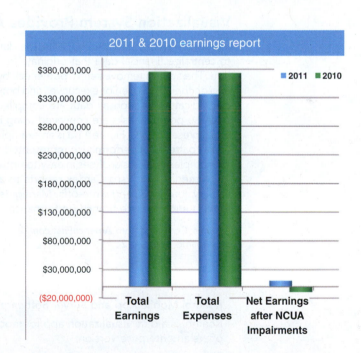

Figure 11.2 Concise visualization of 2011 and 2010 earnings report. Clicking on the bars drills down to detailed data that are shown in the table format.

How Stricter Regulations Were Met

During the recession, pressure to understand the data intensified when the National Credit Union Administration (NCUA) required credit unions to prove that they had sufficient internal controls to monitor and manage risk. America First was facing an NCUA examination within several months. Managers needed:

- A comprehensive view of their key risks
- An assessment of how they are managing each risk
- A sense of how the risks are changing, e.g., increasing, decreasing, or stable.

The Decision Process Leading to Use of Data Visualization for Mobiles

CFO Rex Rollo believed that iPad's portability and familiar touchscreen interface would lead to better risk management. Financial reports could be formatted for mobile screens and presented to principals in a standardized visual format that they would immediately understand. Controller Thayne Shaffer's plan was to feed huge volumes of financial data through a smart visualization app to produce content-rich displays with brief descriptions. Three projected benefits of this plan were:

1. Revenues, risks, costs, and geographic trends would be more easily understood.
2. Management would have a better understanding of the credit union's financial health.
3. Better and faster decisions would improve performance.

Overall, the data visualization system would provide the BI to manage internal controls and risk. Managers would appreciate the **user experience** because visualization app takes advantage of touch screens' hand gestures and accelerometer for rotating between portrait and landscape views. Tablet computers are appealing because of their zero-training interface.

Several free versions of mobile BI visualization tools that work with various types of databases were reviewed and tested: LiveDashBoard, MicroStrategy, Pentaho, PushBI, QlikView, Roambi, and SAS Mobile.

In July 2011, America First deployed the enterprise (server) version of Roambi (roambi.com) that serves 47 users on their iPads. Designed by San Diego mobile app maker MeLLmo, Roambi offers new ways to visually present complex data, and to interact with that data. Roambi integrates inexpensively and easily with the credit union's data systems and engines, including Oracle's Essbase.

Visualization System Provides Additional Benefits

In addition to the expected benefits, the data visualization system also helped America First to centralize financial data that originate from disparate sources throughout its IT infrastructure. The system removes an IT bottleneck by shifting the analysis to business users. With the app on their iPads, senior executives and board members get access to the most recent financial indicators as soon as data are compiled. Credit-related questions are answered faster because potential risks are conveyed using intuitive display features such as heat map-style visual presentations. Figure 11.3 is an example of a heat map. A heat map is excellent for identifying patterns of performance represented by color-codes, area size, and layout. By rendering complex business analyses in easy-to-understand visualizations, more people can use them.

America First uses Cardex reports to assess economic indicators that affect its asset liability, loan risks, and write-offs. Managers also use the system to assess revenue opportunities and measure branch performance.

Sources: Compiled from *AmericaFirst.com* (2012), Eckerson (2011), Kite (2012), Raice & Ante (2010), and *Roambi.com* (2012).

Tech Note 11.1

Roambi Mobile App and Server Software

Roambi is a data visualization app for mobile devices—iPads and iPhones. Roambi also offers an enterprise version.

The free or paid version of Roambi can be downloaded from Apple's App Store and hosted in the cloud for use by anyone or company. For large enterprise customers, MeLLmo installs its Roambi product package on the company's server for $795 per user. The server software extracts data from a company's traditional BI systems, e.g., SAP, IBM, Oracle or *Salesforce.com*, then sends them to the mobile app. Roambi apps include:

- **Analytics:** users convert their spreadsheets into interactive displays.
- **Cardex:** users pull up and flip through pages of reports, for example, to view sales by region or market segment. These reports can be swiped, tapped, or zoomed to drill down into the data, change time frames, or manipulate data.
- **Flow** app embeds visualizations into reports.

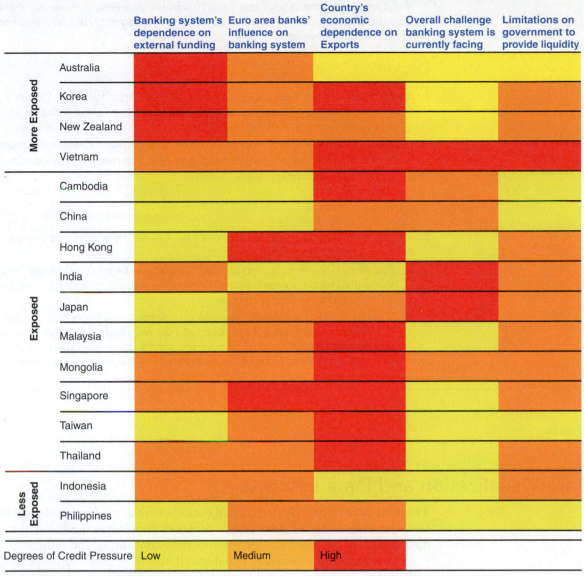

	Banking system's dependence on external funding	Euro area banks' influence on banking system	Country's economic dependence on Exports	Overall challenge banking system is currently facing	Limitations on government to provide liquidity
More Exposed					
Australia					
Korea					
New Zealand					
Vietnam					
Exposed					
Cambodia					
China					
Hong Kong					
India					
Japan					
Malaysia					
Mongolia					
Singapore					
Taiwan					
Thailand					
Less Exposed					
Indonesia					
Philippines					

Degrees of Credit Pressure   Low   Medium   High

Source: Moody's Investors Service

Figure 11.3 Example of a heat map visualization, which is used to convey trends and other information quickly to users. In this example, the colors green, yellow, and red indicate that the risk is "acceptable," "of moderate concern," or "of serious concern," respectively.

Discuss

1. What were the challenges facing the credit union prior to the data visualization reporting system?
2. How did the shift from laptops to tablets and the mobile visualization address or solve each of the challenges in your answer to question #1?
3. Why would managers appreciate the user experience of the new system?
4. In your opinion, how would the user experience influence acceptance and use of the credit union's new system? Explain.
5. How do heat maps convey meaning?
6. The design of a user interface and experience that makes it easy, efficient, and enjoyable to operate the mobile device combined with the use of data visualization to under-

stand complex data quickly can benefit workers immensely. However, there may be downsides to consider. What are potential disadvantages or risks resulting from the use of mobile data visualization apps?

Decide

7. Research and review three mobile data visualization apps for iPads. Download and test their demo versions and watch videos showing how apps are developed.
   a. Using a tablet, compare and contrast the three apps on at least five criteria. Consider price, performance, and ease of developing customized data visualizations.
   b. Based on your analysis, recommend one of these mobile data visualization apps. Explain your recommendation.

Debate

8. Assume you are a manager at America First Credit Union and that you own an iPad, Android, or BlackBerry Playbook.
   a. *iPad owner:* You already own an iPad. Should you be required to use the company-issued iPad for data visualizations? Debate this issue from your personal perspective and the credit union's perspective.
   b. *Android or Playbook owner:* You own an Android. You know that the app also runs on Androids and Playbooks. Should you be required to use the company-issued iPad for data visualizations? Should the credit union also offer the Android and Playbook app? Debate these issues from your personal perspective and the credit union's perspective.

11.1 Data Visualization and Data Discovery

The need to react quickly to changing business climates is forcing managers to make faster business decisions. Answering complex or impromptu questions from company data is critical, but often cost-prohibitive, time consuming, and difficult.

Data visualization—using visual shorthand to present complex data quickly and clearly—makes these tasks easier. **Data visualization** is a broad term referring both to the visual representation of data and to the study of the presentation of data in a visual way. **Data discovery** refers to the process of discovering relationships using data analytics tools, such as statistical software, statistical graphing, and mapping software. Data visualization and discovery have considerable overlap, and their usage is increasing because of the availability of self-service software and mobile apps. For example, *SAS Visual Data Discovery* software (*sas.com/*) provides a point-and-click interface to SAS's analytic capabilities and interactive data visualization.

DATA VISUALIZATION AND TABLETS: DISRUPTIVE TECHNOLOGIES

The ways managers access, explore, and analyze business data are being disrupted by data visualization apps that exploit the high-speed processors, mobile broadband connectivity, and multitouch gesture controls of tablet computers. Enterprise apps for Androids, Apple iPads, and BlackBerry Playbooks are replacing static business reports with real-time data, analytics, and interactive reporting tools. As you read in the opening case, data visualization apps designed for tablet operating systems (OSs) are changing the way people handle and manipulate data. For example, an app can convert an 80-column-by-800-row spreadsheet into an interactive pie graph, chart, and summary table (see Figure 11.4) that the user can tap, swipe, or zoom.

Figure 11.4 Tablets started as consumer media devices, but the combination of tablets and enterprise mobile apps is disrupting how performance management is done.

© Rivi Wickramarachchi/Alamy Limited

DATA DISCOVERY: SELF-SERVICE AND NEXT-GEN ANALYTICS

Quick Demo
Interactive Data Discovery Tool demo *http://www. tableausoftware.com/data- discovery-tool.*

Prior to 2011, data discovery software was viewed as a supplement to traditional BI platforms. But now it is increasingly being used as a viable standalone substitute for these platforms. Today's data discovery technologies provide greater data exploration and ease-of-use to help users find answers to "why" and "what if" questions through self-service analytic apps. Companies are increasingly investing in the latest apps that equip their end users to do their own analytics.

According to the *2011 Gartner Magic Quadrant report*, data discovery software vendors are competing head on with BI mega-vendors Oracle and SAP BusinessObjects. For example, Tableau software (*tableausoftware.com/*) is being deployed at Allstate Insurance Company. Jeff Strauss, the BI architect at Allstate, explained that Allstate is investing in Tableau's data discovery tools so that users throughout the organization could do their own analysis rather than rely on the IT department.

Data Discovery Offers Speed and Flexibility. Data discovery is expected to take on a greater role in corporate decision making. Companies are investing in the latest data discovery solutions largely because of the speed and flexibility that they provide. They allow users and IT experts to unify data from disparate information sources quickly and to explore the data with easy-to-use interactive visualizations and search interfaces. Drill-down paths are not pre-defined, which gives users more ways to view increasingly detailed levels of data.

A powerful feature of several data discovery systems is their ability to integrate with data contained in diverse corporate data stores (Joseph, 2011). When integrating data, the system can automatically extract and organize terms in unstructured content (e-mails, texts, and PDFs) and create tag clouds. These tag clouds give users a quick way to size up a situation and make valuable discoveries.

IT at Work 11.1

eBay Moves to Self-Service Data Discovery

Online retailers are bursting with data. From items that customers add to their online carts to inventory in warehouses, there's virtually no limit to data available for analysis. Since they cannot observe their customers, online retailers depend on logs recording detailed web site activity of visitors, including what links were clicked and how long a visitor remained on a webpage.

With more than 97 million active users globally, eBay is the world's largest online marketplace where just about anything can be bought or sold—and an immense volume of data. eBay collects more than 5 terabytes (TB) of data every day, and the insight they need to run the business is in that data.

At eBay, the trend is toward making sure everyone in the organization can do their own data discovery. David Stone, Senior

Manager Analytics Platform at eBay, described the importance of offering data analytics tools to members of the eBay team. Stone explained:

> When limited to Excel and its million-row limit, it caused us to look at the top three categories instead of the top 40,000 categories and there's so much less data. At eBay that's important because there is more action out in the long tail accumulated than there is in the top three.

Using data discovery software, eBay can dig deep into items in their top 40,000 categories because they no longer face row limits. Employees can now interact and visualize data, and can do data discovery on their own to better manage performance.

Questions

1. In what way is data discovery more critical to online retailers than to retailers with physical stores?
2. How did Excel limit eBay's data analysis?
3. Discuss the impacts of self-service data discovery on eBay.
4. Research the following: How large is a terabyte (TB)?

VISUAL SHORTHAND CAN BE EXTREMELY MEANINGFUL

Rows and rows of data on their own are boring and take a lot of time and effort to understand. Data visualization presents data in engaging ways and helps communicate complex ideas quicker. It also improves data analysis and presents them in a way that allows viewers to discover patterns that might otherwise be hard to uncover. What is considered one of the best statistical graphics ever drawn is the map created in 1869 by Charles J. Minard, shown in Figure 11.5. He portrays the losses suffered by Napoleon's army in the Russian campaign of 1812 using the width of the bands to represents the size of the army at each position. The path of Napoleon's retreat from Moscow is depicted by the dark lower band, along with time and temperature.

Minard also applied visualization to commerce, as shown in Figure 11.6, showing exports of French wines in 1864 with line widths representing the amounts shipped along the distribution paths. Because of the effort and talent that went into creating these visuals, both maps make it easy for the viewer to grasp what occurred. Today's tools practically eliminated the needed effort and talent.

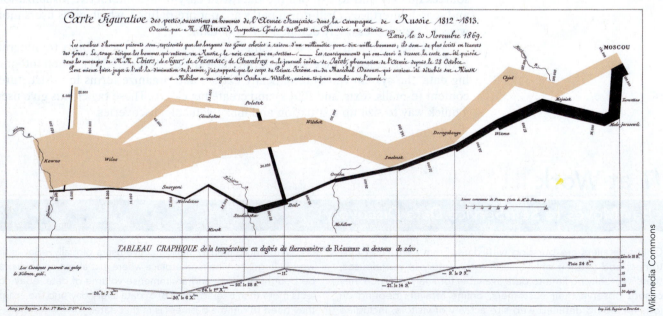

Figure 11.5 Visualization prepared by Charles J. Minard with lines showing losses in men, their movements, and cold temperatures during Napoleon's 1812 Russian campaign.

Wikimedia Commons

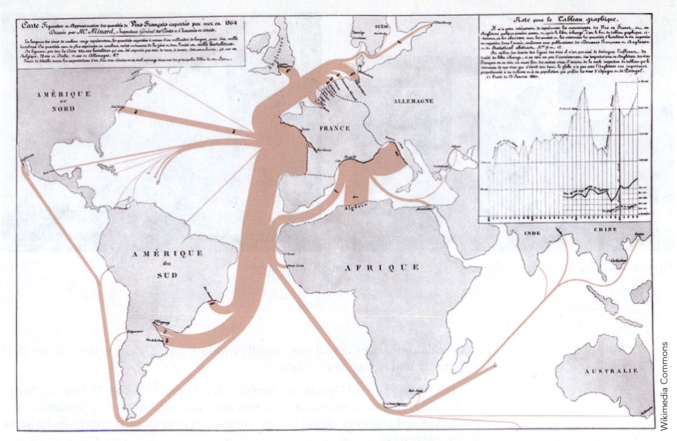

Wikimedia Commons

Figure 11.6 Visualization of the distribution of French wines.

REAL-WORLD EXAMPLES OF DATA VISUALIZATION FOR PERFORMANCE MANAGEMENT

Collecting data is relatively easy. Making sense of that data is not. Here are examples of how companies and or entire industries are using data visualization and interactivity to improve decision speed and performance.

Quick Detection and Decisions in Capital (Stock) Markets. Traders often follow between 100 and 150 stocks, need to quickly understand market trends, and be able to instantly drill down to the micro (detailed) level. Wall Street firms rely on their ability to process and capitalize on market anomalies in real time. Detecting anomalies and making trading decisions requires the analysis of massive amounts of live and historical data. Because of the demanding pace of their decisions, capital markets professionals use visualization for risk analysis, pre-trade and post-trade checks, compliance monitoring, fraud detection, client profitability analysis, research and sales, and portfolio performance (Rodier, 2011).

Traders, wealth managers, risk analysts, and regulators are also using 3D visualization tools to see patterns in disparate sources of worldwide market data, as shown in Figure 11.7. Two examples of 3D visualization tools designed and optimized to help financial market professionals interact with massive datasets are:

1. AlphaVision (*aqumin.com*) apps integrate huge data streams from ThomsonReuters, Bloomberg, the New York Stock Exchange (NYSE), and the Nasdaq to create interactive 3D displays used by traders and managers to interpret financial data faster with greater accuracy.

2. Panopticon (*panopticon.com*) visualization software presents traders with comprehensive views and maps of their portfolios with drill-down capabilities. For instance, Omaha Foreign Exchange (OFX) uses Panopticon's heat maps and other visualizations in its proprietary trading systems to improve traders' ability to

© Cultura Creative/Alamy Limited

© Cultura Creative/Alamy Limited

Figure 11.7 Stock traders' performance depends on visualization technologies.

analyze data and risks in real time, usually within seconds, which is much faster than with traditional reporting methods.

The Chicago Board Options Exchange (CBOE), Gain Capital, JP Morgan, hedge funds, and other asset management firms not only need data visualization—their executives and investors expect the quality and excitement of visuals to make sense of dry financial data.

Prompt Disaster Response by the Insurance Industry. The effectiveness of an insurer's response to a devastating hurricane or other catastrophic event depends on its ability to combine large amounts of data to fully understand the impact. Leading insurers are using web-based data visualization and analysis technologies to better manage their responses to major disasters. In the days and weeks afte a disaster, insurers face analysis and reporting bottlenecks. Analysts capable of creating maps and reports work frantically to respond to requests for information. Because new data continue being generated even after the event, the data have a short life span, and reports need to be regenerated and redistributed.

For example, when an earthquake occurs, workers throughout an insurance company access a web-based data app to visualize and analyze the impact. Users quickly determine which properties were subject to specific shake intensities and can visually build analyses on their own, rather than waiting for a report. The interactive nature and rich visual user experience provide a deeper understanding of data than static reports.

Tech Note 11.2

Data-Driven Documents (D3) Enable Interactive Visualizations in the Browser—Replacing Flash

Interactive data visualizations are now being run natively in web browsers using **D3**—data driven documents. D3 (*http://d3js.org/*) is used by web developers to shape the appearance and structure of web-based documents and to add animation or interaction. D3 is not tied to a proprietary framework. D3 uses open web standards and does not require third-party plugins. **D3.js** is a JavaScript library for manipulating documents that is replacing Flash for interactivity.

TRENDS IN DATA VISUALIZATION

Trends in data visualization indicate more widespread use. Here are three trends:

1. As viz software tools get easier, everyone will be able to design or develop visualizations. Barriers to developing visualizations and interactivity are disappearing. Non-designers and non-programmers will use Google Docs, IBM's ManyEyes, Tableau Public, and many other charting and viz tools.

2. As the need to measure, assess, and report results increase, data viz will become more important in business, health care, society, and government. The trend toward data-driven decisions is driving the trend toward ways to extract the relevant information from huge data sets.

3. Data art will lead to better aesthetics in functional visualizations. Here is a strong connection between art and data visualization. As visualization becomes a larger part of media, reporting, social media, and culture as a whole, this will lead more refined or aesthetic functional visualizations. To compete, data viz vendors will offer features that differentiate their products.

PRINCIPLES OF SUCCESS DATA VIZ DESIGN

Successful data visualizations have three characteristics:

1. Accuracy. Present data in the most appropriate way using proper scales, graph types, and designs.

2. Aesthetically pleasing. Provide an enjoyable user experience.

3. Flexible. Accommodate changes in visual style.

Visualization expert Edward R. Tufte stated: "Excellence in statistical graphics consists of complex ideas communicated with clarity, precision and efficiency" (Henschen, 2011a) The goal is simplicity. Therefore, 3D pie charts and graphics distort the image should not be used because they can make the information harder to read or understand quickly. If a picture is worth 1,000 words, then clear data visualizations are worth more than a stack of spreadsheets or reams of reports.

Questions

1. Define data visualization, and explain its business value.
2. Define data discovery, and explain its business value.
3. Why are data visualization and discovery usage increasing?
4. How are data visualization and tablets disruptive technologies?
5. Explain the ways in which data discovery is changing.
6. Give two examples of data visualization for performance management.
7. What are two trends in data visualization?

11.2 Enterprise Data Mashups

Technically, a mashup is a technique for building applications that combine data from multiple sources to create an integrated experience. In Chapter 8, you read about web mashups. As techniques for creating mashups became easier, companies started using them to build enterprise mashups that supported their business models. Tech-savvy managers realize that they can use mashup apps with their existing data and external services to provide new and interesting views on the data.

In this section, you read about enterprise data mashups. Figure 11.8 shows the general architecture of an enterprise mashup application that integrates data from operational data stores, business systems, external data (economic data, suppliers; information, competitors' activities) and real-time news feeds to generate an enterprise mashup.

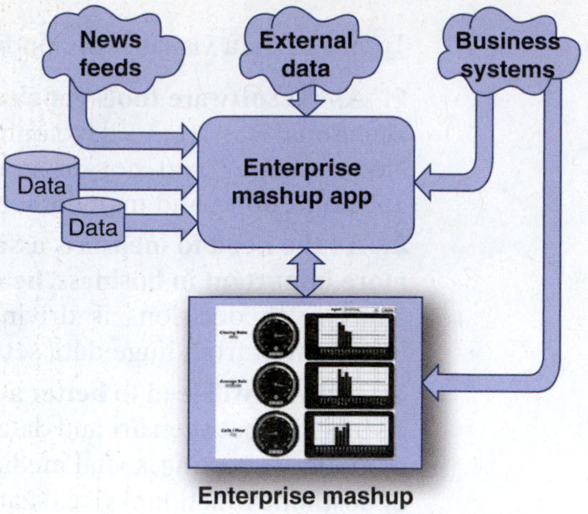

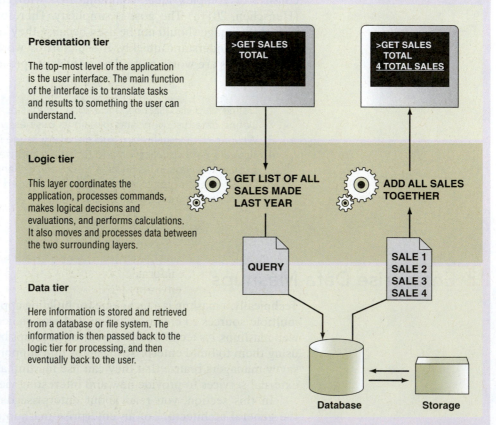

Figure 11.8 Architecture of an enterprise mashup application.

Tech Note 11.3

Mashup apps—The Software That Creates and Delivers the Mashup Experience

Mashup apps themselves are as a combination of service performed by the logic tier and relatively simple business logic (Clarkin and Holmes, 2007). **Business logic** (*logic tier*) manages the data exchange between a database (*data tier*) and the user interface (*presentation tier*), as shown in Figure 11.9. The presentation tier is where the end user interacts with the applications. If this tier is not well thought out and designed for the users' needs—no matter how stable, scalable, and reliable the underlying tiers, it does not enhance productivity of the end user.

Presentation tier

The top-most level of the application is the user interface. The main function of the interface is to translate tasks and results to something the user can understand.

Logic tier

This layer coordinates the application, processes commands, makes logical decisions and evaluations, and performs calculations. It also moves and processes data between the two surrounding layers.

Data tier

Here information is stored and retrieved from a database or file system. The information is then passed back to the logic tier for processing, and then eventually back to the user.

Figure 11.9 Diagram showing a 3-tier application. Presentation tier is the user-interface. Logic tier is the middle tier that increases flexibility by separating the user interface from the data storage locations in the data tier.

Source: http://en.wikipedia.org/wiki/File:Overview_of_a_three-thier_application_vectorVersion.svg.

ENTERPRISE DATA MASHUPS

Mashups source all of their content from existing systems and data sources; they have no native data store. **Enterprise data mashups** are combinations of data from various business systems and external sources, often in real time, and without relying on a middle step of ETL (extract, transform, and load) from a data warehouse. While combining disparate data sources is common for a data mashup, even if there is only a single data source, a mashup can be made by combining data in a way that is not anticipated. End-users and analysts who rely on dashboards and drill-down capabilities benefit from greater access to data, but the mashups remain behind the scenes and invisible. Interactive dashboards and drillable reports can be rapidly built based on mashed up data. Heat maps and tree maps can be created as data visualizations in mashups.

Performance Support Provided by Mashup Apps. The most popular types of mashup apps are those that support self-service, collaboration and sharing, dashboards, and analytics. Table 11.1 lists the most valuable functions and uses of enterprise mashup apps.

For organizations, mashup apps decrease IT implementation costs over traditional, custom software development (discussed in Chapter 12) and significantly simplify business workflows—both increase the ROI (return on investment) of mashup implementations.

WHY BUSINESS USERS NEED DATA MASHUP TECHNOLOGY

Business users have a hard enough time identifying their current data needs. It is not realistic to expect them also to consider all the new sources of data that might be made available to them and the analyses they might do if they had access to that data. With traditional BI and data warehousing systems, data sources have to be identified and some understanding of data requirements and data models is needed.

Realizing that there will always be data needs that cannot be anticipated, the question is whether IT should be in the middle of supporting those requests. Providing business users with self-service enables them to meet their needs more quickly. They also have the opportunity to explore and experiment.

Enterprise mashups improve operational efficiency, optimize the sales pipeline, enhance customer satisfaction, and drive profitability. Within government, mashups have positively impacted strategic areas such as citizen engagement and satisfaction, financial transparency, project oversight, regulatory compliance and legislated reporting. A summary of enterprise mashup benefits are listed in Table 11.2.

ENTERPRISE MASHUP TECHNOLOGY

In a May 2008 report *The Mashup Opportunity*, Forrester Research wrote: "Mashups—custom applications that combine multiple, disparate data sources into something new and unique—hit the web in a big way starting in 2005 . . . and that the enterprise mashup market will reach nearly $700 million by 2013" (Forrester, 2008). Mashup technology leverages organizations' investments in both BI tools and interactive Web 2.0 technologies. A key enabler for achieving self-service BI agility is enterprise mashup technology.

BI systems are very good at filtering and aggregating huge data volumes into information. With mashup technology, for example, users can filter down the data based on their needs so that only the information needed is provided by the available data services.

In an enterprise environment, mashups can be used to solve a wide variety of business problems and day-to-day situations. Examples of these types of mashups are:

TABLE 11.1	Functions and Uses of Enterprise Mashup Apps

Data mashup apps are used in organizations:
- For real-time awareness and data freshness
- To feed data to cross-functional dashboards
- For competitive analysis
- To monitor compliance and manage risk
- For disaster monitoring and disaster response
- To generate external vendor reports

TABLE 11.2 | Enterprise Mashups Benefits

Summary of benefits of mashup technology to an enterprise:

- Dramatically reduces time and effort needed to combine disparate data sources.
- Users can define their own data mashups by combining fields from different data sources that were not previously modeled.
- Users can import external data sources, e.g., spreadsheets and competitor data, to create new dashboards.
- Enables the building of complex queries by non-experts with a drag-and-drop query-building tool.
- Enables *agile BI* because new data sources can be added to a BI system quickly via direct links to operational data sources, bypassing the need to load them to a data warehouse.
- Provides a mechanism to easily customize and share knowledge throughout the company.

Tech Note 11.4

Mashup Self-Service

Many BI systems are designed by the IT department and based on inflexible data sources. The result is a bottleneck of end-user change requests as business needs and data sources change. The solution is self-service mashup capabilities.

Using data mashup apps, nontechnical users can easily and quickly access, integrate, and display BI data from a variety of operational data sources, including those that are not integrated into the existing data warehouse, without having to understand the intricacies of the underlying data infrastructures, or schemas.

1. A customer data mashup that provides a quick view of customer data for a sales person in preparation for a customer site visit. Data can be pulled from both departmental and web sources. This can include information such as contact information, links to related web sites, recent customer orders, lists of critical situations, and more.

2. A logistics mashup that displays inventory for a group of department stores based on some sort of criteria. For example, you can mash current storm information onto a map of store locations, and then wire the map to inventory data to show which stores located in the path of storms are low on generators.

3. A human resources mashup that provides a quick glance at employee data such as profiles, salary, ratings, benefits status, and activities. Can filter data to show only certain pieces of information, for example which employees are paid a certain salary.

Enterprise Mashup Vendors. Several vendors offer mashup capabilities, but not all of them offer enterprise-grade mashup software. Three vendors offering enterprise mashups are IBM (*ibm.com/software/info/mashup-center/*) with Lotus Mashup tools; Serena Software (*serena.com*) with Business Mashups; and JackBe with Presto (*jackbe.com*). These mashup technologies provide visually-rich and secure enterprise apps created from live data. They provide the flexibility to combine data from any enterprise app and the cloud regardless of its location. Users can build apps and dashboards that can be displayed on the web and mobile devices.

Questions

1. Sketch or describe the architecture of an enterprise mashup application.
2. What is an enterprise data mashup?
3. Identify three types of visualizations that can be created in mashups.
4. What are the functions and uses of enterprise mashups?
5. How can enterprise mashups be used to monitor and manage performance?
6. Explain why business workers may need data mashup technology.
7. What are three benefits of mashup technology to the organization?

11.3 Business Dashboards

How do managers get immediate access to clear, understandable metrics to assess and manage business performance in real time? One answer is with business dashboards that end-users can design and build in order to make smart decisions quickly. In this section, the focus is on business dashboards that provide real-time data and alerts—and not simply graphical data displays.

BUSINESS DASHBOARDS

Business dashboards give visual snapshots of an organization's critical operational data or key performance indicators (KPIs) to spot problems, trends, outliers, opportunities, and patterns. Dashboards are performance management tools that apply KPIs, targets, and alerts to measure and monitor business processes and outcomes. Two components of dashboards are:

1. Design. The data visualization techniques, such as informative graphics (infographics) with descriptive captions.

2. Performance metrics. The KPIs and other real-time content displayed on the dashboard. All dashboard data should reflect the current value of each metric.

By looking at the dashboard in Figure 11.10, you notice how color-coded displays can quickly inform the user of the status of KPIs.

Dashboards Are for Real-Time Values of KPIs. Dashboards are often mistakenly thought of as reports consisting of various gauges, charts, and dials. But the purpose of business dashboards is much more specific and directed. The purpose of dashboards is to give users a clear view of the *current* state of KPIs, real-time alerts, and other metrics about operations. Dashboard design is a critical factor because business users need to be able to understand the significance of the dashboard

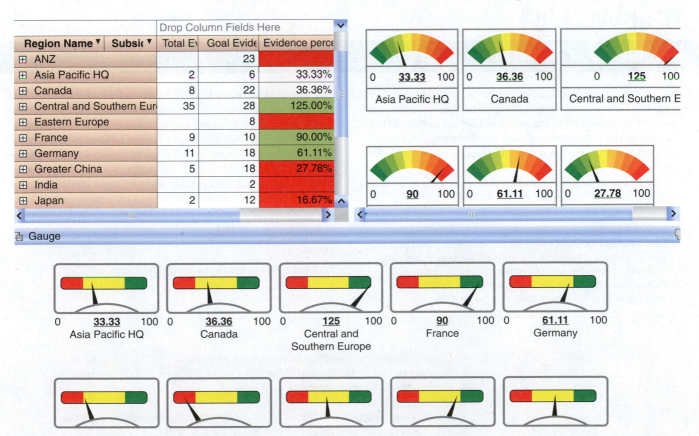

Figure 11.10 Business dashboards display real-time information about KPIs and that can be understood at a glance.

© Luca DiCecco/Alamy Limited

Figure 11.11 Surgeons and medical staff monitor readouts of vital signs to keep informed and be alerted to the need for corrective action.

information at a glance and have the capability to drill down to one or more levels of detail. Having real-time, or near-real time, data is essential to keep users aware of any meaningful changes in the metrics as they occur and to provide information for making decisions in real time. Users can take corrective actions promptly. The best dashboards are optimized for real-time alerts and feedback comparable to what surgeons and surgical staff receive during a procedure, as shown in Figure 11.11.

The latest data visualization platforms make it easier for users to design and build customized business dashboards with high-quality visualizations for mobile screens, advanced analytics, capabilities, and multilanguage support. *IT at Work 11.2* describes dashboards in action Hartford Hospital.

IT at Work 11.2

Dashboards in Action at Hartford Hospital

Health care providers at Hartford Hospital, a 700-bed teaching hospital in Connecticut, were challenged by the shortage of real-time data in useable form, according to Michael Lindbergh M.D., chairman of the department of medicine (Baldwin, 2011). In 2010, Hartford Hospital implemented dashboard technology from CareFx (*CareFx.com*).

Dr. Lindberg uses the dashboard to track data in three key areas that impact the hospital's performance:

1. **Patient data.** Data on patients' length-of-stay and percentage of early morning discharges.
2. **Bed availability.** Data on types of beds open, and percentage of beds not available for patients such as those being cleaned, or beds in a room with a patient in isolation.
3. **Remission rate.** Data about patients who return to the hospital within 30 days of their discharge date.

The dashboard data helps Dr. Lindberg fulfill Joint Commission requirements for ongoing physician evaluations. He can identify trends and compare current to past performance. According to Dr. Lindberg, "We need to have a handle on what physicians are doing. Having a database to drill down to the individual physician goes a long way toward satisfying those requirements." Purely financial data is not yet available on the CareFx dashboard, but Lindberg plans to add indicators such as cost per hospitalization broken down by physician and department to identify doctors who are outliers for test ordering.

Questions

1. What KPIs are displayed on Dr. Lindberg's dashboard?
2. What KPIs will be added to the dashboard?

Questions

1. Describe business dashboards and their functions.
2. How do business dashboards differ from other types of visual reports?
3. Explain the two components of dashboards.
4. Discuss the purpose of dashboards.
5. What design feature enables users to understand dashboards at a glance?
6. What is an important feature of optimized dashboards?

11.4 Mobile Dashboards and Intelligence

Managers and other business users now can run their organization from wherever they are on their device of choice using mobile intelligence apps and dynamic dashboards. For over two decades, BI vendors have tried to sell the concept of *BI for the masses*, but until around 2012, their efforts had limited success. Before then, BI tools were mostly used only by business analysts and other skilled power users.

MOBILE INTELLIGENCE: FROM EXECUTIVES TO STAFF

Tablets, in particular the iPad, are driving enterprise-wide mobile intelligence, according to Joao Tapadinhas, an analyst at Gartner, an IT market research company. Based on his experience, when chief executives see a mobile intelligence dashboard on the iPad for the first time, they want it—and they want their executive team to have the capability, too. When those users see mobile intelligence's potential for line-of-business (LOB) managers and team leaders, the rollout expands—possibly to field engineers, sales executives, and retail staff interacting with shoppers.

In a Gartner survey of over 1,300 companies that use BI tools, only 8 per cent had mobile intelligence in 2011, but 33 percent planned to implement it in 2012, and another 13 per cent planned to test it out by running pilot projects. Businesses already using **mobile dashboards** and intelligence are fashion retailer Guess, insurance company MetLife, and the supermarket chain Whole Foods Market.

Sabre serves travelers, travel agents, corporations and travel suppliers through its four companies: Travelocity, Sabre Travel Network, Sabre Airline Solutions, and Sabre Hospitality Solutions. Sabre is implementing a mobile app that will provide access to its *Sabre Executive Dashboard* via iPhones and BlackBerry phones. The mobile dashboard will provide seamless integration to functional dashboards and enhanced drill down into detailed reporting modules.

Limitations and Challenges, at the Present. Here are current limitation and challenges related to mobile intelligence.

Analytics not available. Most mobile intelligence apps let users view, but not manipulate data. The inability to do analytics will eventually be overcome. Most dashboards allow the user to drill down, but interactive capabilities are less common.

Mobile intelligence linked to BI platform. Typically, mobile intelligence is sold as an add-on module to a specific BI platform. Companies that have more than one BI platform can buy and implement a module for each platform, which can be expensive and complex. A recent alternative is Roambi's mobile data visualization tools, as you read in the Opening Case 1. These tools connect to various BI platforms from SAS, Microsoft, IBM, SAP and Sybase, to display data on iPhones and iPads.

BYOD (bring your own device) policies and practices. Another challenge for organizations is how to integrate mobile intelligence with BYOD policies for employees. The iPad is the device of choice for mobile intelligence, but not everyone uses an iPad. Trying to support iPhones, Android handsets and BlackBerrys, and iPads increases complexity and costs.

Screen size. Naturally, screen size limits what can be displayed, such as being able to show only one data element in a chart. But users' touch-interface speed and agility compensate for that limitation.

Mobile Dashboards. Despite these limitations, BI has gone mobile—and mobile dashboard apps have made it faster and easier to deploy mobile intelligence. Mobile dashboards make it possible to connect to data sources and present metrics from handheld devices.

People won't stop needing to drill down into data, and they won't want to be limited to desktops, or even laptops. Mobile dashboard-supplied intelligence enables

TABLE 11.3	Mobile Dashboard/Intelligence Vendors and Descriptions of Their Products	
Vendor	**Product name**	**Description**
SAS *sas.com*	SAS mobile	A smartphone-based interactive dashboard app.
		Combines the power of SAS with the portability of BlackBerry, Apple iPhone, and Windows-based mobile devices. Users of SAS Mobile applications navigate through displays with interactive graphs, tables, and charts. Alert features notify them of changes in key measures.
SoftwareFX *softwarefx.com*	PowerGadgets Mobile	For authoring and deploying real-time dashboards on mobile devices, including smartphones and tablets.
Shoptech Software Corp. *shoptech.com*	Mobile Dashboard	An ERP mobile app designed specifically for iPads, Tablets, and Smart phones.
		The first mobile app designed specifically for the job shop, make-to-order manufacturer.
WeDo Technologies *wedotechnologies. com/*	RAID Mobile Dashboard	The app provides users with interactive views of current business data straight to their iPhone.
		The module displays revenue and margin assurance, customer experience and operational efficiency information in interactive and analytical dashboards that can be automatically and securely delivered to any iPhone.
BNY Mellon* *Bnymellon.com* *BNY Mellon is an investment management and investment services company.	Performance & Risk Analytics (P&RA) Mobile Dashboard	BNY Mellon's clients can view key portfolio and financial benchmark information on their iPad, including Daily Returns, Historical Returns, Top 10 Positions, Top 5 Overweight Positions, and Top 5 Underweight Positions.
		Results can be viewed as line or bar charts, or in tabular data format. Other features include filters to review investment returns by major asset class, as well as gross or net of fees.
Microstrategy *microstrategy.com*	Mobile Intelligence Platform	Helps companies and organizations build, deploy, and maintain mobile apps across a range of solutions by embedding intelligence, transactions, and multimedia into apps.
Actuate Corp. *actuate.com*	BIRT Mobile Business intelligence for Android devices	Developers can easily deploy custom BI, dashboards, analytics, reports, and interactive content natively on Android mobile devices.
		The application is preloaded with demonstration dashboards, allowing end users to explore and personalize business data on their Android device.

workers to consult their devices as they walk into meetings—and anywhere else. Many apps are too complex for mobile use, but that is no longer a problem for dashboards. Vendors have transported the power of creating dashboards to mobile world devices. Table 11.3 lists mobile dashboard and intelligence vendors and their products.

Executive Acceptance at Alcoa. Because mobile dashboards are a big hit with executives, this technology is expected to progress quickly. For instance, Nancy Wolk, the CIO of Alcoa, a $24.6 billion aluminum manufacturer, explained that Alcoa management decides which projects to invest in based on a simple test to sort ideas. Wolk says: "We think of everything we do in terms of—does it help us grow or help us generate cash?" (Nash, 2012). Management determined that the upcoming project to provide the sales staff with mobile dashboards about customers will help Alcoa grow so the project has the green light. Another project proposal to pilot collaboration tools for problem solving and innovation might boost productivity, but is considered a step or two removed from company growth so it goes into the queue for later implementation.

Questions

1. What is mobile intelligence?
2. What is contributing to enterprise-wide mobile intelligence?
3. Explain how mobile intelligence spreads top-down from executives to LOB managers and staff.
4. Identify and explain the limitations of mobile intelligence.
5. Why did Alcoa's senior management decide to implement mobile dashboards?

Key Terms

business dashboard *334*	data visualization *338*	mobile BI app *334*
business logic *334*	data visualization app *334*	mobile dashboard *349*
D3 *342*	enterprise data mashup *345*	user experience *336*
D3.js *342*	enterprise mashup app *334*	visualization technologies *334*
data discovery *338*	mashup self-service *346*	

Chapter 11 LINK LIBRARY

You find clickable Link Libraries for each chapter on the Companion website.

InetSoft   *http://www.inetsoft.com/*

InetSoft flash demo   *http://www.inetsoft.com/evaluate/demo/flashdemo.jsp*

The Data Warehousing Institute (TDWI)   *http://tdwi.org/*

IBM Cognos 8 BI   *http://www-01.ibm.com/software/data/cognos/*

Oracle   *http://Oracle.com*

SAS BI   *http://sas.com/technologies/bi/*

SAP AG   *http://Sap.com*

Tableau Software   *http://tableausoftware.com/*
   http://www.tableausoftware.com/public/
   http://www.tableausoftware.com/public/gallery

QlikTech   *http://qlikview.com*

iDashboards   *http://idashboards.com*

National park forecast data mashup example   *http://www-10.lotus.com/ldd/mashupswiki.nsf/dx/National_park_forecast_data_mashup_example_imc3*

Periscopic   *http://periscopic.com/hello/*

SAS Visual Data Discovery, Interactive data visualization for analytics   *http://www.sas.com/technologies/analytics/statistics/datadiscovery/*

MicroStrategy Wisdom   *http://www.microstrategy.com/Social-Intelligence/Enterprise/Wisdom/*

Evaluate and Expand Your Learning

IT and Data Management Decisions (see Link Library for links in this section)

1. How people use, access, and discover data in business is being actively disrupted by tablets, which had been designed for consumers. Users have higher expectations for data displays and capabilities. Boring, static graphs, and pie charts are unacceptable. Discuss how performance management—the monitoring of KPIs, for example—may be improved by providing managers with data visualizations. Now consider the opposite. In your opinion, would lack of data visualization hurt the ability to manage performance?

2. Periscopic (*http://periscopic.com/hello/*) is a socially conscious data visualization firm that specializes in using IT to help organizations promote public awareness and action. Their philosophy and tagline is "do good with data." Visit *http://periscopic.com/hello/* and explore their recent work. Then discuss how data is used to do good. How effective is their approach to public awareness and social justice?

3. Visit SAS Visual Data Discovery, Interactive data visualization for analytics at *http://www.sas.com/technologies/analytics/statistics/datadiscovery/*. View the demo. In your opinion, what are the two most important benefits of this data discovery tool? Would you recommend this tool? Explain your answer.

Questions for Discussion & Review

1. Visit *http://www.tableausoftware.com/public/* and click Gallery (*http://www.tableausoftware.com/public/gallery*). Review the posts in the Gallery published by a major business news or sports publisher, such as the *Wall Street Journal*, the *Guardian*, or *CBS Sports*, or related to public policy issue (e.g., The State.) to find different types of data visualizations, interactive graphs, and interactive sites.
   a. Select three of the posts that use different types of data visualizations, interactive graphs, and interactive sites.
   b. Discuss how each of those three posts uses visualization or interactivity and the benefits of their uses.

2. Lots of data are available to retailers to make good decisions—loyalty programs, web analytics, and point-of-sale data. But there's a big gap between having data and being able to leverage them for real-time decision making. How can enterprise mashups close this gap?

3. Opinion Space is a tool for online discussion and brainstorming that uses data visualization to help gather meaningful ideas from a large number of participants. Opinion Space is a United States State Department initiative using the Internet to solicit opinions from people

through a web site. A joint project between the State Department and the University of California's Berkeley Center for New Media, Opinion Space was launched in March 2010 to gain public perspective on foreign policy issues. Visit *http://opinion.berkeley.edu*. Watch the three-minute screencast on how Opinion Space works. Read about the latest version of Opinion Space. Discuss the value of Opinion Space.

Online Activities

1. Visit *http://www.itdashboard.gov/data_feeds*. Use this tool to design your own snapshots of IT Dashboard data. Follow the steps to create, save, and publish your IT dashboard.

2. Visit *http://www.crazyegg.com/*. Explain what Heatmap reports look like.

3. Tableau Software offers a full functioning free trial of Tableau Desktop at *tableausoftware.com/products/trial*. Download the free trial, and use the tool. Discuss how you used the tool. Explain the benefits. Would you recommend its use? Explain.

4. Visit *microstrategy.com/dashboards/*. Explain how enterprise dashboards can lead to better business insights. What are the limitations dashboards?

5. Visit *http://www-10.lotus.com/ldd/mashupswiki.nsf/dx/National_park_forecast_data_mashup_example_imc3*. Follow the directions to complete the National park forecast data mashup example.

Collaborative Work

1. Dashboards that drive business decisions. Each person of the team is tasked with reviewing and reporting on various dashboards. Compile the results into a report for management.
   a. Visit the **Analysis Factory** at *http://www.analysisfactory.com/*.
   b. Click **Gallery** and then select **Custom Solutions.** The URL will be *http://www.analysisfactory.com/gallery/custom-solutions*
   c. Each person tries one or more demos for Performance Trends, Fusion Charts, Manufacturing Performance, College Cost Calculator, and Sales Map Dashboard.
   d. Create a table listing all of the customer solutions for which your team tried the demo in the first column. In the second column, list the departments or functions each customer solution supports. In the third column, list that types of visualizations used in each solution.
   e. In the team report, discuss how dashboards can impact the quality of business decisions.

CASE 2 VISUALIZATION CASE

Are You Ready for Some Football?

Nothing inspires passionate comments among sports fans like pre-season predictions. Brett McMurphy's data visualization looks at how teams ranked in different polls.

1. Visit Preseason Polls & Returning Starters at *http://www.tableausoftware.com/public/gallery/are-you-ready-some-football*.
   a. Interact with the Preseason Polls & Returning Starters visualization.
   b. Select various filters and observe the changes.
   c. Download the workbook by clicking the Download button at the lower-right corner of the display.

2. View and interact with two other sports-related visualizations, such as CBS Sports Defensive Matchup Tracker, Fantasy Closers, and Premier League Points Leaders. Download each.
3. Click the *Business and Real Estate Gallery*. View and interact with two data visualizations in the gallery. Download each.
4. Which visualization was the easiest to understand at a glance? Explain,
5. Which visualization was the most difficult or complicated to understand easily? Explain.
6. What are the benefits and potential drawbacks of interactive visualizations?

CASE 3 VIDEO CASE

Mashup-Driven Dashboards and Reporting

1. InetSoft offers self-service mashups and mashup driven dashboards and reporting.

To do:

a. Visit the InetSoft web site at *http://www.inetsoft.com/*, and click the *View Demo* button. The direct link to the demo is *http://www.inetsoft.com/evaluate/demo/flashdemo.jsp*.
b. View the flash demonstration (6 minutes 25 seconds) of mashup driven dashboards and reporting.

Questions

1. What does the dashboard empower decision makers?
2. Describe the features of the mashup.
3. Does the tool make it easy for users to create, modify, and interact with their dashboards and reports?
4. What is your opinion of this tool?

Data Analysis & Decision Making

Know Your Facebook Fans with Mobile Intelligence

MicroStrategy *Wisdom Professional* enables managers to gain insight from Facebook data and understand who their Facebook fans are and what they like. Wisdom Professional versions are available for the iPad and the Web

1. Visit *http://www.microstrategy.com* and from the **Products** menu, select **Social Intelligence.**
2. Click the icon for MicroStrategy Wisdom. The direct link is *http://www.microstrategy.com/Social-Intelligence/Enterprise/Wisdom/*
   a. Click the "Discover Business Uses" button; then download and read the 4-page report.
   b. View the three videos in the *MicroStrategy Wisdom Professional Demo Library.*
   c. Read *Who should use MicroStrategy Wisdom Professional?*

3. Select on industry sector, such as retail, banking, manufacturing, and so on.
   a. Based on what you learned about how Wisdom Professional, identify and describe the top five benefits of investing in Wisdom Professional for the iPad for the industry sector you selected. The top five benefits are based on your informed opinion and expertise.
   b. State whether each benefit is an operational or strategic benefit.
   c. Identify at least two drawbacks to adopting this type of mobile social intelligence.
   d. Format your analysis into a report for management.

Resources on the Book's Web Site

You'll find additional chapter materials and useful web links. In addition, self-quizzes that provide individualized feedback are available for each chapter.

References

Baldwin, G. "Dashboards in Action." *Health Data Management,* October 20, 2011.

Clarkin, L., & Holmes, J. "Enterprise Mashups." *Architecture Journal,* no. 13, October 2007. *architecturejournal.net.*

Crosman, P. "CSI Launches Data Visualization Tool for Bank Execs." *American Banker,* April 9, 2012.

Baldwin, G. "Dashboards in Action." *Health Data Management* 19, no. 10, October 2011.

Eckerson, W. "Architecting for Mobile BI." *BeyeNetwork,* April 21, 2011.

Gibbs, M. "IT Loses Control—and That's Okay." *CIO Magazine,* November 17, 2011.

Henschen, D. "Data Visualization for the Masses?" *InformationWeek,* March 26, 2012.

Henschen, D. "P&G Turns Analysis into Action." *InformationWeek,* September 19, 2011.

Henschen, D. "Top 15 Data Visualization Tips." *InformationWeek,* January 3, 2011a.

IBM Cognos BI 8. "Leading metal supplier and fabricator introduces efficiency, ease of use to financial planning with IBM Cognos 8 BI and TM1," May 26, 2010.

Joseph, J. "Data Discovery: Next Generation Analytics Brings a New IT Approach." *Dashboard Insight,* July 20, 2011.

Kendler, P. B. "Raising the Stakes." *Insurance & Technology,* May 1, 2011.

Kite, S. "The Whole Bank on an iPad." *American Banker,* April 28, 2012.

Lowe, S. "Quickly create mobile dashboards for your mobile device." *TechRepublic.com,* November 2, 2011.

Maps.google.com.

Markets Media. "Big Data in 3D," March 29, 2012. *marketsmedia.com/sectors/big-data-3-d/*

Nash, K. S. "Business: CIOs and their fellow executives have conflicting priorities on cost and competitors." *CIO* 25, no. 6, January 1, 2012.

Raice, S. & Ante, S. E. "Business Tasks Bring Out Serious Side of Apps." *The Wall Street Journal,* October 27, 2010.

Rodier, M. "Visualizing Success." *Wall Street & Technology*, November 1, 2011.

Savoie, A. "Selected aerospace and defense contracts for Nov. 23, 2011." *Aerospace Daily & Defense Report,* November 29, 2011.

Turban, E., Sharda, R., Delsen, D., and King, D. *Decision Support Systems and Intelligent Systems,* 9th ed. Upper Saddle River, NJ: Prentice Hall, 2011.

Twentyman, J. "iPad tips the balance in favour of giving more data to workers." *Financial Times,* February 27, 2012.

Young, G. O. "The Mashup Opportunity–A Social Computing Report." *Forrester Research.* May 6, 2008.

Chapter

12

IT Strategy, Sourcing, and Vendor Relationships

Learning Outcomes

❶ Describe how the IT strategy supports business strategy, the strategic planning process, and the role of IT steering committees.

❷ Explain the importance, potential impacts, functions, and challenges of IT governance.

❸ Explain the value of aligning the IT and business strategies, and how this alignment can be achieved.

❹ Describe IT operating plans, how sourcing strategies can improve performance, and the risks and challenges of sourcing and offshoring relationships. Identify major types of outsourcing, reasons for outsourcing, and the risks and benefits.

❺ Explain the IT vendor selection and management processes, and how to achieve successful relationships through the use of contracts and service level agreements.

What a company can do depends on what its information systems can do. This principle explains why planning a business strategy in isolation from IT strategic planning will have suboptimal outcomes. As you know, IT is a disruptive force. IT planning helps put the company in a position to positively disrupt how they operate, their business models, and even their industry. CIOs need an IT strategy as well as an operating plan for how the IT strategic plan will be achieved. Two examples of operating plans are in-house development with help from a consulting firm or vendor; and sourcing to a third-party in the same country or offshore. Cloud computing and SaaS are two sourcing options.

By aligning IT and business strategies, companies can build differentiating capabilities—the three or four things that a company does exceptionally well that set it apart from its competitors. This strategic fit is dynamic because keeping the IT and business strategies in alignment is an ongoing process. In the mid-2010s, the process takes into consideration opportunities provided by cloud delivery, software as a service (SaaS) applications, BYOD (bring your own device), consumerization, mobile intelligence, and social media. CIOs evaluate various ways of acquiring or providing new information technologies and services that can drive business growth.

The effectiveness of the IT function relies heavily on relationships with vendors and third-party suppliers and on IT governance. IT governance addresses this question: Are you doing what's right, appropriate, and needed by the business?

CASE 1 OPENING CASE

Consumer Banks Reinvent with New Business and IT Strategies

Customer-centric means that banks design their operations and services around client needs.

Transparency means no surprises—customers know and understand the terms and costs of banking services.

Service-oriented architecture (SOA) is a business-centric IT architecture that makes it faster and easier to develop new apps and ISs because they are built with existing building blocks, called **services.**

Since 2008, the financial crisis and changing marketplace have caused massive disruption in the financial services industry, and consumer banks in particular. Banks also face increasing greater risk and government regulation. Furthermore, as banking processes became more technology intensive, business and IT strategies became inseparable. Bank managers are well aware of the importance of developing an IT strategy that is driven by practical solutions to real problems.

Consumer Banking after the Financial Crisis

Based on a 2011 survey by the IBM Institute for Business Value, researchers conclude that banks need:

1. To move beyond existing organizational silos, infrastructure complexities, and other constraints—and toward an operation centered on customers.
2. To leverage information and analytic tools to better manage risk, pricing, channel performance, and returns.

Need to Reassess Business Strategy

Consumer banks need to reassess their business strategies because of the following pressures and challenges.

- Banks face limited growth opportunities and stronger regulatory constraints related to risk.
- Nonfinancial services organizations and social financing sites, such as PayPal, Mint, and Prosper, are eroding their customer base.
- Most banking products and services have lower operating profits.
- Fierce competition has decreased revenues.

To address these pressures and challenges, consumer banks are devising customer-centric business and IT strategies.

Customer-Centric Business + IT Strategies

A **customer-centric** business strategy gives customers convenience, control, recognition, and transparency. Transparency means "no surprises"—just clear communication of fee structures, terms, restrictions, and deadlines to customers. Six essential customer-centric technologies are:

1. **Mobility** to enable anytime/anywhere connectivity to clients, customers, and employees
2. **High-end analytics** for real-time customer insights
3. **Big data management** to process large volumes of unstructured data from social media and other sources
4. **Next-generation data processing** to manage data from disparate sources and for data driven business intelligence (BI)
5. **Cloud computing** for infrastructure, data, analytics, and applications
6. **Service-oriented architecture (SOA)** for faster development of new apps, which is made possible by the reusability of services or functions. A **service** is a fundamental building block for developing new systems or integrating existing ones. For additional information about SOA, view the flash demo shown in Video 12.1.

Video 12.1
SOA
http://www-01.ibm.com/ software/solutions/soa/flash/ Build03.swf.

SOA reduces business risk and exposure by helping banks comply with regulations, such as the Foreign Corrupt Practices Act (FCPA), Sarbanes-Oxley Act, and the USA Patriot Act.

To make the new business strategy work, consumer banks are investing in new or updated IT architecture, including refining their operating models, governance, and data and application management. Figure 12.1 shows how the IT build-out strategy enables the bank's business strategy.

Sources: Compiled from Chatterjee, Nair, & Tatke (2012), Giridhar, Notestein, & Wagle (2011), Booz.com (2012).

Discuss

1. Visit the PayPal, Mint, and Prosper web sites and identify the financial services that each of them provides to customers. Discuss why customers would use these services instead of a traditional consumer bank. Compare their customer-centric approach to that of consumer banks. What advantage do banks have over Mint and Prosper?

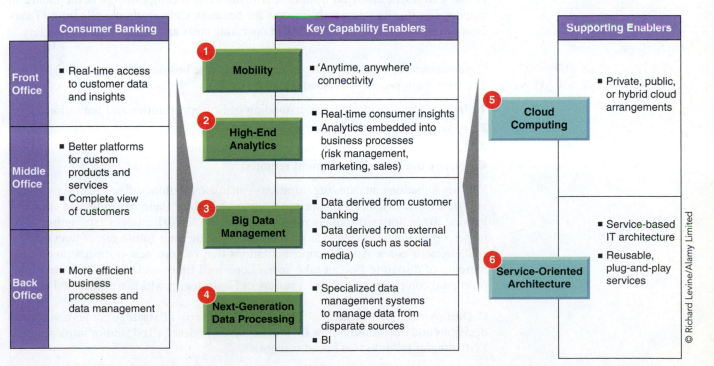

Figure 12.1 Consumer banks are implementing new business and IT strategies to counteract negative pressures and improve profitability. Adapted from Booz&Co, 2012.

2. Explain the pressures and challenges disrupting the consumer banking industry and driving them to reassess their business strategies.

3. Could consumer banks separate their customer-centric business strategy from their IT strategy? Explain.

4. Refer to Figure 12.1. What is the value-added of each of the six technologies to the bank's customer-centric strategy?

Decide

5. Refer to your answer to question 1. Research users' feedback about their experiences with these alternative financial services. Are they an insignificant or serious threat to consumer banks?

Debate

6. "Whatever ITs consumer banks invest in, nontraditional alternatives can also invest in them." Debate the extent to which this statement is accurate. Explain your assumptions and reasoning.

12.1 IT Strategy and the Strategic Planning Process

Can an effective business strategy exist today without IT? Could nonprofits or government agencies fulfill their missions without a technology strategy? Of course not. That's why IT strategy begins and ends with the business—and must be an integral part of the business strategy. Making IT investments on the basis of an immediate need or threat is sometimes necessary, but these reactive approaches won't maximize ROI—and can result in incompatible, redundant, expensive-to-maintain, or failed systems.

Two of the biggest risks and concerns of top management are (1) failing to align IT to real business needs and, as a result, (2) failing to deliver value to the business. Since IT has a dramatic effect on business performance and competitiveness, the failure to manage IT effectively seriously impacts the business. Conversely, payoffs from IT successes include substantial reductions in operating costs and improvements in agility.

IT STRATEGIES SUPPORT THE BUSINESS STRATEGY

Organizations develop IT strategies that support the business strategy and objectives. The four main points of **IT strategic plans** are to:

1. Improve management's understanding of IT opportunities and limitations
2. Assess current performance
3. Identify capacity and human resource requirements
4. Clarify the level of investment required

Various functions in the organization—such as manufacturing, R&D (research and development), and IT—are most successful when their strategies are forward-looking. To be forward-looking means that they do SWOT analysis (strengths, weaknesses, opportunities, threats) to prepare for or create their future rather than react to challenges or crises. And IT implementations that require new infrastructure or the merging of disparate ISs can take years. Long lead times and lack of expertise have prompted companies to explore a variety of IT strategies, which are discussed next.

IT Deployment Strategies: In-House and Sourcing. IT strategy guides investment decisions and decisions on how ISs will be developed, acquired, and/or implemented. IT strategies fall into two broad categories:

1. In-house development in which systems are developed or other IT work is done in-house, possibly with the help of consulting companies or vendors. Typically, ITs that provide competitive advantages, or that contain proprietary or confidential data, are developed and maintained by the organization's own in-house IT function.

2. Sourcing in which systems are developed or IT work is done by a third party or vendor. There are many versions of sourcing, which also had been called *outsourcing*. Work or development can be sourced to consulting companies or vendors that are within the same country, which is referred to as **onshore sourcing.** Or the work can be sourced off-shore to other countries. Sourcing that is done off-shore is also called **offshoring.** Other options are to lease or to purchase IT as services. Cloud computing and software as a service (SaaS) have expanded sourcing options significantly. Tech Note 12.1 discusses a sourcing challenge and solution.

Tech Note 12.1

Sourcing creates its own set of challenges. For example, companies that have multiple outsourcers face the challenges of managing all of those relationships as their operations grow increasingly complex. And as companies increase outsourcing activities, a gap is created in their organizational structures, management methods, and software tools. At that point, companies need to hire an **outsource relationship management (ORM) company.** ORMs can provide automated tools to monitor and manage the outsourcing relationships leading to more productive service level agreements (SLAs), better alignment of business objectives, and streamlined communication.

In the mid-2010s, the critical question is no longer whether or not to use cloud computing for enterprise systems, such as ERP and SCM. Rather, the question is how companies can profit from the capabilities that cloud computing offers.

Organizations use combinations of these IT strategies—in-house, on-shore (domestic) sourcing, offshoring, cloud computing, and SaaS.

IT AND BUSINESS STRATEGY DISCONNECTS

According to a survey of business leaders by Diamond Management & Technology Consultants (*diamondconsultants.com/*), 87 percent believe that IT is critical to their companies' strategic success, but relatively few business leaders work with IT to achieve that success. Other key findings of the Diamond study are the following:

• Only 33 percent of business leaders reported that the IT division is very involved in the process of developing business strategy.

• Only 30 percent reported that the business executive responsible for strategy works closely with the IT division.

• When the IT strategy is not aligned with the business strategies, there is a high risk that the IT project will be abandoned before completion. About 75 percent of companies abandoned at least one IT project, and 30 percent abandoned more than 10 percent of IT projects for this reason.

There are several possible reasons why a high percentage of IT projects are abandoned—the business strategy changed, technology changed, the project was not going to be completed on time or budget, the project sponsors responsible did not work well together, or the IT strategy was changed to cloud or SaaS.

IT AND BUSINESS STRATEGY SUCCESS CASES

Companies that align their business strategy and IT strategy increase their revenues. Here are two cases as examples.

1. At Travelers Companies, Inc., a property and casualty insurance company, a 75 percent increase in new customer sales was realized with the use of a new IS (software) by its independent agents. The success of the software deployment was attributed to the CIO's extensive involvement in strategy development and the close working relationship between the IT division and the responsible business unit.

2. Kraft Foods Inc. launched a master data management (MDM) project to simplify and harmonize its global business processes and enable strategic enterprise information capabilities. Kraft had grown through acquisitions resulting in ISs that could not share data because of differences in the way data was defined—referred to as the master data. For example, most ISs have lists of data that are shared and used by several of the applications that make up the system. A typical ERP system has a Customer Master, an Item Master, and an Account Master. These master data lists enable apps to share data. Because they are used by multiple apps, any errors or inconsistencies in master data cause errors or failures in apps that use them.

Kraft's assessment of its master data situation revealed problems that were negatively impacting its business strategies. According to IT director Marcelo De Santis: "Our master data management program is a key strategic enabler. It is viewed as foundational—data is critical to the business. We have executive sponsorship from the Chief Financial Officer and Executive Vice President of Operations and Business Services." The MDM project was undertaken for several business reasons; for instance, to reduce the complexity of its product portfolio leading to inventory reductions. BI initiatives are also being facilitated by this project—the ability to obtain an integrated sales view of customer and product; higher reliability when measuring and ranking partners; enhanced evaluations of product performance during launches; easily identified category/geographical business opportunities; robust analytics and reporting; and the ability to respond faster to business changes, such as acquisitions, regulatory changes, and customer requirements.

The fundamental principle to be learned is that when organizational strategies change, the IT strategies need to change with them. Both strategies are dynamic. And when people are resistant to change, they create risk because IS success depends on the skills and cooperation of people as well as the design of business processes and IT capabilities.

BUSINESS AND IT STRATEGIES DEFINED

Business strategy has its own terms that are important to know. Those key terms are defined in Table 12.1 and discussed next.

Business strategy sets the overall direction for the business. The **IT strategy** defines *what* information, information systems, and IT architecture are required to support the business and *how* the infrastructure and services are to be delivered.

IT–business alignment refers to the degree to which the IT division understands the priorities of the business and spends its resources, pursues projects, and provides

TABLE 12.1	Business Strategy Definitions

Definitions of key terms related to organizational strategy.

1. Strategy is how an organization intends to accomplish its vision. It's the overall game plan.

2. Objectives are the building blocks of strategy. Objectives set out what the business is trying to achieve. They are action-oriented statements (e.g., achieve a ROI of at least 10 percent in 201x) that define the continuous improvement activities that must be done to be successful. Objectives have the following "SMART" criteria:
- *Specific:* define what is to be achieved.
- *Measurable:* are stated in measurable terms.
- *Achievable:* are realistic given available resources and conditions.
- *Relevant:* are relevant to the people who are responsible for achieving them.
- *Time-frame:* include a time dimension.

3. Targets are the desired levels of performance.

4. Vision statement is an organization's picture of where it wants to be in the future.

5. Mission statement defines why an organization exists.

Figure 12.2 Activists protested the BP Oil Spill at a BP Gas Station in the Soho section of New York City.

© Richard Levine/Alamy Limited

information consistent with these priorities. IT–business alignment includes two facets.

1. One facet is aligning the IT function's strategy, structure, technology, and processes with those of the business units so that IT and business units are working toward the same goals. This facet is referred to as **IT alignment.**

2. Another type of alignment, referred to as **IT strategic alignment,** involves aligning IT strategy with organizational strategy. The goal of IT strategic alignment is to ensure that IS priorities, decisions, and projects are consistent with the needs of the entire business. Failure to properly align IT with the organizational strategy can result in large investments in systems that have a low payoff, or not investing in systems that potentially have a high payoff.

Business and IT strategies depend on shared IT ownership and shared IT governance among all senior managers (Shpilberg et al., 2007). When an IT or any type of failure causes harm to customers, business partners, employees, or the environment, then regulatory agencies—as well as the public—will hold the CEO accountable. See Figure 12.2. A high-profile example is BP CEO Tony Hayward, who is being held accountable to Congress for "The Role of BP in the Deepwater Horizon Explosion and Oil Spill," for the rig explosion that killed 11 workers and caused the subsea oil gusher that was releasing 60,000+ barrels per day into the Gulf of Mexico. Hayward's attempts to claim ignorance of the risks and use the SODDI defense ("some other dude did it") doesn't get him or any CEOs off the hook. *A company can outsource the work, but not the responsibility for it.*

Because of the inter-relationship between IT and business strategies, IT and other business managers share responsibility in developing IT strategic plans. Therefore, a governance structure needs to be in place that crosses organizational lines and makes senior management responsible for the success of key IT initiatives, which is discussed in the next section.

IT STRATEGIC PLANNING PROCESS

CIOs undertake IT strategic planning on a yearly, quarterly, or monthly basis. A good IT planning process helps ensure that IT aligns, and stays aligned, within an organization's business strategy. Because organizational goals change over time, it is not sufficient to develop a long-term IT strategy and not reexamine the strategy on a regular basis. For this reason, IT planning is an ongoing process. The IT planning process results in a formal IT strategy or a re-assessment each year or each quarter of the existing portfolio of IT resources.

Recall that the focus of IT strategy is on how IT creates business value. Typically, annual planning cycles are established to identify potentially beneficial IT services, to perform cost-benefit analyses, and to subject the list of potential projects to resource-allocation analysis. Often the entire process is conducted by an IT *steering committee.* See *IT at Work 12.1* for the duties of an IT steering committee.

IT at Work 12.1

IT Steering Committees

The corporate steering committee is a group of managers and staff representing various organizational units that is set up to establish IT priorities and to ensure the IS department is meeting the needs of the enterprise. The committee's major tasks are:

- **Direction setting.** In linking the corporate strategy with the IT strategy, planning is the key activity.
- **Rationing.** The committee approves the allocation of resources for and within the information systems organization. This includes outsourcing policy.
- **Structuring.** The committee deals with how the IS department is positioned in the organization. The issue of centralization–decentralization of IT resources is resolved by the committee.

- **Staffing.** Key IT personnel decisions involve a consultation-and-approval process made by the committee, including outsourcing decisions.
- **Communication.** Information regarding IT activities should flow freely.
- **Evaluating.** The committee should establish performance measures for the IS department and see that they are met. This includes the initiation of SLAs.

The success of steering committees largely depends on the establishment of IT *governance*, formally established statements that direct the policies regarding IT alignment with organizational goals and allocation of resources.

Figure 12.3 shows the IT strategic planning process. The planning process begins with the creation of a strategic business plan. The *long-range IT plan*, sometimes referred to as the *strategic IT plan*, is then based on the strategic business plan. The IT strategic plan starts with the IT vision and strategy, which defines the future concept of what IT should do to achieve the goals, objectives, and strategic position of the firm and how this will be achieved. The overall direction, requirements, and **sourcing** (outsourcing or insourcing) of resources, such as infrastructure, application services, data services, security services, IT governance, and management architecture; budget; activities; and timeframes are set for three to five years into the future. The planning process continues by addressing lower-level activities with a shorter time frame.

The next level down is a *medium-term IT plan*, which identifies general project plans in terms of the specific requirements and sourcing of resources as well as the **project portfolio.** The project portfolio lists major resource projects, including

Figure 12.3 IT strategic planning process.

infrastructure, application services, data services, and security services that are consistent with the long-range plan. Some companies may define their portfolio in terms of applications. The **applications portfolio** is a list of major, approved IS projects that are also consistent with the long-range plan. Expectations for sourcing of resources in the project or applications portfolio should be driven by the business strategy. Since some of these projects will take more than a year to complete, and others will not start in the current year, this plan extends over several years.

The third level is a *tactical plan*, which details budgets and schedules for current-year projects and activities. In reality, because of the rapid pace of change in technology and the environment, short-term plans may include major items not anticipated in the other plans.

The planning process just described is currently practiced by many organizations. Specifics of the IT planning process, of course, vary among organizations. For example, not all organizations have a high-level IT steering committee. Project priorities may be determined by the IT director, by his or her superior, by company politics, or even on a first-come, first-served basis.

The deliverables from the IT planning process should include the following: an evaluation of the strategic goals and directions of the organization and how IT is aligned; a new or revised IT vision and assessment of the state of the IT division; a statement of the strategies, objectives, and policies for the IT division; and the overall direction, requirements, and sourcing of resources.

Tools and Methodologies of IT Strategic Planning. Several tools and methodologies are used to facilitate IT strategic planning. Most of these methodologies start with some investigation of strategy that checks the industry, competition, and competitiveness, and relates them to technology (*alignment*). Others help create and justify new uses of IT (*impact*). In the next section, we look briefly at some of these methodologies.

Business Service Management. Business service management is an approach for linking KPIs of IT to business goals to determine the impact on the business. KPIs are metrics that measure the actual performance of critical aspects of IT, such as essential projects and applications, servers, the network, and so forth, against predefined business goals, such as revenue growth, reduced costs, and lower risk. For a critical project, for example, performance metrics include the status of the project, the ability to track milestones to budget, and a view of how the IT staff spends its time (Biddick, 2008).

KPIs can be classified into two types. The first type includes those that measure *real-time performance* or *predict future results*. These KPIs assist in proactive, rather than reactive, responses to potential user and customer problems. For example, 80 percent of IT staff may be needed to work on active projects. An evaluation of KPIs may predict that the following month a projected slowdown of project activity will reduce the utilization rate to 70 percent, allowing time to adjust staffing or add more projects. The second type of KPI measures *results of past activity*.

Business service management software tools provide real-time dashboards for tracking KPIs at the executive, functional business areas, services, and operations levels, as you read in Chapter 11. Dashboards make it easier to understand and predict how IT impacts the business and how business impacts the IT architecture.

Business Systems Planning Model. The business systems planning (BSP) model was developed by IBM, and has influenced other planning efforts such as Accenture's method/1. BSP is a top-down approach that starts with business strategies. It deals with two main building blocks—business processes and data classes—which become the basis of an information architecture. From this architecture, planners can define organizational databases and identify applications that support business strategies, as shown in Figure 12.4. BSP relies heavily on the use of metrics in the analysis of processes and data, with the ultimate goal of developing the information architecture.

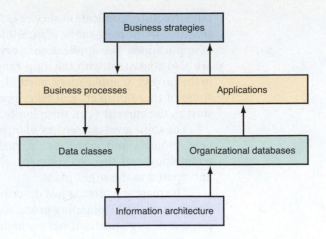

Figure 12.4 Business systems planning (BSP) approach.

Balanced Scorecard. Devised by Robert Kaplan and David Norton in a number of articles published in the *Harvard Business Review* between 1992 and 1996, the **balanced scorecard** is a business management concept that transforms both financial and non-financial data into a detailed roadmap that helps the company measure performance.

Kaplan and Norton introduced the balanced scorecard as a way of measuring performance in companies. The major difference with Kaplan's and Norton's score-card was that it measured a company's performance in other than strictly financial terms. For example, it measures performance from any of the following perspectives:

- Customer perspective
- Internal business process perspective
- Learning and growth perspective
- Financial perspective

The balanced scorecard framework supplements traditional tangible financial measures with criteria that measure four intangible perspectives and address important questions including (Kaplan and Norton, 2007):

1. How do customers see the company?
2. At what must the company excel?
3. Can the company continue to improve and create value?
4. How does the company appear to shareholders?

The balanced scorecard can be applied to link KPIs of IT to business goals to determine the impact on the business. The focus for the assessment could be, for example, the project portfolio or the applications portfolio. As shown in Table 12.2, the balanced scorecard can be used to assess the IT project portfolio of a retail department store

TABLE 12.2	IT Project Balanced Scorecard					
IT Project	**Project's Role in Strategic Business Plan**	**Project's Evolving versus Stable Knowledge**	**Degree of Change Needed in the Project**	**Where the Project Gets Sourced**	**Data's Public or Proprietary Nature**	**Project Budget**
Infrastructure	Efficiency	Stable	Low	Outsourced	Proprietary	Small
Application Services	Customer focus	Evolving	High	ERP software	Proprietary	High
Data Services	Innovation	Evolving	High	Business intelligence software	Proprietary	High
Security Services	Compliance requirement	Evolving	Low	Outsourced	Proprietary	Small

chain. Projects are listed along the vertical dimension, and specific measures, critical to what the organization needs to track, are presented horizontally. The balanced scorecard helps managers to clarify and update strategy; align IT strategy with business strategy; and link strategic objectives to long-term goals and annual budgets.

Critical Success Factors Model. Critical success factors (CSFs) are the most essential things (factors) that must go right or be closely tracked in order to ensure the organization's survival and success. For companies dependent on the price of oil, oil prices would be a CSF. The *CSF approach* to IT planning was developed to help identify the information needs of managers. The fundamental assumption is that in every organization there are three to six key factors that, if done well, will result in the organization's success. The reverse is also true. The failure of these factors will result in some degree of failure. Therefore, organizations continuously measure performance in these areas, taking corrective action whenever necessary. CSFs also exist in business units, departments, and other organizational units.

CSFs vary by industry—manufacturing, service, or government—and by specific industries within these categories. For organizations in the same industry, CSFs vary depending on whether the firms are market leaders or weaker competitors, where they are located, and what competitive strategies they follow. Environmental issues, such as the degree of regulation or amount of technology used, influence CSFs. In addition, CSFs change over time, based on temporary conditions, such as high interest rates or long-term trends.

IT planners identify CSFs by interviewing managers in an initial session, and then refine CSFs in one or two additional sessions. Sample questions asked in the CSF approach are

- What objectives are central to your organization?
- What are the critical factors that are essential to meeting these objectives?
- What decisions or actions are key to these critical factors?
- What variables underlie these decisions, and how are they measured?
- What information systems can supply these measures?

The first step following the interviews is to determine the organizational objectives for which the manager is responsible, and then the factors that are critical to attaining these objectives. The second step is to select a small number of CSFs. Then, determine the information requirements for those CSFs and measure to see whether the CSFs are met. If they are not met, it is necessary to build appropriate applications. See Figure 12.5.

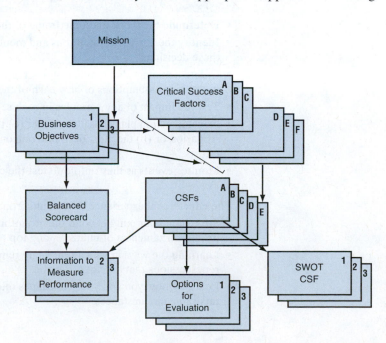

Figure 12.5 Critical success factors—basic processes.

The CSF approach encourages managers to identify what is most important to their performance and then develop good indicators of performance in these areas.

Scenario Planning. Scenario planning is a methodology in which planners first create several scenarios; then a team compiles as many future events as possible that may influence the outcome of each scenario. This approach is used in planning situations that involve much uncertainty, like that of IT in general and e-commerce in particular. Five reasons to do scenario planning are

1. To ensure that you are not focusing on catastrophe to the exclusion of opportunity
2. To help you allocate resources more prudently
3. To preserve your options
4. To ensure that you are not still "fighting the last war"
5. To give you the opportunity to rehearse testing and training of people to go through the process.

Scenario planning follows a rigorous process; the essential steps are summarized in Table 12.3. Scenario planning has been widely used by major corporations to facilitate IT planning (e.g., *ncri.com* and *gbn.com*). It also has been particularly important to e-commerce planning. For instance, creating customer scenarios helps the company better fit the products and services into the real lives of customers, resulting in sales expansion and customer loyalty. National Semiconductor, Tesco, and Buzzsaw.com, for example, have used customer scenarios to strengthen customer relationships, to guide business strategy, and to deliver business value.

A major aspect of IT planning is properly allocating IT resources to the right set of projects. Organizations simply cannot afford to develop or purchase each application or undertake each application enhancement that business units and end users might like. The IT steering committee has an important responsibility in deciding how IT resources will be allocated.

Resource Allocation. **Resource allocation** consists of developing the plans for hardware, software, data communications and networks, facilities, personnel, and financial resources needed to execute the master development plan, as defined in the requirements analysis. Resource allocation can be a contentious process because requests for spending far exceed the available funds. This can lead to

TABLE 12.3	Essential Steps of Scenario Planning

- Determine the scope and time frame of the scenario you are flashing out.
- Identify the current assumptions and mental models of individuals who influence these decisions.
- Create a manageable number of divergent, yet plausible, scenarios. Spell out the underlying assumptions of how each of these imagined futures might evolve.
- Test the impact of key variables in each scenario.
- Develop action plans based on either (a) the solutions that play most robustly across scenarios, or (b) the most desirable outcome toward which a company can direct its efforts.
- Monitor events as they unfold to test the corporate direction; be prepared to modify it as required.

The educational experience that results from this process includes

- Stretching your mind beyond the groupthink that can slowly and imperceptibly produce a sameness of minds among top team members in any organization.
- Learning the ways in which seemingly remote potential developments may have repercussions that hit close to home.
- Learning how you and your colleagues might respond under both adverse and favorable circumstances.

intense, highly political competition among organizational units, which makes it difficult to objectively identify the most desirable investments.

Requests for funding approval from the steering committee fall into two categories. The first category consists of projects and infrastructure that are critical for the organization to stay in business. For example, it may be imperative to purchase or upgrade hardware if the network, or disk drives, or the processor on the main computer are approaching capacity limits. Obtaining approval for this type of spending is largely a matter of communicating the gravity of the problems to decision makers.

The second category includes less-critical items, such as new projects, maintenance or upgrades of existing systems, and infrastructure to support these systems and future needs. Approval for projects in this category may become more difficult to obtain because the IS department is already receiving funding for the critical projects. Generally speaking, organizations set aside funds for the first category of projects and then use the remainder of the IT budget for the second category.

Questions

1. What are the four main points of IT strategic plans?
2. Explain the difference between in-house and sourcing IT strategies.
3. What are the main types of sourcing?
4. What are possible reasons why a high percentage of IT projects are abandoned?
5. Define business strategy and IT strategy.
6. What is the goal of IT–business alignment?
7. Why must IT strategic planning be revisited on a regular basis?
8. Describe the committee that usually conducts the IT strategic planning process? Who is included on this committee? What are the major tasks of this committee? On what is this committee's success dependent?
9. What is the focus of IT strategy?
10. Describe the IT strategic planning process.
11. Describe the project portfolio. Describe the applications portfolio. When are these portfolios developed?
12. What tools and methodologies are available to assist in the IT strategic planning process? How are these methods used to help organizations?
13. What is resource allocation? What are the two types of funding requests?

12.2 IT Governance

The purpose of IT governance is the creation of a management framework that maximizes the value that an organization derives from IT in support of its strategic objectives. In short, IT governance is about doing things right the first time around. IT governance is part of a wider corporate governance activity, but has its own specific focus. The benefits of effective IT governance are reduced costs and damages caused by IT failures; and more trust, teamwork, and confidence in the use of IT and the people providing IT services.

IT GOVERNANCE AND PERFORMANCE

IT governance is concerned with insuring that IT investments deliver full value. As such, **IT performance management**—being able to predict and anticipate failures before it's too late—is a big part of IT governance. IT performance management functions include the following: verifies that strategic IT objectives are being achieved; reviews IT performance, and assesses the contribution of IT to the business. For example, IT performance management assesses outcomes to answer the question: Did the IT investment deliver the promised business value?

In order for IT to deliver full value, three objectives must be met (the first objective you're already familiar with).

1. IT has to be fully aligned to business strategies and direction.
2. Key risks have to be identified and controlled.
3. Compliance with laws, industry rules, and regulatory agencies must be demonstrated.

In light of many corporate failures and scandals, corporate and IT governance have a higher profile today than ever before. Risk management, oversight, and clear communication are all parts of governance.

Individuals Concerned with IT Governance. Individuals who are concerned about IT governance are:

- Top-level business leaders, who are the Board, executives, managers, and especially heads of finance, operations, and IT
- Public relations and investor relations managers
- Internal and external auditors and regulators
- Middle-level business and IT management
- Supply chain and business partners
- Customers and shareholders

As the preceding lists of issues and concerned individuals indicate, IT governance is not just an IT issue or only of interest to the IT function. It is an integral part of corporate governance focused on improving the management and control of IT. Ultimately, it is the duty of the Board of Directors (BOD) to insure that IT and other critical activities are effectively governed.

IT plays a pivotal role in improving corporate governance practices because most critical business processes are automated; and managers rely on information provided by these processes for their decision making.

The governance structure within an organization can either facilitate IT–business alignment—or hinder that alignment. The CIO oversees the IT division and is responsible for the company's technology direction. The CIO is a member of the C-suite of chief officers in the company who share authority in their respective areas of responsibility, such as CEO, chief financial officer (CFO), chief marketing officer (CMO), or chief compliance officer (CCO). To whom the CIO reports is telling of how IT is perceived within the company. For example, if IT is perceived as a strategic weapon to grow revenues and increase operational effectiveness, then the CIO likely reports to the CEO. If IT is perceived as a cost-cutting center, the CIO likely reports to the CFO. Table 12.4 lists the important skills of CIOs.

WHAT IT GOVERNANCE COVERS

IT governance covers IT management and control across five key areas:

1. Supports the strategy: Provides for strategic direction of IT and the alignment of IT and the business.

TABLE 12.4	Skill Set of the CIO

Skills that CIOs need to improve IT governance and the IT-business alignment include:
- *Political savvy.* Effectively understand managers, workers, and their priorities and use that knowledge to influence others to support organizational objectives.
- *Influence, leadership, and power.* Inspire a shared vision and influence subordinates and superiors.
- *Relationship management.* Build and maintain working relationships with coworkers and those external to the organization. Negotiate problem solutions without alienating those impacted. Understand others and get their cooperation in nonauthority relationships.
- *Resourcefulness.* Think strategically and make good decisions under pressure. Can set up complex work systems and engage in flexible problem resolution.
- *Strategic planning.* Capable of developing long-term objectives and strategies, and translating vision into realistic business strategies.
- *Doing what it takes.* Persevering in the face of obstacles.
- *Leading employees.* Delegating work to employees effectively; broadening employee opportunities; and interacting fairly with employees.

2. Delivers value: Confirms that the IT/Business organization is designed to drive maximum business value from IT. Oversees the delivery of value by IT to the business, and assesses ROI.

3. Risk management: Confirms that processes are in place to ensure that risks have been adequately managed. Includes assessment of the risk of IT investments.

4. Resource management: Provides high-level direction for sourcing and use of IT resources. Oversees funding of IT at the enterprise level. Ensures there is an adequate IT capability and infrastructure to support current and expected business requirements.

5. IT Performance management: (Refer also to the beginning of Section 12.2.) Verifies achievement of strategic IT objectives by measuring IT performance and business value.

IT governance, like security, is not a one-time exercise or something achieved by a mandate or setting of rules. It requires a commitment from the top of the organization to instill a better way of dealing with the management and control of IT. IT governance is an ongoing activity that requires a continuous improvement mentality and responsiveness to the fast-changing IT environment. When companies run into legal or regulatory challenges, IT governance is what saves or dooms them.

Questions

1. What is the importance of IT governance?
2. Why is IT performance management a key part of IT governance?
3. In order for IT to deliver full value, what three objectives must be met?
4. Identify four issues driving the need for IT governance.
5. Who is concerned about IT governance?
6. What does IT governance cover?

12.3 Aligning IT with Business Strategy

Alignment is a complex management activity, and its complexity increases as the pace of global competition and technological change increases. IT–business alignment can be improved by focusing on the following activities:

1. Understanding IT and corporate planning. A prerequisite for effective IT–business alignment is for the CIO to understand business planning and for the CEO and business planners to understand their company's IT planning.

2. CIO is a member of senior management. The key to achieving IT-business alignment is for the CIO to attain strategic influence. Rather than being narrow technologists, CIOs must be both business- and technology-savvy.

3. Shared culture and good communication. The CIO must understand and buy into the corporate culture so that IS planning does not occur in isolation. Frequent, open, and effective communication is essential to ensure a shared culture and keep everyone aware of planning activities and business dynamics.

4. Commitment to IT planning by senior management. Senior management commitment to IT planning is essential to success.

5. Multi-level links. Links between business and IT plans should be made at the strategic, tactical, and operational levels.

STRATEGIC ROLE OF IT

Companies must determine the use, value, and impact of IT to identify opportunities that create value and supports the strategic vision. This requires that the CIO, and other senior IT staff, closely interact with the CEO and the senior management in functional areas or business units. And the CIO must be in a position to influence how IT can assume a strategic role in the firm.

COMPETITIVE ADVANTAGE THROUGH IT

Competitive advantage is gained by a company by providing real or perceived value to customers. To determine how IT can provide a competitive advantage, the firm must know its products and services, its customers and competitors, its industry and related industries, and environmental forces—and it must have insight about how IT can enhance value for each of these areas. To understand the relationship of IT in providing a competitive advantage, we next consider the potential of a firm's IT resources to add value to a company.

Three characteristics of resources give firms the potential to create a competitive advantage:

1. Value. Resources are a source of competitive advantage only when they are valuable. A resource has value to the extent that it enables a firm to implement strategies that improve efficiency and effectiveness. But even if valuable, resources that are equitably distributed across organizations are only commodities.

2. Rarity. Resources also must be rare in order to confer competitive advantages.

3. Appropriability. *Appropriability* refers to the ability of the firm to generate earnings from the resource. Even if a resource is rare and valuable, if the firm expends more effort or expense to obtain the resource than it generates through the resource, then the resource will not create a competitive advantage.

Table 12.5 lists the three characteristics necessary to achieve competitive advantage and three additional factors needed to sustain it.

The first three characteristics described in Table 12.5 are used to characterize resources that can create an initial competitive advantage. In order for the competitive advantage to be sustained, however, the resources must be inimitable, imperfectly mobile, and have low substitutability. **Imitability** is the feature that determines whether a competitor can imitate or copy the resource. **Mobility** (or *tradability*) refers to the degree to which a firm may easily acquire the resource necessary to imitate a rival's competitive advantage. Some resources, such as hardware and software, are easy to acquire and are thus highly mobile and unlikely to generate sustained competitive advantage. Even if a resource is rare, when it's possible to purchase or hire the resource, then the resource is mobile and incapable of contributing to a sustained advantage. Finally, **substitutability** refers to the ability of competing firms to utilize an alternative resource.

Information systems can contribute three types of resources: technology resources, technical capabilities, and IT managerial resources, as listed in Table 12.6.

Technology resources include the IT infrastructure, proprietary technology, hardware, and software. The creation of a successful infrastructure may take several years to achieve. Thus, even while competitors might readily purchase the same hardware and software, the combination of these resources to develop a flexible infrastructure

TABLE 12.5	Key Resource Attributes that Build a Competitive Edge
Resource	**Description**
Value	Degree to which a resource helps a firm improve efficiency or effectiveness
Rarity	Degree to which a resource is unique and cannot be duplicated by other firms in an industry
Appropriability	Degree to which a firm can make use of a resource without incurring an expense that exceeds the value of the resource
Imitability	Degree to which a resource can be readily matched
Mobility	Degree to which a resource is easy to transport
Substitutability	Degree to which another resource can be used in lieu of the original resource to achieve value

TABLE 12.6 | IS Resources and Capabilities

IS Resources and Capabilities	Descriptions	Relationship to Resources
Technology resources	Includes infrastructure, proprietary technology, hardware, and software.	Not necessarily rare or valuable, but difficult to appropriate and imitate. Low mobility but a fair degree of substitutability.
IT skills	Includes technical knowledge, development knowledge, and operational skills.	Highly mobile, but less imitable or substitutable. Not necessarily rare but highly valuable.
Managerial IT resources	Includes vendor and outsourcer relationship skills, market responsiveness, IS–business partnerships, IS planning, and management skills.	Somewhat more rare than the technology and IT skill resources. Also of higher value. High mobility given the short tenure of CIOs. Non-substitutable.

is a complex task. It may take firms many years to catch up with the infrastructure capabilities of its competitors.

Technical capabilities include IS technical knowledge such as app development skills; IS development knowledge such as experience with social media or development platforms; and IS operations. Technical IT skills include the expertise needed to build and use IT apps.

Managerial resources include IS managerial resources such as vendor relationships, outsourcer relationship management, market responsiveness, IS-business partnerships, and IS planning and change management.

BUSINESS IMPROVEMENT OPPORTUNITY MATRIX

IT can improve many domains of business activity, as presented in the opportunity matrix shown in Table 12.7.

To ensure that business and IT executives have a common understanding of potential business improvements attainable through the use of IT, each of these benefits should be evaluated in terms of the value to be provided to the business. One or more improvements may be attained through IT. For example, if customer service, number 8 in Table 12.7 is expected to be improved through the use of IT in a

TABLE 12.7 | Business Improvement Opportunity Matrix

Business Improvement with IT	High Impact Value	Low Impact Value	No Value	Description of the Business Value of the Improvement
1. Improve process efficiencies				
2. Increase market share and global reach				
3. Reach new markets, audiences, and channels				
4. Improve external partnering capabilities				
5. Enable internal collaboration				
6. Launch innovative product and service offerings				
7. Improve time to market				
8. Enhance customer service experience				
9. Improve information access and effectiveness in decision-making processes				
10. Bring about new business models				
11. Enable a business to gain, or simply maintain, a competitive advantage				
12. Other				

Sources: Compiled from Kesner (2003) and Center for CIO Leadership (2007).

package delivery service, such an improvement may be regarded as providing high impact value. The description of the business value of enhancing the customer service experience would state:

> *The currently high volume of customer complaints about late delivery of packages will be addressed with an automatically generated personalized e-mail message, to each customer experiencing late delivery, to provide notification of the revised delivery date. This e-mail communication also provides an opportunity for each customer to express any remaining concerns. The external focus on improving customer service will contribute to a positive image of the company.*

This process change to improve customer service may also improve process efficiencies, number 1 in the table, providing low impact value to the business. The description of the business value of this process improvement would state:

> *Customer service agents will be freed from personally attending to all customer complaints, allowing them to focus on resolving the most serious complaints. This improved use of customer service agents' time is expected to improve operational efficiencies and costs.*

Being able to explain how IT adds business value can be facilitated with this matrix. To provide a common understanding, this matrix serves as a tool to discuss and clarify expectations concerning the potential impact of the improvements to the business. Clear, frequent, and effective communication is critical to achieving this potential.

IT DIVISION AND BUSINESS MANAGEMENT PARTNERSHIP

Including the CIO on the CEO's senior management team promotes a partnership between them. For example, at Walgreen Company, a leading drugstore chain, the CIO has been on the top management team since the late 1990s (Worthen, 2007). This arrangement facilitated the delivery of a single IS to connect all Walgreen pharmacies, with continual improvements based on feedback and suggestions from both employees and customers. The CEO recognizes that including the CIO in strategy meetings encourages teamwork. To maintain this mutually beneficial relationship, the CIO must continually educate and update the other executives in the C-suite (chief executive) team about technological advances and capabilities relevant to the business needs.

The partnership between the IT division and business management can extend to fuse with the business, as you read in *IT at Work 12.2*. Such a fusion could be achieved with a new organizational structure, wherein the CIO becomes responsible for managing some core business functions. For example, the CIO at Hess Corporation, a leading energy company based in New York City, is part of a new organizational structure. The CIO began managing several core business functions. Additionally, Hess Corporation is creating a joint IT and business group to develop new operating processes and advanced technologies. Comprised of IT workers with geologists, scientists, and other employees, this unit will report to the senior vice president of oil exploration and production.

Alternatively, the CIO could work directly with other top executives to influence strategic directions, suggest changes in internal business processes, and lead a diversity of initiatives that encompass more than just technology projects. For example, the Vice President of IT at PHH Mortgage, in Mount Laurel, NJ, works alongside the sales managers. This working relationship has fostered a rapport between the CIO and sales executives. In discussions with the sales team about potential changes in some of the mortgage application processes, the CIO is able to take the lead on business improvement opportunities by communicating his understanding of concerns and offering insightful recommendations.

IT at Work 12.2

The Strategic CIO

It is not typical for a CIO to work routinely with business leaders on their strategy and translate it into action, and then be asked by the CEO to manage business strategy worldwide. Nor is it typical that the CEO asks the CIO to run a line of business, in addition to the IT function. A CIO would not be expected to manage the process of opening 10,000 seasonal tax preparation locations and hiring 100,000 seasonal tax preparers, but that's what happened at H&R Block, a tax and financial services company. These responsibilities are typical for CIOs who are responsible for IT governance and supporting the business strategy. We'll refer to them as "strategic CIOs" for clarity.

The strategic CIO is a business leader who leverages IT to add value and gain a competitive advantage. The strategist's focus is on how a company creates shareholder value and serves its customers. Rather than being focused primarily on internal operations, the strategic CIO looks at the company from the outside-in by asking how the company is perceived by customers and how competitors apply IT to compete. The role of strategic CIO is focused on business strategy and innovation. This broader, more business-oriented, and strategic focus is the direction for the CIO role.

Marc West, the senior VP and CIO at H&R Block, began as a "traditional CIO," focusing 95 percent of his efforts on the technology foundation. In preparing for tax season, CIO West was engaged in delivering tax preparation software for the company's seasonal storefront locations. This activity helped him to acquire insight into the core business, operations, and how customers are served. This further led him to compare what H&R was doing against the competition, gaining a big picture perspective of the industry. He shared his strategic insights with the CEO and management team. Encouraged by the CEO, CIO West continued his "outside-inside" strategic assessment, gaining an industry-wide, business-oriented strategic mindset. The CEO then asked CIO West to lead a new line of business, driving growth in the commercial markets.

Sources: Compiled from Ehrlich and West (2007) and *hrblock.com*.

Questions

1. Why has the role of CIO expanded?

2. What are the benefits of this strategic CIO role to the company?

Questions

1. How can the IT-business alignment be improved?
2. What are three characteristics of resources that give firms the potential to create a competitive advantage?
3. Describe the three types of resources that information systems can contribute to a firm.
4. Why is it important for the CIO to be included as a member of the senior management team?

12.4 IT Operating Plans and Sourcing Strategies

The core competencies of many organizations—the things they do best and that represent their competitive strengths—are in retailing, services, manufacturing, or some other function. IT is an *enabler*, and it is complex and constantly changing. IT is difficult to manage, even for organizations with above-average IT management skills. Therefore, many organizations have implemented outsourcing as an IT strategy. Outsourcing can be done domestically or offshore, or via cloud computing or SaaS. Those topics are covered in other chapters, but are mentioned here because they are examples of IT outsourcing strategies.

Cloud computing is not simply about outsourcing the routine computing tasks. It's about the delivery of real business services, enabled by the applications needed to support them, and then powered by computing and network infrastructure to host and deliver them.

SaaS provides an ability to easily extend internal processes outside the organizational boundary to support **business processing outsourcing (BPO)** arrangements and can become a strong competitive advantage for an organization today and in the future. BPO is the process of hiring another company to handle business activities for you.

BPO AND ITES

BPO is distinct from IT outsourcing, which focuses on hiring a third-party company or service provider to do IT-related activities, such as application management and application development, data center operations, or testing and quality assurance.

Originally, BPO consisted of outsourcing standard processes, such as payroll; and then expanded to employee benefits management. Currently, BPO includes many functions that are considered non-core to the primary business strategy, such as financial and administration processes, human resource functions, call center and customer service activities, and accounting.

These outsourcing deals are multi-year contracts that can run into hundreds of millions of dollars. Often, the people performing the work internally for the client firm are transferred and become employees for the service provider. Dominant outsourcing service providers in the BPO fields—some of which also dominate the IT outsourcing business—are IBM, Accenture, and Hewitt Associates in the U.S. and European and Asian companies Capgemini, Genpact, TCS, Wipro and Infosys. Many of these BPO efforts involve offshoring, with India one of the most popular location for BPO activities.

BPO is also referred to as **ITES, or information technology-enabled services.** Since most business processes include some form of automation, IT "enables" these services to be performed.

Andrew Pery, Chief Marketing Officer for document management company Kofax (*kofax.com/*) predicts the BPO market "will likely outgrow all segments of the IT industry. There is increased competition and increased choice."

Why is the BPO industry changing? Don Schulman, General Manager, Finance and Administration for IBM, gives two reasons (Rosenthal, 2010).

1. The economy has triggered a broader group of buyers to consider BPO as a viable option. In an era where companies are challenged to do more with less, buyers are seeking strategic partnerships that enable them to accelerate transformation.

2. The industry has matured. It's no longer about price, cost, and labor arbitrage. The future will be about enterprise business outcomes, process optimization, and cloud computing.

eBay relies on BPO, as you read in *IT at Work 12.3*.

IT at Work 12.3

eBay Challenging Transition to BPO

Since its 1998 IPO, eBay has gone from online experiment in consumer-to-consumer, e-commerce to a Fortune 500 enterprise that sells $60 billion in goods annually. It supports 88 million individual buyers and sellers, plus an expanding list of small businesses. This metamorphosis was not without growing pains. Exploding demand for eBay's services created enviable, but staggering challenges. By 2004, eBay's annual revenues had exceeded $3 billion. Up to then, its accounts payable (AP) function had been able to keep up with the exponentially growing workload. The AP function was a critical system because sellers expected to get paid instantaneously. It was foreseeable that a much larger transaction accounting capacity would be needed than the current IT structure could deliver quickly. eBay's acquisition of several companies with disparate AP processes created additional integration challenges.

Outsourcing Challenges and Lessons Learned

eBay turned to outsourcing for a solution for transaction processing of accounts. In early 2005, eBay migrated all of its AP operations to Genpact. Genpact (*genpact.com/*) is a global leader in business process and technology management. The migration of AP and other business processes to BPO provider Genpact was not without challenges, but was ultimately a success. Six lessons that eBay and Genpact learned from the BPO implementation are the following.

1. Manage change by securing the commitment of senior leaders in an overt fashion, and by recognizing subtle cultural differences that can undermine initial transition efforts.

2. Assess organizational readiness for a BPO transition from a mental and technical standpoint, and set realistic expectations and manage them actively.

3. **Anticipate risks and formulate a plan for mitigating them,** beginning with a strategy for dealing with "loss of control" threats, both real and imagined.

4. **Build project-management infrastructure** that recognizes the "process of transition" needs to be managed as carefully as processes being transitioned. Mapping how the AP process should look post-transition, and how it will be managed end-to-end, and by whom, are important.

5. **Create a governance mechanism** that can discreetly collect feedback from the Transition Project Manager and provide formal executive oversight and guidance. Form an Executive Steering Committee that includes two senior managers from each organization and representation from all business units impacted by BPO.

6. **Properly define how success will be measured,** both qualitatively and quantitatively. Identifying the right benchmarks for success and vigilantly measuring efforts against them over time are critical.

Performance Improvements

The transition was far from perfect at first and hard lessons learned early helped achieve impressive results in time. Year-end 2009 revenues were triple 2004 revenues, and AP transaction volume and headcount doubled, but at a much low cost per volume. On-time payments grew to 30 percent. In other words, more volume is now being handled, and more effectively per AP person. This success paved the way for migration of other eBay transaction accounting processes. From 2006 to early 2008, eBay outsourced its global Vendor/Supplier Maintenance and General Ledger (GL) activities.

Sources: Compiled from Genpact (2010), and *OutsourcingPapers.com* (2010).

Questions

1. Why is the ability to process AP a critical success factor for eBay?
2. Why did eBay choose outsourcing as its IT strategy instead of in-house development?
3. Why did eBay rely on Genpact for its BPO transition?
4. Given that Genpact is a global leader in business process and technology management, why did eBay encounter challenges?

FACTORS DRIVING GROWTH IN SOURCING AS AN IT STRATEGY

Since the late 1980s, many organizations have outsourced the *majority of their IT functions*, rather than just incidental parts. The trend became classic in 1989 when Eastman Kodak transferred its data centers to IBM under a 10-year, $500 million contract. This example, at a prominent multibillion-dollar company, gave a clear signal that outsourcing was a legitimate IT strategy. Since then, many mega outsourcing deals have been announced, some for several billion dollars. The trend, however, has turned away from the mega-deal in favor of the *multi-vendor approach*, incorporating the services of several best-of-breed vendors to meet IT demands.

The major reasons why organizations are increasingly sourcing are:

- To focus on core competency, as you read in the AstraZeneca opening case.
- It's a cheaper and/or faster way to gain or enhance IT capabilities.
- To cut operational costs.
- Offshoring has become a more accepted IT strategy.
- Cloud computing and SaaS have proven to be effective IT strategies.

Increasingly, organizations are leveraging existing *global cloud infrastructures* from companies like Amazon, Google, Rackspace, and Windows Azure. Established companies are more willing to outsource company-critical functions in an effort to reduce costs. And new start-up companies typically outsource and rely on SaaS to avoid upfront IT costs. For example, **S3**, one of Amazon's web services, lets businesses store their data in the cloud, avoiding the need to operate their own servers. S3 is part of the same online infrastructure that Amazon uses to run its own business. Twitter uses S3, as does the *New York Times* to store and deliver articles from its historical archives. Sourcing companies have started to offer some interesting new business models and services around cloud computing. These innovative new IT models have added to the number of options to be considered in IT strategic planning.

CIOs are focusing more on outsourcing to deliver business value, beyond the traditional areas of cost savings and operational efficiencies, in response to an increasingly dynamic environment (IBM, 2008). The environment is characterized by rapid developments in IT; firms that are being transformed by global expansion, mergers and acquisition; and new disruptive business models and mobile capabilities. Benefits of sourcing are listed in Table 12.8.

TABLE 12.8	Benefits of Sourcing

Financial benefits
- Avoid heavy capital investment, thereby releasing funds for other uses.
- Improved cash flow and cost accountability.
- Improved cost benefits from economies of scale and from sharing hardware, software, and personnel.
- Less need for expensive office space.

Technical benefits
- Access to new information technologies.
- Ability to achieve technological improvements more easily.
- Faster application development and placement of IT apps into service.

Management benefits
- Concentration on developing and running core business activity. Improved company focus.
- Delegation of IT development (design, production, and acquisition) and operational responsibility to suppliers.
- Elimination of need to recruit and retain competent IT staff.
- Reduced risk of bad software.

Human resources benefits
- Opportunity to draw on specialist skills available from a pool of expertise.
- Faster career development and opportunities for remaining staff.

Quality benefits
- Clearly defined *service levels*.
- Improved performance accountability.
- Quick response to business demands (agility).
- Ability to handle IT peaks and valleys more effectively (flexibility).

IT at Work 12.4

AstraZeneca Sources R&D, Manufacturing, and IT

British-Swedish company AstraZeneca (*astrazeneca.com/*) is one of the world's leading biopharmaceutical companies. The company focuses on the discovery, development, and commercialization of prescription medicines for six health care areas. AstraZeneca explains its forward-looking business strategy as follows:

> Each year, at the beginning of our business planning cycle, we assess the challenges and opportunities presented by the market, stress test our short and long-term planning assumptions, and critically assess our strengths and weaknesses as an organisation. We do so to assure ourselves that, whatever our past successes, the strategic path we are following is the right one for the future.

Foreseeing a Threat to Its Business

In 2007, management forecasted that the company was going to lose 38 per cent of its revenues over the next five years because patents on its key drug were expiring. Once the patents had expired, competitors could legally produce and sell drugs that AstraZeneca had developed, cutting into their sales and profit. To counter that threat, management launched a radically new business strategy and began major restructuring. David Smith, executive vice-president of operations, was responsible for restructuring to cut costs and improve profitability before the patents expired.

Restructuring from Tightly-Bound to Loosely-Coupled

Smith, who previously worked for cosmetics group Estée Lauder and clothing group Timberland, wanted to follow the restructuring model set years ago in the fashion, electronics, and auto industries. Those industries had shifted away from the traditional tightly-bound model of a vertically integrated company. **Vertically integrated companies** control every part of their business from research and development (R&D) to manufacturing and logistics. Smith shifted AstraZeneca from a vertically integrated biopharmaceutical company to a loosely-coupled organizational model connected by outsourced arrangements and relationships.

Looking to AstraZeneca's new strategy, Smith explained that:

> We would own the IP [intellectual property], the research, branding and the quality and safety issues . . . but [everything else] would be outsourced. The idea is to take out as many stages as you can.

Because of its new business strategy, by 2014 AstraZeneca would have completed its shift toward outsourcing R&D, the manufacturing of active pharmaceutical ingredients, and the IT function. Outsourcing relationships would take several years to complete largely because of complex regulatory hurdles.

R&D and Manufacturing Outsourcing—Radical Changes

The R&D function is the heart of any pharmaceutical company. R&D leads to the discovery of breakthrough drugs that could generate huge profits. So when AstraZeneca cut 7,600 R&D jobs worldwide in 2010, it triggered one of the biggest shake-ups in the industry's history. Jobs were cut because of management's plan to outsource drug manufacturing activities within ten years. Most of AstraZeneca's R&D work was offshored to pharma emerging markets, such as China. According to Smith:

> Manufacturing for AstraZeneca is not a core activity. AstraZeneca is about innovation and brand-building. . . . There are lots of people and organizations that can manufacture better than we can. . . . We are going to go through a model of outsourcing the back-end . . . we don't see manufacturing as core.

Later, the company planned to strip out and outsource more sophisticated manufacturing and supply-chain operations, and logistics activities. These transformations are especially radical because the pharmaceutical industry had been among the most conservative global industries in its attitude towards manufacturing and the supply chain.

IT Outsourcing Arrangements with Multiple Vendors

AstraZeneca depends on its IT capabilities as much as it depends on its R&D—both are crucial. Outsourcing also became a major IT strategy, which was achieved by creating outsourcing relationships with several vendors. Infosys (*infosys.com/*) manages AstraZeneca's manufacturing, supply chain, finance, and human resources applications. Cognizant (*cognizant.com/*) runs the centralized data storage. And IBM (*ibm.com/*) hosts the e-mail and office infrastructure. In 2007, AstraZeneca had signed a seven-year global outsourcing agreement with IBM. Under the deal, IBM provides a single global technical infrastructure for AstraZeneca covering 60 countries. The contract includes server hosting and storage for scientific, network and communications, commercial and supply chain operations. The former infrastructure was limited to major operations in the U.S., U.K., and Sweden. AstraZeneca retains control of its overall IT strategy and development and support of its application systems.

With these outsourcing relationships, AstraZeneca has a single infrastructure linking all functions, regions, and markets. Richard Williams, CIO of AstraZeneca, said the outsourcing deal enables the company to provide greater value to the business by providing a consistent infrastructure across all its global sites. The consistent infrastructure enables it to roll out new technologies, reporting systems, and apps more quickly and efficiently. Williams added: "In allowing IBM greater autonomy on methods of delivery, the agreement will result in cost efficiencies when compared with running in-house systems."

Sources: Compiled from Boyle (2010), Lomas (2007), and Pagnamenta (2007).

Questions

1. What will AstraZeneca look like in 2014 after its restructuring and outsourcing strategies have been completed? That is, which functions will be performed by the company and which ones won't be?

2. What new types of management skills will be necessary?

3. Do you think that this organizational model is the model of the future?

4. IT offshoring is a very controversial issue because it shifts jobs to other countries. At the same time, it has the potential to decrease the organization's costs significantly. Whether offshoring is good or bad for the people of affected countries is an issue of constant controversy. What are the benefits to AstraZeneca of using offshoring as part of its business and IT strategy?

RISK CONCERNS AND HIDDEN COSTS

As companies find their business strategy is increasingly tied to IT solutions, the concerns about outsourcing risks increase. Risks associated with outsourcing are:

- *Shirking:* The vendor deliberately underperforms while claiming full payment. For example, billing for more hours than were worked and/or providing excellent staff at first and later replacing them with less qualified ones.

- *Poaching:* The vendor develops a strategic application for a client and then uses it for other clients.

- *Opportunistic repricing:* When a client enters into a long-term contract with a vendor, the vendor changes financial terms at some point or over-charges for unanticipated enhancements and contract extensions.

Other risks are possible breach of contract by the vendor or its inability to deliver, vendor lock-in, loss of control over data, and loss of employee morale.

Depending on what is outsourced and to whom, an organization might end up spending 10 percent above the budgeted amount to set up the relationship and manage it over time. The budgeted amount may increase anywhere from 15 to 65 percent when outsourcing is sent offshore and the costs of travel and cultural differences are added in.

OFFSHORING

Offshoring of software development has become a common practice due to global markets, lower costs, and increased access to skilled labor. About one-third of Fortune 500 companies outsource software development to software companies in India.

It is not only the cost and the technical capabilities that matter. Several other factors to consider are the business and political climates in the selected country, the quality of the infrastructure, and risks such as IT competency, human capital, the economy, the legal environment, and cultural differences.

Duke University's *Center for International Business Education and Research* studied actual offshoring results. According to their study, Fortune 500 companies reduced costs by offshoring—63 percent of the companies achieved over 30 percent annual savings and 14 percent of them achieved savings over 50 percent. The respondents were overwhelmingly satisfied with their offshore operations. Three-quarters (72 percent) said their offshore implementations met or exceeded their expected cost savings. Almost one-third of the respondents (31 percent) achieved their service level goals within the first five months of their contracts while 75 percent did so within 12 months. The study concluded that "offshoring delivers faster results than average domestic improvement efforts." Even though these are very general results, offshoring success stories ease the fears about the risks of offshoring.

Based on case studies, the types of work that are not readily offshored include the following:

• Work that has not been routinized.

• Work that if offshored would result in the client company losing too much control over critical operations.

• Situations in which offshoring would place the client company at too great a risk to its data security, data privacy, or intellectual property and proprietary information.

• Business activities that rely on an uncommon combination of specific application-domain knowledge and IT knowledge in order to do the work properly.

IT at Work 12.5 gives an example of insourcing becomes preferable to outsourcing.

IT at Work 12.5

JP Morgan Chase Moves from Outsourcing to Insourcing

JP Morgan Chase is one of the world's largest financial institutions. In September 2004, Chase scrapped a seven-year, $5 billion IT outsourcing contract with IBM after its $58 billion acquisition of Bank One. The merger automatically voided the outsourcing contract. As a result, the company carefully evaluated its sourcing options over two to three months and decided to bring IT back in-house, a strategy known as **insourcing**. The acquisition created massive economies of scale, and such a large organization is able to attract and retain talented IT professionals. Furthermore, CIO Austin Adams achieved early career success by building on his ability to integrate bank mergers quickly and make the merged entity more competitive through its use of technology.

People who oppose offshoring declared the "end of outsourcing." As a matter of fact, Adams, who pushed for the scrapping, said that his move was greatly misunderstood by the media who pegged him as a patriot trying to keep IT jobs in the U.S. "I am clearly an advocate of offshoring." While in the case of such a large bank there was a reason for insourcing, mainly to get a better competitive advantage from IT, Adams believes that in smaller organizations, large-scale outsourcing is logical. Further, Adams

manages over 3,000 offshore employees in India, who work in the bank's call center and do basic operations and accounting functions. This offshoring is expected to grow rapidly.

Adams was key in the decision to insource IT at JP Morgan Chase and offers his observations:

• The cancellation was driven mainly by the merger with Bank One, which made the combined bank very large.

• Outsourcing of major parts of mission-critical technologies is not a best solution for a large firm. Technology development should be in-house; support services can be outsourced.

• Four criteria were used to determine what and how much to outsource: (1) the size of the company (should be large enough to attract good IS employees), (2) cost of outsourcing vs. cost of insourcing, (3) the interest level of top management to have and properly manage IT assets, and (4) financial arrangements of the outsourcing.

• It may be difficult to align business and technology objectives when large-scale outsourcing exists.

- The insourcing includes data centers, help desks, data processing networks, and systems development.
- Buying technology directly from vendors saved the bank a considerable amount of money (10 to 15 percent).

Sources: Compiled from Adams (2005) and Strassman (2005).

Questions

1. How can one determine when a company is large enough for insourcing?
2. How important is the financial consideration?
3. What other factors needs to be assessed in the decision?

OUTSOURCING LIFE-CYCLE

The International Association of Outsourcing Professionals (IAOP) has defined 9 critical stages in the outsourcing life cycle that managers need to understand prior to outsourcing (IAOP, 2009).

1. Strategy: Outsourcing is strategic decision that is typically developed at senior levels within a business. It may be part of a larger strategy to move the company to a leveraged business model and to focus on core competencies. Or it may be to save net costs or due to a lack of internal resources. Outsourcing may act as a key differentiator that will give your business a competitive advantage over your competitors. Too few businesses consider taking legal counsel at this stage, but they should. For example, difficulties about licensing, intellectual property rights or a pre-existing contractual or leasing arrangement require legal expertise.

2. Reassessment: This stage is not given enough consideration. But organizations should look again at their business processes, IT capabilities, internal supply, or other problems to see if they could be re-engineered to meet the requirements so that outsourcing is not needed.

3. Selection: This stage involves identifying and defining the work to be outsourced, as well as the selection of the vendors using RFI (request for information) or RFP (request for proposals) processes. The best value outsourcer is selected.

4. Negotiation: In this phase, contracts, schedules, and agreements are negotiated by someone experienced in these issues. Then the final contract is reviewed extensively before signing. This negotiation process must involve adequate resources and senior executives from both sides—the key issues in a long-term relationship, such as outsourcing, are too important not to justify executive engagement from supplier and customer.

5. Implementation: This phase involves the start-up activities of planning the transition and the implementation of the outsourced agreement, as well as establishing the detailed budget and administrative functions needed for its management, and formal launching of the program.

6. Oversight Management: This phase encompasses all ongoing activities required to manage the program, and achieve the contracted results. Specifically, this includes liaison between the customers and the supplier; performance monitoring; contract administration, vendor/partnership management; delivery integration; and vendor transition. Inevitably stresses will develop in a contract, and it is important for both sides to take an adult approach to contract interpretation. Remember that these are long-term relationships that need to flex with time.

7. Build Completion: This phase covers all completion activities of the build phase, including any development program and then acceptance and the introduction of new services.

8. Change: All complex outsourcing contracts will be subject to change and alteration. These are either run as minor changes to the outsourcing contract or major changes, which might involve a re-tendering process. Your contract will—or should—have built into it a contract change procedure to deal with changes that are in the broad scope of the original procurement.

9. Exit: All outsourcing relationships end either because the contract has expired, by mutual agreement, or failure of the outsourcing relationship. The terms of the contract become very important at this time.

1. What is sourcing?
2. What are the major reasons for sourcing?
3. Distinguish between mega outsourcing and the multi-vendor approach to outsourcing.
4. What are the benefits of outsourcing? What are the risks of outsourcing?
5. Discuss the strategies organizations should consider in managing the risks associated with outsourcing contracts.
6. Distinguish between outsourcing and offshore outsourcing.
7. What types of work are not readily outsourced offshore?
8. Describe a tool useful in measuring the business value of outsourcing relationships.

12.5 IT Vendor Relationships

The starting point in building a positive and strong vendor relationship is vendor selection. If a company makes a bad selection, most likely the vendor-provided system software, app, or implementation will fail, and the vendor won't be able to resolve the problems fast enough, if at all.

IT is complex and can be very confusing to those without technical expertise, so there is a high risk of miscommunications between businesses and IT vendors. These miscommunications are the main reason why relationships can turn sour between businesses and IT vendors. It's up to the IT managers keep vendor relationships healthy.

VENDOR SELECTION

To avoid any interpersonal or technical conflicts with IT vendors, businesses need to thoroughly research the vendor. It's very important to ask questions about the services and products the vendor will provide and get as many specifics as possible. Also take the time to verify the vendor's claims about its products and check all its references to make sure that the vendor has a proven track record of success.

When selecting a vendor, two criteria to assess first are experience and stability.

1. Experience with very similar systems of similar size, scope, and requirements. Experience with the ITs that are needed, integrating those ITs into the existing infrastructure, and the customer's industry.

2. Financial and qualified personnel stability. A vendor's reputation impacts its stability.

Of course, for innovative IT implementations, vendors won't have experience and one major failure—and the lawsuit that follows—can create instability. If those criteria are not met, there is no reason to further consider the vendor.

Research by McKinsey indicates that a majority of technology executives want to have stronger relationships with their IT suppliers, but they often act in ways that undermine that goal. In fact, many corporate customers lose out on the potential benefit of close relationships by an overemphasis on costs instead of value. Ideally, a customer/vendor relationship is a mutually-beneficial partnership, and both sides are best served by treating it as such.

Vendors often buy hardware or software from other vendors. In order to avoid problems with the primary IT vendor, check secondary suppliers as well. Ask the primary vendor how they will deliver on their promises if the secondary vendors go out of business or otherwise end their relationship.

Consider a Demo or Trial Run. Vendors may offer the option to test their products or services in a pilot study or a small portion of the business to verify that it fits the company's needs. If the vendor relationship adds value on a small scale, then the system can be rolled out on a larger scale. But if the vendor can't meet the requirements, then the company avoids a failure.

Contracts: Get Everything in Writing. Before entering into any service contract with an IT vendor, get a promise of service in writing. You want a document that spells out every aspect of their services with the company. The contract needs to be reviewed by the IT department to check for accuracy and to make sure the vendor can meet your technology needs; and by the legal department to make sure the company is protected. Businesses need to know what a vendor must do according to the terms of the service-level agreement (SLA), or contract, and to not expect the vendor to do anything more.

The contract should identify the terms clearly before it is signed. The SLA manages expectations so there is no mismatch between what the customer expects to receive and what the vendor is committed to provide. The contract is the only thing a company can count on when there is a problem so it must be understood and aligned with expectations.

Questions

1. Describe the importance of vendor selection.
2. When selecting a vendor, what two criteria need to be assessed? Explain both criteria.
3. What is the risk of an overemphasis on cost when selecting or dealing with an IT vendor?
4. What needs to be done before signing a contract with an IT vendor?

Key Terms

applications portfolio *363*
balanced scorecard *364*
big data management *357*
business processing outsourcing
  (BPO) *373*
business strategy *360*
cloud computing *357*
critical success factors (CSFs) *365*
customer-centric *357*
high-end analytics *357*
imitability *370*
in-house development *358*
insourcing *378*

IT alignment *361*
IT-business alignment *360*
IT governance *367*
ITES (information technology-
  enabled services) *374*
IT governance *367*
IT performance management *367*
IT strategic alignment *361*
IT strategic plan *358*
IT strategy *360*
mobility *370*
offshoring *357*
onshore sourcing *359*

outsource relationship management
  (ORM) company *359*
project portfolio *362*
resource allocation *366*
S3 *375*
scenario planning *366*
service *356, 357*
service-oriented architecture
  (SOA) *356, 357*
sourcing *359*
vertically integrated company *376*
vision statement *360*

You find clickable Link Libraries for each chapter on the Companion website.

FedRAMP   gsa.gov/portal/category/102375

Balanced Scorecard Institute   balancedscorecard.org/

International Association of Outsourcing Professionals' best outsourcing service providers, *The Global Outsourcing 100*   outsourcingprofessional.org/content/23/152/1197/

CIO Insights and Strategy   IBM.com/CIO/

Outsource Blog   theoutsourceblog.com/

Bloomberg Real-time Information Services   bloomberg.com/

Debate Over Offshore Outsourcing   quality-web-solutions.com/offshore-outsourcing-debate.php

IT Governance Institute   itgi.org/

Video interview on SaaS and Outsourcing Relationship Management   janeeva.com/blog/

Association for Computing Machinery (ACM); access their report on "Globalization and Offshoring of Software"   acm.org/globalizationreport

Government Technology, 5 Tips for Managing Successful Vendor Relationships   govtech.com/policy-management/5-Tips-for-Managing-Successful-Vendor-Relationships.html

Strategic Value of Health Information Exchange at UMass Memorial Health Care   *http://www.HealthDataManagement.com/web_seminars/-40414-1.html* **or** *http://bit.ly/UMassHIEWebinar*

Evaluate and Expand Your Learning

IT and Data Management Decisions (see Link Library for links in this section)

1. Vinay Gupta, President and CEO of Janeeva, which sells software to help companies manage outsourcing relationships, gave this advice:

   I would strongly encourage business owners to visit the vendor's facilities. There are a lot of fly-by-night operators, so you want to make sure you have touched and seen the facility before you hand them your business. And I would do at least a 30-day free pilot with the provider. You want to see if it is a good fit and find out who you will be interacting with on a day-to-day basis.

   Not all companies follow this advice.
   a. Discuss why companies would take these precautions when setting up an outsourcing relationship.
   b. Discuss why companies would not take these precautions when setting up an outsourcing relationship.

Questions for Discussion & Review

1. What might be some reasons why companies consider sourcing?
2. What are the benefits and disadvantages of outsourcing work/jobs to other companies within the country?

3. What are the benefits and disadvantages of offshoring work/jobs to other countries, e.g., to China or India? Compare your answers to your answers to questions 1 and 2 about outsourcing and offshoring.
4. What issues does IT governance cover?
5. Why is IT governance the responsibility of the BOD?
6. What does failure to properly align IT with the organizational strategy result in?
7. Why does IT–business alignment continue to be an important issue for CIOs?
8. What does successful IT–business alignment require?
9. Discuss how a CIO might interact with executive management as technology becomes increasingly central to a business.
10. Three characteristics of resources give firms the potential to create a competitive advantage. Discuss the potential of a firm's IT resources to add value to a company.
11. Discuss how the partnership between the IT division and business management can extend to fuse with the business.
12. Describe the IT strategic planning process.
13. What tools facilitate IT strategic planning?
14. Describe strategies for outsourcing.
15. Describe how a company might assess the business value delivered by an outsourcing relationship.

Online Activities

1. Visit *accenture.com* and search on "outsourcing." Describe the IT outsourcing services offered by Accenture. Do the same for two other large international accountancy and professional services firms, such as Deloitte at *deloitte.com*, Ernst & Young at *ey.com*, KPMG at *kpmg.com*, or PricewaterhouseCoopers at *pwc.com*. Create a table that compares the outsourcing services of the three firms.

2. Visit the Government Technology web site at *govtech.com*. Search for "tips for managing successful vendor relationships." Prepare a list of recommendations based on what you learn.

3. Visit the IBM CIO Interaction Channel at *http://www-935.ibm.com/services/ie/cio*. This site showcases insights and perspectives on the issues that matter most to CIOs, including the most important one of all—aligning IT with overall business goals. Select a topic that interests you, read a report on that topic, and summarize the main points of the report.

4. Visit Cognos at *cognos.com* and search on balanced scorecard software. Identify and describe their balanced scorecard software product.

5. Visit FireScope at *firescope.com*. Discuss how business service management software tools provide real-time dashboard views for tracking key performance indicators at the executive, functional business areas, services, and operations levels.

6. Visit the web site for the Association for Computing Machinery (ACM) and access their report on "Globalization and Offshoring of Software" at *acm.org/globalizationreport*. Select two of the case studies presented in Section 4.2 on pages 136–152. Write a report comparing and contrasting the two companies.

Collaborative Work

1. Innovative use of IT has become increasingly important in the global economy. Choose multiple industries and provide an example company for each industry in which IT plays a strategic role by adding value and providing a competitive advantage through innovative application of IT. Now identify competitive counterpart companies for which IT does not play a strategic role. Report on the successes/failures of each pair of companies.

2. Considerable discussions and disagreements occur among IT professionals regarding outsourcing. Divide the group into two parts. One will defend the strategy of large-scale outsourcing. One will oppose it. Start by collecting recent material at *google.com* and *cio.com*. Consider the issue of offshoring.

CASE 2 BUSINESS CASE

Puma Sources Its Billing Department

Collecting customer payments is one of the most important parts of a business. Switching from in-house billing, or accounts payable (A/P), to a third party is a tough decision that companies of all sizes may face. PUMA (*puma.com*), a global sports lifestyle company (Figure 12.6), had strong indicators from customers of problems with its billing department. Its customers range from major buyers like Footlocker to small retailers.

One frustrated customer sent a letter to the billing department saying he hated PUMA's paper invoices and to emphasize his dissatisfaction, he recommended that whoever designed their invoices be fired. However, PUMA's paper billing processes could not be easily or quickly fixed. Table 12.9 lists common customer invoicing problems—and the problems that PUMA faced because of its outdated paper-based invoicing method.

Figure 12.6 PUMA sells to customers worldwide.

© vario images GmbH & Co.KG/Alamy Limited

TABLE 12.9	Customer Invoicing Challenges

Billing is a complex process, and when it's not done correctly, the problems are:

- High cost per invoice (delivery + archiving)
- High invoice processing error rates
- Customer dissatisfaction
- Long delays in cash collections

Billing problems delay the receipt of payments from customers who wait for resolution of billing errors. Delays in collection have a negative impact on cash flow.

Billing Inefficiencies

PUMA has to wait for the U.S. Postal Service and other postal services to deliver its invoices and payments. It was taking a long time to get bills to the customers because PUMA sells its products all over the world, but was mailing invoices from its corporate headquarters in Massachusetts. And postal services kept raising rates.

Criteria for New Billing System

PUMA managers' priority was to meet customers' expectations of being easy to do business with. Their business plan included the following billing improvements:

- Stop aggravating corporate customers and start meeting their needs
- Move to electronic invoicing using e-mail
- Personalize the invoices
- Reduce billing costs by 25 percent

Sending invoices in paper format involved manual production and distribution processes that were having a direct negative impact on the company's cash flow and profitability. However, switching to electronic invoicing would not be easy because of the need to invest in new infrastructure, and because customers would have to approve the new format, the system had to be in compliance with local regulations, and employees would need to be trained in new procedures.

Sourcing Decision

Taking into consideration the business plan and requirements, PUMA decided to source its billing department. Billtrust was the sourcing provider PUMA selected. Billtrust had experience with corporate customers that acquired other companies—and was able to complete the complexities of integrating the billing systems within a few months. That's a big advantage of sourcing.

Within three months, billing processes for the company's two brands–PUMA and Tretorn–were up and running. Six months later PUMA acquired another athletic goods manufacturer, Cobra Golf, whose billing was also taken over by Billtrust.

In 2012, Cobra PUMA Golf has 10,000 active clients. Tretorn has 500 active clients, and PUMA has 2,500. Billtrust can send up to 5,000 invoices a day for PUMA with no issues.

PUMA employees in the finance department no longer spend their time making copies of invoices for customers who misplaced them because now customers can log into their personalized portal and review any errors in the invoice themselves. PUMA's employees make collection calls, which is a more valuable use of their time.

Sourcing Benefits

Billtrust mails PUMA's bills from eight facilities, depending on the recipient's zip or country code to speed up getting the bills to the customers. The quicker turnaround cut 10 days from days sales outstanding (DSO) in the first six months. Customers don't pay any faster, but it's easier for them to pay.

How the New Billing Process Works

As soon as a product leaves the warehouse, PUMA's system automatically electronically transmits the data to Billtrust. The service provider then sends an invoice to the customer in the form they prefer—fax, e-mail, or mail. About 70 percent of customer selected electronic invoices via e-mail.

Every customer logs into the PUMA payment portal. The portal has an online payment tool; customers can pay by credit card or ACH (automated clearing house). The ACH processing network allows customers to pay by online by debiting or credit of checking or savings accounts. Each invoice has its own URL and password. Customers see invoices that are open and account history for up to a year.

Outcomes

By sourcing to Billtrust, PUMA transformed its billing process into a highly efficient, advanced business function that reduced its billing costs and improved cash flow. PUMA's partnership with Billtrust is a contributing factor to the success of the sourcing arrangement. PUMA had prepared for the process transformation by setting clearly defined goals.

PUMA won the *2011 Huntington Bank Accounts Receivable Innovation Award* at Fusion 2011, the annual conference of the Institute of Financial Operations (IFO). PUMA was recognized for its "creative use of technology to produce more efficient results in its accounts receivable department."

Sources: Rosenthal (2012), *puma.com* (2012), and Pitney Bowes (*pb.com*).

Questions

1. Explain the importance of an efficient and effective billing system.
2. What are common customer invoicing problems?
3. What factors contributed to PUMA's inefficient billing and invoicing system?
4. Describe PUMA's sourcing benefits.
5. Describe how PUMA's new billing system works.
6. How does PUMA's new billing system overcome the limitations of its former system?
7. Why did PUMA source its billing process?
8. What impact did sourcing billing process have on the billing department?

CASE 3   WEBINAR CASE

Strategic Value of Health Info Exchange at UMass Memorial

Visit *http://www.HealthDataManagement.com/web_seminars/-40414-1.html* or the short URL *http://bit.ly/UMassHIEWebinar*. Register and watch the Webinar, which is available on demand.

UMass Memorial Health Care Hospital System

UMass Memorial Health Care (*umassmemorial.org/*) is an academic medical center and the largest health care hospital system in Central and Western Massachusetts. UMass Memorial is using the *health information exchange (HIE)* to facilitate patient-centered care. That is, it has aligned its IT with its business strategy to be responsive to the need to share information.

One of the critical components of the HIE is the ability to manage and answer questions about a patient's identity and discover what information is sharable for the patient, no matter where it is stored. Medical privacy legislation, such as the Health Information Portability and Accountability Act (HIPAA), mandates the ability to control access while at the same time to make information sharable for legitimate health care reasons.

All of this is well and good, but if patients, physicians, or anyone involved with the health care ecosystem, doesn't trust the system or have confidence that personal data is protected, it won't be used, and we won't realize any of the potential benefits of the HIE.

Security isn't just about protecting an individual's personal information from hackers and fraud, nor is it merely about complying with new regulations. Security is about ensuring the proper privacy of patients' data while improving the quality and accuracy of care.

This really means that not only should the right patient data be available to the right care giver or care system at the right time, but the system must reliably and continuously build trust for all parties involved.

Obstacles to Information Sharing

With seven hospitals and over 1100 beds, UMass Memorial has 13,500 employees and $1.4 billion in annual revenue, UMass Memorial faced many of the problems plaguing other industries. A lack of information sharing adversely impacted quality, costs, and efficiency—not to mention patient safety.

UMass Memorial turned to master data management (MDM) with a number of objectives, including:

- Knowing patients wherever they are seen in the system
- Enabling seamless interoperability with community health care providers
- Meeting Meaningful Use guidelines defined by the *American Reinvestment & Recovery Act* (ARRA, the Stimulus Bill)
- Facing competitive pressures from other health care systems

Information Sharing and Data Governance Improve Quality of Health Care

The HIE architecture had to enable information sharing across numerous legacy systems while also ensuring data privacy and security. With the right architectural approach and a shared vision, UMass Memorial is overcoming data governance challenges and being seen by others as an innovator.

By modernizing its IT infrastructure, UMass Memorial has improved quality and patient safety, increased efficiency, and enhanced patient satisfaction—all essential for success in today's competitive health care market. With its new patient-centric information architecture, UMass Memorial delivers a comprehensive view of a patient's entire clinical history to physicians and care providers across the health care community, irrespective of the care setting or clinical application being used.

Questions

1. What role does information play in the reputation of UMass Memorial?
2. In the case of health care, what are the consequences of not having data that can be trusted—or one version of the truth?
3. How has UMass Memorial aligned its IT and business strategies?
4. Compare the importance of MDM at UMass Memorial and at Kraft Foods Inc. discussed in Section 12.1. Why do disparate or legacy systems create the need for MDM?

Data Analysis & Decision Making

Third-Party vs. Company-Owned Offshoring

Major companies, such as Citigroup, had wholly-owned offshore service centers. Those types of company-owned offshore centers are called captive models. Captive offshoring models reduce the risk of offshoring. A recent study from the Everest Research Institute estimated the costs of third-party

offshoring and captive offshoring. The estimates are in the chart below.

Create a spreadsheet that totals the average cost of each model for each cost item. For example, average the annual salary based on the range for third parties and also the captives. Then calculate the total cost of ownership (TCO) of each model. The difference is the cost of risk.

Full-time equivalents (FTE) are used to standardize labor costs since workers may be part-time or full-time. For example, two part-time workers equal 1 FTE. The estimates are given in terms of FTE so the conversion is already done.

Based on your results, how much does the Captive Offshoring Model allow for risk? The answer is the difference between the TCOs of the two models.

	Third-Party Offshoring Model	Captive Offshoring Model
Office space: Annual Rental Cost per square foot (assume 10,000 square feet of office space)	$11 to $13	$14 to $16
Base Salary Costs of workers (assume 1,000 FTEs)	$7,770 to $8,200	$9,500 to $10,300
General management staff for every 1,000 FTEs	12 to 14	16 to 18
General Management Salary	$55,000 to $65,000	$70,000 to $90,000
Travel and housing costs per FTE	$280 to $320	$900 to $1,060

Resources on the Book's Web Site

You'll find additional chapter materials and useful web links. In addition, self-quizzes that provide individualized feedback are available for each chapter.

References

Adams, A. "Prominent 'Opponent' of Offshoring, Isn't." *CIO Insight*, March 5, 2005.

Aspray, W., Mayadas, F., and Vardi, M.Y. (eds.). *Globalization and Offshoring of Software*, Report of the ACM Job Migration Task Force. NY: ACM, 2006.

Biddick, M. "Hunting the Elusive CIO Dashboard" *InformationWeek*, March 3, 2008.

Boyle, C. "AstraZeneca to axe 8,000 jobs in global cull." *Times Online*, January 28, 2010.

Center for CIO Leadership. "The CIO Profession: Driving Innovation and Competitive Advantage," October 2007.

Chatterjee, A., Nair, R., & Tatke, R. "The Challenge for the New Bank CIO: How to Achieve Customer-Centricity by Making Better Use of Six Emerging Technologies." *Booz&Co. Report,* March 19, 2012.

Ehrlich, L., and West, M. "The Strategic CIO: Using Leadership Skills and IT to Create Competitive Advantage." *CIO.com*, May 1, 2007.

Farrell, D. "Smarter Offshoring." *Harvard Business Review,* June 2006.

Genpact White Paper. "Six Keys to a Successful BPO Transition," 2010.

Giridhar, S., Notestein, D., & Wagle, L. "From complexity to client centricity." *IBM Global Services*, March 2011.

Hoffman, T., and Stedman, C. "Forget IT-Business Alignment—It's All about Fusion Now, CIOs Say." *Computerworld,* March 12, 2008.

IAOP. "The Outsourcing Life-cycle—9 Stages," 2009. *outsourcingprofesional.org/*.

IBM. "The Outsourcing Decision for a Globally Integrated Enterprise: From Commodity Outsourcing to Value Creation," January 2008.

Kaplan, R.S., and Norton, D. P. "Mastering the Management System." *Harvard Business Review.* 86, no. 1 January 2008.

Kaplan, R.S., and Norton, D. P. "Using the Balanced Scorecard as a Strategic Management System." *Harvard Business Review.* 85, nos. 7, 8 July/August 2007.

Kesner, R.M. "IT Service Delivery: Models and Frameworks." *Enterprise Operations Management*, 42, 2003. Lardi-Nadarajan, K. "Doing Business in Virtual Worlds" *CIO Insight*, March 3, 2008.

Lomas, N. "AstraZeneca signs IBM outsourcing deal." *ZDNet UK,* July 18, 2007.

Luftman, J. "SIM 2007 Survey Findings SIM 2007 Survey Findings." *SIMposium 07*, October 7–12, 2007, *simposium.simnet.org*.

Manter, T., "Smarter Sourcing: Measuring and Communicating the Success of Sourcing Relationships," *CXO Media Inc.*, 2007.

McGee, M.K. "Kimberly–Clark—Virtual Product Center Yields Real Ideas." *InformationWeek*, September 17, 2007.

Ohrstrom, L. "American Apparel Opens Virtual Lower East Side Store." *The New York Observer*, January 10, 2008.

OutsourcingPapers.com, 2010

Pagnamenta, R, "AstraZeneca to Outsource Manufacturing." *Times Online*, September 17, 2007.

Prahalad, C.K., and Krishnan, M.S. "The Dynamic Synchronization of Strategy and Information Technology." *Sloan Management Review,* 43, no. 4. Summer 2002.

Rosenthal, B.E. "Changes in BPO: How Technology Is Changing the Landscape." *Outsourcing Center,* January 2010.

Rosenthal, B.E. "Transforming an Antiquated Billing Process in Three Easy Steps." *Outsourcing Center,* May 15, 2012.

Shpilberg, D., Berez, S., Puryear, R., and Shah, S. "Avoiding the Alignment Trap in Information Technology." *MIT Sloan Management Review* 49, no. 1, Fall 2007.

Strassman, P.A. "Why JP Morgan Chase Really Dropped IBM," *Baseline*, January 13, 2005.

Wailgum, T. "How to Stay Close to the Business," *CIO.com*, January 10, 2008.

Weiss, J. W., Thorogood, A., and Clark, K.D. "Three IT–Business Alignment Profiles: Technical Resource, Business Enabler, and Strategic Weapon." *Communications of the Association for Information Systems* 18, 2006.

Worthen, B., "Business Technology: The IT Factor: Tech Staff's Bigger Role; Increased Input Helps Products Debut Faster, Deals Become Successful," *Wall Street Journal*, December 4, 2007.

Chapter 17

Business Process and Project Management

Learning Outcomes

❶ Describe the structured business process management (BPM) approach, policies, metrics, and software tools to optimize an organization's activities and processes.

❷ Explain the importance of software architecture design to the maintenance and agility of business processes.

❸ Describe IT project identification, justification, and planning; and understand the triple constraints.

❹ Describe the systems development lifecycle (SDLC) and its impact on the acceptance and success of IT implementations.

Being agile—able to change based on market opportunity, economic climate, or competition—comes down to business processes. That is, how fast a company can innovate and redesign its business processes to respond to opportunities or threats. To redesign processes successfully, companies need a sound business process management (BPM) strategy and the right set of tools. BPM is also called continuous process innovation. You read examples of the benefits of agility in each chapter. Managing and redesigning processes are typically very complex and, as a result, risky, which you read about in this chapter. Examples are:

- Accounting: Invoicing, billing, and reconciling accounts
- Finance: Estimating credit risk and terms
- Human resources (HR): Assessing whether business practices are in compliance with laws, regulations, and standards
- Marketing: Designing and implementing sales campaigns

- Management information systems (MIS): Managing big data, cloud services, and BYOD (bring your own device) practices
- Production and operations: Shipping, receiving, and inventory management

BPM is not a point solution to solve problems with one process, but an infrastructure approach to solve multiple process problems. Major consulting and tech firms offer BPM expertise, services, software suites, and tools. For example, Oracle's WebLogic Server Process Edition includes server software and process integration tools for automating complex business processes, like handling an insurance claim.

When new systems are needed, their success depends on IT project management and a coherent systems development process. Project management is a disciplined approach to developing systems and apps to insure that they are completed on time, within budget, and according to specifications.

CASE 1 OPENING CASE

AutoTrader.com's *Order Process Goes from Fragile to Flexible*

BPM, or **business process management,** means looking at what you do and how you do it, and coming up with more efficient processes, usually using automation.

BPM software is used to map processes performed either by computers or manually—and to design new ones. The software includes built-in templates showing workflows and rules for various functions, such as rules for credit approval. These templates and rules provide consistency and high-quality outcomes.

AutoTrader.com is the leading online auto classifieds marketplace listing over 3 million vehicles. The company acts as an intermediary linking buyers and sellers of new and used cars, as shown in Figure 13.1. AutoTrader.com attracts 15 million buyers each month, has over 20,000 customers, and employs more than 2,000 people. Revenues climbed from $626 million in 2009 to $720 million in 2010 and $1.03 billion in 2011.

Autotrader.com topped the ranking of local online ad revenue leaders in 2011, taking in over $1 billion in sales revenues on the strength of a rebounding U.S. auto market. The site edged out the giant AT&T *Yellowpages.com*, with nearly $1 billion in revenue, and newcomer Groupon, at $650 million.

Figure 13.1 *Autotrader.com* Car Search Site.

	Fax	Data Entry	Fulfillment	Quality Assurance	Total Avg
New	2.8 days	.5 day	4 days	1 day	8.3 days
Up-sell	2.8 days	.5 day	2 days	1 day	6.3 days

Contract Signed → ... → Contract Delivered

Figure 13.2 AutoTrader's legacy order fulfillment process had an average cycle time of up to 8.3 days.

Legacy Order Fulfillment Process

AutoTrader processes thousands of orders and contracts each month. Its legacy order fulfillment process was run on *My AutoTrader (MAT),* a system based on Lotus Notes/Domino. MAT took an average of 6.3 to 8.3 days to fulfill orders and process contracts, as Figure 13.2 shows. The order fulfillment process consisted of 100+ coordinated steps had disconnects or hand-offs causing long and error-prone **cycle times**—that is, the process from end-to-end took too long to complete. MAT was a bottleneck that slowed revenue generation and aggravated customers.

Speeding Up the Order Fulfillment Process with BPM

Given its rapid growth in operations, management set goals for the company to be agile, to generate revenues faster, and to increase customer satisfaction. They invested in a BPM solution—selecting webMethods from Software AG (*softwareag.com/*). The BPM software supports the analysis of the current system to learn and document how tasks are performed and then support the design or redesign of the process to simplify and automate; then implementation and execution of the new process, which is then refined to optimize the cross-functional business process.

Using the webMethods BPM Suite (BPMS), *AutoTrader.com* now has an electronic sales order system that compresses the order fulfillment process into about one day, as shown in Figure 13.3.

Impacts of the Enterprise BPM

Creating electronic sales orders is part of a multiyear effort to transform the way sales processes and customer support processes operate. Rob Andrzejewski, AutoTrader's BPM manager, said: "Once an order is entered, we pick it up in BPM, and we handle all the fulfillment orchestration. Right now, it's about 100 orchestrated steps. There are only six human tasks in the process." The process interacts with over 20 different data sources and systems, including the inventory system, the billing system contract fulfillment database, and the CRM platform. The workflow component of webMethods BPMS manages the interaction. The solution is more flexible, more robust, and less prone to errors. Managers are notified instantly when problems arise so that they can correct problems as they occur—rather than find out a day or two later that a contract is stuck in fulfillment.

With BPMS, tasks are assigned immediately to the right people, who are alerted when work is added to their queues. Less than 5 percent of orders need to go back to sales for clarification—a 400 percent improvement. Managers check order fulfillment status anytime using webMethods Optimize for Process, which provides real-time visibility into performance. They can measure key performance indicators (KPIs) in real-time to see where to make improvements.

Figure 13.3 AutoTrader's aim is to process and fill orders within one day.

Submit sales order electronically → Day 1: Live online processing of → Day 2: Order fulfillment

1 day elapsed

TABLE 13.1	Benefits of AutoTrader's electronic sales order system and BPMS

- 70 percent faster order fulfillment
- 100 process steps orchestrated across staff and 20 systems
- 94 percent of process steps now automated
- 400 percent reduction in orders that need clarification
- More satisfied dealers, which represent the largest share of its sales revenue
- Increased productivity—the right people focus on the right tasks
- Proactive alerts enable staff to address issues immediately
- Simpler integration and easier changes after mergers and acquisitions
- Optimized personnel, hardware and software costs

Sources: Compiled from Walsh (2012), SAG (2011), Alesci & Saitto (2012).

Dealers can make changes directly to their contracts, which cut costs for personnel. Software and hardware costs are decreasing as the company retires old systems. Benefits of AutoTrader's electronic sales order system and BPMS are summarized in Table 13.1.

Discuss

1. Rob Andrzejewski commented that by adopting BPM, AutoTrader has *transformed from fragile to flexible*. Discuss what he meant by that statement.
2. Explain AutoTrader's manual order process and its inefficiencies.
3. Discuss how the electronic automated order process supports the company's business strategy.
4. How does the reduced cycle time of the order fulfillment process improve revenue generation and customer satisfaction?

Decide

5. Does reducing the cycle time of a business process also reduce errors? Why or why not? Explain your answer using a few examples.

Debate

6. Consider these two forces:
   a. Many times, companies are driven to transform and improve the way they do business because of customer dissatisfaction and complaints. If companies do not improve their processes, they risk losing customers to competitors and lower sales revenues.
   b. BPM efforts typically involve simplifying processes and then automating them to the extent possible. This transformation reduces the need for human labor and may cost some workers their jobs. Therefore, BPM efforts may be resisted by employees.

   How would you justify BPM investments taking into consideration (a) and (b)?

13.1 Business Process Management (BPM)

BPM, or continuous process innovation as it is also known, is a widely used approach for the design or redesign of enterprise systems. The approach requires every functional area in the company to participate in evaluating and explaining their workflows and how they do things. The existing process needs to be

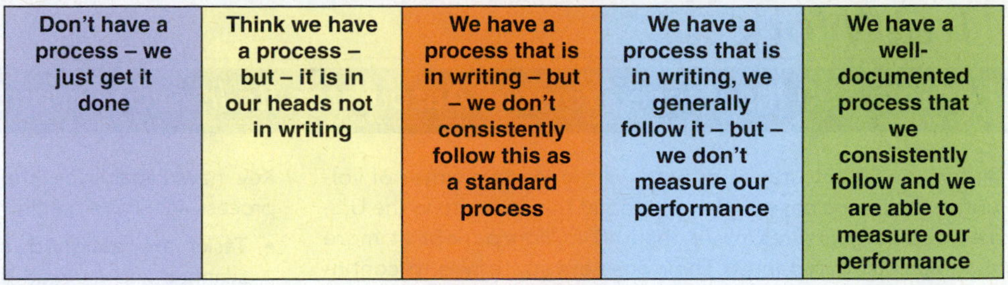

Figure 13.4 *Got process?*
When functional areas are asked to evaluate their processes, their answers range from none to well-documented.

Don't have a process – we just get it done	Think we have a process – but – it is in our heads not in writing	We have a process that is in writing – but – we don't consistently follow this as a standard process	We have a process that is in writing, we generally follow it – but – we don't measure our performance	We have a well-documented process that we consistently follow and we are able to measure our performance

understood to identify gaps, redundancies, bottlenecks, problem areas, challenges, and so on. Before any process can be improved, the desired outcomes need to be clarified as well as the tasks involved in the process. Interestingly, when people in functional areas are asked to evaluate their process, the reactions range from "we don't have a process" to "we have a well-documented process," as shown in Figure 13.4.

Successful process improvement initiatives start with business value. Organizations must understand the business goals and strategy and analyze their current processes to identify the processes that deliver the highest return on investment (ROI).

Enterprise BPM cannot be done effectively without specialized software and vendor support. Appian, IBM, and Oracle each offer BPM solutions and support services.

BPM HELPS ALIGN BUSINESS AND IT

The BPM approach helps to achieve business-IT alignment and improve performance. Here are several examples.

- **Mark's Work Wearhouse.** The mix of manual and automated processes was hard to manage at clothing retailer Mark's Work Wearhouse. The company invested in IBM's WebSphere Business Modeler to help it streamline its inventory management processes. "BPM really came into play because we had some manual-based processes but they weren't integrated. We didn't have a good holistic view of how they all tied together," said Rhett Waley, solution architect at Mark's. "BPM forced us to really analyze our existing processes and look where the bottlenecks were and figure out how we could improve them and generate an automated solution."

- **PDG S.A.,** Brazil's largest construction and real estate company, uses BPM tools to streamline its financing approvals. The redesigned process cuts approval process time from more than a week to a few hours.

- **Horizon BlueCross BlueShield of** (Horizon BCBSNJ) is New Jersey's oldest healthcare insurer, serving more than 3.6 million members with medical, dental, and prescription insurance. The business was established during the manual, paper-intensive era, and virtually all critical processes had remained manual until 2007, when the company launched a business process improvement initiative. To achieve process improvement, Horizon BCBSNJ needed to become more efficient in business process management (BPM) or continued process innovation. As a result of continuous process improvement standard claims are processed 20 to 30 minutes faster, which frees up claims processors to focus on more complex claims. The ROI is estimated at 300 percent for each internal process improvement project.

IT at Work 13.1 describes similar challenges and benefits from BPM at a Fortune 500 company.

IT at Work 13.1

Fortune 500 Insurance Provider Automates Its Invoice Dispute Process

A Fortune 500 insurance provider is the leading writer of voluntary insurance coverage marketed at the work site in the U.S. The company insures more than 40 million people at more than 300,000 companies. Their business strategy is to continually design new policies to help fill the gaps in the existing primary insurance coverage of U.S. consumers and to grow the network of sales associates and coordinators distributing and servicing their policies. Given their huge customer base, product portfolio, and distribution network, the company has numerous different processes to manage, monitor, and improve.

Key Process: Invoice Reconciliation

Invoice reconciliation is an important process for the provider. Each month invoices are sent to corporations billing them for the coverage stipulated by their policy. In any given month, approximately 500,000 invoices are sent out to customers. On average, 30 percent of the invoices, or 150,000 invoices, are disputed in some way each month. The challenge for the Invoice Reconciliation team is to resolve as many of these disputes as possible before the next billing cycle—typically less than 30 days. If not, the customer will dispute the bill the next month—wasting time and frustrating customers.

Key challenges faced by the Invoice Reconciliation team and Research Specialists trying to resolve invoice disputes were:

- **Time-intensive manual routing.** Invoices are mailed back to the insurance provider with notes and questions attached to them. Each dispute had to be reviewed and manually routed to a Research Specialist, which was not always known.
- **Research inefficiencies.** Research specialists collect data from various legacy systems to determine whether or not the dispute is justified; and if it is, the reasons why.
- **No priorities.** With so many requests for reconciliation coming in through e-mail, it was difficult for specialists to prioritize work.
- **No real-time monitoring of the dispute resolution.** The Invoice Reconciliation team wanted the ability to more proactively prioritize work and automatically track deadlines and generate escalations.

Controlling Processes in Real Time

The insurance company selected WebSphere Lombardi Teamworks to gain control over the reconciliation process in 2010. Working collaboratively with IT experts, the team implemented a process that automates routing of disputes, streamlines research timelines, and gives managers real-time control of all disputes being processed.

Key new capabilities after redesigning the dispute resolution process and implementing the BPM solution are:

- **Tasks are assigned automatically.** Disputed invoices are scanned and indexed by an electronic document system and then automatically routed to the appropriate Reconciliation team based on location and company assignments.
- **Disputes are prioritized based on time and value.** Reconciliation tasks are automatically prioritized for specialists according to invoice age and dispute amount. This ensures that the highest-priority invoices are worked on first.
- **Alerts are sent.** Specialists are alerted when a dispute has aged 20 days without resolution. This ensures that disputes do not slip through the cracks.
- **Approval controls can be set.** Reconciliation managers can set the threshold amount at which disputes can be automatically accepted—saving time spent by specialists researching small amount disputes.
- **Real-time performance metrics.** Managers can view real-time process performance reports in the ScoreBoard portal. Metrics include percentage of disputed invoices pending, total outstanding policy items by geography and customer, variance in dollar amount between the original invoice and the resolution, and age and status of every invoice in the system.

Current and Continuous Improvements

The insurance provider deployed the first version of the Invoice Reconciliation process in 90 days. It is projected that the new process of handling electronic records and automation is reducing the amount of workers' time by 80 percent. When rolled out to all 300 users across the Client Services group, the ROI will be significant—even for the single process. The Client Services team is working the next revisions of the process that will help them automate even more of their work. Soon, enterprise BPM will be achieved and deliver ever greater benefits.

Sources: IBM.com (2010) and WebSphere Lombardi Edition (2012).

Questions

1. The company had an invoice dispute rate of 30 percent. How did this problem suggest the need for BPM?
2. Explain how the Fortune 500 insurance company reduced manual work by 80 percent.
3. The first process improvement—dispute resolution—was extremely successful. BPM will be rolled out across the enterprise. How important is the success of the first BPM implementation? Explain your answer.

CHARACTERISTICS OF A PROCESS

A process has inputs and outputs that are *measurable*, and therefore can be managed. Most processes cut across functional areas. For example, the product development process cuts across marketing, R&D, production, and finance (product development needs to be financed). Business processes are becoming more and more complex—composed of interactions across systems and dependent on collaborative

Figure 13.5 Processes that are not optimized are bottlenecks that usually require human intervention to resolve.

© James Steidl/Superfusion/SuperStock

activities between business users and IT. Complex processes often need to be broken into a number of subprocesses for easier management. When processes are designed for maximum efficiency and have no bottlenecks, they are said to be *optimized*. Bottlenecks require human intervention or hand-offs, as depicted in Figure 13.5, which causes delay.

BUSINESS PROCESS LIFECYCLE

As discussed in the cases, business processes integrate ISs and people. Purchase order processing, staff recruitment, patient billing, order fulfillment, and everything else an organization does consist of processes that are performed by employees using ISs. Management of business processes boils down to the management of their lifecycles, as shown in Figure 13.6. Business processes are introduced, modified to the extent possible, and get replaced—the standard format of a *lifecycle*. Changes may require only streamlining tasks or rules of a process, such as changing the sales commission percent. Cross-functional processes need to be reengineered, as you read in the opening case.

Design Stage. The cycle starts with process design. Process design is typically mapped and documented using a modeling tool, such as IBM BPM Blueprint or Microsoft Visio. This model plays a key role and, once finalized, serves as documentation of the entire process.

During the design stage, the team of business analysts and technology experts brainstorm possible solutions to current problem areas or opportunities. The design and functional specifications (specs) are completed at this phase. The *design spec*, also called the *technical spec*, identifies how the business process will be implemented in as much detail as possible. This spec identifies which systems are involved in the process, how they integrate, and the technical details of the implementation. Functional and technical specs can be hundreds of page long, which explains why specialized modeling tools are essential. The deliverables from the design stage are not all technical. The design spec also identifies how process users interact and complete tasks.

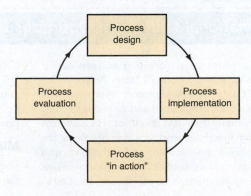

Figure 13.6 Business process life cycle.

Implementation Stage. The business process agreed to in the design stage is delivered. Implementation includes integrating the process with other processes that share inputs or outputs, testing, and verifying that the process works correctly and reliably. Problems may require going back to the process design stage.

Not only is the development of the process important, the testing is equally as critical. Three types of tests are:

1. **User acceptance:** Tests whether the process is designed well from the users' perspective.

2. **Functional acceptance:** Process analysts test whether the process performs its functions.

3. **System acceptance:** Technical experts attest that the process is integrated correctly with inputs and outputs of other processes and data sources and data stores.

After tests and refinements are completed, the process is ready to *go live*.

Process "In Action" and Evaluation Stages. There is enough overlap of these stages to treat them together, at this level of analysis. The process is in production performing its functions. As new processes are added or processes are redesigned or removed, an ongoing process may become problematic. During this stage the process is monitored. Many software vendors that are used to implement business processes, such as Oracle, Microsoft, Cordys, and IBM, include **business activity monitoring (BAM)** functionality. For example, Oracle BAM is an integral part of the BPM suite (*oracle.com/appserver/business-activity-monitoring.html*). It is a message-based, event-driven platform that allows business users to link key performance indicators (KPIs) associated with the process being monitored on a real-time basis, and provides relevant information via dashboards.

Making Processes Predictable. Automation is an important part of BPM because it makes a process predictable, and therefore manageable. The workflow is laid out, step by step, and can be monitored. Manual workflows, on the other hand, are at the mercy of the humans performing them; if someone misses or alters a step, things may go wrong and few will know why.

Businesses of all sizes can profit from BPM techniques, and from some of the technologies developed to help with the process. Vendors who began by addressing big businesses' needs are now offering products sized—and priced—for small- and medium-sized businesses.

In the short term, BPM helps companies improve profitability by reducing waste and costs; and in the long run, BPM helps keep companies responsive to business changes. *IT at Work 13.2* discusses business process optimization at Microsoft International.

IT at Work 13.2

Microsoft International's HR Team Optimizes Business Processes

Microsoft International provides sales, marketing, and services for Microsoft Corporation's locations outside of North America. The Human Resources (HR) team within Microsoft International is made up of approximately 600 employees and provides support for HR management in more than 100 countries. HR performs many legal and staffing functions, and key among them are recruiting, training, employee development, and compliance with regulations, health and safety laws, such as U.K. Employment Law and U.K. Health and Safety Regulations (*direct.gov.uk/*) and OSHA

(Occupational Safety and Health Administration, *osha.gov/*) in the U.S. HR functions also include managing employee benefits and compensation, employee records, and personnel policies. Policies are often in the form of employee manuals, which are posted on the companies' intranets.

Microsoft's HR Business Processes

The HR team uses many global systems and tools across each of the international Microsoft subsidiaries. One key HR objective was to standardize common business processes of all subsidiaries across all Microsoft locations. As each subsidiary developed its own unique business processes, such as training new hires, there was no standardized way to compare, manage, or evaluate the efficiency or effectiveness of the business processes. (As you have read, *you can't manage what you can't measure*.) HR believed that the costs and time required to perform their common activities and train new employees were much higher than they needed to be. Jean O'Connor, HR Project Manager for Microsoft International, explained that:

> Experience with different HR business processes would vary significantly from one location to the next. Without documentation, each new HR employee will need to be trained by someone who may or may not know the process. Teaching new hires an inefficient process can introduce repeatable errors, and decreases our overall effectiveness.

HR Inefficiencies

The lack of standardized business processes and process documentation had a number of adverse impacts on the HR team:

- Increased the time and cost to train new employees as there was no simple way to describe critical HR processes.

- Limited ability to review their business processes and make informed decisions regarding the sequencing of steps and roles and responsibilities involved.

- Decreased business process efficiency, with wide ranges in time to complete tasks across subsidiaries.

Increasing HR Processes Efficiency

The team wanted to find ways to improve process efficiency and effectiveness across subsidiaries. To start, the HR team needed to understand current business processes at each subsidiary and be able to discuss them, which they achieved by diagramming them using Visio modeling software (*visiotoolbox.com/2010/home.aspx*). An example of a diagram of a business process is shown in Figure 13.7. (Visit the Microsoft Visio 2010 web site at *visiotoolbox.com/2010/home.aspx* for more examples of business process modeling.)

After the workflows and information processing involved in a business process are accurately mapped out using standard notation, that process is ready to be analyzed to identify how to improve it. Equally important, these maps (or models) provide the starting point for standardizing the language used to describe their tasks.

Benefits of Business Process Modeling

The HR team used Microsoft Visio Premium 2010—a business process modeling tool—to design templates (also called models) that define and describe the steps in each process. The templates help HR staff understand Microsoft's standardized processes and are used in staff training. Benefits that the HR teams achieved are:

- **Significant savings in labor hours through increased process efficiency.** The models significantly reduced the time required to execute HR processes in all subsidiaries. According to O'Connor, "The key benefit for the HR organization is increased productivity through the creation of standardized process documentation across all of our sales, marketing, and services processes." The increased standardization helps clarify roles and responsibilities across HR employees, and reduces time HR teams spend on administrative tasks. As a result, "the right people are doing the right work at the right time across our business processes," said O'Connor.

- **Decrease in the training time of newly hired employees.** As HR processes are standardized from one subsidiary to the next,

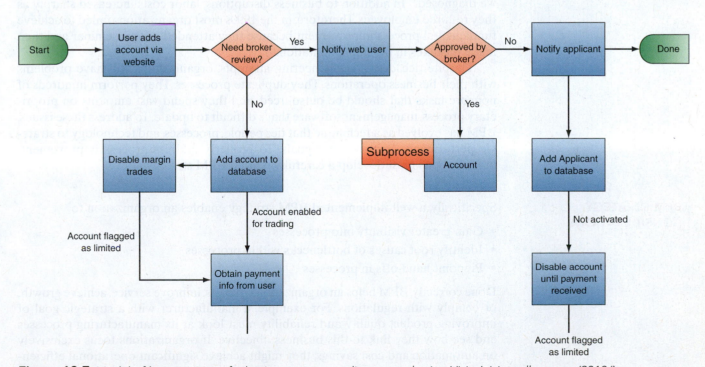

Figure 13.7 Model of key activities of a business process—diagrammed using Visio (*visiotoolbox.com/2010/*)

it's easier for an HR member from one country to move to another because roles, responsibilities, and process steps are similar in all locations. This further reduces the time and cost associated with training.

- **Improved decision making through visual process analysis.** Visual displays make it easier to understand and communicate about processes than using text.

Sources: Compiled from *Microsoft.com* (2010), Visio 2010, and *visimation.com/*.

Questions

1. Why did Microsoft International have inefficient HR business processes—until this HR initiative was completed in 2010?

2. Does it seem strange that a mega-multinational computer software and services company had not been able to "ensure that the right people are doing the right work at the right time across our business processes" until 2010?

3. What may have motivated or pressured Microsoft International to standardize its HR processes?

Business Process Reengineering (BPR). The BPM approach has its roots in **business process reengineering (BPR).** BPR is the radical redesign of an organization's business processes. BPR first attempts to *eliminate* processes that no longer have any purpose, often because of new mobile apps, web services, or other IT. The processes that remain are redesigned and automated to the extent possible.

BPR quickly became a management fad—similar to just-in-time (JIT) inventory management. BPR and JIT were both based on assumptions. And if those assumptions were not met, then they failed to achieve the great expected results. That is, BPR was not understood well enough and was applied incorrectly with terrible results. Many JIT implementations increased inventory costs because it was based on the assumption that warehousing costs were extremely high, as they were in Japan where JIT was initiated by Toyota. Why? Because JIT increases transportation and ordering costs. The increase in the costs must be offset by an even larger drop in warehousing costs. If not, JIT is more expensive. With BPR, first companies had to analyze and understand the inefficiencies in their business processes. Then they had to figure out how to drive out waste and streamline processes and design them to minimize the risk of errors that led to re-work. Then, and only then, should remaining processes be designed and automated. Many companies skipped the beginning steps and jumped to downsizing—firing employees. A manager at one of the major telecoms, in a discussion with one of the authors, lamented that "we amputated before we diagnosed." In addition to business disruptions, labor costs increased sharply as they re-hired employees. Therefore, in the 1990s most organizations failed to achieve fundamental process improvement because they attended a BPR seminar and then made mistakes in the implementation.

Despite decades of reengineering attempts, organizations still have problems with their business operations. They duplicate processes. They perform hundreds of noncore tasks that should be outsourced, and they spend vast amounts on proprietary process-management software that's difficult to update. To address these issues, BPM has evolved as a technique that ties people, processes, and technology to strategic performance improvement goals. To properly address process improvement, organizations must develop a carefully crafted BPM strategy.

BPM STRATEGY CONSIDERATIONS

Specifically, a well-implemented BPM strategy enables an organization to

- Gain greater visibility into processes
- Identify root causes of bottlenecks within processes
- Pinpoint hand-offs in processes

Done correctly, BPM helps an organization cut costs, improve service, achieve growth, or comply with regulations. For example, a manufacturer with a strategic goal of improving product quality and reliability must look at its manufacturing processes and see how they link to this business objective. If organizations focus exclusively on automation and cost savings, they might achieve significant operational efficiencies but lose their competitive edge and fall short of their performance targets, as

TABLE 13.2	SOA Defined

SOA is an architectural style for building software applications that use services available in a network such as the web. It promotes loose coupling between software components so that they can be reused. Applications in SOA are built based on services. A service is an implementation of well-defined business functionality, and such services can then be used by clients in different applications or business processes.

SOA allows for the reuse of existing assets where new services can be created from an existing IT infrastructure of systems. In other words, it enables businesses to leverage existing investments by allowing them to reuse existing applications, and promises interoperability between heterogeneous applications and technologies. SOA provides a level of flexibility that wasn't possible before in the sense that:

- Services are software components with well-defined interfaces that are implementation-independent. An important aspect of SOA is the separation of the service interface (the what) from its implementation (the how). Such services are consumed by clients that are not concerned with how these services will execute their requests.
- Services are self-contained (perform predetermined tasks) and loosely coupled (for independence).
- Services can be dynamically discovered.
- Composite services can be built from aggregates of other services.

Sources: See *java.sun.com/developer/technicalArticles/WebServices/soa/*.

British Telecom (BT) and UAL did when they failed to link strategic goals with their BPM initiatives.

Once the assessment is complete, it is necessary to develop a process performance plan that documents the ways in which the identified operational processes contribute to strategic goals. If a strategic goal is customer satisfaction, for example, appropriate process benchmarks should be established to accurately and consistently analyze progress of your BPM initiative. In improving an order-to-fulfillment process, although order throughput and on-time delivery are important, other measures might have a direct impact on customer satisfaction, such as fulfillment accuracy.

Finally, processes must be prioritized with highest priority being given to those processes that are determined to have the greatest potential impact on strategic objectives.

SERVICE-ORIENTED ARCHITECTURE

Service-oriented architecture (SOA) was introduced in Chapter 12 and is discussed in this section because SOA and BPM are both valuable approaches to improve business performance. SOA is a confusing concept, even for practitioners. SOA is mistakenly described like BPM. *Services* are like reusable software programs, or modules. You might even compare it to a macro in Excel. You can use and reuse the macro instead of writing code to perform common functions.

Oracle offers a technical explanation of SOA, which you find in Table 13.2. *IT at Work 13.2* shows the value of SOA.

IT at Work 13.3

Financial Industry Regulatory Authority (FINRA) SOA Project

The Financial Industry Regulatory Authority (FINRA; *finra.org/*) is the largest independent regulator for all securities firms doing business in the U.S. FINRA oversees nearly 4,700 brokerage firms, about 167,000 branch offices, and approximately 635,000 registered securities representatives. FINRA was created in July 2007 through the consolidation of NASD (National Association of Securities Dealers) and the regulatory and enforcement functions of the New York Stock Exchange (NYSE). FINRA protects investors and market integrity through effective and efficient regulation and complementary compliance and technology-based services (*finra.org/AboutFINRA/*).

FINRA SOA Project

The FINRA SOA project consolidated the NYSE Member Regulation systems with the NASD Member Regulation information systems. The primary challenges were:

- Consolidation of the two organizations' application portfolios that support the member regulation business. Each application portfolio was sizable and heterogeneous. At the onset FINRA had 160 applications and NYSE Member Regulation had 86 applications.
- Reconciliation of two sets of legacy business processes into a final-state business process.
- Final-state business processes must seamlessly integrate new systems and existing systems from both legacy organizations. The existing systems required enhancements.
- Business teams were distributed across the U.S. in district office locations. The development team was located in New York City and the Washington D.C. area.

The three key objectives were:

1. The final-state business processes of the merged company required seamless operation.
2. The team needed to ensure a continuity of business operations while transitioning in phases to the new final-state business processes.
3. Performance and reliability of the systems were key requirement in maintaining core mission success.

SOA selection criteria were:

- The size and complexity of the project required multiple teams in different locations working effectively in parallel to meet the aggressive schedule.
- A SOA approach reduced risks presented by the large team size.
- The end-state systems had to be flexible so changes in business process can be made without breaking the architecture.
- It was anticipated that the approach would deliver significant savings in both cost and time when compared to competing approaches.

ROI of the SOA approach

The Member Regulation function of FINRA benefited greatly from the new system. Broker regulation tasks were simplified and accelerated, as well as delivered cost savings for the business. The key business values achieved are:

1. *Time to Market.* Project delivery was greatly accelerated by allowing development teams to conduct parallel development of 10 major services with minimal interaction and dependencies.

The service-oriented approach and detailed overall vision allowed each team to rapidly deliver individual services that were seamlessly integrated and tested by the system team.

2. *Reduced Risk.* The SOA approach mitigated many of the risks associated with large development teams (100+ staff) by facilitating parallel development while minimizing team interdependencies and setting clear team responsibilities. The key to reducing risk is the early definition of business service interfaces and responsibilities.

3. *Cost Savings.* The modular SOA architecture of the new system consolidated business functions into a common set of business services that are leveraged across many business processes, resulting in cost savings for construction, deployment, and maintenance of the system.

4. *Improved Agility.* The business-centric service design and modularity of the SOA approach provides flexible deployment to support current business processes and to rapidly adapt to support future business process. Current business centric services include data sourcing, analytic surveillance, and case management.

5. *Resilience.* Fault-tolerant business-continuity is achieved using guaranteed message delivery, as individual business services are moved off-line for maintenance and restored.

6. *Process Optimization.* Technology duplication is eliminated through the consolidation of functionality into discrete standardized business services. This also provides a uniform approach and consistent results across all the business processes.

SOA Lessons

Understanding the underlying business problems and processes is crucial to creating well-defined services that are reusable and exhibit the correct level of granularity. The payoff for this is a flexible business process that can change and grow without changing the architecture. Effective governance, along with well-defined services with clear functions and interfaces, are essential.

Sources: Compiled from FINRA (*finra.org/AboutFINRA/*, 2010), SOA Consortium (*blog.soa-consortium.org/*, 2009), and CIO Magazine (*cio.com*).

Questions

1. How tolerant of business disruption or errors do you think FINRA would be? Explain your answer.

2. How many legacy systems needed to be integrated after the merger? Why would those systems be considered valuable assets?

3. Why was this implementation a success? Do you think that cost was one of the most important concerns? Why or why not? Assuming that it was not *cost*, what do you think was the most important criterion during the implementation?

BPM and SOA: Business Optimization. BPM and SOA both promise to help companies create new value from existing IT investments. They reuse IT programming efforts (think macros or modules) across many other processes. They also enable greater agility, lower cycle time, and lower cost structures. They offer many of the same benefits. SOA focuses on creating a more flexible IT architecture, while BPM has a pure focus on optimizing the way actual work gets done. SOA has delivered business value to very large corporations, but almost all SOA in practice are used only in web services, application integration as middleware, and business-to-business (B2B) solutions.

BPM Mashups through Web Services. Business processes are not self-contained. They need information from people and ISs (data stores) across departments and business areas. Many business processes even require information to be shared with external partners, clients, and providers. Web services can expand the functionality of the BPM system. A **web service** is a set of technologies used for exchanging data between applications. Web services can connect processes with other systems across the organization and with business partners. The resulting integrated BPM systems are called **BPM mashups.**

Mashups are pre-configured, ready-to-go integrations between different business software packages. They streamline information sharing among systems. For example, a BPM system can leverage web services to share customer data with CRM (customer relationship management). Budget and cost data from an ERP (enterprise resource planning) can be shared with the BPM, both in order to approve or deny an expense report filed using the BPM and subsequently to update the ERP once the expense report is complete. Web services can be used to share information with any other system that uses web services. Mashups make the sharing process easier by providing the systems integration and streamlining the way that the two systems work together.

Questions

1. What is a business process? Give three examples.
2. What are the stages in the business process lifecycle?
3. Define business process management.
4. Why is BPM important?
5. What is a BPM mashup?

13.2 Software Architecture and IS Design

An organization's software architecture refers to the structure of its apps. Like roads and bridges, IT architecture determines what is possible and the ease with which changes can be made to systems and processes.

AN OVERVIEW OF COUPLING IN SOFTWARE APPS

Long ago, business apps were written in COBOL software. These apps were one large piece or tightly coupled programs that performed many functions. *Tightly coupled* means that the programs and the data they processed and reports they generated were hardwired. Changes to these apps are tedious and time-consuming. The preferred software design is loosely coupled and built using modules or code that performs only one or two functions. For example, software code might calculate federal taxes as part of payroll.

Loosely Coupled. *Loose coupling* refers to way in which components in a system or network are connected. Loosely connected components have minimal dependence on each other. This simplifies testing, maintenance, and troubleshooting procedures because problems are easy to isolate and unlikely to spread or propagate. The extent or "tightness" to which the components in a system are coupled is a relative term. A loosely coupled system can be easily broken down into definable elements.

The goal of loose coupling is to reduce dependencies between systems. Benefits of loose coupling include flexibility and agility. A loosely coupled approach offers unparalleled flexibility for adaptations to changing landscapes. Since there are no assumptions about the landscape your application is running against, you can easily adapt the composite application as needed.

Another aspect to consider is the probability of landscape changes during the lifetime of the application. Due to mergers and acquisitions and system consolidations, the landscape underneath the application is constantly changing. Without loose coupling, organizations are forced to adapt or rewrite their apps again and again.

Maximizing architecture flexibility. An organizations' software architecture can also be designed for greater flexibility by using a tiered model. An example of a three-tier architecture model is shown in Figure 13.8.

Notice the modular architecture. The 3-tier architecture is intended to allow any of the three tiers to be upgraded or replaced independently as business requirements or technology change. For example, a change of OS (operating system) in the presentation tier would only affect the user interface code.

The middle tier does the processing and coordinating of the data. The middle tier may be multi-tiered itself, which is called an n-tier architecture.

Three-tier architecture has the following three tiers:

1. **Presentation or client tier.** This is the topmost level of the application, an example of which is your web browser. The presentation tier displays information related to such services as browsing merchandise, purchasing, and shopping cart contents. It communicates with other tiers by outputting results to the browser/client tier and all other tiers in the network.

2. **Application or business logic tier.** Detailed processing is performed in this tier. This middle tier consists of **middleware**. *Middleware* refers to a broad range of software or services that enable communication or data exchange between applications across networks. Specifically, middleware enables the data exchange by translating data requests and responses between clients and servers. This type of software is often

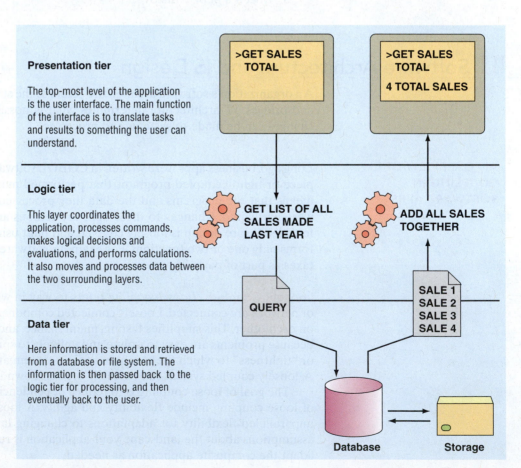

Figure 13.8 Overview of a three-tier software architecture design.

Source: Courtesy of Bartledan (Wikipedia, 2009).

described as "glue" because it connects or integrates business-critical software applications to other applications. By performing some of the tasks that an application would have performed, middleware eliminates the need for an application that is shared by multiple clients to function differently for each different type of client.

With today's networked-based applications—especially ERP, SCM, CRM, B2B, and B2C e-commerce—business operations depend upon middleware providing secure data transfers between these applications.

3. Data tier. This tier consists of the data sources, such as the database and data warehouse servers. Here information is stored and retrieved. This tier keeps data neutral and independent from application servers or business logic. Giving data its own tier also improves scalability and performance.

Conceptually the three-tier architecture is linear. A fundamental rule in a three-tier architecture is that the presentation tier never communicates directly with the data tier; all communication must pass through the middleware tier.

With this understanding of tiered architecture, you will now read about the IT acquisition process. Recall from Chapter 12, which focused on sourcing strategies, that developing ISs in-house was the alternative option.

IT ACQUISITION PROCESS

The acquisition process of an IT application has five major steps, which are shown in Figure 13.8.

Step 1. Planning, Identifying, and Justifying IT-Based Systems. IT systems are usually built as *enablers* of some business processes. Therefore, their planning must be aligned with the organization's overall business plan and the specific tasks it intends to support. Often processes may need to be redesigned or restructured to fully reap the benefits of the supporting IT applications. Also, the systems may need to be justified, for instance, by cost-benefit analysis. Both of these activities may be complex, especially for systems that require a significant investment to acquire, operate, and maintain—or that are cutting-edge.

The output of this step is the decision to invest or not invest in a specific application and a timetable, budget, and assigned responsibility. This step is usually done in-house, with consultants as needed. All other steps can be done in-house or outsourced.

The importance of a realistic evaluation cannot be overstated. Many projects pass this stage because of political reasons or fear of taking an unpopular position. Managers may hope that the system will work out. *Hope is not a plan*—it's a risk. *IT at Work 13.4* describes the multibillion dollar failure of the plan by the U.S. Census to collect data using handheld devices.

IT at Work 13.4

High-Tech Census Project Fails—An Analysis

U.S. Secretary of Commerce Carlos M. Gutierrez issued the following official statement explaining (in an obscure way) why the Census Bureau was scrapping its $600 million project that was to collect data using 500,000 handheld devices. The Bureau had contracted to use handheld devices from Harris Corp., but mismanagement, cost overruns, and poor planning helped derail the plan.

Over the last month or so, a clear sense has emerged: to have a fully successful 2010 Census, we must immediately revamp some programs, refocus priorities and get on top of the challenge.

According to a Press Release (*census.gov/*):

Multiple internal and external reviews have identified continuing Census challenges across a number of areas, including adequate planning over key systems requirements, key technology requirements, specification of operational control system characteristics and functions and regional center technology infrastructure. . . . Gutierrez said that the Census Bureau will need an additional $2.2 to $3.0 billion in funding over the next five years to meet the replan needs. . . . The *life cycle cost for the Reengineered 2010 Census was estimated at $11.8 billion in the FY 2009 Budget Request, including $1.8 billion for the American Community Survey which replaced the long-form. The new estimated life cycle cost for the 2010 Census is $13.7 to $14.5 billion.*

In summary, the Census Bureau had planned to issue more than 500,000 handhelds to temporary employees to collect personal data on Americans who do not return census forms in the mail. The handhelds were being developed under a $600 million contract awarded to Harris Corp. in 2006. Stumbling over this multibillion-dollar plan for a high-tech census, the government reverted to counting the nation's 300 million people the old-fashioned way: with paper and pencil. Poor management—not poor technology—caused the government to spend an additional $3 billion for the next census.

Was the Failure a Surprise?

Senator Susan Collins, ranking member of the Committee on Homeland Security and Governmental Affairs, wasn't surprised by the failure. "This committee is unfortunately no stranger to tales of federal projects and contracts that have gone awry, often at a heavy cost in taxpayer funds," she said. Collins listed the usual failure reasons:

- Poorly defined initial requirements, and

- Inability or unwillingness of management to control "requirements creep" and cost overruns.

Something larger than poor project management was at work. It was the failure of top management in the bureau to assess and mitigate the risks inherent in such a major project. "It should be noted that the problems with this contract seemed apparent to everyone except the Census Bureau," said Sen. Tom Coburn (D-Okla.).

Analysis of the Handheld Project Failure

The 2010 census was to have been the first true high-tech count in the nation's history. The Census Bureau had awarded a contract to purchase 500,000 of the computers, plus the computer operating system, at a cost of more than $600 million. The contract ballooned to $1.3 billion, even though the Bureau scaled back its purchase to only 151,000 handheld computers. The higher expenditure was due to cost overruns and new features ordered by the Census Bureau on the computers and the OS. Gutierrez blamed many of the problems on "a lack of effective communication with one of our key contractors."

Census officials were being blamed for doing a poor job of spelling out technical requirements to the contractor, Harris. In addition, the handhelds proved too complex for some temporary workers who tried to use them in a test in North Carolina, and the devices were not initially programmed to transmit the large amounts of data necessary.

Harris spokesman Marc Raimondi said the cost of the contract increased as the project requirements increased. "The increased funding is required to cover additional sites, equipment, software and functions added by the bureau to the program."

Rep. Alan Mollohan, chairman of the appropriations subcommittee, said the Census Bureau and Harris "contributed to today's crisis." The Census Bureau's failure to address problems with the computers early on has "turned the crisis into the emergency that we now face."

Sources: Compiled from U.S. Census (census.gov/2008), Hogue (2008), and Holmes (2008).

Questions

1. What went wrong? Make a list of things that went wrong and classify them as technology-related, management-related, and/or project-related (due to changes in the scope of the project).

2. Consider the statement: "hope is not a plan." Does that statement apply to this project failure? Explain why or why not.

Step 2. Creating IT Architecture. IT architecture is a plan for organizing the underlying infrastructure and applications of the IT project. The architecture plan includes the following:

- Data required to fulfill the business goals and vision
- Application modules that will deliver and manage the information and data
- Specific hardware and software on which the application modules will run
- Security, scalability, and reliability required by the applications
- Human resources and procedures for implementing the IT project

See Figure 13.9.

Various IT tools and methodologies are used to support the creation of an IT application architecture. The results obtained from step 2 are routed to the strategic planning level; for instance, to a steering committee. Based on the results of step 2, the application portfolio (a portfolio is *a set of applications*) or a specific project may be changed. For example, the steering committee may scale down a specific project because it is too risky at that time. Once the architecture is compiled and the project gets final approval, a decision about *how* to acquire the specific IT application must be made.

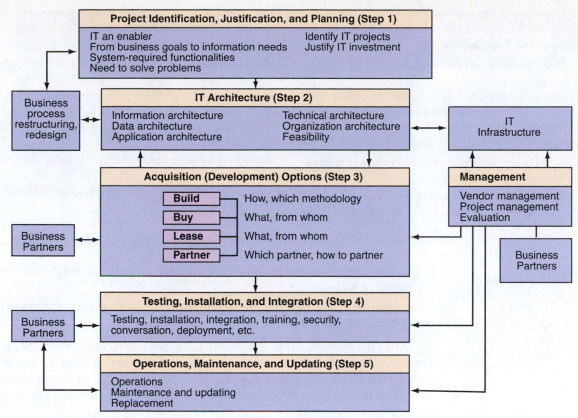

Figure 13.9 The process of IT application acquisition.

Step 3. Selecting an Acquisition Option. IT applications can be:

- Built in-house. In-house development using the systems development life cycle (SDLC) approach is covered in section 13.4.
- Custom-made by a vendor.
- Bought and customized, in-house or through a vendor. See Table 13.3 for a list of advantages and limitation of the *buy option*.
- Leased from an application service provider (ASP), or leased through a software-as-a-service (SaaS) arrangement, as you read in Chapter 12.
- Acquired via a partnership or alliance that will enable the company to use someone else's application.

Once an option is chosen, the system can be acquired. At the end of this step, an application is ready to be installed and deployed. No matter what option is chosen, you most likely will have to select one or more vendors and consulting companies.

Step 4. Testing, Installing, Integrating, and Deploying IT Applications. Once an acquisition option has been selected, the next step involves getting the application up and running on the selected hardware and network environment. One of the steps in installing an application is connecting it to back-end databases, to other applications, and often to partners' information systems. This step can be done in-house or outsourced. During this step, the modules that have been installed need to be tested. A series of tests are required:

- *Unit testing*: testing the modules one at a time
- *Integration testing*: testing the combination of modules interacting with other applications

TABLE 13.3	Advantages and Limitations of the Buy Option
Advantages of the Buy Option	**Disadvantages of the Buy Option**
• Many different types of off-the-shelf software are available. • Much time can be saved by buying rather than building. • The company can know what it is getting before it invests in the software. • The company is not the first and only user. • Purchased software may avoid the need to hire personnel specifically dedicated to a project. • The vendor updates the software frequently. • The price is usually much lower for a buy option.	• Software may not exactly meet the company's needs. • Software may be difficult or impossible to modify, or it may require huge business process changes to implement. • The company will not have control over software improvements and new versions. (Usually it may only recommend.) • Purchased software can be difficult to integrate with existing systems. • Vendors may drop a product or go out of business.

- *Usability testing*: testing the quality of the user's experience when interacting with the portal or web site
- *Acceptance testing*: determining whether the application meets the original business objectives and vision.

After the applications pass all of the tests, they can be rolled out to the end users. Here developers have to deal with issues such as conversion from the old to the new system, training, changes in priorities affecting acceptance of the application, and resistance to changing processes to maximize the benefit from the application.

Step 5. Operations, Maintenance, and Updating. It usually takes as much time, effort, and money to operate and maintain an application as it does to acquire and install it in the first place. For the maximizing of its continual usage, an application needs to be continually updated. Software maintenance can be a big problem due to rapid changes in the IT field. Operation and maintenance can be done in-house and/or outsourced.

Managing the IT Acquisition Process. The IT acquisition process most likely will be a complex project that must be managed properly. Except for small applications, an IT project team is usually created to manage the process, budget, costs, and vendors. Projects can be managed with *project management* software, such as Microsoft Project. Three criteria that are used to evaluate the effectiveness of IT project management are performance, time, and cost. That is, was the IT project done right, on budget, and on time?

Standard project management techniques and tools are used by project managers to manage project resources to keep them on time, on budget, and within performance specifications. Finally, implementing an IT project may require restructuring one or more business processes.

IN-HOUSE DEVELOPMENT: INSOURCING

A third development strategy is to develop or build apps in-house. Although in-house development—*insourcing*—can be time consuming and costly, it may lead to IT apps that better fit an enterprise's strategy and vision, and differentiate it from competitors. The in-house development of IT apps, however, is a challenging task, as most applications are novel, and may involve multiple organizations.

Options for In-House Development. Three major options exist for in-house development:

1. Build from scratch. This option should be considered only for specialized IT applications for which components are not available. This option is expensive and slow, but it will provide the best fit to the organization's needs.

2. Build from components. The required applications are often constructed from standard components. Commercially packaged and homegrown components must integrate tightly for component-based development to meet its requirements. This is especially critical for real-time applications and for e-business systems. The scope of component integration and code reuse is broadening, too.

3. Integrating applications. The application integration option is similar to the build-from-components option, but instead of components being used, entire applications are employed. This is an especially attractive option when IT applications from several business partners need to be integrated. Integration methods such as Web Services or Enterprise Application Integration (EAI) can be used.

Insourcing requires specialized IT procedures and resources. For this reason, most organizations rely on packaged apps or vendors for app development and maintenance.

Methods Used in In-House Development. Several methods can be used when you develop IT applications in-house. Three major development methods are:

1. Systems development life cycle (SDLC). Large IT projects, especially ones that involve infrastructure, are developed according to the SDLC methodology using several tools. Details about this approach are provided in section 13.4.

2. Prototyping methodology. With a prototyping methodology, an initial list of basic system requirements is defined and used to build a prototype. The prototype is then improved in several iterations, based on users' feedback. This approach can be very rapid. The prototype is then tested and improved, tested again, and developed further, based on the users' feedback. The prototyping approach, however, is not without drawbacks. There is a risk of getting into an endless loop of prototype revisions, as users may never be fully satisfied. Such a risk should be planned for because of the rapid changes in IT and business models.

3. Web 2.0 or Application 2.0 methodology. This development approach involves quick, incremental updates with close user involvement. For new application developments, a beta (prototype) version is developed and then refined—also in very close collaboration with users.

Questions

1. What is the advantage of loosely coupled software design?
2. Explain the functions of middleware.
3. What is IT architecture?
4. What testing needs to be done on an application?
5. List the major acquisition and development strategies.
6. Compare the buy option against the lease option.
7. List the in-house development approaches.

13.3 IT Project Management

A **project** is collection of tasks to achieve a result, such as implementing a new JIT inventory management system. Projects have a defined beginning and end; a scope, resources, and a budget. Projects are approved before they are allocated resources. *Projects* differ from *operations* or *business as usual* because of their uniqueness. Characteristics of projects are shown in Table 13.4.

The management of projects is enhanced by computerized project management tools such as the *program evaluation and review technique* (PERT) and the *critical path method* (CPM). For example, developing a social media campaign can be a major project, and several IT tools are available to support and help manage the tasks.

Successful organizations perform projects that produce desired results in established time frames with assigned resources. Projects are not limited to IT, but can

TABLE 13.4	Distinguishing Characteristics of Projects

Projects have these characteristics.
- Are unique endeavors.
- Have a high degree of uncertainty with respect to costs and completion times due to the generally long length.
- Involve participation of outsiders, which is difficult to control.
- Requires extensive interaction among participants.
- May compete and conflict with other business activities making changes in planning and scheduling difficult.
- Involve high risk of delay, failure, and costly changes, but also has high profit potential or benefit.

apply to most all functions of the organization. The project management principles and practices discussed in this section, apply to any type of project.

Projects are managed by managing the triple constraints, which are:

1. Scope: The project scope is the definition of what the project is supposed to accomplish—its outcomes or deliverables. Scope is measured in terms of the project size, goals, and requirements.

2. Time: A project is made of up *tasks*. In defining the tasks, they should start with an active verb, such as: *purchase servers*, *apply for permits*, and *interview vendors*. Each task is assigned a duration—which is the difference between the task's start date and its end date. The project's time is determined by task durations and task dependencies. Some tasks are dependent on other tasks being completed before they can begin. For example, in construction, a hole must be dug before the pouring of concrete can start. Task durations and task dependencies determine the time required to complete the project.

3. Budget: Projects are approved subject to their costs.

These constraints are interrelated, so they must be managed together for the project to be completed on time, within budget, and to specification (spec).

After the project scope has been defined, it is used to estimate a realistic timeline and budget based on the availability of necessary resources. Resources include the people, equipment, and material needed to complete the project. The result is a project plan that is specified in a **Work Breakdown Structure (WBS).** Figure 13.10 shows a screen shot of Microsoft Project, with a WBS on the left-side and a Gantt chart on the right-side. A **Gantt chart** is a type of bar chart that illustrates a project schedule. Gantt charts illustrate the start and finish dates of the terminal elements and summary elements of a project. Terminal elements and summary elements comprise the work breakdown structure of the project. Project resources must be managed according to the WBS.

Scope Creep. It is absolutely imperative that any change to the scope of the project explicitly include compensating changes in the budget, the deadline, and/or resources. **Scope creep,** which refers to the growth of the project after the scope has been defined, is a serious issue. Scope creep is the piling up of small changes that by themselves are manageable, but in aggregate are significant. IT projects, particularly one as complex as implementing an ERP or CRM, can take a long time to complete.

During the project, it's almost guaranteed that requests will be made that change the scope. If the project scope is to build an accounting app for processing expense reports with a budget of $100,000 and four-month duration, the project manager is expected to do that. However, if the scope is changed to also include processing of sales commissions, the project manager must obtain an appropriate change in budgeted resources and time. If the budget is not adjusted, the smart project manager

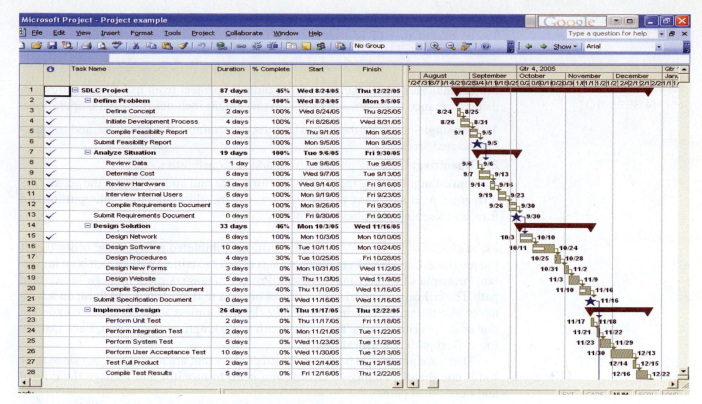

Figure 13.10 Microsoft Project screen shot of WBS (left-side) and Gantt Chart (right-side).

will refuse to agree to the change in scope. Make sure any requested change, no matter how small, is accompanied by approval for a change in budget or schedule or both.

WHO'S ACCOUNTABLE FOR IT FAILURE?

IT failures are a management crisis. They are often of serious proportions. An estimated 70 percent of IT projects fail in some important way (Krigsman, 2012).

Two experts calculated the worldwide economic impact of IT failure. Gene Kim, founder and former CTO of Tripwire, Inc., and Mike Orzen, author of Lean IT. They estimated that the global impact of IT failure as being $3 trillion annually. They explained:

> *For just the Standard & Poor 500 companies, aggregate 2012 revenue is estimated to be $10 trillion. If 5 percent of aggregate revenue is spent on IT, and conservatively, 20 percent of that spending creates no value for the end customer—that is $100 billion of waste.*

Both IDC and Gartner projected that in 2011, 5 percent of the worldwide gross domestic product will be spent on IT (hardware, services and telecom). In other words, in 2011, approximately $5.6 trillion was spent on IT. Assuming conservatively that 30 percent of IT spending is for capitalized projects, and that 30 percent of those projects will fail, that's $252 billion of waste.

IT projects fail when managers lack experience or commitment, hire the wrong people, and ignore red flags that warn of problems. While project managers may be partly responsible for failure, senior executives are responsible for allowing the conditions for failure to exist in the first place. Three underlying reasons for IT project failure are:

1. Expectations that are unrealistic. Executives often expect technology can magically solve business problems

2. Conflicts of interest among customers, vendors, and integrators. Implementing enterprise software typically involves multiple groups, each with its own set of interests, goals, and measures of success.

3. Corporate structure or culture that does not encourage innovation and success. To the extent that IT is disconnected from lines of business, the conditions for failure intensify.

Project management is the process of guiding a project from its beginning through its performance to its closure. Project management includes three basic operations:

1. Planning: Specifying the desired results, determining the schedules, and estimating the resources.

2. Organizing: Defining people's roles and responsibilities.

3. Controlling: Tracking the planned performance and budget against the actual performance. Also managing people's performances, addressing problems, putting out fires, and keeping priorities well-known.

Managing the Critical Path. Tasks must be completed in a specific order to get the job done. Certain tasks make up what is called the **critical path,** which is an important principle of project management. Project managers must manage the critical path. The **critical path** consists of activities or tasks that must start and finish on schedule or else the project completion will be delayed–unless action is taken to expedite one or more critical tasks. The critical path is the length of the project. Each task on the critical path is a **critical task.**

There are noncritical paths composed of tasks that are not critical, but since their status could easily change to critical, you need to monitor and manage the critical and noncritical paths.

The purpose of the **critical path method (CPM)** is to recognize which activities are on the critical path so that you know where to focus your efforts. You use critical tasks to identify or prioritize tradeoffs.

Project Manager Success Skills. The success of a project manager depends on:

• **Communication:** Clear, open, and timely sharing of information with appropriate individuals and groups. Since people are often reluctant to admit bad news, extra effort is needed to insure that news about anything that will delay or compromise the project is reported promptly. Without truthful and complete communication during the project, it will fail.

• **Information:** No surprises. Accurate, timely, and complete data for the planning, performance monitoring, and final assessment.

• **Commitment:** Team members' personal promises to produce the agreed upon results on time and within budget.

Questions

1. Define triple constraint.
2. What is the project scope?
3. What is scope creep?
4. Why does scope creep increase project risks?
5. Who's accountable for IT failure?
6. What is the critical path?
7. What do project managers do?

13.4 Systems Development

The **systems development life cycle (SDLC)** is the traditional systems development method used by organizations for large IT projects such as IT infrastructure. The SDLC is a structured framework that consists of sequential processes by which information systems are developed. As shown in Figure 13.11, these processes are

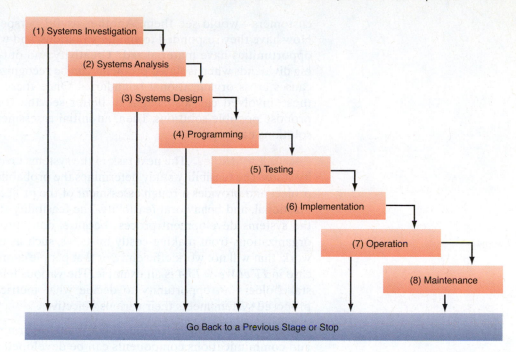

Figure 13.11 An eight-stage system development life cycle (SDLC).

investigation, analysis, design, programming, testing, implementation, operation, and maintenance. The processes, in turn, consist of well-defined tasks. Large projects typically require all of the tasks, whereas smaller development projects may require only a subset of the tasks.

Within the SDLC, there is an iterative feature. *Iteration* is the revising of the results of any development process when new information makes this revision the smart thing to do. Iteration does not mean that developments should be subjected to infinite revisions, but it does mean that developers should adjust to new relevant information. Recall scope creep that tends to happen to projects. IS design is highly susceptible to scope creep as users ask for additional features or try to keep up with new the latest mobile technologies. Social media, viral marketing, and e-commerce development are susceptible to scope creep because these systems constantly evolve.

Systems development projects produce desired results through team efforts. Development teams typically include users, systems analysts, programmers, and technical specialists. *Users* are employees from all functional areas and levels of the organization who will interact with the system, either directly or indirectly. **Systems analysts** are information systems professionals who specialize in analyzing and designing information systems. Programmers are information systems professionals who modify existing computer programs or write new computer programs to satisfy user requirements. Technical specialists are experts on a certain type of technology, such as databases or telecommunications. All people who are affected by changes in information systems (e.g., users and managers) are known as systems stakeholders, and are typically involved by varying degrees and at various times in the systems development.

SDLC STAGE 1: SYSTEMS INVESTIGATION

Systems development practitioners agree that the more time invested in understanding the business problem or opportunity, in understanding technical options for systems, and in understanding problems that are likely to occur during development, the greater the probability that the IS will be a success. For these reasons, systems investigation begins with the *business problem* or *opportunity*.

Problems and opportunities often require not only understanding them from the internal point of view, but also seeing them as organizational partners—suppliers or customers—would see them. Another useful perspective is that of competitors. How have they responded to similar situations, and what outcomes and additional opportunities have materialized? Creativity and out-of-the-box thinking can pay big dividends when isolated problems can be recognized as systemic failures whose causes cross organizational boundaries. Once these perspectives can be gained, those involved can also begin to better see the true scope of the project and propose possible solutions. Then, an initial assessment of these proposed system solutions can begin.

Feasibility Studies. The next task in the systems investigation stage is the feasibility study. The feasibility study determines the probability of success of the proposed project and provides a rough assessment of the project's technical, economic, organizational, and behavioral feasibility. The feasibility study is critically important to the systems development process because, done properly, the study can prevent organizations from making costly mistakes, such as creating systems that will not work, that will not work efficiently, or that people cannot or will not use. The Census case in *IT at Work 13.4* is an example. The various feasibility analyses also give the stakeholders an opportunity to decide what metrics to use to measure how a proposed system meets their various objectives.

- *Technical Feasibility.* Technical feasibility determines if the hardware, software, and communications components can be developed and/or acquired to solve the business problem. Technical feasibility also determines if the organization's existing technology can be used to achieve the project's performance objectives.
- *Economic Feasibility.* Economic feasibility determines if the project is an acceptable financial risk and if the organization can afford the expense and time needed to complete the project. Economic feasibility addresses two primary questions: Do the benefits outweigh the costs of the project? Can the project be completed as scheduled?

Three commonly used methods to determine economic feasibility are return on investment (ROI), net present value (NPV), and breakeven analysis. Return on investment is the ratio of the net income attributable to a project divided by the average assets invested in the project. The net present value is the net amount by which project benefits exceed project costs, after allowing for the cost of capital and the time value of money. Breakeven analysis determines the point at which the cumulative cash flow from a project equals the investment made in the project.

Determining economic feasibility in IT projects is rarely straightforward, but it often is essential. Part of the difficulty stems from the fact that benefits often are intangible. Another potential difficulty is that the proposed system or technology may be cutting edge, and there may be no previous evidence of what sort of financial payback is to be expected.

- *Organizational Feasibility.* Organizational feasibility has to do with an organization's ability to accept the proposed project. Sometimes, for example, organizations cannot accept a financially acceptable project due to legal or other constraints. In checking organizational feasibility, one should consider the organization's policies and politics, including impacts on power distribution, business relationships, and internal resources availability.
- *Behavioral Feasibility.* Behavioral feasibility addresses the human issues of the project. All systems development projects introduce change into the organization, and people generally fear change. Overt resistance from employees may take the form of sabotaging the new system (e.g., entering data incorrectly) or deriding the new system to anyone who will listen. Covert resistance typically occurs when employees simply do their jobs using their old methods.

Behavioral feasibility is concerned with assessing the skills and the training needed to use the new IS. In some organizations, a proposed system may require mathematical or linguistic skills beyond what the workforce currently possesses.

In others, a workforce may simply need to improve their skills. Behavioral feasibility is as much about "can they use it?" as it is about "will they use it?"

After the feasibility analysis, a Go/No-Go decision is reached. The functional area manager for whom the system is to be developed and the project manager sign off on the decision. If the decision is No-Go, the project is put on the shelf until conditions are more favorable, or the project is discarded. If the decision is Go, then the systems development project proceeds, and the systems analysis phase begins.

SDLC STAGE 2: SYSTEMS ANALYSIS

The systems analysis stage produces the following information: (1) strengths and weaknesses of the existing system; (2) functions that the new system must have to solve the business problem; and (3) user information requirements for the new system. Armed with this information, systems developers can proceed to the systems design stage.

There are two main approaches in systems analysis: the traditional (structured) approach and the object-oriented approach. The traditional approach emphasizes *how*, whereas the object-oriented approach emphasizes *what*.

SDLC STAGE 3: SYSTEM DESIGN

Systems analysis describes what a system must do to solve the business problem, and *systems design* describes *how* the system will accomplish this task. The deliverable of the systems design phase is the technical design that specifies the following:

- System outputs, inputs, and user interfaces
- Hardware, software, databases, telecommunications, personnel, and procedures
- How these components are integrated

This output represents the set of *system specifications*. Systems design encompasses two major aspects of the new system: **Logical system design** states what the system will do, using abstract specifications. **Physical system design** states how the system will perform its functions, with actual physical specifications. Logical design specifications include the design of outputs, inputs, processing, databases, telecommunications, controls, security, and IS jobs. Physical design specifications include the design of hardware, software, database, telecommunications, and procedures. For example, the logical telecommunications design may call for a wide-area network connecting the company's plants. The physical telecommunications design will specify the types of communications hardware (computers and routers), software (network operating system), media (fiber optics and satellite), and bandwidth (e.g., 100 Mbps).

When both of these aspects of system specifications are approved by all participants, they are "frozen." That is, once the specifications are agreed upon, they should not be changed. However, users typically ask for added functionality in the system (called *scope creep*). This occurs for several reasons: First, as users more clearly understand how the system will work and what their information and processing needs are, they see additional functions that they would like the system to have. Also, as time passes after the design specifications are frozen, business conditions often change, and users ask for added functionality. Because scope creep is expensive, project managers place controls on changes requested by users. These controls help to prevent *runaway projects*—systems development projects that are so far over budget and past deadline that they must be abandoned, typically with large monetary loss.

SDLC STAGE 4: PROGRAMMING

Systems developers utilize the design specifications to acquire the software needed for the system to meet its functional objectives and solve the business problem. Organizations may buy the software or construct it in-house.

Although many organizations tend to purchase packaged software, many other firms continue to develop custom software in-house. For example, Wal-Mart and Eli Lilly build practically all of their software in-house. The chief benefit of custom development is systems that are better suited than packaged applications to an organization's new and existing business processes. For many organizations, custom software is more expensive than packaged applications. However, if a package does not closely fit the company's needs, the savings are often diluted when the information systems staff or consultants must extend the functionality of the purchased packages.

If the organization decides to construct the software in-house, then programming begins. **Programming** involves the translation of the design specifications into computer code. This process can be lengthy and time-consuming because writing computer code remains as much an art as a science. Large systems development projects can require hundreds of thousands of lines of computer code and hundreds of computer programmers. In such projects, programming teams are used. These teams often include functional area users to help the programmers focus on the business problem at hand.

In an attempt to add rigor to the programming process, programmers use structured programming techniques. These techniques improve the logical flow of the program by decomposing the computer code into *modules*, which are sections of code (subsets of the entire program). This modular structure allows for more efficient and effective testing because each module can be tested by itself. The structured programming techniques include the following restrictions:

- Each module has one, and only one, function.
- Each module has only one entrance and one exit. That is, the logic in the computer program enters a module in only one place and exits in only one place.
- GO TO statements are not allowed.

For example, a flowchart for a simple payroll application might look like the one shown in Figure 13.12. The figure shows the only three types of structures that are

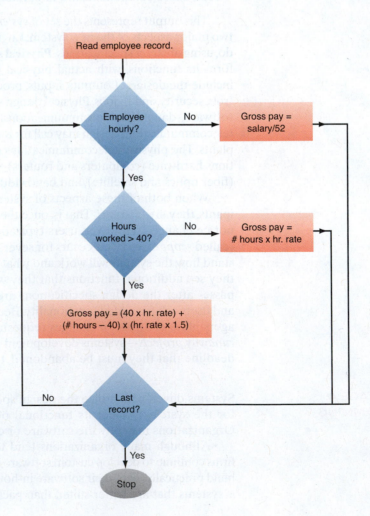

Figure 13.12 Flowchart of a payroll application.

used in structured programming: sequence, decision, and loop. In the *sequence* structure, program statements are executed one after another until all of the statements in the sequence have been executed. The *decision* structure allows the logic flow to branch, depending on certain conditions being met. The *loop* structure enables the software to execute the same program, or parts of a program, until certain conditions are met (e.g., until the end of the file is reached, or until all records have been processed).

As already noted, structured programming enforces some standards about how program code is written. This approach and some others were developed not only to improve programming, but also to standardize how a firm's various programmers do their work. This uniform approach helps ensure that all of the code developed by different programmers will work together. Even with these advances, however, programming can be difficult to manage.

SDLC STAGE 5: TESTING

Thorough and continuous testing occurs throughout the programming stage. Testing verifies that computer code works correctly under various conditions. Testing requires a lot of time, effort, and expense to do properly. However, the costs of improper testing, which could possibly lead to a system that does not meet its objectives, are enormous.

Testing is designed to detect errors (bugs) in the computer code. These errors are of two types: syntax errors and logic errors.

1. *Syntax errors* (e.g., a misspelled word or a misplaced comma) are easier to find and will not permit the program to run.

2. *Logic errors* permit the program to run but result in incorrect output. Logic errors are more difficult to detect because the cause is not obvious. The programmer must follow the flow of logic in the program to determine the source of the error in the output.

To have a systematic testing of the system, we must start with a comprehensive *test plan*. There are several types of testing: In *unit testing*, each module is tested alone in an attempt to discover any errors in its code. *String testing* puts together several modules, to check the logical connection among them. The next level, *integration testing*, brings together various programs for testing purposes. *System testing* brings together *all* of the programs that comprise the system.

As software increases in complexity, the number of errors increases, making it almost impossible to find them all. This situation has led to *"good-enough" software*, software that developers release knowing that errors remain in the code but believing that the software will still meet its functional objectives. That is, they have found all the "show-stopper" bugs, errors that will cause the system to shut down or will cause catastrophic loss of data.

SDLC STAGE 6: IMPLEMENTATION

Implementation (or deployment) is the process of converting from the old system to the new system. Organizations use four major conversion strategies: parallel, direct, pilot, and phased.

In a **parallel conversion,** the old system and the new system operate simultaneously for a period of time. That is, both systems process the same data at the same time, and the outputs are compared. This type of conversion is the most expensive, but also the least risky. Most large systems have a parallel conversion process to lessen the risk.

In a **direct conversion,** the old system is cut off and the new system is turned on at a certain point in time. This type of conversion is the least expensive, but the most risky if the new system doesn't work as planned. Few systems are implemented using this type of conversion, due to the risk involved.

A **pilot conversion** introduces the new system in one part of the organization, such as in one plant or in one functional area. The new system runs for a period of time and is assessed. After the new system works properly, it is introduced in other parts of the organization.

A **phased conversion** introduces components of the new system, such as individual modules, in stages. Each module is assessed, and, when it works properly, other modules are introduced until the entire new system is operational.

Enterprise application integration (EAI) is often called the *middleware*, which you read in section 13.2. Interfaces were developed to map the major packages to a single conceptual framework that guides what all these packages do and the kinds of information they normally need to share. This conceptual framework could be used to translate the data and processes from each vendor's package to a common language. It is the only way to implement collaborative supply chain sharing of information.

XML is the technology that is being used by many EAI vendors in their cross-enterprise applications development. It can be thought of as a way for providing variable format messages that can be shared between any two computer systems, as long as they both understand the format (tags) that is (are) being used.

SDLC STAGES 7 AND 8: OPERATION AND MAINTENANCE

After conversion, the new system will operate for a period of time, until it no longer meets its objectives. Once the new system's operations are stabilized, *audits* are performed during operation to assess the system's capabilities and determine if it is being used correctly.

Systems need several types of maintenance. The first type is *debugging* the program, a process that continues throughout the life of the system. The second type is *updating* the system to accommodate changes in business conditions. An example would be adjusting to new governmental regulations (such as tax rate changes). These corrections and upgrades usually do not add any new functionality; they simply keep the system functioning as needed. The third type of maintenance *adds new functionality* to the system—adding new features to the existing system without disturbing its operation.

Questions

> 1. Define the eight stages of the SDLC.
> 2. What is the difference between logical and physical design?
> 3. Explain logic errors and syntax errors.
> 4. Explain the feasibility tests and their importance.
> 5. Discuss the four conversion methods.

Key Terms

You find clickable Link Libraries for each chapter on the Companion website.

ARIS Express, free business process modeling software *http://ariscommunity.com/aris-express*

Oracle BPM Suite 11g *http://oracle.com/us/technologies/bpm/*

Oracle SOA Suite 11g *http://oracle.com/us/technologies/soa/*

Project Management Institute *http://pmi.org/*

Fastforward BPM blog *http://fastforwardblog.com/2010/06/26/social-bpm-business-process-management-enters-the-21st-century/*

Open source BPM and workflow *http://processmaker.com/*

BPM/SOA Community Insights *http://blog.soa-consortium.org/*

Adaptive Planning demo for budgeting, forecasting, reporting, and analysis *http://adaptive planning.com/*

IBM BPM *http://www-01.ibm.com/software/info/bpm/*

IBM BPM Blueprint demo (download the demo) *http://www-01.ibm.com/software/integration/bpm-blueprint/*

ITBusinessEdge BPM *http://itbusinessedge.com/topics/show.aspx?t=482*

Oracle Business Activity Monitoring (BAM), integral part of the BPM suite *http://www.oracle.com/us/products/database/index-090604.html*

InfoSys Research BPM, SOA, and enterprise architecture; and Centers of Excellence *http://infosys.com/research/*

Gartner *http://gartner.com/technology/research/content/business_process_improvement.jsp*

Evaluate and Expand Your Learning

IT and Data Management Decisions

Visit the BMP website at *http://www.bpm.com/*. Click the Vendor Guide tab.

1. Review the vendors listed in the guide. Then select three of the vendors.
2. Research each of the vendors using information from their websites and white papers or reports.
3. Prepare a comparison of the vendors. Specify the types of software and services they provide. Do any of the vendors identify their experience in specific industries, types or sizes of firms?
4. Consider each vendor's BPM suites. For which type of organization would you recommend each vendor? Why?

Questions for Discussion & Review

1. What is a business process?
2. Why is it important for all business managers to understand business processes?
3. Why did many early BPR efforts fail?
4. Explain the relationship between BPM and SOA.
5. Why does BPM begin with understanding current processes?
6. Discuss the reasons why end-user-developed IT systems can be of poor quality. What can be done to improve the situation?
7. Explain the 3-tier IT architecture.
8. What is the critical path?
9. Explain the triple constraint.
10. Explain the stages of the SDLC.
11. Why are feasibility tests done?

Online Activities

1. *Linkedin Discussion Group.* Visit the BPTrends Discussion Group on Linkedin where members and visitors exchange ideas on a wide variety of BPM-related topics. Join the BPTrends Discussion Group. Describe three topics of current interest.
2. Visit *www-01.IBM.com/software/info/bpm/* and download the IBM BPM eKit. After reviewing the eKit, explain how BPM and enterprise architecture improve business outcomes.
3. Research open-source BPM software vendors. Create a table that lists five of these vendors, the software applications they provide, and their features.

4. Visit Gartner at *gartner.com/technology/research/content/business_process_improvement.jsp.* Click "Get the Report" under the heading FEATURED RESEARCH. Describe three lessons that you learned from the report.

5. Search recent material on the role BPM software plays in support of BPM. Select two vendors' software products and download/view their demos. In your opinion, how useful were the software products. For example, would they be helpful for both simple processes and complex processes? What skill level was needed to use the tools? Where they easy to learn *how to use*?

6. Explore project management software on vendors' web sites. Select a single project management package, download the demo, and try it. Make a list of the important features of the package. Be sure to investigate its web, repository, and collaboration features. Report your findings to the class.

Collaborative Work

1. As a group, design an information system for a startup business of your choice. Describe your chosen IT

resource acquisition strategy, and justify your choices of hardware, software, telecommunications support, and other aspects of a proposed system.

2. Managing a project with Microsoft Project is often the approach to IT project management. But many users prefer to use Microsoft Excel instead. The main reasons are that MS-Project is too expensive, wastes too much time to set up and keep updated, and is tough to use. The debate between Excel and Project has valid arguments for either approach. Each of two groups takes one software tool—Excel or Project—and debates the advantages of their tool.

3. Examine some business processes in your university or company. Identify one process that needs to be redesigned to eliminate waste or inefficiencies. Diagram the existing tasks/activities in the process; and then diagram an improved process. Use modeling tools in Microsoft Word or one of the free BPM or workflow software tools.

CASE 2   BUSINESS CASE

Pep Boys' IT Planning Process

Pep Boys (*pepboys.com/*) is a $2 billion publicly held company and the only aftermarket retail and service chain in the U.S. capable of serving all four segments of the automotive aftermarket: the do-it-yourself, do-it-for-me, buy-for-resale, and replacement tires. The company operates 582 stores in 35 states and Puerto Rico, is headquartered in Philadelphia, and has approximately 18,000 employees.

Budget Process Supported by Adaptive Planning Software

Pep Boys used Adaptive Planning (*adaptiveplanning.com/*) to prepare the budgets for its 580-plus automotive-service stores for its 2009 and 2010 fiscal years. The company previously had its budget information on Excel spreadsheets, which were sent to the store owners for changes, then to area directors for review, then back to headquarters for more changes, and, ultimately, a consolidation.

"It was an administrative nightmare to create all those files, get them out there, follow up on their status, and collect them," according to Phil McAllister, director of budgeting and internal reporting.

With all users now accessing a single system running on top of a relational database and thus able to view updated information in real time, Pep Boys is saving 600 person-hours of effort per budgeting cycle compared with its former cumbersome procedure.

Selection Criteria

Pep Boys selected Adaptive Planning because it didn't need the largest vendors' more-sophisticated software for purposes

of its individual store budgets. McAllister notes, it hasn't even come close to using all of the software's features.

A shorter implementation time frame was also appealing, since the decision to seek a more collaborative budgeting process was made too late in 2008 to accommodate a drawn-out installation of an on-premise system. It took about six weeks for Adaptive Planning to create templates incorporating all the store-budget information and get the service up and running.

Adaptive Planning service's list price is $600 to $800 per user per year. Pep Boys has about 650 users, including the stores, area directors, division vice presidents, and administrators.

Sources: Compiled from *adaptiveplanning.com/index.php/* (2010) and *pepboys.com/about_pep_boys/* (2010),

Questions

1. Diagram the process by which Pep Boys had collected data during its budget planning process.

2. View Adaptive Planning's pre-recorded online demo at *adaptiveplanning.com/demo_recorded.php/.* This demo covers Expense Planning, Personnel Planning, Sales Planning, Reporting, and Administration. How does this software improve the various planning processes?

3. Evaluate Pep Boys software vendor selection process? The outcome was successful, but given the selection process, what risks did they take?

4. In your opinion, why did the Adaptive Planning company provide Pep Boys with excellent service and support?

CASE 3   VIDEO CASE

BlueWorksLive

1. Visit *http://www.Blueworkslive.com* and read the Overview.
2. Click "Watch a Video Walkthrough" and watch the video (2:06). Describe what you learned.
3. Return to *http://www.Blueworkslive.com*. Click the Features tab, and read about the BPM features. Click "See>>" under each section for more information.

   a. After clicking *Discover, document . . .,* and *See,* explain why the software is simple for everyone to get started quickly.
   b. After clicking *. . . and automate . . .,* and *See,* explain how companies gain visibility and control.
   c. After clicking *. . . collaboratively . . .,* and *See,* explain how realtime collaboration is possible.

Process Modeling Using ARIS Express and Blueprint

Modeling a Business Process and Brainstorming a Strategy

ARIS Express is a BPM modeling tool based on industry standards. A free downloadable featured-rich version is available from *http://www.ariscommunity.com/aris-express/how-to-start*. Support features on the web site are installation instructions, quick reference, and video tutorials.

1. To get started with ARIS: download and install ARIS Express.
2. Visit *ariscommunity.com* and click Videos. From the site *ariscommunity.com/aris-express/tutorials*, select and view the video tutorial "How to model business processes" to learn how to model process steps in ARIS Express, and understand the meaning of symbols used in the "Business process" model type. View other tutorials, as needed.
3. Create a new model type. Select business process as the model type.

4. Design and develop a model of a business process. Review your model for any missed steps or other omissions. Edit as needed.
5. Download the BPM Blueprint 30-day Trial and the Demo from *http://www-01.ibm.com/software/integration/bpm-blueprint/*. Model the process you'd completed in #4 with this software tool.
6. Which BPM modeling tool did you prefer? Why?
7. Visit *ariscommunity.com* and click Videos. You will be at the site *ariscommunity.com/aris-express/tutorials*. Select and view the video tutorial "How to model a whiteboard" to learn how to structure ideas and tasks with a Whiteboard model. Then use the Whiteboard to model a brainstorming session related to business plan. For example, you could brainstorm ideas about how to manage a new project to use for social media and 2D tags to market a new product or service. To what extent did the Whiteboard tool make planning the project easier? Explain.

Resources on the Book's Web site

You'll find additional chapter materials and useful web links. In addition, self-quizzes that provide individualized feedback are available for each chapter.

References

Alesci, C., & Saitto., S. "*AutoTrader.Com* Said To Be In Talks About Possible IPO Of Buyer-Seller Site." Bloomberg, February 4, 2012.

Aris Express. *ariscommunity.com/aris-express/how-to-start/*

CIO Magazine. "SOA Consortium and CIO Magazine Announce Winners of SOA Case Study Competition," 2009. *soa-consortium.org/*.

Fheili, M. I. "Information technology at the forefront of operational risk: Banks are at a greater risk." *The Journal of Operational Risk.* Summer 2011.

Financial Industry Regulatory Authority (FINRA). *finra.org/*.

Hogue, F. "Handling the Census Handheld Debacle." *Baseline.com,* April 15, 2008.

Holmes, A. "Census program to use handheld computers said to be in 'serious trouble.'" *GovernmentExecutive.com,* January 2, 2008.

Krigsman, M. "Who's accountable for IT failure?" *ZDNet,* April 16, 2012.

Oracle BAM. 2010. *oracle.com/appserver/business-activity-monitoring.html*.

SAG (Software AG). "Orders are in the Fast Lane at *Autotrader.com*— Thanks to BPM." *SoftwareAG.com,* 2011.

SOA Consortium. *blog.soa-consortium.org/*

Walsh, M. "*Autotrader.com* Tops in Local Online Ad Dollars." *MediaPost.com,* April 3, 2012.

IT Ethics and Responsible Conduct

Learning Outcomes

❶ Explain how the IT industry and users can reduce carbon emissions and global warming that harm the earth's ecosystem by implementing green business practices that conserve natural resources.

❷ Debate the tradeoffs between conveniences and competitive advantages that IT offers and responsible conduct.

❸ Describe the impacts of *constant connectivity* and distractions on quality of life, business, safety, and interpersonal relationships.

❹ Describe the IT-business trends for the next three to five years.

Are you prepared to deal effectively with ethical challenges that social, search, mobile, and mining technologies create in business? Anecdotal research suggests that individuals—both professionally and personally—often do not even recognize when ethical issues are present. If people cannot recognize them, it is hard to imagine how they could deal responsibly with ethical challenges.

IT ethics is discussed in this chapter, which also presents the challenges of identifying responsible conduct related to IT and acting accordingly. Most major retailers rely on predictive analytics to understand consumers' shopping habits and also their personal habits to more efficiently market to them. Using information and processing power to gain a competitive edge in

ways that managers try desperately to keep secret from customers or regulators is a solid indicator of ethical misconduct. Not all misuse or abuses of information are so obvious.

Key issues you read in this chapter are social discrimination; the impact of present practices on the ecosystem, society, and environment of the future; and what the entire range of IT is doing to quality of life. Mobile technology helps reduce travel-related energy consumption and yet contributes to environmental deterioration. There are no easy fixes, clear-cut judgments, answers, or solutions. The goal is to recognize the crucial ethical and ecological issues to better manage IT and tip the balance toward better conduct and sustainability.

CASE 1 OPENING CASE

Recognizing Corporate Social Media Discrimination

Social recruiting refers to use of social media to find, screen, and select job candidates. Often it entails searching information the job candidate did not want considered.

Discrimination, or bias in recruitment, hiring, and employment based on certain characteristics, such as age, gender, and genetic information, is illegal in the U.S.

Protected classes are characteristics identified by law that cannot be used in the hiring process.

Social media sites are a big part of the in-house and sourced recruiting, screening, and candidate selection process, known as **social recruiting.** Many U.S. companies and recruiters look at Facebook, YouTube, Twitter, Flickr, and blogs to get a clearer picture of job candidates. Recruiters see LinkedIn as the world's largest resume database. Tools like Wink are used to do keyword searches across social networks and to create lists of desirable candidates who are further investigated. Depending on how job candidates control their privacy and how much they reveal by checking in and posting (Figure 14.1), recruiters learn a great deal of information that should *not* be used in their decision to interview, recommend, or hire someone.

Protected Classes and Information

According to Federal Equal Employment Opportunity (EEO) Laws (*eeoc.gov*) discriminatory practices are prohibited. Title VII of the Civil Rights Act of 1964, the Age Discrimination in Employment Act of 1967 (ADEA), the Americans with Disabilities Act of 1990 (ADA), and Genetic Information Nondiscrimination Act of 2008 (GINA) make it illegal to discriminate in any aspect of employment, including recruitment, hiring and firing. GINA, the latest of these laws, was passed when results from the human genome project (*genomics.energy.gov/*) started raising ethical dilemmas. **Protected class** is a term used in these laws to describe characteristics that cannot be targeted for discrimination and harassment. Protected classes include age, disability, gender, religion, genetic information, race, national origin, and pregnancy.

With high unemployment rates hurting the recruiting industry, fiercer competition is driving recruiters to use unprecedented access to social information to do what they

Figure 14.1 (a & b) Via their own posts and check-ins, people deliver information to potential employers and recruiters that are forbidden by law when deciding whether or not they are a good fit for the job and company.

(a)

(b)

Discrimination

The prejudicial treatment or consider of a person, racial group, minority, e based on category rather than indivi excluding or restricting members of on the grounds of race, sex, or age

© Ivelin Radkov/Alamy Limited

Figure 14.2 Discrimination is the result of prejudicial treatment based on protected information rather than a person's qualifications.

consider that best possible job to keep their clients loyal and survive the downturn. But when information about protected classes is used to weed out candidates, it can lead to **corporate social media discrimination.** Discrimination is not always black-and-white because it is prejudicial treatment (see Figure 14.2) that may be tough to prove. There may not be any high-profile cases yet, but social media discrimination is going on. Within a few years, there likely will be several lawsuits.

Social Media Discrimination Scenario

Imagine that an employer reviews a candidate's activity on social media platforms and discovers the following information about her:

1. The candidate checks in via Foursquare at Woodsman Gym once or twice a day usually around 7 a.m., noon, or 6 p.m.
2. She shared many Occupy Wall Street twitpics.
3. Her Facebook album has lots of party photos, like the one in Figure 14.3, showing what might be excessive drinking.
4. Based on the college graduation date, her resume suggests that she's about 35 years old, but her social profile indicates a birth date that makes her real age 43 years.
5. Twitter conversations with friends joke about the night she was arrested, and her considering becoming Buddhist.
6. Her blog talks about her family's serious medical condition and the financial stress caused by the condition.

Like many other job seekers, this candidate is posting, tweeting, and blogging information she would not want a recruiter or prospective employer to know about. If she is rejected because of her age, religion, or genetic condition, the company has committed social media discrimination and is very likely in violation of the laws and regulations cited earlier.

Figure 14.3 Party photos might not show illegal behavior, but when posted on a social network could influence a potential employer's evaluation of a job applicant, as well as disclose information about race, gender, age, and other protected characteristics.

© Bubbles Photolibrary/Alamy Limited

Legal Ethics—Finding the Line between Must Do & Cannot Do

Employment law attorneys have advised organizations to avoid using social media in their hiring and recruitment process to avoid legal risk. But that's not realistic. In 2011, 36.6 million U.S. job seekers used social media according to *Jobvite.com*. By opting out of social media, recruiting firms would lose a lucrative way to find candidates, which could cost them millions of dollars. And background checks are needed to manage hiring risks.

Almost all employers do some form of background screening in order to avoid the risk of **negligent hiring.** Negligent hiring is a claim made by an injured party against an employer who knew or should have known facts about an employee's background that indicate a dangerous or untrustworthy character. Employers have a legal obligation to make the best effort to protect their employees and customers when they hire. Max Drucker, president of Social Intelligence explains that:

> *Employers are in a tough spot—on the one hand, if they do not review applicants' publicly available social media, they expose the organization to workplace risks and negligent hiring. On the other hand, if they conduct the screening internally, they are exposed to a lot of information not legally allowable for hiring such as religion, sexuality orientation, and health status that may lead to a discrimination lawsuit.*

Social Intelligence (*socialintel.com*) performs social media searches and screens candidates for a limited number of things, namely aggressive or violent acts or assertions, unlawful activity, discriminatory activity such as racist remarks, and sexually explicit activity. For examples of social media background screening reports, visit *gizmodo.com/5818774/this-is-a-social-media-background-check* (also see the *Chapter 14 Link Library*).

In 2011, the Federal Trade Commission (FTC) ruled that companies that research how you spend your personal time, hobbies, and the like do not violate your privacy. "When someone puts their public life out there publicly, it's there to be evaluated," says Kim Harmer, a partner at Harmer Associates, a Chicago-based recruiting firm (Waters, 2011).

Avoiding Social Discrimination

Steps companies can take to manage social media recruiting risks are:

1. **Ask candidates to sign a disclosure statement.** Let candidates themselves disclose information found on social media—and, if necessary, explain the information or circumstances.
2. **Create a standard process and document it.** A consistent and well-documented process is needed to insure and show compliance if there is an EEO employment investigation.
3. **Avoid coercive practices.** Make sure recruiters do not pressure applicants to disclose protected information via social media by requiring them to disclose passwords or relax privacy settings for purposes of review by the employer.
4. **Training.** This may sound like a no-brainer, but training and recurring reminders are important to emphasize that management intends to be in compliance with laws and regulations related to social recruiting.

Sources: Miller-Merrell (2012), Sturmer & Tincup (2010), Waters (2011), *Jobvite.com* (2012), *Socialintel.com* (2012), and *EEOC.gov* (2012).

Discuss

1. Why do companies and recruiters continue to engage in social recruiting?
2. Visit two or more social media sites and review information that people have posted about themselves—or their friends have posted about them. What types of protected class information did you find? Give examples.
3. When organizations source their hiring to recruiting firms, how might that increase or decrease the risk of social media discrimination?
4. Consider Max Drucker's statement about employers being in a "tough spot." Explain the two risks that employers face.

Decide

5. Social media discrimination is now a serious consideration for employers. Managers can evaluate vendor options such as *LinkedIn Recruiter* to limit liability and to remove protected information from profiles. Venture-funded startup BranchOut offers a similar tool for Facebook recruiting called *RecruiterConnect*.
   a. Visit the websites of *Recruiter* and *RecruiterConnect*. Review these vendor options. Describe their key features and benefits.
   b. Do *Recruiter* and *RecruiterConnect* protect against social discrimination? Explain your answer and give examples.

Debate & Brainstorm

6. Refer to the discrimination scenario containing the six types of information found by the person checking out the candidate. For each of the six types of information, debate whether or not it should be used to determine whether or not to hire this person.

7. In a brainstorming session, try to agree on the meaning of *responsible conduct* with respect to the use of social media for screening purposes. In your session, consider the FTC's 2011 rule stating companies that research how you spend your personal time, hobbies, and the like do not violate your privacy. Was an agreement on the meaning of *responsible conduct* with respect to the use of social media for screening purposes possible? If yes, what is the agreed upon meaning? In not, what were the list of meanings? Why was no agreement possible?

14.1 Can IT Cut its Global Carbon Footprint? Can Users?

YouTube reports that 48 hours of video are uploaded every minute, totaling 8 years of content each day. The Consumer Electronics Association (*ce.org*) estimates that in 2013, the average U.S. household has 2.5 times as many digital media devices (computing, gaming, consumer electronics, and mobile devices) in use as in 2008. BIA/Kelsey (*biakelsey.com*) and *eMarketer.com* predict that U.S. mobile ad spending will grow from $1.8 billion in 2012 to $4.4 billion in 2015, with locally targeted mobile ads increasing from 51 percent of overall U.S. mobile ad spending to 70 percent by 2015. Fossil fuels burned and other energy sources consumed to power today's life style harm the environment, unless corrective action is taken.

GREENHOUSE GAS (GHG) EMISSIONS HIT RECORD HIGHS

Heat-trapping **greenhouse-gas (GHG)** emissions worldwide hit record highs in 2011, according to the International Energy Agency (*IEA.org*), the energy analysis group. The IEA's preliminary estimates indicate that global emissions of carbon-dioxide (CO_2) from fossil-fuel combustion spiked to 31.6 gigatonnes (Gt) in 2011, an increase of 1 Gt or 3.2 percent from the 2010 level (Lemonick, 2012). One Gt equals one billion metric tons.

> **Tech Note 14-1**
>
> **Carbon Counter, in Real-Time:**
>
> *http://www.dbcca.com/dbcca/EN/*
>
> To see what CO_2 emissions in the atmosphere looks like in real time, view Deutsche Bank's carbon counter, which logs the accumulated weight at dangerously close to 4 trillion metric tons.

Video
Watch 131 Years of Global Warming in 26 Seconds
climatecentral.org/videos/web_features/nasa-finds-2011-ninth-warmest-year-on-record/.

Global Temperature Is Rising Too Much Too Fast. At the United Nations' 2009 climate conference in Copenhagen, climatologists estimated that countries must keep global mean temperature (GMT) from rising by more than 2 degrees Celsius (3.6 degrees Fahrenheit) above the pre-industrial GMT in order to avoid profound

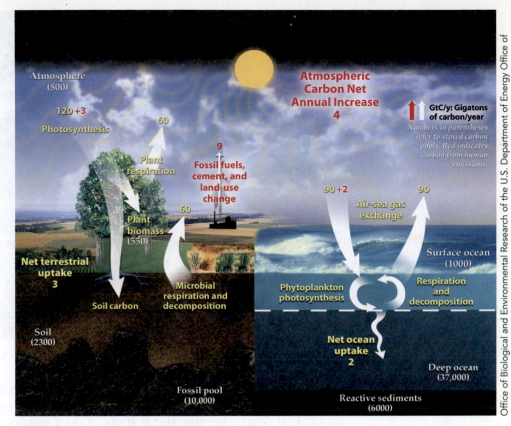

Office of Biological and Environmental Research of the U.S. Department of Energy Office of Science. science.energy.gov/ber/

Figure 14.4 Carbon cycle. One of the most daunting challenges of the 21st century is predicting the response of Earth's ecosystems to global climate change. The global carbon cycle plays a central role in regulating atmospheric carbon dioxide (CO_2) levels and thus Earth's climate. Courtesy of *genomicscience.energy.gov/*

Figure 14.5 Illustration of the earth's greenhouse effect.

IT'S ROLE IN GLOBAL WARMING

damage to life on Earth. Damage includes water and food scarcity, rising sea levels, and greater incidence and severity of disease. Only three years later, GMT already increased by 0.7°C, or 1.3°F. In 2012, IEA chief economist Faith Birol warned that this trend is perfectly in line with a temperature increase of 6 degrees Celsius by 2050, which would have devastating consequences for the planet.

Global Warming. **Global warming** refers to the upward trend in GMT. It is one of the most complicated issues facing world leaders. Figure 14.4 shows the relationship of fossil fuel, soil, water, atmosphere, etc. in the carbon cycle. Even though the global carbon cycle plays a central role in regulating CO_2 in the atmosphere and thus Earth's climate, scientists' understanding of the interlinked biological processes that drive this cycle is limited. They know that whether an ecosystem will capture, store, or release carbon depends on climate changes and organisms in the Earth's biosphere. The **biosphere** refers to any place that life of any kind can exist on Earth and contains several ecosystems. An **ecosystem** is a self-sustaining functional unit of the biosphere; and exchanges material and energy between adjoining ecosystems. Global warming occurs because of the **greenhouse effect,** which is the holding of heat within Earth's atmosphere as illustrated in Figure 14.5. GHGs such as CO_2, methane (CH_4), and nitrous oxide (N_2O) absorb infrared radiation (IR), as diagrammed in Figure 14.6.

The IT industry sector is called the *information and communications technology*, or ICT, in emission reports. ICT has certainly supported economic growth in developed and developing countries and transformed societies, businesses, and people's lives. But what impacts do our expanding IT and social media dependence have on global warming? How can business processes change reduce GHGs? And what alternative energy sources can be used to power the increasing demands for telecommunications (telecom)? Here are several reports and initiatives to help answer these questions.

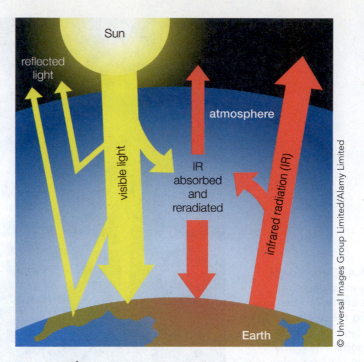

Figure 14.6 Greenhouse gases absorb infrared radiation (IR) emitted from Earth and reradiate it back, thus contributing to the greenhouse effect.

Global e-Sustainability Initiative and the SMART 2020 Report. The Climate Group's **SMART 2020 Report** (*theclimategroup.org/programs/ict/*) is the world's first comprehensive global study of the IT sector's growing significance for the world's climate. On behalf of the **Global e-Sustainability Initiative** (GeSI, *gesi.org*) Climate Group found that ICT plays a key role in reducing global warming. Transforming the way people and businesses use IT could reduce annual human-generated global emissions by 15 percent by 2020 and deliver energy efficiency savings to global businesses of over EUR 500 billion, or US $800 billion. And using social media, for example, to inform consumers of the grams (g) of carbon emissions associated with the products they buy could change buyer behavior and ultimately have a positive eco-effect. Like food items that display calories and grams of fat to help consumers make healthier food choices, product labels display the CO_2 emissions generated in the production of the item, as shown in Figure 14.7. By 2020, not only will people become more connected, but "things" will too—an estimated 50 billion machine-to-machine connections in 2020. A benefit of machine-to-machine connections is that they can relay data about climate changes that make it possible to monitor our emissions.

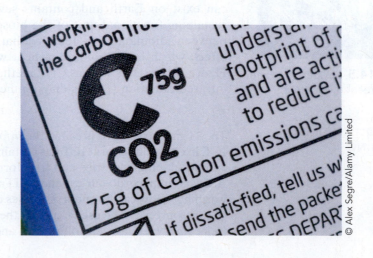

Figure 14.7 Label showing the amount of CO_2 emission generated by the production of a bag of Walkers crisps in the United Kingdom.

Recommended Actions for the IT Sector. Analysis conducted by management consultants McKinsey & Company concludes the following:

• The IT sector's own footprint of 2 percent of global emissions could double by 2020 because of increased use of tablets, smartphones, apps, and services. To help, rather than worsen, the fight against climate change, the IT sector must manage its own growing impact and continue to reduce emissions from data centers, telecom networks, and the manufacture and use of its products.

• IT has the unique ability to monitor and maximize energy efficiency both within and outside of its own industry sector to cut CO_2 emissions by up to five times this amount. This represents a saving of 7.8 Gt of CO_2 per year by 2020, which is greater than the 2010 annual emissions of either the U.S. or China.

The SMART 2020 Report gives a picture of the IT industry's role in addressing global climate change and facilitating efficient and low carbon development. The role of IT includes emission reduction and energy savings not only in the sector itself, but also by transforming how and where people work. The most obvious ways are by substituting digital formats—telework, video-conferencing, e-paper, and mobile and e-commerce—for physical formats. Researchers estimate that substituting physical products/services with their digital equivalents would provide 6 percent of the total benefits the IT sector can deliver. Greater benefits are achieved when IT is applied to other industries. Examples of those industries are smart building design and use, smart logistics, smart electricity grids, and smart industrial motor systems. "Smart" means that wasted energy and materials are minimized; and procurement, manufacturing, distribution, service, and recycling are done in an environmentally-friendly manner.

GREEN IT AND MOBILE SOLUTIONS IN DEVELOPED AND DEVELOPING NATIONS

Sustainability refers to the concept of using things at a rate that does not deplete their availability in future generations. In environmental terms, a process or industry is *unsustainable* when it uses up natural resources faster than they can be replenished. The following examples give you a wider perspective on how mobile initiatives and changes in behavior and business processes are reducing GHG and soot emissions worldwide.

• Isotrak's (*isotrak.com/*) fleet management system is designed to help U.K. businesses cut fuel costs and CO_2 emissions, reduce fleet size, and save staff time. Isotrak's fleet management system combines satellite tracking and onboard telematics data sent over the Vodafone mobile network using standard SIM cards. This IS enables businesses to monitor their fleets remotely and plan more efficient logistics based on where vehicles travel, what they carry, and how they are driven. Isotrak estimates that by changing driving styles, for example, fuel efficiency is improved up to 15 percent.

• Using fleet management systems, the U.K. supermarket chain Asda's fleet saved 29 million road kilometers and 28 Kt (kilotonnes) of CO_2, and cut fuel costs by 23 percent over three years. Asda drivers have changed their behavior to improve fuel efficiency by 6.6 percent, and the system is also enabling Asda to haul more waste and recyclable materials between stores and distribution centers, minimizing the number of trucks running inefficiently without full loads.

• To reduce fossil fuel consumption by telecom operators, solar, wind, and **sustainable biofuels** are replacing diesel fuel. Diesel emits less CO_2 than gasoline, but 25 to 400 times more black carbon and organic matter (soot).

Solar, wind, and sustainable biofuels alternative energy sources have been successful at reducing harmful emissions and global warming.

TELECOM INDUSTRY CAN LEAD THE LOW CARBON REVOLUTION

The CO_2 emissions of various segments in telecom chain are shown in Figure 14.8. As the telecoms market continues expanding so does its emissions, unless or until countermeasures are implemented. There are four carbon hotspots where significant CO_2 savings can be achieved. The first two hotspots are under the control of

Distribution of the carbon (CO$_2$) footprint

Figure 14.8 Components of the carbon footprint in the ICT sector.

telecom operators and vendors. The other two hotspots are under the control of users—and hopefully will motivate you to reduce your carbon emissions. End-users account for a substantial 16 percent of the telecom footprint.

Data centers. IT equipment that runs networks effectively and manages their client-bases are energy-guzzlers. IT equipment vendors now offer much greener equipment, and overall data center management, cooling, and recycling can significantly reduce costs and CO$_2$ emissions. Data centers are discussed later in this chapter.

Radio base stations. Millions of mobile radio base stations have to run at full power 24/7/365/worldwide. Equipment vendors are developing smart solutions to reduce power consumption. As you read, off-grid solutions are using alternative fuels.

Fixed network access equipment. Routers, switches, and modems operated by end users are inefficient machines that could be significantly greener. Household broadband modems, built at the lowest possible cost, are power guzzlers. Users can invest in eco-friendly equipment and take the responsibility to switch off their equipment manually when it is not in use.

Mobile handsets. Mobiles consume very little electric power, but are a threat to the environment because millions of phones are produced and disposed of. Recycling practices are very poor with only 5 percent of discarded handsets properly disposed of. If users slowed their renewal rates (which is unlikely) or ensured that their old equipment was properly recycled, this carbon hotspot could be reduced.

BOTTOM LINE OF GREEN COMPUTING

Green computing, the study and practice of eco-friendly computing resources, may be in companies' best financial interests. High energy costs together with the growing power consumption of computing and communications technologies are having a negative impact on many businesses' bottom line. There is also growing interest among consumers to shrink their carbon consumption (like switching to vehicles with higher miles per gallon or kilometers per liter) and increase the use of recycled and recyclable materials. But the business case for green computing is not always compelling—or compelling enough to invest in it and make the necessary process changes. *IT at Work 14.1* discusses the three myths about green IT.

While not often recognized, there are financial benefits associated with becoming a sustainable company. Three leading benefits are:

1. Cost savings by limiting waste and consumption of natural resources.
2. New business opportunities through environmentally-friendly product innovations.
3. Enhanced brand value and reputation with customers and partners, and others.

Virtualization in Data Centers. At the heart of the "Next Generation Data Center" strategy is the ability to deliver and support secure IT applications through virtualization. Virtualization enables efficient use of available resources. With energy and power costs increasing as the size of IT infrastructures grows, holding expenses to a minimum is a top priority for many CIOs. Data center virtualization means that servers are consolidated (integrated) so that they can be shared. Most stand-alone servers are highly underutilized. Virtualization technology optimizes the capacity and

IT at Work 14.1

Three Green IT Myths

All hardware manufacturers offer systems that meet stringent standards for efficiency and sustainable manufacturing. Lead and toxic materials are eliminated or minimized and data centers are consuming less energy. While it may seem that going green is a common goal, it's the actual execution that matters.

Myth 1: Business case for green IT is clear. Trying to quantify the cost savings of green IT may be impossible or nonapplicable if cloud computing is used. The beneficiary of energy-efficient servers is not the company, but their outsourcer. For in-house servers and other hardware, energy costs may not be broken down enough for anyone to know what the savings would be. So the issue of who realizes the cost benefits is unclear, and that makes it tricky to pinpoint the real payback drivers for a given green project. Once a company can track the energy use of specific equipment, and break it down by business units, it becomes possible to incentivize and recognize those departments (like IT) that drive improvements.

Myth 2: Green IT is an achievable outcome. Green IT is an ongoing process and includes policies that define a way of operating over the long term. Companies don't achieve green and then quit. Energy efficiency and environmentally responsible manufacturing need to be made a part of hardware procurement policy. Industry standards like EPEAT and ENERGY STAR (discussed in this chapter) change. As green technology evolves, so do the standards, making green IT a continuous improvement process.

Myth 3: Everyone cares about green IT. The Society for Information Management (SIM) surveyed CIOs and IT executive leaders about their top priorities for 2010, based on a list of 20 IT and business concerns. Green IT wasn't one of them. The two top priorities were *cost reduction* because of the recession and alignment of IT and the business. Companies are concerned with costs—and so are the public and nonprofit sectors. Green IT initiatives should be described in terms of reducing waste and inefficiency to get management's attention. But even that tactic may be a tough sell if prior IT investments touted as reducing waste and inefficiency did not achieve those objectives.

Sources: Compiled from Alvares (2010) and Chickowski (2009).

Questions

1. Discuss the implications of these three myths.

2. If you can't sell *green IT* as a concept to management, identify a way to package and present the concept. Viewing the slideshow *CIO Priorities for 2010* on *Baseline.com* at baselinemag.com/c/a/IT-Management/CIO-Priorities-for-2010-706071/may be helpful.

---

processing power of servers so that fewer servers are needed to provide the necessary processing power. Two examples are:

1. Microsoft's commitment to green technology heavily leverages virtualization because of their massive data centers. Data centers are where virtualization can have the greatest impact, and that's where leading companies in the virtualization market are investing their resources. Virtualized, dynamic data centers lower energy consumption, reduce the number of servers needed, and extend server life. The benefits of longer server life are less manufacturing and less toxic materials in landfills.

2. By consolidating and moving to more efficient data centers, Sun increased processing power by over a 450 percent with about one-half the servers and over a 240 percent increase in storage capacity with about one-third the storage devices.

Telework. Telework can minimize damaging the environment or depleting natural resources by reducing pollution. Also called telecommuting or virtual work, it offers many green benefits, including reducing rush-hour traffic, improving air quality, improving highway safety, and even improving healthcare. Table 14.1 lists telework benefits.

Questions

1. What is green computing?
2. Explain global warming and the greenhouse effect.
3. What are some low carbon alternatives to fossil fuels?
4. What is the role of virtualization in green data centers?
5. What are the benefits of telework?

TABLE 14.1	Benefits of Telework	
Individuals	**Organizations**	**Community and Society**
• Reduces or eliminates travel-related time and expenses • Improves health by reducing stress related to compromises made between family and work responsibilities • Allows closer proximity to and involvement with family • Allows closer bonds with the family and the community • Decreases involvement in office politics • Increases productivity despite distractions	• Reduces office space needed • Increases labor pool and competitive advantage in recruitment • Provides compliance with Americans with Disabilities Act • Decreases employee turnover, absenteeism, and sick leave usage • Improves job satisfaction and productivity	• Conserves energy and lessens dependence on foreign oil • Preserves the environment by reducing traffic-related pollution and congestion • Reduces traffic accidents and resulting injuries or deaths • Reduces the incidence of disrupted families when people do not have to quit their jobs if they need to move because of a spouse's new job or family obligations • Increased employment opportunities for the homebound • Allows the movement of job opportunities to areas of high unemployment

14.2 Responsible Conduct

Does the availability of information justify its use? Can shoppers keep their buying habits private? Can people keep their entertainment, online gaming, and other legal activities confidential? Do media have the right to publish or post highly private text messages of politicians and celebrities? Questions about data access and capture, mining, tracking, monitoring, privacy, and profiling are examples of IT capabilities that have ethical considerations. Here are cases of taking the power of information and analytics too far.

CASES OF QUESTIONABLE OR IRRESPONSIBLE CONDUCT

1. Credit card companies: Divorce in the future?   Using analytics and monitoring, credit-card companies try to figure out whether customers may be headed toward divorce. They look for indicators knowing that divorce increases the risk that customers will skip or stop paying their bills. Paying for marriage counseling with a credit card is an obvious indicator that credit card companies react to by decreasing the credit limit.

When companies can see inside bodies or bedrooms is that too invasive or a smart use of IT? When customers learn the truth, there may be backlash. Depending on how intrusive, companies may face investigations and fines. An example is Google's Street View Wi-Fi scandal—dubbed *Wi-Spy*.

2. Google: Disturbing FCC Report on Google's Street View Wi-Spy Snooping Scandal.   Beginning in 2007, Google's Street View cars (Figure 14.9) began driving on U.S. streets—and later in Europe, Canada, Mexico, and everywhere else—collecting a stream of images to feed into Google Maps (*maps.google.com*). Google's engineers realized the cars could be used for **wardriving**—driving around sniffing out and mapping the physical location of the world's Wi-Fi routers. Wardriving is also a hacking technique, an invasion of privacy, and an information security risk.

Creating a database of Wi-Fi hotspot locations would make Google Maps more useful on mobile devices. Mobiles without GPS chips could use the database to approximate their physical location, and GPS-enabled devices could use the system to speed up their location-monitoring systems. When Google was building its system, a few startups already had created their own Wi-Fi mapping databases. But Google

Multimedia Graphic
How Google Collected Data from Wi-Fi Networks
nytimes.com/interactive/2012/05/23/business/How-Google-Collected-Data-From-Wi-Fi-Networks.html?ref=technology

Figure 14.9 Google vehicle with camera attached to photograph images used in Street View maps.

was not only recording the location of people's Wi-Fi routers. When a Street View car encountered an **open Wi-Fi network**—a non-password protected router—it recorded *all the digital traffic traveling across that router.* That is, when the car was within range of someone's open router, Google captured personal data, including login names and passwords, the full text of e-mails, Internet histories, people's medical conditions, online dating searches, streaming movies, and all other traffic.

According to the FCC (Federal Communications Commission; *fcc.gov*) report, French investigators reviewed the data Google collected, and found "an exchange of emails between a married woman and man, both seeking an extra-marital relationship" and "Web addresses that revealed the sexual preferences of consumers at specific residences." In the U.S., Street View cars collected 200 gigabytes of private data between 2008 and 2010. The sniffing stopped only when regulators discovered the practice. Google denied any wrongdoing.

The FCC posted the following on its website: "Google's behavior also raises important concerns. Whether intentional or not, collecting information sent over Wi-Fi networks clearly infringes on consumer privacy."

The FCC determined that Google's actions were not technically illegal because snooping on unencrypted wireless data is not prohibited by the Wiretap Act. Given that Google manages so much of our personal data, this privacy invasion is an example of irresponsible conduct.

But the story did not end with the FCC's decision. In May 2012, the FCC's investigation into Google's mapping project was itself being investigated. The renewed attention followed release of a mostly unredacted version of the FCC's findings in the case. The unredacted findings appear to contradict Google's claim that it inadvertently intercepted "payload data," or the content of individuals' Internet communications, in the process of gathering information from Wi-Fi networks across the globe for the Street View project. The document shows that, during preparations for the Street View effort, a Google engineer shared e-mails with colleagues at the firm revealing that he had designed software for the project that was capable of collecting payload data. The new revelations have prompted *Consumer Watchdog,* a Washington-based advocacy group, to call for a hearing by the Senate Judiciary Subcommittee on Privacy, Technology and the Law.

Business Case 2 describes how Target's aggressive and intrusive use of data mining triggered customer backlash—and forced management to change its marketing tactics.

These cases highlight contentious ethical issues and possibly irresponsible data-driven business practices. There may be no easy answers to these dilemmas.

Competing Responsibilities. To market more efficiently, most major retailers, from supermarket and drug store chains to major investment banks rely on predictive analytics to understand consumers' shopping habits and their personal habits. There are competing interests and tradeoffs at work when the issue is privacy. And there's not a clear-cut framework for deciding what is ethical and what's not. The personal privacy vs. public's security debate is a prime example. Typically, privacy invasion is considered unethical. An ethically conscious corporate attitude sounds politically correct, but managers also have responsibility to stakeholders. Monitoring may be (or seem to be) the responsible thing to do. And with intense competition, marketers naturally want to use every tool or technique to gain an edge or nullify a risk.

Globalization, the Internet, and connectivity have the power to undermine moral responsibility because it becomes relatively easy to ignore harm. Despite the challenges and lack of clear answers, ethics is important because relying on the law alone to safeguard civil rights and society is insufficient. The law has its limits in large part because it changes so slowly.

FREE SPEECH VIA WIKIS AND SOCIAL NETWORKS

Free speech and privacy rights collide in a world populated by anonymous critics, vengeful people, personal agendas, and malcontents. But the attacks are not always from competitors or others outside the company. Because of the nature of the Internet, at times we may become our own worst enemies personally and professionally based on the content or images we post on blogs, or the friends we keep on social networking pages. *IT at Work 14.2* describes irresponsible and illegal conduct of the CEO of Whole Foods. The lesson to be learned from this case is that companies need to make sure that when managers and employees post in the blogosphere, they know what they can and cannot say about business information.

Questions

1. Why might credit card companies use data analytics and monitoring tools?
2. How can data analytics reduce risk for credit card companies?
3. Distinguish between presence and location. Give an example of each.
4. Where and why do free speech and privacy rights collide?

IT at Work 14.2

CEO's Blogging Is a Federal Crime

The CEO of Whole Foods Market, John Mackey, was blogging on the Yahoo! Finance message boards (*messages.yahoo.com*) anonymously as *Rahodeb*. Whole Foods Market (*wholefoodsmarket.com*) is the world's largest retailer of natural and organic foods, with stores throughout North America and the United Kingdom. As Radodeb, the CEO told the world that "Whole Foods Is Hot, and Wild Oats is NOT." He did not disclose that he was hoping to purchase Wild Oats Market.

Whole Foods eventually completed the controversial $565 million purchase of Wild Oats, which closed in August 2007 after a six-month battle with the FTC. When the FTC had audited Whole Foods, they discovered the CEO's deceptive blog posts. The blogging caused significant problems for the acquisition. Manipulating or influencing financial markets is a

federal crime. Therefore, blogging to influence financial markets may be deemed by the FTC or SEC as a federal crime, particularly when done by the CEO posing as someone else. The takeover also led to an investigation by the Securities and Exchange Commission (SEC) following the revelation that "Rahodeb" had been secretly promoting his company's stock and disparaging his rival's management team in postings in the Yahoo! stock message board. The investigation led to the suspension of Mackey's blogging privileges until the SEC and the Whole Foods board completed their investigations of Mackey's ill-considered blog outbursts.

While the acquisition was eventually approved, Whole Foods and the CEO suffered damage to their reputations and huge legal fees and fines.

14.3 Connectivity Overload and a Culture of Distraction

Consider your daily sources of information and what you check on your mobile or the Internet. Tweets, texts, feeds, posts, voice messages, Facebook, LinkedIn, sport sites, Web cams, Skype, and dozens of apps. You probably haven't noticed the increase in the amount of information that you receive or check routinely. How many more things do you check today compared to a year ago? How long can you go without checking your mobile or computer without experiencing some anxiety? How many browser tabs do you have open right now, as you read? When do you put down your mobiles and concentrate on one thing at a time? Even if you're not aware of it, your answers indicate information or connectivity overload and your tolerance for distractions.

People adapt to new ITs—many of which become *must have* and *can't function without* gadgets rather quickly. This situation is not limited to only digital natives. Studies show that adults are just as distracted as teenagers, which can also be confirmed with a casual glance at offices, airports, cafes, and so on.

OVERLOADS AND DISTRACTIONS

IT's capability to introduce ever-growing amounts of data into our lives can exceed our capacity to keep up with the data, leading to **information overload.** Business users are more likely to suffer from too much data, rather than from data scarcity. Finding the information they need in massive collections of documents can be complicated, time consuming, frustrating, and expensive.

Maggie Jackson, author of *Distracted: The Erosion of Attention and the Coming Dark Age* (2008) suggested: "We're really facing the limit of human ability to cope with stimuli in our environment." University of California—San Diego researchers found that on average, Americans hear, see, or read 34 gigabytes worth of information a day—about 100,000 words from TV, Internet, books, radio, newspapers and other sources. And *Bloomberg BusinessWeek* (2008) reported that knowledge workers are distracted every three minutes at work—answering the phone, checking e-mail, responding to a text, or checking YouTube or Facebook. The consequence is that people are continuously paying partial attention to everything—skimming instead of being fully engaged. But there are also financial costs. According to Basex, a business research company in New York City, distractions take up to 28 percent of the average U.S. worker's day, including recovery time, and sap productivity to the cost of $650 billion a year.

To be effective at solving the problem of information overload, information systems must differentiate between the data that can be safely summarized and the data that should be viewed in its original form. This is a difficult problem to solve.

INFORMATION QUALITY—MANDATED BY FEDERAL LAWS

As organizations and societies continue to generate, process, and rely on rapidly increasing amounts of information, they begin to realize the importance of **information quality.** Information quality is a somewhat subjective measure of the utility, objectivity, and integrity of gathered information. To be valuable, both data and information must possess a number of essential characteristics, such as being complete, accurate, up to date, and consistent with the purposes for which they are used. The value and usability of data and information that do not satisfy these requirements are severely limited.

Information quality is mandated by several legislations. The Data Quality Act of 2001 and the Sarbanes-Oxley Act of 2002 impose strict information quality requirements on government agencies and companies. For example, one of the provisions of the Sarbanes–Oxley Act makes chief executive and financial officers personally responsible and liable for the quality of financial information that firms release to stockholders or file with the Securities and Exchange Commission (SEC). This provision emphasizes the importance of controlling and measuring data quality and information quality in business intelligence (BI), corporate performance management, and record management systems.

Problems with information quality are not limited to corporate data. Millions of individuals face information quality issues whenever they search for information online, whether on publicly available web pages or in specialized research databases, wikis, blogs, and newsfeeds.

Among the most common problems that plague online information sources is omission of materials. A number of online "full-text" periodicals databases may omit certain items that appeared in the printed versions of their publications. In addition, online sources of information leave out older documents, which are not available in digital form. Thus, one cannot be assured of having access to a complete set of relevant materials. Even materials that are available from seemingly reputable sources present information quality concerns. Information may have been incorrectly reported, whether intentionally or unintentionally, or it may have become out of date. These and other information quality issues are contributing to the frustration and anxiety that for some people have become the unfortunate side effects of the Information Age.

IMPACTS ON INDIVIDUALS

Pervasive IT has caused changes in structure, authority, power, and job content, as well as personnel management and human resources management. Details of these changes are shown in Table 14.2. Together, the increasing amounts of information and IT use impact job satisfaction, dehumanization, and information anxiety as well as health and safety. Although many jobs may become substantially more enriched with IT, other jobs may become more routine and less satisfying.

Questions

1. What is information overload?
2. What are the consequences of connectivity or information overload?
3. What are the consequences of constant distractions?
4. What is information quality? Name one law that requires companies to ensure their information quality.
5. What are the impacts of pervasive IT?

TABLE 14.2	Impacts of IT on Structure, Authority, Power, and Job Content
Impact	**Effect of IT**
Flatter organizational hierarchies	IT increases *span of control* (more employees per supervisor), increases productivity, and reduces the need for technical experts (due to expert systems). Fewer managerial levels will result, with fewer staff and line managers. Reduction in the total number of employees, reengineering of business processes, and the ability of lower-level employees to perform higher-level jobs may result in flatter organizational hierarchies.
Change in blue-collar-to-white-collar staff ratio	The ratio of white- to blue-collar workers increases as computers replace clerical jobs, and as the need for information systems specialists increases. However, the number of professionals and specialists could *decline* in relation to the total number of employees in some organizations as intelligent and knowledge-based systems grow.
Growth in number of special units	IT makes possible technology centers, e-commerce centers, decision-support systems departments, and/or intelligent systems departments. Such units may have a major impact on organizational structure, especially when they are supported by or report directly to top management.
Centralization of authority	Centralization may become more popular because of the trend toward smaller and flatter organizations and the use of expert systems. On the other hand, the web permits greater empowerment, allowing for more decentralization. Whether use of IT results in more centralization or in decentralization may depend on top management's philosophy.
Changes in power and status	Knowledge is power, and those who control information and knowledge are likely to gain power. The struggle over who controls the information resources has become a conflict in many organizations. In some countries, the fight may be between corporations that seek to use information for competitive advantage and the government (e.g., Microsoft vs. the Justice Dept.). Elsewhere, governments may seek to hold onto the reins of power by not letting private citizens access some information.
Changes in job content and skill sets	*Job content* is interrelated with employee satisfaction, compensation, status, and productivity. Resistance to changes in job skills is common, and can lead to unpleasant confrontations between employees and management.

14.4 On the Verge of a New Tech Revolution

Accenture's Technology *Vision* (*Accenture.com*) is an analysis of key IT trends that are expected to impact businesses over the next three to five years. The *Vision* is updated yearly to help organizations set their IT strategy and investment priorities.

Accenture's *Technology Vision 2012* trends and descriptions are:

1. Context-based services. Where you are (your context) and what you are doing will drive the next wave of digital services.

Industry uses RFID sensors and tags to supply contextual data about product locations, time, temperature, and much more. In the next five years, the increased number and types of sensors will add context to other services. Services will integrate real-time signals from the physical world with location data, online activities, social media, and many other types of contextual inputs. For example, services may support a pharmaceutical sales rep with context about doctors she will be meeting and drugs she's selling. It could be data made available to a technician at an oil refinery, customized to the equipment he's servicing and what its downtime history looks like. Or a shopping app that gives a customer fast access to data about new snowboards whose quick response (QR) codes he's scanned in the store; tells him how far he is from stores that carry them, alerts him to his available credit; and gets instant opinions, via Facebook, from friends about the board. iPhone, for instance, contains Bluetooth Smart technology—a new standard that supports connections to sensors that consume very little power.

2. Converging data architectures. Successfully rebalancing the data architecture portfolio and blending structured with unstructured data are key to turning data into new streams of value. IT needs to find ways to converge all forms of data, sometimes using bridge technologies. One large high-tech company uses Hadoop to process and import data into traditional systems in ways that wouldn't be possible with technology designed for structured data, The Hadoop framework acts as a preprocessing engine for analyzing raw data to extract important events before feeding the data to other systems. Data are integrated with existing reporting in such a way that they minimize the impact on the rest of the enterprise.

3. New approaches to data management. The ability to share data will make it more valuable if it is managed differently. Businesses looking for ways to extract more value from their data will increase data sharing. New approaches to data management will be needed to centralize the processes and tools needed for data sharing.

4. Social-driven IT. Realize that social media is not just a bolt-on marketing channel. It will have true business-wide impact. Facebook, LinkedIn, Twitter, and other social media are not just new communication channels to customers. They are powerful catalysts changing how customers, employees, and partners use IT to interact with the world around them. Few organizations are leveraging social media in new ways to take full advantage of it. Within five years, they will.

The social media question for businesses has changed from "What should I be posting to Facebook?" to "How do my customers want to interact with my services?" Social transforms our way of interacting with the world; it has its own language, taboos, interaction styles, communication channels, customs, habits, preferences, and pace. It provides businesses with new interactions, services, customers, forms of loyalty, and sales revenue. Those not actively engaged with or experimenting with social, or planning ways to move it beyond marketing are putting themselves at risk.

5. PaaS-enabled agility. The platform-as-a-service (PaaS) market is shifting the emphasis from cost cutting to business innovation, supporting business processes that need continuous change.

Managers are identifying the business processes and apps that will matter most to their organizations—and that are best suited to a platform-as-a-service model. PaaS is not just a tool for squeezing cost out of IT; PaaS will provide an environment that can support rapid evolution for key business processes that need continuous change.

6. **Orchestrated analytical security.** Organizations will have to accept that their networks and databases will be breached. They need to prepare their second line of defense—*data platforms*—to mitigate the damage caused by attacks that get through firewalls and other end-points.

Attacks on organizations' information systems are out of control, and threat levels are skyrocketing as sophisticated, targeted forms of cybercrime emerge. Information security is no longer only about solo hackers and occasional malware. It's about increasingly professional attacks. Although most companies have huge IT security systems investments, they are still largely unprepared for the scope, severity, and sophistication of today's attacks or for the growing list of exposed entry points that highly skilled attackers can now exploit. Governments and organized crime groups are being added to the lists of hackers. Cars, assembly lines, pumps, and mobile phones are quickly becoming new vulnerability points for hackers to target as those systems and devices get connected to corporate IT.

NEXT WAVE OF DISRUPTION WILL BE MORE DISRUPTIVE

High-performing business leaders now accept that their organizations' future success is tied to their ability to keep pace with technology. Accenture reports that their clients tell them that technology is more important than ever to their business success. Some sense that we are on the verge of a new technology revolution that will be even more disruptive than previous ones. The flexibility of new technologies and architectures will naturally change how IT makes it easier for organizations to innovate.

Questions

1. Explain context-based services.
2. Explain converging data architectures.
3. Describe why data architectures need to converge.
4. Explain why the social media question for businesses has changed from "What should I be posting to Facebook?" to "How do my customers want to interact with my services?"
5. Explain PaaS-enabled agility.
6. How have information risks changed? What information security is needed to defend against the latest risks?

Key Terms

You find clickable Link Libraries for each chapter on the Companion website.

Accenture Technology Vision 2012 *accenture.com/us-en/technology/technology-labs/Pages/insight-accenture-technology-vision-2012.aspx?c=tech_tgpfy12_10000007&n=ilc_0112*

Watch 131 Years of Global Warming in 26 Seconds *http://www.climatecentral.org/videos/web_features/nasa-finds-2011-ninth-warmest-year-on-record/*

Social Intelligence report examples. *I Flunked My Social Media Background Check. Will You?* *http://gizmodo.com/5818774/this-is-a-social-media-background-check*

Carbon counter, in real-time *http://www.dbcca.com/dbcca/EN/*

Internet World Stats *http://internetworldstats.com/stats.htm*

Green IT *http://greenit.net/*

Google Earth *wirelessintelligence.com/green-power/*

SMART 2020, enabling a low carbon economy *smart2020.org/*

Green Student U *http://greenstudentu.com/*

Green Power for Mobile (GPM) of the GSMA *http://www.gsma.com/developmentfund/welcome-to-the-new-green-power-for-mobile-webpage/*

3D view of mobile Green Power deployments/solutions *http://wirelessintelligence.com/green-power/*

Google Earth plug-in *earth.google.com/plugin/*
Or *http://www.google.com/earth/explore/products/plugin.html*

Stop Climate Change, European Free Alliance *http://stopclimatechange.net/*

U.S. Global Change Research Program *http://globalchange.gov/*

Demanding Facebook Passwords May Break Law, Say Senators *http://abcnews.go.com/Technology/facebook-passwords-employers-schools-demand-access-facebook-senators/story?id=16005565#.T8FBjVK_7VA*

Employers requiring Facebook passwords may be investigated by feds *http://agbeat.com/real-estate-technology-new-media/employers-requiring-facebook-passwords-may-be-investigated-by-feds/*

Expert says policy requiring employee to give employer Facebook password is bad idea *http://www.employmentlawdaily.com/index.php/news/expert-says-policy-requiring-employee-to-give-employer-facebook-password-is-bad-idea/*

PBS Newshour video titled "How Will FCC's Google Street View Fine Shape Data Rules?" *youtube.com/watch?v=wMO7TPRhaEk*

How Google Collected Data From Wi-Fi Networks *http://www.nytimes.com/interactive/2012/05/23/business/How-Google-Collected-Data-From-Wi-Fi-Networks.html?ref=technology*

Evaluate and Expand Your Learning

IT and Data Management Decisions

1. Investments in energy-conserving data centers or other computing facilities can reduce the long-term costs of ownership and maintenance. But organizations need to pay upfront premiums to invest in green computers that are both energy efficient and environmentally responsible.

Organizations that have invested in green hardware find that the energy savings, extended product lifecycle, positive public image, and other benefits exceeded the additional costs of that hardware—improving net profit.

a. Given this situation, in your opinion, why wouldn't companies invest in energy-saving IT and business practices?

b. In your opinion, why aren't managers more concerned with global warming and the greenhouse effect? That is, why aren't all levels of management concerned enough about the health of current and future generations and the planet to make investments to reduce GHGs?

c. What can you do to reduce your carbon footprint and still meet your responsibilities? (Skipping class to reduce driving would not meet both those criteria.) What would motivate you to take the actions?

d. Why is reducing your carbon footprint so difficult?

2. To increase payback from its green initiatives, customers would have to learn that the company was green, and they'd also need to be concerned about the dangers of global warming. What would be a cost-effective way for companies to promote their green public image and convince customers of the value of green efforts?

Questions for Discussion & Review

1. What is the relationship between GHG emissions and global warming?

2. How can carbon footprints be reduced by users and by organizations?

3. In your opinion, have mobiles, the Internet, and social media changed the way we communicate with each other and get news about our friends and family?

4. How has IT changed the way you communicate?

5. What changes do you predict in the way we communicate with each other in future?

6. If you were an employee in a company that offered telecommuting options, would you prefer to work from home, from the office, or some combination of both? Explain your answer.

7. Clerks at 7-Eleven stores enter data regarding customers' gender, approximate age, and so on into a computer system. However, names are not keyed in. These data are then aggregated and analyzed to improve corporate decision making. Customers are not informed about this, nor are they asked for permission. What problems do you see with this practice?

8. Discuss whether information overload is a problem in your work or education. Based on your experience, what personal and organizational solutions can you recommend for this problem?

9. Discuss how IT will change or influence organizations in the future.

Online Activities (find links in the Chapter 14 Link Library)

1. Visit *wirelessintelligence.com/green-power/* and download the Google Earth plug-in at *http://earth.google.com/plugin/* or *http://www.google.com/earth/explore/products/plugin.html*. Then take the 3D view of mobile Green Power deployments/solutions. Describe what you learned.

2. Assume that you read about a new non-alcoholic drink discovery called "Don't-forget-a-thing." This remarkable drink, being marketed to students for $9.99 plus shipping and handling, would give the perfect recall of what he or she had read in the textbook in preparation for the exam. How would you verify the truth and accuracy of this drink—or any new drink or drug treatment—before ordering it or ingesting it? Identify five sources of trusted health, medical, or drug information.

3. Visit Climate Central's site at *climatecentral.org/videos/web_features/nasa-finds-2011-ninth-warmest-year-on-record/* and click "Watch 131 Years of Global Warming in 26 Seconds" Describe what you learned.

4. Visit *gizmodo.com/5818774/this-is-a-social-media-background-check* and read the article *I Flunked My Social Media Background Check. Will You?* Describe what you learned.

5. Visit *abcnews.go.com/Technology/facebook-passwords-employers-schools-demand-access-facebook-senators/story?id=16005565#.T8FBjVK_7VA* and read "Demanding Facebook Passwords May Break Law, Say Senators." Explain why demanding Facebook password might break the law.

6. Visit *agbeat.com/real-estate-technology-new-media/employers-requiring-facebook-passwords-may-be-investigated-by-feds/* and read "Employers requiring Facebook passwords may be investigated by feds." Describe the issues and make policy recommendations based on the article.

7. Visit *employmentlawdaily.com/index.php/news/expert-says-policy-requiring-employee-to-give-employer-facebook-password-is-bad-idea/* and read "Expert says policy requiring employee to give employer Facebook password is bad idea." Describe the important business issues.

Collaborative Work

1. Research the Google Street View investigation by the FCC. How did Google respond to the allegations and investigation? Explain why Google's management responded the way they did. Then research the investigation of the FCC's investigation, as called for by *Consumer Watchdog,* which wanted a hearing by the Senate Judiciary Subcommittee on Privacy, Technology and the Law. What was the outcome?

2. The State of California maintains a database of people who allegedly abuse children. (The database also includes names of the alleged victims.) The list is made available to dozens of public agencies, and it is considered in cases of child adoption and employment decisions. Because so many people have access to the list, its content is easily disclosed to outsiders. An alleged abuser and her child, whose case was dropped but whose names had remained on the list, sued the State of California for invasion of privacy. Debate the issues involved. Specifically:

a. Who should make the decision or what criteria should guide the decision about what names should be included, and what the criteria should be?

b. What is the potential damage to the abusers (if any)?

c. Should the State of California abolish the list? Why or why not?

CASE 2   BUSINESS CASE

Target's Big Data Analytics Know Too Much

An angry man went into a Target store near Minneapolis insisting on talking to a manager: He handed a Target promotion that had been mailed to his daughter to the manager saying: "My daughter got this in the mail. She's still in high school, and you're sending her coupons for baby clothes and cribs? Are you trying to encourage her to get pregnant?" The confused manager had no idea what was going on. The mailer had been sent by Target and addressed to the man's daughter; and it contained specials for maternity clothing, and nursery furniture. A few days later he called the father to apologize again. Instead, the father apologized to the manager explaining that he has since learned that his daughter was pregnant.

Big Data Analytics Too Invasive

How did Target know? Using big data, models of buying habits, predictive analytics, and her purchase history, Target had figured out (with about 87 percent probability) that she was pregnant. But Target informed her family before she did. A lesson that Target discovered fairly quickly is that knowing about pregnancies in advance creeps out people and can be a public-relations disaster (Duhigg, 2012). While Target assures compliance with all privacy laws, not breaking the law does not mean it's in the company's best interest to invade customers' privacy.

How Does Target Make Such Accurate Predictions?

Target assigns every customer a Guest ID number that is linked to her credit card, name, e-mail address, social media profile. Guest ID becomes a bucket to store everything she's bought and demographic data. Linked to Guest ID are demographic data including age, marital status, number of kids, address, how long it takes to drive to the store, estimated salary, whether the person moved recently, other credit cards, and visited web sites. Using their own predictive models, Target identifies customers who are pregnant.

Why Does Target Invest in Predictive Analytics?

Target's strategy is to capture a greater share of spend on baby items by being first to reach and promote to prospective parents. Waiting for public birth records is too late because by then parents are bombarded with offers and incentives from competing companies. Not everyone appreciates Target's strategy.

Questions

1. Are Target's data mining and predictive analytics a success or failure? Explain your answer.
2. How does Target create profiles of customers?
3. Is Target's "pregnancy predictor" a competitive advantage? Explain.
4. How can this predictor upset families who receive the promotions?
5. How does Target make such accurate predictions?
6. Why does Target invest in predictive analytics?

CASE 3   VIDEO CASE

Backlash against Google Street View

View the PBS Newshour video titled "How Will FCC's Google Street View Fine Shape Data Rules?" The *YouTube* link is *youtube.com/watch?v=wMO7TPRhaEk*. The video is 10 minutes.

1. How can people protect their privacy from Street View?
2. What does it mean that rules are in a grey area? Why are they in a grey area?
3. Why wasn't Google transparent about the type of data it was collecting?
4. Did Google violate any Wiretapping laws by capturing data from non–password protected wireless routers?
5. Why is it so easy to snoop and sniff data?
6. What is the "right to be forgotten"?
7. Why do wiretapping laws need to be reviewed and updated?
8. Name two of the issues discussed in the video that you find most disturbing. Explain why.

Simulation: Global Warming Calculator

1. Visit http://timeforchange.org/mitigation-global-warming-calculator to download the Excel file attachment Global-warming-calculator-Excel.xls. The Global Warming Calculator is an interactive simulation.
2. Input data for three different scenarios in the section: *What would happen if everyone was like you?*
3. Explain what you learned and make two recommendations to organizations about how to reduce their impact on global warming.

Resources on the Book's Website

More resources and study tools are located on the Student Website. You'll find additional chapter materials and useful Web links. In addition, self-quizzes that provide individualized feedback are available for each chapter.

References

Accenture Technology Vision 2012: Emerging Technology Trends for IT Leaders. *accenture.com/us-en/technology/technology-labs/Pages/insight-accenture-technology-vision-2012.aspx.*

Alvares, M. "The Three Biggest Myths about Green IT." *Greenbiz.blog,* June 22, 2010. *greenbiz.com/blog/2010/06/22/three-biggest-myths-about-green-it.*

Boyd, G. "Assessing Improvement in the Energy Efficiency of U.S. Auto Assembly Plants." *Duke University Environmental Economics Working Paper Series.* Working Paper EE 10-01, June 2010. *nicholas.duke.edu/institute/Duke_EE_WP_10-01.pdf.*

Carbon counter, in real-time. *http://www.dbcca.com/dbcca/EN/.*

Center for Nanoscale Materials. *nano.anl.gov/index.html.*

Chickowski, E. "CIO Priorities for 2010." Baseline, September 28, 2009. *baselinemag.com/c/a/IT-Management/CIO-Priorities-for-2010-706071/.*

Duhigg, C. "Psst, You in Aisle 5." *The New York Times,* February 19, 2012.

Finley, K. "Monitoring Employees Online Behavior—When They're Not at Work." ReadWriteWeb, October 13, 2010.

Gonsalves, A. "Despite the Internet, Google Generation Lacks Analytical Skills." *InformationWeek,* January 18, 2008.

International Energy Agency. IEA.org.

Lemonick, M.D. "Greenhouse-Gas Emissions Across Globe Hit Record High." *Climate Central,* May 25, 2012. *climatecentral.org.*

Manjoo, F. "Is It Time To Stop Trusting Google?" *Slate Magazine,* May 1, 2012.

Miller-Merrell, J. "Risky Business," *HRO Today,* Vol. 11, no. 1. January/February 2012.

Sturmer, S., & W. Tincup. "A Recruiter's Forbidden Fruit." *HRO Today,* Vol. 9, no. 9, November 2010.

U.S. Global Change Research Program, *globalchange.gov/.*

Waters, J. "Facebook Is Fun for Recruiters, Too." *The Wall Street Journal,* July 24, 2011.

Glossary

3G Third-generation mobile network standard.

4G Fourth-generation mobile network standard.

Acceptable use policy (AUP) Policy that informs users of their responsibilities, acceptable and unacceptable actions, and consequences of noncompliance.

Ad hoc report Unplanned reports generated on request to provide more information about a situation, problem, or opportunity.

Administrative controls Deal with issuing guidelines and monitoring compliance with the guidelines, policies, and procedures.

Advanced persistent threat (APT) attack.

Adware Software that automatically displays advertisements while running a program.

Affiliate marketing An arrangement whereby a marketing partner (a business, an organization, or even an individual) refers consumers to the selling company's Web site.

Agile enterprise A firm that can identify and capture opportunities more quickly than its rivals.

Agility An EC firm's ability to capture, report, and quickly respond to changes happening in the marketplace.

AJAX (Asynchronous JavaScript and XML) A group of technologies that create Web pages that respond to users' actions without requiring the entire page to reload.

Android OS Google/Open Hardset Alliance mobile OS.

Application controls Safeguards that are intended to protect specific applications.

Applications portfolio Major information systems applications, such as customer order processing, human resource management, or procurement, that have been or are to be developed.

Application Programming Interfaces (APIs) A toll that allows programs to talk to or interact with one another.

Artificial intelligence (AI) The branch of computer science that is concerned with making computers behave and "think" like humans.

Asynchronous javascript

Auction A competitive process in which either a seller solicits consecutive bids from buyers or a buyer solicits bids from sellers, and prices are determined dynamically by competitive bidding.

Audit or Auditing Investigation that is an important part of any control system.

Augmented reality An app that involves computer-generated graphic images superimposed over photos of real things.

Avatar A cyberbody that a user creates when using an online 3-D virtual world.

B2B gateway A Suite of software products that support internal and external integration and business processes.

Back-office operations The activities that support fulfillment of sales, such as accounting and logistics.

Balanced scorecard A performance measurement approach that links business goals to performance metrics.

Bandwidth A measure of the speed at which data is transmitted.

Barriers to entry How easy or difficult it is to enter an industry.

Batch processing Processing system that processes inputs at fixed intervals as a file and operates on it all at once; contrasts with *online* (or *interactive*) processing.

Blackberry OS Made by Research in Motion. This is currently the dominant smart phone OS in the U.S.

Blog Web log where users post information for others to read.

Blogosphere Blogs that exist together with similar interests as a connected community.

Botnet Collection of computers infected by software robots, or bots.

BPM mashup Preconfigured, ready-to-go integrations between different business software packages.

Brick-and-mortar organizations Organizations in which the product, the process, and the delivery agent are all physical.

Broadband Short for broad bandwidth. A measure of a network's capacity or throughput.

Buffer stock Extra inventory in case of unexpected events. Also called *safety stock*.

Bullwhip effect Phenomenon that occurs when companies significantly cut or add inventories.

Business activity monitoring (BAM) A message-based, event-driven tool that allows business users to link KPIs (key performance indicators) associated to the process being monitored on a real-time basis and provides relevant information via dashboards.

Business analytics Provides models, which are formulas or algorithms and procedures to BI.

Business continuity plan Plan that outlines the process by which businesses should recover from a major disaster. Also known as a *disaster recovery plan*.

Business impact analysis (BIA) A method or exercise to determine the impact of losing the support or availability of a resource.

Business intelligence (BI) Category of applications for gathering, storing, analyzing, and providing access to data to help enterprise users make better decisions.

Business model A method by which a company generates revenue to sustain itself.

Business process A collection of activities performed to accomplish a clearly defined goal.

Business process management (BPM) A popular management technique that includes methods and tools to support the design, analysis, implementation, management, and optimization of operational business processes.

Business process outsourcing (BPO) The process of hiring another company to handle business activities.

Business record A document that records business dealings such as contracts, research and development, accounting source documents, memos, customer/client communications, and meeting minutes.

Business process reengineering (BPR) The radical redesign of an organization's business, where one takes a current process and makes changes to increase its efficiency and create new processes.

Business strategy Defines the business objectives and long-term direction of an organization.

Business-to-business (B2B) E-commerce in which both the sellers and the buyers are business organizations.

Business-to-consumers (B2C) E-commerce in which the sellers are organizations and the buyers are individuals; also known as *e-tailing*.

Buy-side marketplace B2B model in which organizations buy needed products or services from other organizations electronically, often through a reverse auction.

Channel conflict Possible conflicts between the online selling channel and the traditional physical channel may be internal (e.g., regarding pricing or advertisement), or between a company that wants to sell direct to customers and its existing distributors.

Circuit switching Older technology that was used for telephone calls. A circuit cannot be used by any other call unti the connection has ended.

Click-and-mortar organizations Organizations that do business in both the physical and digital dimensions.

Client/server network Consists of user PCs, called *clients*, linked to high-performance computers, called *servers*, which provide software, data, or computing services over a network.

Cloud computing Technology that is rented or leased on a regular, or as-needed basis.

COBIT (Control Objectives for Information and Related Technologies) An internationally accepted IT governance and control framework that aligns IT business objectives, delivering value and managing associated risks.

Collaborative planning, forecasting, and replenishment (CPFR) Project in which suppliers and retailers collaborate in their planning and demand forecasting to optimize flow of materials along the supply chain.

Commodity Basic things that companies need in order to function, like electricity and buildings.

Comparison shopping engine Search engine that compares prices and finds great deals for certain brands and products.

Competitive advantage An advantage a company has over its competitors, which is gained by providing consumers with greater value through product or service offerings.

Competitive forces model A business framework devised by Michael Porter, depicting five forces in a market (e.g., bargaining power of customers), used for analyzing competitiveness.

Computer-integrated manufacturing (CIM) Integrates several computerized systems, such as CAD, CAM, MRP, and JIT, into a whole, in a factory.

Content indexing A searchable index of all content.

Content marketing A type of marketing where valuable information is shared with current or prospective clients. Blogs are a key tool of this.

Corporate governance Rules and processses ensuring that the enterprise adheres to accepted ethical standards, best practices, and laws.

Corporate procurement Buying products and services for operational and functional needs. Also called *corporate purchasing*.

Critical path Activities or tasks that must start and finish on schedule or else the project completion will be delayed unless action is taken to expedite one or more critical tasks.

Critical path method (CPM) The purpose of this method of project management is to recognize which activities are on the critical path so that you know where to focus your efforts.

Critical success factors (CSFs) The most essential factors that must go right or be closely tracked in order to ensure an organization's survival and success.

Critical task Each task on the critical path.

Crowdsourcing A model of problem solving and idea generation that marshals the collective talents of a large group of people.

CSS (Cascading Style Sheets) A style sheet language used to enhance the appearance of Web Pages written in a markup language.

Customer relationship management (CRM) The entire process of maximizing the value proposition to the customer through all interactions, both online and traditional. Effective CRM advocates one-to-one relationships and participation of customers in related business decisions.

Dashboard A BI tool that provides a comprehensive, at-a-glance view of corporate performance with graphical presentations, resembling a dashboard of a car. These graphical presentations show performance measures, trends, and exceptions, and integrate information from multiple business areas.

Data The raw material from which information is produced.

Data centers Facilities containing mission-critical ISs and components that deliver data and IT services to the enterprise.

Data entity Anything real or abstract about which a company wants to collect and store data, such as customer, vendor, product, or employee.

Data mart Small data warehouse designed to support a department or SBU.

Data mining Process of analyzing data from different perspectives and summarizing it into useful information (e.g., information that can be used to increase revenue, cuts costs, or both).

Data tampering An attack wherein someone enters false, fabricated, or fraudulent data into a computer, or changes or deletes existing data.

Data visualization Ways to depict data to make it easier for users to understand data.

Data warehouse A specialized type of database that is used to aggregate data from transaction databases for data analysis purposes, such as identifying and examining business trends, to support planning and decision making. See *enterprise data warehouse*.

Database Repository of enterprise data that business applications create or generate, such as sales, accounting, and employee data. An organized logical grouping of related files.

Database management systems (DBMS) Programs used to create, manage, and access databases.

Decision support system (DSS) Computer-based information system that combines models and data to solve semistructured and some unstructured problems with intensive user involvement.

Demand management Knowing or predicting what to buy, when, and how much.

Denial of Service (DoS) attack Occurs when a server or Web site receives a flood of traffic—much more traffic or requests for service than it can handle, causing it to crash.

Direct procurement Procuring materials to produce finished goods.

Dirty data Poor quality data. .

Disintermediation The elimination of intermediaries in EC; removing the layers of intermediaries between sellers and buyers. Effective for technological forecasting and for forecasting involving sensitive issues.

Document management systems (DMS) Hardware and software to manage and archive electronic documents and to convert paper documents into e-documents, and then to index and store them in an organized way.

Dot-com era (bubble) Period from 1995–2005 when number of Internet users sharply increased and during which countless Internet companies rode an enormous wave of enthusiasm.

E-commerce Process of buying, selling, transferring, or exchanging products or services or information via the public Internet or private corporate networks.

E-government The use of e-commerce to deliver information and public services to citizens, business partners, and suppliers of government entities, and those working in the public sector.

E-procurement Purchasing by using electronic support.

E-sourcing Electronic procurement of products.

Economic order quantity (EOQ) Inventory model that is used to determine when and how much to order of stock.

Electronic data interchange (EDI) The electronic transfer of specially formatted standard business documents, such as bills, orders, and confirmations, sent between business partners.

Electronic funds transfer (EFT) Electronic payments and collections.

Enterprise 2.0 The strategic integration of social computing tools (e.g., blogs, wikis) into enterprise business processes.

Enterprise application integration (EAI)   A middleware that connects and acts as a go-between for applications and their business processes.

Enterprise resource planning (ERP)   Software that integrates the planning, management, and use of all resources in the entire enterprise; also called *enterprise systems*.

Enterprise risk management (ERM)   A model for IT governance that is risk-based integrating internal control, the Sarbanes-Oxley Act mandates, and strategic planning.

Enterprise search   Offers the potential of cutting much of the complexity accumulated in applications and intranet sites throughout an organization.

Enterprise social network   A social network within an enterprise that allows employees to communicate, collaborate, and set up virtual worlds in which they can meet like-minded colleagues within the company and exchange ideas with them to improve productivity.

Exception report   Report generated only when some unusual event or deviation has occurred.

Executive information system (EIS)

External supply chain   Business or supply chain partners, such as customers or suppliers.

Extract, transform, and load (ETL)   Process that moves data from multiple sources, reformats, cleanses, and loads them into another data warehouse or data mart for analysis or another operational system to support a business process.

Extranet   Private, company-owned network that uses IP technology to securely share part of a business's information or operations with suppliers, vendors, partners, customers, or other businesses.

Firewall   System or group of systems that enforces an access-control policy between two networks.

Fixed-line broadband   Either cable or DSL Internet connection.

Forward auction   An auction that sellers use as a selling channel to many potential buyers; the highest bidder wins the items.

Front-office operations   The business processes, such as sales and advertising, that are visible to customers.

Gantt chart   A type of bar chart that illustrates a project schedule.

Gateway   An entrance point that allows users to connect from one network to another.

General controls   Protects the system regardless of the specific application.

Geocoding   Process of finding geographic coordinates from other data, such as zip codes or addresses.

Geographical information system (GIS)   Computer-based system that integrates GPS data onto digitized map displays.

Giant global graph   Concept that illustrates the connections between people and/or documents and pages online.

Global positioning systems (GPS)   Wireless devices that use satellites to enable users to detect the position on earth of items (e.g., cars or people) the devices are attached to, with reasonable precision.

Global warming   The upward trend in global mean temperature (GMT).

Government-to-business (G2B)   E-commerce in which a government does business with other governments as well as with businesses.

Government-to-citizens (G2C)   E-commerce in which a government provides services to its citizens via EC technologies.

Government-to-government (G2G)   E-commerce in which government units do business with other government units.

Greenhouse effect   The holding of heat within the earth's atmosphere by certain GSGs—such as CO_2, methane, and nitrous oxide—that absorb infrared radiation (IR).

Groundswell   A spontaneous movement of people using online tools to connect, take charge of their own experience, and get what they need from each other.

Hard ROI metrics   A method for businesses to measure the hard return on investment by evaluating various data.

Hotspot   A specific geographic location in which an access point provides public wireless service to mobile users.

HTML (Hypertext Markup Language)   Predominant language for Web pages. Provides a means to create structured documents by denoting structural semantics for text, such as headings, paragraphs, and lists, as well as for links, quotes, and other items.

Implementation   All organizational activities involved in the introduction, management, and acceptance of technology to support one or more organizational processes.

In-house development   When systems are developed or other IT work is done in-house.

In-store tracking iOS   Apple's mobile OS.

Inbound logistics   Incoming materials are processed in this activity.

Indirect procurement   Procuring materials and products for daily operational needs.

Information   Data that have been organized so they have meaning and value to the recipient.

Information overload   The inability to cope with or process ever-growing amounts of data into our lives.

Information quality   A subjective measure of the utility, objectivity, and integrity of gathered information based on its being complete, accurate, up-to-date, and fit for the purpose for which it is used.

Information technology (IT)   The technology component of an information system (a narrow definition); or the collection of the computing systems in an organization (the broad definition used in this book).

Information technology architecture   High-level map or plan of the information assets in an organization; on the Web, it includes the content and architecture of the site.

Insourcing Development and management of IT services within the organization.

Integrated Social Media (ISM)   Social media services that are integrated into social networks.

Interactive marketing   Online marketing, facilitated by the Internet, by which marketers and advertisers can interact directly with customers, and consumers can interact with advertisers/vendors.

Internal control   Process designed to provide reasonable assurance of effective operations and reliable financial reporting.

Internal control environment   Work atmosphere that a company sets for its employees.

Internal supply chain   Internal functions that take place within a company.

Internal threats   Threats from those within the organization, such as employees, contractors, and temporary workers.

Interoperability   Connectivity between devices. Refers to the ability to provide services to and accept services from other systems or devices.

Intranet   Network designed to serve the internal informational needs of a company, using Internet tools.

Intrusion Detection System (IDS)   Technology tool that scans for unusual or suspicious traffic.

IP network   Internet Protocol-based network that forms the backbone that is driving the merger of voice, data, video, and radio waves by digitizing content into packets that can be sent via digital networks.

IP telephony   Voice communication over a network using the Internet Protocol. Also called VoIP.

IT-business alignment   Refers to the degree to which the IT division understands the priorities of the business and spends its resources, pursues projects, and provides information consistent with these priorities.

IT governance   Supervision monitoring and control of an organization's IT assets.

IT infrastructure   Provides the foundations for IT applications in the enterprise. It is shared by many applications throughout the enterprise and made to exist for a long time.

IT performance management   Being able to predict and anticipate failures before it's too late.

IT strategy   Defines what information, information systems, and IT architecture are required to support the business and how the infrastructure and services are to be delivered.

IT strategic planning   Plans and strategies that support the business strategy and objective.

ITES (information technology-enabled services)   See *Business process outsourcing (BPO)*.

JavaScript   An object-oriented language used to create apps and functionality on Web sites.

Just-in-time (JIT)   An inventory scheduling system in which material and parts arrive at a work place when needed, minimizing inventory, waste, and interruptions.

Knowledge   Data and/or information that have been organized and processed to convey understanding, experience, accumulated learning, and expertise.

Legacy system   Application that has been used for a long period of time and that has been inherited from languages, platforms, and techniques used in earlier technologies.

Location-based commerce (l-commerce)   M-commerce transactions targeted to individuals in specific locations at specific times.

Logistics   The operations involved in the efficient and effective flow and storage of goods, services, and related information from point of origin to point of consumption.

Malware   Any unwanted software that exploits flaws in other software to gain illicit access.

Management information systems (MISs)   Systems designed to provide past, present, and future routine information appropriate for planning, organizing, and controlling the operations of functional areas in an organization.

Mashup   An application or Web page that pulls information from multiple sources, creating a new functionality.

Master data entity   Main entities of a company, such as customers, products, suppliers, employees, and assets.

Master data management (MDM)   The integration of data from various sources or enterprise applications to provide a more unified view of data.

Master reference file   File that stores consolidated data from various data sources, which then feeds data back to the applications to create accurate and consistent data across the enterprise.

Metadata   Way of describing data so that it can be used by a wide variety of applications.

Metrics   A specific, measurable standard against which actual performance is compared.

Microblogging   Sending messages up to 140 characters.

Micropayment   Payment of small sums using a mobile device.

Mobile commerce (m-commerce)   Any e-commerce done in a wireless environment, especially via the Internet.

Mobile intelligence (MI)   Information access via mobiles that far exceed desktop or laptop information access.

Mobile social networking   Social networking where one or more individuals of similar interests or commonalities, conversing and connecting with one another, use mobile devices, usually with cell phones, and in virtual communities.

Mobile supply chain management (MSCM)   Technology that monitors supply networks by observing specific events, disruptions, and exceptions in real-time alerts if problems occur and offers solutions.

Model   Simplified representation or abstraction of reality. Models are often formulas.

MRO   Products used for maintenance, repair, and operations.

Multichanneling   Integrating online and offline channels for maximum reach and effectiveness.

Net neutrality   The absence of restrictions or priorities placed on the type of content carried over the Internet by carriers.

Newsgroups   An area on a computer network devoted to the discussion of a specific topic.

Offshoring   See *offshore outsourcing*.

On-demand CRM   CRM *hosted* by an ASP or other vendor on the vendor's premise; in contrast to the traditional practice of buying the software and using it *on-premise*.

Online analytical processing (OLAP)   Systems that contain *read-only data* that can be queried and analyzed much more efficiently than OLTP application databases.

Online communities   Social networks of individuals who interact through specific media.

Online transaction processing (OLTP)   A transaction processing system where transactions are executed as soon as they occur.

Onshore sourcing   Using vendors who are in the same country.

Open graph OWL (Web Ontology Language)   An initiative proposed by Facebook that will link other Web sites to Facebook.

Operational data store   Database for transaction processing systems that uses data warehouse concepts to provide clean data.

Operational risk   The risk of a loss due to inadequate or failed internal processes, people, and systems or from external events.

Order fulfillment   All of the activities needed to provide customers with ordered goods and services, including related customer services.

Outbound logistics   Products are prepared for delivery (packing, storing, and shipping).

Outsource relationship management (ORM)   Provides automated tools to monitor and manage outsource relationships.

Packet   A small unit of data.

Packet switching   The path of the signal is digital and is neither dedicated nor exclusive.

Payment Card Industry Data Security Standard (PCI DSS)   Data security standard created by Visa, MasterCard, American Express, and Discover that is required for all members, merchants, or service providers who store, process, or transmit cardholder data.

Payment Card Industry Security Standards Council (PCI SSC)   Organization founded by American Express, Discover Financial Services, JCB International, MasterCard Worldwide, and Visa, Inc.

Performance management   These help to monitor business metrics and key performance indicators (KPIs).

Periodic report   Report created or run according to a preset schedule (daily, weekly, or quarterly).

Personal data assistant (PDA)   A small, handheld wireless computer.

Personalization   The user's personal characteristics that impact how relevant the 3Cs—content, commerce, and community—are to the individual.

Phishing   Deceptive attempt to steal a person's confidential information by pretending to be a legitimate organization.

Physical system design   States how the system will perform its functions, with actual physical specifications.

Planners Lab   Software for building a DVD. It is free to academic institutions.

Podcast   Video file transferred over a network.

Primary activities   In Porter's value chain model, those activities in which materials are purchased and processed to products, which are then delivered to customers. Secondary activities, such as accounting, support the primary ones.

Private cloud   Cloud owned by a large company or government agency with multiple locations when data confidentiality is required.

Produce-to-stock   The manufacture of products to stockpile inventory so the company is ready to respond to future demand.

Project portfolio   IT resources, such as infrastructure, application services, data services, security services, to be developed.

Protocol   The standard or set of rules that govern how devices on a network exchange and how they need to function in order to "talk" to each other.

Radio-frequency identification (RFID)   Generic term for technologies that use radio waves to automatically identify individual items.

Real-time system   An information system that provides real-time access to information or data.

Reintermediation   Occurs where intermediaries such as brokers provide value-added services and expertise that cannot be eliminated when EC is used.

Resource allocation   Consists of developing the plans for hardware, software, data communications and networks, facilities, personnel, and financial resources needed to execute the master development plan, as defined in the requirements analysis.

Response hierarchies   Model that busniness use to set measurable objectives. Stages include: awareness, knowledge, liking, preference, and purchase.

Reverse auctions   Auction in which the buyer places an item for bid (*tender*) on a request for quote (RFQ) system, potential suppliers bid on the job, with the price reducing sequentially, and the lowest bid wins; primarily a B2B or G2B mechanism.

Reverse supply chain   Products that are returned.

RSS reader   A place where RSS feeds allow users to aggregate regularly changing data, such as blog entries, news stories, audio, and video.

Safety stock   Extra inventory kept in case of unexpected events. Also called *buffer stock*.

SAR (specific absorption rate)   A way of measuring the quantity of radio frequency energy absorbed by the body.

SCM 2.0   The use of social media tools to increase effectiveness of this communication, and enhancement of the acquisition of information necessary to make optimal decisions.

SCM software   Applications programs specifically designed to improve decision making in segments of the supply chain.

Scalability   Being able to add additional capacity incrementally, quickly and as needed.

Scenario planning   A methodology in which planners first create several scenarios; then a team compiles as many future events as possible that may influence the outcome of each scenario.

Search engine optimization (SEO)   The process of improving the volume or quality of traffic to a Web site from search engines via unpaid search results.

Sell-side marketplace   B2B model in which organizations sell to other organizations from their own private e-marketplace and/or from a third-party site.

Semantic Web   An evolving extension of the Web in which Web content can be expressed not only in natural language but also in a form that can be understood, interpreted, and used by intelligent computer software agents, permitting them to find, share, and integrate information more easily.

Service packs   Microsoft's releases to update and patch vulnerabilities in its operating systems or other software.

Service-level agreements (SLAs)   A written legal contract between a service provider and client wherein the service provider guarantees a minimum level of service.

Service-oriented architecture (SOA)   An architectural concept that defines the use of services to support a variety of business needs. In SOA, existing IT assets (called services) are *reused* and *reconnected* rather than the more time consuming and costly reinvention of new systems.

SharePoint   An integrated suite of capabilities that provides content management and enterprise search to support collaboration.

Short codes   A code of only five or six characters.

Shortage   The absence of inventory.

Short message service (SMS)   Technology that allows for sending of short text messages on some cell phones.

Single sign-on   Needing only one password, entered one time, to enter a Web site.

SMART 2020 Report   The world's first comprehensive global study of the IT sector's growing significance for the world's climate.

Social engineering   Collection of tactics used to manipulate people into performing actions or divulging confidential information.

Social graph   The global social network that reflects how we are all connected to one another through relationships.

Social media   The online platforms and tools that people use to share opinions and experiences, including photos, videos, music, insights, and perceptions, with each other.

Social media metrics   The data-driving measurements that evaluate the effectiveness of social media efforts.

Social media monitoring services   Services that use IT to track online content and then feed summary statistics into dashboards that can be used by their clients.

Social media ROI   This approach attempts to monetize the return on the cost of implementing social media strategies.

Social network analysis (SNA)   The mapping and measuring of relationships and flows between people, groups, organizations, animals, computers, or other information or knowledge processing entities. The nodes in the network are the people and groups, whereas the links show relationships or flows between the nodes. SNA provides both a visual and a mathematical analysis of relationships.

Social networking service (SNS)   A primarily Web-based service that uses software to build online social networks for communities of people who share interests and activities or who are interested in exploring the interests and activities of others. These services provide a collection of various ways for users to interact, such as chat, messaging, email, video, voice chat, file sharing, blogging, discussion groups, and so on.

Software-as-a Service (SaaS)   Also referred to as *on-demand computing, utility computing,* or *hosted services.* Instead of buying and installing expensive packaged enterprise applications, users access applications over a network, with an Internet browser being the only absolute necessity.

Sourcing   Organizational arrangement instituted for obtaining IT products and services, and the management of resources and activities required for producing these services. These arrangements include insourcing, outsourcing, and offshore outsourcing.

Spam   Use of e-mail to send unsolicited bulk messages.

Spot sourcing   Purchasing indirect materials on an as-needed basis.

Spyware   Software that obtains information from a user's computer without the user's knowledge or consent.

Standard Operating Procedure (SOP)   A clearly defined and mandatory procedure to be followed without deviation to complete a process or function.

Structured decisions   Decisions that are routine and repetitive problems for which standard solutions exist.

Supply chain   A pipeline composed of multiple companies that perform any of the following functions: procurement of materials, transformation of materials into intermediate or finished products, distribution of finished products to retailers or customers, recycling or disposal in a landfill.

Supply chain management (SCM)   The management of all of the activities along the supply chain, from suppliers, to internal logistics within a company, to distribution, to customers. This includes ordering, monitoring, and billing.

Support activities   Business activities that do not add value directly to a firm's product or service under consideration but support the primary activities that do add value.

Sustainability   Refers to the concept of using things at a rate that does not deplete their availability in future generations.

Sustainable biofuels   Energy source that will not be depleted in future generations.

SWOT analysis   Involves the evaluation of strengths and weaknesses, which are internal factors, and opportunities and threats, which are external factors.

Symbian OS   Symbian Foundation mobile OS.

Systematic sourcing   Direct materials are traded in large quantities in an environment of a long-term relationship.

Systems development lifecycle (SDLC)   Large IT projects, especially those that involve infrastructure, are developed according to this methodology.

Tactical metrics   A way an organization can define and measure their objectives.

Tags   Identifier to describe various aspecsts of a Web page.

Tag clouds   Graphic representations of all the tags people have attached to a particular page.

TCP/IP (Transmission Control Protocol/Internet Protocol)   Internet protocols created by U.S. Department of Defense to ensure and preserve data integrity and maintain communications in the event of catastrophic war.

Text mining   The application of data mining techniques to discover actionable and meaningful patterns, profiles, and trends from documents or other text data.

Time-to-exploitation   Elapsed time between when a vulnerability is discovered and the time it is exploited.

Tool-based metrics   Measurements designed to identify information about specific applications.

Total quality management (TQM)   A management strategy aimed at embedding awareness of quality in all organizational processes.

Trackback   A type of hyperlink that is inserted into one's blog.

Transaction processing system (TPS)   An information system that processes an organization's basic business transactions such as purchasing, billing, and payroll.

Tweets   Text posts to the Twitter Web site using the Web, phone, or IM. Tweets are delivered immediately to those signed up to receive them via the same methods.

Two-factor authentication   System to verify a user's identity based on two pieces of information, such as a password and smart card.

Unstructured decisions   Decisions that involve a lot of uncertainty for which there are no definitive or clear-cut solutions.

URI (uniform resource identifier)   One of the features that allow data to be used by multiple applications.

Usenet   Network that provided initial platform for online communities to make it possible for users to exchange messages on various topics.

Value chain model   Model developed by Michael Porter that shows the primary activities that sequentially add value to the profit margin; also shows the support activities.

Vendor-managed inventory (VMI)   Strategy used by retailers of allowing suppliers to monitor the inventory levels and replenish inventory when needed, eliminating the need for purchasing orders.

Vertical search   A search strategy that focuses on finding information in a particular content area, such as travel, finance, legal, and medical.

Vertically integrated companies   Companies that control every part of their business from research and development to manufacturing and logistics.

Virtual community   A group of people with similar interests who interact with one another using the Internet.

Virtualization   A concept that separates business applications and data from hardware resources, allowing companies to pool hardware resources, rather than dedicate servers to application and assign those resources to applications as needed.

Virtual private network (VPN)   Connects remote sites or users together privately using "virtual" connections routed through the Internet from the company's private network to the remote site or employee.

Vision statement   An organization's picture of where it wants to be in the future.

VoIP (Voice over Internet Protocol)   Voice communication over a network using the Internet Protocol. Also called IP telephony.

WAN (wide area network)   Network that covers a large geographic area, such as a state, province, or county.

Wardriving   Stealth search for wireless local area networks by driving around a city or elsewhere.

Web 2.0   The second generation of Internet-based services that let people collaborate and create information online in perceived new ways—such as social networking sites, wikis, and blogs.

Web 3.0   A term used to describe the future of the World Wide Web. It consists of the creation of high-quality content and services produced by gifted individuals using Web 2.0 technology as an enabling platform.

Web Services   Modular business and consumer applications, delivered over the Internet, that users can select and combine through almost any device, enabling disparate systems to share data and services. These are software systems designed to support machine-to-machine interactions over a network.

Widget   A small application that can be installed and executed within a Web page by an end user.

Wi-Fi   Technology that allows computers to share a network or Internet connection wirelessly without the need to connect to a commercial network.

Wiki   Software program, discovery tool, collaboration site, and social network.

WiMAX   A wireless standard (IEEE 802.16) for making broadband network connections over a large area.

Wireless access point (WAP)   Device that allows wireless communication devices to connect to a wireless network.

Wireless LAN (WLAN)   LAN without the cables; used to transmit and receive data over the airwaves, but only from short distances.

Work Breakdown Structure (WBS)   A project plan where the project scope is defined, and is used to estimate a realistic timeline and budget based on the availability of necessary resources.

World Wide Web Consortium (W3C)   Group working on programming standards to make it possible for data, information, and knowledge to be shared even more widely across the Internet.

WWANs (wireless wide area networks)   WAN for mobile computing.

XBRL (eXtensible Business Reporting Language)   Version of XML for capturing financial information throughout a business's information processes.

Zombies   Computers that are infected.

Organization Index

Name Index

Subject Index